Sri Lanka

the Bradt Travel Guide

Royston Ellis

edition
5

www

Bradt Trav
The Globe

D0267423

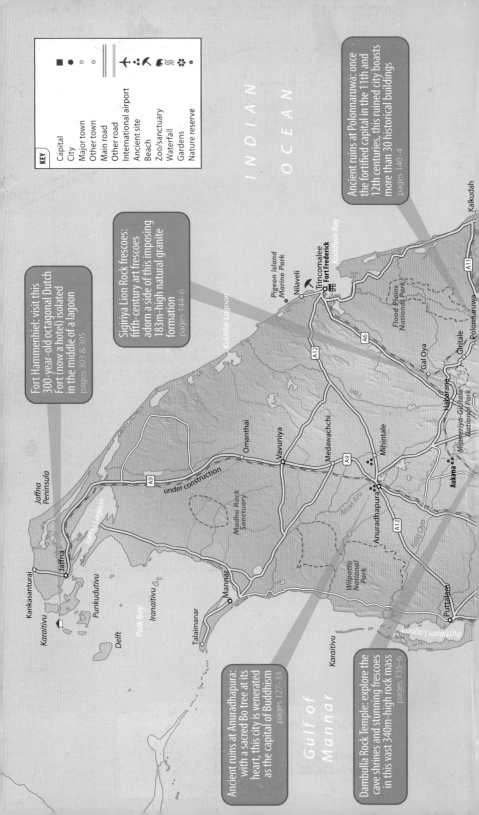

KEY

■ Capital
● City
○ Major town
○ Other town
║ Main road
║ Other road
✈ International airport
∴ Ancient site
Ψ Beach
⌂ Zoo/sanctuary
≋ Waterfall
❀ Gardens
• Nature reserve

Fort Hammenhiel: visit this 300-year-old octagonal Dutch Fort (now a hotel) isolated in the middle of a lagoon
pages 303 & 305

Sigiriya Lion Rock frescoes: fifth-century art frescoes adorn a side of this imposing 183m-high natural granite formation
pages 144–6

Ancient ruins at Polonnaruwa: once the fortified capital in the 11th and 12th centuries, this ruined city boasts more than 30 historical buildings
pages 140–4

Ancient ruins at Anuradhapura: with a sacred Bo tree at its heart, this city is venerated as the capital of Buddhism
pages 127–33

Dambulla Rock Temple: explore the cave shrines and stunning frescoes in this vast 340m-high rock mass
pages 135–6

INDIAN OCEAN

Gulf of Mannar

Jaffna Peninsula

Kankasanturai
Karaitivu
Jaffna
Punkudutivu
Iranaitivu
Delft
Polk Bay
Mannar
Talaimanar
Karaitivu

Jaffna Lagoon
Kokkilai Lagoon
Puttalam Lagoon

under construction
A9
Omanthai
Vavuniya
Medawachchi
A9
Mihintale
Anuradhapura
A12
Kala Oya
Puttalam
A11

Madhu Rock Sanctuary
Wilpattu National Park
Aruvi Aru

Pigeon Island Marine Park
Nilaveli
Trincomalee
Fort Frederick
Koddiyar Bay
A6
A12
Gal Oya
Habarana
Aukana
Minneriya-Giritale National Park
Flood Plains National Park
Giritale
Polonnaruwa
Kalkudah

Temple of the Tooth: this spectacular temple in Kandy is the sacred site of the tooth relic of Buddha *pages 119–20*

Royal Botanical Gardens: approximately 61ha dedicated to the flora of Sri Lanka, this peaceful eden in Peradeniya is a must-see *pages 122–4*

Elephant Orphanage: a national treasure, this sanctuary in Pinnawela provides shelter and care for abandoned and orphaned elephants *pages 194–5*

Galle Face Green: a popular evening promenade spot in the heart of Colombo *page 94*

Galle Fort: recognised as a World Heritage Site, the fort is the best preserved colonial sea fortress in Asia *pages 265–6*

Bradt

50km
30 miles

Laccadive
Sea

Batticaloa
Ampara
Arugam Bay
Senanayake Samudra
Gal Oya
Maduru Oya Reservoir
Maduru Oya National Park
Maduru Oya
Lahugala Kitulana National Park
A4
Yala East Strict Natural Reserve
Ruhunu National Park (Yala)
Kataragama
Kirinda
Bundala National Park
Kehelula
Mahiyangana
A5
Badulla
Kirindi Oya
Wellawaya
A26
Bandarawela
Haputale
Lunugamvehera National Park
Tissamaharama
Mattala
Hambantota
A2
Knuckles 1863m
Mahaweli Ganga
Wasgomuwa National Park
Mahaweli Ganga
Udawalawe National Park
Tanamalwila
Kalametiya
Ukuwela
Udawatte Kalle Sanctuary
Kandy
Nuwara Eliya
Hakgala Botanical Gardens
Ella
Belihul Oya
Walawe Ganga
Tangalle
Matale
A9
Peradeniya
Ramboda Falls
Pussellawa
A5
St Clair Falls
Nanu Oya
Horton Plains
World's End
Falls
A4
Dondra Head
Matara
A6
Yapahuwa
Munneswaram
Kurunegala
Polgahawela
Maha Oya
Ambepussa
Pinnawela
A1
Kadugannawa
A21
Kitulgala
Avissawella
A4
Adam's Peak 2243m
Ratnapura
A8
Kalu Ganga
Sinharaja Forest
Galle
Unawatuna
Gampaha
Chilaw
Deduru Oya
A3
Negombo
Gampaha
Ragama
Kelani Ganga
SRI JAYAWARDENEPURA KOTTE
A2
Kalutara
Beruwala
A2
Bentota
Ambalangoda
Hikkaduwa
Hikkaduwa Marine Park
Colombo
Dehiwela
Mt Lavinia

Sri Lanka
Don't miss...

Temple of the Tooth, Kandy
A must-see in the delightful town of Kandy, this famous temple houses the sacred Tooth Relic of Buddha
(S/S) pages 119–20

Sigiriya
Climb the vertiginous stairway on the sheer rock face to gaze at the well-preserved 5th-century frescoes
(TM/S) pages 145–6

below
Pinnawela Elephant Orphanage
Not a national park, but a national treasure, this famous orphanage is the only one of its kind
(H/D) pages 194–5

Galle Fort
The best preserved colonial sea fortress in Asia, this imposing walled fort is a UNESCO World Heritage site
(WPTB) pages 265–6

Ancient ruins of Polonnaruwa
Containing more than 30 shrines, this ancient ruined city was the capital in the 11th century
(J/D) pages 143–4

Sri Lanka in colour

above   Sri Lanka's international cricket stadium in Colombo on the final night of the ICC Twenty-20 World Cup clash between the West Indies and the home team (JC/D/C) pages 13–14

left   The modernist exterior of the new world-class Nelum Pokuna Mahinda Rajapaksa Theatre (DH/ISL) pages 12 & 94

below   The National Museum in Colombo has a striking Neoclassical design (SS) page 94

above Sri Lankans strolling along the promenade and flying kites in the breeze on the Galle Face Green (NP/J/C) page 94

right Galle Fort's distinctive white lighthouse at the end of the peninsula (I/S) page 265

below Colonial-period buildings surrounded by coconut palms, Bentota (KFS/FLPA) pages 237–43

above Surfing is popular at Weliwala Beach, Hikkaduwa on the west coast and Arugam Bay on the east coast (KK/I/FLPA) pages 248–51 & 299

left Head to Udawalawe National Park for guided jeep excursions to see the largest living land animals in Asia – the Asian elephant (DH/FLPA) pages 199–201

below Sri Lanka's rivers, particularly Kitulgala (where *Bridge on the River Kwai* was filmed), are well suited to white-water rafting (N/D) pages 207–9

AUTHOR

Royston Ellis is a novelist, travel writer and erstwhile beat poet, born in Britain, who has lived in Sri Lanka since 1980. He has contributed hundreds of articles about Sri Lanka to UK newspapers and magazines, to airline in-flight magazines, and to Sri Lankan publications, including *Explore Sri Lanka*, of which he was editorial consultant for 16 years, and to the *Sunday Times* (Colombo) for whom he reviews Sri Lankan hotels. In 2012 he was appointed by the chairman of the Western Province Tourist Board as editorial consultant for *Amazing Sri Lanka*, a  quarterly magazine, and he also produces a weekly newsletter about Sri Lanka with a readership of over 240,000 (*www.roystonellis.com/blog*).

He is the author of *Sri Lanka by Rail* and *India by Rail* (both out of print) and original author of Bradt's *Maldives* and *Mauritius, Rodrigues & Réunion*. He has written several locally published coffee-table books on Sri Lanka, including a guide for investors, a history of the Ceylon Planters Association, a book about organic tea and a garment industry review. As Richard Tresillian, he is the author of a score of historical novels, some of which are set in Sri Lanka, and he is currently working on a Ceylon tea plantation saga. *Gone Man Squared,* a collection of beat poetry he wrote and performed in England in the 1960s, was published in 2013 in New York by Kicks Books.

Since 2003 Royston has been the voluntary British Consular Warden for the Southern Province of Sri Lanka, appointed by the British High Commission in Colombo, responsible for keeping in touch with British residents of the area. When he is not writing about Sri Lanka he relaxes at his colonial-period cottage on the island's west coast.

AUTHOR'S STORY

'But don't you ever go back to England?'

When visitors ask me that, I wonder what they have sensed about me that strikes them as odd. I'm content in my cottage in a coconut and papaya garden overlooking the Indian Ocean, but they seem uncertain. 'Don't you miss the theatre? Marmite?' They really mean 'Life in the West as we are accustomed to it'.

I tighten my sarong and shake my head. I tell them that I get Marmite (it's actually produced in Sri Lanka too), as well as jolly good New World wines, and all the culture I want from books, films and CDs ordered through the internet. My old friends and relatives from England visit me from time to time, and my new friends are Sri Lankans. Perhaps it's my serenity as I relax on my veranda with legs hooked over the extended arms of a planter's chair, a cup of tea to hand and a smile of bliss as I watch the sun set, that worries them.

They give me the impression that my living in the tropics is somehow disreputable, or perhaps they are simply envious and wonder how they could adapt too. This guide might help. In spite of the setbacks (tsunami, terrorism) many people who visit Sri Lanka as tourists long to spend more time here, even settling down as I have. When you discover Sri Lanka you'll understand why.

PUBLISHER'S FOREWORD — Adrian Phillips, Publishing Director

Bradt readers love Royston, and Royston loves Sri Lanka – indeed, he has lived there for over three decades, his enthusiasm for its charms undiminished despite the turmoil the country suffered during times of terrorism and tsunami. Of course, the longstanding violent conflict between the government and Tamil separatists ended in 2009 with the bloody crushing of the Tamil Tigers that made headlines around the world. Since then the country has made significant efforts to attract tourists. As Royston makes clear, it has so much to offer – whether you're a wildlife fan or a cricket nut, an independent traveller or a visitor on an organised tour.

Fifth edition published January 2014   First published 2002

Bradt Travel Guides Ltd
IDC House, The Vale, Chalfont St Peter, Bucks SL9 9RZ, England
www.bradtguides.com
Print edition published in the USA by The Globe Pequot Press Inc,
PO Box 480, Guilford, Connecticut 06437-0480

British Library Cataloguing in Publication Data
A catalogue record for this book is available from the British Library

Photographs 4Corners Images: Massimo Ripani (MR/4CI); Corbis: Jiti Chadha/Demotix (JC/D/C), Nigel Pavitt/JAI (NP/J/C), Philip Brown/Reuters (PB/R/C); Dhammika Heenpella/Images of Sri Lanka (DH/ISL); Dreamstime: Ekrystia (E/D), Enjoylife25 (En/D), Honzahruby (H/D); Jurquijophoto (J/D), Nastiakru (Na/D), Nazar1980 (N/D); FLPA: Christian Hatter/Imagebroker (CH/I/FLPA), David Hosking (DH/FLPA), Imagebroker (I/FLPA), Karl F Schöfmann/Imagebroker (KFS/I/FLPA), Katja Kreder/Imagebroker (KK/I/FLPA), Kevin Schafer/Minden Pictures (KS/MP/FLPA), Martin B Withers (MBW/FLPA), Stefan Auth/Imagebroker (SA/I/FLPA); Shutterstock: Anton Gvozdikov (AG/S), bobby20 (b/S), erandamx (e/S), foryouinf (f/S), itsmejust (i/S), Jorg Hackermann (JH/S), leoks (l/S), SurangaSL (S/S), Suranga Weeratunga (SW/S), suronin (s/S), Tatiana Morozova (TM/S), Vidu Gunaratna (VG/S); SuperStock (SS); Western Province Tourist Board of Sri Lanka (WPTB)
Front cover Sigiriya (Lion) Rock, Central Province (MP/4CI)
Back cover Drummers at a Buddhist festival in Colombo (SS); Fishing boats on the beach (AG/S)
Title page Scorpion orchid (f/S); Buddha wall painting in Mulgirigala Temple, Mulgirigala (SA/I/FLPA); Decorated masks are worn in low country dance rituals (SS)

Maps David McCutcheon FBCart.S; relief map base by Nick Rowland FRGS

Typeset from the author's disc by Wakewing
Production managed by Jellyfish Print Solutions; printed in India
Digital conversion by the Firsty Group

Acknowledgements

As in all the previous editions of this guide, I reiterate my thanks to all the hotel, restaurant, bar, guesthouse, resthouse, nightclub, tavern, museum, station, supermarket, shop, plantation, historical-site and travel-agency staff who had to put up with my questions and suggestions, and who handled me with exceptional charm and understanding. In other words, my thanks are due to every single Sri Lankan I have ever met for being Sri Lankan and proud of it. For their contributions to this edition, I am grateful to Gehan de Silva Wijeyeratne (author of *Sri Lankan Wildlife*; Bradt, 2007) and, for his take on Colombo after dark, Rehan Mudannayake.

Thanks too to the many readers who wrote with tips, updates and corrections, including Anne Beal, John and Elisabeth Cox, Andrew and Monica Forsyth, Richard Jones, Margaret Sheldon, Derek Wren; Eric J Butler for his comments on water conservation and Chinese massage (not at the same time); and to my great-nephew, Tom Ellis. To my stalwart companions, Neel Jayantha, my manager since 1982, and B Kumarasiri, my house manager since 1998, my thanks because without their help and insight this guide would never have been written. Thanks also for his advice, comments and photos to my colleague, award-winning AP photojournalist in Sri Lanka, Gemunu Amarasinghe and to Udara Chinthaka who helped with research and updating contact details for this new edition. I thank, too, my friends who are at the tourism frontier: Selvam (aka Eddie) the doyen of freelance guides based in Nuwara Eliya, and Loga, who dispenses advice (and sells his own brand of fresh, High Grown estate tea) from his internet café in Haputale. Thanks especially to Andrew Jebaraj of www.webwizard-lk.com who helped greatly with research for the previous fourth edition and who publishes my weekly newsletter about Sri Lanka, available by free subscription from www.roystonellis.com/blog.

Some parts of this book have previously appeared in *Sri Lanka by Rail* and in my articles published in *Explore Sri Lanka* and in *Open Skies*, the in-flight magazine of Emirates Airlines, and in other magazines, to whose publishers I am grateful for permission to reproduce extracts here. Some material has also appeared in my weekly email newsletter.

Royston Ellis
(*www.roystonellis.com*)
Induruwa, Sri Lanka

Contents

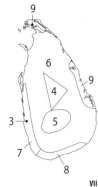

LIST OF MAPS

HOW TO USE THIS GUIDE

MAPS

Keys and symbols Maps include alphabetical keys covering the locations of those places to stay, eat or drink that are featured in the book. On occasion, hotels or restaurants that are not listed in the guide (but which might serve as alternative options if required or serve as useful landmarks to aid navigation) are also included on the maps; these are marked with accommodation (⌂) or restaurant (✖) symbols. Note that regional maps may not show all hotels and restaurants in the area: other establishments may be located in towns shown on the map.

Grids and grid references Several maps use gridlines to allow easy location of sites. Map grid references are listed in square brackets after listings in the text, with page number followed by grid number, eg: [103 C3].

ATTENTION WILDLIFE ENTHUSIASTS

For more on wildlife in Sri Lanka, check out Bradt's *Sri Lankan Wildlife*. Go to www.bradtguides.com and key in SRILANKAWILD40 at the checkout for your 40% discount.

FEEDBACK REQUEST AND UPDATES WEBSITE

At Bradt Travel Guides we're aware that guidebooks start to go out of date on the day they're published – and that you, our readers, are out there in the field doing research of your own. You'll find out before us when a fine new family-run hotel opens or a favourite restaurant changes hands and goes downhill. So why not write and tell us about your experiences? Contact us on ☎ 01753 893444 or e info@bradtguides.com. We will forward emails to the author who may post 'one-off updates' on the Bradt website at www.bradtupdates.com/srilanka. Alternatively you can add a review of the book to www.bradtguides.com or Amazon.

Introduction

'Warm, friendly people.' The hackneyed phrase flows easily from the travel writer's pen when describing Sri Lanka. So, too, does 'tropical paradise' and, I must confess, those were words I used when I visited the country first in 1980.

I was on my way to Sarawak where I planned to write a novel about the white rajah, James Brooke. Somehow, Sri Lanka's spell enchanted me, as it does most visitors. I wanted to stay, and I did. I never wrote the novel but was soon ensconced in a cottage attached to a guesthouse in Bentota writing other novels, travel guides and magazine articles, and living the carefree life of my dreams. After 20 years I decided to stay and bought my own colonial cottage on a small hill overlooking the railway line, road and sea.

Fortunately, the dream has not become a nightmare, despite Sri Lanka's troubles that frequently erupted to turn this 'tropical paradise' into a festering hell.

Neither has it become impossibly expensive as a place for the perfect holiday. For foreign visitors, by a quirk of the world's economy, many things in Sri Lanka are actually cheaper now than 30 years ago. The Sri Lankan rupee floats against major foreign currencies. In the 1980s, a rice and curry lunch cost 35 rupees, which was the equivalent then of about £1 sterling. In 2013, a rice and curry lunch could still be had for the equivalent of £1 and it was possible to stay in a room in some guesthouses near the beach or in the interior for the equivalent of around £10 a night.

However, I do not want to imply that Sri Lanka is the place for a cheap holiday. It isn't. In addition to the high room rates of boutique and mainstream hotels and on lower-priced guesthouse room rates, a guest must pay the service charge and various taxes, which add a further 25% or more to the quoted room rate. My advice is to regard Sri Lanka as a country where a holiday can bring unexpected bonuses, not as a low-budget destination.

The slogan chosen by the Tourist Authority to promote Sri Lanka as a destination to appeal to all visitors was 'Sri Lanka: a land like no other'. It was apt, perhaps in a way not originally intended. For where else is there a country – so blessed with nature's bounties – seemingly so intent on destroying itself?

The slogan was obviously intended to present Sri Lanka as a holiday destination that would suit everyone. It is. Whatever the visitor seeks in Sri Lanka can be found there. This book, although the outcome of my having resided in Sri Lanka for three decades, necessarily reveals only a little of this 'land like no other'. You will get a sense of the country after a few days, but a deep understanding would take a lifetime. No wonder that the Tourist Authority now bills Sri Lanka as 'The Wonder of Asia'.

While this guide will tell you all you need to know as an introduction to the country, if what you see intrigues you, then do read locally published books too. Through different eyes you will see a different version of the country. I have tried in this book to guide you to what I think are places of good value, whether it's something to see or somewhere to eat or stay. Deliberately, I have not mentioned every restaurant and guesthouse, nor every place to visit.

This led to Richard Jones of the UK writing to say that, while he found this guide generally helpful and informative, he – being interested in Buddhism – was 'a little disappointed by the relative paucity of information on the sites of religious importance'. Were I to write in more detail on Buddhist sites I should necessarily include more information on Hindu, Muslim and Christian sites. I have written this as a general introduction to Sri Lanka because extreme enthusiasts, whether interested in religion or ecology, mask-making or tea manufacture, can obtain more detailed insight of their particular passions on the spot.

If you want basic facts and no opinions, a travel agent's brochure or a Sri Lankan website will give you that. This is the land I like and I make no apologies for steering you to what I enjoy. You, however, need not worry; if what suits me doesn't suit you, I'm sure you'll find what you like, serendipitously.

My favourite things and places in Sri Lanka conform to no particular pattern. I have been enraptured sitting in the moonlight in my garden watching the leaves of a palm tree quivering in the breeze, and then been astonished to see that graceful movement emulated by dancers of a local ballet troupe performing in the lobby of Colombo's five-star Galadari Hotel.

I am as thrilled by the defiant seediness of the dining room of the Olde Empire Hotel in Kandy as I am by the sparkle of the fine-dining restaurant of the Taj Vivanta resort in Bentota. A leisurely paddle in a hollowed-out tree-trunk catamaran crossing the Bentota River is as exciting to me as the harried ride by three-wheeled, auto-rickshaw taxi ('tuk-tuk') through the chaos of Colombo's Pettah bazaar district.

Perhaps the pattern to experiences and places that intrigues me in Sri Lanka can be defined with one word: contrast. The romantic may envisage Sri Lanka as a land of serenity (it is, usually) while the sports fan sees it differently, as the home of dynamic cricket. There are rolling hills clad in close-cropped tea bushes in the frosty chill of nearly 2,000m (6,561ft) above sea level. Yet they are only a morning's drive from the surf-lapped beaches of the Indian Ocean, where temperatures sizzle at 30°C or more.

In those hills are granite bungalows that could have been transported from an Edwardian Surrey. They have fireplaces in the drawing rooms and retainers who call honoured guests 'master' as they serve tea. And on the beach there are hotels of brisk, modern design with air conditioning in every bedroom and eager young stewards propelling visitors towards groaning buffet tables.

In Kandy, the country's erstwhile royal capital, the contrasts are side by side. The Temple of the Tooth there is the exotic symbol of Sri Lanka's Buddhist history. Close by its railed compound is another faith-inspired building: the Gothic 19th-century St Paul's Church.

However, Sri Lanka is not solely a contrast of the colonial and the quixotic. National parks provide the visitor with the chance to see herds of wild elephant in their protected natural habitat. Yet you can also marvel at the sight of a domestic elephant plodding calmly through Colombo's traffic on the way to take part in a *perahera* (procession).

And the people! A guidebook in the 1920s described the Ceylonese (as Sri Lankans then were) as 'tropical Italians'. You will encounter more diversity in manner and appearance in a few days in Sri Lanka than you will in a lifetime in England (or in Italy). The eyes have it. A Sri Lankan will look where others will only glance. The effect on visitors can be devastating; they find the people handsome, and invariably charming. Countless are the visitors who have fallen in love, not just with the country, and returned home exhilarated, soon to be followed by their new-found Sri Lankan partner. Sex tourism has reared its ugly head in Sri Lanka, but that can be contrasted with the lasting bonds of friendship that are forged between locals and visitors.

Sri Lanka has become associated through legend and copywriter's plagiarism with serendipity. It is an easily acceptable word that conjures up the serenity of old Ceylon with the rapidity of change in the modern Sri Lanka. Serendipity is defined by the dictionary as 'the faculty of making happy and unexpected discoveries by accident'. It is attributed to Horace Walpole who coined the word, in a letter written in January 1754, from the title of 'a silly fairy tale called The Three Princes of Serendip' that he had read as a child.

Some writers mistake Walpole as the author of that book when listing 'serendipity' as one of the delights of a holiday in Sri Lanka. The author of the story, according to Richard Boyle, writing in the Colombo *Sunday Times* (30 July and 6 August 2000), was in fact an Italian, Michele Tramezzino, who published the book in Venice in 1557. The first version in English appeared in 1722. Boyle explains that the news of the introduction of Christianity in 1554 to what was then 'a strange and far off land variously known as Ceilao, Zeylan, Taprobane and Serendip' would have made the setting for the story topical as well as tropical.

Boyle cites a more recent use of the word 'serendipity' as adequately conveying its meaning. In *The Last Voyage of Somebody the Sailor* (New York, 1991), John Barth writes: 'You don't reach Serendip by plotting a course for it. You have to set out in good faith for elsewhere and lose your bearing serendipitously.'

My 18-year-old great-nephew, Tom Ellis, who visited in 2007, later wrote about his trip for his Canadian university newspaper. 'Sri Lanka is truly a tropical paradise in every sense, yet the ethnic tension hurts the country in many ways, from the high number of lives lost in the conflict to the bad international press it receives. My trip showed a friendly, diverse and exciting country with much to offer, yet sadly for political reasons many people will likely miss out on the adventure of a lifetime.'

Sri Lanka is going through a complex period during which it is variously wooing, defying, registering and misunderstanding visitors. When war reigned, the country had to be content that a nucleus of some 200,000 visitors came annually. Most were repeat guests (and their friends) who adored Sri Lanka for various reasons, not always altruistic, and found a niche for their self-designed holiday in the country. They toured the safe areas, stayed in low-budget guesthouses or modest package hotels, and bought gems and souvenirs, knowing that their mere presence helped the local economy, even if at times they were inconvenienced by discourteous private hotel security guards, hassled by peddling predators and petty officialdom. Sri Lanka, during those difficult war years, was still a beautiful, fascinating country refreshingly without pretension – and it suited them.

The change began in 2005, following the 26 December 2004 tsunami. The tragedy attracted a wave of do-gooders armed with good intentions as well as collected alms. Some of those foreigners who came to aid Sri Lanka saw potential in the country for their own ambitions and created a new niche of 'boutique' tourism by investing in and creating tourism establishments themselves, in their own image.

The arrival of the charitable followed by their affluent cliques who flocked to stay in their trendy properties, didn't go unnoticed. The tourist product island-wide began to edge to a higher – and more expensive – level. With the end of the terror (in 2009), old hotels underwent refurbishment and fashionable rebranding. The country in 2013 confidently awaited an onslaught of high-spending visitors, with ambitious government plans to welcome 2½ million visitors by 2016.

In 2012, there were about one million visitors but, oddly, the hotels desperate to host those visitors found their rooms stayed empty. Even during the high season in

2012 and throughout 2013, Sri Lankans were being offered discounts of as much as 50% to stay in hotels that previously had spurned their custom. What had happened to the foreign tourists?

It seems that prices had climbed too high as cheaper, or better-value, holidays were available in other Asian destinations. Also, while the infrastructure had been expensively renovated, the staff standards had been neglected and did not match the new sparkle. Sri Lankan hotels, from package to boutique, were regarded as 'not worth it' by discerning travellers.

Meanwhile the simple guesthouses and family-run bed-and-breakfast establishments – the 'informal sector' as the regulators uncertainly dubbed it – thrived. They were discovered and enjoyed not solely by impecunious foreign students but also by middle-aged travellers seeking an agreeable holiday experience at a reasonable price. These mature backpackers were discerning individuals who came not on 'all-inclusive packages', but as FITs, free independent travellers.

Perhaps unintentionally, Sri Lanka has been transformed into a destination catering for all kinds of visitors. While strenuous efforts are being made to entice the Indian and mid-European tourists to stay in the formula, factory-style hotels, and quality niche marketing of such things as extreme sports holidays and temple tours is developing, the FITs soldier on, discovering that Sri Lanka is still an enchanting place to visit independently – thus perhaps perfect for the Bradt traveller.

Although I have lived in Sri Lanka since 1980, I am continually astonished by the changing facets of this country, shining like a gemstone when the light is right. It really is a country for everyone, from what nature and history offer to the standard of accommodation and food. The charm is that visitors don't have to limit themselves to high-end beach hotels or slip downmarket to family-run guesthouses in the remote countryside, or travel extravagantly in an air-conditioned hired van with an English-speaking Sri Lankan driver or risk crowded train travel. Now they have a broad choice: to stay and travel as they please.

This is a guidebook and not a catalogue so I couldn't possibly feature every monument, temple, hotel and restaurant in Sri Lanka. They are all there for visitors to discover at leisure. Instead, I have tried to focus on some of the places that a responsible, curious visitor might appreciate. This book is intended as an introduction to this fascinating country and is updated in this, the fifth edition, in the hope that it will guide visitors to experiences they will enjoy, as well as entice them to return and find out more about amazing Sri Lanka for themselves.

I don't recommend that, like me, you plan to fly to Sarawak and land in Sri Lanka instead. I do suggest, though, that you visit Sri Lanka before it is overwhelmed. Make your own arrangements and tour the country independently, or come as part of an organised group. Once in Sri Lanka, let serendipity take its course. This guidebook will help you begin.

Part One

GENERAL INFORMATION

Country The Democratic Socialist Republic of Sri Lanka, formerly Ceylon. It became Sri Lanka – and a republic – in 1972, with the addition of 'Sri', meaning 'resplendent', to an ancient name for the island, 'Lanka'.

Location An island off the southern tip of India, 880km north of the Equator; latitude 5°55' to 9°50'N, longitude 70°42' to 81°52'E

Area 65,525km² (25,299 square miles)

Topography Flat on the coastal areas and northern half of the island with the central and south-central areas being hilly and mountainous

Climate Tropical in lowlands with average temperatures of 27°C. Cooler in hills with average of 16°C. Monsoon in southwest May–July; in northeast, December–January.

Capital Sri Jayewardenepura. Commercial capital Colombo; population of Colombo district 2.3 million (2012).

Government The executive consists of an elected president who is head of state, commander-in-chief of the armed forces, and head of the cabinet of ministers drawn from a parliament of 225 elected members

Population 20.26 million (2012 estimate), of whom 74.9% are Sinhalese, 11.2% Sri Lankan Tamil, 4.2% Indian Tamil, 9.2% Moors, with the balance being Malays, Burghers (descendants of Dutch colonists) and others

Population distribution Urban 21.5%, rural 72.2%, estate 6.3%

Literacy rate 92%

Life expectancy at birth Males 69 years; females 74 years

Economy Main foreign-exchange earners: emigrants' remittances, tea, tourism (1,000,000 visitors in 2012) and locally manufactured garment exports

Gross domestic product (GDP) 6% real growth rate

Gross national product (GNP) Rs7.5 million (2012)

Average per capita income US$1,160 per annum

Languages Official languages are Sinhala and Tamil, with English as the official link language

Religion Buddhist 69.3%, Hindu 15.5%, Christian 7.6%, Muslim 7.5%, others 0.1%

Currency Rupee (Rs)

Rate of exchange £1 = Rs210, US$1 = Rs131, €1 = Rs178 (October 2013)

International dialling code +94

Time GMT +5 hours 30 minutes

Electricity 230 volts AC

Weights and measures Metric

Flag Two equal stripes of green and yellow alongside the Lion Flag of King Sri Wickrama Rajasinghe

Public holidays See pages 59–60

1

Background Information

GEOGRAPHY

Sri Lanka is about half the size of England. Its length from north to south is 435km (271 miles) and its greatest width is 240km (149 miles). A stretch of water 48km (30 miles) wide, known as the Palk Strait, separates the island from India. It is so shallow that ocean-going vessels cannot pass around the north of the island. Although the distance from Sri Lanka to India is slight (and probably in prehistoric times the two were joined), the difference is great in all respects.

Most of the island is low-lying and flat, but the south-central part is mountainous and has nine peaks over 2,133m (7,000ft) high. The highest mountains are Pidurutalagala at 2,524m, Kirigalpota at 2,395m, Thotupola Kanda at 2,357m, Kudahagala at 2,320m and Sri Pada (Adam's Peak) at 2,243m. Of the many rivers, the longest is the Mahaweli Ganga at 335km, double the length of the next longest, the Aruyi Aru at 164km. The island has about 100 waterfalls, of which the highest is Bambarakanda at 263m, followed by Diyaluma at 220m and Kurundu Oya at 206m. Sri Lanka has 113 islands dotted around its coast.

The land and sea areas total 554,235km², based on a land area of 65,525km² plus internal waters (1,570km²), historic waters (12,060km²), territorial sea (18,060km²), contiguous zone (19,620km²) and the economic exclusion zone (EEZ) amounting to 437,400km².

CLIMATE AND SEASONS

Being close to the Equator, Sri Lanka's seasons are not well defined, and there is no winter. Daylight is almost regular in length throughout the year, the difference in Colombo being only 48 minutes between 22 June and 22 December.

Sri Lanka's climate ranges from an average low of 12°C in Nuwara Eliya to a high of 33°C in Trincomalee.

The average rainfall varies from about 1,000mm (39in) over a small region in the arid parts of the northwest and southeast to over 5,000mm (197in) at a few places

AVERAGE TEMPERATURES (°C)	Jan–Apr	May–Aug	Sep–Dec
Colombo	30–22	30–24	29–22
Kandy	31–17	29–21	28–18
Nuwara Eliya	21–12	18–16	18–15
Trincomalee	32–24	33–25	33–23

in the Kegalle and Nuwara Eliya districts (on the southwestern slopes of the central hills). The monsoonal rains generally cover the southwestern and northeastern parts in their seasons although sometimes the rains fail, causing not only droughts but also power cuts as the hydro-electric supply suffers water shortage.

Traditionally the best time to visit is from October to March, if you plan to stay on the west coast. The east coast is best from April to September. However, tradition can no longer be relied on as a guide to the weather. In practice it will never be cold enough for snow and, even when it rains, you would find an umbrella more useful than a raincoat because the humidity makes wearing heavy clothes uncomfortable. In general, every day is a sunny one somewhere in the country.

NATURAL HISTORY AND CONSERVATION

For more on wildlife in Sri Lanka, check out Bradt's Sri Lankan Wildlife. See page VI for a special discount offer.

Two hundred years ago almost the entire island was covered by natural forest complemented by an abundance of flora and fauna common to a tropical monsoon climate. Unfortunately, very little thought was given to conservation by the pioneers of the plantation development of the country. Forest cover has rapidly declined and is now less than 30% of the land. This amounts to 1.58 million hectares of closed-canopy natural forest cover or dense forest, with sparse forest cover raising the total coverage to about two million hectares.

There is a brighter side to the picture. For a country with one of the highest population densities in the world, Sri Lanka is remarkable in having 13% of its land area designated for wildlife and nature conservation. With 242 known species of butterflies, 435 recorded birds, 92 species of mammals, 107 species of fish, 54 species of amphibia, 74 species of tetrapod reptiles and 81 species of snakes, Sri Lanka is one of the most biodiverse eco-travel destinations. There are 830 endemic flowering species, of which 230 are so rare they are in danger of extinction. The richest area for flora, not only in Sri Lanka but also in all of south Asia, is the southwestern lowland where more than 90% of the endemic species are concentrated in a small region of about 15,000km². For details of Sri Lanka's wildlife, see pages 183–5.

Alongside efforts to sustain the ecology, there are programmes to improve the yield of agricultural land based on irrigation schemes started over 2,000 years ago. An area of concern is the erosion of the coast. It has been calculated that the west, southwest and south coastline, which is 685km long, is being eroded at the rate of 0.3mm to 4mm a year. Environmental policy matters and international affairs relating to the environment are handled by the Ministry of Environment, and there is a Central Environment Authority with powers to enforce environmental regulations to preserve the island's natural resources.

The effects of the tsunami of December 2004 – which left some 35,000 people dead and 800,000 displaced – can still be seen along the west and south coasts from Kalutara to Yala and up the entire east coast. Sri Lankans displayed a remarkable resilience in adapting to the disaster. Building of new villages by various sponsors for those who lost their homes has resulted in a new landscape with coastal areas opened up and settlements inland on higher ground.

HISTORY

It is probable that the island was inhabited 500,000 years ago. Since it was a lush and fertile island of forests, plains and animals, with rivers abundant with fish, it would have been an attractive place for wandering prehistoric man to settle. The domestication of plants, broadening the food supply of hunting people, may have occurred in Sri Lanka some 12,000 years ago.

If southeast Asia was the cradle of human civilisation, Sri Lanka would have benefited from the development of agriculture, pottery making and the fashioning of stone tools introduced by seafarers from neighbouring archipelagos like the Philippines and Indonesia. Evidence from Stone Age cultures has been unearthed and it is believed that Stone Age recluses survived in the island's unexplored jungles up to 1,000 years ago. Today the Veddahs (see box, page 6) are regarded as a living link with the original inhabitants.

Sri Lanka's recorded history began 2,500 years ago. There exist texts, begun 1,500 years ago by Buddhist monks, called the *Mahavamsa* and its sequel, the *Culavamsa*, containing details of a rich and colourful past. The *Mahavamsa* confidently determines the coming of the Sinhalese race with the arrival of Vijaya, 1,000 years earlier.

Sri Lanka was actively involved in trading with other countries long before the birth of Christ, and was regarded as an island of great bounty. For traders, the island was regarded as the granary of Asia. Greek merchants came during the time of Alexander the Great (335–323BC) to trade in precious stones, muslin and tortoise shells, and the island was known as a source of ivory as well as rice. There were trade links with the Roman Empire during the Anuradhapura period, which flourished for 14 centuries, until 1017.

Buddhism was introduced to the island 246 years before the birth of Christ. The kingdom was overrun by the Chola army which had conquered southern India under Rajaraja the Great (985–1018). This resulted in the setting up of a new powerbase, with Polonnaruwa as the centre of the kingdom. Conquest of the Cholas eventually came under forces led by Vijayabahu I (1055–1110) who restored Buddhism to prominence after the Cholas' Hinduism.

His nephew, Parakramabahu I (1153–86), is remembered not only for unifying the island but also for his splendid buildings (now in ruins at Polonnaruwa) and his irrigation work. His death led to dynastic disputes and gradually the island fractured. There were five different capitals from 1253 to 1400. Eventually a new kingdom grew from a powerbase at Kotte, near Colombo, which is where the modern parliament and today's declared capital, Sri Jayewardenepura, are located. With the death of Parakramabahu VI (1412–67) there was a scramble for control that was diverted by the arrival in 1505 of the Portuguese.

Whether it was due to a premonition about the impact of foreign rule that was to last for 443 years, or to simple caution, the King of Kotte led the first of the Portuguese invaders a merry dance. Hearing reports of these strange people who were dressed in iron clothes (armour), appeared to eat stones (bread), drank from bottles of blood (wine) and had sticks that cracked like thunder and lightning (firearms), the king must have been desperate to delay any encounter with them. He directed the strangers be brought to him by a roundabout route so they would not realise how close (13km) his kingdom was to Colombo, and hence vulnerable to their attack.

The ruse did not work since the noise of cannons fired from the ship, and the seamen's knowledge of navigation, let the reconnoitring party know its position. To this day, the Sri Lankan expression for 'taking people for a ride' is 'like taking the Portuguese to Kotte'. At the time, the Portuguese were interested only in trade, wanting to take over the shipment of camphor, sapphires, elephants and cinnamon controlled by the King of Kotte.

That might have been the end of Portuguese involvement but for internal dissensions among the Sinhalese. The rulers of Kotte hoped to take advantage of the presence of the Portuguese, so they were allowed to settle and build strategic forts along the coast. This resulted, however, in Portuguese entrenchment throughout the island, with the notable exception of the Kingdom of Kandy. In 1617, the Kandyan king agreed to a treaty with the Portuguese, but this led to Portuguese incursions into the Kandyan ports of Batticaloa and Trincomalee. Then King Rajasinghe II (1635–87) formed an alliance with the Dutch against the Portuguese.

The Dutch were powerful in the region through their pursuit of the spice trade in the East Indies. They were not slow to take advantage of the promise of a monopoly of the island's spice trade in return for help in ridding the island of the Portuguese. They took Batticaloa and Trincomalee for the Kingdom of Kandy, but kept the ports of Galle and Negombo, which they captured in 1641, for themselves. In 1656 they took over the fort in Colombo from the Portuguese and, with the capture of Jaffna in 1658, brought the Portuguese occupation to an end. The Dutch, to the dismay of the Kandyans, were not keen to leave Sri Lanka and contrived to stay for 138 years.

A breach between the Dutch and the British during the Napoleonic Wars resulted in the annexation of Dutch settlements in the East by Great Britain. The first phase of British takeover began with a siege of Colombo. This resulted in the Dutch surrendering the town and ceding the Dutch East India Company possessions in Ceylon to Britain in 1796. However, the Kingdom of Kandy atop the Central Highlands defied British attempts to tidy up the country into a neat package they could call their own.

The British tried, and failed disastrously, to conquer the kingdom by military means in 1803. Diplomacy and duplicity were then employed as weapons, and Sir John D'Oyly (see page 121) was one of those who connived with disaffected Kandyan chiefs, enabling the British to take the kingdom. The king, Sri Wickrama Rajasinghe (1798–1815), was bundled off to India and a convention was signed between British rulers and the Kandyan chiefs.

Having a convention did not mean the British had Kandy, and there was resistance that was marshalled into organised rebellion in 1817–18. The British retaliated ruthlessly and at last the administration was set on a neat and tidy

VEDDAHS

The Veddahs (literally 'hunters') are the aboriginals of Sri Lanka. They survive in defiance of government attempts to assimilate them, and tourists' attempts to patronise them. Their culture has been affected by the interest of tourists who sometimes turn up at their settlements in coachloads to gaze at – and be photographed with – near-naked men armed with axes and bows. Naturally, this involves a reward of money (or even alcohol) with its corresponding effect. Instead of relying on the jungle that they once considered their home – and to which access is often restricted – many have become virtual performance artists to satisfy the local and foreign tourists.

There are thought to be only a few hundred Veddahs left, although their community comprises a few thousand families as many have become mixed through marriage with Sinhalese. While the Veddahs and their close-to-nature lifestyle may seem fascinating to us, it is probably better to leave them in peace than make a sport of visiting them.

course of government. For the first time since the kingdoms of Parakaramabahu (1153–86) and Nisanka Malla (1187–96), Sri Lanka was governed in its entirety by one power.

Having conquered the island, the British energetically set about colonising it. It became a plantation economy, first with coffee and then tea, with young Britons (many from Scotland) emigrating to open up the countryside to tea plantations. Some commentators see the plantocracy as a colonial subterfuge to plunder, exploit and enslave 19th-century Sri Lanka and its people. However, that ignores the benefits and progress that the British colonial presence not only fostered but also financed through the success of the plantation industry.

Its success rubbed off on to Sri Lankans too. A new indigenous aristocracy grew up by involvement in capitalist enterprises. It was the springboard to an enhanced social status. Sinhalese and Tamils together, coupling lucrative freelance initiative with an embrace of British ways, became wealthy through their commercial ventures. The British presence remained until 4 February 1948, when the Duke of Gloucester, representing King George VI, ceremonially conferred independence on Ceylon. This was recalled with a ceremony attended by the current Prince of Wales in Colombo 50 years later.

GOVERNMENT AND POLITICS

Perhaps it was the placid, tolerant nature of the people that enabled Britain to administer the country without having to face any major traumatic local crises. There were riots in 1915, on the centenary of the fall of Kandy, that stemmed from the development of radical movements of protest. Moderate attitudes were developing too and the Ceylon National Congress, a political party of a conservative nature, was founded in 1919. Under the leadership of Don Stephen Senanayake the Congress lobbied steadily for constitutional reforms. The British complied by granting a system of territorial representation as an initial measure for internal self-rule. In addition, the British introduced universal adult suffrage, with every Sri Lankan over the age of 21, male or female, entitled to vote. This was the first time that such suffrage was permitted in a British colony, and came only two years after Britons themselves achieved it.

With all over-21s in Sri Lanka entitled to vote, a new freedom of expression and responsibility was in the air. Buddhist nationalism emerged, as did some working-class movements. The British hoped for a gradual transition to independence in a manner that would not antagonise those who were not part of the Sinhalese Buddhist dominance. In 1944, a new constitution was proposed by D S Senanayake that was intended to guarantee the state's religious neutrality. A commission led by Lord Soulbury arrived at a similar conclusion and espoused internal self-government. However, popular feeling was for complete independence and this was granted, so avoiding the traumas experienced by India.

D S Senanayake, as leader of the United National Party (UNP), formed a coalition government with members of independent groups, to become the first prime minister of independent Ceylon, after 152 years of British rule. The country became a member of the Commonwealth of Nations and, in 1955, a member of the United Nations. In 1956, Mr S W R D Bandaranaike, leader of the opposition Mahajana Eksath Peramuna (MEP) Party, became prime minister after a general election. He pursued a nationalisation programme, forming state monopolies, but was assassinated in 1959. In 1960, his widow, Mrs Sirimavo Bandaranaike, as leader of the Sri Lanka Freedom Party, became prime minister, the first woman in

1

the world to hold such a post. She continued the policy of nationalisation until an election defeat in 1965, being returned to power in 1970.

With a new constitution ending Ceylon's dominion status, the Republic of Sri Lanka came into existence on 22 May 1972. The first general election after that resulted in the UNP gaining power in 1978 under Junius Richard Jayewardene, who subsequently amended the constitution and became the first executive president of the Democratic Socialist Republic of Sri Lanka. He was succeeded by Ranasinghe Premadasa who was elected as president in 1988 and the UNP won the general election in 1989. Premadasa was assassinated in 1993.

In 1994, the People's Alliance (PA) won the general election and formed the government under the leadership of Mrs Chandrika Bandaranaike Kumaratunga, daughter of two prime ministers and who herself became prime minister. She was elected as president in 1995 and was re-elected in 1999. Her party won a slim majority at the general election the next year, losing its majority by the crossing over to the opposition of some members of one of her coalition parties in June 2001.

The general election held in December 2001 resulted in a win for the UNP and its allies who had previously been the opposition, and Ranil Wickremesinghe, a former prime minister and nephew of former president, J R Jayewardene, became prime minister. He immediately set up negotiations to achieve a political solution to end the terrorism initiated by the Liberation Tigers of Tamil Eelam (LTTE), popularly known as the Tamil Tigers.

The conflict had its roots in the Tamil population losing their chances for advancement when Sinhala was declared the national language in the 1970s. In July 1983 the LTTE killed 13 government security personnel and this led to ethnic clashes in Colombo, Jaffna and several other cities, and is regarded as the date Sri Lanka's sweet future turned sour. Despite attempts at both conquest and peace, the LTTE actively survived with a culture of assassinations and their most dramatic incident was the bombing in July 2001 of military and civilian planes parked at the international airport.

As a result of the new government's efforts a formal truce was signed in February 2002. Gradually tensions eased, roadblocks were removed and life throughout the country returned almost to normal. Foreign investment and tourism picked up. However, having a president (and cabinet head) from one side of the great political divide and a government from the other eventually resulted in a showdown, with President Kumaratunga dissolving parliament and new elections being held in April 2004.

Although the president's party and its JVP (Marxist) allies did not win an outright majority, they were able to form a government while the UNP and allies formed the opposition, headed by Ranil Wickremesinghe. A presidential election held in November 2005 resulted in victory over Ranil Wickremesinghe for then prime minister, Mahinda Rajapaksa. Rajapaksa's party and its allies went on to form the new government in February 2007, having, with more than 50 ministers, the world's largest cabinet. With members of the opposition joining the government as ministers, and government MPs joining the opposition, party politics continued to be a nebulous affair into 2008.

An increase in terrorist activity in 2007 brought about the reintroduction of vigorous security checks at police and military roadblocks throughout the country, especially in Colombo. The formal ceasefire agreement (which had by then collapsed) was abrogated by the government in January 2008 and military action against the LTTE was intensified. Random bombing, said to be by LTTE terrorists, took place in the southeastern interior of the country as well as in Colombo and its suburbs.

A surge in the military effort under General Sarath Fonseka and government determination resulted in the annihilation of the LTTE militarily in 2009. This was followed by a presidential election in which Mahinda Rajapaksa was returned to power, beating the opposition candidate, General (by then retired) Fonseka. Rajapaksa's party and allies won the subsequent general election while Fonseka was court-martialled, stripped of his rank and jailed. He was released in 2012. The next presidential election is expected to be held in 2015.

The executive consists of the president, as head of state and commander-in-chief of the armed forces, elected by the people at a presidential election. The president is responsible to parliament and is a member and head of the cabinet of ministers. Parliament consists of 225 members elected by a complicated system that includes majority winners, proportional representation winners and nominated members. The person who is most likely to command the confidence of parliament is appointed by the president as prime minister. The chief justice, who is appointed by the president, heads the judiciary.

ECONOMY

Although the country is primarily an agricultural one (the chief crop is rice, in which there is almost a self-sufficiency), its income is mainly based on the manufacture and export of garments, on remittances from Sri Lankans working overseas, on the production and export of tea, and on tourism. The emphasis in recent years has been to diversify by increasing the export of manufactured goods and to export agriculture commodities in processed forms.

The main export markets for goods from Sri Lanka are the USA, the UK and Japan. (The main source countries for imports are Japan, India and China.) Sri Lanka is the world's largest exporter of black tea. Other agricultural exports include: areca nut (betel nut), baby corn, baby okra, betel leaf, cantaloupe melon, cardamom, cashew nut, cinnamon, citronella oil, cloves, cocoa, coconut, coffee, cut flowers, decorative foliage plants, fresh fruits, fresh vegetables, gherkins, mace, mushrooms, nutmeg, oil of cinnamon bark and leaf, papain, pepper, rice, rubber, sesame (gingerly) seed and tobacco.

Industrial products that are exported include aviation and marine fuels, canned fruit, cement, ceramic ware, chemicals, computer software, cosmetic accessories, dairy products, diamonds (re-exported cut and polished), electric and electronic appliances, fertiliser, footwear, fruit juices, furniture, garments, gloves, handicrafts, industrial pumps, jewellery, leather goods, machinery, paper, paper products, petrol, pharmaceuticals, plywood, porcelain figurine ornaments, PVC pipes, refrigerators, rubber goods, silk flowers, steel, sugar, textiles (cotton/synthetic), toys/sports requisites, tyres, water purification units, wooden products and yarns (cotton/synthetic).

Also exported are gems and minerals, timber (ebony, mahogany, satinwood and teak), and marine products such as aquarium fish, bêche-de-mer, crab, fish maws, lobsters, prawns, seashells, shark fin and shrimps.

Sri Lanka supplies the export services of bunkering, cargo transhipment, computer data entry, computer software development, construction/consultancy, entrepôt trade, lapidary, manpower, printing, ship chandlery, ship registry, ship repair/maintenance and tourism.

The **Colombo Stock Exchange** (*4-01 West Block, World Trade Centre, Echelon Sq, Colombo 1;* ☏ *011 2356456;* e *info@cse.lk; www.cse.lk;* ⏰ *09.30–12.30 working w/days*) is the country's sole stock exchange. There are no taxes imposed on share transactions, except for a 15% withholding tax on dividends for non-residents.

NATIONAL FLAG

The national flag of Sri Lanka has an ancient link. To the design of the Lion Flag of King Sri Wickrama Rajasinghe, which was taken to Britain in 1815, were added two stripes, one green and the other yellow, to form the national flag. Each of these stripes is equal to one-seventh of the size of the flag.

When Sri Lanka became a republic in 1972, the traditional *Bo* leaves depicted on the national flag were changed to resemble natural Bo leaves. This version of the flag was first unfurled at the Republic Day celebration held on 22 May 1972. The flag continues in use today, its design incorporated in the constitution.

PEOPLE

The total population in 2012 was estimated at about 20.26 million spread over nine provinces with the Western Province being the most populated (5,821,710 people) and the Northern Province (1,058,762 people) the least. The majority (74.9%) are Sinhalese, with 11.2% Sri Lankan Tamils and 4.2% Indian Tamils. The majority of the remainder (9.2%) are Moors, being descendants of Arab settlers. There are also Sri Lankans of Malaysian, Chinese, Dutch (the Burghers) and distant Portuguese ancestry, plus a few Eurasians and some small Indian communities like Parsis. The Veddahs were originally a forest-dwelling aboriginal group of whom there are now a few hundred since most have inter-married with Sinhalese. The Sinhalese are of Aryan stock while the Tamils are Dravidian. There is no easy visible way for a visitor to distinguish between a Sinhalese and a Tamil. For visitors, all are Sri Lankan.

LANGUAGE

Sinhala is the language spoken by most of the population. It is a language of Indo-Aryan origin. The constitution now designates Sinhala and Tamil as the official languages and English as the link language. English is becoming more widely spoken, after a lull when it was not used as a medium of education; it is the main language of the mercantile sector and the hospitality industry. Place names and signboards are usually in English and Sinhala or English and Tamil; sometimes all three.

RELIGION

Buddhism arrived on the island around 2,300 years ago, giving birth to a cultural revolution. In the wake of this cultural revolution came an era of unsurpassed achievement. It fashioned lifestyles, fostered the arts and inspired the creation of *dagobas* (stupas), temples, monasteries, statues, vast manmade reservoirs and irrigation systems. Even 23 centuries after its arrival in the island, Buddhism is still preserved in its purest form: Theravada Buddhism.

Buddhism's doctrine of peace and tolerance has left its gentle mark on the land and its people. Different religions and ethnic groups live side by side in total harmony in a democratic society.

Those words from a tourist board leaflet may have been hard to swallow in the climate of terrorism that prevailed from 1983. However, the strife of the country was not a religious one.

The Buddha was named Siddhartha and was a member of a north Indian family, born about 624BC. He was married and had a son but renounced his life of ease and luxury out of compassion for human suffering. He took up a life of self-denial and, at the age of 35, on the full-moon day of Vesak, seated under a Bodhi-tree at Bodh-Gaya (in India), he realised the Ultimate Truth. He became known thereafter as the Buddha, the Enlightened or Awakened One, and began to teach the Dhamma (truth) to the world.

Buddha taught that a human being is constantly reborn into the world as a result of desire, and this is the root cause of suffering. The cycle can only be broken when one reaches nirvana or the State of Supreme Enlightenment. The Noble Eightfold Path of right belief, right aims, right speech, right action, right means of livelihood, right effort, right concentration and right meditation is the way to deliverance.

If a Buddhist renounces his home, his family and the world, he can join the Sangha (the order of monks). There is an equivalent order for women. Traditionally a monk should own only eight items of property, earn his living by begging, and rigorously follow the rules of the order.

Reader Richard Jones has this clarification:

> I feel the use of the word 'begging' to describe a monk's way of 'earning his living' is a little misleading. A monk does not 'earn his living', he adopts a lifestyle that is dependent on the lay community for the provision of the four 'requisites' (food, clothing, shelter and medicine). These are usually supplied willingly and gladly by the lay community, who regard it as a highly meritorious deed to make gifts to monks, who are living examples of high virtue and moral leadership. To describe this as 'begging' introduces connotations that degrade the status of the monk.

Is Buddhism a philosophy or a religion? The answer usually given is that it is both, for all the principles of Buddhism blend into a way of life with an ideal: nirvana. Buddhists in Sri Lanka are deeply 'religious', following rituals and beliefs and being devoted to the Buddha, not as a god but as a supremely enlightened being who shows them the way to the ideal.

In Sri Lanka there are days that are special to Buddhists, and important events are started at auspicious times as determined by a monk. Although Sri Lanka is not exclusively Buddhist, the influence is what visitors see. Hinduism, Islam and Christianity are flourishing and it is really an island of religious freedom and tolerance. Those of one faith frequently take part in the religious observances of other faiths, and all enjoy the holidays of all religions.

EDUCATION

Education is important in Sri Lanka, and it is said to have begun informally in Buddhist *pirivenas* (schools attached to temples) over 500 years before the birth of Christ and eventually formalised by the British until independence. Now it's overseen by a Ministry of Education and one of Higher Education. The proud boast that the literacy rate is around 92% does not take into account that this would be in Sinhala or Tamil and not in English, although some schools do teach through the medium of English.

Education is free at government schools and there are also fee-charging kindergarten and 'international' schools. Primary education lasts for five to six years, after which children proceed to the junior secondary level for four years, followed by two years in preparation for the General Certificate of Education exams at Ordinary Level. At 16 children can leave school or stay on to study for Advanced Level.

Top students in the A-level examinations can apply to proceed to undergraduate education in one of the country's 15 state universities.

CULTURE

The mixed heritage of today's Sri Lanka results in a varied and vibrant culture, combining influences from Buddhist, Hindu and Islamic cultures as well as colonial lifestyles. There is a thriving artistic tradition in painting, music, dance and theatre and, perhaps surprisingly, architecture. The varied building styles are easily visible on any drive through the country and add diversity to the city, suburban, coastal, agricultural and forest landscapes.

Individual Sri Lankans, whatever cultural background has influenced them, appear dedicated and determined, while preserving a somewhat orthodox outlook on life. Agriculture is regarded as a respected profession and many Sri Lankans are lifelong vegetarians or decline to eat a particular meat because of individual belief. Cricket is followed religiously. Sri Lankan culture is enhanced by frequent rest days either for religious or government decreed holidays.

TOURISM

Tourism in Sri Lanka is big business. Independent travellers who get to Sri Lanka on their own initiative may not like the idea of being lumped together with organised tourists, but for the purpose of statistics a tourist in Sri Lanka is 'a person who stays one night or more away from the usual place of residence'.

This, of course, includes even Sri Lankans who are on a few days' trip to discover the delights of their own country. Sri Lankans are great travellers and think nothing of hopping on a bus or train, or hiring a minibus with a group of friends, to see for themselves sites familiar from local television programmes. They usually don't stay in the hotels built for foreign tourists, although that is changing as empty hotels drop their prices in an effort to attract 'locals'. **World Travel Centre** (*16 Grenier Rd, off Cotta Rd, Colombo 8;* \ *011 2690500; www.totaltravel.lk*) organises coach tours of the country, mainly for Sri Lankans. There are many advertisements directed at Sri Lankan and foreign tourists about unusual accommodation and tours in the free *HIT* magazine issued every week with the *Sunday Times of Sri Lanka* (*www.sundaytimes.lk*).

The word 'tourist' is used in English by Sri Lankans to describe any obvious foreigner. Many Sri Lankans believe the word means 'white person'. I resented this pigeon-holing and even considered having a T-shirt printed with a slogan in Sinhala saying: 'I am not a tourist. I live here. Please charge me the proper price.' Now I have accepted the fact that, even after more than three decades of living in Sri Lanka, I am still a 'tourist'. Living here may have given me a better understanding of Sri Lankans than a visitor on holiday, but for Sri Lankans I will always be a guest in their country.

This insistence that tourists are different from locals gives rise to many complaints, especially when visitors are charged more than residents. Although the letter that follows was written in July 2001, nothing has changed. An English visitor, David Mansfield, expressed the feelings of many when he wrote to the *Daily News* (Colombo):

I must draw your attention to an injustice being perpetrated by your authorities on foreign tourists. Fees for tourists are much higher than for Sri Lankan natives. For example, when I visited the Botanical Gardens at Gampaha (see page 206), I had to pay Rs150 but native Sri Lankans pay only Rs15.

This practice would cause a terrible scandal if it occurred here. There would be a storm of indignation if, for example, the Tower of London tried to charge Sri Lankans £375 (about Rs71,250) for a family ticket, instead of £37.50 (about Rs7,125) which they charge everyone else.

Visitors to your country should be treated like welcome guests. Hostile, even racist, pricing will discourage them from taking their holidays in Sri Lanka, and from recommending the same to their friends. The principle is wrong even if foreign visitors all had plenty of cash (and many do not).

Although it does not seem politically correct to visitors, especially those from the West, what tourists are charged compared with what locals pay is rarely the same. Whether it is an official distinction – as at national parks where a tourist is charged the day's rupee equivalent of the admission fee quoted in US dollars and a local pays about a tenth of that price in rupees – or unofficial, as when a souvenir seller doubles his price when he sees you coming, it is an accepted way of life in Sri Lanka (and in India too). (However, the authorities do recognise a difference in tourists and foreign residents by letting those foreigners with resident visas pay the local price.)

If foreign visitors are seen as a source of income it is because that's what we are. The argument runs that the extra charged to foreigners to visit state-owned properties helps to subsidise a lower price for locals. (Perhaps it would be more palatable to visitors who feel they are being discriminated against, if only the tourist price were listed at tourist sites in English, with a small-print explanation in Sinhala/Tamil that a discount is available on request for locals.)

Tourism's history in Sri Lanka has been chequered. It began to be organised as an industry in the 1960s, and in the 1970s areas were officially designated for the development of tourist infrastructure. Typical was the organised development of Bentota as a National Tourist Resort, which spared it the higgledy-piggledy growth of the cluttered beach resorts of Hikkaduwa and Unawatuna.

Tourism did very nicely, with affluent independent travellers following in the wake of hippies to holiday in the island's sunshine. The industry was growing at a rate of 33% a year until the outbreak of ethnic troubles in 1983. Up to then many tourists were independents, staying in family-run guesthouses on the periphery of the beach-hotel compounds and making their own way around the country.

Tourists mostly stayed away during the 1980s. Those who did visit were regulars who came every year because of their contacts with locals; they knew what to expect despite the bad news. The tide turned slowly during the 1990s as new hotels were built and new marketing strategies – which saw a growth in low-cost, all-inclusive packaged group tourism – were successful.

In December 2010, the Tourism Authority proudly announced the arrival of the 600,000th tourist for 2010, a great improvement over the numbers (usually around 400,000) who had visited during the earlier years of this decade. India was the main source of tourists in 2010, with Britain second. The total number of visitors grew to one million in 2012 and the government looked to a total of 2½ million in 2016.

For many years Germany provided the most visitors and it was thanks to the German connection that tourism as an industry was able to stagger on during the difficult 1980s. Then, with the relaxation of the advance visa requirement for Indian visitors, the top source for tourist arrivals each year became India, although in years when England played cricket in Sri Lanka, there were an extra 10,000 British visitors, pitching the UK to the top of the list for visitor arrivals.

The tourist board – thinking in terms of numbers – released a five-year plan effective from 2005 to boost the number of arrivals to one million by 2010. That happened in 2012. However, while India and the new market of China were targeted to make up those numbers, the industry was aware that the upmarket (and niche) traveller – read Big Spender – does not come from those countries.

Niche tourism is seen locally as catering to visitors coming for reasons other than the beach and round-trip tour, including health and spa breaks, 'wellness' holidays, shopping or adventure holidays, or eco- and wildlife-based itineraries.

While foreign tourists, especially those from colder climes, make the beach the heart of a good holiday, domestic tourists have different priorities. They will make a trip to Sigiriya to climb the rock there, and to the Royal Botanical Gardens at

SRI LANKAN CRICKET   *Adrian Phillips*

In Sri Lanka, cricket is embraced with an intensity rarely to be found elsewhere in the world. When the international team is playing, the whole island is enthralled; when it isn't, flat pieces of wasteland are dotted with children immersed in fiercely competitive games using any equipment which comes to hand. Successful players attract adulation, and significant victories are met with lively celebration and dancing in the streets. If you visit between January and April, take the opportunity to watch a match at the Kettarama Stadium in Colombo, or at Asgiriya in Kandy, and experience the colourful atmosphere. Cricket is the first, the truest, the most enduring love of all Sri Lankan sports fans.

Such unfettered passion belies its roots in the more refined and stolid version of the game to be found in England. You are unlikely to come across stands full of trilbied spectators wrapping themselves around salmon and champagne. Nevertheless, English influence has played a conspicuous role in many of the defining moments in Sri Lanka's cricketing history. The sport was introduced by British officers in 1832, and it was against the team of an Englishman, G F Vernon, that the All Ceylon Eleven competed in their first 'unofficial Test' at Kandy in 1889. Indeed, England were the opponents in 1982 when Sri Lanka finally contested a match as a nation with Test status. It was several years before the newcomers won a Test match (against India in 1985). But in 1996 they emphatically, gloriously, announced themselves as a force on the world stage by winning the World Cup Final in Lahore.

This victory was by no means undeserved, for Sri Lanka not only play with an extravagance ideally suited to the one-day game, but have had some truly outstanding players. The courageous Anura Tennekoon, the elegant Aravinda de Silva and the nonchalant Arjuna Ranatunga all brought lustre and swagger to the team. Later players do not suffer by comparison. Mahela Jayawardene and Chaminda Vaas both set world records during 2001, and the beguiling off-spinner Muttiah Muralitharan retired in 2010 as the bowler with the highest number of career wickets, assuring his place in cricket's pantheon.

The path, though, has not always been smooth for Sri Lankan cricket. Its board has been dogged by accusations of financial mismanagement. Muralitharan has been branded a cheat and a 'javelin thrower' by some for his unorthodox bowling action. But one senses that the spirit with which the islanders approach the game will prevail in the face of such difficulties. It is just this spirit – this combination of flair and grit, commitment and pleasure – which has made the Sri Lankan team so popular abroad as well as at home.

Readers John and Elisabeth Cox wrote to add 'It was a pleasure to see that most local teams play in traditional whites', and that 'a great place to watch a match is from the Old Fort Ramparts in Galle'. Test cricket was first played again at the Galle ground in December 2007, three years after the tsunami flooded it and destroyed buildings.

Peradeniya (a favourite place for courting couples). The Dehiwela Zoo is popular with local families with young children.

The hill station of Nuwara Eliya is crowded with domestic tourists in August, the season for upcountry visits, and also during the Sinhalese/Tamil New Year holiday in April. Local devotees make pilgrimages to climb Adam's Peak between December and April, while June is traditionally the month for visiting Anuradhapura and Polonnaruwa. August is the month of *peraheras*, with the one in Kataragama attracting attention from locals while foreign tourists head for the world-famous one at Kandy.

A study under the sponsorship of the World Tourism Organisation (WTO) and the United Nations Development Programme (UNDP) was prepared by the tourist board and resulted in the Sri Lanka Tourism Master Plan of 1993. Although this is now a historical document, it is interesting for the 14 recreational zones that it identifies, and for telling us what the experts think tourists want to see.

TOURIST DEVELOPMENT REGIONS

1 **Colombo City** Mount Lavinia Beach, Dehiwela Zoological Gardens, BMICH conference centre, World Trade Centre, Fort area, parks, historic monuments, religious sites and shopping centres.

2 **Colombo region** Henerathgoda Botanical Gardens and popular watersports at Bolgoda Lake.

3 **West coast (north of Colombo)** Beaches, some old Christian and Catholic churches and festivals, and colonial fortresses in Negombo and Chilaw.

4 **West coast (south of Colombo)** Swimming, surfing, boating, Hikkaduwa Marine Sanctuary, Kechchimalai Mosque, Kalutara temple complex, mask making at Ambalangoda, low-country dancing, turtle hatcheries and *madal* fishing operations.

5 **South coast (Galle to Hambantota)** Beaches and marine activities including scuba diving at Weligama and Unawatuna, Galle Fort, Kudawella blowhole, Devalaya at Dondra, Matara star fort, archaeological museum of ancient paintings, and wildlife.

6 **Southwest inland** The Rakwana-Bulutota hill range, Sinharaja tropical rainforest, Bopatha Ella waterfalls, Wavulpane lime caves, Maduwanwela Walauwa, Samanalawewa reservoir and Ratnapura.

7 **Southeast region** Pilgrim centres of Kataragama, Tissamaharama, Maligawila, Buduruwagala, archaeological sites at Galbedda Udaganawa Habessa, Mahagama Tank, Ruhunu National Park, Bundala National Park and Kirinda.

8 **East coast region** Coral reefs and off-shore attractions like wrecks of ships for scuba diving, resorts at Passikudah and Nilaveli.

9 **East inland region** National parks, sanctuaries, reserves, pilgrim centre (Mahiyangana), thermal springs (Kanniya) and Westminster Abbey rock formation.

10 **Hill country region** Nuwara Eliya, Hakgala Botanical Gardens, Adam's Peak, Horton Plains and World's End, tea estates, spice gardens, scenic passes in Ramboda, Ginigathena, Ella and Ohiya and waterfalls.

11 **Kandy region** Sacred tooth relic of Lord Buddha at Dalada Maligawa Temple, the king's palace and audience hall, the king's and queen's museum, seven *devalayas* and Kandy Lake. The Esela perahera festival during July/August. Kandyan craft villages such as Embekke and Kalapura. Ancient temples such as Lankathilaka, Gadaladenya, Hindagala, Degaldoruwa, Gangaramaya and Dodanwela. James Taylor tea museum at Loolecondera estate, elephant bathing at Katugastota and Peradeniya Botanical Gardens.

12 **Ancient cities region** World Heritage Sites of Anuradhapura, Polonnaruwa, Dambulla and Sigiriya. Mihintale rock temple and monastic complexes; the Aukana Buddha statue. Poson festival at Anuradhapura and Mihintale. Resorts at Habarana and Sigiriya; sanctuaries and nature reserves. The reservoirs built by Sinhalese kings: Tissawewa, Kalawewa, Nuwarawewa, Parakrama Samudra and Minneriya Wewa.

13 **Northwest inland region** Ruins of old capital cities such as Panduwasnuwara, Yapahuwa and Dambadeniya. The Wilpattu National Park.

14 **Northern region** Hindu temples and festivals at Nallur, Jaffna, Kanksanthurai and in the islands. Archaeological and pilgrim sites at Nagadeepa, Kantharodai, Vallipuram, and stone inscriptions of Parakramabahu the Great. Madhu Road church, Portuguese churches and Dutch fort in Jaffna. Giant's Tank, Madhu Road and Chundikulam sanctuaries and springs at Keerimalai.

The list is heavy on what Sri Lankans are themselves proud of, rather than what would actually appeal to the international tourist.

In March 2008, the then chairman of the Tourism Advisory Committee, industry veteran Cornel Perera, told me he wanted the industry to target improved standards rather than improved numbers. His view was that Sri Lankan hotels should be encouraged to raise their standards for the guests' benefit, so that the improved quality would lead to a greater spend per person. He felt this would help the industry to improve and be competitive with other destinations, whereas simply chasing after more guests would be detrimental to the industry. Under his leadership, minimum room rates were set in 2008 for Colombo hotels, whose guests were mostly business, official or NGO-funded visitors and not holiday tourists, which resulted in an immediate rise in income, both for the hoteliers and the staff, through an increased service charge. Happier staff earning more through the service charge brought about better service, which in turn created happier guests. 'With a better product governed by higher standards,' said Perera, 'the industry will do better at maintaining around 600,000 visitors a year, than by targeting more guests than we can handle.'

The key focus, according to tourism expert Renton de Alwis, speaking prophetically in 2001, was on 'ensuring sustainable product development for tourism, enhancing its yield, bringing benefit to communities, and creating positive vibes for peace and harmony'.

I like the bit about 'positive vibes for peace and harmony'. It seems to be a philosophy left over from the hippy invasion of the 1970s. And why not? While the tourism industry works 'to build Sri Lanka's image and brand through a Sri Lanka Inc strategy', let guests, wherever they come from and for whatever reason, contribute their mite, not just in dollars and rupees, but also in helping sustain those positive vibes.

2

Practical Information

WHEN TO VISIT

The rule used to be that October to March was the best time to stay on the west coast (the sea is calm then and the beach broad). April is the spring season in the hill country, and May to September is the time to be on the east-coast beaches north and far south of Trincomalee when the sea there is at its best. Now the seasons are not so predictable, the rule can be broken. Visit whenever you can; chances are that at any time of the year you will find the climate that suits you somewhere on the island.

If the cost is the main factor, then consider the so-called 'off season' of May to September which – except for August – will yield cheaper west-coast hotel rates. The rainy season? Well, that's why May to September is cheaper on the west coast, but it seldom rains monsoon-style for the whole day, so it's worth a chance. The sea, however, is rougher on the west coast then and not pleasant (safe) for swimming, but beach hotels all have swimming pools.

Another plan would be to visit when hotels are cheaper on the east coast, which is from October to March, and stay there with tours inland. But only do that if you like 'out of season' holiday resorts. The east coast is never very lively at the best of times and you might find it as dull as the weather then, which is why it's cheaper than the west coast.

HOW LONG?

Because the attractions of Sri Lanka are so many, and the flight to get there from anywhere but India so long, allow as much time as possible to enjoy the country. The period given at the airport for a holiday visit is 30 days, which is adequate to explore and spend some time on the beach. If you only have two weeks, or less, then at least try to fit in trips by hired minibus (it's also possible to go by train to most sights) to Kandy and Galle if you want to see more of Sri Lanka than a beach or hotel buffet restaurant.

HIGHLIGHTS

To Sri Lanka's comfortable and moderate climate, rich biodiversity of flora and fauna, tropical rainforests and botanical gardens, add its varied land forms, with mountains, valleys, lakes and waterfalls contrasting with sandy, palm-fringed beaches and blue seas with coral reefs to explore.

Evidence of the island's 2,300-year-old hydraulic civilisation through manmade reservoirs remains alongside ruins of ancient cities that have been declared UNESCO World Heritage Sites. These include Anuradhapura (which flourished from the 5th century BC to the 10th century); Sigiriya (5th century); Polonnaruwa (9th to 14th century); and Kandy (16th to 19th century).

The island's glorious, and sometimes turbulent, past is represented by hundreds of dagobas, temples, monasteries and gardens, and by paintings, sculptures, carvings and ancient as well as colonial architecture, such as the World Heritage Site of Galle Fort. Religious and cultural festivals are living monuments, to be seen alongside more modern rituals, such as cricket with Sri Lanka's feisty team, and even rugby matches, horse racing and billiard tournaments.

Every visitor's 'must see' list would probably include the following:

- Temple of the Tooth, Kandy
- Royal Botanical Gardens, Peradeniya
- Elephant Orphanage, Pinnawela
- Galle Fort
- Sigiriya
- Ancient ruins at Anuradhapura and Polonnaruwa
- Tea gardens and gem mines

Of the hundreds of buildings with religious connections, those of particular interest are:

- Embekke Temple, near Kandy
- Dambulla Rock Temple
- Munneswaram, near Chilaw
- Jumi-Ul-Affar Jummah Mosque, Pettah
- Holy Trinity Church, Nuwara Eliya

SUGGESTED ITINERARIES

After a long flight you owe it to yourself to rest a day or two to recover and also to adjust to the heat and the way of life. I suggest getting the trip to Colombo over and done with on arrival, so from the airport head straight for the city, check in and relax. The next day you could explore the city and attend to any travel business (booking tours, banking, buying rail tickets, etc).

BY TRAIN Although trains do not go everywhere in Sri Lanka, they cover the most interesting parts of the island. Using trains and taxis would enable you to see most of the country without doubling back. However, the railway system in Sri Lanka suffers from lack of maintenance and journeys are an adventure rather than a comfortable way of travelling. Here are two rail/road itineraries to see a lot during a two-week stay:

Colombo to Kandy By intercity train, you could take a day train to the hill country via Nanu Oya (for Nuwara Eliya), day train to Haputale or Bandarawela, taxi to Tissamaharama, jeep hire for Yala safari, three-wheeler to Matara, train to Galle, train to Hikkaduwa or Bentota (for beach stay), train to Colombo or taxi direct to the airport for departure. This could also be done in reverse if you prefer to relax on the beach before exploring.

To include the Cultural Triangle by train and road, try:

Colombo to Anuradhapura By train, you could take a taxi to Polonnaruwa, Sigiriya and Matale, train to Kandy, train to Nanu Oya (for Nuwara Eliya), train to Bandarawela, taxi to Tissamaharama, jeep for safari to Yala, three-wheeler to Matara, train to Hikkaduwa or Bentota for beach stay, taxi to airport.

BY BUS The above itineraries can be followed using intercity and local buses instead of trains. Long-distance bus travel is even more uncomfortable than by train and is not recommended for visitors unless resiliently young and travelling with a companion, and unfazed by reckless driving, occasional roadblocks and sometimes passengers of dubious demeanour.

BY ROAD By hiring a car or minibus with a driver you are free to set your own itinerary. My suggestion for a 13-night stay is below. Reverse the itinerary if you want to start in Colombo and finish at the beach.

- Airport to west or south-coast beach resort by taxi to stay two nights
- Beach resort (via Galle) to Yala (two nights)
- Yala to Ella (one night)
- Ella to Nuwara Eliya (two nights)
- Nuwara Eliya to Kandy (one night)
- Kandy to Giritale (one night)
- Giratale to Sigiriya (one night)
- Sigiriya to Anuradhapura (one night)
- Anuradhapura to Colombo (two nights)
- Colombo to airport

TOUR OPERATORS

A number of international tour operators sell holidays to Sri Lanka in the UK. There are also many mainstream local tour operators who create and run the tours that are sold by overseas travel agents. A few international and local operators arrange specialist or unusual tours (such as ecotours and adventure sports), either for groups or couples, and these are included below with a note on their expertise.

Many hotels are owned and operated, or managed and marketed, by the same local companies. This makes reserving rooms easier since it can be done through the head office, and also guarantees a certain consistency in standard. Some options are given below.

INTERNATIONAL
Bales \0844 488 1386; www.balesworldwide.com
Cox & Kings \0845 564 1327; e cox.kings@ coxandkings.co.uk; www.coxandkings.co.uk
Elite Vacations \01707 371000; e info@ elitevacations.com; www.elitevacations.com
First Choice \0871 200 7799; www.firstchoice. co.uk
Hayes & Jarvis \0843 636 2797; www. hayesandjarvis.co.uk
Kuoni Travel \0844 488 0266; www.kuoni.co.uk
Prospect Music & Art Tours \01227 743307; e bookings@prospecttours.com; www. prospecttours.com

Sri Lanka Holidays \020 7439 0944; www. srilanka-holidays.co.uk
Thomas Cook/Airtours www.thomascook.com
Thomson Holidays \0871 231 4691; www. thomson.co.uk

SPECIALIST
Audley Travel New Mill, New Mill Lane, Witney, Oxon OX29 9SX; \01993 838000; e mail@ audleytravel.com; www.audleytravel.com. Highly recommended by Tim & Marion Gowing (whom I met in Bentota in Feb 2008) for the tour the company put together so they could stay & travel exactly where they wanted.

CaroLanka Rowden Hse, Brentnor, nr Tavistock, Devon PL19 0NG; ☏ 01822 810230; e carolanka@ btconnect.com; www.carolanka.co.uk. Deals with independent travellers & prepares individual itineraries. Also has a portfolio of villas to rent.

Discover the World Arctic Hse, 8 Bolters Lane, Banstead, Surrey SM7 2AR; ☏ 01737 214250; e enquiries@discover-the-world.co.uk; www. discover-the-world.co.uk

Explore Worldwide Nelson Hse, 55 Victoria Rd, Farnborough, Hants GU14 7PA; ☏ 0845 013 1537; e webmaster@explore.co.uk; www.explore.co.uk

Indus Tours & Travel Harrow Exchange, 2 Gayton Rd, Harrow, Middx HA1 2XU; ☏ 020 8901 7320; e holidays@industours.co.uk; www. industours.co.uk

On the Go Tours 68 North End Rd, West Kensington, London W14 9EP; ☏ 020 7371 1113; e info@onthegotours.com; www.onthegotours.com

Red Dot Tours Ltd Orchard Hse, Folly Lane, Bramham, W Yorks LS23 6RZ; ☏ 0870 231 7892; e enquiries@reddottours.com; www.reddottours. com. A great favourite for new & regular visitors to Sri Lanka because of the company's knowledge & extra care. See ad, colour page 16.

The Traveller 51 Castle St, Cirencester, Glos GL7 1QD; ☏ 01285 880931; www.the-traveller.co.uk

World Big Cat Safaris ☏ 01273 691642, (US toll free) +1 866 357 6569, (Australia toll free) +1 800 066 8890; e sales@worldbigcatsafaris.com; www. worldbigcatsafaris.com. Offers handcrafted, eco-friendly safaris to Sri Lanka, with a donation from each safari sold going towards the conservation of big cats across the globe.

LOCAL
Tour operators

Aitken Spence Travels (Pvt) Ltd 4th Flr, Aitken Spence Tower, 315 Vauxhall St, Colombo; ☏ 011 2308308; e astonline@aitkenspence.lk; www.aitkenspencetravels.com. A major tour & hotel operator; soft adventure, birdwatching, nature trails, trekking, culture & wildlife ecotourism.

Bird & Wildlife Team 71 C P de Silva Mawatha, Kaldemulla, Morutuwa; ☏ 011 3181519; e birdteam@sltnet.lk; www.birdandwildlifeteam. com. Specialising in nature tours with both birding & wildlife watching, this outfit can also arrange pelagic tours to watch marine wildlife, including whales.

Columbus Tours (Pvt) Ltd 221/2 Dharmapala Mwatha, Colombo 7; ☏ 011 2687719; e info@columbustourssrilanka.com; www. columbustourssrilanka.com. Trekking, mountain biking, rafting, rock climbing, wilderness camping.

Delair Travels (Pvt) Ltd 101 Vinayalakara Mawatha, Colombo 10; ☏ 011 7729900; e inquiries@delairtravel.com; www.delmege.com. Birdwatching, trekking, camping, paragliding, canoeing, kayaking.

Diethelm Travel Lanka (Pvt) Ltd 6th Flr, Hemas Hse, 75 Braybooke Pl, Colombo 2; ☏ 011 2313131; e inquiries@lk.diethelmtravel.com; www.hemtours.com. For birdwatching, trekking, rafting, cultural heritage & rainforest programmes.

Ecowave Travels (Pvt) Ltd Main St, Arugam Bay, Pottuvil; ☏ 0094633730404; e info@ ecowavetravels.lk; www.ecowavetravels.lk. See ad, page 286.

Jetwing Eco Holidays Jetwing Hse, 46/26 Navam Mawatha, Colombo 2; ☏ 011 2381201; e enquiries@jetwingeco.com; www.jetwingeco. com. Part of the Jetwing group which has its own hotels of character; good for birdwatching, wildlife safaris, expeditions, adventure sports, cultural travel. Jetwing also operates www. srilankaluxury.com as a booking website for luxury properties & tours & is behind the cut-price Hotel J (*www.hotelj.lk*), the first of which opened in Negombo in 2013.

J F Tours & Travels 58 Havelock Rd, Colombo 5; ☏ 011 2589402; e inquiriesjft@sltnet.lk. Runs tours on the *Viceroy Special* steam train, & private rail tours as well as wildlife & nature tours in 4x4 vehicles & limousine transfers. Also specialises in arranging upmarket guesthouse, villa & bungalow holidays & boutique hotels. Operates Cranford Lodge near Bandarawela & Galapita Eco Lodge.

Leopard Safaris (Pvt) Ltd 45 Colombo Rd, Katunayake; m 071 3314004, 077 7314004; e noel@leopardsafaris.com; www.leopardsafaris. com. Not just leopards & other wildlife but unique mobile tented accommodation, gourmet camp meals & especially adapted 4x4s for the personalised safaris escorted by the personable Noel Rodrigo, former Sri Lanka motorcycle & 4x4 rally champion, ex-Sri Lankan Airlines' purser & wildlife photographer. An extraordinary experience in capable hands for getting to know Sri Lanka in the wild. See ad, colour page 16.

Quickshaws Tours Ltd 3 Kalinga Pl, Colombo 5; 011 2583133; e tours@quickshaws.com; www. quickshaws.com. Individual attention for nature tours, trekking, diving, birdwatching, cultural tours.

Red Dot Tours 011 7895810; e enquiries@ reddottours.com; www.reddottours.com. Good for little-known & charming retreats & individually planned tours to suit all tastes.

Serendib Leisure Management Ltd 5th Flr, Hemas Hse, 75 Braybrooke Pl, Colombo 2; 011 4790500; e inquiries@serendibleisure.lk; www.serendibleisure.com. With its own hotels, a good company for birdwatching, jungle safaris, snorkelling, surfing, diving, cultural ecotourism.

Sri Lanka In Style 011 2396666; e holidays@ srilankainstyle.com; www.srilankainstyle.com. An agency that combines the offers of some upmarket companies to arrange a holiday that is 'unique, independent, unexpected, exotic, memorable', taking in the best of Sri Lanka whether by *Viceroy Special* or balloon, staying in luxury private villas or in tented safaris.

Tangerine Tours Ltd 236 Galle Rd, Colombo 3; 011 2422518; e tangerinetours2@mi.com. lk; www.tangerinetours.com. A hotel group with arrangements for trekking, hiking, watersports, birdwatching.

Tea Trails (Pvt) Ltd 46/38 Nawam Maratha, Colombo 2; 011 7745700; e manager@teatrails. com; www.teatrails.com. Tours to plantation bungalows – each one unique – enabling guests to journey on a time trail, from British-colonial to post-colonial Sri Lanka.

Walkers Tours Ltd 117 Sir Chittampalam A Gardiner Mawatha (Cinnamon Lakeside Hotel), Colombo 2; 011 2306306; e info@ walkerstours.com; www.walkerstours.com. A major tour operator with programmes for trekking, birdwatching, deep-sea fishing, diving, cycling.

Wayfarers Ltd 6 Boyd Pl, Colombo 3; 011 2306306; e wayfar@eol.lk; www.wayfarers-srilanka.com. A small family company good for plantation-bungalow stays as well as white-water rafting, camping, jungle treks, safaris & local homestays.

World Travel Centre 16 Grenier Rd, off Cotta Rd, Colombo 8; 011 2690500; e tours@wtccolombo; www.totaltravel.lk or www.coachtourssrilanka. com. Pioneers of tours for locals, operating special tours to Kandy, Haputale & Knuckles for camping & wildlife, & adventure tours for visitors too.

Hotel operators

Aitken Spence Hotels Level 5, Aitken Spence Tower II, 315 Vauxhall St, Colombo 2; 011 2308408; e ashmres@aitkenspence.lk; www. aitkenspencehotels.lk. Has luxury, moderate-rate & some all-inclusive properties: Heritance Kandalama, Dambulla; Heritance Tea Factory Hotel, Kandapola; Heritance Ahungalla; Earl's Regency & Hilltop hotels, Kandy; Bandarawela Hotel; The Sands, Kalutara; & Ayurveda Maha Gedara Beruwala.

Amaya Resorts & Spas Level 27, Unit 3, East Tower, World Trade Centre, Colombo; 011 4767800; e sales@amayaresorts.com; www. amayaresorts.com

Asia Leisure 21-1 West Tower, Echelon Sq, World Trade Centre, Colombo 1 011 5769500; e marketing@asialeisure.lk; www.asialeisure.lk. A new hotel investment company with 3 medium-range smart, small hotels (Park Street Hotel, Colombo; The River House, Balapitiya; Tamarind Hill, Galle), & scheduled to open 2 new hotels (in Balapitiya & Wadduwa) early 2014.

Ceylon Hotels Corporation Regency Wing, Galle Face Hotel, 2 Galle Road, Colombo 2; 011 5585858; e information@ceylonhotels.net; www.ceylonhotelscorporation.com. Formerly government owned, now private-sector (under the umbrella of the Galle Face Hotel-owning company); runs resthouses under different names at Ambepussa, Belihuloya, Dambulla, Habarana, Hanwella, Kitulgala, Medawachchiya, Pussellawa, Polonnaruwa, Sigiriya & Weligama, Hotel Mihintale, Ella Resthouse, the Lake, Polonnaruwa & the Heritage Tissamaharama. Also in its portfolio are the Surf Hotel, Bentota, the Hotel Suisse & Queen's Hotel in Kandy & a restaurant (Avanhala) near Ambepussa.

Colombo Fort Hotels Ltd 53 1/1 Sir Baron Jayatilleke Mawatha, Colombo 1; 011 2381644; e marketing@forthotels.lk; www.forthotels.lk. A diversified group running 3 popular hotels: Club Palm Bay, Marawila; Sigiriya Village, & The Palms, Beruwela; as well as 2 eco-cabins: Hermitage Rock Cabin & Stonycliff Log Cabin at Kotagala & 4 tea-plantation bungalows for paying guests: Thotalagala, Sherwood, St Andrew's & Rosita.

Connaissance Holdings Level 12-02, East Tower, World Trade Centre, Echelon Sq, Colombo 1; 011 4706400; e cdctrv@connaissance.lk; www. connaissance.lk. Owners &/or operators of the

Amaya Reef, Amaya Lake & Amaya Hills, Amaya Hunas Falls & other resorts (e sales@amayaresorts. com; www.amayaresorts.com).

Jetwing Hotels Ltd Jetwing Hse, 46/26 Navam Mawatha, Colombo 2; ☎011 2345700; e hotels@jetwinghotels.com; www.jetwing.com. For hotels of character: Lighthouse Hotel & Spa, Galle; St Andrew's, Nuwara Eliya; the Warwick Gardens bungalow in Ambewela &, in Negombo, The Beach, Blue & Lagoon & Ayurveda Pavilions hotels. Also the ecotourist resort of Vil Uyana, Sigiriya & the new brand name 'Hotel J' for lower-priced rooms.

John Keells Hotels Cinnamon Lakeside Hotel, Colombo 2; ☎011 2306600 e reservations@ johnkeellshotels.com; www.johnkeellshotels.

com. Operate good-value, top- & medium-rate hotels rebranded as Cinnamon properties (www.cinnamonhotels.com): Cinnamon Grand, Cinnamon Lakeside (both in Colombo); Cinnamon Citadel, Kandy, Cinnamon Lodge, Habarana; & Cinnamon Yala; & Chaaya properties (www.chaayahotels.com) including: Chaaya Tranz Hotel, Hikkaduwa; Chaaya Blu, Trincomalee; & Chaaya Village, Habarana & Bentota Beach Hotel, Bentota.

Tangerine Group 236 Galle Rd, Colombo 3; ☎011 2422518; e info@tangerinehotels.com; www.tangerinehotels.com. Comprises hotels from moderate to luxury rate: Royal Palms & Tangerine Beach hotels, Kalutara; Grand Hotel, Nuwara Eliya; & Nilaveli Beach Hotel, Trincomalee.

TOURIST INFORMATION The head office of the successor to Sri Lanka Tourism and the Ceylon Tourist Board is the **Sri Lanka Tourism Development Authority** (*80 Galle Rd, Colombo 3;* ☎ *011 2437055;* e *info@srilanka.travel; www.srilankatourism. org*). Tourism promotion is currently handled by the **Sri Lanka Tourism Promotion Bureau** (*80 Galle Rd, Colombo 3;* ☎ *011 2426900;* e *info@srilanka.travel; www. srilanka.travel.net*) although the tourism bureaucracy was undergoing changes at press time. There is an information centre (☎*011 2437059;* ⊕ *08.30–16.15 Mon–Fri, closed Sat, Sun & public holidays*) in the building, which is opposite the Cinnamon Grand (formerly Lanka Oberoi) Hotel. There are also information centres in Kandy and at the Bandaranaike International Airport (☎ *011 2252411, ext 6652*). International addresses are as follows:

📧 **France** Ms Marie Caroline Willaume; ☎+33 01 53 25 04 25; e mcaroline.willaume@ interfacetourism.com

📧 **Germany** Mr Tobias Bandara; ☎+49 89 2366 2111; e t.bandara@srilanka.travel.com

📧 **India** Mr Sanjit Shastri; ☎+91 22 666 11339; e sanjit@beehivecommunications.com

📧 **Japan** Sri Lanka Tourist Promotion Bureau; ☎+81 47441 7207; e director@srilanka-kankou. travel

📧 **Middle East** Mr Ajay Rajguru; ☎+97 1433 2088; e info@biz.com.ae

📧 **UK** Sri Lanka Tourism Promotion Bureau, 1 (3rd Flr) Devonshire Sq, London EC2M 4WD; ☎+44 845 880 6333; e infouk@srilanka.travel

📧 **USA** Sri Lanka Tourism Promotion Bureau, 379 (6th Flr) Thornall St, Edison, NJ 08837; ☎+1 732 608 2676; e dilan@srilankanusa.com

RED TAPE

VISAS Entry into Sri Lanka has been streamlined for the cyber age. Whatever your nationality you can now get an Electronic Travel Authorisation (ETA) online that guarantees you an entry permit as a tourist for 30 days upon arrival. The details and the current cost (payable online by credit card) are available on the website www. eta.gov.lk. An ETA is required by every visitor, except those holding Singaporean or Maldivian passports, or those who are in transit. If you haven't got an ETA (it's a document you must download and print to show at the immigration counter) then you will have to join a tiresome queue at a special desk upon arrival to pay your fee and get one there.

At the immigration desk, a sticker will be placed in your passport showing until what date you are allowed to remain in Sri Lanka.

If you intend to stay longer than 30 days it helps to have obtained a visa for the required period from a Sri Lankan consulate abroad before arriving. However, extensions up to 90 days from the date of arrival are possible upon application in Colombo. If you are visiting on business then a visa is required from the Sri Lanka mission in your home country.

Staying on It is possible to extend a 30-day-visit visa on application in person to the visit-visa section of the **Department of Immigration and Emigration** (*41 Ananda Rajakaruna Mawatha, Punchi Borella, Colombo 10;* ⍉ *011 5329000;* e *controller@immigration.gov.lk; www.immigration.gov.lk*). The department has an excellent website explaining the procedures and fees and has a map showing how to get to its office by train or bus. Visa application forms can be downloaded from the site. An extension of a visit visa up to 90 days from date of arrival is possible. In all cases you are expected to show a confirmed air ticket out of Sri Lanka and evidence of having exchanged enough funds (based on an average of US$30 a day) for the entire length of your proposed stay, not just for the days you have already spent in the country. Take along the exchange receipts.

There are forms to fill in and rupees to pay – the fees differ according to your nationality; Brits pay more than Germans. In theory you are not supposed to have extensions totalling more than six months in any one year. Some travellers who long to linger in Sri Lanka pop over to India or the Maldives for a few days, then apply for another ETA to be granted another 30-day permit on entry. However, now it's all computerised, the number of visits a traveller makes to Sri Lanka is monitored very carefully.

A residence-visa scheme with a (renewable) two-year validity especially for retirees was introduced in 2008 requiring a fixed bank deposit in Sri Lanka of US$15,000 and a guaranteed income remitted from overseas of US$1,500 per month.

Longer, leading to permanent, residence is possible in conjunction with an investment (upwards from US$150,000) in a Board of Investment (BOI)-approved project. However, if you are a foreign professional with a skill unavailable in, or of benefit to, Sri Lanka, and can show a monthly flow into Sri Lanka of at least US$1,500, a resident guest visa (renewable very year) is possible. Information is available from the Board of Investment (*Ministry of Economic Development, 464/A T B Jaya Mawatha, Colombo 10;* ⍉ *011 2681973;* e *edmediaunit@gmail.com; www.investsrilanka.com*).

A new service has opened which is a boon both to tourists wanting to extend their stay and to others who need visas or extensions for various reasons. **Migration Lanka Services (Pvt) Ltd** (MLS) (*5a Aloe Av, off Galle Rd, Colombo 3;* ⍉ *011 2375972;* e *service@migrationlanka.com; www.migrationlanka.com*) provides advice and submits applications for tourist visas, other purpose visit visas, multiple-entry visas, residence visas and permanent residence visas as well as for all types of extensions. A service fee starting at Rs5,000 is charged depending on the visa or extension required on top of the fees levied by the Department of Immigration. Since a personal appearance at the immigration office is not required, this is a great help for genuine applicants.

EMBASSIES AND HIGH COMMISSIONS

If you intend to stay for more than 30 days, even only on holiday, it would be advisable (although not obligatory) to register your presence and address with your home country's embassy or high commission. Some of the prominent ones are listed here.

There are many international organisations represented in Sri Lanka. Some of them are included below. Other international agencies include the Asian Development Bank, World Bank, United Nations Industrial Development Programme, International Monetary Fund, United Nations Development Programme, World Health Organisation (WHO), Food and Agriculture Organisation, International Labour Organisation, Colombo Plan Bureau, South-Asia Co-operative Environment Programme, International Water Management Institute and Commonwealth Development Corporation.

EMBASSIES

❸ Australia High Commission of Australia, 21 Gregory's Rd, Colombo 7; ☎ 011 2463200; e austcom@sltnet.lk; www.srilanka.embassy.gov.au

❸ Canada High Commission of Canada, 33A 5th Lane, Colombo 3; ☎ 011 5226232; e clmbo-cs@international.gc.ca; www.canadainternational.gc.ca/sri_lanka/visas/index

❸ France Embassy of France, 89 Rosmead Pl, Colombo 7; ☎ 011 2639400; e ambfrclb@sltnet.lk; www.ambafrance-lk.org

❸ Germany Embassy of the Federal Republic of Germany, 40 Alfred Hse Av, Colombo 3; ☎ 011 2580431; www.colombo.diplo.de

❸ India High Commission of India, 36–38 Galle Rd, Colombo 3; ☎ 011 2421605; e hc.colombo@mea.gov.in; www.hcicolombo.org

❸ Italy Embassy of Italy, 55 Jawatta Rd, Colombo 5; ☎ 011 2588388; e ambasciata.colombo@esteri.it; www.ambcolombo.esteri.it

❸ Japan Embassy of Japan, 20 Gregory's Rd, Colombo 7; ☎ 011 2693831; e cultujpn@co.mofa.go.jp; www.lk.emb-japan.go.jp

❸ Netherlands Royal Embassy of the Netherlands, 25 Torrington Av, Colombo 7; ☎ 011 2510200

❸ Norway Royal Embassy of Norway, 34 Ward Pl, Colombo 7; ☎ 011 2469611

❸ Russian Federation Embassy of the Russian Federation, 62 Sir Ernest de Silva Mawatha, Colombo 7; ☎ 011 2573555; e rusemb@itmin.net; www.russianembassy.net

❸ Switzerland Embassy of Switzerland, 63 Gregory's Rd, Colombo 7; ☎ 011 2695117; e col.vertretung@eda.admin.ch; www.eda.admin.ch

❸ UK British High Commission, 389 Baudhaloka Mawatha, Colombo 7; ☎ 011 5390639; e colombo.general@fco.gov.uk; http://ukinsrilanka.fco.gov.uk/en/

❸ USA Embassy of the United States of America, 210 Galle Rd, Colombo 3; ☎ 011 2498500; e consularcolombo@state.gov; www.srilanka.usembassy.gov

ORGANISATIONS

The British Council 49 Alfred Hse Gdns, Colombo 3; ☎ 011 4521521; e info.lk@britishcouncil.org; www.britishcouncil.org/srilanka.htm

European Commission Delegation of the European Commission, 26 Sir Marcus Fernando Mawatha, Colombo 7; ☎ 011 2674413

United Nations 202–4 Bauddhaloka Mawatha, Colombo 7; ☎ 011 2580691; e info.lk@undp.org; www.un.lk

GETTING THERE AND AWAY

BY AIR Colombo airport (CMB) is served by various airlines from Europe, the Middle and Far East, and India. The major carriers are SriLankan (UL – the only one with non-stop flights from London), BA (via Maldives), Emirates (EK – with aircraft change in Dubai). Other airlines with scheduled flights include Aeroflot (SU), Air Arabia (G9), Air Asia (AK), Air India Express (IX), Air Italy (I9), Air Italy Polska (AEI), Air Sahara (S2), Austrian (OS), Cathay Pacific (CX), China Eastern Airlines (MU), Condor (DE), Eurocypria (ECA), Erofly (GJ), Etihad (EY), First Choice Air (TOM), Fly Dubai (FZ), Gulf Air (GF), Indian (IC), Iran Air (IR), Jet (9W), Jet Lite (S2), Kingfisher (IT), Kuwait (KU), LTU (LT), Malaysian (MH), Martin Air (MP), Mihin Lanka (MJ) (see below), Oman (WY), Qatar (QR), Royal Jordanian (RJ), Saudi Arabian (SV), Singapore (SQ), Spice Jet (SG), State Transport Co Russia (FV), Thai (TG) and Turkish (TK).

To Mattala Rajapaksa International Airport (HRI) there are at press time flights by Fly Dubai (from Dubai) and SriLankan (from Riyadh, Bangkok & Male').

The national carrier is **SriLankan Airlines**, descended from Air Ceylon, which became Air Lanka in 1979. A new name was introduced in 1999 after the management was taken over by Emirates Airlines of Dubai on an agreement which expired in March 2008. Then it became wholly Sri Lankan managed. It has an all-Airbus fleet with direct services to London, Paris, Rome, Frankfurt and Moscow; Singapore, Bangkok, Hong Kong, Shanghai, Beijing, Canton, Kuala Lumpur and Tokyo; Kuwait, Damman, Riyadh, Jeddah, Doha, Abu Dhabi, Muscat and Dubai; Malé (Maldives), and a network linking Colombo with cities in India, including Bangalore, Chennai (Madras), Delhi,

Kochi (Cochin), Trichy, Trivandrum, Mumbai (Bombay) and Karachi. The planes are comfortable with each seat having individual in-flight movie screens and controls, including a telephone. Business class (there is no first) has reclining seats in a 2x2x2 layout, which means it is more spacious than its former partner airline, Emirates, whose business class is 2x3x2. The cabin crew are all Sri Lankan and passengers are greeted on boarding with the traditional *ayubowan* ('may you have long life'). If you have a chance to talk with the crew you will surely enjoy the flight since they are great ambassadors for their country.

There is also a budget airline operated by a government concern, **Mihin Air (MJ)** which was started in 2007 and subsequently closed down for a few months for a revamp and which at press time was operating scheduled flights to Dubai, Sharjah, Bahrain and India (Varanasi, Gaya, Madurai and Trichy), as well as to Dhaka and Jakarta.

Contact details of the main carriers in Sri Lanka are listed below. To Colombo there are one-stop Emirates flights (change planes in Dubai) between Houston, New York, San Francisco, São Paulo and Toronto; otherwise, travellers from America have to fly via Europe, or via Tokyo or Singapore, as do travellers from Australia and New Zealand.

✈ **Aeroflot** 7A Sir Ernest de Silva Mawatha, Colombo 7; ☏011 2671201; www.aeroflot.ru

✈ **Air Arabia – Nawaloka Aviation (Pvt) Ltd** General Sales Agent for Air Arabia in Sri Lanka, Air Arabia Bldg, 73 Sir James Peiris Mawatha, Colombo 2; ☏011 5777999; e reservations@nawalokaav.com

✈ **Air India** Bristol Complex, 4 Bristol St, Colombo 1; ☏011 2323136 e mgria@sltnet.lk

✈ **Air India Express** 108 Y M B A Bldg, Sir Baron Jayathilaka Mawatha, Colombo 1; ☏011 2422249; e AirIndiaExpress.Airport@aviation.hayleys.com

✈ **British Airways** Cinnamon Lakeside Hotel, Sir Chittampalam Gardiner Mawatha, Colombo 2; ☏011 4767767

✈ **Cathay Pacific** 186 Vauxhall St, Colombo 2; ☏011 2334145

✈ **China Airlines** 35 Edward Lane, Colombo 3; ☏011 2598184; e randy@pership.com

✈ **Emirates** GSA office: 7th Flr, Hemas Hse, 75 Braybrooke Pl, Colombo 2; ☏011 4704070; www. emirates.com/lk. Serves Colombo via Dubai (about

4hrs' flying time). The stopover in Dubai to change planes usually takes about 3hrs.

✈ **Etihad Airways** Level 3, WTC, Colombo 1; ☏011 4766500; e cmbtkt@ethiad.ae

✈ **Flydubai** No. 28, St Michael's Road, Colombo 3; ☏011 2371000; e flydubai.assistance@ travelguard.com

✈ **Gulf Air** 1 Justice Akbar Mawatha, Colombo 2; ☏011 2359888; e gulfaircmb@keells.com

✈ **Jet Airways** 1 Justice Akbar Mawatha, Colombo 2; ☏011 2475375; e jetairways.mal@ keells.com

✈ **Kuwait Airways** South Asian Travels Ltd, Ceylinco Hse, 69 Janadhipathi Mawatha, Colombo 1; ☏011 2445531; e cmb@kuwaitairways.com

✈ **Malaysian Airlines** 81 York St, Colombo 1; ☏011 2344322; e malaysiaairlines@hemas.com

✈ **Mihin Air** EML Bldg, 61 W A D Ramanayake Mawatha, Colombo 2; ☏(24hrs daily) 011 2002255; e info@mihinlanka.com; www. mihinlanka.com

✈ **Oman Air** 400 Deans Rd, Colombo 10; ☎011 4462222; e CMB.CTOStaff@omanair.com

✈ **Qatar Airways** WTC, West Tower, 2nd Flr, Colombo 1; ☎011 5570000; e cmb-resv@lk.qatarairways.com

✈ **Royal Jordanian** 40A Cumaratunge Mawatha, Colombo 3; ☎011 2301621; e CMBTS@RJ.com

✈ **Saudi Arabian Airlines** 6 Joseph Lane, Bambalapitiya, Colombo 4; ☎011 2577241

✈ **Singapore Airlines** 315 Vauxhall St, Colombo 2; ☎011 2499690; e lk_feedback@singaporeair.com.sg

✈ **Spice Jet** 140A Vauxhall St, Colombo 2; ☎011 4732489; e spicejet@jetwing.lk

✈ **SriLankan Airlines** [76 B1] Ticket Office, Level 3, East Tower, World Trade Centre, Echelon Sq, Colombo 1; ☎(reservations) 019 7335500; (flight information) 019 7335555 or 019 7331377; e ulweb@srilankan.aero; www.srilankan.aero. There are also ticket offices at the BIA airport (☎24hrs daily 019 7332424) & at Galle (☎091 2246942), Kandy (☎081 2232495), Ratnapura (☎045 5678787), & Trincomalee (☎026 2221101).

✈ **Thai Airways** JAIC Hilton, Union Pl, Colombo 2; ☎011 2307100 e info@thaiairways.com.lk

✈ **Turkish Airlines** 35 Edward Lane, Colombo 3; ☎011 2598184 e CMBSales@thy.lk

Air fares The availability of discount tickets to Sri Lanka depends on demand (or lack of it) and can best be researched through the travel advertisements in newspapers of the country from which you are flying to Sri Lanka. Colombo used to be a good place to purchase onward airline tickets but this is no longer the case, so come with your return or onward ticket (as required by immigration anyway).

As an example of airfares, the website of SriLankan Airlines (*www.srilankan.com*) was quoting a round-trip economy-class fare from London to Colombo of £561.65, and a business-class return ticket for £2,038.65 for travel in January 2014.

Arrival On the plane you should be given an Arrivals Card prior to disembarkation. If not, you will find one in the arrivals hall and have to fill it out while passengers with ready-filled cards get ahead of you in the queue. The usual passport information is required. You must give your address in Sri Lanka. If you don't have one because you haven't made a hotel reservation, choose a hotel from this book and put that down as your hotel address. If you are Sri Lankan you no longer need an Arrivals Card.

The main international airport is at Katunayake, 32km from Colombo, and known as the **Bandaranaike International Airport** (*flight enquiries* ☎*011 2252861 or 019 7335555; www.airport.lk*). The airport has undergone massive extension work with the happy result that arriving and departing queues now flow smoothly and most planes are served by corridor connections, instead of passengers having to be ferried to and from planes by bus. But this means a long walk from aircraft to immigration so keep hand luggage bearable as there are no hand-luggage trolleys. The first trolleys you'll see are hidden away in the duty-free shopping mall; if you find one you'll need to take an elevator with it down to the customs hall; otherwise there is an escalator (no trolleys permitted).

To reduce the agony of arrival after a long flight, the **Silk Route Lounge** (with complimentary drink and snack, newspapers, internet and television) is located at the arrival terminal. Passengers who subscribe to this service in advance of their arrival (☎ *011 2256067; www.airport.lk; US$50*) will be met as they leave the aircraft and escorted through immigration and customs, with porter assistance available, and have the opportunity to relax and freshen up in the lounge. This service is also available for departing passengers with a separate VIP check-in lounge where luggage is collected by the lounge's porters at the kerb and taken the few steps to the check-in desk. Passport formalities are also handled in the lounge, after which passengers are escorted, away from the crowds, into the main departure lounge, where Executive Lounge access is available at US$15. The cost of using the Silk Route Lounge on departure is US$50 (payable in advance online) but there is no charge for SriLankan Airlines business-class passengers.

In the no-man's-land of the arrivals/departure area (which means you must either have arrived from a flight, be in transit, or have checked in for one) is the airport's **Serenediva Transit Hotel** (\ *019 7334111;* e *serenediva@srilankancatering.com; www.srilankancatering.com;* **$$**). Opened in September 2010 and managed by Sri Lankan Catering (the SriLankan Airlines-owned company that provides the food on contracted airlines using the airport), it has 24 air-conditioned rooms and is located on the second level above the main pier of the airport terminal. Rooms of various sizes (single, double, family) are available on six-hour occupancy, starting at US$35. They all have satellite television with flight information, IDD telephone, complimentary tea/coffee, Wi-Fi high-speed internet access, laundry and dry cleaning and 24-hour room service.

The peak time for arrivals is 05.00 to 10.00 with Sunday being the quietest day. For the long hike along the corridor to the terminal there are moving walkways, as well as toilets at strategic points. Wheelchair passengers who have requested wheelchair assistance in advance will be met at the plane's doors. At the immigration desk, observe the yellow line and don't cross it until the previous passenger has been processed. A computer-generated sticker giving the date of arrival will be put in your passport showing how many days you are permitted to stay.

There is a mall of duty-free shops for arriving passengers after the immigration desks. These cater for returning Sri Lankans, which is why there are domestic appliances like refrigerators and televisions on sale. There are also two bright supermarket-style stores side by side stacked with duty-free alcohol and perfumes but no cigarettes since the importation of duty-free cigarettes, cigars and tobacco is officially not permitted. (And there is only a limited range of brands of international cigarettes available in the country, so smokers usually end up trying the locally manufactured product.) There are some (free) luggage trolleys available on this level but most of them are to be found in the ground-floor baggage hall, after descending to it by escalators or elevator. Luggage is delivered on one of the carousels. If it doesn't turn up, there are counters to register reports of lost baggage. Porters are available. If you can't find your luggage on the designated conveyor belt, look around all sides of the belt carefully as some zealous baggage handlers might have pulled your bags off to make a separate pile.

Customs The customs (*www.customs.gov.lk*) desks are at the exit to the baggage hall. If you have only hand luggage, you will be spared the agony of waiting for your baggage and can head straight for the green channel. There are frequent checks, even at the green channel, so be prepared to open luggage on request or to put it in the X-ray scanner. The duty-free allowance for tourists is: 1½ litres of spirits and two bottles of wine (Campari and Pernod pass as wine); 2oz perfume and ¼ litre of eau de toilette; no tobacco products.

The smuggling of drugs can lead to the death penalty and the authorities are very watchful. Unlimited amounts of foreign exchange can be brought into the country but if it's more than US$10,000 in cash you should declare it to customs – so you can prove you brought the cash in with you if you want to take it out again.

Arrivals hall From the baggage/customs hall you emerge into a hall where there are bank counters and then process to the main arrivals hall, where there is an official tourist information counter (\ *011 2252411;* ⏲ *24hrs*) and where members of the public (who have bought an entry ticket for Rs150) greet incoming passengers. This is where you will also find representatives of hotels waiting for you with your name on a board, if you have pre-booked with them, or your tour rep will be there gathering his flock. If you want to make a hotel booking at the designated desks, that is possible and the hotel rep will arrange a hotel car to drive you there. If you do not have transport pre-arranged through your tour operator or hotel, it is advisable to do it at the official taxi desk before you leave the terminal rather than get into a haggling match with the freelance drivers hanging around outside.

If you are **going independently to Colombo**, head down the mall-like corridor to the exit. There is no dedicated airport bus service but there are some public buses. To find one, when you get out of the exit mall, turn left and walk about 200m to cut around the car park and exit the airport property. Cross the access roads and gardens to reach the main road. There is a shelter on the opposite side for buses to Colombo. Bus No 187 goes there and the journey will take more than an hour and will be quite an experience. It is not a good idea to try it unless you are feeling fit and really have the lightest and smallest of luggage.

At press time there was no dedicated airport passenger train service in operation.

Once you start walking away from the airport terminal you will be accosted by all manner of 'helpful' people, offering transport and hotels and doing their best to convince you that they have been sent especially to meet you. If the offer of transport by one of these hustlers sounds appealing, inspect the vehicle – and the driver (he may not be the person you negotiate with) – first. If you have doubts about either, change your mind. Expect to pay at least Rs2,500 to Colombo.

If you fly in on a pre-paid package tour, the transfer from the airport to your hotel will be included. Look for the tour operator representative with a sign board indicating the tour company as you emerge from customs. You may be given a car to yourself or be put on a coach that seems to stop at every hotel but your own for the next three hours. At least it's a way of seeing the coastal resorts at no extra charge.

Some independent travellers have complained that as they are about to load their luggage on to a taxi, a person pretending to be a porter grabs the bags and tries to do it for them. Accept that service and you will end up paying for it. Just be firm and tell the person offering help that you will load your bags yourself. The real porters have identification vests and don't hang around for passengers leaving the airport, although they are available in the baggage hall for arriving passengers.

Departure Reconfirmation of return reservations is no longer required. If you have a reservation and don't intend to use it, remember to cancel it so that someone on the waiting list can travel instead. The check-in procedure is operated by SriLankan Airlines on behalf of all carriers. Economy-class passengers should check in three hours ahead of the departure time shown on the ticket (two hours ahead for business class). Although it adds to your total journey time, it is worth checking in early to be ahead of the queues (including one to get into the airport) and to make sure you get a seat (flights are routinely overbooked). Both SriLankan and Emirates Airlines have an online check-in facility on their websites, which means that if you check in online you have to get to the airport 90 minutes, instead of three hours, before departure.

There are more options for getting to the airport than getting from it. Many independent travellers take the train from their beach resort to Colombo and then catch a taxi or a three-wheeler to the airport. If you have a lot of luggage, travelling by bus will not be comfortable, nor is it reliable or convenient since it will take a long time. All the major Colombo hotels have their own liveried taxis with fares to the airport from Rs2,500. It can be done for less in a privately hired taxi. From resorts where transfer is not provided by the tour operator, minibus taxis can be hired. Official drivers should have a rate sheet so best to check that and then see what unofficial drivers (ie: not attached to a hotel) will charge, and decide accordingly. With the new expressway link between Colombo and the airport that was due to open in October 2013, the journey time and travel experience should be greatly improved.

If you want to stay close to the airport the night before an early morning departure there is a somewhat seedy hotel 100m from the airport entrance; the **Goodwood Plaza Hotel** (*55 AC rooms; Airport Rd, Katunayake;* ☏ *011 2252561;* e *hotelgoodwood@ mymail.lk;* **$$**). Much more upmarket with a free shuttle service (five-minute drive) to the airport is the **The Gateway Hotel Airport Garden** (formerly Taj Airport Garden Hotel) (*120 AC rooms; 234/238 Negombo Rd, Seeduwa;* ☏ *011 2252950;* e *gateway.colombo@tajhotels.com; www.thegatewayhotels.com;* **$$$**). Another option is to spend the last night at Negombo where there are popular package holiday resorts that also accommodate independent tourists, as well as boutique-type guesthouses and from where it's only a 20-minute drive to the airport.

From the kerbside drop-off you have to queue to be frisked by Air Force personnel. The trick here is to spurn the luggage trolley and hire a porter instead (officially Rs100 a bag but worth double). He knows the drill and somehow gets you to the head of the queue and speedily through all the other queues. He will steer you through the baggage X-ray and to the right check-in desk and then wait with you to unload the luggage on to the airline scales. Only passengers with tickets to travel or those with entry permits (bought for Rs150 at a nearby counter) are allowed into the airport building.

If for some reason you don't have an airline ticket, there is a SriLankan Airlines ticket office, open 24 hours, by the entrance to the check-in security area and that's where you can buy one. There's another SriLankan Airlines office there where passengers who have requested wheelchair or other assistance must wait while ground-staff personnel come to help. (Wheelchairs are only available if ordered in advance of arrival.)

There is then a long covered mall to the public lobby where last-minute shopping can be done (there is a supermarket, a counter catering to travellers' needs, a nut shop and a snack counter) while waiting to pass through the barrier to the check-in counters. Friends who have come to see you off can accompany you only this far. (Before reaching the departure terminal there is also a kind of stadium overlooking the runway where families congregate to watch flights depart.)

The validity of your ticket will be checked by security before you are allowed to approach the airline check-in desks. All baggage must be put through the X-ray scanners, not for security purposes but for customs officers to see if you are taking anything out of the country illegally (such as a 2,000-year-old Buddha statue).

At busy times there will be long queues to check in, even at the dedicated desks for business- and first-class passengers and airline club members. Departing foreign passengers no longer need to fill in a Departure Card, but Sri Lankans do. The embarkation tax is no longer payable in cash as it would have been included in your ticket cost. Your boarding pass and passport will be checked again before you are allowed into the main departure hall. Luggage trolleys cannot be used once you have checked in and the porter, if you have one, will whisk it away.

The secure area (don't go there until your flight is called) is on the right for some flights but most now use the departure gates at the end of the long walkway upstairs. There are a few shops but you'll find the new and rather glamorous ones are upstairs. As well as a self-service section with perfume, cigarettes, liquor and confectionery, there are shops selling tea, jewellery, electronics and books and there's even a branch of Odel, Colombo's premier department store. Purchases can be paid for only with foreign currency or credit card.

As well as a café specialising in coffees, there are dedicated lounges for premium-class passengers, including a smart one exclusively for SriLankan Airlines business-class passengers. This has a free ayurveda massage parlour, eight internet computers, four day rooms, a smoking room, a television with the volume turned down and headphones provided, showers in the toilets, and a buffet with hot meals according to the time of day. There is a self-service drinks bar with champagne and premium drinks. There is a separate lounge for gold and silver members of the Skywards (Emirates) and FlySmiles (SriLankan) frequent flyers club who are not travelling in business class, as well as premium-class lounges for other airlines, and one with paid admission for economy-class passengers.

The boarding gates are down the long corridor with bridges to the aircraft doors. There is an X-ray of hand baggage and a hand search of passengers before you are allowed through to the secure boarding lounge. The usual rules relating to what can be carried on the aircraft apply for all flights, so don't have any unsealed liquids. Passengers are usually told to remove their shoes too and put them to be X-rayed. At the entrance to the boarding lounge there is a passport and ticket inspection and then the ticket counterfoil is torn off, leaving you with the boarding card. (Keep the boarding card until after you have left the airport at your destination in case of a surprise check, or just to claim mileage points.) Sometimes there is a surprise check in the boarding lounge by European or North American immigration personnel intent on trapping illegal immigrants bound for their countries.

For information about Sri Lanka's second international airport, the Mattala Rajapaksa International Airport near Hambantota in the deep south, see page 279.

BY SEA Going to Sri Lanka by sea is almost impossible. There is no ferry service from India, and no regular sailings by passenger ships from anywhere. However, sometimes cruise liners of the Silverseas and Seabourn lines drop in for the day and it might be possible to cruise on them and disembark in Colombo. Disembarking at the Colombo port is a hassle; so many documents have to be supplied (by the ship's agent to the authorities) and there is also a tiresome customs check (no green channels). Some cargo/passenger ships call in too. If you are determined to come by sea, a good way might be as a crew member on one of the few private sailing yachts that occasionally visit Galle.

The port itself has very few facilities for visiting cruise passengers although temporary stands displaying souvenirs, gems and tea will be set up for the arrival of a cruise ship. Passengers are obliged to take a taxi into town (no shuttle buses) and the taxi drivers, who are hoping for full-day tours, are reluctant to take passengers on short runs unless tipped outrageously. However, it is worthwhile hiring a taxi in the port for the day as it will have a permit to enable it (and you) to get back in again. If you walk to the port gates (often a long hike) you'll have to walk back again from the gates after your journey as outside taxis aren't allowed inside the port. There are no ATMs, post office, IDD telephones or dining facilities available in the port.

HEALTH *with Dr Felicity Nicholson*

BEFORE YOU GO As nothing is required by law (unless you are coming from a yellow fever area), whether you have the usual cocktail of inoculations recommended for visits to tropical countries is up to you. Since you may be travelling throughout the country and experiencing different locations and being with different people every day, we suggest you have just what the doctor orders. Evidence of a **yellow fever** vaccination (or an exemption certificate if you are unable to take the vaccine), valid for ten years, will be demanded *en route* if you visit Sri Lanka within ten days from sub-Saharan Africa or South America.

Vaccinations against **diphtheria, tetanus and polio** (given as the all-in-one vaccine Revaxis) and **hepatitis A** are recommended for trips of any length. For longer trips and definitely for those working in hospitals or with children, **hepatitis B** is recommended. A course of **rabies** vaccine should ideally be taken by everyone, as treatment for rabies is not always easy to come by (see page 33). Hepatitis B and rabies vaccinations comprise a course of three injections given over a minimum of 21 days, so it is essential to go to your GP or specialist travel clinic (see page 32) well in advance of your trip. If you are under 16 then the minimum time for three doses of hepatitis B vaccine is eight weeks.

There are occasional reports of **cholera** and as there is now a more effective vaccine available in the UK, those travellers with debilitating long-term medical conditions or those working in high-risk areas should take the vaccine (Dukoral). For people aged six years and over, two doses should be taken between one and six weeks apart and at least one week before entering the affected area. No food or drink should be consumed an hour before or after taking the vaccine. Even if you don't take the vaccine and are unlucky enough to catch the disease it is usually mild in well-nourished people and is treatable with antibiotics anyway.

More adventurous travellers who intend to spend time in more rural areas, especially in the north, should consider being vaccinated against **Japanese encephalitis**. This disease is mosquito-borne and occurs throughout the year. The course of vaccine (Ixiaro) comprises two doses given ideally 28 days apart but 24 days is allowed if time is short. Ixiaro is licensed for those aged two months and over.

Malaria prevention The risk of malaria, predominantly Plasmodium vivax, exists throughout the year in most districts but the main risk is in the north of the country – an area where most visitors are unlikely to venture. Unless you are going to the far north then you will not be advised to take malaria tablets as the risk of catching malaria in the rest of the country is considered low. That said, it is always wise to take precautions against being bitten by mosquitoes so ensure that you use a mosquito repellent that contains around 50–55% DEET (eg: Repel), and if you are outside cover up from dusk till dawn with trousers and long-sleeved tops, and make sure your sleeping accommodation is mosquito-proof. For those going to the malarial area of Sri Lanka then a combination of Chloroquine and Proguanil will be recommended unless there are medical reasons for not taking this. The tablets should be started a week before you go, taken whilst you are in the malarial area and continued for four weeks thereafter. They are best taken in the evening with food and washed down with plenty of fluids. Tell your doctor if you have a fever over 38°C and you feel unwell during the year after leaving Sri Lanka regardless of where you have been in the country – remember the majority of the country is low risk, not no-risk. Malaria is treatable if it is caught early. Also remember that there are other mosquito-borne diseases (eg: dengue fever and Chikungunya) that can be spread by day-biting insects, so use repellents in the daytime too. In fact dengue fever is more likely to be a problem than malaria and unfortunately there are no tablets or vaccines to prevent the illness.

TRAVEL CLINICS AND HEALTH INFORMATION A full list of current travel clinic websites worldwide is available on www.istm.org. For other journey preparation information, consult www.nathnac.org/ds/map_world.aspx (UK) or http://wwwnc. cdc.gov/travel/ (US). Information about various medications may be found on www.netdoctor.co.uk/travel. All advice found online should be used in conjunction with expert advice received prior to or during travel.

IN SRI LANKA Minor health problems should always be treated with respect, in case they become major. Most common illnesses are the same as at home – colds, respiratory infections, minor ear, nose and throat infections, gastro-intestinal upsets, skin irritations and accidents. Prickly heat is common and will probably stay with you once you've got it, until you reach a colder and less humid climate. Hangovers are likely since you may be tempted to drink more than usual

LONG-HAUL FLIGHTS, CLOTS AND DVT

Any prolonged immobility including travel by land or air can result in deep vein thrombosis (DVT) with the risk of embolus to the lungs. Certain factors can increase the risk and these include:

- Previous clot or close relative with a history
- People over 40 but greater risk over 80 years
- Recent major operation or varicose veins surgery
- Cancer
- Stroke
- Heart disease
- Obesity
- Pregnancy
- Hormone therapy
- Heavy smokers
- Severe varicose veins
- People who are very tall (over 6ft/1.8m) or short (under 5ft/1.5m).

A deep vein thrombosis (DVT) causes painful swelling and redness of the calf or sometimes the thigh. It is only dangerous if a clot travels to the lungs (pulmonary embolus). Symptoms of a pulmonary embolus (PE) include chest pain, shortness of breath, and sometimes coughing up small amounts of blood and commonly start three to ten days after a long flight. Anyone who thinks that they might have a DVT needs to see a doctor immediately.

PREVENTION OF DVT
- Keep mobile before and during the flight; move around every couple of hours
- Drink plenty of fluids during the flight
- Avoid taking sleeping pills and excessive tea, coffee and alcohol
- Consider wearing flight socks or support stockings (see *www.legshealth. com*).

If you think you are at increased risk of a clot, ask your doctor if it is safe to travel.

because of the heat, excessive socialising or trying to match the locals in arrack consumption. Guard against them – and dehydration – with lots of mineral water before you sleep.

HIV HIV is a risk in Sri Lanka and can be transmitted through unprotected sex and by infected blood and blood products. The best precaution is sexual abstinence and this is not difficult because tempting offers of sex are unlikely, despite scandalous press speculation about child prostitution. However, there are beach boys in the habit of making themselves available to clients of both sexes, and professional ladies of the night, mostly from other countries, lurking in Colombo's hotel lounges and casinos. If you do decide to experience romance make sure you are prepared. Condoms of various styles are obtainable, even in villages; however, you would still be wise to take your own from home that are quality-controlled. You are best off taking your own needles and syringes to guarantee sterility should you need an injection or stitches. These can be obtained from some travel clinics and the larger pharmacists (eg: Boots) in the UK.

Rabies Rabies is carried by all mammals and is passed on to man through a bite, scratch or a lick of an open wound. You must always assume any animal is rabid, and seek medical help as soon as possible. Meanwhile scrub the wound with soap under a running tap or while pouring water from a jug for a good 15 minutes. Find a reasonably clear-looking source of water (but at this stage the quality of the water is not greatly important), then pour on a strong iodine or alcohol solution of gin, whisky or rum. This helps stop the rabies virus entering the body and will guard against wound infections, including tetanus.

Pre-exposure vaccinations for rabies are ideally advised for everyone, but are particularly important if you intend to have contact with animals and/or are likely to be more than 24 hours away from medical help. Three doses should be taken over a minimum of 21 days which will change the treatment that you then need. Contrary to popular belief these vaccinations are relatively painless.

If you are bitten, scratched or licked over an open wound by a sick animal, then post-exposure prophylaxis should be given as soon as possible, although it is never too late to seek help, as the incubation period for rabies can be very long. Those who have not been immunised will need rabies immunoglobulin (RIG), preferably human (but horse will do if there is nothing else), and five doses of vaccine. It is important to get RIG but is often very hard to come by in Asia and is also expensive (around US$800 a dose). If you have had the pre-exposure doses of vaccine then you no longer need RIG and only need two more doses of vaccine three days apart. Take any written evidence that you have had the rabies vaccine to make your and the doctor's life easier.

Travellers' diarrhoea Visiting Sri Lanka carries a fairly high risk of getting a dose of travellers' diarrhoea; perhaps half of all visitors will suffer and the newer you are to exotic travel, the more likely you will be to suffer. By taking precautions against travellers' diarrhoea you will also avoid typhoid, paratyphoid, cholera, hepatitis, dysentery, worms, etc. Travellers' diarrhoea and the other faecal-oral diseases come from getting faecal bacteria in your mouth. This most often happens from cooks not washing their hands after a trip to the toilet, but even if the restaurant cook does not understand basic hygiene you will be safe if your food has been properly cooked and arrives piping hot. The most important prevention strategy is to wash your hands before eating anything. You can pick up salmonella and shigella from toilet door handles and possibly bank notes. The maxim to remind you what you can safely eat is:

PEEL IT, BOIL IT, COOK IT OR FORGET IT.

This means that fruit you have washed and peeled yourself, and hot foods, should be safe but raw foods, cold cooked foods, salads, fruit salads which have been prepared by others, ice cream and ice are all risky, and foods kept lukewarm in hotel buffets are often dangerous. That said, plenty of travellers and expatriates enjoy fruit and vegetables, so do keep a sense of perspective: food served in a fairly decent hotel in a large town or a place regularly frequented by expatriates is likely to be safe. Another sensible precaution is to drink only bottled water, even if it is advertised that local water is safe to drink. If bottled water is not available then you may have to resort to boiling the water for ten–15 minutes and if the water is coming from a river or looks contaminated then you should filter it as well. **Remember to clean your teeth in bottled water too** and to use an alcohol-based hand rub after washing your hands.

It is dehydration that makes you feel awful during a bout of diarrhoea and the most important part of treatment is drinking lots of clear fluids. Sachets of oral rehydration salts give the perfect biochemical mix to replace all fluids you are losing but other recipes taste nicer. Any dilute mixture of sugar and salt in water will do you good: try Coke or orange squash with a three-finger pinch of salt added to each glass (if you are salt-depleted you won't taste the salt). Otherwise make a solution of a four-finger scoop of sugar with a three-finger pinch of salt in a 500ml glass. Or add eight level teaspoons of sugar (18g) and one level teaspoon of salt (3g) to one litre (five cups) of safe water. A squeeze of lemon or orange juice improves the taste and adds potassium, which is also lost in diarrhoea. Drink two large glasses after every bowel action, and more if you are thirsty. These solutions are still absorbed well if you are vomiting, but you will need to take sips at a time. If you are not eating you need to drink three litres a day plus whatever is pouring out of you into the toilet. If you feel like eating, take a bland, high carbohydrate diet. Heavy greasy foods will probably give you cramps.

If the diarrhoea is bad, or you are passing blood or slime, or you have a fever, you will probably need antibiotics in addition to fluid replacement. A dose of norfloxacin or ciprofloxacin repeated twice a day until better may be appropriate (if you are planning to take an antibiotic with you, note that both norfloxacin and ciprofloxacin are available only on prescription in the UK). If the diarrhoea is greasy and bulky and is accompanied by sulphurous (eggy) burps, one likely cause is giardia. This is best treated with tinidazole (four x 500mg in one dose, repeated seven days later if symptoms persist).

Protection from the sun It is important not to let the sun go to your head and cause you to do silly things. When sunbathing, remember how close you are to the Equator. Even in the chill of the hill country, the sun that seems so pleasant is actually just as fierce as on the beach.

Give some thought to packing suncream. Keep out of the sun during the middle of the day and, if you must expose yourself to the sun, build up gradually from 20 minutes per day. Be especially careful of exposure in the middle of the day and of sun reflected off water, and wear a T-shirt and lots of waterproof suncream (at least SPF15) when swimming. Sun exposure ages the skin, makes people prematurely wrinkly and increases the risk of skin cancer. Cover up with long, loose clothes and wear a hat when you can. The glare and the dust can be hard on the eyes, too, so bring UV-protecting sunglasses and, perhaps, a soothing eyebath.

Insect bites Walking barefoot anywhere (even if the locals do it) is bound to lead to trouble. Creepy crawlies to worry about include the ubiquitous cockroach, which may be unpleasant but not a direct health risk. More dangerous are centipedes – six-inch long, fat monsters – whose bite can swell up and be painful for a couple of days. Take care, too, in long wet grass for leeches. If one latches on to you, it can be removed by soap, salt or, better still, iodine drops which will make it drop off of its own accord. The hole could fester if you scratch it.

Yes, there are poisonous snakes but you are unlikely to be bitten by one unless you are really off the beaten track, perhaps sleeping on a mat on the floor of a mud hut.

Most snakes are harmless and even venomous species will dispense venom in only about half of their bites. If bitten, then, you are unlikely to have received venom; keeping this fact in mind may help you to stay calm. Many so-called first-aid techniques do more harm than good: cutting into the wound is harmful; tourniquets are dangerous; suction and electrical inactivation devices do not work. The only treatment is antivenom. In case of a bite that you fear may have been from a venomous snake:

- Try to keep calm – it is likely that no venom has been dispensed
- Prevent movement of the bitten limb by applying a splint
- Keep the bitten limb BELOW heart height to slow the spread of any venom
- If you have a crêpe bandage, wrap it around the whole limb (eg: all the way from the toes to the thigh), as tight as you would for a sprained ankle or a muscle pull
- Evacuate to a hospital that has antivenom.

And remember:

- NEVER give aspirin; you may take paracetamol, which is safe
- NEVER cut or suck the wound
- DO NOT apply ice packs
- DO NOT apply potassium permanganate.

If the offending snake can be captured without risk of someone else being bitten, take this to show the doctor – but beware: even a decapitated head is able to bite.

Local health care If you do need medical attention, doctors in the resorts are good for typical tourist maladies and will prescribe lots of tablets and charge around Rs2,000 for the consultation. For advice on how to find a doctor, ask the people where you are staying. There are plenty of pharmacies everywhere for basic medicines.

Doctor home visits, ambulance patient transport and home nursing care can be arranged in the west-coast tourist areas by telephoning (24hrs) m 077 3043576 or ☎ 060 2153999. If you have to be hospitalised, there are several private hospitals and clinics in Colombo as well as in Colombo's suburbs to the north, and ones at Kalutara and Galle in the south.

Every town, even small ones, has a government hospital where visitors can receive emergency treatment for a fee. Below is a list of the major private (fee-charging) hospitals. There are private doctors with clinics open all day throughout

Sri Lanka who will treat visitors for a fee (usually more than a local would pay). There are also pharmacies in every town, some in supermarkets, where trained pharmacists will provide standard medicines without a prescription as well as medicines by prescription.

✚ **Nawaloka Hospital** 23 Deshamanya H K Dharmadasa Mawatha, Colombo 2; ☎ 011 2544444; e nawaloka@sltnet.lk; www.nawaloka.com. The island's largest private hospital is very crowded with outpatients & visitors.

✚ **Oasis Hospital** Near Narahenpita railway station, 18A Muhundhiram D Dabare Mawatha, Narahenpita, Colombo 5; ☎ 011 5506000; e care@oasishospital.lk; www.oasishospital.lk. Is new, has a host of clinics & crowds are small. The 6th floor has private wards with TV, mini fridge & AC.

✚ **Lanka Hospitals** 578 Elvitigala Mawatha, Narahenpita, Colombo 5; ☎ (emergency) 1566 or 011 5530000; e info@lankahospitals.com; www.lankahospitals.com. Newish & descended from the Indian-run Apollo Hospital, has a variety of thorough health checks available at a fraction of the cost for the same thing in Western countries.

✚ **Durdans Hospital** 3 Alfred Pl, Colombo 3; ☎ 011 5410575; e contactus@durdans.com; www.durdans.com. Specialists in heart care.

SAVING WATER

Sri Lanka's climate is so diverse there can be floods in one part of the island at the same time that there is a drought in another. Since water comes from wells, not from catchments, the source can run dry when there is excessive demand, as in tourist areas. So it is wise always to remember that extravagant use of water while staying in a hotel could result in the well of a nearby village suddenly drying up. This happens frequently in Bentota where the villagers suffer from the beach hotels' demand. (Perhaps someday beach resorts will be obliged to manufacture water from the sea, as resorts do in the Maldives.)

From my bathroom at Cinnamon Lodge, Habarana, I have copied this advice on saving water since it's well worth remembering.

		Do	**Don't**
1	Brushing teeth	Use a tumbler of water, rinse briefly (*Only half litre used*)	Let tap run for five minutes (*45 litres used*)
2	Washing hands and face	Half-fill basin (*2 litres used*)	Wash under a running tap for two minutes (*18 litres used*)
3	Shaving	Use mug of water (*Quarter litre used*)	Let tap run for two minutes (*18 litres used*)
4	Shower	Rinse, turn off tap, soap up, rinse down (*20 litres used*)	Let tap run while soaping (*90 litres used*)
5	Leak	Report immediately (*Slow drip 400 litres*)	Let leak persist (*Fast drip 3,000 litres*)

Eric J Butler writes that he is 'slightly resentful at the printed notices displayed in many hotel bathrooms which imply that the guest is responsible for water waste when often the main culprit is the hotels themselves, with the widespread use of (inefficient) pop-up wash-hand basin plugs which mean having to keep the tap running as the basin drains before ablutions are completed'.

While there are a few public toilets in Colombo, they are not for the squeamish. In Colombo, hotels, upmarket restaurants and shopping malls are convenient instead. While travelling by road, however, where there is no such option, look for a major supermarket, like a Cargills Shopping Centre where there will be a clean toilet available for customers. Some restaurants, resthouses and bars in the countryside levy a fee (Rs20) for using their toilets if you are not actually a paying customer.

⊞ Hemas Hospital 389 Negombo Rd, Wattala; \011 7888888; e info@hemashospitals.com; www.hemashospitals.com. Covers the area from Colombo to Negombo.

⊞ Hemas Southern Hospital 10 Wackwella Rd, Galle; \091 4640640; www.hemashospitals. com. Newly opened in a purpose-built building in Galle, this hospital is exceptional for its dedicated medical & nursing teams, comfortable private rooms, cheerful staff &, surprisingly, good food

& low charges. Has a dental surgery & optician & operates a loyalty scheme.

⊞ New Philip Hospital On the way from Colombo to Galle, 225 Galle Rd, Kalutara South; \034 2222888; e inquiries@philiphospitals.com. This small outfit is the most convenient private hospital serving the main tourist areas of the west coast. There's a new wing, & 24hr attention available from resident doctors & visiting specialists.

Before being admitted to any hospital, check (or have someone do it) with your insurance company about bill payment. (Don't dare visit Sri Lanka without adequate travel insurance!) You will also be expected to pay a deposit when you are being admitted, and this can be done with a credit card. For emergency dental treatment (although there are village dentists still using drills with a foot pedal), modern equipment, skill and reassuring attention is available in Colombo from a UK-qualified dental surgeon, **Dr Asoka Ratnayake** (*207/8 Dharmapalà Mawatha, Colombo 7;* *011 2692562*).

SECURITY AND SAFETY

After an attack on the airport in July 2001, a lot of attention was paid to the Travel Advisories listed by foreign missions for the benefit of their nationals. Naturally, they were cautious. The result was that overseas tour companies cancelled package holidays because of their potential insurance liability if something happened to their clients. The decision of independent travellers about coming to – and staying in – Sri Lanka is theirs, not their government's, who can only advise. However, private travel insurance may not be effective for nationals of a country that has officially advised its citizens against going to specific areas.

There was a similar situation after the tsunami in 2004 when foreign governments (and travel companies) advised their nationals holidaying in Sri Lanka to leave because of the uncertain situation. Those who stayed on were overwhelmed by the continued welcome they received and found their presence was a morale-booster.

There is occasional criticism in Sri Lanka by the government and press (and hoteliers) when foreign governments advise their citizens about the dangers of visiting certain areas. While terrorism has been eliminated, crime has not. Foreigners, whether visitors or resident, are especially attractive to robbers, and there have been a few cases reported recently about tourists being raped and murdered. To check the latest situation, but as seen by government officials who

Ayurveda (pronounced *ae-ur-vay-dah*) is the natural medicine of Sri Lanka, an alternative to Western medical lore, which has an efficacy proven by 3,000 years of care and cure. It is nature's way to good health because of its reliance on natural plants, herbs and oils.

As the name implies (*ayur* = life; *veda* = knowledge), ayurveda is the 'Knowledge of Life' or 'the art of healthy living'. According to the leaflet provided by the Neptune Ayurveda Village, it is the oldest complete medical system in the world.

These traditional medications were developed by ancient sages through keen observation of life and its functions. Ayurvedic philosophy postulates that the development of each of us from birth is governed by the varied combination of the five basic forces of nature – Water, Fire, Air, Earth and Ether.

Treatment comprises not only potions made from fresh, natural ingredients, but also oil massages, steam baths and bathing in herbal waters. Treatments are particularly beneficial for patients suffering from migraine, insomnia, arthritis and gastritis, but can also help in cases of paralysis and practically any affliction. The *Panchakarma* method has a great distinction in ayurveda as it uses the five elements of medicinal herbs – leaves, flowers, barks, roots and berries – to cleanse the blood and the body's system of impurities.

Ayurveda treatment not only cures, it provides immunity too, so patients are both those in need of a cure for a particular ailment, and those who want to follow a course to stimulate and maintain good health. Treatment by nature cannot be hurried; it is not nature's aspirin.

While locals are likely to consult a renowned village practitioner, tourists can have a course of treatment from a government-licensed practitioner while staying at a holiday resort. Popular, particularly with clients from Germany, are Aida's two Holistic and Ayurveda hotels and the Ayurveda Walauwa, all in or close to Bentota. These are exclusively ayurveda hotels with treatment supplemented by specially prepared meals recommended by a resident physician.

---

have to be cautious, go to either the UK website (*www.fco.gov.uk*) or the US version (*www.travel.state.gov/sri_lanka.html*).

If the advisories put you off and you are in doubt about whether to go, phone a Sri Lanka tourism office for an opinion from the tourist viewpoint.

If you are travelling in a vehicle, occasionally your driver will be flagged down at **police checkpoints**. Usually all that will be required is for the driver to present his driving licence and for the vehicle's registration number to be logged. You may also be asked where you are going and for some proof of identity. Always carry your passport with you or a photocopy of the relevant pages (including the page with your entry permit sticker).

Tourists are advised not to linger at places where they could be at risk, even though accidentally, such as at political meetings, protest marches and where over-enthusiastic Sri Lankans are celebrating something.

Theft is not as rampant as you might expect but, of course, you should not encourage it by leaving your handbag open on a train seat, wallet peeping out of your hip pocket or camera by an open window. Pickpockets are a hazard on buses, especially with passengers standing so close to each other. Razor blades are used to slash holes in bags or to cut the strap and remove the bag from a shoulder. Better to leave valuables sealed in the hotel safe or in the mini safe in your room. Also, it might not be prudent to venture into unknown territory at night with newly met companions. Street or beach muggings, however, are not yet part of the culture.

Do not interpret a Sri Lankan's insatiable curiosity as a threat. On a train or bus you may be the first opportunity the Sri Lankan passengers have had of observing a foreigner at close quarters. Everything about you will be as fascinating to them as they are to you. Those stares are because they are trying to understand what makes you tick, not how to get your watch. When someone asks 'Where are you from?' it could be because the person has a relative living in England and wonders if you know him. It is also a conversation ploy, to break the ice.

There is no need to get paranoid about your personal safety. If you do, your fear will show and somehow what you dread will actually happen. Take normal, simple precautions and relax. If you do get robbed and intend to claim from your insurance company, make a report to the police and get a copy of the report from them as proof of your loss.

WOMEN TRAVELLERS There have been letters in the local press from female foreigners complaining of 'sexual harassment' from men who pester them in the street or 'accidentally' touch them on buses. Male foreigners and mixed couples are also subjected to this nuisance in tourist areas. It begins with the question 'Where are you going?' as a kind of hello that does not really need an answer. Foreigners, trying to be polite, usually respond, which the pesterer will use to start a conversation. Just keep quiet if you don't want it to go further; cutting remarks have little effect.

A woman sunbathing on the beach will attract attention, which can be annoying when she wants to be alone. However, some women prefer company and they're the ones the lads on the beach are hoping for. If being ogled and chatted up is offensive to you, remember it's not intended to be threatening.

DISABLED TRAVELLERS There are few of the facilities for disabled travellers that exist in some countries, although public buildings are now supposed to be accessible to wheelchair occupants. At the two international airports wheelchairs and assistance in boarding and disembarking from planes are available. Because of the difficulties in boarding trains and lack of space within carriages, train travel by the disabled would be difficult. Yet beggars without limbs know how to get on board, and blind singers – usually with a child as guide – patrol the aisles. Sri Lankans are generally very considerate to a foreigner who has special needs and one could expect help from strangers in an emergency.

TRAVELLING WITH CHILDREN Travellers with babies will attract a lot of friendly attention since Sri Lankans love kids. However, babies may feel the heat. Children should be watched in case they wander off alone. There are half-price entrance tickets to most places for children.

SOLO OR GROUP TRAVEL? Travel alone and you will have a great trip; travel with someone else and the experience will be influenced by the state of your relationship with that person. It is often by travelling overseas with someone you have known for years that you really get to know that person – but that is not why you go to Sri Lanka. If the relationship with your travelling companion breaks down, it could turn the whole trip sour.

Solo travelling in Sri Lanka is both practical and enjoyable. Go alone anywhere in the country and people will talk if you want, so you will hardly feel lonely. The encounters can be rewarding, the kind you might not experience so deeply if you have a companion wanting to do something else. You might also have a chance to make real Sri Lankan friends whose kindness and graciousness will make what you hear about the calculated approach of some Sri Lankans towards tourists seem absolute nonsense.

If you do travel with a companion, your individual costs will be lower since you can share the cost of accommodation (double and single room rates are usually the same) and taxi fares, as well as experiences and jokes. While being an exclusive group of two may give you a feeling of confidence and is convenient, it could also shelter you from adventures, if your companion is not the outgoing type.

If you want to be organised, then visit with a group, on a pre-planned package tour. It will give you a wonderful introduction to the country so that you can return again by yourself for your next holiday. If you come with a group and don't like it, or want to stay longer somewhere than scheduled, then inform the tour guide and drop out. You won't get a refund and you will have to meet up with the group for the return flight, but that way you would have combined solo and group travel, and done what you want.

When I stated in an article in *Explore Sri Lanka* (a monthly magazine available free in Sri Lanka) that 'tourists on all-inclusive packages don't have as much fun as independent travellers', I received an indignant letter from Anne Beale of the UK, a reader of this guide, who visited on a 'package' and said:

My husband and I have just returned from a wonderful first holiday in Sri Lanka. After visiting the historic cities and sites where, celebrating my husband's 80th birthday, we climbed to the top of Sigiriya unaided and rode on the neck of an elephant, plus Kandy, we retreated to the pampered seclusion of the Bentota Beach Hotel. From there we walked across the bridge several times to poke around and make purchases in the shops and markets in Alutgama: did a raft trip on the Bentota River; took a tuk-tuk (three-wheeler taxi) to Brief Garden; took the train (an experience) to Galle, walked the Fort ramparts circuit and spent several absorbing hours wandering the narrow streets with their ghosts of past centuries and beautiful decaying buildings. Finally we visited the Kosgoda turtle hatcheries and took a glass-bottomed boat out to the coral reef at Hikkaduwa. (On reflection, probably not a good idea, conservation-wise.) So we package tourists don't all travel thousands of miles to sit on a beach and make no attempt to discover the country and its people.

WHAT TO TAKE

Really, hand luggage – that you can carry on the plane with you – is enough. Most of us take far too much on the 'just in case' principle. You don't even have to bring much in the way of clothes.

There is an appalling habit you will encounter among local children in tourist areas. They have learned that tourists are a soft touch and will come running after you crying 'school pen' or 'bon-bon'. If you feel that distributing ballpoint pens and sweets encourages cordial relations, bring them and try it. What to give gracious hosts and their children is often a problem, but don't try to solve it by bringing gifts in your luggage. Cakes bought locally may not have the cachet of being something from abroad but will nevertheless be a welcome gift that will delight.

Books, and notebooks, can be bought in local shops; so can a torch. However, bring a strong water bottle in which to store mineral water as the local plastic bottles could puncture. A penknife with bottle opener is handy, but will be removed by airline security if it is packed in your hand baggage. Take whatever gadgetry (iPod, radio, digital camera, laptop, mobile phone) you would feel lost without, though be warned the sea breeze is corrosive and sensitive equipment may seize up. Decent walking shoes you have already broken in are important; you can buy good sandals locally.

You can get practically everything in Sri Lanka (including the latest iPod) but suncream may be expensive and the brand you like may be difficult to find. Bring prescription medicines. If you wear spectacles it would be advisable to carry a spare pair in case of loss, although computerised eye testing is available so you could have a replacement pair made up.

Following advice to bring quantities of tampons, soap, shampoo, toilet paper, spare padlocks, etc, will only fetter you. Buy what you need at the village shops as you go; the experience of shopping locally will add to your fun and understanding of local life. A local supermarket chain (Cargills Food City) has over 150 well-stocked outlets in Sri Lanka, making shopping even more fascinating. They're a good source of packed spices and teas too at local prices, as is the rival chain of Keells Super which has around 50 branches including popular ones at the Crescat and Liberty Plaza shopping malls in Colombo and an emporium in Galle.

You will not need a sleeping bag, sleeping sheet, camping equipment (it is not advisable to camp except at organised campsites arranged through tour operators), towel, photo albums of your family and dog. Carry necessary addresses on a sheet of paper folded in your purse or wallet, rather than a huge address book. You don't even need to take a raincoat (it will be too hot to wear one) since you could buy a locally made collapsible brolly if it rains.

Do not take anything that you value highly and would be devastated to lose. If it is a document, bring a photocopy; if it is anything else, leave it at home. Take photocopies of your passport, air ticket and insurance policy and keep them separately from the originals, in case of loss. You will need insurance, both for yourself and your belongings. If you plan to go on to India from Sri Lanka, get your Indian visa at home. (It is possible to get a visa to enter India from the Indian High Commission in Colombo, but it involves delay for reference back to your home country and other hassles.) If you plan to drive, take an international driving licence so you can apply for a temporary local licence through the AA office in Colombo.

If you belong to any organisation (Lions, Rotary, etc) that has branches in Sri Lanka, bring your membership card if you want to make contact. A student – or other – ID card could be useful since gate security personnel at some establishments like you to leave your passport or an ID card when you enter their premises and you collect it when you leave. Even an ID card you make up with a small photograph and laminate yourself is better than having to part with your passport.

If you have credit cards, bring them, since they are widely accepted in Sri Lanka. However, check first where you plan to use them, even if you see a MasterCard or

READERS' TIP

Andrew and Monica Forsyth suggest taking some seal-easy plastic bags. 'These are excellent for keeping passport/air tickets/money dry and safe for when you get rained on, fall into rivers, sink into mud, etc.' These, however, can be bought in local supermarkets.

Visa sign in the window, since some establishments show the stickers just to lure you in. ATMs are everywhere but not all of them can cope with foreign-issued credit or debit cards.

Photographers using non-digital cameras should bring the film they like. Printing of photos from digital cameras can be done easily in most towns. If you smoke you will have to buy cigarettes locally, or declare them and pay import duty, since duty-free cigarettes are not allowed. If you use exotic perfume or make-up, or something that is hard to obtain even in your own country, then take it too, although mainstream international brand-name products are available in Colombo at such outlets as Odel.

The post-tsunami period saw tourists turning up with clothes, kitchen utensils, medicines, etc, to distribute to displaced families. While the thought is good, it is far better to bring extra cash (not secondhand clothes) either to give directly to those obviously in need or to use to purchase locally made items (such as a fridge, gas stove, mattresses, furniture) when you discover families in need. (If someone approaches you in the street claiming to be a tsunami victim and you feel like helping, do check first to see if the person is genuine and not just using a ploy to beg.)

WHAT TO WEAR

Sri Lanka is mostly hot and humid, which means cotton T-shirts and trousers or loose-fitting frocks are enough. There are some great shops in Colombo selling Western fashions at Third-World prices (a third of what you would pay in the West). These are made locally for export so you could travel light and stock up. Or you could have cotton shirts and slacks made up in a few hours by a village tailor.

If you plan to spend some time in the hill country, you will need a sweater, but even warm clothes are made in the local garment factories so you could buy something fashionable as well as warm in Colombo or in the clothes bazaar in Nuwara Eliya.

Clothing needs to be practical for everyday use. Long trousers, especially ones with lots of zippered pockets to stash cash, loo paper and passports, are better than shorts, which might cause offence in religious places. Women should have loose-fitting garments (also with hidden, zippered pockets) for greater comfort. Scanty clothing is fine for the beach and pool, but not for street wear unless you want to get propositioned. Clothes dry quickly so you won't need many changes of clothes since you can wash dirty ones as you go along, or give the job to the hotel laundry.

It really is advantageous to have one smart outfit in your travel wardrobe, since you may want to dine in style or accept an unexpected invitation to a cocktail party. Perhaps that's what you should wear on the plane to keep your luggage to a minimum. If the invitation for a formal function says 'Lounge' it means a suit. A locally made safari suit could serve the purpose for a man while for a less formal evening a good shirt (perhaps one with a tropical design) and trousers are fine. For a woman, a blouse and skirt, or a cocktail dress, looks good. You'll find Sri Lankans (especially the women) dress beautifully for parties and you won't want to look scruffy.

MONEY

The currency is the rupee and it comes in coins of Rs1, Rs2, Rs5 and Rs10 (anything smaller has little use). There are notes of Rs10, Rs20, Rs50, Rs100, Rs200, Rs500, Rs1,000, Rs2,000 and Rs5,000. At press time, there were three different designs and colours of currency notes in circulation while the newest design, smaller than the older notes, is replacing the former currency. Check the value of each note carefully as different values share colours that are similar. Rupees are written on bills in figures with Rs before the number of rupees, then a stroke followed by the number of cents, if any (there are 100 cents to the rupee). Rs15/- indicates 15 rupees exactly, while Rs15/20 indicates 15 rupees and 20 cents. (You'll hardly ever see cents.)

CHANGING MONEY Travellers' cheques are not used so much since ATMs now proliferate. But they are best not only for security but also because they garner a higher rate of exchange than cash does. Pounds sterling and US dollars are the most common, although banks are now accustomed to euro cheques. There are commercial-bank exchange counters in the arrivals hall of the airport, and also in the check-in hall. (Get rid of unwanted rupees there as they can't be used for purchases after checking in.) The airport bank exchange counters give the same rate as their parent banks in Colombo so, to save hassles later, change all you need at the airport on arrival. Hotel exchange rates are significantly lower.

Do not expect to change travellers' cheques with ease outside of Colombo or the resort areas. If you are going on a tour it is better to change money in advance so you have enough. I always carry Rs10,000 in cash with me (squirreled in different pockets) in case of unexpected emergencies. It is advisable, too, to build up a collection of low-denomination notes as shops rarely have change for Rs1,000 or Rs2,000. Keep cash and travellers' cheques in several places on your person, having small notes for each day's spending in one purse, spare cash in another and cheques elsewhere. That's why you will need lots of zippered pockets. (Money belts are favoured by some but are itchy in the heat; remember they could slip off in the loo and are an embarrassment when you need sequestered cash in a hurry.)

Readers Andrew and Monica Forsyth commented that: 'small notes quickly get hoovered up by tips, temple donations, entrance fees and snacks. Make sure you get plenty of small notes when you change money, and get hotel cashiers to break down your big notes whenever you can, even if you have plenty of small notes on hand.'

You need your passport for changing travellers' cheques. Street people will offer to change money, but it's a con. There is no black market as such but you might get an extra chip or two above the bank rate if you play with dollars in a casino. There are licensed money changers in the main towns.

Cash can be obtained from bank machines if you have the right card and the right PIN. The control panel has an option in English. Remember with ATMs in Sri Lanka: you need to press a button to retrieve your card after you have received the cash. The card isn't ejected automatically so don't just grab the cash and leave the card in the machine. If you need funds to be transferred to you from overseas, choose a bank that appeals to you (the World Trade Centre branch of the Hatton National Bank is never crowded and is familiar with transactions for foreigners). Ask the bank what procedure it recommends for transferring funds to you quickly, then send that information to the remitter. Transfer from overseas to country-district banks can take ages, since it has to go via the bank's head office in Colombo. Keep the foreign-exchange chits in case you finish up with too many rupees (highly unlikely) and want to change them to another currency on departure. The chits are needed to prove you have changed foreign funds.

The exchange rate fluctuates daily. The rates are given in the daily newspapers or are available on www.xe.com/ucc. In October 2013, they were approximately £1 = Rs210; US$1 = Rs131; €1 = Rs178.

Banking There are more than 25 different banks in Sri Lanka, with the local People's Bank and the Bank of Ceylon having the most branches island-wide.

Other local banks include the Commercial, Hatton National, Sampath, Seylan, Pan Asia, Nations Trust and Union. There is also a National Savings Bank and a State Mortgage and Investment Bank. International banks, mostly with a single branch in Colombo, but some with branches in the suburbs and Kandy, include: ABN Amro, American Express, Citibank, Deutsche, Standard Chartered and HSBC. Banking hours are from 09.00 to, variously, 13.30 or 15.00, Monday to Friday. Some banks open on Saturdays too and branches of Nations Trust Bank keep longer hours than the others and are open 365 days a year.

There is usually at least one bank in every town, and ATMs can be found on their premises, sometimes guarded by uniformed security personnel.

BUDGETING

The immigration requirement (if you want to extend your one-month visa) is a minimum of US$30 exchanged per day. It is possible to survive on that amount (as long as you've covered your full-board accommodation cost in the holiday package). You are not obliged to spend that amount and, if you are not extending your visa, you don't even have to change that amount. In fact, if you are on a pre-paid holiday, and pay for your hotel extras with a credit card, you will need less cash. However, do allow for unexpected cash-only expenses like craftsman-made souvenirs, a jeep or boat safari, or a few beers in a local pub.

Because there are so many options in Sri Lanka, whether it's transport, meals or accommodation, it is impossible to predict what to budget per day as it depends on the level of luxury and convenience required. Transport could cost from US$1 a day for bus or train travel to US$100 a day for a hired minibus with driver/guide. Accommodation ranges from US$25 for two in a beachside guesthouse to US$200 for a double room in a city five-star hotel, to US$500 a day and more in a modern 'over-the-top' boutique-style hotel. Meals in a local café could be had for about US$5 each, or buffet lunch for US$15 to US$30, while a super meal could be at least US$40 per person. Bottled mineral water costs the equivalent of about US$0.50, and soft drinks about half that from a shop but double and more if ordered in a hotel or restaurant.

When thinking of how much to bring, remember that hotels as well as restaurants are obliged to add various government and local taxes which push the bill up by about 17%. On top of that there is the customary 10% service charge. Some restaurants absorb the taxes in their menu prices, in which case it advertises that prices are Nett. Where a price is, eg: Rs1,234+++ it indicates that government and local taxes and service charge will be added to the quoted price.

TIPPING In a commercial establishment a tip helps to reward and encourage good service; in a restaurant I suggest adding about half of the quoted service charge (ie: 5%). Tip in cash if you are paying the bill by credit card, otherwise it will never filter through to the server, and give the tip directly to the person you want to reward. Where you want to reward a hotel's doorman or porter, tip Rs100–200. For the room boy (or chambermaid in some places), it depends on the time you are staying in a place, perhaps Rs200–500 just for one night or Rs100 a day if you are staying longer and are pleased with your room's cleanliness. If you go to a cocktail party (even in a private house) and a steward looks after you diligently, reward him with Rs500, but discreetly in case the host is offended. Tip in rupees, not foreign currency, except in a major hotel, as it could be difficult (embarrassing) for the recipient to change. Don't tip in the major casinos.

Hotel and restaurant staff share in the accumulated service charge at the end of each month on a points basis according to their tenure of service, and this is essential to boost their take-home pay. In a gourmet restaurant in Spain, when I asked whether service was included, I was told that service was indeed included, but the tip wasn't. So it is in Sri Lanka, where wages are so low and the cost of living mounting. A tip given in Sri Lanka is a delightful gesture that really does work wonders for all concerned.

Opportunist characters and professionals such as snake charmers will expect a tip if you want to photograph them, or just to make them go away. Arrange the price first, like a modelling fee; however, usually people are happy to pose and would not expect a tip for so doing. Keep a few Rs50 notes for buskers, lads who direct your vehicle to a parking space, the boy who carries your supermarket shopping to your taxi, and the chap who presses a packet of mothballs into your hand (better than begging; at least he's trying to sell something).

GETTING AROUND

There is a school of thought which suggests that when you visit a Third-World country, you should travel the way the locals do. The idea is that you will then experience life in the raw, as the locals do. In Sri Lanka, forget it. You are there on holiday, so why subject yourself to the horrors of the cheapest local public transport?

You see, if you do try to travel the cheapest possible way, you might be depriving a Sri Lankan, who cannot afford any other method of travel, of a place on that bus, or a seat in that third-class carriage. The argument that travelling by public transport helps the economy is spurious. You would be contributing more, and more effectively, to the local economy by hiring a car with a driver for a private tour.

However, the main reason for hiring your own transport is convenience. You will be able to see all you want in the short time you have available, and you will be able to stop whenever you want. If you are on a bus and see a pretty spring bridge or a couple of copulating porcupines you want to photograph, you haven't got a chance.

Tourists on organised coach tours suffer in a different way; they are stuck with the stops decreed by the guide. His motivation often depends on getting his passengers to purchase something (overpriced spices, suspect gems, vulgar batiks) so he can earn a commission. It may be a strain on your holiday budget, or against the grain of your thrifty outlook but – believe me! – hiring an air-conditioned car with driver/guide is a worthwhile investment for a few days' touring.

BY AIR The opening in 2013 of Sri Lanka's second international airport at Mattala, in the deep south of the country, has brought with it scheduled domestic flights (although not every day) by SriLankan Airlines with seats available on the international flights that touch down at Mattala Rajapaksa International Airport.

✈ **SriLankan Airlines** (see page 26)
✈ **Helitours** Sir Chithampalam Gardiner Mawatha, Colombo 2; ☏ 011 3144944; e helitourstickets@slaf.gov.lk; www.helitours.lk. A branch of the Sri Lanka Air Force has scheduled fixed-wing plane services between Ratmalana airport (Colombo) & Palaly (Jaffna), Trincomalee, Batticaloa, Ampara & Mattala, as well as helicopters for chartering.

✈ **FitsAir** 6 Joseph Lane, Colombo 4; ☏ 011 2555156; e fitsair@fitsair.com; www.fitsair. com. Another domestic carrier with daily scheduled flights, Sri Lanka's pioneering domestic air service has daily scheduled flights between Ratmalana (Colombo) & Palaly (Jaffna). For more details, see page 302.
✈ **Cinnamon Air – Saffron Aviation (Pvt) Ltd** 11 York St, Colombo 1; ☏ 011 2475451;

e sales@cinnamonair.com; www.cinnamonair.com. A combined wheel & float plane flies daily between BIA & Water's Edge, Kandy, Sigiriya, Trincomalee, Koggala, Dickwella & Batticaloa.

✈ **Simplifly** (formerly Deccan Air) The Landmark, 385 Galle Rd, Colombo 3; m 077 7703703; e sales@simplifly.com; www.simplifly.com. Operates helicopters, planes & seaplanes on charter.

BY TRAIN For travelling independently by public transport, trains provide the most enjoyable means of getting around. Buying a ticket is simple. You turn up at the station at least ten minutes before the train is scheduled to depart (or earlier so you can secure a seat if you are boarding at its originating station), go to the counter for second- or third-class travel (there may be a short queue), pay your money and collect your ticket. Reserved accommodation, booked no more than ten days in advance, is available on some trains.

Although the departure and arrival times quoted in this guide are based on the current timetable, intending passengers should check with the departure station for changes owing to rescheduling. There is a railway tourist information service on ☏011 2421281, ext 336. There is also an efficient timetable enquiry service run, not by the railways, but by the government (*see www.gov.lk*), which gives train times and fares. However, it does not list trains that go through Colombo (such as the Vavuniya/Matara/Vavuniya service) so some stitching together of connections and/or departures is necessary.

There are fast, daily Intercity Express (ICE) trains serving Kandy, Anuradhapura and Galle from Colombo. Colombo's main railway station is **Colombo Fort** [76 C1]; the other station is **Maradana** [76 F2], which is also a terminus for trains on the Coast line. Except where stated all trains have second and third class.

TRAIN TIMETABLE: SERVICES TO AND FROM COLOMBO

These are some of the main daily trains from and to Colombo Fort station. For up-to-date details of schedules, try the government website www.gic.gov.lk/gic/?option=com_findnearest&task=train.

MAIN DAILY TRAINS FROM COLOMBO FORT RAILWAY STATION

Train No	Departure	Destination	Arrival time
4001	05.45	Vavuniya	11.21
1005	05.55	Badulla	16.06
6011	06.05	Batticaloa	14.20
8050	06.55	Matara	10.53
1009	07.00	Kandy	09.31
1007	08.30	Badulla	17.55
8040	08.35	Matara	11.50
1015	09.45	Badulla	19.23
1019	10.35	Kandy	13.52
8056	14.25	Matara	17.48
1029	15.35	Kandy	18.06
8058	15.50	Matara	18.20
4003	16.20	Vavuniya	21.16
1035	16.35	Kandy	19.36
8760	17.25	Galle	20.03
1039	17.45	Kandy	20.58
6079	19.15	Batticaloa	04.00

A recent – and welcomed by tourists – introduction is a complement of air-conditioned carriages marketed by two private companies and attached to major trains.

Exporail Level 12, East Tower, World Trade Centre, Colombo 1; 011 5225010; e reservations@ exporail.lk, www.exporail.lk. Exporail operates an AC carriage on a daily basis attached to trains running between Colombo & Kandy, Badulla, Vavuniya & Trincomalee, & all scheduled stops in between. Seats can be reserved online with tickets having to be collected from the departure station. Snacks are included in the fare. For an account of the service between Colombo & Kandy, see page 106.

Rajadhani Express Blue Line Company, 75A Kynsey Rd, Colombo 7; m 071 0355355; e info@ rajadhani.lk; www.rajadhani.lk. An AC 48-seat carriage with all seats bookable, attached to regular train services between Colombo & Kandy (on a daily basis), Badulla (6 days a week), & Matara (not Thu). Seats can be reserved online with collection of tickets at the company's agents throughout Sri Lanka.

Taking a cue from the private sector, Sri Lanka Railways had plans in 2013 (not in place by press time) to introduce a one-class (first) all-air-conditioned train with seats reservable from one month in advance on the Colombo–Kandy line. At the start this was to be a weekend-only service with the train stopping on the way at Peradeniya, Ragama and Gampaha.

Throughout the country the railway service is slowly improving. The line down the west coast from Colombo via Galle to Matara has been relaid allowing trains to go faster and thus reduce the journey time. New rolling stock has been introduced too, including 13 sleek Diesel Multiple Units (DMU) from China. Seven of them have been designated for the hill country line to operate with eight coaches and

1045	20.00	Badulla	07.10
7083	21.00	Trincomalee	05.10
4089	22.30	Vavuniya	05.08

MAIN DAILY TRAINS TO COLOMBO FORT RAILWAY STATION

Train No	Departure	Time	Arrival time in Colombo
7084	Trincomalee	19.30	04.05
6080	Batticaloa	20.15	04.55
1046	Badulla	18.00	05.17
8059	Matara	06.05	08.43
1030	Kandy	06.15	08.52
4004	Vavuniya	05.45	10.25
8085	Matara	10.15	13.30
1016	Badulla	05.45	15.27
6012	Batticaloa	07.15	15.25
1006	Badulla	08.30	18.57
4022	Vavuniya	13.30	18.35
4018	Vavuniya	15.10	19.15
8039	Matara	13.35	17.20
1010	Kandy	15.00	17.36
8051	Matara	14.10	18.05
1008	Badulla	10.00	20.25

two engines. Four DMUs are on the Kelani Valley line with six coaches and one locomotive, serving commuters. Two DMUs are 'AC luxury sets' (according to the railways) for Railway Tourism, and they consist of five coaches, one restaurant coach and two locomotives.

The latest developments of Sri Lanka Railways are posted on the railway website www.railway.gov.lk.

BY BUS The dedicated bus traveller has plenty of choice, although it is confusing. Basically there are two types of bus operation. The buses that look like buses, with an entry at one end and an exit at the other, rigid seats, and a high roof with room for passengers to stand, are run by a nationalised concern in different forms. They are still sometimes referred to as CTB (Ceylon Transport Board) buses and are generally a grubby aluminium and red or yellow in appearance. Where I mention these in the text, I refer to them as 'local buses' since they are more appropriate for short journeys from one village to the next than for long-distance trips.

The other kind are private buses, mostly of the coach type, built in Japan, with padded seats including some which flop down in the aisle, and rarely enough leg or head room. Some of these are air-conditioned intercity buses running between major towns, which do not (well, sometimes they do) stop to pick up passengers *en route*. Fares on these cost more than on stopping buses. (On all buses be sure to collect a ticket or receipt of some sort when you pay; there is a fine for ticket-less travel, even if you have paid.)

There was a proposal in 2013 to have all new public buses painted red, new private ones blue and new school buses yellow. There is also a system in operation of coloured destination boards (and a strip on the side near a bus's entrance) signifying what kind of bus it is.

- **Yellow** with yellow number on maroon background – normal service, normal fare
- **Blue** with blue number on white background – semi-luxury, 1½ times the normal fare
- **Green** with green numbers on white background – luxury service, twice the normal fare
- **Purple** with purple number on white background – super luxury, three times the normal fare

There are two separate bus stations in major towns for the former CTB buses and the private ones. It is better to board a bus at its starting point than on the way, if you want a seat on a long journey. You will often come across the extraordinary sight of a bus with half-a-dozen passengers hanging on to its side and the whole bus canting to its left.

Information on the departure of buses is difficult to obtain, and often unreliable, since departure depends on a bus arriving in the first place. When one of my Sri Lankan friends sought a timetable he was sent to the Transport Commission and told to submit a letter explaining why he wanted to know the times. However, people at bus stations are very helpful and will direct you to the bus you need when you explain where you want to go. Do check with the conductor for confirmation that the bus does go where you want, since other passengers might not know, and buses with the same numbers go to different places.

It is possible (although my view is that it is not advisable because of the scary driving) to travel by air-conditioned (AC) intercity buses between Colombo and the main towns. Readers John and Elisabeth Cox wrote to say they travelled several times by bus and they found it to be quite satisfactory. 'Use the AC buses, they are only slightly more expensive. The style of driving is different, but it works. Luggage space is minimal; if you are carrying a lot it may be best to pay for an extra seat and pile everything on it.'

It is possible, although not recommended because of discomfort and roadblocks requiring all passengers to get down, be searched and troop back on again, to travel from Colombo by bus to most parts of the country. All the main Colombo bus stations are within five to 15 minutes' walk of the Colombo Fort railway station. They are:

Central bus station [76 D1] Off Olcott Mawatha, adjoining Bodhiraja Mawatha, to the right of the railway station as you leave it, next to the Pettah Bo tree (there is a temple there); (information) 011 2328081. This is for government-run buses, formerly known as the CTB bus station.

Bastian Road bus station To the right of Fort railway station, next to Manning Market, the main fish, vegetable, fruit & meat market in Pettah; Private Omnibus Operators Association; 011 2421731. For private buses only.

People's Park bus station Behind the CBS. Was formerly Saunders Place bus station & is now for private buses.

Olcott Mawatha bus stops outside the Fort railway station are served by both private and government buses. There are also bus stops throughout the city for suburban buses.

There are two websites with details of bus services: **Sri Lanka National Transport Board** (*www.sltb.lk*) and the **National Transport Commission** (*www.ntc.gov.lk*).

BY ROAD The road network is good and extensive and the main highways are generally well maintained, although country lanes are very bumpy. By 2013, upgrading to most main highways throughout the country had been completed, although work was still underway on the A7 linking Colombo with Nuwara Eliya and on the A9 to Jaffna at the time of going to print. The opening of the (toll fee payable) Southern Expressway from the southern Colombo suburb of Kottawa to Galle has reduced the travel time from over two hours to just one hour. The country's second expressway, linking the international airport at Katunayake with the northern Colombo suburb of Kelani, opened late 2013.

Not all minibuses that take tourists have good springs, which adds to the agony of a long journey along country lanes. Traffic and other police wear brown uniforms and will suddenly step out into the road and blow a whistle to order a vehicle to stop, either because of speeding or some other perceived traffic violation. The driver is given a charge sheet detailing the fine payable for the offence he is deemed to have committed and must surrender his licence. The fine has to be paid to any post office, a receipt obtained, and the driver has to go back to the police station nearest to where he was stopped and collect his licence. Very tiresome if the driver is stopped far from home and has to make another trip back just to retrieve the licence. However, there was a proposal mooted in 2013 for a system of spot fines instead.

Car hire Unless you are experienced with tropical Asian driving skills (or lack thereof), do not even think about hiring a self-drive car as you will encounter a skill of driving that is heart-stopping. You are on holiday, so avoid stress. On your first experience, as you are being driven from the airport, you may wish you had an airline eye-mask to avoid seeing every near-miss. If you try to drive in Sri Lanka either you or the car will be a wreck before the day is out. Anyway, self-drive cars are more expensive to hire and drive than the much more relaxing option of hiring one with a driver.

A car, or a minibus, with a driver, can be hired at a specific price per kilometre for a long journey but more usually at a fixed price per day (think Rs12,000) plus an overnight allowance (Rs200–500), but meals and accommodation for the driver are generally provided by the establishment where you stop.

Some journeys such as a day trip to Kandy are at fixed rates, and the driver (if attached to a hotel) will have a printed tariff. If you are planning to hire a driver and a vehicle you don't know, try a short hire first (perhaps to a nearby temple or turtle farm) to see if you could put up with several days of him and it. If not, there are plenty of other drivers touting for business both outside hotels and in town centres.

When you are calculating the total cost of your own independent tour with a hired car or minibus with driver, remember to add to the hire cost the extra expenses of hotel and admission charges, meals, driver's allowance, amazing things sold wayside that you simply must have, and tips for helpful (or to get rid of unhelpful) people. If your driver says he wants to bring along a guide (perhaps because the driver himself doesn't speak your language very well), see if the guide has some experience so what he tells you is accurate and not made-up-to-please-the-guest fantasy. Courses are being held for guides with licences granted on successful completion and it is planned that licences (and hence some correct knowledge) will become compulsory for all those who are guiding tourists.

By taxi In Colombo there are radio taxis and the major hotels also have their own cars, with hotel logo, for hire by the hour or by the journey (hotel cars have fixed-price lists and the fee can be added to the room bill for paying by credit card). The rate for taxis in Colombo (but bound to increase) is from Rs68 per kilometre, with a 3km minimum charge.

For short journeys around Colombo, a new service has been introduced using Indian-made Nano cabs: small mini cars. They're a bit cramped if you're tall especially in the back seat, but cheap and cheerful and more comfortable than the ubiquitous three-wheeler taxis. They are metered so if the meter's working you'll have a journey priced at less than a hotel's hired car.

The major taxi firms whose cars can be booked by telephone are:

🚗 **ACE Cabs** Pepelliyana; ☏011 2818818
🚗 **Airport Express** Colombo 5; ☏011 2554343
🚗 **Airport Link** Colombo 5; ☏011 5336666
🚗 **City Cabs** Colombo 6; ☏011 2552222
🚗 **Colombo Cabs** Dehiwela; ☏011 4203303
🚗 **Emcee Travels** m 077 7329292
🚗 **Excel Cabs** Kotte; ☏011 2889889

🚗 **GNTC** Colombo; ☏011 2688688
🚗 **Ideal Cabs** ☏011 7700700
🚗 **Kangaroo Cabs** Colombo 4; ☏011 2501501
🚗 **Kango Cabs** Colombo 3; ☏011 2577577
🚗 **Radiant Cabs** Colombo 3; ☏011 2556556
🚗 **Unique Cabs** Mount Lavinia; ☏011 2733733

In the resorts, the usual form of transport will be by private minibus that can be hired through the hotel for touring. Arrangements can be made independently and the drivers will usually have a fixed-price list for standard tours.

By three-wheeler Colombo and all towns and villages have clusters of three-wheelers. Called a ground-helicopter in Hikkaduwa, this is what is known as a *tuk-tuk* in Thailand, or an *auto*, short for auto-rickshaw in India, and also a trishaw. They have three wheels and are noisy; breezy too since they don't have side panels.

They can be hailed whenever you see an empty one. It is wiser, though, to look for one that is parked so you can agree on the price before boarding, as not all have meters (or the meter might be 'out of order'). The official minimum fare will be Rs50. You can bargain if you have the energy; don't bother to tip though, as the driver will include a tip in the fare he quotes you. Some drivers will tell you to pay what you think is a fair fare. You'll soon know if you haven't paid enough.

Tuk-tuks with meters are more easily available in Colombo where the first kilometre incurs a charge of Rs50, with subsequent kilometres at Rs32. Regulations were being introduced in 2013 for all tuk-tuks to have meters.

While some tuk-tuk drivers own their own vehicles, others hire them from a boss to whom they must pay a fixed rental each day. In Colombo most of the drivers will speak a little English and some of them (especially those regularly parked near the major hotels) are knowledgeable about the city and make good guides. If you have a lot of places to visit in Colombo, it is often worthwhile to hire a three-wheeler for the whole morning. They always seem to be able to find somewhere to park (which a hotel car might not). When you do find a good driver whose fares are reasonable and who knows his way around, encourage him by using him again.

Three-wheeler drivers in Colombo not only serve the city but will also accept hires out of town, such as to the airport. It is not a comfortable ride and may not be cheaper than a hotel taxi, but it can be fun. Away from tourist resorts, the three-wheeler drivers seem more laid-back, prepared to quote a reasonable fare even for long journeys like Matara to Tissamaharama, or Sigiriya to Dambulla. They are the best alternative to bus travel (when there are no trains) and, for one or two people with light luggage, are ideal since you can stop wherever you want on the way.

The driver will usually start a long journey by pulling into a petrol station and asking you to give him an advance on the fare to pay for fuel. Remember to deduct it when you pay the final amount. Remarkably few of these vehicles are involved in major accidents, possibly because they are easily manoeuvrable and an alert driver can avoid an accident in the way a car could not. Some versions have half-doors, which seems an unnecessary refinement. Some owner-driven three-wheelers boast a music system while others have a kind of altar as well as a dashboard. They have sides that can be rolled down from the canopy top when it rains.

By motorbike Motorbikes and motorscooters can be hired, usually on an informal basis, in resort towns like Hikkaduwa. If you do rent one, be sure to check it thoroughly, perhaps with a test drive. As well as the fee in advance, by negotiation, you will be asked to leave your passport as security. If you have an accident, the repair bill will be at your expense, which you'll have to pay to get back the passport. You will often see local families on motorbikes with the father driving while a youngster sits on his lap, and the wife rides pillion with a couple of kids between the two of them. Crash helmets are compulsory for both driver and pillion rider.

By bicycle Bicycles can be hired in resort areas and are great for discovering what lies down the country lanes away from the beach, or for pedalling around Anuradhapura. Unfortunately, they are real bone-shakers and, if they do have brakes that work, then something else will be wrong. Visitors who bring their own bikes seem to fare pretty well and, on country lanes away from the madness of the main roads, may even enjoy it. **Walkers Tours** (*www.walkerstours.com*) organise cycling holidays with accommodation and motor vehicles to transport guests and bikes between cycling bases.

Guided tours   Local tour operators have standard tours that make discovering Sri Lanka much easier.

For the first-time visitor, a good organised tour is the best introduction to the island as it gives a chance to visit, without hassles, a lot of the country and one can return later independently to any place that seems worth a second look.

Standard tours commence with pick up of guests at the airport and then a few days' touring before they are dropped off at a beach hotel to relax and recover. This has the advantage of a guest being met on arrival and, thanks to the presence of a Sri Lankan tour guide, includes lectures on wheels of all that's intriguing.

The price of such a tour covers overnight stay with breakfast (but lunch and dinner are usually extras paid direct), transfer by air-conditioned car or minibus, entry permits (but not the cost of video camera permits) and entrance fees, an English-speaking guide plus driver, and government taxes.

When booking a tour do consider the shape you will be in on arrival in Sri Lanka. If you are arriving on a long-haul flight you will probably want to rest close to the airport, rather than set out on a gruelling seven-hour drive at the start of a tour. That will put you in a bad mood from which you will never recover during your holiday, and won't leave you in a fit state to appreciate the ruins, the scenery... and the traffic.

If your time is limited and you are eager to tour, then spend the first night close to the airport at Negombo. Or head for a beach resort to spend a few days getting over jetlag before starting a tour. This will not only help you to acclimatise but will also introduce you to Sri Lanka's very different culture and mindset, so you will become familiar with the lifestyle and this will help you appreciate the tour to the interior even more.

While local tour operators and their drivers, who usually work under contract rather than being tour agency employees, like to stick to a regular routine, most operators will design a tour to reflect your own interests. Not all the websites of local tour operators show their prices. Actually, it is very easy to arrange your own tour from your resort hotel by finding a licensed tour driver/guide (and a vehicle) you are comfortable with, and letting him put together a tour based on where you want to go and the style of accommodation you fancy.

For an introduction to Sri Lanka, **Red Dot Tours** (*www.reddottours.com*) offers good tours for all budgets from guesthouse to boutique-hotel accommodation. A recent innovation is scheduled coach tours that can be booked locally via **World Travel Centre Coach Tours** (*16 Gremier Rd, Colombo 8;* ☏ *011 2685100;* e *tours@ wtccolombo.com; www.coachtourssrilanka.com*), with daily tours from Colombo to Kandy and on Wednesdays, a Classical Tour; on Thursdays a Cultural Tour and a Jaffna Tour; on Saturdays a Galle Tour; on Sundays a Kitulgala Tour. On Thursdays, Fridays and Saturdays there are two more tours from Colombo: a Misty Hills and Sandy Beaches Tour and a Kingdom Tour.

ACCOMMODATION

Sri Lanka is one of those delightful destinations where you do not need to book accommodation in advance of your arrival if you are travelling independently without a travel agent's help. There is always a guesthouse (or a house with a guestroom) that will be willing to offer accommodation at the going rate (probably around Rs2,500 for a double with bathroom en suite). The 'going rate' will depend on demand. At the height of the season, say Christmas and January (and at Kandy in July/August during the perahera), demand is good so prices are going to be higher.

Tour operators contacted locally (either in advance or after your arrival) will take care of hotel reservations. On the other hand, you could do it yourself. Don't expect replies when you write from overseas; it's far better to check on the internet about availability and current room rates and fill in the 'contact us' form for a quotation. If that doesn't bring results, don't worry unduly as bookings can usually be arranged after you've arrived in Sri Lanka (as long as it's not a peak time).

Fear not, however. If you are arriving in Sri Lanka without any accommodation, the major Colombo hotels have desks at the airport, and the tourist board counter can also suggest places with vacancies. It makes sense to stay the first couple of nights in a decent Colombo hotel since it's only an hour's drive from the airport and will give you a chance to get over the long-haul flight, to acclimatise and to enjoy upmarket hospitality at a pretty reasonable rate (from US$85 at a three-star property), while planning your exploration of the country.

Plans are in hand to be able to cater for 2½ million tourists by 2016, which seems optimistic although one million visitors did arrive in 2012. Not all stayed in registered properties as there are dozens of unregistered private guesthouses in the areas popular with tourists (like Kandy, Nuwara Eliya, Negombo, Bentota, Induruwa, Hikkaduwa, Galle, Unawatuna, Tangalle), and these are super for walk-in guests, usually because the hosts/staff are helpful – even if untrained – and the experience is just the sort that independent travellers enjoy.

According to the *Accommodation Guide* issued by the Tourist Development Authority, there are 288 registered hotels open for business throughout the island. Of those, 115 are classified as star-class hotels, meaning they have facilities designed for international tourists. Fourteen of them are five-star properties, 15 four-star, 16 three-star, 36 two-star and 34 one-star. There are many more unclassified hotels. They were either awaiting classification or declined to be classified as their owners prefer to be graded by the tour operators selling their rooms overseas. Some are colonial properties whose infrastructure is hardly star-class but which have a five-star reputation as 'hotels of character'. The 'Boutique Hotels & Villas' section in that guide lists 52 properties but, even so, such highly desirable bungalow accommodation such as The Lavender House (see page 180) are not included.

In addition to the hotels, the *Accommodation Guide* lists over 400 approved guesthouses and paying-guest accommodation.

There are many places to stay, particularly in the beach and resort areas, which operate informally and are not on the tourist-board books. They exist for, and because of, the independent traveller who turns up and asks for a room. The price of such places would usually be around US$25 a night for a double with breakfast. Their presence makes touring around Sri Lanka without booking anywhere to stay in advance such a pleasure, giving a chance for serendipitous discoveries. On the other hand, at the top end of the price scale, private villas around Bentota and Galle, and some tea plantation bungalows, rent for US$500 a night.

Curiously, the hotels located inland which are generally visited on a 'round-trip tour' usually have a better infrastructure for guest comfort – and are more interesting to stay in – than properties on the beach. This is odd because visitors touring the interior stay no longer than a couple of nights in such hotels. Invariably guests want to stay longer, especially when they find that the beach resort where they are to spend a week or more has little of the appeal of the inland properties.

Inland hotels of the major local hotel groups have rooms that are well designed and well appointed, in villas or cottages in parkland settings, whereas in most beach resorts rooms are in storeyed blocks and pared down to the basic luxuries. Service, too, seems more obliging in the inland hotels, perhaps because the staff come from local villages, and do not have the chance to get too familiar with guests. They also have more opportunities for daytime in-house training since the inland hotels are generally empty during the day as guests are touring.

Since most inland properties of good standard have a swimming pool in a beautiful location, where guests can relax without being disturbed by roaming strangers, as well as lots of activities available in the vicinity, it's worthwhile arranging a stay of more than a couple of nights. That's not usually possible on a pre-organised tour, but if you leave the arrangements until you are in Sri Lanka and hire a chauffeur-driven car or minibus, you can plan a few nights staying somewhere different.

BOUTIQUE HOTELS

In his book *Words in Indian English* S Muthiah, who hails from Ceylon, defines 'boutique' as 'a small wayside shop in Sri Lanka that's part tea/coffee shop, snack bar and sales counter for sundries'. A more embracing, Western definition is 'a business that serves a sophisticated or specialised clientele'. Michael Meyler notes in his fascinating *Dictionary of Sri Lankan English* that the word is 'pronounced with the stress on the first syllable in Sri Lankan English, and the second syllable in British Standard English'.

In Sri Lanka there are boutiques that are village shops selling basics, and boutiques that are hotels offering the priciest bedrooms in the country. No-one is likely to mistake one for the other.

Boutiques are good business for Sri Lanka, whether shop or hotel. One keeps the villagers going, the other is boosting the economy at the upper level. The opening of boutique hotels throughout the country (the beach isn't a necessary ingredient) is changing the image of Sri Lanka as a cheap destination for package tourists to an eco-chic port of call for the new jetsetter.

Boutique hotels, where a suite can cost over US$500 a night, plus taxes and without food, are the new momentum of tourism in Sri Lanka, discovered by the incognito wealthy and kept as a secret from the rest of us. Their surprising success (thriving when conventional hotels are empty) has resulted in some very ordinary beach establishments declaring themselves to be 'boutique hotels' in an effort to attract high-net-worth guests. The result is pure disappointment for those seeking a holiday of cachet, not cliché.

To find a genuine boutique hotel in Sri Lanka look for one with no more than 12 rooms, in a rural or distinctive location, and with plush, creative interior décor that is not a blatant copy of 1980s-style severe architecture. The hotel should be idiosyncratic and fun. The service, since the place is small and intimate, should be courteous and caring and the food, since it is prepared on demand from the day's purchases, should be healthy, prettily presented and enjoyable. Among the real boutique hotels I recommend are:

Casa Colombo Colombo (see page 78)
Colombo Courtyard (see page 79)
Fits Margosa Pavilion Jaffna (see page 303)
Galle Fort Hotel Galle (see page 261)
Galle Fort Printers (see page 264)
Kandy House Kandy (see page 114)

Nisala Arana Bentota (see page 239)
Saman Villas Induruwa (see page 243)
Tintagel Colombo (see page 78)
Turtle Bay Kalamatiya (see page 277)
Vil Uyana Sigiriya (see page 144)

There are guesthouses wherever there are hotels. Do not despair if the only information you have before reaching a place is about 'Tourist Board Approved' hotels that are beyond your budget or simply not your cup of tea. You will be amazed at how easy it is to find places that suit both your pocket and your mood.

Obviously it is better to arrive in a strange town before dark so you have a chance to look around. And if the guesthouse you stay in at first is not really what you want, don't worry. Find another the next day and check out of the first one. Lads who want to guide you can sometimes come up with a super place you would never find yourself.

When business at a guesthouse is slack, a lowering of the price you are first quoted is possible, but do not make this a condition of your stay in a place if otherwise it is just what you are looking for. You might not find somewhere else as good. Ask to see a room before you commit yourself, and make sure you understand what is (and what isn't) included in the price. And prices can still be low. In October 2013 there were still places offering double rooms for two at around US$25 a night.

An amazing source of information, with photographs of the guesthouses showing their facilities, is the *Hit Ad* magazine published free as part of the *Sunday Times* (Colombo) every Sunday. In this 120-page magazine, after pages devoted to advertisements of cars, properties and oddities, there are eight pages advertising guesthouses and bungalows, some with amusing typos, such as 'an efficient management to make you stress tree', and 'surrounded by mash'. One states 'marketing officer's are reasonable packages'.

When touring independently, however, choose hotels belonging to the main groups or those recommended here so you know what you're getting. The owner of a place that calls itself, for example, 'Guest House and Restaurant' will be as surprised as you are if you try to stay there. Such places cater for local tourists or travelling salesmen, and are not geared up for instant response to a foreign visitor's demands, even if they claim recognition by the tourist board. Other places to avoid are the shacks that call themselves 'Hotel' but are actually no more than a wayside eatery and don't have accommodation at all.

The good news is that even when you stay in what I define as a **Basic** rate (**$**) guesthouse, you can expect a bathroom en suite ('attached'). It will have a shower and a toilet. However, there will be no hot water and no toilet paper, although there might be a towel, on request, and soap. The bedroom will have a hook or two, or even a rack, from which to hang clothes. The bed will have a sheet and a pillow. Sometimes an extra sheet with which to cover yourself will be provided. There will probably be a ceiling fan that moves sluggishly. Even if there is a mosquito net, be sure to light a mosquito coil (buy locally), as mosquitoes will find a way of getting in. Don't expect a light that's bright enough to read by.

Reviews in this guide are listed in descending price order. The **Luxury** (**$$$$**) grading refers to places that are special in some way (location, room design, ambience, exclusivity) and charge appropriately for it. Alas, some do not live up to the high price they charge since often the management and staff fall short of the pretensions of a place. In others, the staff and food might be pleasing but the architecture and design aren't. A **Deluxe** rate (**$$$**) hotel can either be an

Most of the hotels in Sri Lanka were built – and cater for – mass-market tourism. Older ones survive from the days when travel was more leisurely and the guest was exactly that, a 'guest', not a tour operator's 'pax'. Not all old hotels of character are without shortcomings, and if you really do want hot water and air conditioning, you should stick to the newer properties. That's why I have included some of the newer ones as well in this list.

Some of the new hotels have an appeal because they are original and offer something different. Generally, the independent traveller will be better served by hotels that were not created for group tourism, but for individuals. Boutique hotels fall into that category and I have listed some of them here as well as elsewhere.

Amangalla (formerly New Oriental Hotel) Galle (see page 261)
Amanwella Tangalle (see page 277)
Bandarawela Hotel Bandarawela (see page 157)
Closenberg Hotel Galle (see page 264)
Deer Park Hotel Giritale (see pages 136–7)
Ella Adventure Park Ella (see page 160)
Fits Margosa Pavilion Jaffna (see page 303)
Fort Hammenhiel Jaffna (see page 303)
Galle Face Hotel Colombo (see page 79)
Galle Fort Hotel Galle (see page 261)
Grand Hotel Nuwara Eliya (see page 173)
Grand Oriental Hotel Colombo (see page 80)

Helga's Folly Kandy (see page 112)
Heritage Tea Factory Kandapola, Nuwara Eliya (see page 174)
Hill Club Nuwara Eliya (see page 175)
Hotel Glendower Nuwara Eliya (see page 176)
Queen's Hotel Kandy (see page 113)
Royal Bar & Hotel Kandy (see page 113)
Saffron Hill House Bandarawela (see page 158)
Saman Villas Induruwa (see page 243)
St Andrew's Hotel Nuwara Eliya (see page 175)
Sun House Galle (see page 264)
Turtle Bay Kalamatiya (see page 277)
Vil Uyana Sigiriya (see page 144)

overpriced moderate one or, indeed, a luxury property that delivers everything that a tourist expects. A **Moderate ($$)** establishment is usually one of good value with a few refinements (toilet paper, mosquito coil, extra sheet) and even some pretence at being a hotel.

In the first edition of this book, I noted a failure of most hotels was the hard pillows. Now that has changed and pillows are usually comfortable and the linen is crisply laundered. However, even the newer hotels copy the older ones in having dimly lit bedrooms. If you want to read, then you must use the loo where the light is brighter. New hotels have lighting systems that are very technical with hidden switches, and sometimes it's necessary to call for help to find out how to turn them off.

Tim and Marion Gowing observed of their visit in February 2008 that the staff did not always match the purported standard of the hotel and they identified the problem as lack of proper and concentrated training and supervision. Unfortunately, the paucity of tourists (and consequently no service charge to boost the meagre wages) led staff in some hotels and restaurants to lose interest in their jobs. On the other hand, where staff are keen enough but haven't been trained by an expert (such as in the smaller, privately owned properties), service can be a shambles because they don't know what to do. It's best to keep expectations low and then be pleasantly surprised, and reward good service accordingly.

Since room rates change constantly, to indicate an approximate room rate I have classed hotels according to price, using the words Basic, Moderate, Deluxe and Luxury, but this does not apply to their standard of comfort. In fact, some Basic rate hotels offer a standard of personal attention that is better than in a Luxury rate hotel.

The room rates are the minimum for two in high season in a twin or double bedroom with breakfast, unless otherwise stated. Single rooms may occasionally be more per person than half the double room rate.

Expect the addition of ++ or +++ after the room rate in tariffs quoted by the hotels. This means that the following will be added to the quoted price: a service charge of 10% (+); government tax (++); and other extra taxes (+++), such as a Tourist Development or Regional Authority Tax. Taxes and service charge can add as much as 25% to the room rate. Where the room rate is declared as Nett, all the service charge and taxes have been included in the quoted price.

ACCOMMODATION PRICE CODES

Standard double room per night in high season (October–April west coast; April–October east coast; August hill country):

$$$$	Luxury	US$250+
$$$	Deluxe	US$100–250
$$	Moderate	US$50–100
$	Basic	<US$50

EATING AND DRINKING

The staple diet is **rice and curry**. This is not a misnomer (for curry and rice) since rice is the centrepiece and main point of the meal, with a number of different curries served in dishes to go with it. The Westerner might prefer curries and a little rice, but for the Sri Lankan a heap of rice is essential. Not all the curries are spicy hot since the word 'curry' refers to the sauced accompaniment rather than to something fiendishly fiery. Devilled is the word for that, as in devilled fish, which is fish smothered in chillies and served with chopped leeks, tomatoes and flame-red chilli sauce. Curries are actually best savoured when they are not hot in temperature, which makes them ideal for buffet service, or when the dishes are allowed to remain on the dining table to cool before you are called to eat.

The best rice and curry meals are those that are home cooked, preferably in a rural kitchen in clay pots over a wood fire. The second best are those served in country resthouses for local guests. Of course, some curries are hot and if they are not hot enough, fried and crushed raw chillies will be provided to add more fire. The addition of coconut milk will tame them a bit. If they should be too hot for your palate, try a slice of pineapple to counteract the fieriness. (A desperate Sri Lankan will ask for a teaspoon of sugar to soothe the taste buds.) Or you could try a banana, which will remove the pieces of chilli where they have settled between your teeth. Water doesn't help.

You will have a wonderful time trying to identify the ingredients of curries. You will be amazed not only at the different kinds of plants, tubers and leaves that can be eaten, but also how good it all tastes. The adventurous could try eating in village cafés, those shacks with a few tired cakes in a glass showcase, for a real rural rice and curry. Although such places sometimes call themselves hotels, they do not have rooms. The less adventurous should try a real hotel's rice and curry buffet; a little of everything to find out what tastes good.

Another attraction of Sri Lankan cuisine is the **light snacks**, some of which are called *short eats* (little bites). These range from savoury patties to deep-fried hard-boiled eggs with a lentil mix where the yolk should be, battered rolls stuffed with vegetables or a bun with a fish stew baked in it. Add to this a kind of pancake called a *hopper* (or *egg hopper* if an egg is fried in it), *string hoppers* (like a nest of vermicelli) and all kinds of *roti* (pancake-style bread) and you have the ideal food for travelling, since it can be popped in a bag to eat on the way.

On the **sweet** side there is a kind of crème caramel called *wattalapam* and something which will make yoghurt forever seem insipid: buffalo curd. This is eaten with treacle, the natural sweet sap from a kitul palm tree. Sri Lankan fruits are delicious, as well as unusual. They can be bought from street vendors or markets.

A popular drink is *thambili*, the golden-hued coconut you'll see on sale beside the coastal road to Galle. The vendor will chop off the top so you can drink the water from within. He'll even provide a straw. Ask him to cut open the nut when you've finished, so you can scoop out the flesh (it looks like the white of a poached egg) to taste young coconut at its most succulent.

There are several varieties of locally produced mineral water available from about Rs75 for a 1½-litre bottle. For easy carrying, so the bottle does not split, decant its contents into your own water bottle. Good soda water – at Rs26 (from a shop, over Rs100 in a hotel) for a 400ml bottle – is refreshing if you want to avoid sweet drinks, like Coca-Cola (about Rs30 a bottle). A great local fizzy drink is Elephant House ginger beer, at about the same price.

Sri Lanka's answer to Scotland's whisky or France's cognac is called **arrack**. There are many brands available, ranging in price for a 750ml bottle from Rs810. The purest is coconut arrack made with distilled toddy (the sap extracted from a coconut palm). Since there is not enough toddy, most brands of arrack only have a percentage of the toddy distillate blended with neutral spirit. Connoisseurs drink arrack neat or on the rocks or perhaps with soda water. Others, to disguise its smell and taste, drown it with cola or Sprite (like lemonade). Its alcohol strength is about 36.8% by volume and Sri Lankans prefer to finish a bottle in a sitting rather than leave some for another time.

Imported spirits are available everywhere although expensive because of the duty. A bottle of imported whisky, gin, rum, vodka, etc, will cost from Rs4,000 but at the airport duty-free shop for incoming passengers the price will be about half the tax-paid price. Hotels and bars sometimes add as much as 300% mark-up on the wholesale price to arrive at their list price for wines and spirits either by bottle or measure.

It is possible to buy locally produced spirits by the bottle and in bars at about a quarter of the price of imported spirits. The local gin (at around Rs1,230 a bottle) is excellent but the whisky lacks refinement.

Wine costs from around Rs1,000 a bottle, retail, for a basic New-World red or white, but from three-times that in most hotels. French wines in the same price range are, unfortunately, not as good. A glass of house wine, usually

RESTAURANT PRICE CODES		
Price range for eating out (no wine) per person:		
$$$	Gourmet	US$25+
$$	Moderate	US$7.50–25
$	Basic	<US$7.50

April–June Avocado
(eaten with sugar), jak (also
September–October), mango
(also November–December)
May–July Durian
June–August Mangosteen
June–January Pineapple
July–August Rambattan
Year-round Papaya

Californian poured from a flagon, will cost at least Rs500 for 150ml. There is a local winery, Montanari (*Fullerton Estate, Bombuwela, Kalutara;* 034 2281497; e *lwine@slt.lk*), that produces Villa Ortensia Italian wine from imported concentrate. Party-type red, white and rosé wines cost half the price of imported wines.

Locally brewed **beer** is excellent, although if you like the popular Lion Lager brand then you probably won't like its competitor, the German-influenced Three Coins. You can get draught Lion Lager at pubs in Colombo and at the Lion Pub in Nuwara Eliya, where it was originally brewed, and at branches of the Machang chain of pubs in Alutgama, Ambalangoda, Dambulla, Diyawanna, Ekala, Homagama, Induruwa, Kandana, Kandy, Koswatta, Kurunegala, Minuwangoda, Nawala, Negombo, Panadura and Ratnapura. Carlsberg is also readily available brewed locally.

Eating out beyond Colombo's boundaries is usually best done in hotels, although resort areas do have some independent restaurants. Colombo has everything, from fast-food franchises to upmarket gourmet restaurants that cater for the connoisseur. The five-star hotel lunch and dinner buffets are superb for overdoing it, at around US$25 a head. In most cases, the price of a dish quoted on a restaurant's menu will be subject to 10% service charge (+) and the government tax (++) and a local levy (+++) which can add as much as 25% to the bill. Where the prices are quoted as Nett, the service charge and taxes are included.

A comment on amazon.com about the previous edition of this book said that I give the impression that if you don't eat in your hotel, you will go hungry. Of course, that's not the case. However, as a writer I have to consider the reality of what most visitors want. While every town and village has snack shops where pastries (short eats) and rice-and-curry meals are available, are they of a standard suitable for travellers to eat day after day? Unfortunately, Sri Lanka does not yet have much of a restaurant culture outside Colombo.

PUBLIC HOLIDAYS AND FESTIVALS

When you are feeling hot, tired and thirsty after a day's outing, it is not only frustrating but also weird that you can't have a beer to quench your thirst because the moon will be full that night. *Poya* Day, as the day of the full moon is called, is celebrated by Buddhists as a day of worship. Consequently it is a dry day with all liquor shops, pubs, casinos and even hotel bars closed. True, some places will serve tourists clandestinely with beer in a teapot and cups, or in the backroom of a resthouse. In a hotel you would be able to get a drink on room service or from your minibar. Many Sri Lankans, even those who are Buddhist, will drink in the privacy of their homes on days when alcohol is not sold. Strangely, since it is a Christian festival, the sale of alcohol is sometimes banned by government fiat on Christmas Day but that doesn't seem to happen every year.

As well as Poya days there are other national holidays when everything grinds to a halt, and it usually takes a couple of days to crank into action again. If a holiday falls on a Thursday, some people will take the Friday off too to extend the holiday into the weekend. There are other combinations, such as Monday off if the Poya day is a Tuesday. If a holiday coincides with a weekend, then an extra day off during the week is expected. The official holiday for the national New Year in April is two days but many house and shop staff take two weeks off, since that is the traditional time of the year to return to one's village home.

There are also occasional bank holidays. With about 26 public holidays a year and an entitlement of 45 paid days leave a year as well as every Saturday and Sunday off work, Sri Lanka really is a holiday island.

PUBLIC HOLIDAYS The following is the list of public holidays during 2014. When the official holiday falls on a Saturday or Sunday other days may be given as additional holidays. Where a date is in bold it is fixed at the same date every year; holidays marked with a * are variable (usually according to the moon) and the dates change from year to year. Poya holidays are observed on the day of each full moon.

14 January	Tamil Thai Pongal Day*
14 January	Milad un-Nabi (Holy Prophet's Birthday)*
15 January	Duruthu Full Moon Poya Day*
4 February	**National Day**
14 February	Navam Full Moon Poya Day*
27 February	Maha Sivarathri Day*
16 March	Madin Full Moon Poya Day*
13 April	**Day prior to Sinhala and Tamil New Year**
14 April	**Sinhala and Tamil New Year Day**
14 April	Bak Full Moon Poya Day*
18 April	Good Friday*
1 May	**May Day**
14 May	Vesak Full Moon Poya Day*
15 May	Day following Vesak Full Moon Poya Day*
12 June	Poson Full Moon Poya Day*
12 July	Esala Full Moon Poya Day*
29 July	Eid al-Fitr (End of Ramadan)*
10 August	Nikini Full Moon Poya Day*
8 September	Binara Full Moon Poya Day*
5 October	Eid al-Adha (Hadji Festival Day)*
8 October	Vap Full Moon Poya Day*
22 October	Deepavali Festival Day
6 November	Il Full Moon Poya Day*
6 December	Unduvap Full Moon Poya Day*
25 December	**Christmas Day**

FESTIVALS
December–April
Sri Pada Pilgrimage Season Sri Pada (Adam's Peak), in the southwest corner of the Central Highlands, is 2,243m high. Thousands of pilgrims of many faiths climb the mountain to pay homage and make observance commencing from the full-moon day of December to the full-moon day of April the following year. Buddhists believe that it enshrines the footprint of Gauthama Buddha at the summit. Hindus, Muslims and Christians also make the pilgrimage for their own religious reasons.

Duruthu Perahera A colourful religious pageant with caparisoned elephants, torch-bearers and dancers at the Kelaniya Temple, 12km from Colombo.

Tamil Thai Pongal Thai Pongal is an ancient thanksgiving harvest festival celebrated by Hindus the world over. Houses are decorated with mango and plantain leaves and the hearth is decorated with rice flour. The festival is important for farmers to share happiness with nature.

Navam Perahera A colourful traditional perahera organised by Gangaramaya Temple in Colombo with parades of dancers, elephants and whip crackers.

Sinhalese and Tamil New Year The two main ethnic groups, Sinhalese and Tamil, celebrate a common traditional New Year at what was originally a harvest thanksgiving festival that marks the passage of the sun from Pisces to Aries. It occurs on 13 and 14 April. Games customary to the time and other rituals take place, and it is two days of fun for everyone.

Vesak This is a thrice-blessed day for Buddhists as it commemorates the birth of Prince Siddhartha, his attaining enlightenment and his passing away into nirvana as Gauthama Buddha. The day is devoted to religious observances and charity as well as being celebrated with illuminations, pageants and *pandals* (decorated and electrified hoardings). Celebrants set up wayside stalls to distribute food and refreshment to pilgrims and passers-by.

Poson This commemorates the advent of Buddhism in Sri Lanka and the day is celebrated with religious observances as well as illuminations and processions.

Esala festivals The main festival is in Kandy where a spectacular pageant is held for ten nights climaxing with Kandyan dancers and drummers, chieftains in court dress, elephants, torch-bearers and whip crackers in a splendid procession of processions, the real perahera. Kataragama, where a jungle shrine is dedicated to the god Skanda, is a popular pilgrim centre for Buddhists and Hindus and the season is commemorated by fire-walking. At Dondra, a shrine dedicated to the god Vishnu is the centre of celebrations featuring Kandy and low-country dancing. In Bellanwila a perahera features low-country folk dancing as well as Kandyan dancers. At Munneswaram there is fire-walking.

August
Vel Colombo's main Hindu festival (but not an official holiday) takes place with the ornately decorated Vel Chariot making its annual trip from one temple to another.

Deepavali The festival of lights celebrated by all Hindus.

Sangamitta Day: Unduvap This day commemorates the bringing from India of the shoot of the sacred Bo tree under which Gauthama Buddha attained enlightenment.

TIME

Time in Sri Lanka has changed three times in the past two decades as different governments have adjusted the clocks in an effort to maximise daylight usage.

Sri Lanka is now back in the same time band as India, that is 5½ hours ahead of GMT, or 4½ hours ahead of BST (British Summer Time) and 3½ hours ahead of continental Europe time. It is the same time as India, and 30 minutes ahead of time in Maldives, 2½ hours ahead of Dubai and 2½ hours behind Singapore. You will find time shown using the 12-hour and 24-hour clocks. In this book, I have used the 24-hour clock.

Sri Lankans are not obsessed with punctuality except where an auspicious time has to be observed for the start of a new undertaking. Meal times are flexible, with lunch taken from 11.30 to 14.00 depending on a person's employment. The evening meal is generally taken late, just before going to bed.

BUSINESS HOURS Government concerns and most private businesses observe a five-day week, although travel agents and airlines may also be open on Saturday morning. Commercial office hours are 08.00–17.00. Government offices are open from 09.00 to 17.00 but staff often leave earlier to catch their train or bus home. Shops in Colombo open from 10.00 to 20.00; many also open at the weekend. Out of Colombo, shops in towns open from 09.00 and in villages seem to be open all day and every day, except at the Sinhalese–Tamil New Year. In Colombo some shops are open 24 hours a day.

Bank hours depend on the branch but banks are generally open from 09.00 to 13.00 or 15.00, Monday to Friday. Some are also open at the weekend.

Hotel bars are open from 11.00 to 23.00, discos and nightclubs usually from 21.00 to 02.00. Places with pub licences sometimes close for a break in the afternoons (14.00–17.00), and close at 23.00. Restaurants open from 12.00 to 15.00 and from 18.00 to 23.00 but hours are flexible to suit diners. Casinos are open 24 hours a day, closing only on Poya days, but they keep to standard hours for alcoholic drinks service.

SHOPPING

The best shops are in Colombo while the resorts will have a few souvenir shops specialising in crafts such as batiks, lace and woodwork. There will also be gem shops. Towns and villages are a wonderful jumble of local shops from grocers to florists (actually funeral parlours). A visit to a village market is fascinating, and great for photography of odd goods and characters. Tom Ellis liked the marketplaces but commented: 'Based on personal experience, I would say it is necessary to haggle extensively, as prices are greatly inflated for foreigners.' In catering specifically for tourists the prices quoted could be triple what the vendor is prepared to accept.

CRAFTS Sri Lankan handicrafts are the products of age-old techniques and tools, and of natural, indigenous raw materials, fashioned in the cottages of craftsmen and women, or in rural craft centres, and incorporate a legacy of centuries of skill. The ancient Indo-Aryan social system assigned certain trades and pursuits to specific socio-economic groups, or castes. It was within these castes that historical skills were preserved with a high degree of purity and a distinct ethnic identity.

Traditional handicrafts have vivid colour combinations (mainly red, green, yellow and black) and bold design. Items are made of silver and brass; reed, rush, bamboo and rattan; coir (coconut fibre); lacquer ware; batik, handloom fabrics and lace. Also there are drums and other musical instruments, pottery, wood carvings including demon masks, papier-mâché dolls, embroidered garments and linen.

ARTS AND ENTERTAINMENT

Local artists flourish and several hold exhibitions either in hotel lobbies or in galleries. Popular private galleries in Colombo are **The Gallery Café** (*2 Alfred Hse Rd*) and **Barefoot** (*704 Galle Rd*), and there is also a **National Art Gallery** [76 E4] (*106 Green Path*). An open-air one-day-only art exhibition for any artists who want to exhibit their work is held annually in Colombo and many amateur artists from towns and villages display their work. In Kandy, Thilanka Hotel has a perpetual but ever-changing exhibition of local artists' paintings that can be bought through reception. Also in Kandy, the new Amaara Sky Hotel has over 80 paintings by local artists hanging on its walls. Sri Lankan paintings, in general, are uninhibited with a bold use of colour, although many seem to be copies of other local artists' work.

There are several dance performing groups whose shows can be seen at tourist hotels in Colombo and on the coast. There are also occasional performances by local classical (both Western and oriental) orchestras and by choirs, particularly at Christmas. As well as many groups who play bland and ancient pop music in hotel lobbies and casinos, there is a small coterie of heavy-metal musicians, and some jazz too. Local pop music tends to be rather melodramatic, harping on unrequited love, while traditional airs have a bouncy rhythm that soon gets people dancing. Beach hotels sometimes feature musicians in silly straw hats warbling popular songs like 'Yellow Bird'. There are discos, too, either temporary ones for hotel guests or major ones in Colombo.

PHOTOGRAPHY

Be careful what you photograph and avoid any sensitive subject such as military people and installations like checkpoints, airports, ports, railway stations and even museums. People generally don't mind having their photograph taken, but do ask first – although asking permission will often have them posing like mad, instead of the natural shot you were hoping for.

Photo permits are required for photography at the Kandy Temple and cost Rs50 for a still camera and Rs250 for a video camera. The cost of a photographic permit is included in the entrance fee of US$12 to the main archaeological sites but not at Dambulla (entrance Rs400) where photography is not allowed.

MEDIA AND COMMUNICATIONS

FILMS The latest films (copies) can be hired in digital form from outlets in every town. DVDs are available at low rates in Colombo's shopping malls. There are cinemas in Colombo (see box, page 86) and the towns, which show imported films as well as locally produced ones.

INTERNET The internet is as ubiquitous in Sri Lanka as it is elsewhere, and there is broadband in the main areas as well as Wi-Fi. While Colombo has many internet cafés, there are also bureaux throughout the country where you can surf the internet and send emails. Hotel business centres also provide the same service, perhaps in pleasanter surroundings, but these are likely to be more expensive. There are several internet service providers. The domain code for Sri Lanka is lk.

POST The General Post Office is in Colombo by the back entrance of the Fort railway station in D R Wijewardene Mawatha (℘ *011 2326203*), having been relocated there from its grand 19th-century building opposite the President's House for security reasons.

It is open 24 hours a day, every day, but only for the sale of stamps outside regular hours. General opening hours are: registered letters 08.00–16.00; money orders 09.00–15.00; poste restante 07.00–21.00; philatelic bureau 09.00–15.00; stamps (large denominations) 07.00–18.00; telex, fax, telegrams and overseas calls 09.00–15.00. The philatelic bureau stocks a collection of intriguing first-day covers for sale.

There are 4,737 post offices on the island which, in theory, means there is one post office for every 14km radius. Every town has its own government post office and villages have sub post offices. In Colombo and major towns there are also privately operated agency post offices. The postal service is generally good, with blue-shirted postmen on bicycles delivering the mail door to door once a day, except on Sundays and public holidays. The outgoing mail service is quick too. Rates increase frequently; at the time of going to press an airmail letter cost Rs75 to England, and a local letter Rs5, or Rs15 if a business letter.

Courier services For important mail it is preferable to use courier services since this provides a tracking system, by internet, of where the package is, and there is less chance of it going astray. There are over 30 courier companies represented in Colombo including the main ones of **DHL** (*148 Vauxhall St, Colombo 2;* \ *011 2304304*) and **FedEx** (*300 Galle Rd, Colombo 3;* \ *011 4522222*). They pick up through their local offices anywhere in Sri Lanka.

There are also internal courier services including ACE Xpress (*315 Vauxhall St, Colombo 2;* \ *011 2308444*), which has branches in Fort, Ratmalana, Biyagama, Katunayake, Jaffna, Kandy and Nuwara Eliya. Other courier services can be found on www.shiplink.lk/sri-lanka-courier.html.

PUBLICATIONS There are three major daily newspapers published in English. The *Daily News* is run by a government-owned company and hence the news has a government-of-the-day slant. The *Island* and the *Daily Mirror* are independent. All carry agency and English newspaper reports. There are four major Sunday newspapers in English: the *Observer*, part of the same government group as the *Daily News*; the *Sunday Times*, part of the same group as the *Daily Mirror*; and the *Sunday Island* and *Sunday Leader*.

Two monthly magazines deal with business: *LMD* (*Lanka Monthly Digest*) which is motivational in tone, and the respected *Business Today* covering local enterprises. A free magazine that contains interesting features and bags of tips for visitors (including a map and a monthly timetable of all passenger flights in and out of Colombo) is *Explore Sri Lanka* (*2 Temple Lane, Colombo 3;* \ *011 2597991; e esl@btoptions.com; www.btoptions.com*). It is available by subscription or free in some hotel bedrooms. Published quarterly by the Western Province Tourist Board is a free magazine of features and facts called *Amazing Sri Lanka*, whose editorial consultant is the author of this book (*www.wptb.lk*). The glossy magazine *Hi!!* (*Wijeya Newspapers, 8 Hunupitiya Cross Rd, Colombo 2;* \ *011 5330812; e subs@wijeya.lk; www.hi.lk*) features over 150 pages of photographs of Sri Lanka's smart set and breathless text, and is eagerly snapped up when it appears every few weeks.

International news magazines are available at hotel bookshops and Colombo supermarket outlets, as is the *International Herald Tribune*. There is no regular supply of daily newspapers from Britain.

Books Colombo has some very good bookshops and there are also bookshops in the major hotels. All the bookshops have sections dedicated to books on Sri Lanka. For some of the books about Sri Lanka that might be useful, see *Appendix 3*, page 111. For secondhand books, either to buy or to borrow for a fee against a deposit, visit the well-stocked **bookstalls** [76 E2] by the roundabout where D R Wijewardene Mawatha joins T B Jayah Mawatha near Maradana railway station in Colombo.

Barefoot Bookshop 704 Galle Rd, Colombo 3; ☎011 2589305; e merchandiser.barefoot@gmail.com; www.barefootceylon.com. Specialises in books with a local theme; also coffee-table books & books on photography & architecture.

Bookland 430–432 Galle Rd, Colombo 3; ☎011 2565284. A general bookstore with a well-organised Sri Lanka section.

Lakehouse Bookshop 1st Flr, Liberty Plaza Shopping Complex, R A De Mel Mawatha, Colombo 3; ☎011 2574418. There are also branches in Dehiwela & Nugegoda.

M D Gunasena 217 Olcott Mawatha, Colombo 11; ☎011 2323981; e info@mdgunasena.com; www.mdgunasena.com. With branches in Avissawella, Bambalapitiya, Bandarawela, Borella, Galle, Gampaha, Hulftsdorp, Kandy, Kalutara, Kiribathgoda, Kurunegala, Matara, Negombo, Panadura, Piliyandala & Ratnapura, this popular family bookseller is also a well-respected publisher of notable Sri Lankan books.

Odel 5 Alexandra Pl, Colombo 7; ☎011 4722200; e info@eodel.com; www.odel.lk. On this department store's mezzanine floor is an attractive layout of illustrated books with a large section devoted to books about Sri Lanka, in a pleasant atmosphere for browsing.

Taprobane 720 Galle Rd, Colombo 3. A pioneering bookshop with outlets at hotels, including the Galadari.

Vijitha Yapa Bookshop Unity Plaza, Galle Rd, Colombo 4; ☎011 2596960; e vybunity@gmail.com; www.vijithayapa.com. An innovative bookseller, with branches at Crescat Bd, Nugegoda, Kandy, Galle, Matara, Negombo, Colombo 7 & at the transit lounge at the airport often featuring bargain-priced books as well as their own published works.

Maps The bookshops have commercially produced maps on sale. Simpler are the ones produced by the **Survey Department** (*Kirula Rd, Colombo 5;* ☎ *011 2585111; www.survey-dept.slt.lk*). The compact 52cm x 36cm map is at a scale of 1:1,000,000, which means 10km to 1cm (ten miles to five-eighths of an inch). The Survey Department's road map is much larger (scale of 1:500,000 or 5km to 1cm) and has town plans of Nuwara Eliya, Anuradhapura, Polonnaruwa, Kandy, Colombo and Sri Jayewardenepura, as well as a distance chart, resthouse locations and railway lines.

An invaluable book for finding your way around is *Arjuna's A-Z Street Guide* (*Arjuna Consulting Co Ltd, 60 School Av, Dehiwala;* e *arjunaco@slt.lk*). The latest edition has 112 pages with street maps not just of Colombo and suburbs but also of Galle, Kandy, Nuwara Eliya, Negombo, Anuradhapura, Polonnaruwa, Trincomalee, Batticaloa and Jaffna. The maps are in colour and there is an alphabetical street index as well as easy grid referencing.

There is an excellent A4-size book, *Sri Lanka Road Atlas*, covering the entire island with street maps of major towns published by Sarasavi Publishers (*30 Stanley Thilakaratne Mawatha, Nugegoda*) with a scale of 1:250,000 (about 2½km or four miles to one inch).

RADIO The government-owned Sri Lanka Broadcasting Corporation is based in Colombo and serves the whole island through various channels in English, Sinhala and Tamil. BBC World Service news is relayed in English. There are several independent radio stations that specialise in pop-music broadcasting.

IMPORTANT AREA CODES

Colombo	011	Gampola	081	Monaragala	055
Ampara	063	Hambantota	047	Nawalapitiya	054
Anuradhapura	025	Hatton	051	Negombo	031
Avissawella	036	Kalmunai	067	Nuwara Eliya	052
Badulla	055	Kalutara	034	Polgahawela	037
Bandarawela	057	Kandy	081	Polonnaruwa	027
Batticaloa	065	Katana	031	Puttalam	032
Chilaw	032	Kegalle	035	Ratnapura	045
Dikoya	051	Kurunegala	037	Tangalle	047
Galle	091	Matale	066	Trincomalee	026
Gampaha	033	Matara	041	Vavuniya	024

Dialog Axiata: area code plus 4 plus six-digit number
Lanka Bell: area code plus 5 plus six-digit number

TELEPHONE To phone Sri Lanka from overseas, dial whatever you need to get into your country's international system, usually 00, followed by 94 as the Sri Lanka country code. Follow this with the area code or the mobile phone code, which is a three-digit number beginning with zero. Do not dial the zero. Thus my area code is 034, but from overseas I would dial 94 34. My manager's mobile phone code is 077, and from overseas I would dial 94 77 to reach him. The Tourist Authority's Travel Information Centre number is 011 2437059; from overseas it is 94 11 2437059.

All telephone numbers in Sri Lanka were changed during 2003 and 2004 to make them ten-digit numbers beginning with 0. This has created considerable confusion since then and if you are confronted with an old number that you dial unsuspectingly, the operator's advice is in Sinhala or Tamil so you still won't know what to do. When there is a recording in English, it is a haughty voice saying 'The number you dialled is not in use'.

Some important area codes are listed in the box above, but not all codes are included. You will need to dial the area code when phoning from one area to another, but not within the area. Thus if you are phoning me from Colombo, you need to dial 034 first. I need to dial 011 to phone any Colombo number. However, when I am phoning my neighbour, I do not dial 034, just the number. When using a phone in Colombo omit 011 if phoning someone in Colombo.

To call someone with a mobile phone, those with 07 as part of the three-digit area code, you dial the number in full. When calling any number from a mobile phone the three-digit area code (such as 011 for Colombo) and the number or the full mobile number must be dialled.

There are three fixed-phone (landline) systems: Sri Lanka Telecom, Lanka Bell and Dialog Axiata (formerly Suntel). There are five mobile-telephone companies: Etisalat (formerly Celltel, then Tigo), Mobitel, Dialog, Airtel and Hutchinson. There are various pre-paid calling cards for calls using mobile phones. Mobile phones can be rented for short periods from the various companies and there are mobile phone counters at the airport.

Useful telephone numbers

Sri Lanka Telecom ☏ 011 2329711; e pr@slt. lk; www.slt.lk

Directory Assistance ☏ 1231 (National), 1234 (International)

IDD Inquiries ☎011 2449216	**Emergency telephone numbers**

IDD Inquiries ☎011 2449216
Fault reporting ☎1241
Time (in English) ☎1294
Lanka Bell ☎011 5375375; www.lankabell.net
Dialog Axiata ☎011 4747474; www.suntel.lk
Airtel m 075 5555555; www.airtel.lk
Etisalat m 072 3123123; www.etisalat.lk
Mobitel m 071 2755777; www.mobitellanka.com
Dialog m 077 7678678; www.dialog.lk
Hutchinson m 078 8632632; www.hutch.lk

Emergency telephone numbers
Police emergency number ☎119
Emergency rescue service ☎110
Government Information Service ☎1919;
www.gic.gov.lk
Accident service ☎011 2691111, ext 544
Bomb disposal ☎011 2434251
Fire & ambulance ☎011 2422222
Police ☎011 2433333
Flight information ☎019 7332677/011 2252861

For phoning overseas there are call boxes of different phone companies that can be used by purchasing a phonecard, usually from a shop nearby. The access code is 00. When phoning from a hotel, you would need the hotel's access code first, usually 9, then 00. Hotel telephone rates are high, so it's worth buying a phonecard and finding a phone booth, or use a locally acquired mobile phone service.

Every town and village has a fax bureau from where it is possible to fax home or make overseas telephone calls.

TELEVISION There are several television channels, some of which relay CNN, BBC World and Sky TV. Much of the programming consists of local musical talent shows, slow-moving tele-dramas in Sinhala and fast-moving Indian movies in Tamil or Hindi. International TV programming is available by satellite.

BUSINESS

The major hotels in Colombo have their own business centres to handle what a secretary usually does. Assistance with arranging conferences can be obtained through the **Sri Lanka Convention Bureau** (*4th Flr, Hotel School Bldg, 78 Galle Rd, Colombo 3;* ☎*011 4865050;* e *slcb@sltnet.lk; www.visitsrilanka.net*).

BUYING PROPERTY

Foreigners can and do buy property in Sri Lanka but it involves considerable patience as well as expense. Do not assume that a property has a clear title. In many cases, if the property has not changed hands for many years, there may not actually be a surveyed plan and title. So that has to be arranged, during which process many unknown owners might turn up for a share of the proceeds with the result that the price rises. There is also a 100% tax payable by foreigners. Good, professional advice will certainly be needed, especially as the law relating to land (and apartment) purchase by foreigners seems to change frequently.

Many foreigners who say they own a property in Sri Lanka in fact only lease it (usually on an informal basis) from or through a Sri Lankan contact. For foreigners who are not planning to spend the whole year in Sri Lanka, but only the winter months, informal arrangements can be useful, since someone is there to look after the property when the foreigner is absent. Alternatively, renting a property (even a suite in a boutique hotel or guesthouse) for a few months can be a sensible alternative to actually owning a property and not living in it year-round. Also, what happens to property owned by foreigners when they die is a grey area. As desirable as Sri Lanka might seem for retirement, it is not easy in terms of obtaining resident visas or for people who are accustomed to a different culture.

There are only a few real-estate agents; details can be found on www. lankapropertyweb.com/agents/estate_agents.php. Villas can be rented through agents (see pages 268–9).

CULTURAL ETIQUETTE

Sri Lankans are tolerant of breaches in social etiquette by foreigners, so do not let your anxiety to conform and not give offence deter you from enjoying your holiday. It is accepted that you, as a foreigner, might not be privileged to know very much about local habits.

The major culture shock will come when you are invited to eat in a Sri Lankan home and find there is no cutlery. Thus you discover that the technique of eating with your fingers is not as easy as it looks. You use only your right hand, letting your fingers and thumb mix the food together into a convenient-sized morsel, which you then pop into your mouth using your thumb as a guide. You do not pick up chicken by the bone and gnaw it as you would at a barbecue. You use your fingers (right hand only) to peel the chicken off the bone; usually meat will be of a convenient bite size anyway. If you can't manage, you won't cause offence if you ask for a spoon and use that instead.

The next shock comes when you go to the loo and there's no toilet paper. The secret is always to carry a few sheets of tissues with you. However, if you have forgotten, then you must use the traditional method, which is to splash yourself clean with water using the utensil provided, and your left hand. The passing of anything to another person should always be done with the right hand.

The Sri Lankan all-purpose greeting is *ayubowan*, uttered while keeping one's own hands with palms together at chest height. It means 'may you have long life' and if you are greeted in that manner, respond in kind. Handshaking is an acceptable greeting, but do not offer your hand to a monk.

Many Sri Lankans, whether Buddhist or Hindu, do not eat beef, and Muslims do not eat pork. So, if you are inviting Sri Lankan friends for a meal, choose your menu or the restaurant with that in mind. All restaurants have a good vegetarian selection.

Modesty in dress will always be appreciated. A male tourist who feels like 'going native' by adopting the Sri Lankan man's traditional garb of a sarong, will be regarded with amusement if he wears it other than on the beach or in bed. The sarong is a length of waist-to-ankle cloth with its ends sewn together to form a kind of cloth tube. It is donned by pulling it over the head and draping it around the waist and legs. Secure it by tying it around your waist as you would a beach towel. A sarong is the ideal garment to wear in bed as it can act as a covering sheet when no such sheet is available. Shorts, whether worn by women or men, are frowned upon for temple visits, which is when you might find yourself wrapped in a sarong. Female visitors who learn from Sri Lankan friends how to wear a sari for social occasions will be much admired.

Perhaps it is the colonial instinct of many visitors from Western countries – an urge to educate and reform – which inspires many foreigners to explain to Sri Lankans how things should be done. I once had to listen to an English couple at a nearby table telling their Sri Lankan driver all about England while they completely ignored the wondrous beauty of the scenery and the serenity of the river flowing past the restaurant's garden. I urge visitors to forget the way things are done 'at home' and accept and appreciate all Sri Lanka has. And listen patiently to what you are being told. Even if the manner in which a local is doing something is neither logical nor efficient, is too slow or unhygienic, and perhaps even sick-making, it is not necessary

At the Chaaya Tranz Hotel in Hikkaduwa, a town where tourists and locals inevitably mix, this notice offering good advice appears in each guest room:

IN RELIGIOUS PLACES:

Remove your hat and shoes Shoes should always be removed and left outside the main worship area. A pile of shoes is an obvious indication of where to leave them.

Show respect Turn off mobile phones, remove headphones, lower your voice, avoid inappropriate conversation and no smoking or chewing gum.

Cover yourself Shoulders should be covered and long pants worn rather than shorts.

Respect the statues Never touch, sit near, or climb on a statue. Get permission before taking photographs and never do so during worship.

Don't point Pointing at things or people around the place is considered extremely rude.

Stand up If you happen to be sitting in the worship area when monks or nuns enter, stand to show respect; wait until they have finished their prostrations before sitting again.

IN PUBLIC PLACES:

Kissing, hugging and public demonstrations of intimate behaviour is considered impolite. If you must demonstrate your love for your partner, please be respectful and mindful of the social environment you are in.

Alcoholism, drug usage (illegal) and smoking (banned in public places) causes poverty, ill health and other negative social issues. Please try to make and be a good role model and be an example to local people through your own behaviour.

Prostitution is prohibited, and guests shall not bring any illegal thing into the hotel.

for you, the visitor, the guest, to try to change or even comment on it. Sri Lanka is not the same as your home country; better to leave it that way and to learn from it.

Do not be surprised if someone speaks perfect English, even with a better vocabulary than you. English is a national language and many Sri Lankans speak it all the time and won't take it as a compliment if congratulated on how well they speak what is their mother tongue.

A scourge for tourists that seems to be increasing is hassling by touts and beggars. These are persistent. The best way to deal with them, unless what they are offering appeals, is to ignore them completely, however rude your behaviour may seem to you. You may also find yourself shadowed in a shop by an assistant desperate to sell you something, when all you want to do is 'look around'. If that's annoying, just leave the shop.

The following remarks are taken from a leaflet issued by the tourist board:

Mode of dress in public and sacred places   Visitors to shrines, temples and other places of worship should be modestly attired. A knee-length dress is appropriate in these places. Footwear and head-gear must be removed before entering a Buddhist or Hindu shrine. Photography is allowed with prior permission, but posing alongside or with religious statues is not permitted. Please also note that swimwear is not acceptable attire in public places.

Nudism and topless bathing   Nudism is prohibited, as is topless bathing by females.

Drugs   Import/export, possession or trafficking in narcotics and dangerous drugs are strictly forbidden by law and carry heavy penalties.

Child abuse   Sri Lanka is determined to stamp out the crime of child abuse. In this it is co-operating with the international community. Recent amendments to existing legislation in the Penal Code of Sri Lanka imposed severe and deterrent penalties for all acts of child abuse. In terms of this legislation, children are defined as persons below the age of 18. Punishments for sexual abuse range from a mandatory sentence of seven to 20 years of imprisonment with fines and a payment of compensation to child victims.

Prostitution and pornography   Male and female prostitution, sexual exploitation, homosexuality, and all forms of pornography are offences punishable by law in Sri Lanka.

A 204-page book has been published with the title *Culture Shock! Sri Lanka* (see page 311). Mainly intended for the expatriate who is taking up residence in Sri Lanka, it has much good advice for the adventurous visitor too. 'Sri Lanka,' the authors warn, 'is not what it initially appears to be.'

Eric J Butler of London, an experienced traveller, wrote of his visit to Colombo:

For me (I am 75 years of age) probably the most serendipitous moment to date was on the first evening of my arrival in the lounge of a Colombo five-star hotel when I was approached by a very pretty Chinese hooker from Beijing who wanted to come to my room to give me a massage. We had a very pleasant talk (in the lounge) before she drifted away. 'Never in the field of human conflict etc' have I had an experience of this sort in a major hotel abroad. I have to say I rather enjoyed it even without the 'massage' as the lady concerned said she was only 27 years old. Long live serendipity!

STUFF YOUR RUCKSACK – AND MAKE A DIFFERENCE

www.stuffyourrucksack.com is a website set up by TV's Kate Humble which enables travellers to give direct help to small charities, schools or other organisations in the country they are visiting. Maybe a local school needs books, a map or pencils, or an orphanage needs children's clothes or toys – all things that can easily be 'stuffed in a rucksack' before departure. The charities get exactly what they need and travellers have the chance to meet local people and see how and where their gifts will be used.

The website describes organisations that need your help and lists the items they most need. Check what's needed in Sri Lanka, contact the organisation to say you're coming and bring not only the much-needed goods but an extra dimension to your travels and the knowledge that in a small way you have made a difference.

Part Two

THE GUIDE

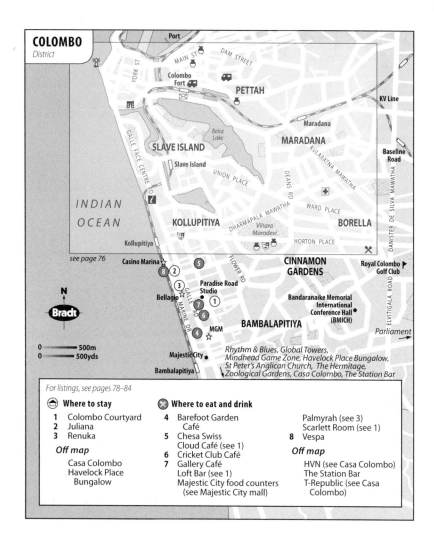

COLOMBO
District

Port

MAIN ST

DAM STREET

YORK ST

Colombo Fort

PETTAH

KV Line

Maradana

Beira Lake

MARADANA

Baseline Road

KULARATNA MAWATHA

GALLE FACE CENTRE RD

SLAVE ISLAND

Slave Island

UNION PLACE

DEANS RD

DHARMAPALA MAWATHA

WARD PLACE

DANISTER DE SILVA MAWATHA

INDIAN OCEAN

KOLLUPITIYA

Kollupitiya

Vihara Maradevi

HORTON PLACE

BORELLA

see page 76

Casino Marina

8 2

5

CINNAMON GARDENS

Royal Colombo ▶ Golf Club

FLOWER RD

3

Paradise Road Studio

Bellagio

7   1

6

Bandaranaike Memorial International Conference Hall ● (BMICH)

ELVITIGALA ROAD

GALLE RD

MARINE DR

MGM

4

BAMBALAPITIYA

Parliament

N

Bradt

0 ———— 500m
0 ———— 500yds

Majestic City ●

Bambalapitiya

Rhythm & Blues, Global Towers,
Mindhead Game Zone, Havelock Place Bungalow,
St Peter's Anglican Church, The Hermitage,
Zoological Gardens, Casa Colombo, The Station Bar

For listings, see pages 78–84

🛏 **Where to stay**

1 Colombo Courtyard
2 Juliana
3 Renuka

Off map

 Casa Colombo
 Havelock Place
  Bungalow

🍴 **Where to eat and drink**

4 Barefoot Garden
  Café
5 Chesa Swiss
 Cloud Café (see 1)
6 Cricket Club Café
7 Gallery Café
 Loft Bar (see 1)
 Majestic City food counters
  (see Majestic City mall)

 Palmyrah (see 3)
 Scarlett Room (see 1)
8 Vespa

Off map

 HVN (see Casa Colombo)
 The Station Bar
 T-Republic (see Casa
  Colombo)

3

Colombo

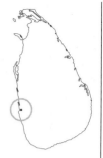

Not many world travellers would admit to Colombo being their favourite city, but it is mine, especially so as the authorities work hard to restore buildings and make the city greener and tidier. Facing the Indian Ocean and stretching 14km along Sri Lanka's western shore, it has within its boundaries an astonishing variety of people, historical monuments, simple temples, gleaming hotels, trendy restaurants, glittering casinos, fascinating department stores, tree-lined boulevards, mysterious lanes, old and new markets, shopping malls, and even skyscrapers. It never disappoints, although on a hot, hectic day it is certainly tiring.

It is not a city of romance like Paris, or of ruthless commerce like Hong Kong, nor is it dedicated to progress like Singapore, or to fun like Bangkok. Colombo has no such pretensions, being simply an ancient maritime settlement that has burgeoned into a modern metropolis.

The traffic is heavy in the day, thins out late evening, and then the streets seem eerily deserted at night. There are no central squares but the city has its areas of character: Fort and Pettah; Galle Face Green and the neon-lit gaming clubs of the Galle Road; and clusters of theme restaurants revitalising colonial houses.

In the 1920s it was known as the Garden City of the East and visitors stayed for weeks. Now it's a city of traffic chaos and most visitors only pass through on their way to and from their beach resorts. It used to be bombs going off that threw the city into occasional confusion; now it's the unexpected temporary closure of roads because a politician is on the move and wants priority for his motorcade. A rash of one-way streets has broken out too, often resulting in a long and frustrating detour wherever you are heading.

HISTORY

Colombo's history starts later than that of the Cultural Triangle (see page 99). It was used as a port in the 8th century by Arab traders. The settlement there was referred to by a Chinese traveller in 1330 as Kao-lan-pu. Even today, the Sinhalese call it Kolomba, which seems similar.

The settlement was fortified by the Portuguese in the 16th century with a wooden stockade, which the Dutch improved. The British, who came in 1796, extended the city south and east beyond the fort's limits, leaving a legacy of wide streets and spacious buildings, as though they knew that two centuries later they would be required to accommodate far more traffic and people than existed then. The resident population of Colombo city is estimated to be 752,993 (2012). The fort itself has completely vanished, but the area is still called, in Sinhala, Kotuwa, meaning Fort.

GETTING THERE AND AROUND

BY TRAIN If you are staying in a beach resort, it is possible to make an independent day trip to Colombo by train and, of course, Colombo is the starting point for train journeys to explore the country. However, there is no train service dedicated to moving people around the city.

There are two major stations: **Colombo Fort** [76 C1] and **Maradana** [76 F2]. Trains for the south (except those in transit from the north) start at Maradana, while trains for the north (unless they are in transit from Matara in the deep south) start at Fort. The majority of Sri Lankans, as well as visitors, whether they are going north or south, board their trains at Fort station.

Like Maradana, Fort is actually a through station, and has only two platforms that are termini; these are used by trains on the Puttalam line and the Intercity Express to Kandy. Trains originating at Fort station come in from the yard, which is actually at Maradana.

Considering the traffic that flows around it, and the people who lurk in its environs, Fort station is kept quite clean. With its wooden-faced awning stretching its length to give waiting passengers shade and shelter, it has a traditional railway-station ambience. Under the awning are the various ticket counters. There is also a place called **Railway Tours** (\ *011 2440048*), which is not the official train enquiry counter (that's inside the station; \ *011 2434215*) but serves to assist independent travellers, particularly those who might be interested in the *Viceroy Special* (see box, page 96).

At the **Berth Reservations Office** (\ *011 2432908;* ⊕ *06.00 –14.30 Mon–Sat, 06.00–12.00 Sun & hols*) reservations can be made up to 14 days in advance on trains to Anuradhapura, Badulla, Kandy, Trincomalee and Batticaloa. It is also the place where passengers who booked online to travel in the Exporail or Rajadhani air-conditioned carriages get their tickets. A new system for making seat reservations on intercity train services was introduced in 2013, which entails telephoning 365 by a local Mobitel mobile phone up to 28 days before the proposed journey. There is a website (*www.railway.gov.lk*) with all sorts of interesting information about train fares, fees for hiring trains and for photographing in stations (quoted as Rs2,000 per photo!).

There are footbridges linking the platforms and one carries on across all the lines to the station's back entrance on D R Wijewardene Mawatha. An old steam loco is permanently parked on this side of the station. Painted black and maroon with some yellow stripes, it is a cheerful sight for commuters. Built by Hunslet in 1908, it is a 4–6–0 class, No 135. The station also has other bygones of the steam age. Hanging by the stationmaster's office on Platform 3 are ancient wooden frames containing photographs of views of the railway of long ago.

Colombo's other railway station, Maradana, is to the northeast of Fort, and is not usually used by visitors. It is located away from the main area (and bus stations) in Colombo 10, but is by no means quiet. Maradana Road and the road junctions and flyover close to the station are clogged with traffic. A system of elevated walkways with shops on one side, and footbridges over the roads, helps passengers gain access without having to dodge through the traffic.

The station building retains its colonial lines even though it is hemmed in by footbridges. The main entrance faces Maradana Road with a small courtyard in front, behind railings. As you enter the station, the booking counters are grouped in a semicircle ahead of you. There is another entrance to the station across the road from the Elphinstone Theatre.

There is one other station in central Colombo. Called **Secretariat Halt** [76 C2] because of its proximity to the Presidential Secretariat, it is the stop for some commuter trains in the morning and evening. It is close to the Galadari and Hilton hotels.

Travel by train within Colombo is not practical although it would be possible to take a train from Fort to Maradana or vice versa. The Kelani Valley line (see map, page 204) has trains from Fort station to the suburbs of Baseline Road, Cotta Road, Narahenpita and Nugegoda.

BY ROAD Colombo's street plan is not as easy to follow as it should be, even though the core of the city is on the coast. Try driving through the city and you – or your driver – will become hopelessly lost because of the imposition of one-way streets, and sudden diversions when politicians are on the move. A good guide to the streets is *Arjuna's A–Z Street Guide* (see page 311).

> **TRAVELLING BY BUS?**
>
> See page 49 for a list of the bus stations in Colombo. See also page 95 for details of the popular Sundays-only city bus tour by a former 1956 London Transport double-decker Routemaster bus.

Colombo-based **taxis** and **three-wheelers** are best for seeing the city because their drivers know which roads are closed, and are generally pretty knowledgeable about the whereabouts of streets whose names you can barely pronounce. Also some street names have been changed from the ones marked on maps.

Air-conditioned taxis are available through the town's major hotels and have fixed rates for getting from one major hotel to another, or from one part of Colombo to another, or for morning or whole-day hires.

Colombo also has some radio-controlled taxis with meters and these have to be booked by telephone. Allow at least 30 minutes for pick up. Taxis do not roam the streets looking for hires and the only real taxi ranks are those attached to the major hotels.

Three-wheeler auto-rickshaw taxis buzz around ubiquitously and will stop even before you hail one, if you happen to be walking along a street minding your own business. Drivers cannot bear the sight of a foreigner walking instead of riding in their vehicles. Many have meters or the fare will depend on your bargaining powers. As a foreigner you won't be able to go anywhere for less than Rs100. If you do not agree to what the driver wants to charge you (before you get in his three-wheeler), walk away (in the opposite direction to the one he is going) and look for another. It helps then not to understand Sinhala.

Colombo is a flat city so walking is reasonably easy even if you will have to watch your step where the pavements are uneven. In the daytime the streets will be crowded as the city's population during the working day is over two million, swelled with commuters and others from out of town. At weekends and at night the crowds and their cars disappear and you can stroll the streets and stand and stare (but not for too long in case you attract the attention of the security guards) without disrupting the flow of pedestrians and traffic.

WHERE TO STAY

The Ministry of Tourism has divided Colombo's hotels into six categories for the setting of *minimum* room rates for fully independent travellers. The city's six

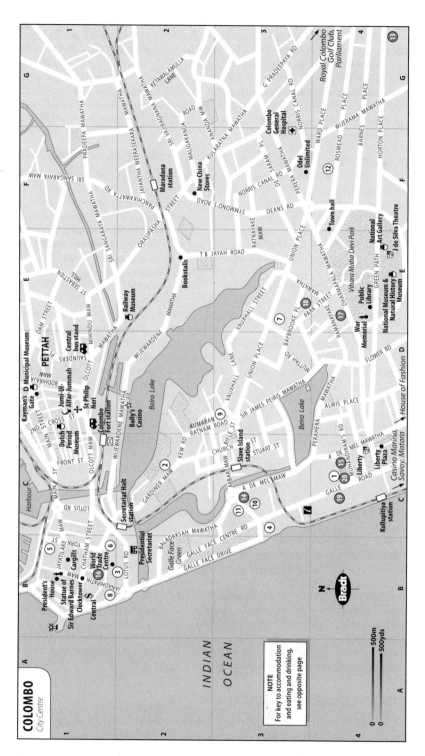

COLOMBO
City Centre

A

INDIAN

OCEAN

NOTE
For key to accommodation
and eating and drinking,
see opposite page

0   500m
0   500yds

N

Bradt

B

President's
House
Statue of
Sir Edward Barnes
Clocktower
Cargills
Central
JAYATILAKE MAW
YORK ST
CHATHAM STREET
JANADHIPATHI MAW
World
Trade
Centre
LOTUS RD
Presidential
Secretariat
Secretariat Halt
station
BALADAKSAH MAWATHA
Galle Face
Green
Galle Face Centre RD
Galle Face Drive
Harbour
MAIN ST
LOTUS RD
FRONT ST

C

Kayman's D Municipal Museum
Gate
Jumi-Ul-
2ND CROSS ST Alfar-Jummah
MAIN STREET
Dutch
Period
Museum
Colombo
Fort station
St Philip
Neri
BODHIRAJA
MAW
PETTAH
DAM STREET
MIHINDU MAW
OLCOTT MAW
WIJEWARDENE MAWATHA
Bally's
Casino
Beira Lake
GARDINER MAW
KEW RD
GALLE FACE CENTRE RD

D

Railway
Museum
Central
bus stand
SAUNDERS P
OLCOTT
WIJEWARDENE
MAWATHA
Bookstalls
Beira Lake
KUMARAN
RATNAM ROAD
CHURCH
ST
Slave Island
station
STUART ST
AKBAR MAW
A DE MEL MAW

PETTAH

ORASIPASHA

T B JAYAH ROAD

VAUXHALL STREET
VAUXHALL
LANE
UNION PLACE
BIRFLE ST
Casino Marina,
Savoy, Matara

E

SRI SANGARAYA MAWATHA
ST SEBASTIEN
HILL
MAWATHA
WIJEWARDENE

JAYANTHA WEERASEKARA
MAWATHA
SYMOND'S ROAD

DEANS RD

RATNAYAKE
MAW
UNION PLACE
BAYBROOKE PL
PARK STREET
MUTTAH RD
SIR JAMES PEIRIS MAWATHA
ALWIS PLACE
PERAHERA
DHARMAPALA MAWATHA
RAMANAYAKE
MAWATHA

New China
Stores
NORRIS CANAL SARAM PL
DE RD
PERERA MAWATHA

Maradana
station
KETAWALAMULLA
LANE
ROAD
MALIGAKANDA
SRI VAJRAGNANA MAWATHA
KULARATNA MAWATHA

F

SRI SANGARAYA MAW
PRADEEPA MAWATHA
PANCHIKAWATTA RD

G PRADEEPAYA RD
Colombo
General
Hospital
NORRIS CANAL MW
Odel
Unlimited

Town hall

National History
Museum
Public
Library
War
Memorial
Vihara Maha Devi Park
National Museum &
Natural History
Museum
GREEN PATH
National
Art Gallery
J de Silva Theatre
FLOWER RD

WARD PLACE
ROSMEAD
HORTON PLACE
BARNES
PLACE
WIJERAMA MAWATHA

Royal Colombo
Golf Club,
Parliament

G

House of Fashion
Liberty
Plaza
Liberty
ROAD
A DE RAM'S RD
MUHANDIMEL MAWATHA
GALLE
Kollupitiya
station

⑤ ⑥ ③ ⑧ ① ④ ⑪ ⑩ ⑭ ② ⑨ ⑦ ⑱ ⑰ ⑫ ⑳ ⑮ ⑲ ⑯ ⑬

five-star properties are those in Bands 1, 2 and 3; Galle Face Regency is rated as equivalent to a five-star property in minimum price but is actually the wing of the Galle Face Hotel, which is itself three-star.

The categories are Band 1: Cinnamon Grand, Colombo Hilton, Cinnamon Lakeside; Band 2: Taj Samudra, Galle Face Regency; Band 3: Galadari, The Kingsbury (formerly Ceylon Continental/Intercontinental); Band 4: Ramada, Mount Lavinia, Galle Face Classic; Band 5: Renuka, Grand Oriental; Band 6: Colombo City, Palm Beach, Pegasus Reef, Janaki, Indra Regent, Berjaya Mount Royal, Pearl City, Juliana, Sapphire, Hilton Colombo Residencies, Global Towers.

I cannot quote the actual (as opposed to enforced) minimum prices, as properties in all bands are charging as much above the minimum room rate that the market will bear. And even the minimum rate for other bands has shifted upwards as demand improves. The best rates for budget travellers would be those in Band 6, with a hotel like the Juliana quoting a double room rate of US$65 in June 2013.

Colombo's boutique hotel properties have not been categorised, and not all the hotels in the list above are reviewed in this section.

On a tight budget, US$125 (the minimum room rate for a top five-star hotel) a night might seem expensive, especially when you can find beach guesthouses out of town for a quarter of that. However, it costs less to stay at the best properties in Colombo than it does to stay in the best properties on the beach. And the Colombo hotels offer a variety of restaurants as well as experienced service and the proximity to shops and entertainment that their beach equivalents don't have. Budget hotels are few in Colombo and generally not as good as budget hotels (which are used to tourists) in the beach areas. The cheapies in Colombo are for Sri Lankans on a visit from their villages, perhaps to see a job agent or apply for a passport or petition a government minister.

Apartments are an attractive alternative to staying in a hotel, especially if you want to cater for yourself or entertain a lot; apartments can be rented by the day, week or month.

COLOMBO City Centre
For listings, see pages 78–84

Where to stay

1	Cinnamon Grand	C4	6	Hilton Colombo	B1
2	Cinnamon Lakeside	C2	7	Hilton Colombo Residences	E3
3	Galadari	B2	8	Kingsbury	B1
4	Galle Face	C3	9	Nippon	D3
5	Grand Oriental	B1	10	Ramada	C3
			11	Taj Samudra	C3
			12	Tintagel	F4

Where to eat and drink

	1864	(see 4)
13	Bay Leaf	G4
	Café 64	(see 3)
	California Grill	(see 3)
14	Castle Hotel	C3
	Cheers Pub	(see 1)
	Chinese Restaurant	(see 11)
	Chutneys	(see 1)
15	Crescat Boulevard food courts	C4
	Curry Leaf	(see 6)
16	Dutch Hospital	B1
	Echelon Pub	(see 6)
	Emperor's Wok	(see 6)
	Harpo's Colombo Fort Café	(see 16)
	Heladiv Tea Club	(see 16)
	Il Ponte	(see 6)
	In On the Green	(see 4)
	Indian Restaurant	(see 11)
	Lagoon	(see 1)
	Latitude	(see 11)
	London Grill	(see 1)
	Long Feng	(see 2)
	Ministry of Crab	(see 16)
17	Paradise Road Café	E4
18	Park Street Mews Café	E3
19	Raja Bojun	C4
	Royal Thai	(see 2)
	Seaspray	(see 4)
	Semondu	(see 16)
	Sky	(see 8)
	Spices	(see 6)
	Spoons	(see 6)
	Steak & Grill	(see 11)
20	Sugar Bistro & Wine Bar	C4
	Tao	(see 1)
	Taphouse by RnR	(see 16)
	Union Bar & Grill	(see 7)
	WIP	(see 16)

For a new arrival's first night in Colombo, the expense of a reliable, top-grade hotel is worth it, especially as the city can be enervating and exasperating after stepping off a long-haul flight. A reliable, comfortable and friendly hotel is essential to start with – you can cope with the cheapies later on. My advice would be to choose a hotel from the bands listed above for your first night or two.

Fortunately, Colombo's luxury hotels do not duplicate each other's ambience, and all are distinctive. The Hilton, Galadari and Kingsbury hotels form a hospitality triangle all within a few minutes' walking distance of each other, near the Presidential Secretariat and overlooking the Indian Ocean. All listings are included on the Colombo city centre map, page 76, unless otherwise noted.

LUXURY

⌂ **Casa Colombo** [map, page 72] (12 AC suites) 231 Galle Rd, Bambalapitiya, Colombo 4; ☏ 011 4520130; **e** reservations@casacolombo. com; www.casacolombo.com. Describes itself as a 'retro-chic designer hotel' with a 'blend of edgy, elegant chic interiors housed within a charming older building'. It is a remarkable conversion of 200-year-old Moorish mansion into a breathtaking, fun & decidedly individualistic place to stay. Such a soothing contrast to the clamour of Colombo, with every guest attended by a personable, personal 'casa domo' & endearingly eccentric suites equipped with Wi-Fi, laptops, gadgets & non-stop music. With an alfresco tapas restaurant, a grand dining room, a tea garden & a pink swimming pool, Casa Colombo is a surprising, inspiring experience to find down a suburban side road. **$$$$**

⌂ **The Kingsbury** (207 AC rooms, 21 suites, 1 Presidential Suite) 48 Janadhipathi Mawatha, Colombo 1; ☏ 011 2421221; **e** info@ thekingsburyhotel.com; www.thekingsburyhotel. com. This hotel began life on the Colombo seafront as the Ceylon Intercontinental, had a period as plain Ceylon Continental & now, taken over by one of Sri Lanka's oldest & largest conglomerates, Hayleys, has been enthusiastically renovated into a hostelry of bling catering for guests who want everything upfront. With live décor of tropical fish swimming up one of the columns in the lobby & lively restaurants (buffet, seafood & Chinese) & topped by Sky, a rooftop bar half-open to the sky, this is Colombo's flashiest hotel & a fun place to stay. **$$$$**

⌂ **Tintagel** (10 AC suites) 65 Rosmead Pl, Colombo 7; ☏ 011 4602060; **e** info@ tintagelcolombo.com; www.tintagelcolombo. com. Tintagel opened in 2007, & quickly became the best address in town. It is created with taste & style from a famous 1930s villa (it was the home of 3 prime ministers of the Bandaranaike family) by Shanth Fernando, the designing genius behind the Paradise Road stores & the Gallery Café. It is classic in its furnishings with crystal chandeliers, a large antique Parisian gilded mirror & a library of 500 leather-bound volumes, with contemporary excitement like the statue-lined interior swimming pool & the bar lounge with red lacquered walls. The décor of the lavishly appointed bedrooms is rich in relaxing hues & delightful *objets d'art*. The food, served in the outdoor courtyard or indoor dining room, matches the sophistication of the hotel. **$$$$**

⌂ **Cinnamon Grand** (501 AC rooms) 77 Galle Rd, Colombo 3; ☏ 011 2437437; **e** grand@ cinnamonhotels.com; www.cinnamonhotels. com. The former Lanka Oberoi is now managed as part of the Keells group. The old staid hotel has been transformed, beginning with a glittering glass lobby that sets the tone of a hotel geared to cater for a demanding & sophisticated holiday- &-business clientele. The original wing has been recently rebuilt with Singaporean design flair, while the former new wing retains a solid dignity. To complement its increased popularity, new restaurants (see page 81) & bars & a trendy outlook have added extra sparkle. A favourite of British visitors, it is located on the Galle Road, close to the tourist office & the Indian High Commission & US Embassy. **$$$$–$$$**

⌂ **Cinnamon Lakeside** (359 AC rooms) 115 Sir Chittampalam A Gardiner Mawatha, Colombo 2; ☏ 011 2491000; **e** lakeside@cinnamonhotels.com; www.cinnamonhotels.com. Overlooks the Beira Lake, & resembles a fortress. Now part of the Keells group of top properties, it has been revamped in Singaporean 'lite' style with a bright lobby & additional restaurants. Its rooms are furnished in a dignified, gentleman's-club style. There are executive floors with dedicated elevator access & a club on the lobby floor reserved for executive-floor guests & members. Leading off the lobby at one side of the swimming pool & garden courtyard is an avenue of excellent restaurants (see page 81). $$$$–$$$

🏠 **Hilton Colombo** (384 AC rooms) 2 Sir Chittampalam A Gardiner Mawatha, Colombo 2; 📞 011 2492492; e colombo@hilton.com; www. colombo.hilton.com. The city's main international chain hotel is set in a fine location & rooms have a view of the Beira Lake or the city. The hotel is somewhat corporate having lost the sparkle it once had. As well as its luxury standard rooms (**$$$**), there are 2 grades of executive rooms (**$$$$**) on its top floors where breakfast & happy-hour drinks are included in the room rate. $$$$–$$$

DELUXE

🏠 **Colombo Courtyard** [map, page 72] (14 AC suites, 12 AC rooms) 32 Alfred Hse Av, Colombo 3; 📞 011 4645333; e info@ colombocourtyard.com; www.colombocourtyard. com. Smack in the centre of the action & within easy reach of everything the business or leisure visitor needs to see & do while in the city with a convenient location, at the corner of Albert Hse Av & R A De Mel Mawatha (Duplication Rd), close to shops, restaurants & casinos. Each of the suites not only has complimentary Wi-Fi but also a 21in iMac computer. There is also a separate cyber lounge to serve the deluxe rooms. This deftly designed hotel's bedrooms are for living in, not just for sleeping, although they do feature large, plump, modern 4-poster beds, plenty of power points, TV, minibar, etc, & even a retro hand-operated juicer (plus a bowl of oranges on the coffee table). Each landing has a lounge area & every suite has a parlour useful for private meetings. The bathrooms have cement bathtubs & twin washbasins with a separate waterfall shower corner emphasising the hotel's trendsetting, boutique character. The hotel's décor is refreshingly different with fascinating climbing sculpture made out of old bicycle parts, the walls of shaved railway sleepers & a cobbled entrance courtyard. With a wine lounge off the courtyard & a restaurant wing with Scarlet Room Restaurant, & a long Loft Bar with signature cocktails & an alcove for smokers, & rooftop Cloud Café there is no real need to venture out to the city to eat or drink at night. $$$

🏠 **Galadari** (300+ rooms) 64 Lotus Rd, Echelon Sq, Colombo 1; 📞 011 2544544; e galadari@sri. lanka.net; www.galadarihotel.com. Has some of Colombo's best doormen, who welcome guests into the businesslike lobby. The entrance is easily accessible by the roundabout at the northern end of Galle Face Green Road. The hotel is popular with repeat guests & demanding business visitors. The rooms are large & comfortable, with large beds & simple, not too elaborate, furnishings. There is an executive floor with breakfast & complimentary drinks included in the reasonable room rate. See page 81 for restaurants. $$$

🏠 **Galle Face** (65 AC Classic rooms, 80 AC Regency rooms) 2 Galle Rd, Colombo 3; 📞 011 2541010; e reservations@gallefacehotel.net; www. gallefacehotel.com. This is Colombo's most venerable hotel, commanding a magnificent view of Galle Face Green & the ocean. Opened in 1864, it retains the ambience of more gracious days. Its suites are bigger than most hotels' dining rooms & it's a historical treat to stay in one, even if only for a night. It now has 2 wings: the newly refurbished Classic (**$$$**) & the established Regency (**$$$$**) with a separate entrance & grand style, a cellar wine bar & a restaurant for trenchermen (see page 81). $$$

🏠 **Havelock Place Bungalow** [map page 72] (3 suites, 3 dbls) 6–8 Havelock Pl, Colombo 5; 📞 011 2585191; e manager@havelockbungalow. com; www.havelockbungalow.com. Ideal for those seeking solace after a surfeit of slick, modern city hotels, or who don't have time to discover the charm of hill-country bungalow hostelries. Resembling a quiet country retreat, yet within a 3-wheeler ride of the city's action, it has a swimming pool with jacuzzi, a gourmet restaurant (Asian-fusion menu) & broadband internet with Wi-Fi facility. Suites & rooms have 4-poster beds, wooden floors & individual patios. It's a place of comfort & character that its regulars would like to keep a secret. $$$

🏠 **Ramada** (94 AC rooms) 30 Sir Mohamed Macan Markar Mawatha, Colombo 3; 📞 011 2422001; www.ramadacolombo.com. Formerly the Holiday Inn, tucked away behind the Taj Samudra, it offers convenience & comfort at lower prices than 5-star hotel rates & is a friendly, informal place to stay. It was being given a much-needed refurbishment at press time. $$$

🏠 **Taj Samudra** (300 AC rooms) 25 Galle Face Centre Rd, Colombo 3; 📞 011 2446622; e samudra.colombo@tajhotels.com; www.

tajhotels.com. Part of the Indian-operated Taj Group. It stands in magnificent grounds overlooking Galle Face Green & the Indian Ocean with a bright, if large, lobby with a coffee lounge, sports bar & several restaurants (see page 82). There are 2 wings of rooms, which include an executive floor. **$$$**

MODERATE

⌂ **Grand Oriental** (74 AC rooms) 2 York St, Colombo 1; ☏011 2320320; e info@grandoriental. com; www.grandoriental.com. Built at the port gates as an army barracks in 1837 & opened as a hotel in 1875, this was a popular place to stay on arrival in the days of sea travel. It has been refurbished & long-abandoned rooms reopened to revitalise it while retaining bags of character. It is a lower-cost option for staying in the centre of the city. **$$**

⌂ **Juliana Hotel** [map, page 72] (52 AC rooms) 316 Galle Rd, Colombo 3; ☏011 2542056. A few doors north of the Renuka, occupancy here often exceeds 100% because its large but basic rooms can be booked for day-use too. **$$**

⌂ **Renuka** [map, page 72] (80 AC rooms) 328 Galle Rd, Colombo 3; ☏011 2573598; e renukaht@renukahotel.com; www.renukahotel.

com. In the shopping centre area of the Galle Road, this is a favourite with both business & holiday visitors on a budget since it offers good value, comfort & convenience. See page 82 for its restaurant. **$$**

BASIC

⌂ **Nippon** (30 rooms) 123 Kumaranratnam Rd, Colombo 1; ☏011 2431887. Downtown & downmarket, this Edwardian-built hotel reeks of character. With flowers hanging from its wrought-iron balcony it looks like a New Orleans bordello. **$**

APARTMENTS

⌂ **Hilton Colombo Residences** (165 AC apts) 200 Union Pl, Colombo 2; ☏011 2300613; e colomboresidence@hilton.com; www.hilton. com. These apartments are worthy of any major city; they are spacious (2 or 3 bedrooms plus maid's quarters), beautifully furnished & with all you need (washing machine, fridge, cooker, etc) for self-catering. They have the advantage of a good supermarket next door, whose delivery boys will bring your groceries into your kitchen. There is a swimming pool, bar & restaurant exclusively for residents' use. **$$$$–$$$**

In the street (Sellamuttu Avenue) leading down to the sea behind the Renuka Hotel, there are some small self-catering, basic (**$**) apartments available in different locations through three different operators. These are **Mrs Niri Rockwood** (*9A Sellamuttu Av, Colombo 3;* ☏ *011 2437220;* e *rockwood@eureka.lk*); and those at **14, 19 and 21 Sellamuttu Avenue** (☏ *011 2573533*). For others, ☏ 011 2588340; e ramana@mail.ewisl.net.

There are also more cheapie (**$**) places to stay in Pettah and off the Galle road, where it heads south through Kollupitiya, Bambalapitiya and Wellawatte, and in the recently opened ocean-side Marine Drive.

✗ WHERE TO EAT AND DRINK

The theory that **hotel restaurants** are not the best places to dine, as is the case in some cities, is not applicable in Colombo. In an effort to attract loyal local clientele hotels have diversified their appeal and operate several restaurants featuring different cuisines within their premises.

Hotel restaurants are complemented by several fine **independent restaurants** that are well patronised, which means interesting menus and fresh ingredients. There are scores of rice-and-curry cafés filled with city office workers at lunchtime, but for the visitor who wants to try typical Sri Lankan cuisine, the best bet would be a hotel's buffet or the Palmyrah at the Renuka Hotel, mentioned above. Except where stated, restaurants listed here are open all day, every day. All listings are included on the Colombo city centre map, page 76, unless otherwise noted.

HOTEL RESTAURANTS

✗ **Casa Colombo** [map, page 72] 231 Galle Rd, Bambalapitiya, Colombo 4; ☎011 4520130; e mail@casacolombo.com; www.casacolombo.com. In contrast to its glamorous conversion of a former grand mansion, this boutique hotel features meals that are surprisingly moderately priced (menus are posted on the website). **HVN** ($$) is its bright dining room (formerly the main hall of the mansion) with scrumptious fusion-style food at the lower end of the price scale. The late Dr Alistair Smith, a retired Scottish resident of Sri Lanka, commented after having dinner at HVN: 'Décor reminiscent of a whorehouse for departed Indian gurus but sensible menu & food simple, well prepared & nicely presented. Friendly, competent service which didn't send the hormones into orbit.' The **T-Republic** ($) on the lawn specialises in tea & other non-alcoholic beverages & light snacks.

✗ **Cinnamon Grand** 77 Galle Rd, Colombo 3; ☎011 2437437. Has expanded & been revitalised since its years as the Lanka Oberoi & has jazzed up its dining options. These include a poolside garden evening restaurant called **Tao** ($$) that specialises in Asian fusion cuisine in an original & pleasantly palatable manner. **The Lagoon** ($$) specialises in seafood, chosen by guests from an iced fish-market counter for lunch & dinner. My favourite restaurant in Colombo for a traditional night out, however, remains the hotel's secret, the **London Grill** ($$$). Looking like a 1950s steakhouse, it is the preferred place to dine for celebrating expats & those nostalgic for, well, London steakhouses. Pub grub & a good time are to be had at the **Cheers Pub** in the basement ($). Its upmarket canteen-style restaurant, **Chutneys**, specialises in veg & non-veg south Indian dishes that are as good as, if not better than, any in India ($$). Rural Sri Lankan food in an especially created reproduction village setting is available in the garden ($).

✗ **Cinnamon Lakeside** 115 Sir Chittampalam A Gardiner Mawatha, Colombo 2; ☎011 2491000. Oriental cuisine is featured in the speciality restaurants of the Cinnamon Lakeside (formerly Trans Asia). **The Royal Thai** ($$) is usually packed every night for dinner; it also serves an à la carte lunch of exciting Thai dishes. Its adjoining **Long Feng** ($$) Singaporean restaurant has a menu & genteel atmosphere designed for the discerning. The lobby coffee shop ($$$) is set in its own glass-walled pavilion as part of the lobby.

A Mediterranean bar restaurant ($$) has been added for open-air dining by the lake.

✗ **Galadari** 64 Lotus Rd, Echelon Sq, Colombo 1; ☎011 2544544. The **California Grill** rooftop restaurant ($$$) offers superb views of the sea & the city to complement formula cuisine with an American hint, & a dance band. At the lower end of the price scale, & on the ground floor with outdoor terrace, the hotel's pastry shop **Café 64** is popular with office workers & tourists ($).

✗ **Galle Face Hotel** 2 Galle Rd, Colombo 3; ☎011 2541010. Boasts a popular open-air seafood restaurant, **Seaspray** ($$). The buffet rice-&-curry lunch on the hotel's terrace, overlooking the sea, is a must if you are only in Colombo for a day. With its own entrance on the Galle Road, **In On The Green** features a selection of imported & local beers, & great pub grub, including a beef & Guinness pie that expats adore ($). The Regency Wing of the hotel houses a club-like restaurant, the **1864**, & a wine bar cellar, & serves a combined buffet/set menu lunch with fine dining in the evening ($$$). On the wing's 1st floor, in the hotel's museum, is a marvellous, & discreet, pastry shop ($) with monthly low-priced specials like Baked Alaska.

✗ **Hilton Colombo** 2 Sir Chittampalam A Gardiner Mawatha, Colombo 2; ☎011 2492492. Its fine-dining Gables Restaurant was being challenged by other city hotels, so they ditched it in favour of **Spoons** ($$$) – a relentlessly modern venue with matey service, show-kitchen with chefs in caps instead of hats & formula food. It is located off the lobby at the Hilton, alongside the **Echelon Pub** ($$). With TV & video screens, & a cheerful ambience, this pub is popular with expats & visitors who don't want the rough & tumble of lesser watering holes. The Hilton's buffet restaurant, **Spices** ($$), features an enormous choice of all-you-can-eat for breakfast, lunch & dinner buffets, as well as a traditional coffee-shop menu. Adjoining it, Chinese food fans delight in the **Emperor's Wok** ($$). In the garden, a restaurant, **Curry Leaf** ($$), serves genuine Sri Lankan food in a leisurely atmosphere at night. Across the road by the bridge, next to the swimming pool & gymnasium, is **Il Ponte** ($$), which specialises in Italian cuisine.

✗ **Hilton Colombo Residences** 200 Union Pl, Colombo 2; ☎011 2300613. Has the **Union Bar & Grill** ($$), which offers elaborate buffets with action stations where the food is prepared to diners' commands. The adjoining bar is a hangout for the young at heart, & frequently features enthusiastic bands in the evenings.

✘ **Renuka** [map, page 72] 328 Galle Rd, Colombo 3; ☎ 011 2573598. The **Palmyrah Restaurant** ($$) has good Sri Lankan cuisine, with a comprehensive range of dishes that are not all super-spicy. Long established, with a good bar & décor of local scenes, the restaurant enables guests to appreciate Sri Lankan cuisine (including Jaffna dishes from the north) in a refined yet relaxed atmosphere.

✘ **Taj Samudra** 25 Galle Face Centre Rd, Colombo 3; ☎ 011 2446622. There is a **Chinese restaurant** ($$) here, & as one would expect, a good **Indian restaurant** ($$). The hotel's **Steak & Grill** ($$$) restaurant is also popular for traditional dishes served with aplomb. The coffee shop, **Latitude** ($$), is appealingly contemporary.

INDEPENDENT RESTAURANTS

✘ **Barefoot Garden Café** [map, page 72] 706 Galle Rd, Colombo 3; ☎ 011 2553075; e barefoot@eureka.lk. This informal eatery is part of the Barefoot enterprises, including the Barefoot Gallery (☎ 011 2505559) of Sri Lanka's famous photographer Dominic Sansoni. Access is through the Barefoot store or from the back car park. It's a good place to relax after the hectic tempo of the city while enjoying a light meal. $$

✘ **Cricket Club Café** [map, page 72] 34 Queens Rd, Colombo 3; ☎ 011 2501384. Has a simple formula of fast-served & well-cooked pub grub, as well as speciality dishes. Consistently good.

You can dine on the terrace, in AC dining rooms, or nosh at the bar where smoking is allowed & TVs play cricket matches endlessly. It's usually busy. $$

✘ **Gallery Café** [map, page 72] 2 Alfred Hse Rd, Colombo 3; ☎ 011 2582162. Elegant & close to the Cricket Club Café, this café is part of the oft-copied Paradise Road phenomenon originated by designer & entrepreneur Shanth Fernando. Fernando has turned his winning skill as a creator & retailer of irresistible knick-knacks into a restaurant that attracts the cognoscenti. Set in the garden & patio of what was once the studio of architect Geoffrey Bawa, the café is ideal for a leisurely light snack, or to linger over a meal in the company of like-minded souls. $$

✘ **Raja Bojun** At Ceylino Seylan Towers, opposite the Cinnamon Grand, 90 Galle Rd, Colombo 3; ☎ 011 4716171. Has a good buffet experience of 'spicy, traditional Sri Lankan food' with a sea view. $$

✘ **Sugar Bistro & Wine Bar** Crescat Bd, Colombo 3; ☎ 011 2446229; ⏱ 08.00–midnight daily. At the Galle road entrance to the Crescat Shopping Mall attached to Colombo's Cinnamon Grand Hotel, this is more of a boulevard café since it overlooks the road, & you can't even see a bottle of wine, although the wine list is extensive & wine is available by the glass. So are reasonably priced cocktails. There is a good menu too with breakfast, lunch, dinner & everything in between. Free Wi-Fi. Décor is simple & striking, with air ducts coated in silver foil & 9 odd clocks, all working, on the back wall. Sugar's arrival, with its obliging staff (one steward's called Royston) has added a much–needed, conveniently located, pleasant café to Colombo's day & night scene. $$

The cuisine in **Chesa Swiss** [map, page 72] (*3 Deal Pl, Colombo 3;* ☎ *011 2573433; www.chesaswiss.com;* ⏱ *for lunch & dinner daily except Poya days;* $$$) is relentlessly Swiss, with Swiss wines too. It was long renowned as one of Colombo's top restaurants for many years but is facing stiff competition in service and food standards from newer and livelier establishments.

WINE

A word about wine in Colombo's upmarket hotels. Although reasonable New World wine can be bought from Rs1,000 in Colombo's retail liquor shops, when the same wine appears on a hotel's wine list it will have tripled in price. Independent restaurants exercise less of a mark-up but a bottle of wine with a meal will still push the final price from the $$ range into the $$$ bracket.

The **Bay Leaf** (*79 Gregory's Rd, Colombo 7;* ✆ *011 2695920;* ⏰ *11.00–23.00 daily;* $$) is a favourite haunt of foreigners working in nearby embassies or for NGOs. Created in a colonial house whose rooms and veranda lend themselves ideally to pleasant dining, the restaurant serves coffee and pastries as well as Italian-themed dishes. Pleasingly informal or smart, whatever guests wish. There is a lively cocktail bar.

For just a coffee, a snack or light meal in genteel surroundings while shopping, there are several outlets. At **Paradise Road** (*213 Dharmapala Mawatha, Colombo 7;* ✆ *011 2686043;* $), there is a tiny café in the balcony overlooking the town hall with, according to one world traveller, 'the best chocolate cheesecake I've ever tasted'. It is expensive, though.

While there are plenty of mid-range restaurants and low-cost local eateries throughout the city, there is also a chance to try a variety of cuisines in shopping malls. In the basement of **Majestic City** (*Station Rd, Colombo 4;* ✆ *011 2508673;* $) and **Crescat Boulevard** (*89 Galle Rd, Colombo 3;* $) (see page 88), there are several counters serving different kinds of food in a Hawker Street atmosphere (you queue to buy what you want from the counters and then sit in the central dining area to eat it).

An action-packed café can be found at **Park Street Mews** (*50/1 Park St, Colombo 2;* ✆ *011 2300133;* e *parkstreetmews@harpoog.com; www.harposonline.com;* ⏰ *09.00–22.00 daily;* $$) with space to lounge as well as to enjoy snacks or full meals. It's located at the entrance to a cobbled mews of converted warehouses. There's an ayurveda spa there too, **Spa Ceylon** (*Park St Mews;* e *info@spaceylon. com; www.spaceylon.com;* ⏰ *10.00–23.00 daily*).

Although it calls itself a shopping precinct, the conversion of the **old Dutch Hospital** building [76 B1] (in Echelon Square, opposite Colombo's twin-towered World Trade Centre) into a modern mall, has yielded an amazing range of restaurants, including one serving airline food, as well as some twee boutiques. Dating back to 1677, the building is among the oldest in Colombo, and its former wards and barracks around two courtyards have been converted with care to preserve its historical features.

The first of its restaurants, on the left of the entrance arch, is **Semondu** (✆ *011 2441590;* ⏰ *10.00–15.00 & 19.00–23.00 daily;* $$). This is proudly run by SriLankan Airlines serving menus based on in-flight cuisine and presented on a tray. Surprisingly, it works for an uncomplicated meal. Wines and beer are also available at a counter with a view of the kitchen. On the opposite side of the arch is **WIP**, short for 'Work In Progress' (✆ *011 2441275;* ⏰ *11.00–23.00 daily;* $$), a café/restaurant run by the Colombo Hilton Hotel. It also has a small cocktail bar, and the restaurant has service to tables set up on the cobbles of the interior courtyard.

A popular evening drinking haunt before dinner is **The Brewery By O** (✆ *011 2436462;* ⏰ *10.00–23.00 daily;* $), except Poya Day where busy stewards deliver draught beer by the tower and snacks to drinkers at tables in the back courtyard. Overlooking the main courtyard, **Harpo's Colombo Fort Café** (✆ *011 2434946;* ⏰ *11.00–22.30 daily;* $$) specialises in pub grub with a Mediterranean touch and cocktails in an informal atmosphere. Next door to it, the ambience is more sophisticated with plush sofas for enjoying cocktails, bottled beers, spirits, wines, tea and dessert, in the **Heladiv Tea Club** (✆ *011 5753377;* ⏰ *09.30–01.00 daily;* $$). It's the perfect bar to end a convivial evening of wining and dining therapy.

The main attraction, however, is the judiciously named **Ministry of Crab** (✆ *011 2342722;* ⏰ *every evening except Poya (full moon) day;* $$$). This establishment has kept all the original 17th-century building features intact, including the high-beamed ceiling, wooden shutters and the flagstone floor. Its three owners are two former captains of the Sri Lanka cricket team, Kumar Sangakkara and Mahela Jayawardene, and the renowned Sri Lankan/Japanese restaurateur, Darshan Munidasa.

Munidasa explains that the two cricketers have not just lent their names to the Ministry of Crab Restaurant; they are actual 'Crabinet' ministers. 'When we were deciding who should be chairman of the company,' says Munidasa, 'I invited them to toss a coin for it as they would at the start of a cricket match. Mahela won and he has to sign orders, pay sheets, etc, if I am unavailable. They have a say in everything and often eat at the restaurant with their teammates and visiting cricketers too.'

The crabs, which are delivered fresh every day from Sri Lanka's northwest and northeast lagoons, are kept alive in a tank at the back of the open kitchen and guests are welcome to view their dinner before it's cooked. All are export quality, the kind that has been exported to, and delighted diners in, Singapore for many years. Only freshly ground herbs and no imported manufactured flavour enhancers are used, to produce an authentic, purely Sri Lankan culinary delight.

The restaurant concentrates on crab creations (with pepper, chilli, butter, garlic or curry) with the price based on size. Bibs are provided for diners who are encouraged to tuck into the crab using fingers. Even the water in the finger bowls at the end of the meal, is a purely Sri Lankan creation. It's actually cold tea to cleanse the oiliness from the fingers, mixed with *veniwelgeta*, a Sri Lankan herbal disinfectant, and garnished with *iramusu* flowers for fragrance.

DOWNBEAT BARS   *Rehan Mudannayake*

Away from the tourist beat of glitzy hotels and cocktail bars in Colombo, there are some pubs with more of a local ambience. All are open daily except Poya Day. All listings are included on the Colombo city centre map, page 76, unless otherwise noted.

Castle Hotel Masjid Jamiah Rd, Colombo 2; ⏰ 10.00–14.00 & 17.00–23.00. The finest of Colombo's dodgy bars, Castle Hotel is the place to head to if you're keen on a few cheap drinks with or without the friendly local crowd. A charming old building in Slave Island, do not be put off by the crumbling insides: this is all part of its old-world charm. Attracts a loud male clientele, who, if you're lucky, may begin serenading you with folk songs. Situated in Slave Island, around the corner from Burger King. A real hidden treasure. $

The Station [map page 72] 1/41 Wasala Rd, Dehiwela; ⏰ 10.00–22.00. Faces out onto Dehiwela Beach, next to the railway tracks. Fancy watching the waves crash & the trains whiz past as you sip your beer? The alcohol is cheap & the bar tends to be packed with locals, though the quieter kind. Sometimes a *baila* (local polka) band plays. The place to head to if you're in the mood for a (fairly) quiet night out at a low price. $

Vespa [map, page 72] Sea Av, Colombo 3; ⏰ 11.00–14.00 & 17.00–22.00. A haven for drinking & dining alfresco, a dilapidated old building with a small bar & a large car park – where people usually sit. As in all these kinds of bar throughout Sri Lanka, it's male dominated so female travellers/drinkers should be accompanied by men. The staff are friendly, & the drinks & bites relatively cheap. A strong sea breeze permeates Vespa, keeping it just the right temperature for a lunchtime drink on a warm day. Night-time on a Friday or Saturday night attracts a host of loud customers, many of whom blast chart music out of their Jeeps & frequently dance along to it. A great place to pre-lash before a club! $

In the middle of all this wonderful choice of restaurants, bars and cafés, Colombo has its Pizza Huts, Kentucky Fried Chickens and McDonald's. There are also innumerable eating houses where office workers will snatch a snack or rice and curry, and where budget travellers can try local fare at low prices.

ENTERTAINMENT AND NIGHTLIFE

Strangely, no-one thinks of Colombo as a fun city; action is not nightly and, even on a Saturday night, some discos may seem dull. Perhaps it is because the number of locals who can afford the time and money to go out on the town at night is small. However, some places will be packed, if you pick the right night (usually a Saturday or the night before a national holiday) and follow the crowd.

You may be amazed at the amount of money Sri Lankans are prepared to spend on a good night out: bottles of premium whisky and good champagne on the table; chips worth thousands of rupees stacked on the roulette table.

Extra-curricular activities are not a feature of the city's nightlife, although there have been news stories of Thai and Russian goodtime girls being rounded up and deported. As well as Sri Lankans, fellow night revellers are likely to be expatriate workers, many from the Orient, and the occasional tourist out for a night on the town. It all seems pretty respectable.

As in other cities, **nightclubs** in Colombo go in and out of fashion pretty quickly. The word at the time of writing is that the one at **Hotel Galadari** [76 B2] (*64 Lotus Rd, Colombo 1;* ✆ *011 2544544*) attracts clubbers of all ages, but it can be quiet midweek unless it's a holiday eve. Beyond the hotels and somewhat cliquish, with regular patrons who seem to size up each newcomer, is **Rhythm & Blues** (*19/1 Daisy Villa Av, off Duplication Rd, Colombo 4;* ✆ *011 5363859; $$*). There is live music most evenings and the pool tables are a draw. People like to hang out in the outside area where there are tables and chairs.

Other established haunts of night owls include **B52** at the Grand Oriental Hotel [76 B1] (*York St, Colombo 1;* ✆ *011 2320320*), **The Library** at the Cinnamon Lakeside Hotel [76 C2] (*115 Sir Chittampalam A Gardiner Mawatha, Colombo 2;* ✆ *011 2491925*), the karaoke bar **Sopranos** (*29 Maitland Crescent, Colombo 7;* ✆ *011 2300133*), and the hostess bar **Boss** (*16 Sir Ernest de Silva Mawatha, Colombo 3;* ✆ *011 5545553*).

Colombo must be unique in the number of **casinos** it has, yet few people know about them. There are not many gamblers from overseas jetting in just to try their luck at the city's gaming tables, yet the best casinos are pretty classy. They are open every day except on the Poya Day full moon holiday.

In the casinos, as long as you are a player, all drinks, food and even cigarettes are free. Some tourists have been known to take the money they would spend in a hotel on drinks and dinner, and gamble it in a casino instead. If you go to the casinos recommended here at around 21.00 there will be a buffet dinner, as well as premium-quality drinks, so even if you lose, the cost of a good night out is still worth it. As well as roulette, there are blackjack, baccarat and other gaming tables. The minimum stake for roulette is Rs100, but be prepared to change at least Rs10,000 to join in. Membership is not necessary.

The following three are all run by the same management to a high standard with excellent service and refreshments. On Galle Road, near the Majestic City shopping complex, is the **MGM** [map page 72] (*772 Galle Rd, Colombo 4;* ✆ *011 2591319;* ⏰ *24hrs*). Livelier is **Bellagio** [map page 72] (*430 R A De Mel Mawatha, Colombo 3;* ✆ *011 2575271;* ⏰ *24hrs*). Behind the Fort railway station a short three-wheeler ride

There are only a few cinemas in Colombo that show films in English. If you venture into them, dress warmly as they are like glorified freezers. All cinemas are closed on Poya days. Where admission charges are not shown, admission charge depends on the film being screened.

Majestic Cineplex Majestic City, Galle Rd, Colombo 4; ☎011 2581759; ⏰ daily. The country's only multiplex, comprising 4 cinemas – Platinum (⏰ *10.30–13.30 & 16.15–19.00*); Superior (⏰ *10.30–13.30 & 16.15–19.30*); Ultra (⏰ *10.45–13.45 & 16.45–19.30*); and Gold (⏰ *10.30–13.30 & 16.15–19.00*). Platinum & Superior are 3D cinemas, the former a sizeable screen usually showcasing the most recent action films & the latter a smaller, more intimate room usually screening the latest Pixar hits. The other 2 – Ultra & Gold – are 2D cinemas which usually screen current & (somewhat) recent blockbusters. Service is great: one is politely shown to one's seat by ushers. Reserve seats via credit card up to 7 days in advance on www.ticketslk. com. Admission from Rs500.

Savoy Cinema 12 Savoy Bldg, Galle Rd, Wellawatte, Colombo 6; ☎011 7444400; ⏰ 10.30–13.30 & 16.15–19.00 daily. The newly refurbished Savoy Cinema is made up of the main 3D screen – Savoy 1 – & a much smaller 2D screen – Savoy 2. It screens a mixture of Sri Lankan, Bollywood & Hollywood (animation & blockbuster) flicks, providing a welcome alternative to the Majestic–Liberty duo. There is no usher, so arriving early might be a good idea. The new design is state of the art as is the sound quality: the cinema is illuminated by blue & red spotlights & blasts crisp Dolby Digital GTS sound. It is possible to reserve seats up to 10 days in advance on www.eapmovies.com. Beer is available; clean bathrooms too.

Liberty Cinema [76 C4] 65 Dharmapala Mawatha, Colombo 3; ☎011 7444477; ⏰ 10.30–13.30 & 16.15–19.00 daily. Established in 1965, Liberty is the oldest English-language cinema in Colombo, with a stench to prove it. A relic of a past age, it has 401 seats upstairs & 185 seats downstairs. Screening a range of Sinhala, Hindi & Hollywood action & horror films, it offers a cheaper alternative to its modern counterparts. Arrive late & an usher will help you find your seat. Tickets can be reserved 10 days in advance via www.eapmovies.com.

Liberty Lite [76 C4] 37A Dharmapala Mawatha, Colombo 3; ☎011 2325533; ⏰ 10.30–13.30 & 16.15–19.00 daily (21.30 on Fri & Sat). Despite its name & location next to the Liberty Cinema, Liberty Lite is no relation. A smaller but more recently built 2D cinema, it features the latest Hollywood blockbusters. It has 140 seats, a 35mm projector & Dolby DTS sound, an impressive feat for a cinema of its size. Tickets can be reserved online via www.ticketslk.com.

from the major hotels (don't bother with a tip; the driver will get commission; a free taxi will take you back to the hotel) is **Bally's Casino** [76 D2] (*34 D R Wijewardene Mawatha, Colombo 10;* ☎*011 2331150;* ⏰ *24hrs*). All three casinos have the unusual distinction of having the best guest toilets in the whole of Sri Lanka, as well as being easy-going and enjoyable places for gambling.

Casino Marina [map page 72] (*30 Marine Dr, Colombo 3;* ☎*011 4219988;* e *info@ marinacolombo.com; www.marinacolombo.com;* ⏰ *24hrs daily, except Poya days*) is a new casino (opened in 2013) with a view built on Colombo's new thoroughfare, Marine Drive, with classic style in the hope of attracting high rollers from overseas to play roulette, blackjack, baccarat and poker. With constant service of free drinks and snacks, an Indian/Chinese buffet restaurant, music by foreign bands, special draws and fashion shows, the Casino Marina bills itself as an entertainment hub with three extra floors of gaming (for package groups, VIPs and VVIPs) as well as the ground-floor mall of action-packed tables.

SHOPPING

To reach most of the places described here you will need a taxi. Colombo is full of unusual places so if you do not find what you want in the air-conditioned shopping malls, see if your hotel doorman or taxi driver can suggest something. For instance, for shirt materials, I head for Maradana where the **New China Stores** [76 F2] (*12 Deans Rd, Colombo 10;* \011 2699313) is one of several shops grouped together with a satisfying selection of the brightest cottons for shirts, frocks and tropical safari suits.

BOOKSHOPS If you are looking for reduced-price paperbacks to read on the beach or rare volumes on Ceylon's history, head for the secondhand bookstalls grouped on one side of the road by the D R Wijewardene Mawatha roundabout (about five minutes' walk from Maradana station). What a trove of magazines, paperbacks and collector's items! I once bought a decade's worth of 1950s *Reader's Digest* magazines there as well as old volumes of *Ferguson's Directory* that list British tea planters in the island in the 1930s. From **Sarath Books & Communications (Lending Library)** (*D R Wijewardene Mawatha;* \011 2679832) books can also be borrowed.

UNUSUAL SOUVENIRS

Colombo resident Rehan Mudannayake lists ideas for unusual local souvenirs easily obtainable at stores in Colombo.

JEWELLED ELEPHANTS Wooden elephants dextrously covered with colourful beads, mirrors and sparkling colours make a bright pachyderm present.

WOODEN SPOONS Spoons made of sanded coconut shell with painted wooden handles are fun for the kitchen.

DOOR STOPPERS Wooden door stoppers amusingly decorated with figures of Ceylon colonials bedecked in moustaches, sarongs and saris.

FLOATING CANDLES Flower-shaped candles in yellow and white modelled on the (araliya) frangipani blossom and purple and yellow lotus shapes, to light and float in a bowl of water.

KITUL PLACE MATS Mats made from polished strips of *kitul* (sugar palm) wood.

HANDMADE NATURAL SOAP Soap made and scented with natural ingredients such as cinnamon, sandalwood, coconut, eucalyptus, aloe and peppermint.

HANDWOVEN SARONGS Handwoven sarongs make a startling fashion statement in glorious colours, particularly the vibrant orange matching the colour of a monk's robe, and deep greens and blues.

SOFT TOYS Locally made cuddly geckos, monkeys and elephants make a tropical alternative to the teddy bear.

BEERALU LACE Lace tray- and tablecloths with daintily decorated edges that tourist souvenir purchasing will keep alive.

For quality books on all subjects, but especially on local folklore, art, music, dance and architecture that you might not find elsewhere, check the bookshop at **Barefoot** (*704 Galle Rd, Colombo 3;* ✆ *011 2589305*). For more details on bookshops, see page 87.

CLOTHES For fashionable clothes at a fraction of what you would pay for the same garment (made in Sri Lanka) overseas, join the crowds that flock to **Odel Unlimited** [76 F3] (*5 Alexandra Pl, Lipton Circus, Colombo 7;* ✆ *011 7722200; www.odel.lk;* ⊕ *daily*). Starting as a warehouse store, this has blossomed into an attractive shopping complex with sections specialising in brand-name goods and household items as well as bargain-priced fashions and imported desirable knick-knacks. For cheaper stuff, there is **House of Fashion** [76 D4] (*28 R A De Mel Mawatha, Colombo 3*), a glittering glass-walled emporium.

SHOPPING MALLS The city's first shopping mall (it opened in the 1980s) was **Liberty Plaza** [76 C4] (*cnr R A De Mel Mawatha & Dharmapala Mawatha;* ✆ *011 2575935*), and it shows its age. On two floors (with a supermarket in the basement), it contains shops that specialise mostly in imported items and there are a couple of shops selling wine. It is followed in style by **Majestic City** [map page 72] (*Station Rd, Colombo 4;* ✆ *011 2508673*), which is livelier and with a better standard of shop. More upmarket is the shopping complex called **Crescat Boulevard** [76 C4] (*89 Galle Rd, Colombo 3, adjacent to the Cinnamon Grand Hotel*). In its basement and

---

WHERE TO WORSHIP

There are a number of places of worship in Colombo that are interesting places for the faithful or the curious to visit. Sri Lankans of all faiths actually enjoy the ritual and festivals (and holidays) of religions other than their own.

These are some of the main churches, temples, *kovils* (Hindu temples) and mosques in the city.

ROMAN CATHOLIC The Church of St Philip Neri [76 D1] (*157 Olcott Mawatha, Colombo 11*); St Mary's Church (*Lauries Rd, Colombo 4*); St Lawrence's Church (*Galle Rd, Colombo 6*); St Mary's Church (*Galle Rd, Dehiwela*)

ANGLICAN St Peter's Church [76 B1] (*Mission to Seamen; 26 Church St, Colombo 1*), a fascinating colonial church next door to the Grand Oriental Hotel; Christ Church (*Galle Face, Colombo 3*); St Michael and All Angels (*1 Cameron Pl, Colombo 3*); Cathedral of Christ the Living Saviour (*368/3 Bauddhaloka Mawatha, Colombo 7*); St Paul's Milagiriya (*299 Galle Rd, Colombo 4*); Christ Church (*Galle Rd, Dehiwela*); Church of St Francis of Assisi (*Hotel Rd, Mount Lavinia*)

INTERDENOMINATIONAL St Andrew's Church [76 C4] (*73 Galle Rd, Colombo 3*) is the church favoured by expats and visitors, next to the Cinnamon Grand Hotel

DUTCH REFORMED (*724 Galle Rd, Colombo 3; 363 Galle Rd, Colombo 6; Station Rd, Dehiwela*)

METHODIST (*6 Station Rd, Colombo 3; 10 1st Chapel Lane, Colombo 6; Hotel Rd, Mount Lavinia*)

open daily is **Keells' supermarket**, sometimes featuring imported specialities (like cheeses and patés) unavailable elsewhere. There is also a food court ($) for low-priced self-service meals from different themed outlets (Chinese, Thai, Korean, Indian, Sri Lankan, etc).

TRENDSETTERS It is difficult to categorise those stores in Colombo that deserve to be a must on every visitor's shopping list, since they sell so many things you'd love to have, as well as items you'd be appalled to be given. So I've called them trendsetters even though most of them specialise in versions of items that are traditional rather than trendsetting.

The vogue started many years ago with **Barefoot** [map page 72] (*704 Galle Rd, Colombo 3;* ✎ *011 2589305; www.barefootceylon.com;* ✆ *10.00–20.00 daily*) and its dedication to local handwoven fabrics in colourful, hippy-style designs. It has expanded to include all that's bright and beautiful, as well as books, art, crafts and hundreds of delightful household items.

The real trend, though, for Colombo to become the city for fun-filled, treasure-trove shopping was set in motion by **Paradise Road** [map page 72] (*213 Dharmapala Mawatha, Colombo 7;* ✎ *011 2686043; www.paradiseroadsl.com;* ✆ *daily*). Walk into this converted 19th-century mansion (previously called Fin Castle; see its name in ceramic chips on the entrance steps) and you'll feel as though you have found Aladdin's cave. You can amble through avenues of candles and crazy cutlery, discover basketry and sculpture, go upstairs for stylish sarongs, tableware and

BAPTIST (*120 Dharmapala Mawatha, Colombo 7*)

PENTECOSTAL (*41 Greenpath, Colombo 3; 78/5 W A Silva Mawatha, Colombo 6; 123 High Level Rd, Colombo 6*)

JEHOVAH'S WITNESS (*711 Station Rd, Wattala*)

ASSEMBLY OF GOD (*160/30 Kirimandala Mawatha, Colombo 5*)

BUDDHIST TEMPLES Asokaramaya (*Thimbirigasyaya Rd, Colombo 5*); Dipaduttaramaya (*159 Kitahena St, Colombo 13*), built in 1806; Gothami Viharaya (*Colombo 8*) with murals influenced by famous Sri Lankan artist, George Keyt; Issipatanaramaya (*Colombo 5*); Paramanada Purana Viharaya (*Colombo 13*); Vijiraramaya (*Colombo 4*)

HINDU TEMPLES Sri Bala Selva Vinayagar Moorthy Kovil (*D R Wijewardene Mawatha, Colombo 10*), with shrines dedicated to Shiva and Ganesh; Sri Siva Subramania Swami Kovil (*Kew Rd, Slave Island, Colombo 2*), used by Indian soldiers during British times; Sri Muthumariamma Kovil (*Kotahena, Colombo 13*); Kathiresan Kovil (*Sea St, Colombo 11*)

MOSQUES Grand Mosque (*New Moor St, Colombo 12*); Maradana Mosque; Kollupitiya Mosque; Bambalapiyiya Mosque; the Boarah Mosque (*Pettah*); Military Mosque (*Slave Island, Colombo 2*); Jumi-Ul-Alfar Jummah Mosque [76 D1] (*Pettah*)

modern versions of Victoriana and even find genuine antiques as well as copies. At home I am proud to have a wooden butler table, a wooden blotter-roller and a bottle carrier from Paradise Road. It's the sort of shop worth visiting every few weeks to check out what's new, or rather old, in store.

There are branches of Paradise Road in the **Gallery Café** (see page 82) and at **Paradise Road The Villa Bentota** (see page 238). Rather more super is the same owner's **Paradise Road Studio** [map page 72] (*12 Alfred Hse Gdns, Colombo 3;* ✆ *011 2506844;* ⊕ *daily*), where opera soothes as you gaze in amazement at household furnishings and fittings and select tiny items worth taking home for yourself or others.

For colonial reproduction furniture as well as genuine antique prints, maps and postcards, and beautiful things from India, there is **The Hermitage** [map page 72] (*28 Gower St, Colombo 5;* ✆ *011 2502196;* ⊕ *daily*).

OTHER PRACTICALITIES

BANKS Some of the main banks, many of which have branches throughout the island, are listed here. They are all open on weekday (non-holiday) mornings from 09.00, while some are also open during the afternoon and even on holidays and weekends.

$ **Bank of Ceylon** 4 Bank of Ceylon Mawatha, Colombo 1; ✆ 011 2446790; www.boc.lk

$ **Deutsche Bank** 86 Galle Rd, Colombo 3; ✆ 011 2447062; www.db.com/srilanka

$ **Hatton National Bank** HNB Towers, 479 T B Jayah Mawatha, Colombo 10; ✆ 011 2664664; www.hnb.net

$ **HSBC** PO Box 73, Colombo; ✆ 011 4472200; www.hsbc.lk

$ **Nations Trust Bank** 242 Union Pl, Colombo 2; ✆ 011 4711411; www.nationstrust.com

$ **People's Bank** 75 Sir Chittampalam A Gardiner Mawatha, Colombo 2; ✆ 011 2327841; www. peoplesbank.lk

$ **Standard Chartered** 37 York St, Colombo 1; ✆ 011 2480000; www.standardchartered.com

BEAUTY SALONS Beauty culture and hairdressing are a fine art in Sri Lanka and Colombo has many hairdressing salons in the five-star hotels, in shopping malls and beauty boutiques throughout the city.

INTERNET CAFÉS All the five-star hotels have business centres where those who are not hotel residents can use the facilities, including the internet, in the calm reserved for guests. They serve coffee through the hotel room service.

There are internet cafés of varying degrees of efficiency along Galle Road. The **Mindhead Game Zone** (*78 Galle Rd, Dehiwela;* ✆ *011 2716346*), as its name suggests, has games as well. There is a much-used internet facility in the Crescat Boulevard shopping mall [76 C4].

LAUNDRY SERVICES Colombo's five-star hotels have counters where non-guests can get their laundry done; there are also outlets at the Crescat shopping mall [76 C4].

MEDICAL Below is a selection of hospitals and emergency services, as well as some of Colombo's 24-hour pharmacies.

Government hospitals in Colombo (see also pages 36–7)

✚ **Cancer Institute** Maharagama; ✆ 011 2850252

✚ **Castle Street Maternity Hospital** Dudley Senanayake Mawatha, Colombo 8; ✆ 011 2696231

✚ **Eye Hospital** Deans Rd, Colombo 10; ✆ 011 2693911

Lady Ridgeway Hospital Baseline Rd,
Colombo 8; 011 2693711
National Hospital 10 Regent St, Colombo 10;
011 2691111
Sri Jayawardenepura Hospital
Thalapathpitiya, Kotte; 011 2778610

Ambulance services
Ceylinco Swiftcare 598 Nawala Rd,
Rajagiriya; 011 2867000
Durdans 3 Alfred Pl, Colombo 3; 011 2564566
Lanka Hospitals 578 Evitigala Mawatha,
Colombo 5; 011 5431088
National Hospital 10 Regent St, Colombo 10;
011 2691111
Oasis 18A Muhandiram Dabare, Colombo 5;
011 2369113
Sri Lanka Red Cross 307 T B Jayah Mawatha,
Colombo 10; 011 2691095

St John's Ambulance 65/11 Sir
Chittampalam A Gardiner Mawatha; 011
2341736

Pharmacies
Asiri 181 Kirula Rd, Colombo 5; 011
2500608
Durdans 3 Alfred Pl, Colombo 3; 011 2575205
Lanka Hospitals 578 Evitigala Mawatha,
Colombo 5; 011 5430000
Laugfs Supermarket 252 Havelock Rd,
Colombo 5; 011 5364112
Nawaloka 23 Sri Saugathodaya Mawatha,
Colombo 2; 011 2304444
Oasis 18A Muhandiram Dabare Mawatha,
Colombo 5; 011 2369113
Osusala 255 Dharmapala Mawatha, Colombo
7; 011 2694716

POST OFFICE The **General Post Office** [76 C1] (011 2326203; 24hrs for the sale of stamps) is located on D R Wijewardene Mawatha, behind the Colombo Fort railway station (see also pages 63–4).

TOURIST INFORMATION Tourist information counter [76 C3] (Ground Flr, Sri Lanka Tourism HQ, 80 Galle Rd, Colombo 3; 011 2426900; e info@srilanka.travel; www.srilanka.travel; 08.30–16.15 Mon–Fri, closed w/ends & public holidays; see pages 59–61 for more details). Tourist information is also available by dialling 1912 from any phone within Sri Lanka. (This brings a real person answering the phone with a 'hello' and no other greeting but who confirms it's the tourist information office when pressed, and then transfers the call to 'the reception unit'.)

WHAT TO SEE AND DO

It is best to tour the city early, before the sun has a chance to raise temperatures too high, and while the streets are still empty. Starting from Colombo Fort station (if you are visiting by train for the day) is ideal for walking, since you can cross the main road in front of the station and plunge straight into the colourful chaos of the area known as **Pettah**.

This is Colombo's haunt of the streetwise, a bazaar spreading over several city blocks where everything you have ever wanted, and most things you will never need, can be found. Pettah was a select residential area during the Dutch and early British periods, although later British inhabitants regarded it as 'the native quarter'. A jungle of streets is jammed with bargain hunters, herds of trucks, cars and bullock carts, and accompanied by the klaxons of three-wheelers and the shouts of porters telling you to move out of their way. The contents of the various hardware shops, garment stores and groceries flow over on to the pavement.

The road facing the station is Olcott Mawatha, named after Henry Steel Olcott, an American-born Buddhist crusader whose **statue** stands in the station car park. Cross the road to Pettah and you will find Maliban Street parallel to Olcott Mawatha (*mawatha* means avenue or street), and the **St Philip Neri Church** [76 C1], 1859.

The candy-striped **Jumi-Ul-Alfar Jummah Mosque** [76 D1] deeper in Pettah dates from 1909.

Also in Olcott Mawatha is the **Railway Museum** [76 E2] (*Olcott Mawatha, Colombo 10; www.railwaymuseum.lk;* ⊕ *08.00–16.00 daily except public holidays & w/ends; admission Rs500*). Colombo's collection of steam engines used to be a source of amazement to steam and rail enthusiasts who were occasionally allowed to view them in the rail yard at Dematagoda. Now, after many years and various attempts, a small but fascinating railway museum has opened to the public near the Fort railway station.

The museum consists of a hall with some railway station furniture, including a Tyers Patent Train Tablet Apparatus over 100 years old, and a station platform called Colombo Terminus. An enormous narrow-gauge crane dominates the space, but the main attraction is the three locomotives at the platform. The first is a cute saddle tank steam engine (Class 040ST), probably from the Oil & Fats Corporation, perhaps dating to 1894. The second steam engine is identified as Class 20601 but there was no other information available. The third, Number 727, is a remarkable diesel hydraulic Y1 Class Shunting locomotive – remarkable because it was originally designed and built locally, and then long lay abandoned until rehabilitated (see also www.youtube.com/watch?v=tNe-QmVCx3c).

In Prince Street, parallel to Maliban, is a 17th-century colonnaded Dutch townhouse that has survived the gutting of progress around it. In its time it has served as an orphanage, a private residence, a hospital, the headquarters of the Ceylon Volunteers, a police training school and a post office. Restored in 1980, it is now a **museum** [76 D1] (⊕ *09.00–17.00 except Fri; admission Rs500*) devoted to the **Dutch Period**, 1658–1796.

Continue northwards up to Main Street and turn right. About 50m from the old town hall junction stands a restored **belfry**, complete with bell and crows nesting in it, a forgotten link with Pettah's past. The bell is believed to have been salvaged from the ruins of a 16th-century Portuguese church. It is all that remains of **Kayman's Gate** [76 D1] and is placed where crocodiles from Beira Lake once scavenged for food. Public executions were held at its foot; now electricity board transformers block access to it.

The **old town hall** is almost submerged by the waves of vendors of vegetables and machine parts surging around it. Its yard has been turned into the unexpected **Municipal Museum** [76 D1] (⊕ *09.00–17.00 Sat–Thu; admission Rs500*) featuring assorted bygones of city life: cast-iron water pumps and drinking fountains, a manhole cover, a signpost, a city father's official robes, bits of machinery, a massive steamroller and an ancient steam lorry emblazoned with the council's crest. Potted plants brighten the exhibits. Built in 1873, it was the seat of city government until 1928, when the yard became a public market before being turned into a museum in 1984.

Gabo's Lane, not marked on the maps, is a street of remarkable shops specialising in the ingredients of ayurveda (herbal) remedies. Outside the New Royal Fireworks & Medical Store and its neighbouring ayurveda merchants are sacks of twigs, strips of bark, dried herbs and leaves that, properly mixed, offer an age-old alternative to modern Western medicine. **Sea Street**, close by, deals in gold and jewellery.

Back along Main Street, in the direction of Fort, you come to a **clocktower** in the centre of a roundabout. This commemorates the life of one Framjee Bhikkajee Khan, and was erected in 1923 by his sons on the 45th anniversary of his death. It marks the division of Pettah and Fort.

From Pettah, across a bridge where ships' masts peep over the tops of shops hiding the harbour views, and the portside freight railway line, the road forks. To the right, it leads past the entrance to the harbour; to the left, it brings you to the shopping and commercial area of York Street.

Colombo's oldest store, **Cargills** [76 B1], established in 1844, with its broad, puce stone walls, is a contrast to the façade of more modern architecture. Looking up, you can see the balustrade typical of Colombo's older buildings, and plaster horns of plenty bursting with bounty that decorate its walls.

If you could take the road westwards alongside Cargills (now controlled by security) you would arrive at Janadhipathi Mawatha (once Queen Street) with the splendid colonial building that was until 2001 the General Post Office. The street and the post office are closed to the public now while the president is resident in **President's House** [76 B1]. Built in the 18th century by the last Dutch governor, it was formerly known as King's or Queen's House. Now the official residence (not just for entertaining) of the president, it is hidden behind a wealth of trees and heavily guarded.

Almost hidden by the trees that shade him where he stands permanently on guard is the **statue of Sir Edward Barnes** [76 B1], which bears the inscription 'Erected by the European and Native inhabitants of Ceylon and Friends in England and India to testify their respect and affection for this person'. Barnes, governor from 1820 to 1822 and 1824 to 1831, was responsible for much of the development of the island, including its roads. All road distances from Colombo to the outstations are measured from this statue.

THE GREEN FLASH

It's not the name of a cocktail served on the veranda of the Galle Face Hotel, but the Galle Face Green is an ideal place to watch for the Green Flash. The first glimpse of it usually happens by accident. Tourists on the beach, whether in Bentota or Negombo, peering at the horizon as the sun dips towards the sea in a flaming orange ball, rub their eyes in disbelief at the sudden prick of green emphasising the majestic beauty of the setting sun's bright orb.

There are those who maintain the Green Flash doesn't exist because they have never seen it. However, just because the Green Flash can only be seen on a cloudless horizon doesn't mean it's a fable. Sunsets seen from Sri Lanka's western shores are sensational. Even when there are clouds gathering along the horizon, watching the sun descend gracefully at dusk is a breathtaking experience. And if the sky is clear, a fraction of a second after the crown of the sun has sunk below the horizon, there it is: the Green Flash. It can be just a pinprick of turquoise green, or a lingering wink of a jade-eyed sea monster.

There have been several scientific papers written about the Green Flash. It has been described as an astronomical or rather an atmospheric event caused by a scattering of light by molecules in the atmosphere. It is light refracted by air. One expert (imagine being an expert in Green Flashes!) describes it as the last bit of sun coloured green when the sun sinks below the horizon. The top rim of the sun appears green and red on the horizon; when the sun sets the green rim is the last to disappear.

Another expert points out that the actual Green Flash, a green flame above the point where the sun sets below the horizon a few seconds after sunset, is 'extremely rare'. Anyway, it's fun to watch out for it in Sri Lanka, where the sunsets are memorable and sometimes do, indeed, end with a Green Flash.

Where Chatham Street intersects Janadhipathi Mawatha stands a city landmark, the **clocktower** [76 B1], visible not only from parts of Fort but also from the sea. It served as a lighthouse until the 1950s, perhaps the only one in the middle of a city. The tower was built in 1857, although it was not until 1914 that the clock with four faces – to show the time north, east, south and west – was installed.

Walk towards the sea (but this is a high security area so don't pause) and you will see on your left, by the pavement behind railings in front of the building opposite the Kingsbury Hotel, a small **domed cell** with a roof of red scalloped tiles. A plaque in English and Sinhala says that Sri Wickrama Rajasinghe, last King of Kandy (1798–1815), was imprisoned 'in this specific chamber'. An effigy of the king behind bars glowers at passers-by who never notice his jail.

Turn right at the roundabout by the **Kingsbury Hotel** and you may be able to walk along the waterfront drive up to the **lighthouse** [76 B1] built in 1951 to function instead of the one in Chatham Street. Below it is a natural seawater swimming pool in the rocks where colonial governors and their ladies were wont to bathe. Known as the **Governor's Bath**, it was restored in 1991.

At the other side of the roundabout is the former parliament building, now the **Presidential Secretariat** [76 B2], its forum-style brownstone lines an antidote to the brightness of the mirror-glass skyscrapers of the headquarters of the **Bank of Ceylon** that towers behind the **Galadari Hotel** [76 B2]. Its twin-tower neighbour is Colombo's own **World Trade Centre** [76 B1]. The Secretariat stands at the northern end of Galle Face Green.

Although it is often more brown than green, the restored (in 2001) **Galle Face Green** [76 B2] is a popular promenade at dusk, with the venerable **Galle Face Hotel** [76 C3] commanding the southern end, where the road and railway head down to Galle. When the sun and the heat have gone, it is fun to stroll along the waterfront, as the citizens of Colombo do, enjoying the breeze, the camaraderie and the night-time hawker snacks, and even buying a kite and having a go at flying it. An inscribed stone at the sea's edge stated that Galle Face Walk was commenced by Sir Henry Ward in 1856, completed in 1859, and 'recommended to his successors in the interest of the Ladies and Children of Colombo'. The original stone is in the old town hall (municipal) museum in Pettah.

Although it is not within walking distance, you will probably catch a glimpse of the neoclassical 'new' **town hall** [76 F4] (*F R Senanayake Mawatha, Colombo 7*) when you are driving around the town by taxi. This is supposed to be modelled on Washington, DC's Capitol building. Opposite is the **Vihara Mara Devi** (formerly Victoria) **Park** [76 E4], which is open to the public. It survives from the time when this area, known as **Cinnamon Gardens**, really did consist of cinnamon gardens.

At the other side of the park, the palatial building in its own grounds is the **National Museum** [76 E4] (*Sir Marcus Fernando Mawatha, Colombo 7;* ✆ *011 2694366; admission Rs500 & fee for photography*) and behind that is the **Natural History Museum** [76 E4] (*Sir Marcus Fernando Mawatha, Colombo 7;* ✆ *011 2691399; admission Rs300*). Both are open 09.00–17.00 every day except Friday. The National Museum houses an extraordinary collection of what may seem dull objects but which give an insight into the cultural history of the country. It was purpose-built to display the nation's treasures and opened in 1877.

Also in the prestigious Colombo 7 area you will see the especially prestigious **Bandaranaike Memorial International Conference Hall (BMICH)** [map page 72] (*2–101 Bauddhaloka Mawatha, Colombo 7;* ✆ *011 2696364; www.bmich.gov.lk*), which has been the site of many important international conferences. Close to it is the **Independence Memorial Hall** (*Independence Av, Colombo 7*), built in the ancient forum style. This was erected to commemorate the formal signing of the independence declaration that took place in 1948.

The new **Parliament Building** [76 G4] (*Parliament Rd, Sri Jayewardenepura, Kotte*) is also an impressive sight, set in the middle of the Diyawanna Lake. Further afield, south of Colombo at Dehiwela, you will find the **Zoological Gardens** (*Dharmapala Mawatha, Dehiwela; ☏ 011 2712752; www.colombozoo.gov.lk; ⊕ 08.00–18.00 daily; admission Rs2,000/Rs1,000 adult/child; see page 229 for further information and details*).

An amazing contrast to the clutter of the city is to be found at the **Royal Colombo Golf Club** [map page 72] (*223 Ven Pelpola Vipassi Himi Mawatha, formerly Model Farm Rd, Colombo 8, Borella; ☏ 011 2695431; www.rcgcsl.com*). This 18-hole, 5,770m-long (par 71) course defies the suburban buildings crowding it and gives a welcome breath of fresh air and greenery to Colombo's citizens and visitors. The course is flat with broad fairways, which look simple to beginners, but there are water hazards and bunkers that quickly change the opinion. Trains on the Kelani Valley line cut through the course periodically. Temporary membership is available to visitors and equipment can be hired. There is a restaurant and bar ($$), as well as a practice and exercise ground.

DAY TRIPS If you are in Sri Lanka for a day, either in transit while changing flights, or as a cruise passenger, there are plenty of things to do. Colombo itself is rewarding as a city of good restaurants and a few good shops, with a little bit of culture and entertainment thrown in.

The most enjoyable morning trip is the **Colombo Bus Tour** (*www.colombocitytour. com; Sun only; 4hrs*). A genuine 1950s London Transport Routemaster double-decker bus, with roof cut off its upper deck for easy viewing, takes guests on a delightful ramble through Colombo's quiet streets every Sunday morning, revealing much of the backstreets of Colombo as well as the impressive sights of the Beira Lake, a temple, kovil and church; and visits to Independence Square and the National Museum (*admission charge included*). An expert guide is on board with a running commentary in English and to answer questions; sandwiches and mineral water are included, and there are umbrellas available.

The tour is a project by the national bus company (formerly CTB), the Sri Lanka Tourism Promotion Bureau and Ebert Silva Tours (*www.ebertsilva.lk*). It's worth planning to be in Colombo on Sunday as this is a definite 'do not miss' experience.

Although only a few cruise ships call in at Colombo, they stay 12 hours or longer when they do. This is to enable passengers to take the organised excursion by road to the Elephant Orphanage, Kandy (including the Botanical Gardens), and back. It makes a tiring day, almost entirely spent in the air-conditioned coach (over six hours there and back) or waiting for other passengers to find their way back to the coach after stops. It is not recommended. However, the same itinerary by independently hired car is possible on a day's visit to Colombo, whether you come by sea or are in transit at the airport.

Cars wait where the ship docks and their driver/guides are well prepared for bargaining with passengers. If your journey is only to be a short one into the city, wait until the excursion and other passengers have disembarked before attempting to negotiate a fare. (This is because drivers want the longer hires on which they can make more money, but if the prospect is no hire at all, the fare will drop.) All taxis that have managed to get into the port have had to pay to get there and so are entitled to charge more than a taxi hired outside the port. The smarter ones have tariffs that they will show on request.

A day out to the **Elephant Orphanage** and **Kandy** by hired car (called 'hiring car' in Sri Lankan English) is worth it for the instant insight it brings of industrial, rural, religious and natural Sri Lanka. The driver will know which restaurants, spice gardens and batik factories to stop at since he has taken tourists there before and knows where the toilets are tolerable. However, on the road to Kandy there are several places you will want to linger at, so be firm with the driver and stop where you want, rather than where he thinks you want to stop. For more details, see pages 194 and 102 respectively.

The other excursion usually provided for cruise-ship passengers is the **Colombo city tour**. If you just want to sample the city, this is a good way to do it, perhaps returning in the afternoon by taxi for a second look at places that intrigue you.

The main problem for ship passengers is that cruise liners are usually obliged to tie up at quays far from the port gates. This makes walking into town, or even to the port gates to find independent taxis, quite a task, especially in the hot sun. Those passengers who find themselves at the **Queen Elizabeth Quay** are luckier. There is a duty-free shop in the customs hall, and it is not far to walk to the port gates where there are usually some three-wheelers available. They will charge whatever you are prepared to pay to take you into town. If you are a good walker, keep going; eventually you will be out of the port security area and can pick up a three-wheeler at the usual rate (starts at Rs100).

Many cruise passengers who make their way independently into town go to the Galadari, Kingsbury or Hilton hotels (the nearest to the main port gates) and hire hotel cars from there for their touring. While this is a good option, the problem will be getting back to the ship since those cars can't go within the restricted area around the port, so you'll have a long walk back.

Colombo lends itself conveniently to a day's exploration and shopping. Three-wheeler taxis are the best for negotiating the traffic; however, a hotel taxi will be air conditioned and, since it has the hotel's logo on its side, has the standard of the

VICEROY SPECIAL: STEAM TRAIN TOURS

The *Viceroy Special* is a steam-hauled train that makes special trips, from Colombo to Kandy and back, as part of a package deal marketed by travel agents. The package usually includes a visit to the Elephant Orphanage at Pinnawela (reached by tour bus from Rambukkana station) and a tour of Kandy, as well as meals on the train, and hotel accommodation with meals.

It is not possible to buy a ticket just to travel to Kandy on the train, but it is worth contacting the train operators, **J F Tours & Travels** (*58 Havelock Rd, Colombo 5;* \ *011 2589402;* e *inquiriesjft@sltnet.lk; www.jftours.com*) in case they can suggest something. They can also give the times the train will be at certain stations if you want to photograph it.

The *Viceroy Special* consists of four coaches, all painted in the bright red livery of the former Ceylon Government Railway, and outlined in gold with the CGR crest displayed on the body panels. The train has accommodation for 48 passengers in air-conditioned coaches with reclining seats; there is also a restaurant car and a bar.

Four steam engines, all British built, have been brought out of retirement to pull the *Viceroy Special*. The main one, *Sir Thomas Maitland*, No 251, was built in 1928; the oldest, No 213, in 1922; No 240 in 1927; and the newest, No 340, in 1945.

hotel to guide it. You can choose what to see by consulting the section on pages 91–5 and then lunching perhaps on the terrace of the Galle Face Hotel (see page 81) or in the Old Dutch Hospital (see page 83).

The five-star hotels in Colombo all have super swimming pools (the Hilton's by the Beira Lake is especially attractive) that can be used by non-residents by arrangement. Those hotels also have day rooms so you could make a luxury hotel your base from which to explore, even on foot, as well as having a swim and doing lunch.

If a **beach** is the main objective, head for the Mount Lavinia Hotel where there are facilities for beach enjoyment and a variety of restaurants. Although there are no organised excursions to the beaches of the west coast, it is feasible to go there if your stay is ten hours or more. Allow two hours for the drive to Bentota's broad beach, basing yourself at the Bentota Beach Hotel or, more downmarket, at Hotel Susantha's. A pleasant option at Bentota is to make the riverside Hotel Aida your base and take a river cruise, have lunch, and even shop for gems, since Aida himself is a renowned and trusted gem dealer (see page 239).

Northwards from Colombo (and the best beach option if you are based at the airport) you can go to **Negombo** for the day where several beachside guesthouses have day rooms. From Colombo harbour, though, the drive is fraught with traffic and not as fascinating as the drive south.

The determined could make a day trip from Colombo to **Galle Fort** (allow seven hours for the journey there and back). It is not possible, however, to visit Anuradhapura or the tea gardens of the hill country on a day trip. It may not look far on the map, but there is simply not enough time.

Since many cruise ships do not leave Colombo until late evening, there is a chance to sample the city's pubs or casinos (which are open all day).

If you want to try a **train ride**, this is possible using the local passenger services from Colombo Fort station. A brief trip could be made to Maradana and back, but for something more exciting try the Kelani Valley line. This runs through the suburbs and you could alight at Nugegoda or Homagama and take a three-wheeler back to town. Another option would be to take the scenic route by train down the west coast to Bentota and then hire a minibus for the trip back to Colombo.

Whatever you do during the day, allow extra time for unexpected happenings, whether it's a religious procession holding up the traffic, a diversion because of road closure, or simply because you're enjoying yourself so much you don't want to leave.

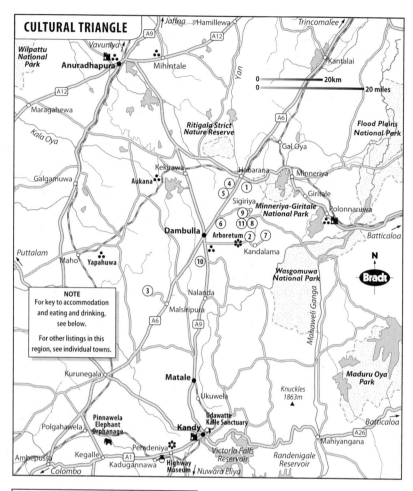

CULTURAL TRIANGLE

For listings, see pages 133–5, 138 & 144–5

Where to stay and eat

1 Acme Transit
2 Amaya Lake Resort
3 Brook Boutique
4 Chaaya Village
5 Cinnamon Lodge
6 Gimanhala Transit
7 Heritance Kandalama
8 Hotel Sigiriya
9 The Elephant Corridor
10 Thilanka Resort
11 Vil Uyana

4

The Cultural Triangle

Whoever named the interior north of Kandy as the 'Cultural Triangle' has created an intriguing image. For visitors whose interest in ancient kingdoms and religion is minimal, it helps to have a defined area where they can go for a dash of culture. They take a quick sortie around the Triangle to salve their consciences, then drive back to lotus-eating on the beach or elephant-adoration at Pinnawela.

Actually, the Cultural Triangle is not all culture. There are elephants and birds galore within its perimeters, and hotels that are better than those on the beach for original architecture and hassle-free comfort. For most tourists, the holiday reaches its zenith with a visit to the Cultural Triangle. It is what makes Sri Lanka unique.

The points of the Triangle are three ancient capitals. The southern point is **Kandy**, the last capital of the Sinhalese kings, in the hills, 116km (72 miles) from Colombo. To the north is **Anuradhapura**, founded in the 5th century BC and venerated as the capital city of Buddhism. **Polonnaruwa**, to the northeast of Kandy, was the medieval capital, where art, architecture and engineering were revived to a cultural intensity that is a monument to the country's renaissance.

Contained within the Triangle are **Sigiriya**, with its rocky abode and water gardens built in the 5th century, and **Dambulla**, the largest cave monastery in the country, with a history going back to the 1st century BC. Included are **Mihintale** where Mahinda, son of the Indian emperor Ashok, preached Buddhism in 246BC; the wildlife reserve of **Minneriya–Giritale**; and hotels at home with nature at **Habarana** and **Kandalama**.

The Cultural Triangle Project to excavate and preserve monuments within the defined area was launched in 1978 by the Ministry of Cultural Affairs in association with the United Nations Educational, Scientific and Cultural Organisation. The Central Cultural Fund was set up to finance the work, and the income from entrance fees to the sites within the Triangle goes to the fund.

If your time is limited, it is possible to make a one- or two-day trip from Colombo to visit the sites. However, that is not recommended as travelling by road is tiring and won't put you in the best frame of mind to view the ruins and temples. Driving time from Colombo to Kandy is three hours; to Dambulla 3½ hours; to Sigiriya four hours; to Anuradhapura or Polonnaruwa, 4½ hours. It would be more feasible to make Kandy your base and visit the other sites on day trips from there.

HISTORY

Of the eight World Heritage Sites in Sri Lanka declared and listed by UNESCO, five of them, spanning 2,500 years of history, are within the Cultural Triangle, as is the Knuckles Conservation Forest, part of the newly recognised (since 2010) Heritage Site, the Central Highlands:

- The sacred city of Anuradhapura (5th century BC)
- The medieval capital of Polonnaruwa (10th century AD)
- The cave temples of Dambulla (1BC)
- The Sigiriya rock fortress (5th century AD)
- The royal city of Kandy (17th century)
- The Dutch fortifications at Galle (17th century)
- Sinharaja Forest Reserve
- The Central Highlands (Peak Wilderness, Horton Plains, Knuckles Conservation Forest)

The recorded history of Sri Lanka began when Buddhism gave birth to a cultural revolution more than 2,000 years ago. It was at **Mihintale**, 12km from Anuradhapura, which was itself founded in the 5th century BC, that Buddhism was first introduced to the island. **Anuradhapura** is venerated as the capital city of Buddhism. The sacred Bo tree, grown from a sapling of the tree under which the Buddha attained Enlightenment, is the oldest living tree in documented history.

The rock temple at **Dambulla** with its carvings and statues is as old as the Christian world, dating from the 1st century BC. **Sigiriya** commemorates some of the turbulence of Sri Lanka's history, while **Polonnaruwa** with its well-preserved 12th-century ruins and impressive stone culture recalls an inspired past. More recent in its fall from glory is **Kandy**, the last capital of the Sinhalese kings.

A complete understanding of the diverse history and culture of Sri Lanka can be gleaned from visiting this geometrical package: the Cultural Triangle.

GETTING THERE AND AWAY

BY TRAIN There is no one train that links all the points of the Cultural Triangle, either with each other or with Colombo. Each of the apex cities of Anuradhapura, Polonnaruwa and Kandy are on different lines. So the only way that trains could be used to visit all of them is by doubling back. Thus, after travelling by train from Colombo to Anuradhapura, you would have to take a train back to the junction station of Maho and from there catch a train to Habarana (for Sigiriya) or to Kaduruwela (for Polonnaruwa). Next would be a Colombo-bound train from Habarana or Polonnaruwa to change at Polgahawela for a train to Kandy. A shorter way would be to take a bus from Habarana or Polonnaruwa to Matale. From Matale there are trains to Kandy, and from Kandy an intercity train will bring you back to Colombo.

BY BUS Intercity buses serve Anuradhapura (Nos 4 and 15), Kandy (No 1) and Polonnaruwa (No 48) from Colombo.

BY ROAD The Cultural Triangle is most conveniently visited by hiring a chauffeur-driven vehicle and driving from site to site. The driver will act as guide. Cheaper might be to join others on an organised guided tour. This shouldn't be scorned by the independent traveller as such tours have guides who know the ruins and where to find them, and every other dodge to make the trip stress-free, as well as including accommodation, fees and permits in the price (for further details, see pages 49–50).

With a chauffeur-driven car you could have a do-it-yourself tour around the Cultural Triangle staying at, say, Anuradhapura and visiting Mihintale, then Aukana and on to Polonnaruwa for lunch, sightseeing and overnight, then an early start to climb Sigiriya Rock Fortress, drive to Kandy and visit the Temple of the Tooth and overnight in Kandy. Spend the final day of sightseeing in Kandy, with a visit to the Royal Botanical Gardens and Elephant Orphanage at Pinnawela, before finishing up at a Colombo or beach hotel. This three-night and four-hectic-day tour (800km), using basic/moderate rate accommodation and eating local meals, and with entry fees, permits, car hire and tips included, would cost about US$1,500 for two people.

GETTING AROUND

To visit the monuments and ruins in the Cultural Triangle, you will need a permit (see box below). Keep the permit with you, especially if you are riding a bicycle in Anuradhapura or walking around the ruins in Polonnaruwa, as a security guard might ask if you've got one.

BY BUS There are cross-country buses linking the apex cities. From Anuradhapura, there are buses to Kandy (Nos 42-2 and 43) and to Polonnaruwa.

BY ROAD To do it without hassle, a group tour or hiring a car with driver/guide is the best way of getting around all areas of the Cultural Triangle, not just to its points.

CULTURAL SITES

The special sites of the Cultural Triangle, as administered by the **Central Cultural Fund** (*212/1 Bauddhaloka Mawatha, Colombo;* \ *(help desk) 011 2587921;* e *gen_ccf@sri.lanka.net; www.ccf.lk or www.cultural.gov.lk;* ⊕ *08.30– 16.00 Mon–Fri*), are the Jetavana and Abhayagiri monastery complexes at Anuradhapura; the Alahana Pirivena monastic university and the royal city and palaces at Polonnaruwa; the city, palace and gardens at Sigiriya; and the painted cave temples at Dambulla.

An inclusive ticket (permit) for admission to all sites (except Dambulla and the Sri Dalada Maligawa, Temple of the Tooth) costs US$50 per person with children's tickets at half price. Permits are obtainable from the **Cultural Triangle Office** (*Atapattu Bldg, 11 Independence Av, Colombo 7;* \ *011 2587912*) or at any of the sites; they can also be obtained in advance through the website www.ccf.lk. Payment must be in rupees, at the rupee equivalent of the US dollar price, as set by the selling office.

Adult tickets for individual sites cost as follows (tickets for children aged six–12 are half price):

Anuradhapura	US$25	Madirigiriya	US$8
Polonnaruwa	US$25	Nalanda	US$5
Sigiriya	US$30	Ritigala	US$5
Kandy	US$12	Kataragama Museum	US$5

The Cultural Triangle sites of the Sri Dalada Maligawa (Temple of the Tooth) in Kandy and the cave temple at Dambulla are administered by the temple authorities, and tickets have to be purchased separately to visit them. Local residents pay a special discounted price to visit all the sites. The admission ticket also covers fees for photography, recording and vehicle parking.

Kandy is blessed not only with the sacred Temple of the Tooth, but also with a name, Kandy, so sweet it is irresistible. It is the one place on the itinerary of every visitor, and it doesn't disappoint. Its location, the temple, the ambience, the royal history, the lake – everything about the town is delightful.

It is a pleasant town to amble through, but unfortunately an organised tour doesn't allow enough time for that. After seeing the temple, it's back on the bus to head for somewhere else. However, since Kandy is easy to visit by train, even for just a day trip from Colombo, it is possible to make the journey independently.

A three-wheeler will take you from the station to the temple square. The driver will do his best to entice you to take a tour with him, or to stay where he recommends. If you like him, keep him. Having one guardian tuk-tuk driver stops the others hounding you. He'll wait patiently while you visit the temple and then take you on a city tour.

Try a walk along the lakeside. Here you will meet people in a more leisurely mood than those in Colombo. A school of young monks in bright saffron robes might file religiously past while you gaze at the golden roof of the temple complex. A gaggle of giggling girls try to suppress their amusement at the sight of curious tourists. Vendors sit quietly by the pavement hopefully offering balloons and sunglasses to anyone who looks their way. At your feet the bathroom scales belong to a man holding a placard which says, in English, that he will measure your weight for a few rupees.

HISTORY Kandy was founded by Vikrama Bahu, who ruled his part of the country from Gampola during 1474–1511. Legend attributes many reasons for him choosing to move his capital to what was first called Senkadagala. The region formed a sub-kingdom known as Kanda-uda-pas-rata (the five *ratas*, or districts on the hills) or the *uda-rata* (hill district). It became known by Europeans as Kanda and, thus, Kandy. The Sinhalese called it Maha Nuwara (the big town).

In 1592, the sacred tooth relic (that had arrived in the island in AD331) was brought to Kandy. Its presence confirmed Kandy as the capital, despite the presence of the Portuguese on the littoral. By 1658, when the Portuguese were ousted by the Dutch, the kingdom was able to coexist, albeit uneasily, with the new occupiers. The British, however, wanted the island in its entirety and conquered Kandy in 1815. The king, Sri Wickrama Rajasinghe (1798–1815), was exiled.

GETTING THERE
By train The well-modulated voice over the loudspeaker – 'The train now standing on Platform two …' – announces the departure from Colombo Fort station of the Intercity Express for Kandy twice a day. The excitement rises as the late arrivals hurry to board the train. Although the guard does not shout 'All-abooooard' as he would do in the USA, he blows his whistle and waves his green flag vigorously, and the train pulls out on time.

The opening of the line to Kandy in 1867 was the start of railways in Sri Lanka. (That must have been an auspicious year since it was also the year that the tea industry started.) It was the culmination of years of speculation, negotiation and ingenious engineering, a feat that was considered a masterpiece of railway construction.

The line reached Ambepussa in 1864 and up to Polgahawela in 1866. Then heavy rock-cutting, especially at Sensation Rock, was carried out for the line to top the incline to Kadugannawa by March 1867. Ten tunnels were built in 19km on a steady

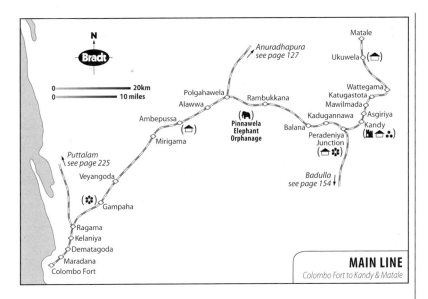

MAIN LINE
Colombo Fort to Kandy & Matale

gradient of 1 in 44. It was this pioneering enterprise by the railway that opened up the country to change and prosperity.

You can sample the journey easily by buying a ticket to ride on the Intercity Express (ICE). Seats can be reserved in Colombo for the return at **Fort station** [76 C1] (*intercity enquiries* \ *011 2434215; www.railway.gov.lk; reservation counters* ⏲ *06.00–17.00 daily*). Reservations may be made up to ten days in advance and also on a 'space available' basis on the day of travel. Reservations for the return journey up to 14 days from the arrival date can also be made there. Round-trip tickets purchased in this manner show a saving of 50% over two separate one-way tickets. Tickets are marked with train number, coach number, seat number and date of travel.

The train is all second class, apart from an observation saloon at the end of the train, which is first class. It is possible to upgrade a second-class ticket to sit in the observation saloon while on the train, but see the guard before sneaking into it.

The one-way fare by intercity between Colombo and Kandy is Rs340 for a reserved seat in the observation car, and Rs190 second class in a normal express.

The train is scheduled to take 155 minutes for the 116km rail journey, with one stop at Peradeniya Junction. On paper it does not seem very fast but on board the train it certainly does. The carriages sway and clatter as the train rushes along the track laid over concrete sleepers, making conversation impossible.

Try to get a seat on the right-hand side of the train, facing the engine for the best views (left-hand side, facing engine for the journey from Kandy). The spectacular scenery is a blur as the train speeds through the mainline stations until it slows for the climb after Rambukkana. The views of distant hills and terraced paddy fields at the base of lush valleys are stunning.

For a more intimate introduction to the countryside, take an ordinary 'express' from Fort station. The experience is low-key at the start as the train winds its way out of the web of lines surrounding the abandoned rolling stock on the outskirts of **Maradana** station, just after Fort.

Two luxury carriage services have been introduced to/from Kandy and tickets can be purchased online but the printout has to be validated at the station (or train

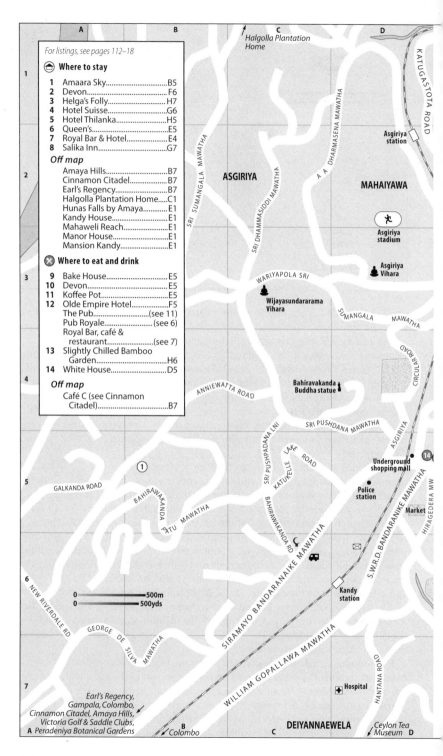

For listings, see pages 112–18

⌂ Where to stay

1	Amaara Sky	B5
2	Devon	F6
3	Helga's Folly	H7
4	Hotel Suisse	G6
5	Hotel Thilanka	H5
6	Queen's	E5
7	Royal Bar & Hotel	E4
8	Salika Inn	G7

Off map

Amaya Hills	B7
Cinnamon Citadel	B7
Earl's Regency	B7
Halgolla Plantation Home	C1
Hunas Falls by Amaya	E1
Kandy House	E1
Mahaweli Reach	E1
Manor House	E1
Mansion Kandy	E1

✖ Where to eat and drink

9	Bake House	E5
10	Devon	E5
11	Koffee Pot	E5
12	Olde Empire Hotel	F5
	The Pub	(see 11)
	Pub Royale	(see 6)
	Royal Bar, café & restaurant	(see 7)
13	Slightly Chilled Bamboo Garden	H6
14	White House	D5

Off map

Café C (see Cinnamon Citadel)	B7

ASGIRIYA

MAHAIYAWA

Halgolla Plantation Home

KATUGASTOTA ROAD

Asgiriya station

A A DHARMASENA MAWATHA

SRI DHAMMASIDDI MAWATHA

SRI SUMANGALA MAWATHA

Asgiriya stadium

Asgiriya Vihara

WARIYAPOLA SRI

SUMANGALA MAWATHA

Wijayasundararama Vihara

CIRCULAR ROAD

ANNIEWATTA ROAD

Bahiravakanda Buddha statue

SRI PUSHDANA MAWATHA

SRI PUSHPADANA LNI

ASGIRIYA

Underground shopping mall

KATUFELLE LAKE ROAD

Police station

GALKANDA ROAD

BAHIRAWAKANDA PATU MAWATHA

BAHIRAWAKANDA RD

HIRAGEDERA MW

Market

S. W. R. D. BANDARANAIKE MAWATHA

①

Kandy station

NEW RIVERDALE RD

0 ──── 500m
0 ──── 500yds

GEORGE DE SILVA MAWATHA

SIRAMAYO BANDARANAIKE MAWATHA

WILLIAM GOPALLAWA MAWATHA

Hospital

HANTANA ROAD

Earl's Regency,
Gampala, Colombo,
Cinnamon Citadel, Amaya Hills,
Victoria Golf & Saddle Clubs,
Peradeniya Botanical Gardens

Colombo

DEIYANNAEWELA

Ceylon Tea Museum

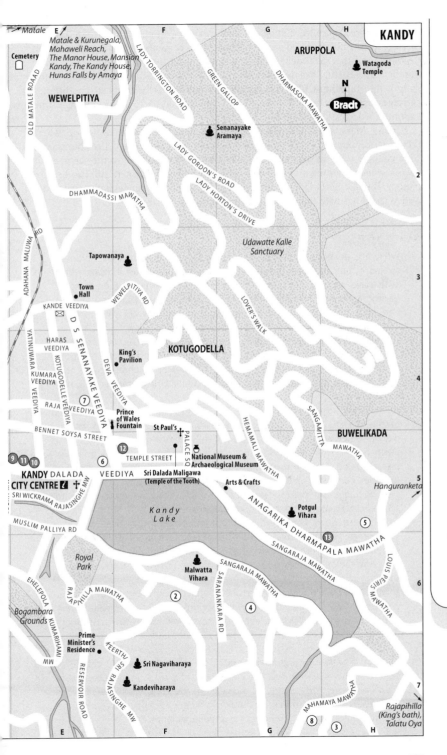

KANDY

ARUPPOLA

WEWELPITIYA

KOTUGODELLA

BUWELIKADA

The Cultural Triangle KANDY

agency) before departure. **Exporail** (*www.exporail.lk*) operate an air-conditioned carriage with only reserved seating attached daily to the 07.00 departure from Colombo and the 15.00 departure from Kandy (the Intercity Express; ICE, train number 1009/1010). The fare is Rs1,450 one-way. Operating in the reverse direction daily is the **Rajadhani Blue** carriage (*www.rajadhani.lk*) with its air-conditioned carriage attached to the ICE from Kandy departing at 06.15 and to the ICE from Colombo at 15.35. The fare is Rs1,100 one-way.

Beyond Maradana is the **Dematagoda** running-shed and workshop where retired steam engines can be glimpsed peeping out of the shed. The countryside soon changes to rural with silhouettes of women bent parallel to the earth, ankle deep in water, planting single blades of paddy by hand. Farmers still use oxen to plough. Bullock carts laden with firewood jingle along jungle trails, past mud-walled dwellings with thatched palm fronds.

EXPORAIL

While it is possible to book online for the Exporail carriage from Colombo to Kandy, unfortunately the seat diagram shown does not indicate which seats have windows (not all do, so avoid 9D) and which are the best for photographers, with small windows that can be opened (I suggest 4D, 11A and 11D). Avoid Row 1 with limited legroom and Row 12 with constant annoyance from the closing of the sliding door to the galley.

Next comes the catch. The printout downloaded from the website is NOT the ticket. This printout has to be swapped for an e-ticket by joining the long queue of all passengers planning to travel by reserved seat on the Intercity Express to Kandy, snaking around a tiny, airless office at Colombo Fort station.

The train arrives at Platform 2 at Colombo Fort station 20 minutes before departure and people surge aboard. However, the engine (on the day I travelled a diesel electric loco M6 790 built in 1980 by Henschel, West Germany) has to be uncoupled so it can shunt to the front of the train and be re-coupled for the journey. The rake (number of railway carriages coupled together) consists of an observation car at the rear of the train, three second-class carriages, one pantry car with third-class seating, a luggage van with second-class seating, and the Exporail luxury carriage.

This carriage is converted from a regular passenger one, with the addition of air conditioning, two video screens, a luggage rack by the entrance doors, overhead closed luggage lockers, 48 slightly reclining seats with tray tables, a galley and, worth the premium alone, a clean, sweet-smelling lavatory.

Mercifully the only video screen that was functioning had the sound turned down very low. The show began with captions that I thought were meant to be funny, such as: 'Do not lean on or read over your fellow passenger's shoulder'; 'Avoid consuming smelly food'; 'Do not panic'; 'Do not lean close to the generator.'

Because of the air conditioning, the doors of the carriage had to be kept closed, so there was none of the excitement of a rail journey in second or third class when the sounds (and smells) of the countryside pervade the carriages and people stroll up and down looking for friends. But it makes for a more comfortable rail journey in a traditional manner.

Train	Colombo–Kandy	Train	Kandy–Colombo
1005	05.55–08.42 (to Badulla)	1046	02.36–05.17 (from Badulla)
1009	07.00–09.35 (ICE)	1040	05.10–08.17
1015	09.45–12.19 (to Badulla)	1030	06.15–08.52 (ICE)
1019	10.35–13.52	1036	06.30–09.45
1023	12.40–16.04 (to Hatton)	1024	10.30–13.52 (from Nanu Oya)
1029	15.35–18.06 (ICE)	1016	12.50–15.27 (from Badulla)
1035	16.35–19.36	1010	15.00–17.36 (ICE)
1039	17.45–20.58	1020	15.30–18.55
		1006	16.06–18.57 (from Badulla)

Some trains make a stop at **Ragama**, an important junction where stopping trains heading northwards to Negombo and Puttalam branch off. **Gampaha**, the next major station, is the stop for the Henarathgoda Botanical Gardens, the closest (32km) gardens to Colombo.

At **Veyangoda** station, 35km from Colombo, express trains connect with local ones stopping at all stations to Polgahawela and back; good for a glimpse of lowland rural life. The stationmaster at **Mirigama** (48km) kept rabbits in a cage built around the trunk of a tree on the platform when I last stopped there. Golden husks of *thambili* (king coconuts) drained of water by thirsty travellers littered the track.

Few trains stop now at **Ambepussa**, 54km from Colombo, the halt for the first-ever train on the line, which arrived there in 1864. **Alawwa** is a small station before the major junction of **Polgahawela**, where trains to the north leave the line to Kandy. This also marks the end of the dual track from Colombo. Train traffic is one-way from now on.

The excitement of the ascent through the hills begins at the next station, **Rambukkana**. Alight here for the Elephant Orphanage at **Pinnawela**. Some trains to Kandy have an extra engine (banker) attached to them at Rambukkana to push them up the climb from 116m to Kadugannawa station, 517m above sea level. Maximum speed on this stretch is 32km/h and the trains seem to dawdle along, but fortunately the view of lush vegetation, deep valley and mountain streams is spectacular.

The banker engine that pushes the train through a warren of tunnels and a tangle of tropical jungle is uncoupled at **Kadugannawa** station. The journey from there to Kandy is actually a descent (from 517m to 488m). The slim **column** like a lighthouse, which can be glimpsed from the platform, is a monument erected in 1832 to (and named after) Captain Dawson, who built the Colombo to Kandy road.

As befits the station closest to the Royal Botanical Gardens, the platforms at **Peradeniya** are attractively disguised by potted plants. From this junction trains either go to Kandy or continue the long haul to Badulla. The last lap is a run of 6km through rural suburbs and stations to the terminus.

Kandy station [104 D6] has four platforms and is bright and clean. The line running from Platform 1 is the branch to **Matale**. There are various restrooms and toilets on the main concourse, as well as a fish tank. The kiosk selling refreshments, newspapers and mineral water is pleasant for a snack before departure. Locomotives are detached here and manoeuvred to the other end of the train for the return or onward journey.

On the left after the exit is a bookshop and the ticket windows in a semicircle. The window where intercity bookings are made is on the right of the exit (⏰ *05.30–16.00*). Two other windows sell tickets for first-, second- and third-class journeys.

The Cultural Triangle KANDY

4

The station is not the original 1880 building but has charm with its mock-Kandy architecture. It is possible to walk (take the road straight ahead) to the Temple of the Tooth, but eager tuk-tuk drivers will offer you a ride.

Train times, listed in the box on page 107, should be checked before travelling in case of rescheduling.

By bus There are intercity buses (No 1) to and from Kandy with departures from Colombo every 15 minutes.

By road Jungle and junk, cashew nuts and cane furniture, steam rollers and flying foxes; not the usual roadside sights, but the Kandy road has them all and more. As the A1 highway from Colombo to Kandy, the road is one of the country's busiest. On its 116km journey from the metropolis – from lowland fields glistening with paddy to misty vistas of hills and valleys – the road reveals much of Sri Lanka's lore and lifestyle. In 1926, Frances Parkinson Keyes wrote:

> If I could take only one drive in a tropical country, I believe I would choose this drive from Colombo to Kandy, for here in the space of a few hours can be seen a greater variety of scenery, rich in concentrated beauty, of vegetation and of humanity than can be seen in double or treble that time in any other place.

Over 85 years after Mrs Keyes, wife of a US senator, took her trip by motorcar to Kandy, the road is still fascinating. Along its length a skein of memorable sights is gradually unravelled as the road climbs from sea level at Colombo to 488m at Kandy.

The road officially begins outside President's House in Colombo, although that area is now closed to the public. There, in isolation, is a statue of Sir Edward Barnes that marks the point from which all road distances from the city are measured. Barnes was governor (1820–22 and 1824–31) of the then Ceylon and believed administration of the country would be better achieved by the building of roads instead of forts. Construction started in 1820 and the road was opened to traffic in 1825.

Before it was built, it took six weeks to travel from Colombo to Kandy, mostly in single file along jungle trails. The opening of the road reduced the journey to ten days by bullock cart. In 1832, a horse-drawn mail coach ran to Kandy three times a week, with a maximum speed of 6mph. The opening of a passenger train service to Kandy in 1867 brought the stagecoach era to an end.

It is difficult to imagine those days while sitting in an air-conditioned taxi or intercity bus zipping along the broad, modern highway to complete the journey in three hours. Once when I wanted a leisurely jaunt so I could see everything the road had to offer instead of racing along with places and people becoming a blur, I hired a tuk-tuk. It took a day to get to Kandy.

As the three-wheeler wove its way through the suburban traffic, I quickly discovered its disadvantages: exhaust fumes from buses belched directly at face-level; a skittering progress that left me shaky and exhausted. However, seated in the back with sides open to the road, I was able to look people in the eyes and stop easily when something unusual took my fancy.

A lot of trading is done at the roadside. The first taste of it is at 16km from Colombo, where roadside stalls offer pineapples for sale, stacked on shelves like paperback books, or peeled and quartered and ready to serve with a sprinkling of salt and pepper. From pineapple country, the Kandy road gives access to the region's first rubber plantation where, at **Miriswatta**, 27km from Colombo, a road to the left leads to the Henarathgoda Botanical Gardens. The first rubber trees in Asia were planted there, after being smuggled in from South America, via London's Kew Gardens.

At **Horagolla**, there is a park laid out in the gardens of the ancestral home of Solomon West Ridgeway Dias Bandaranaike, prime minister from 1956 to 1959 and father of Mrs Chandrika Bandaranaike Kumaratunga, who was president from 1994 to 2005. His wife, Sirimavo, who died in 2000 and is buried there, was prime minister three times and the world's first female prime minister. Columns and a memorial commemorate Bandaranaike's life while on the other side of the road, on a hillock, there is a pavilion erected in memory of his grandfather, Don Solomon Dias Bandaranaike.

After the road junction at **Pasyala**, girls in colourful blouses with bare midriffs and ankle-length wraparound cloths wave at motorists to get them to halt. This area is known as Cadjugama, or **Cashew Village**, with dozens of stalls where shelled and roasted cashews are offered for sale by village belles. Rare is the driver who can resist their blandishments to stop and buy some cashews. The nuts are baked and shelled in shelters beside the highway, by women deftly tapping each nut twice with a stone.

The graceful curves and wide sweep of the road at **Radawadunna** provide an ideal setting for another village enterprise: the selling of basketware and cane furniture. Shops line both sides of the road offering cane chairs and laundry baskets, and oddities like swizzle sticks and food covers. Stuffed pillows of patchwork and locally made brooms are also on sale.

Flat wooden trays containing what look like shrivelled cigars are laid out to dry in the sun at several places along the road. These indicate the village *beedi* factories, where old men roll tobacco into a slim, cone shape using a fragrant outer leaf, called *tendu*, imported from India. This is a cheap cigarette substitute much appreciated by country folk.

After passing through the town of **Warakapola**, the road grows a branch, the A6, which shoots off northeastwards to Kurunegala and Trincomalee. At **Ambepussa**, the resthouse (recently re-renovated and renamed Heritage Rest) marks the halfway point of the journey. It was for long a traditional stop for a snack and the owning company has opened a pastry shop called Avanhala, on the opposite side of the A1 by the Warakapola junction. Tradition is alive there in the 'short eats' (small snacks) served at old-fashioned (low) prices ($).

The pungent odour drifting from palm-thatched stacks with blue smoke heavy above them, comes from roadside lime kilns. Thick tangles of trees thrive in groves beside the road wherever there is a break in the shimmering green fields of young paddy. Porcupines can be seen there too; pets proudly held and paraded by their owners for tourist cameras.

At times the road runs beside a river, or crosses one. In his book *Ceylon*, published in 1859, Sir James Emerson Tennent, formerly colonial secretary of Ceylon, wrote:

> In the numerous streams which are passed on this route, the Sinhalese are to be seen all hours of the day, indulging in their passion for the bath.

Nothing has changed. Boys with sarongs hoicked up like loincloths leap in the rapids while ladies bathe more demurely at the river's edge.

Abandoned cars of 1950s vintage in the hedgerow hint at a treasure trove of classic car parts to be discovered in the breakers' yards between **Galigomuwa** and **Ranwala**. Sheds packed with chrome hubcaps and bumpers stand beside the bulbous bodies of mid-20th-century British, French and American motorcars, and the salvaged doors and assorted panels of crashed Japanese minibuses.

Kegalle, 79km from Colombo, is a bustling market town whose only link with the rest of Sri Lanka is this road, since the railway bypasses it. A turn-off to the left after the town leads to the Pinnawela Elephant Orphanage. What seems to be a ruined castle atop a hill, viewed straight ahead, is actually a natural rock formation. It served as home for a 19th-century highway robber called Sardiel, whom legend has transformed into Sri Lanka's Robin Hood. The hill is called Utuwankanda and can be seen on the left as the road climbs.

Platoons of clay pots guard both sides of the road at **Molagoda**, where some 200 families are engaged in pottery making. Their main product is earthenware jars classically curvaceous in their simplicity, and used for storage by rural folk or for interior design statements by Colombo trendsetters. The clay comes from fields in the area and the craftsmen keep to traditional patterns.

Fruit of all kinds, according to season, and sweet corn boiled or roasted over a log fire, are sold the length of the road. As it climbs to more fertile land, the road enters the territory of spice gardens. Each of them has a sign with a number to distinguish it from its neighbours, such as Hollywood 100. Visitors are shown spices and herbs growing in the back gardens of these wayside residences and are urged to buy samples as souvenirs. If you really want spices, it would be better to pop into a local supermarket, as the housewife does, and pay a fixed, marked price.

The brave are tempted in the village of **Hingula**, and elsewhere along the road, to taste durian. Protected by its spiky skin and rampant pong, its flesh is ambrosia to addicts and nauseating to others. Its season is May to August.

VINTAGE AND CLASSIC CARS

Motorcars as old as 50 years and more are still driven on Sri Lanka's roads, especially in rural districts where they are sometimes found outside country railway stations as taxis. Morris Minors are quite common but classic cars such as Austins and Rileys are more likely to be owned by enthusiasts, while cars in the vintage group come out only for rallies.

British planters and wealthy Ceylonese brought the first motorcars to the island. There were several Daimlers and Rolls-Royces as well as cars with names that conjure up the 1920s, such as Napier and Graham Paige (now seen in rallies). The oldest motor vehicles in running condition are an Albion Murray lorry with solid tyres, dating from 1908, and a small open two-seater Paltney car registered in 1913. A Robey steam lorry from the 1920s and an open-sided Chevrolet bus of 1935 vintage also take part in rallies.

The value of vintage and classic cars is appreciated by Sri Lankan enthusiasts who hunt in tea plantations and jungles of the interior for vehicles to restore. Their export is forbidden by law so it is possible to see priceless 1920s Mercedes-Benzes, Daimlers and Austin Sevens, as well as BSA motorbikes, on the road and not in museums.

A vintage motorcar is one with a registration number preceded by a letter of the alphabet from A to Z. The letter indicates where the car was registered, not the year. Colombo was assigned the letter C, while X and Y indicated all-island registration. The system was changed in the 1930s.

Classic cars are those registered between then and 1950. A pair of letters, such as CE or CY or EN, derived from Sri Lanka's colonial name of Ceylon, was used in front of numbers for registration.

Mawanwella, where the road bridges the Maha Oya, is the place to see flying foxes. Resembling dark fruit, they hang head downwards from branches of trees on the river's banks. As the road climbs, there are views to the right of the rolling landscape, including a curious, flat-topped hill, dubbed **Bible Rock** by the British who likened it to an open Bible.

The scenery becomes wilder, with deep canyons on the right and sheer faces of rock on the left. Tennent wrote:

> The last 30 miles (48km) of this wonderful road pass through scenery which combines the grandeur of the Alps with the splendour of tropical vegetation. It is an Oriental Simplon, climbing hills, crossing torrents; and following the windings of ravines, till it reaches its extreme altitude at the pass of Kadugannawa, one of those romantic glens which the kings of Kandy guarded as an entrance from the low country.

It is guarded now by boys wielding hoses tapped to the stream above the rock face, providing a natural gravity supply for washing cars and buses beside the road. A relic of ancient times is the *ambalama*, an open wayside pilgrim shelter with columns and a peaked, tiled roof typical of Kandyan architecture. Enterprising women selling jewellery made of coir (fibre spun from coconut husks) greet travellers who stop at the fruit stalls overlooking the gorge.

Tennent reports it was prophesied that the Kandyan kingdom would perish 'when a horseman rides through a rock'. The kingdom fell to the British in 1815 and the road that was begun by Barnes in 1820 took 11 years to build. The original path does, indeed, burrow through a rock, although the new road skirts around it now.

The making of the road and the man who designed it, Captain W F Dawson of the Royal Engineers, are remembered by the white tower like a slender lighthouse that soars 38m into the sky from a bluff where the railway line joins the road at **Kadugannawa**. It can be climbed if you can find the man with the key to open the door at the back of the tower. You'll have to climb 110 wooden steps, clinging to the central wooden column for support, to reach the top. An inscription in English at the base praises Dawson 'whose science and skill planned and executed this road and other works of public utility'.

A more recent monument to public utilities is the **Highway Museum** complex at **Pilimatalawa**. Opened in 1986, it is a yard beside a level crossing with a collection of green-and-red painted steamrollers and other old road-building equipment. A few metres down the road leading to **Hendeniya** is the original Kandy road where a grand brick bridge, now closed to traffic, bears the date 1826.

A much larger bridge, over the Mahaweli River, carries the road on to Kandy, while the road to the right leads to the Royal Botanical Gardens at **Peradeniya**. The road becomes the Dalada Veediya as it cuts through the town to skirt the north shore of Kandy Lake on its approach to the Temple of the Tooth.

GETTING AROUND It is pleasant to stay right in Kandy itself, either in one of the hotels overlooking the lake, or in those near the temple compound. If you do that, then the best way to get around is to walk. Kandy is a fascinating town to explore on foot, especially as it is smaller and more laid-back than Colombo. It has colonial buildings to wonder at, as well as all the excitement of an Asian bazaar. There are plenty of three-wheelers too.

WHERE TO STAY Because of its popularity with local tourists, there are plenty of places to stay in Kandy (over 800 rooms) at prices ranging from around US$40 a double up to US$250 and beyond (such as US$500 for the Penthouse Suite at the Amaara Sky). There is no need to book in advance, except during the perahera season (July/August), when demand can cause room rates to double. Several top-class hotels have been opened in recent years on the outskirts of Kandy. All listings are included on the map, pages 104–5.

City centre

⌂ **Amaara Sky Hotel** (10 AC rooms, 2 suites) 72/22A B Damunupola Mawatha, Kandy; ✆081 2239888; e res@amaarasky.com; www.amaarasky.com. This hotel is appropriately named as it soars into the sky atop a hill overlooking Kandy. Somehow 12 well-appointed rooms including a split-level Penthouse Suite, all with balconies, are neatly packed into this new boutique property which also has a spa in the sky with jacuzzi, sauna & steam bath & therapists experienced in ayurvedic treatments. The restaurant with a view is open to non-residents & there is a long terrace for evening alfresco dining too. With over 80 stunning paintings by local artists hanging on the walls of the public areas & bedrooms, this is a bright & delightful place to stay while exploring Kandy. It's 2km from the city centre, up the road that's opposite the Kandy police station. **$$$$–$$$**

⌂ **Cinnamon Citadel** (117 AC rooms, 2 suites) 124 Srimath Kuda Ratwatte Mawatha, Kandy; ✆081 2234365; e reservations@cinnamonhotels.com; www.cinnamonhotels.com. Before reaching Kandy from Colombo there is a signposted turn-off to the left that leads to the Cinnamon Citadel. The road goes past the very neatly kept Kandy War Cemetery (1939–45) & then a clutch of small hotels & a fenced-off, privately run, riverside elephant park. Cinnamon Citadel itself, surrounded by paddy fields, is built on the bank of the Mahaweli River, on an open plan allowing a breeze to waft through the building. The reception lobby leads to the bar, which is open to the swimming pool with the river flowing in the background. Its Café C fine à la carte restaurant (🕐 *19.30–23.00 daily;* **$$$**) is available to non-residents. **$$$**

⌂ **Helga's Folly** (25–40 AC & non-AC rooms, 1 suite) 32 Frederick E de Silva Mawatha, off Mahamaya Mawatha, Kandy; ✆081 2234571; e chalet@sltnet.lk; www.helgasfolly.com. Its brochure proudly proclaims that 'We do not do package tours'. This hotel smacks of appropriate arrogance for a place where the creator, Helga de Silva Blow Perera, has been quoted in *Condé Nast*

Traveler as saying: 'I call it an anti-hotel. It's more of a home & I don't like it full; it spoils the family feeling.' Don't worry. Anything less like family & home (unless yours is something out of *Kind Hearts and Coronets*) is hard to imagine. Having taken over the boring & aptly named Chalet Hotel from her parents in the mid 1990s, Helga threw everything at it & it stuck. Visitors fed up with the soulless design & concrete-column architecture of modern hotels will find solace in the tat & outrageous colours that adorn this long building. Every room has a view of Kandy, its lake, the temple & the dramatic scenery of the Knuckles & Hunnasgiriya mountains. The hotel has enough fantastic décor to satisfy the inner child. 'If this is folly,' wrote a stunned guest in one of Helga's voluminous guest books, 'it's foolish to be wise.' Helga, who presides over her erstwhile home with the grace of a princess, has created a fantasy with outrageous colour schemes & candle-lit parlours of antiques & whimsy. Even the swimming pool garden has an air of magic & is probably, says Helga, the haunt of fairies. 'It's tongue-in-cheek,' she says to startled guests, 'staying here should be fun.' It's an attitude that has made the place popular with cosmopolitan trendsetters. The food is as memorable as the over-the-top décor, with such dishes as fish poached in tea. Appropriately, this amazing place has a style of service with a hint of Fawlty Towers, thanks to staff who cheerfully mock its extravagances as they amble around the clutter that fills every nook & cranny & even creeps into the bathrooms. A stay there is great fun, & a welcome break from the tourist trail. It is a 10min walk downhill to Kandy town, but decades removed from present-day Sri Lanka. Try it without hesitation – as an antidote to too many temples & ruins seen in the Cultural Triangle – since high camp is a kind of culture too. Beware! If your taxi driver or guide insists that Helga's Folly is fully booked or unsuitable, or he doesn't know it, don't believe him. There are no drivers' quarters at the hotel (Helga directs drivers & guides to a nearby guesthouse to preserve guests' serenity) so they try to deter guests from staying there. Readers John & Elisabeth Cox did stay at Helga's Folly &, alas, found it 'different – but we would describe our room as shabby, dilapidated & overpriced; interesting for a meal (must book) but that may be long enough'. **$$$**

⌂ **Hotel Suisse** (85 AC rooms) 30 Sangaraja Mawatha, Kandy; ☏ 081 2233024; e hotelsuisse@ sltnet.lk; www.hotelsuisse.lk. Sister hotel of the Queen's Hotel, it has adapted its colonial image & architecture to accommodate a steady throughput of tourists doing the round-trip tour. Its origins stem from the changes wrought by a Swiss lady who bought the original building, Haramby House, from its British army officer owner & started taking paying guests. With its Edwardian façade & rooms reeking of the 1950s, it still has the ambience of a snootier place than it really is. Refurbishment has brought TVs & minibars into some rooms. There is a suite dedicated to Lord Mountbatten, whose HQ the building was from 1943 to 1945. There is a swimming pool in its garden overlooking the lake. **$$**

⌂ **Hotel Thilanka** (87 rooms) 3 Sangamitta Mawatha, Kandy; ☏ 081 4475200; e thilankah@ sltnet.lk; www.thilankahotel.com. One of the pioneers in providing accommodation in Kandy for the impecunious tourist on an independently arranged tour, or for the visitor on a mainstream package holiday. Its reception lobby is in the original building (look at the grand period floor tiles) from when it began as a guesthouse. It seems never to cease growing &, while it looks formidable from the exterior where it has taken over a hillside, it is charming within. Some rooms have been transformed into arbours of Kandyan character with murals & Kandyan costumes in glass display cabinets, complementing the modernism of titanium, polished cement bathrooms. Other deluxe rooms are entered through a tiny patio garden behind latticework, giving them privacy as well as a pleasing aspect. There is a swimming pool set into the hillside & a spa at the foot of the Udawatte Kalle rainforest behind the hotel. The hotel's success over the years seems to be based on giving guests more than they expect at a reasonable price. While other hotels have opened up to challenge Thilanka as a popular place to stay while touring, they lack the polish, flair & friendliness that characterises the Thilanka. There is a sister hotel, Thilanka Resort & Spa, at Dambulla (see pages 134–5). **$$**

⌂ **Queen's Hotel** (75 AC rooms) Dalada Veediya, Kandy; ☏ 081 2222813; e queenshotel@ sltnet.lk; www.queenshotel.lk. The most central hotel in Kandy, & the oldest (established 1844), is on a prestige site. It stands opposite the end of the garden square in front of the Temple of the Tooth. It is at the head of the town's main street & overlooks the lake built in 1812 by the last king of Kandy. An authentic 19th-century hotel that is recovering from neglect, it soldiers on, albeit rather sluggishly, despite modernisation. Its refurbished rooms still have a colonial feel with the contemporary touch of tiles, AC, tiled floors & glass shower cabinets. There are hints of how grand the hotel must have been in its ballroom-size dining room, huge lobby & long corridors with creaking floorboards. It's a pleasant surprise to find a swimming pool in the secret garden of its interior. With its genuine planters' bar & gentle ambience, the hotel seems to be waiting to become popular again. **$$**

⌂ **The Royal Bar & Hotel** (5 rooms) 44 King's St, Kandy; ☏ 081 2224449; www.royalbarandhotel. com; bar & restaurant ⊕ 11.00–14.00 & 17.00– 23.00 daily, except Poya days. In King's St (behind the Queen's Hotel) this is a colonial building with high pitched tiled roof & swing doors, an elegant replica from Kandy's noble past. A licensed tavern since 1860, it's been beautifully converted into a mansion with 5 stylish bedrooms & no hint of boutique snobbery. It has a public bar with a black- &-white tiled floor & a teak & mirror display cabinet, a cobbled courtyard café, & a 1st-floor restaurant with a 1930s ambience & jolly good food (**$$**). The charm of the place is its mix of clientele: Kandyans popping in for a quick snifter & chat with friends, expat residents gossiping & tourists gawping at the memorabilia & welcome friendliness of the ambience. The bedrooms have 4-poster beds, plenty of pillows & stylish bathrooms; no TVs but Wi-Fi & tea/coffee-making facilities. Kept a secret from the mainstream tourist, its reputation has spread solely by word of mouth. A great find & superb value as it costs less than you'd think. **$$**

⌂ **Salika Inn** (4 AC rooms) 27/1 Rajapihilla Mawatha, Kandy; ☏ 081 2222365; e info@ salikainn.com; www.salikainn.com. With great views of the lake, town & temple, this small inn is stylish, simple & well run; a sister of the Salika Restaurant in Kegalle. A good base for a few days while touring the area. **$**

Outskirts of the city

🏠 **The Kandy House** (9 suites) Amunugama Walauwa, Gunnepana, Kandy; ☎ 081 4921394; e info@thekandyhouse.com; www.thekandyhouse.com. It is a difficult drive to reach it with several turnings along a bumpy road from Kandy & at first sight seems low-key in both appearance & ambience. This *walauwa* (manor house) was originally built in 1804 as the home of the last chief minister to the last king of Kandy. Its low, clay-tiled roof, entrance arches & deep verandas surrounding the house conceal an astonishing transformation to a hotel that has become popular with discerning independent travellers who like an exclusive, unusual place to stay. The main doors open on to a hall & formal dining area with a long table, & on to a courtyard where suites are spread over 2 floors. The upper rooms have the original wooden floorboards & all bedrooms have polished titanium cement bathrooms as a contrast to the traditional furnishings & fittings. There are chairs & tables throughout all the verandas & in the cloisters of the courtyard for relaxing or dining. The patio garden has mirrored walls that give it a delightful depth & brightness. Beyond the trees at the garden's edge is an infinity swimming pool in a lush setting above a paddy field. The table d'hôte meals are as memorable as the hotel's design & with a young staff of 20 to care for them, guests feel happily pampered, & loath to leave. **$$$$**

RESTHOUSES

One of the joys for those who decide to travel independently in Sri Lanka is the availability of resthouses throughout the country. As places for travellers to rest for the night, they were developed by the British colonial administration, who extended the network of bungalows for travelling officials begun by the Dutch. They were usually built in superb locations, each within a day's march, or horseride, from one another. More than 100 remain, ranging from the luxury of the one at Tissamaharama (now upgraded to The Safari), to the basic, cowshed architecture of municipal properties deep in the heartland. Some are charming, while some are not.

Resthouses are government-owned, leased either to urban councils or government organisations to manage or, through the Ceylon Tourist Board, to private companies. A major operator is the **Ceylon Hotels Corporation** (*www.ceylonhotelscorporation.com*), whose resthouses are run to a high standard and are accustomed to accommodating visitors from overseas. They have been upgraded as 'Prestige' and 'Heritage' properties with new facilities and their prices for food or accommodation have been upgraded as well.

Resthouses of the old school are distinguished by the service provided by stewards in their white sarongs and starched white tunics, who treat every visitor as an honoured guest. A typical example is the one at Hambantota (see page 280). A feature of the old resthouses is that they have a very well-deserved reputation for providing authentic, rural cuisine and local spirits.

If you want to enjoy a meal in a resthouse, here are some hints to make the process smooth and stress-free:

- To save time, order your meal as soon as you sit on the veranda, since it may have to be cooked especially for you.
- Do not order drinks until after the steward has given your meal order to the kitchen.
- If you are in a hurry at lunchtime, order rice and curry. This will have been prepared that morning, will be fresh and tasty, and cheap compared with other items on the menu. (Some resthouses feature rice and curry as a buffet, which is good if you're in a hurry.)

⌂ **Amaya Hills** (formerly Le Kandyan) (100 AC rooms) Heerassagala, Kandy; ☏ 081 4474022; e amayahills@amayaresorts.com; www. amayaresorts.com. A 3km drive uphill from the Botanical Gardens. This is a breezy, action-oriented hotel, & the favoured retreat for sportsmen competing in Kandy. The upper-floor billiard saloon has a collection of mementoes from international cricket & rugby teams who have stayed there. Rooms are in wings linked to the central reception area by open-sided corridors & much of the hotel is square columns & passageways open to the elements. There are mock-Kandyan touches; even the beds have bulbous faux-lacquered legs. The reception area is open on all sides & the centre of much hustle & bustle. There is a tea lounge with 40 different teas available; drinks from the bar next to it can be consumed in the comfort of the lounge. The dining room is vast. Fun is to be had on Sat in the underground disco, called the Garage, which is like a motorcar junkyard in design, & great for forgetting where you are. **$$$**

⌂ **Earl's Regency** (100 AC rooms) Kundasale, Kandy; ☏ 081 2422122; e res@earlsregency.lk; www.aitkenspencehotels.com. One of those hotels where you'll probably feel like staying longer. It is built amid a high-rise of cliffs & boulders near the Tennekumbura Bridge over the Mahaweli River. It is 4km from Kandy, on a good road, & about 15mins' drive from the Victoria Golf Club. Its central

- Do not request chicken curry unless the steward says it is already prepared; if a frozen bird is cooked in a hurry you may find it won't be cooked properly.
- Because you are a foreigner, the curries may have extra coconut milk added to tame them for your palate. If you want your curry local-style, insist on the real thing when ordering.
- If you have a driver he will usually be able to eat free – or at a nominal local rate – with the staff, so you don't have to invite him to dine with you at the tourist price for the same food.
- Some resthouses charge more for foreigners than locals, even if you all sit together and eat the same dishes. If this worries you, find out before you order.
- Relax on the veranda with a drink until you are called into the restaurant to eat. Then you will find the table set up with curries in different dishes, surrounding a huge plate of rice. The steward will serve the rice; you help yourself, and fellow diners close to you if you like, to the curries.
- The choice for non-vegetarians is usually either fish or beef, and rice and curry. For two people dining together, order one fish and one beef as you will usually get more, and certainly a better choice, than by ordering two fish or two beef.
- Beware of the offer of anything not actually presented on the table, such as mango chutney, as this will be an extra over the set fee for rice and curry. However, empty dishes of curry will often be replenished free of charge.
- If you want to eat with your fingers, use only the right hand; but nobody will mind if you stick to cutlery: a spoon and fork is better than a knife and fork.
- When it comes to paying the bill, some resthouses keep up the old tradition of presenting you with a register in which you are supposed to enter your name, nationality and address. Your name will then appear on the bill, which will be large in size (but usually not in amount). Every item, including occupation (cover) charge, will be itemised with beer listed in millilitres not bottles. A service charge of 10% and the government taxes will be added to the bill. Tipping is up to you, but you will usually have had such superb service and a great rice and curry meal, that a tip of another 5% will seem reasonable.

edifice, designed with a high-pitched roof of deep eaves in the Kandyan style, rises several storeys. This houses the hotel's public areas where its walls of glass give glimpses of activity on its 3 floors. Inside it has the spaciousness of an atrium with a gallery bar on its upper floor & restaurant & coffee shop leading from it. A graceful bridge, strongly influenced by the design of the Bogoda Bridge at Hali Ella, soars out to the hotel's south wing. Each room there has a balcony or veranda & is furnished with good taste & solid wood, with a granite luggage bench & all the accoutrements expected of a tourist-board-graded 5-star property. The northern wing, reached by elevator, has carpeted interior corridor & rooms with polished-wood floors. The gardens of the hotel are a combination of the manicured & the romantically rustic. This preserves its identity as a city-style hotel (it has an internet den) while capitalising on its rural location. There is a tennis court, a swimming pool, a gym built into the cliffside, & an ayurveda centre as well as an eco-park. **$$$**

🏠 **Hunas Falls by Amaya** (28 AC rooms, 3 suites) Elkaduwa, Kandy; 📞 081 2470041; e sales@ amayaresorts.com; www.hunasfallskandy.com. If there were ever a contest for the most scenic jogging trail at a hotel, a leading contender would be the one that runs around this establishment. The hotel is 26km from Kandy off the road that twists & turns into the Matale district. You drive through a tea plantation to reach the hotel, surrounded by hills & tropical woodlands at 1,097m above sea level. For the active there are hiking trails, golf (6 holes), pony riding, mountain biking, fishing in the hotel's own lake or boating on it, as well as jogging. The track is edged with feathery bamboo where it runs around the lake, crossing it by 2 bridges, one of which is at the very lip of the waterfall. It leads through the golf course, past a duck pond, & back into the hotel's prettily maintained gardens. A gentle tranquillity pervades the hotel itself, in contrast to the building's austere exterior. There is a library with deep-wing chairs for dozing over a dull book after a good lunch. Overlooking the heated swimming pool, the Herbal Health Centre offers herbal massage & steam baths. Teenagers have their own clubroom with pool table, football & computer machines. There is a snooker table in the lounge, where the granite-topped bar counter is complete with brass rails. Although isolated in

the hills, the hotel has a fully equipped conference hall. Rooms each have TV, minibar, telephone, balcony or terrace & gorgeous bathrooms with the kind of brightly lit mirrors a Hollywood star would have in her dressing room. The Katsura Suite has Japanese décor & a private putting green & garden at its door, while the Highlander Suite is pleasantly eccentric with Gothic arched windows, imitation fireplaces, a galley with a collection of copper pots & pans, & its own hot spa, as well as dining room, lounge & plush bedroom. **$$$**

🏠 **Mahaweli Reach Hotel** (112 AC rooms) 35 P B A Weerakoon Mawatha, Kandy; 📞 081 4472727; e reserve@mahweli.com; www.mahaweli.com. A 5-star hotel off the Katugastota road (just 5km from the town centre), that is privately owned & operated. By the banks of the Mahaweli River, it is a complex of spacious rooms in mansions grouped around a large swimming pool, with garden or river views. The hotel has expanded over 3 decades from a family guesthouse (the original parlour adjoins the reception lobby) to a homely 5-star resort of character. Service is impressive & recent refurbishment has added a sparkling new business centre & a dynamic-looking gym. Popular with package groups, it is nevertheless ideal for an independent visitor to spend a few lazy days in style by pool & river. **$$$**

🏠 **The Manor House** (6 rooms, 4 suites) Nugawela, Kandy; 📞 081 5638062; e reservation@srimalgroup.com; www. manorhousekandy.com. Bills itself as a boutique hotel but its attraction is in being a restored 19th-century mansion that somehow managed to survive while around it the monstrous cement box houses of a Kandy suburb were being built. The twin towers surmounting its 2 wings are a reminder of the building's original importance when they conveyed to the populace the status of its original owner, a Kandyan aristocrat. The house has been restored at the behest – & expense – of a Sri Lankan living in the USA who had seen its gradual dilapidation as a boy. Its rooms are comfortable while its public areas, including a reception area with a restored copper ceiling, are grand & chintzy. With Wi-Fi, business centre, beauty parlour, billiard hall & garden swimming pool, it has modern facilities to complement its traditional style. **$$$**

🏠 **The Mansion Kandy** (11 rooms) 213 Katugastota–Kurunegala road, Aladeniya, Kandy;

081 2463166; e reservations@mansionkandy; www.mansionkandy,com. To experience the home life of a Kandyan grandee, drive to Katugastota & then 6km along the Kurunegala road to the village of Aladeniya (10km from Kandy). From there an unmetalled track leads to the Mansion Nugawela, now marketed as The Mansion Kandy. Built in 1917 by a British architect as a grand Sri Lankan family's residence, this huge mansion (*walauwa*) has been meticulously cared for over the years & now opened to paying guests. The original fittings & furniture (including a billiard table) remain, with an astonishing collection of Edwardian/oriental embellishments on ceilings, walls & doors. There is a cupola of stained glass casting light on the twin teak staircases leading up from left & right of the dining hall. Guests can lounge on the tiled terrace or dip in the (new) swimming pool. Other new additions to this magnificent mansion are telephone & TV in the bedrooms. All bathrooms have hot water, & some have the original bathtubs with lion's-paw legs. **$$**

Halgolla Plantation Home (2 rooms) Galagedera, near Kandy; 081 3808007; e emil@halgollaplantationhome.com; www. halgollaplantationhome.com. B&B Sri Lanka style in the residence of a third-generation Sri Lankan whose ancestor's portrait hangs proudly on the bungalow wall. 2 lounges linked to the dining area & a separate kitchen in an adjoining building mean guests can either be alone or enjoy the hospitality & conversation of the mature Sri Lankan couple who live there & have restored the bungalow, where a handmade stained-glass window installed in 1890 shines light on old bookcases & rural antique furniture. Meals (delicious & fragrant) as well as breakfast can be provided. Super place for the contemplative as well as trekkers. Set in a plantation of 45 acres north of Galagedara off a trail through tropical wilderness close to the 17km marker on the Kurenegala to Kandy road. Reflects the heart & soul of Sri Lanka in congeniality, scenery & tranquillity. **$**

✗ **WHERE TO EAT AND DRINK** Kandy's main street (Dalada Veediya) has several eating places whose concern is to cater for locals, but which have glass cabinets displaying the food available, so ordering is possible by pointing. By the People's Bank, cross the road to the Bake House complex for a variety of outlets. All listings are included on the map, pages 104–5.

✗ **Slightly Chilled Bamboo Garden** 29a Anagarika Dharmapala Mawatha, Kandy; 081 2238267; e slightlychilled@hotmail.com; www. slightly-chilled.com; 11.00–23.00 (no bar service 14.00–17.00) daily, except Poya days. Enchantingly called Slightly Chilled, which – since it's half open to the elements – it does get in the evenings from Oct to Jan. It's on the 1st floor above a cheapie guesthouse with staggering views of the lake & the sprawl of Kandy town. It's different from most bars in Sri Lanka as it is owned & operated by a Brit, Michael, who is very hands-on – & not ashamed to hand out leaflets in Kandy's main street to attract customers, or to serve them himself if his plentiful staff are too busy. Its attraction is not just the view & the drinks but also the food with a genuine Chinese touch (Michael's wife is Chinese & suggests intriguing recipes to the local chefs), prepared in an open kitchen where diners can see how clean it is. It's also a lot of fun as Michael performs the role of 'Mine Host' in assured & hospitable form. Michael explains how to get

to Slightly Chilled, which is situated below Hotel Thilanka: 'Easiest & laziest way from town is to take a tuk-tuk. From Queen's Hotel it takes 10mins depending on traffic. Otherwise it takes about 20–25mins walking from the Queen's Hotel. Cross the road & walk left along the lake going past the Temple of the Tooth. Go past the old baths & you will come to the back entrance of the temple. On your left you will see flower stalls & a short flight of steps. Go up the steps & turn right. Walk straight for about 15mins. Go past the hospital on your left & go past the History Restaurant (they will try their best to get you in). Above the History you can see an old building with Slightly Chilled at the front of the building. Keep walking & there is a small lane on your left going up that has a sharp incline. If you are coming from the Kandy dance hall, turn left & walk about a minute. On your left there are some old stalls and a small place for cars to park. On the far right there is a Fuji advertisement board. Behind that there are some steps that take you up to the main road. Follow the road going up and away from town. Go past the hospital and look up on the left after History.' Phew! – you'll certainly need a drink after that trek. $$

✗ **Olde Empire Hotel** (15 rooms) 21 Temple St, Kandy; ☎081 2224284; ⏲ 08.00–20.00 daily. Exactly what you expect it to be with a name like that: packed with atmosphere. When I was writing *Sri Lanka By Rail* in 1994 & wanted to recommend this as a great place to stay, the owner begged me not to do so. He said he couldn't cope with more business. So I won't suggest that you stay in this boarding house in the square in front of the Temple of the Tooth. Its bedrooms are basic & its bathrooms are mostly common (ie: communal). Its balcony overlooking the square has become a meeting point for travellers. However, by not staying there you will miss one of the best places for making contact with young adventurers, even if you make the owner happy that he doesn't have to modernise his simple place & add more bedrooms. (A plaque at its entrance says it is a conserved building as part of Kandy's status as a World Heritage city.) Anyway I do recommend that you eat there. It is in front of the Queen's Hotel, on the left side (the Kandy Lake is on the right) as you face the Temple of the Tooth. A few steps lead up to the closed-in veranda where a reception desk is on the left. A sarong-clad steward will greet you & usher you into one of the dining rooms on the ground floor for rice & curry. No alcohol served. $

✗ **Devon** 11 Dalada Veediya; ☎081 2223947; ⏲ 10.00–21.00 daily. A popular restaurant that has spawned a hotel the other side of the lake, also called **Devon** (*25 AC rooms; 51 Ampitiya Rd, Kandy;* ☎*081 2235164;* $). Foreigners are ushered upstairs to the AC restaurant where there is a balcony overlooking the main drag. This is a good place for short eats as well as devilled dishes. The pastry shop is at road level. $

⌨ **Koffee Pot** 36 Dalada Veediya; ☎081 2234341; e admin@koffeepot.com; ⏲ 08.00–20.00 daily. A cyber café that actually serves food. The display cabinet has a selection of light, healthy-looking sandwiches; hot chocolate, espresso & cappuccino are also available. In its cramped & somewhat gloomy backroom are 16 terminals for internet surfing. The **Bake House** pastry shop is next door. $

✗ **The Pub** 36 Dalada Veediya; ☎081 2234868; www.koffeepot.com; ⏲ 17.00–24.00 daily. Above the Koffee Pot, with its dart room, pool tables & video games, this is especially popular in the evenings, although more as a restaurant than a pub. It has a broad gallery overlooking the street, an extensive menu & draught beer by the litre. $

♀ **Pub Royale** Dalada Veediya; ⏲ 16.00–24.00 daily. Tucked away at the end of the veranda walkway of the Queen's Hotel, is a unique bar that is sure to bring shivers of nostalgia to the colonial buff. Its Victorian counter, brass rails, teak bar shelves, antique mirror & moulded ceiling conjure up images of roistering tea planters. Now it caters for locals sipping arrack in dignity or intrepid visitors in search of a beer in a time warp. Go there soon in case it is born again as, heaven forbid, a fast-food outlet. $

✗ **White House** 21 Dalada Veediya; ☎081 2223395; ⏲ 08.30–23.00 daily. On the same side of the street as Devon, with similar fare. It also boasts a side room called the Golden Wok as an 'authentic Chinese restaurant'. $

FESTIVALS The **Kandy Esala Perahera** is held in honour of the tooth relic (which is not actually paraded, but a casket does the rounds instead) and of its four guardian deities. These are Natha, Vishnu, Kataragama and Pattini. During a preliminary five days, the perahera is held within the precincts of each temple in the Temple of the Tooth (see page 120). The public peraheras then begin, taking place at night; five are known as *kumbal* peraheras, while the final five are *randoli* peraheras.

The final five nights are the most spectacular with men cracking whips leading the parade, followed by men bearing flags of the various provinces of the former Kandyan kingdom. You will also see jugglers and fire-eaters as well as elephants of varying stature. The parade lasts at least three hours.

Seats are sold at strategic points for the public to watch. The perahera was shown on a live webcast for the first time ever in August 2001. The Temple of the Tooth has a good website with information about the rituals, religious ceremonies and charitable projects with which it is associated: www.daladamaligawa.org.

SHOPPING Kandy has plenty of places for shopping in a leisurely fashion. There are alleys with small shops selling clothes, and an occasional glimpse of old craftsmen at work, either cleaning silver or pedalling a contraption with a bicycle wheel to turn a grinding stone to sharpen knives.

Newly opened is the **Kandy City Centre Commercial and Shopping Complex** [104 E5] (*5 Dalada Veediya, Kandy;* ◟ *081 2202844; www.kandycitycentre.lk*), with several banks, a post office counter, a tourism information counter and fashionable shops.

Under the roundabout at the beginning of the main street (Dalada Veediya) is a fountain in the centre of an **underground shopping mall** [104 D5] used by pedestrians to get from one side of the road to the other. Both sides of the road have lots of pastry shops for the peckish.

OTHER PRACTICALITIES

Banks There are branches of the **Bank of Ceylon** and **People's Bank** as well as several private banks such as **HNB** in Kandy, and ATMs are easy to find; try Kandy City Centre (see details above for more information).

✚ **Lakeside Adventist Hospital** ◟081 2223466
✚ **Suwa Sevana Hosital** ◟081 2236404

Post office
✉ Level 1, Kandy City Centre

Medical
✚ **National Hospital** ◟081 2222261
✚ **Kandy Nursing Home** ◟081 2222041
✚ **Kandy Private Hospital** ◟081 2234338

Tourist information
🛈 Level 1, Kandy City Centre; ◟081 2222661;
🕐 10.00–18.00 daily

WHAT TO SEE AND DO

Temple of the Tooth The bombing of the **Temple of the Tooth** [105 F5] (Sri Dalada Maligawa) in February 1998 was the end of innocence for visitors to the temple. Now it is something of an ordeal as well as a solemn pilgrimage. It begins with the disgorging of passengers by the various tour buses in the narrow space opposite the Queen's Hotel at the entrance gates to the compound. Any atmosphere of reverence is dispelled by the insistent chimes of the bicycle carts of vendors selling ice cream.

Notices say: 'All visitors entering the Sri Dalada Maligawa sacred area are kindly requested to refrain from wearing headdresses, mini-skirts, short trousers, sleeveless jackets, so to maintain the sanctity of the holy place.' All visitors are searched, males and females in separate cubicles, before entering the park in front of the temple. There is an admission fee charged (*Rs1,000*), with extra payable for a camera or a video camera. Before entering the temple itself all visitors are obliged to remove their shoes, which can be deposited for safekeeping, and retrieved on payment of a tip. The main shrine is one floor up and its doors are opened during *puja* (offering) times (06.30, 10.00 and 18.00 daily) when the casket containing the sacred tooth is visible.

The tooth is an object of veneration to Buddhists, and of curiosity to visitors. You don't actually see it. Tradition states that it was taken from the ashes after the cremation of Gauthama Buddha at Kusinara in India in 543BC, eventually being smuggled to Sri Lanka in the 4th century, hidden in the hair of a princess from Orissa.

It was lodged in many places, as a symbol of nationhood, until coming to rest in Kandy in 1592 when the king at the time, Wimala Dharma Suriya I (1591–1604), built a two-storey shrine where the present temple stands. The two-storey temple that replaced it is now the Inner Temple. The golden canopy constructed over the relic chamber was added at the end of the 20th century.

Every year, on the occasion of the Esala month (July/August), public honour is paid to the sacred tooth relic with a ten-day public perahera, which culminates on Poya (full moon) Day.

The Sinhala term 'perahera' has come to mean a procession of musicians, dancers, acrobats and other performers accompanied by elephants parading the streets in celebration of a religious or secular person or event. It is not confined to Kandy and, indeed, at the same time a perahera is held in Kataragama. Peraheras can also be seen in Colombo in February and even in the tourist resort of Bentota in December.

Museums and temples Associated with the Temple of the Tooth is a new **temple museum** [105 F5] (☉ 09.00–17.00 *daily; admission Rs500*) at one side of the Sri Dalada Maligawa where jewellery presented as homage over the years is on display, together with ornaments and paintings. Raja, the majestic elephant that used to carry the casket in procession during the perahera season, is preserved in a lifelike stance.

The **four *devales*** (temple or shrine with residing deity) associated with the Sri Dalada Maligawa and the royal palace can also be seen. The **Natha Devale** is the oldest of the four. It directly faces the Sri Dalada Maligawa and dates from the 14th century. In front of its main gate is the **Vishnu Devale**. The palanquin used in the Esala perahera is kept in its main hall.

The **Pattini Devale** lies to the west of the main temple complex. It is probably 400 years old and is said to hold the golden anklet of the goddess Pattini. The **Kataragama Devale** at Kotugodelle Videeya (the street on the right after the Queen's Hotel) is the only one of the four devales where Hindu Brahmins are the officiating priests. Its importance stems from the god Kataragama being the guardian god of Sri Lanka.

Admission to the devales is covered by the Cultural Triangle ticket. The ticket can be purchased at the Cultural Fund office, which is close to the Pattini Devale (in the old building with veranda that was once a courthouse) next to the Prince of Wales Fountain. The ticket also allows admission to the National and Archaeological museums in Kandy (see box, page 101).

Around town The Prince of Wales **Fountain** [105 E4] is worth a second glance. Rich in Rococo cherubs, it was erected 'by the coffee planters of Ceylon' to commemorate the visit to Kandy of Edward, Prince of Wales, the eldest son of Queen Victoria, in 1875. An extravagant memorial in front of the Pattini Devale, it seems to have been a deliberate attempt to perpetuate a little acceptable frivolity into the solemnity of its surroundings.

It is a wonderful, although woefully spurned, work of the Victorian foundryman's art. Cast-iron cherubs made in Glasgow ride crocodiles and water jugs. When the fountain works, water gushes from the crocodile mouths and jars into scallop shells set below to trickle into the fountain's pool. In the pool's centre, a narcissus of coral-like blooms opens up to support jolly fishes spouting water, while above them cast-iron cranes dip their beaks and refresh themselves. Incorporated throughout this joyful design are plumes representing the emblem of the Prince of Wales. Walk a few yards down the street and gaze to the left at what remains of an imposing Edwardian building spattered with lawyers' signboards advertising their names and qualifications. This used to be a barracks with soldiers quartered on the first floor and their horses stabled below. It has 15 arches downstairs filled in with doors and windows and with lawyers sitting at desks where horses were once groomed.

Historical buildings With the identification of Kandy as a World Heritage Site, some of the city's buildings have been reviewed and categorised to aid conservation, with buildings that are to be conserved with nothing changed put into a special category. This includes the buildings in Dalada Veediya (street) as well as the Olde Empire Hotel, the building housing the Central Cultural Fund and the **Muladeniya Mandiriya** open-sided pavilion.

Also in Dalada Veediya is a steadfast reminder of the British presence: **St Paul's Church** [105 F4/5], built in 1846 and still going strong. Associated with it is the **Garrison Cemetery**. You can find this at the edge of the Udawatte Kalle sanctuary bordering Kandy, just behind the Temple of the Tooth and some 200m beyond St Paul's vicarage.

The sanctuary is a vast virgin primeval forest at 1,600m covering 104ha and with more than 150 species of plant life. It makes a wonderful respite from the heat of the city to stroll through this protected forest reserve (see page 201).

The graves of British pioneers and settlers crowd what remains of the space allocated for the cemetery with 130 graves listed now but an inventory in 1914 showed 163. The disappearance of 33 graves is symbolic of the decline in importance of the cemetery. Yet it is here that one of those indefatigable Britons who was instrumental in the final conquest of Kandy is buried. He was Sir John D'Oyly, born Sussex 1774, died Kandy 1824. His tomb describes him as:

> Resident of the Kandyan provinces and one of the members of His Majesty's Council
> of this island whose meritorious service to the Government from the year 1802 and
> his talents during the Kandyan War stand recorded in the archives of this Government
> and in the Office of the Secretary of State for the Colonies.

D'Oyly seems to have been an intriguing character, almost a 19th-century hippy who went native, for he learned and spoke Sinhala fluently, and was described by contemporaries as 'a Cingalese hermit ... a native in his habits of life ... an uncouth recluse'.

It is fascinating to read the headstones and see the graves of such pioneers as the last European to be killed by an elephant, or that of Captain Lardy who explored the Mahaweli Ganga, or that of the unfortunate David Findley, killed in 1861 when his house collapsed on him. The cemetery is no longer used and is maintained by donations through the church.

Signs of the British presence can still be seen in colonial buildings and spotting them is part of the fun of exploring the town. While many have been converted some still languish for want of restoration and many bear a plaque in three languages saying: WORLD HERITAGE CITY KANDY – CONSERVED BUILDING.

The very energetic could walk (but it's probably wiser to take a tuk-tuk) through Kandy to climb up to the Bahirawakanda Buddha statue for a high panoramic view of the town. Apart from the many new buildings added to the town, the magnificent sight of the Kandy Lake and the dome of the Dalada Maligawa hasn't changed much since the British days of the 19th century.

Museums There are two museums concentrating on Kandy, both within the vicinity of the temple. The **National Museum** [105 F5] (⊕ *09.00–17.00 Sat–Thu*) is east of the temple on a small hill overlooking the lake, housed in what were once the quarters of the royal concubines. The **Archaeological Museum** [105 F5] (⊕ *08.00–16.00 Wed–Mon; admission Rs300*) is in what little remains of the splendid royal palace.

Also worth a visit is the **Audience Hall**, behind and to the north of the temple, with its carved pillars of characteristically Kandyan design. It was begun in 1784 by King Rajadhi Raja Sinha but not completed until 1820. It was there that the Kandyan Convention, ceding the territories of the kingdom to the British, was signed on 2 March 1815.

Around Lake Kandy The essence of tranquillity is enhanced by the **lake**. It was constructed by the last king of Kandy, Sri Wickrama Rajasinghe (1798–1815), who is remembered for that as well as for losing his throne. He built the lake in 1810–12 by damming a stream that ran through marshes skirting the town. He is said to have been delighted when fish thrived in it and he used to feed them with boiled rice.

Two of the most important monasteries are on opposite sides of the lake. The chief incumbents are the senior ecclesiastics of the Buddhist order. The **Malwatta Vihara** [105 F6] on the southern side, across the lake, is embellished with 18th-century architectural design and planning. The **Asgiriya Vihara** [104 D3] is situated to the western side of the city and contains the cremation ground of Kandyan royalty. There is a gigantic statue of the recumbent Buddha in one of its shrine rooms. The higher ordination of the *sangha* (monks) takes place annually in both temples.

Inevitably, as a visitor, you will be invited to a **cultural show**. This is included in organised tours and, even if you visit Kandy independently, your driver or a freelance guide will suggest a show. There are a couple of rival performances put on every evening for visitors, and they are a good introduction to local dances and folk culture.

They include displays of typical Kandyan dances by men, where the participants wear elaborate costumes with an extravagance of silver ornaments on ears and bare chests, and a juggling performance involving intricate twirling of lacquered wooden plates. There is usually some energetic fire-eating and a mask dance representative of low-country dancing. The music by a trio of dervish-style drummers is frenetic. Admission can cost about US$5.

Full information on Kandy and its attractions is available from the very helpful staff of the **Tourism Promotion Bureau** desk (✆ *081 2222661;* ⊕ *08.30–17.00 daily*), opened in 2010 in the glass-fronted mall known as Kandy City Centre (see page 119). It's in the main street (Dalada Veediya) next to the Cargills Food City complex.

Gardens No visit to Kandy is complete without seeing the **Royal Botanical Gardens** at Peradeniya, 6½km south from the town, on the Colombo road. Its origins go back to the reign of King Kirti Sri Rajasinha (1747–80) when it was a royal residence and park. It formally became a botanical garden in 1821 when the redoubtable Edward Barnes was governor. The first tea seedlings to be grown in Ceylon were planted in the gardens at Barnes's behest in 1824, although it was 50 years later that tea showed its potential as a viable commercial crop.

The gardens consist of nearly 61ha dedicated to the flora of Sri Lanka with a spectacular arboretum that includes many endemic trees. There are over 110 endemic plants, as well as major collections of palms, bamboo, cacti, flowers and orchids in a delightful orchid house. There are more than 200,000 dried and preserved specimens in the **Herbarium**, collected during the 180 years the gardens have been in existence. There is also a biotechnology laboratory engaged in the mass propagation of ornamental, rare and endemic plants. A striking feature is the avenue of royal palms (*Roystonea regia*) begun in 1905. In the medicinal herb garden grow some of the herbs used in ayurveda medicine.

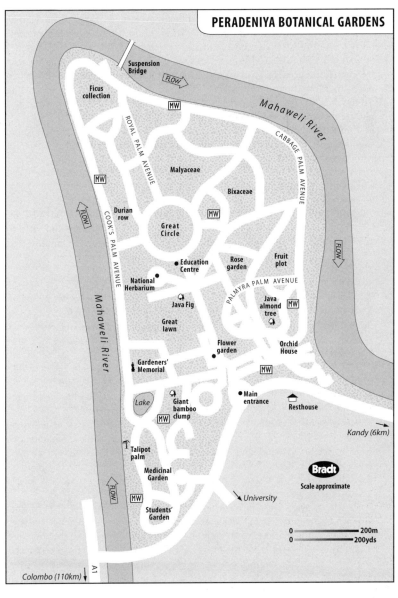

PERADENIYA BOTANICAL GARDENS

Suspension Bridge

FLOW

Ficus collection

MW

Mahaweli River

ROYAL PALM AVENUE

CABBAGE PALM AVENUE

MW

Malyaceae

Bixaceae

Durian row

COOK'S PALM AVENUE

FLOW

MW

Great Circle

Education Centre

Rose garden

Fruit plot

National Herbarium

Java Fig

PALMYRA PALM AVENUE

Java almond tree

MW

Great lawn

Mahaweli River

Flower garden

Orchid House

Gardeners' Memorial

MW

Lake

Giant bamboo clump

MW

Main entrance

Resthouse

Kandy (6km)

Talipot palm

Bradt

Scale approximate

Medicinal Garden

FLOW

MW

University

Students' Garden

0 — 200m
0 — 200yds

Colombo (110km) A1

The entire area of the gardens is embraced by the Mahaweli River, curving around it like an elbow. At an altitude of 550m it has a mean temperature of around 26°C. To avoid the heat of the day, the best time to visit the gardens is between 08.30 and 10.00, or in the afternoon from 16.00.

Admission tickets are issued from 08.00 to 17.00; the cost is Rs1,000. You should keep your ticket until leaving the gardens. A notice at the entrance advises visitors to be properly clad when entering the gardens. There is a kiosk selling books on cut flowers, on bamboo as house plants, and on the wayside trees and wild flowers of Sri Lanka.

AROUND KANDY Off the Peradeniya–Kadugannawa road, 16km from Kandy, there are three incredible shrines, all dating from the 14th century. **Gadaladeniya** is built of stone and sits scenically on a rock. The seated Buddha image, lacquered doors, wall murals and carved stone friezes are fascinating and the temple shows a south Indian influence. The **Lankatilaka Viharaya** stands out because of its Rococo design; a brick building with a flourish of red-tiled hipped roofs, shining white against the blue sky. It consists of three storeys, and has painted doors of wood and bright frescoes on walls and ceilings, with a seated image of the Buddha.

The **Embekke Temple** is more rustic and is dedicated to the god Kataragama. It is renowned for its forest of wooden pillars, each one carved with squares of intricate designs, depicting the activities of wrestlers, dancers, musicians and legendary beasts and birds. There are some stalls at its entrance, some of which sell brass made in the village foundries close by.

The harnessing of the waters of the **Mahaweli Ganga**, the country's longest river, was the prime purpose of the Accelerated Mahaweli Programme (AMP) begun in 1977. The motives were not only to generate hydro-electric power but also to provide irrigation for dry-zone cultivations, and settlements for the landless and

TEA

Tea was first grown in Ceylon in 1824 at the Botanical Gardens at Peradeniya when a few plants were brought from China; more were introduced from Assam in 1839. In 1867 (the year the railway reached Peradeniya), a Scottish planter, James Taylor, planted tea seedlings on 8ha of forest land which had been cleared for coffee growing.

Taylor's foresight was remarkable because two years later a blight wiped out the country's coffee crop. The island's planters turned to tea and had 400ha flourishing by 1875. In 1965, Ceylon displaced India as the world's biggest tea exporter, and tea is one of the major foreign-exchange earners for Sri Lanka.

The large tea (and other) estates were nationalised in 1972, leaving individual owners with only 20ha. The process was reversed 20 years later and plantations were leased to management companies and the private sale of tea allowed (instead of exclusively through the weekly tea auction). The industry is going through a period of streamlining, with the result that more specialist (single estate, organic and green) teas are available.

The best Ceylon teas are known as 'High Grown', from plantations at heights above 1,200m, where the climate has a crucial effect on quality. The finest teas, from the Uva district, are produced in the middle of the year when that region is swept by very dry winds and the tea takes on its characteristic refreshing flavour. Teas from the other, western side of the main range of hills, from Nuwara Eliya, Dimbula and Dickoya, show their best quality in January and February after the northeast monsoon, when dry weather and cold nights predominate. The flavour of Nuwara Eliya tea is quite distinct from Uva, though the two districts are neighbours, which illustrates how sensitive tea is to soil, environment and climate.

'Low Grown' teas, mostly produced on private estates in the Matara, Galle and Ratnapura districts of southern Sri Lanka and bought more for leaf appearance than taste, grow at sea level up to 600m. 'Medium Grown' teas, which produce a liquor with a rich, mellow taste and good colour, are grown at heights of between 600m and 1,200m.

unemployed through the development of physical and social infrastructure for human habitation.

The UNDP/FAO was involved in the preparation of a master plan for the project. By 1995, the settlement programme was substantially completed, with over 80,000 families settled in various sections of the entire project. Special attention was focused on wildlife and forest conservation with four national parks and two nature reserves established, covering 45% of the land area included in the AMP.

The vision can be seen in reality at the **Victoria Dam**, where the Victoria-Randenigala sanctuary covers 4,600ha. The dam is located below the Polgolla diversion barrage and above the Victoria rapids on the main stream of the Mahaweli River. The dam's concrete arch of staggering proportions was completed in 1985. It has created a storage reservoir of 730 million cubic metres and a power capacity of 210MW. The storage level of 438m of water corresponds to a crest level of 442½m above sea level. The height of the dam above the lowest foundation level is 118m. To reach it, take the A26 from Kandy.

Mired in controversy before it was built and still attracting criticism as a modern intrusion on the environment, the **Victoria Golf and Country Resort** (*Rajawella*,

The journey from bush to tea taster's spoon takes 24 hours, although it could be months before the same tea is used to make one of the billion cups brewed around the world every day.

The tea bush is actually an evergreen tree called Chinese camellia (*Camellia sinensis*), which could grow 10m high if not pruned every two or three years. The pruning encourages the repeated growth of a 'flush' of fresh young shoots throughout the year. These shoots, of two top leaves and a tender bud, are plucked every six to ten days.

On arrival at the tea factory from the field, the leaves are spread out in troughs to wither until they lose their moisture and go limp. The 100kg of green leaf in each trough is reduced to 50–55kg during this period. The withered leaves are fed into a rolling machine, which crushes their cell structure, releasing the natural juice and enzymes that give tea its flavour. The leaves emerge from the machine in twisted, sticky lumps. Oxidisation, called fermentation, takes place then in about three hours, changing the pulverised green leaf into a light, coppery shade through the absorption of oxygen. Firing (drying) in a hot-air chamber for about 20 minutes halts the 'fermentation', kills off any bacteria, dries the tea and preserves it, further reducing the original 100kg to 24kg.

The fired leaf is left to cool before being sifted. The main commercial leaf grades are Orange Pekoe (OP), Pekoe (Pek) and Flowery Pekoe (FP). Broken leaf grades are Broken Orange Pekoe (BOP), Broken Pekoe (BP), Fannings (F) and Dust. BOP grades are used in traditional packet blends, while Fannings and Dust find their way into tea bags. CTC tea, so called because the leaf is cut, torn and curled by machine instead of rolled, is also produced in Sri Lanka as tea-bag-quality tea.

While tea is sold at auction in Colombo to traders who buy different grades and qualities for export and blending, it is now possible to buy pure, unblended estate teas in shops in Colombo. The major retail outlets for speciality teas (packed in gift containers) are the Mlesna shops to be found in the Crescat, Liberty Plaza and Majestic City shopping centres, as well as in Beruwala, Bandarawela, Nuwara Eliya, Kandy and the airport departure lounge.

Kandy; ✆ *081 2376376;* ℮ *gm@victoriagolf.lk; www.golfsrilanka.com*) is a 40-minute drive from Kandy via Kundasale, Digana and Teldeniya. As well as the golf club it has houses for rent and sale. This 18-hole championship golf course set in a 209ha site by the Victoria reservoir was designed to USPGA specifications by golf architect Donald Steel. He has described it thus:

> Some golf courses have a splendid undulating terrain over which the holes are routed.
> Some golf courses have a scenic backdrop of hills and lakes which excite the senses.
> However, the Victoria Golf Course is blessed with both attributes.

Stately trees and avenues of coconut palms lend the course an air of maturity although it was established only in 1999. Impressive natural outcrops of rock are a distinctive feature as well as a hazard of the course. Its brochure says: 'Measuring 6,879 yards at its full championship length, Victoria's par-73 layout has four par-5 holes of which three are over 500 yards long. There are four excellent par-3 holes ranging from the very short, but tricky, 5th of 124 yards, to the testing 210-yard 13th hole, a great par-3.'

There is a clubhouse with changing rooms, showers and food service, a golf shop with facilities for hiring golf clubs, golf caddies and fore caddies, a practice fairway and year-round golf in a cool, sunny climate 457m above sea level. At the same location, there are birdwatching and nature trails, bike riding, horseriding, canoeing, croquet, paddle tennis and boules. Visitors are welcome to play. Clubs, shoes, caddies and ball spotters can be hired.

Associated with the golf club is the **Victoria Saddle Club** (✆ *081 2421459*) adjoining the golf course. There is a riding school here where beginners are welcome and the one-hour pony ride through the lush, tropical countryside is popular.

The roots of Sri Lanka's tea industry are to be found, literally, at **Loolecondera**, the estate where Scotsman James Taylor in 1867 planted the first 8ha of tea seedlings. He planted them in field No 7, which still exists with abandoned tea bushes growing wild where jungle has reclaimed its territory. The foundations of Taylor's original log cabin also remain.

You get to the estate on the road from Kandy, past Peradeniya and climbing steadily through tea plantations for 34km to **Deltota**. There a signposted road leads to Loolecondera, at 1,098m (3,600ft) above sea level. At the estate there are people who still speak of James Taylor with the affection normally shown a recently departed relative. This is because some of the estate employees have descended from those who worked on the estate during Taylor's long tenure, from 1852 to 1892. Even his funeral is recalled because he was a heavy man who had to be carried all the way to Kandy, where he is buried in the **Mahayaya** cemetery.

Taylor was acknowledged even during his lifetime as the founding pioneer of the tea industry. He was 16 when he arrived in Ceylon in 1852. Within six weeks he settled at Loolecondera Estate and made it his home for 40 years. He began by clearing the land, opening it up for coffee growing, and building a homestead. His youth and lack of plantation knowledge seems to have helped him; he tackled tasks experienced men would have avoided.

After a decade of successful coffee cultivation, he became interested in growing other crops. He grew chincona (for quinine) with great success but it had limited export potential. The popular myth is that Taylor experimented with growing tea on his own initiative. However, he had the support of the Botanical Gardens at Peradeniya from where he obtained seedlings.

And so, in 1867, within a few weeks of the arrival of the first steam train at Kandy, he cleared 8ha of stone-strewn rugged hillside and began the first successful commercial planting of tea in Ceylon. It was six years before Loolecondera tea was shipped to London, and nearly 15 years before Ceylon tea began to win market favour. It was fortuitous that the railway came to Kandy at the same time, thereby providing the means to transport the tea to Colombo for shipment to England.

The remains of the brick chimney and the foundations of the log cabin James Taylor built and lived in for 40 years are at 1,250m above sea level. A notice says Taylor 'made his first tea on the verandah of his log cabin. The leaf was hand-rolled on tables.' A kilometre or so away is a bench of granite commanding views across the vast valley of the Victoria reservoir, and a body of hills known as the Sleeping Warrior because of its profile. On the left is the Knuckles range. It is enthralling to sit there and imagine how James Taylor must have felt about living a life of such fulfilment.

Some of Taylor's belongings are displayed at the **Ceylon Tea Museum** (*Hantene;* ✆ *060 2803204;* e *info@ceylonteamuseum; www.ceylonteamuseum.com;* ☉ *08.30– 16.30 Tue–Sun except Poya days; admission Rs500; guided tours on demand*), easily accessible by three-wheeler or bus from close to the Kandy railway station, up the Uduwella road, and past the Bogambara junction to the old four-mile post. (See also box, page 181.)

ANURADHAPURA *Population: 63,208 (2012 estimate)*

Anuradhapura is a sacred city, venerated as the capital of Buddhism. At its heart is the sacred Bo tree, reputed to be the oldest living tree in documented history, having been brought as a sapling to Sri Lanka in the 3rd century BC. In the vicinity of the shrines surrounding the tree are the remains of the Brazen Palace, the towering Ruwanwelisaya Dagoba, the seated Buddha, temples, palaces and parks. They may have lost their vibrance and become historical monuments, but nevertheless they bear testimony to a proud past.

By the middle of the 3rd century BC, the fame of Anuradhapura as the capital (it was founded a century earlier) was known as far away as the Mediterranean. Three centuries later a trade delegation from the capital presented its credentials to Claudius Caesar in Rome and met Pliny the Elder. Within another three centuries, a connection was established eastwards with China.

According to the *Mahavamsa* (the Sinhala Buddhist chronicle), Anuradhapura was a model of city planning, although hierarchical. Precincts were set aside for huntsmen and scavengers, and even for heretics and foreigners, so those belonging to the establishment were not disturbed. There were cemeteries for high and low castes, and also hospitals. Reservoirs were constructed to assure a regular water supply. The city remained the capital until the 10th century, when its position was weakened by internecine struggles for the royal succession. The final blow came in AD993 when the Chola king, Rajaraja I, conquered the island, burning and looting the capital. Anuradhapura was abandoned and the capital moved to Polonnaruwa.

While its importance diminished, buildings crumbled into ruin and the jungle closed in, communities of dedicated Buddhists remained, many as guardians of the Bo tree. The British conquerors of the island were intrigued by tales of a ruined city and it was 'discovered', then chosen in 1833 to be the seat of local government. It was designated in 1873 as the capital of the new North Central province. In the 1950s, a new town was begun on the outskirts of the ancient capital.

GETTING THERE
By train There are trains between Colombo and Anuradhapura that have a first-class air-conditioned observation saloon. The air-conditioned coach is ideal if you

4

want to sleep your way through the scenery, but it isolates you from the real world of rail travel. Neither breezes nor vendors penetrate. It is best to use this coach as a base during the journey, wandering through the train when you get bored, although if it is crowded you would be better off enjoying what you have paid for.

It is possible to catch a train (No 8085/4085, the *Rajarata Rajini*) from the southern terminus of Matara to Anuradhapura. At 410km, this is the longest through-train ride in Sri Lanka; the second-class fare is less than US$5.

Exporail (*www.exporail.lk*) operates an air-conditioned carriage with reserved seating and refreshments leaving Colombo at 16.20 as part of Train 4003; returning at 06.40 as part of Train 4004; the fare is Rs1,500 one-way.

(Train times should be checked before travelling in case of rescheduling.)

The original length of the Northern line was 412km from Colombo, via Anuradhapura, to Jaffna and on to Kankesanturai. At present, rail travellers can only travel as far as Kilinochchi (but the line is expected to reach Jaffna in March 2014). The Northern line actually begins at Polgahawela, where it branches up to the north from the main line to Kandy.

Trains first reached **Kurunegala** in 1894 and then Anuradhapura in 1903. After the train leaves Kurunegala, it speeds through coconut plantations ringed with hills and past phantom stations that are just nameboards and thus not shown in the timetable. There are glimpses of lily ponds blinking in the early morning sunlight on one side of the line and brilliant green paddy fields on the other.

When the train does stop, the platforms are not long enough and the atmosphere is overwhelmingly relaxed. At **Timbiriyagedara** (131km from Colombo), you learn from the signboard that it is only 79m above sea level. You feel it should be higher after coming all that way.

Maho, 5km further on and built in 1899, is called the Crewe of Sri Lanka: the junction for trains heading north, east and south. It is modest considering the number of trains it deals with. Prettier, and a prize winner, is the next station on the Northern line, **Ambanpola**, while the one after it, **Senarathgama**, is lent charm by the temple trees (frangipani) on its platform. The lushness of the scenery begins to evaporate to dry-zone forest and scrub, but watch out for the colonial cottage-style stations of **Tambuttegama** and **Talawa** in the midst of trees.

TRAIN TIMETABLE: COLOMBO FORT TO ANURADHAPURA

Train	Colombo Fort	Anuradhapura
4001	05.45	09.40 (to Omanthai)
4017	06.50	10.02 (to Vavuniya)
4452	10.00	15.52
4085	13.45	18.40 (from Matara to Vavuniya)
4003	16.20	20.06 (to Vavuniya)
4089	22.30	03.40 (to Omanthai)

Train	Anuradhapura	Colombo Fort
4086	05.00	10.10 (from Vavuniya to Matara)
4004	06.40	10.25 (from Vavuniya)
4868	09.15	15.05
4002	14.35	18.35 (from Omanthai)
4018	16.00	19.15 (from Vavuniya)
4090	23.30	04.35 (from Omanthai)

A contrast comes with the depressing cowshed architecture of **Anuradhapura New Town**, 200km from Colombo. Don't get down here but continue to the main station of **Anuradhapura** [130 B6], originally built in 1904. The only buildings remaining from that period are the colonnaded railway cottages that house the colony of railway residents surrounding the station. The new station opened in 1963 and is built with a frontage of columns to resemble the temples of the ancient city.

By bus There is an intercity bus service (No 15) leaving Colombo every 30 minutes to travel via Dambulla. Bus No 4-3 travels from Colombo via Puttalam to Anuradhapura.

By road To enable a stop at Dambulla on the way to Anuradhapura, you need to take the A1 (the Kandy road) from Colombo. This bifurcates at **Ambepussa** with a branch becoming the A6 via Kurunegala to Dambulla, and on to Trincomalee. At Dambulla the A9 takes you straight to Anuradhapura. If you drive instead to Sigiriya to overnight, then you pick up the A11 at the Habarana junction to head northwest before joining the A9 at **Maradankadawala**.

The road from Kurunegala is attractive, particularly where it passes through a kilometre-long nave of trees that provide shade and a semblance of spirituality contrasting with the rough tarmac of the road. At wayside kiosks shielded by spreading branches, corn on the cob is offered for sale: raw, boiled or barbecued.

After the serenity of the cathedral of trees, plots of land beside the road have been cleared and demarcated as building lots. On the right can be glimpsed the jagged peaks of hills, part of the mountains of the Matale district. The checkpoint in the forest is to root out timber smugglers.

Internet bureaux are conspicuous among the village shops at **Dambulla**, where the A9 heads northwards away from the A6 to Habarana and Trincomalee. On the A6, just after Dambulla, near the **Mirisgon Oya** junction, are roadside stalls selling a remarkable collection of pulses and grain, from soya beans to sesame seeds. Included are gooey sweets in egg-size balls and sugar-lump cubes that are so moreish you'll wish you had bought more. Bottles of thick, treacly ghee and of a rich bronze bee honey stand alongside cushion-sized plastic bags packed with round, dried red chillies.

The road to Green Paradise Hotel and the Kandalama Wewa (reservoir) is on the right. The next turning of importance is at **Inamadula** junction where

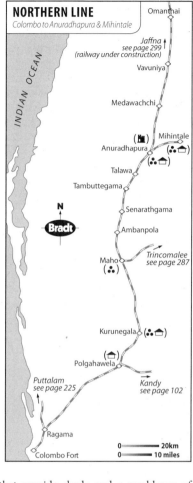

4

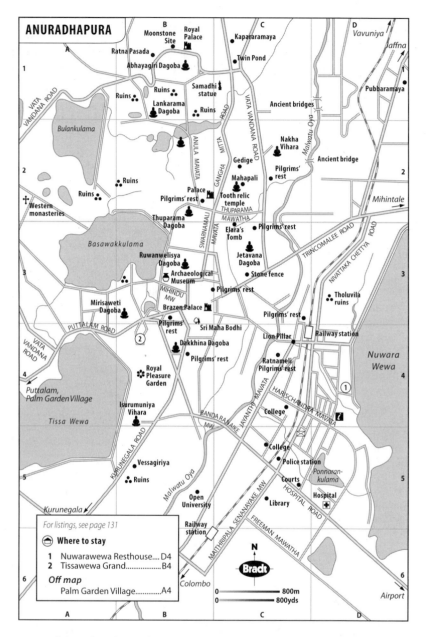

ANURADHAPURA

Vavuniya
Jaffna

B — Moonstone Site
Royal Palace
Kaparaaramaya

A
Ratna Pasada
Twin Pond
Abhayagiri Dagoba
Pubbaramaya

1

Ruins
Samadhi statue
Ruins
Lankarama Dagoba
Ancient bridges
Nakha Vihara
Ancient bridge

Bulankulama

Gedige
Pilgrims' rest
Ruins
Mahapali
Palace
Pilgrims' rest
Tooth relic temple
THUPARAMA MAWATHA
Mihintale

2

Ruins
Ruins
Western monasteries
Thuparama Dagoba
Elara's Tomb
Pilgrims' rest
Jetavana Dagoba

Basawakkulama

Ruwanwelisya Dagoba
Archaeological Museum
Stone fence
Pilgrims' rest
Tholuvila ruins

3

Mirisaweti Dagoba
MIHINDU MW
Brazen Palace
Pilgrims' rest
Pilgrims' rest
Railway station

PUTTALAM ROAD
Pilgrims' rest
Sri Maha Bodhi
Lion Pillar
Nuwara Wewa

Dakkhina Dagoba
Ratnameli Pilgrims' rest

4

Puttalam, Palm Garden Village
Royal Pleasure Garden
Pilgrims' rest

Tissa Wewa
Isurumuniya Vihara
BANDARANAIKE MW
College

Vessagiriya
College
Police station
Ponnaran-kulama

5

Ruins
Courts
Library
Hospital

Kurunegala
Open University

For listings, see page 131
Railway station

Where to stay
N
Bradt

1 Nuwarawewa Resthouse.... D4
2 Tissawewa Grand................. B4
Colombo
0   800m
0   800yds
Airport

Off map
Palm Garden Village..............A4

a roundabout bristles with signs advertising various hotels at Sigiriya, where the road heads. The A6 continues to Habarana, giving a view of Sigiriya on the right, mango orchards on the left, and roadside stalls abrim with shaddocks and small melons.

Elephants are parked beside the road as it draws into Habarana. These are tame, owned by entrepreneurs who lease them to local people who organise the elephant safaris into the surrounding jungle. The road from Habarana, until it joins the A9 at Maradankadawala, passes paddy fields where sun-baked farmers in loin cloths stumble in slurries of mud behind ploughs pulled by truculent buffaloes. Homes there are wattle-and-daub or clay-walled huts with thatched roofs. Maradankadawala has its communications bureaux too while, lining the road outside this small town, neatly stacked piles of firewood are for sale. Look out for the lotus pond at **Thirapanne**.

At **Galkulama** the road forks into the A9 to Mihintale, and beyond to Jaffna. More paddy fields and then the Nuwara Wewa expanse of water glistens in the sunlight, and flamboyant trees bedazzle with their outrageous crimson flowers by a junction where both roads lead to Anuradhapura.

GETTING AROUND The best way to explore the ruins of the ancient city (the modern town is not up to much) is by bicycle, available for hire from the resthouses. Make sure you have a viewing permit for the Cultural Triangle (see box, page 101), as inspectors might leap out and demand it even as you ride your bicycle innocently along a byway.

 WHERE TO STAY AND EAT All listings are included on the map opposite.

Palm Garden Village Hotel (10 AC suites, 40 AC rooms) Pandulagama, Anuradhapura; ☎ 025 2223961; e pgvh@sltnet.lk; www. palmgardenvillage.com. For comfortable extravagance drive 3km on the road to Puttalam, past the Open Prison Camp, to this hotel. Few palm trees but tame deer & birds, & other chance wildlife, abound in this 15ha park adjoining a jungle watering hole. Accommodation is in detached villas split into 2, 3 or 4 units, warm with polished wood furniture & fittings. Traditional, colonial rattan-&-wood lounge chairs have been reproduced with an Italian flair, giving the hotel an upmarket look. **$$**

Nuwarawewa Resthouse (70 AC rooms) New Town, Anuradhapura; ☎ 025 2222565; e hotels@quickshaws.com; www.quickshaws.com. Closed for renovation at press time.

Tissawewa Grand Hotel (20 rooms) Old Town, Anuradhapura; ☎ 025 2222299; e hotels@ quickshaws.com; www.quickshaws.com. For recent decades known as Tissawewa Resthouse, before reverting to its original name as the Grand Hotel in 2006 when it was fine for the discerning, independent traveller being set in the precincts of the **Royal Pleasure Garden** [130 B4] & endearingly dated. However, it was closed for renovation at press time.

OTHER PRACTICALITIES
➕ **Suwa Shanthi Hospital** [130 D5] ☎ 025 22236360

WHAT TO SEE AND DO The sacred **Bo tree** [130 B3] (Sri Maha Bodhi) should be a must-see for nature lovers as it is such an object of veneration. Surely a country whose people worship a tree qualifies as an eco-destination? Grown from a sapling, from the tree under which Buddha obtained Enlightenment in 528BC, and brought to Anuradhapura in the 3rd century BC, the sacred Bo tree (*Ficus religiosa*) lures pilgrims. Outside the compound where the tree grows surrounded by shrines, stalls sell coconut saplings and candles for devotees.

Inside the compound is a counter where shoes have to be left (and retrieved on payment of a tip) before a walk of 100m to a shrine behind which can be seen a branch of the tree, garlanded with cloth. The tree is surrounded by a gold-plated fence added in 1966.

Ficus religiosa trees are known to live for a long time and are remarkably hardy. This tree has been protected and nurtured throughout its 2,250 years by (it is said) the descendants of the guardians appointed by King Tissa (250–210BC) who received the sapling. It is surrounded by other Bo trees that have grown from its roots.

In ancient times there was a channel leading from the Tissa Wewa around the Bo tree to a reservoir by the Brazen Palace, and this watered the tree. Fa Xien, the Chinese explorer who visited in AD413, noted, 'as the tree bent over to the southeast, the king feared it would fall, and therefore placed a prop to support it'. The tree is still supported in the same way.

When invaders from India destroyed most of the city, they left the Bo tree as it is also a sacred tree for Hindus. When the city was abandoned, and jungle returned, the guardians burnt fires at night to keep away wild animals from the tree. A wall was built around the tree in 1803 by the last king of Kandy to protect it from them. Now the health of the tree is monitored by the director of the Royal Botanical Gardens at Peradeniya and the Ministry of Agriculture.

The chapter house, built by King Tissa in the 3rd century BC for the monks who were guardians of the tree, was made into the Loha Pasada or **Brazen Palace** [130 B3] by King Dutugemunu (161–137BC). He built a nine-storey building with 1,000 rooms and a roof of copper tiles, which gave the palace its name. In the central pavilion there was an ivory throne inlaid with a sun in gold, a moon in silver and stars in pearls. This was because the symbol of the Buddha, up to the introduction of Buddha image-worship in AD1, was an empty throne and the representation of his footprints.

All that remains as a link with this splendid building are 1,600 pillars, since the original palace, which was made of wood, burnt down in a fire 15 years after it was built. The pillars are actually the remains of restoration work done by Parakramabahu the Great (1153–86) and had evidently been collected from other buildings. In the southeast corner of the palace is a group of columns with friezes of happy dwarves.

The building of the **Ruwanwelisaya Dagoba** [130 B3], known as the Mahathupa, began in 144BC. The foundations of this stupa (domed building erected as a Buddhist shrine) were dug to 1½m and filled with stone stamped down by elephants and reinforced with plating in copper then silver.

The story is that the architect, who won the competition to design the shrine, when asked for his design, called for a golden bowl full of water. He scooped water into his hand and let it fall into the bowl where it formed a perfect bubble. Thus the bubble shape was chosen for the stupa. Different restorations over the centuries have changed its shape.

To the east of the Mahathupa can be seen an enormous brick stupa known as the **Jetavana** [130 C3]. This was originally 120m high, making it the third-largest building in the world at the time (AD3; the two taller buildings were Egyptian pyramids). It has a concrete base and foundations of brick at 12m deep. Clustered around it were monastery buildings (now in ruins) of the image house, chapter house, living units and refectory and the remains of a rectangular pond that was the central reservoir for the monastery.

If you do not have time to view all the stupas and ruins of Anuradhapura, a visit to the museums and visitor information centres there could compensate. There are now two opened as part of the UNESCO–Sri Lanka Cultural Triangle Project. These are in the Abhayagiri complex – the **Mahatissa–Fa Xien Museum** [130 C3] – and in the Jetavana complex – the **Archaeological Museum and Treasure Room** [130 B3] (⊕ *08.00–17.00 daily except public holidays*).

There are other interesting cultural relics in the area around Anuradhapura, and all of them are best reached by road. The closest is **Mihintale**, a large rock once inhabited by thousands of monks.

Aukana is 50km southeast of Anuradhapura, and can be reached by a road that runs along the dam of the Kelawewa reservoir. There is a station at Aukana (174km from Colombo) but not all trains stop there. Another way would be to leave the Trincomalee-bound train at Kelawewa, which is where all trains on the line stop. Then it is a journey by road. There is a colossal statue of Buddha carved out of solid rock at Aukana, and it is possible to walk there from the railway station. Another massive image, but not so impressive, is at **Saseruwa**, 10km beyond Aukana. But, according to reader Andrew Forsyth, 'Saseruwa is a fascinating place, with an incomplete rock Buddha of the same dimension as that at Aukana, and a cave containing a large reclining Buddha. The reclining Buddha is carved from rock, and is actually clad in cotton robes. Fee payable.'

Southeast of the city, about 40km away, is Ritigala mountain massif. The site has a large group of forest monasteries and the mountain is, in legend, associated with healing plants. It is also a natural reserve. At Tantrimala, about 40km north of Anuradhapura, are a large seated Buddha and a recumbent figure, both of which are carved out of solid rock.

DAMBULLA *Population: 68,821 (2012 estimate)*

Here is the renowned rock temple on a hill 340m high containing many carvings and statues. It was founded by King Valagam Bahu in the 1st century BC in gratitude for the shelter he found in the cave while fleeing from Malabar invaders.

GETTING THERE
By train Train is not an option since the railway does not go to Dambulla. The nearest station is Habarana, from where it is possible to get a bus. The best way by train would be to take the intercity from Colombo to Kandy and then get a bus from there.

By bus There are buses (No 15) from Colombo to Anuradhapura that stop in Dambulla. No 549 links Dambulla with Kurunegala.

By road The drive to Dambulla from Colombo is along the A1 (Kandy road) to Ambepussa and then the A6 via Kurunegala. From Kandy, the A9 heads directly north through Matale to Dambulla.

WHERE TO STAY AND EAT Upmarket tour groups and travellers with a nose for something different stay on opposite sides of the Kandalama reservoir at one of two hotels designed with pleasing eco-eccentricity, and also at one new contender. Those who like one usually loathe the others; they are so different in their approach to 'getting back to nature'. Yet all three by the lake appeal to visitors craving an unusual ecological experience without forsaking creature comforts. All listings outside Dambulla are included on the map, page 98. Green Paradise and Dambulla Heritage are in the town centre.

Heritance Kandalama (formerly Kandalama Hotel) (152 AC rooms) Kandalama, Dambulla; 066 5555000; e kandalama@ heritancehotels.com; www.heritancehotels. com. Before this hotel was built on the fringe of 2,000ha of primary forest overlooking the Kandalama Wewa (reservoir), there was a rumpus over its possible effect on the environment. Now it is praised as a model of hotel development within an ecologically sensitive area. It is still a shock to see it, apparently locked to a cliff face with the jungle vegetation, & monkeys, gradually claiming it, which is what the architect, Geoffrey Bawa, intended. It is an experience to stay there, sometimes a trying one since it is a kilometre long & requires stamina to get from bedroom to bar, if you can find it. Its effect on the environment is now seen as sustaining. For guests there are all manner of things to do, like jungle trekking, canoeing on the lake, safari by river, birdwatching & horse, pony & bullock cart rides. There are also, sometimes, hot-air balloon voyages floating over treetops & viewing wildlife & the Kandalama Tank, as well as the Sigiriya Rock. The hotel's rooms are architecturally cute (the clothes cupboard gives a view into the bathroom) with trendy fittings. **$$$$**

⌂ **Amaya Lake Resort** (formerly Culture Club) (95 rooms & suites) Kandalama, Dambulla; ☏066 4468100; e amayalake@amayaresorts.com; www.amayaresorts.com. This hotel not only blends into the environment of wilderness, birds & butterflies by the Kandalama reservoir, with ease of access to all points of the Cultural Triangle, it also provides a fulfilling holiday experience. A 16ha park conceals elegant AC cottages, some of them individual units, others as pairs or groups of 4 units sharing a private lounge. Room décor includes a kingly figure in bas-relief in an alcove, upholstered stone couches, & doors adorned with paintings of a bearded royal guard holding aloft a mighty sword. 11 'eco cottages' are built of wattle & daub like village houses, but with all mod cons. There is a sense of spaciousness & an acceptable proximity to nature. The blue of the swimming pool, modelled on ancient baths at Mihintale, contrasts with the lush green of ornamental paddy fields. Activities include elephant safaris, canoe cruises to view birds on the lake & guided nature walks. The Veda Madura ayurveda natural health centre has become so popular that guests stay for several days just for the herbal baths & steam treatments. The reception area is large & open-sided, furnished with smoothly crafted reproductions of typical Sri Lankan colonial furniture, & some intriguing wooden sculptures. Village women joyfully pound wooden kettle drums to welcome each new day, & a flautist serenades at dusk. Meals are buffets, laid out against a backdrop of serenity inspired by the lakeside setting. **$$$**

⌂ **Brook Boutique Hotel** (10 AC units), Madahapola Rd, Alipallama, Malsiripura; ☏066 7500500; e res@brook.lk; www.brook.lk. In a

jungle wilderness where you least expect it lies Brook Hotel, as sophisticated a resort as any in a city, with sumptuous accommodation in individual villas with musical bathrooms, lavish, colourful décor & privacy in a 70-acre tropical woodland & orchard where mango, cashew, soursop, woodapple, passion fruit & coconuts grow. There's a hilltop infinity swimming pool, a menu featuring local produce to delight gourmets, a spa, veranda & dungeon bars & a wine cellar. Everything needed for an upmarket stay away from it all, in this case 10km from Malsiripura, a small town on the road linking Kurunegala with Dambulla. A sign indicates the turn then another one comes 8km later as you go deeper into the wilderness. No kids allowed. **$$$**

⌂ **Green Paradise Agro Eco Hotel** (67 AC chalets) Kubukkadanwala, Dambulla; ☏066 2286300; e reservation@greenparadise.net; www.greenparadise.net. Much more elegant & sophisticated than the formidable term 'Agro Eco Hotel' implies, this complex of terraced deluxe chalets & semi-detached garden villa suites lies in wilderness near Kandalama Lake, with its own nature trail to a mini lake, huge boulders to climb, & kids' & adults' swimming pools (33m long), gym & spa, open-sided bar & dining pavilions. Timber beams, high roofs, wooden floors & a sense of community (chalets are grouped around a park) are the hallmarks of this newly built country retreat where 'agro' & 'eco' concepts are pursued but not thrust in guests' faces. There is no 'hard' music at night for instance, but a sensitive flautist playing solos or a violinist or an oriental mandolin player. It's the kind of place that merits more than a one-night transit stop as each room is creatively designed with an attic for sitting room or kids, huge wardrobe, Italian fittings & birdsong chorus accompanying perfect peace. Access to the hotel is from the A9 just before the junction with the A6 at Dambulla, 14km along the signposted road to Kandalama. **$$$**

⌂ **Thilanka Resort** (24 AC rooms) Godawelyaya, Moragollawa, Dambulla; ☏081 4475200; e thilankar@sltnet.lk; www.thilankaresorts.com. This hotel seems a bold architectural statement in such flat wilderness & is one of the new generation of unusual resort properties, contemporary in style with gourmet cuisine. It has a connection with an old favourite of tourists 'doing the Cultural Triangle', the Hotel

Thilanka in Kandy, & has a similar no-nonsense approach to accommodation, but at higher prices. Its rooms are set as 2 down & 2 up in blocks happily distanced from each other by vegetation. The interiors have lots of polished grey cement as a counterpoint to the vibrancy of the fabrics & paintings & the jungle scenery outside their windowed walls. The resort is defined by a bridge-like deck supported by square columns protruding from the reception & restaurant area where a 36m-long swimming pool stretches into the garden like a giant's bathtub. There is also a spa. Set in a 10ha orchard of mangoes & coconuts & paddy fields stretching 1km to a river, this refreshingly different resort is easy to find, being 3km out of Dambulla on the right side of the road to Matale, just past the cave temple. **$$$**

⌂ **Dambulla Heritage** (formerly Resthouse) (4 rooms) Matale Rd, Dambulla; 📞066 2284799. Billed as the ideal stopover, it is a good place to eat traditional resthouse fare of quick-served set-meal rice & curry. Rooms are basic. **$**

⌂ **Gimanhala Transit Hotel** (17 AC, 5 non-AC rooms) 754 Anuradhapura Rd, Dambulla; 📞066 2284864; e gimanhala@sltnet.lk. Pleasant but no more than it pretends to be: a transit hotel. Alert service & a garden layout (with swimming pool), lunch buffets & à la carte restaurant make this a handy low-cost base to overnight. **$**

WHAT TO SEE AND DO As if the hedonism of the hotels in the region and the chance to indulge in broadening one's environmental awareness were not enough reason to visit Dambulla, there is a cultural one too. The **rock temple** here dates from the 1st century BC. It is a vast isolated rock mass 340m high and 1.6km round the base. The caves in the area sheltered King Valagam Bahu during 14 years of exile from Anuradhapura, 65km distant. When he regained the throne he set about creating rock temples in the caves, turning them into shrines.

In the first cave is an image of a recumbent Buddha that is 15m long and cut out of the rock. Deities associated with Buddhism surround it. Some of the wall paintings that have been discovered seem to date from earlier times. However, the frescoes on the walls and ceilings are from the 15th to 18th centuries. In the second cave, considered the finest, are 150 life-size images of the Buddha. The ceiling is covered with frescoes depicting great events in the life of Buddha as well as notable landmarks in the history of the Sinhalese.

Reader Andrew Forsyth writes:

The best way to enjoy this place is to take a long time looking at all the caves, and then get an official guide. By the time you get the guide, you will have plenty of questions about the various paintings and statues, which the guides will be happy to answer.

There is a car park in front of the stylish building fronting the steps which climb up to the **rock temple** (⊕ 07.00–19.00 daily; admission Rs1,100). John and Elisabeth Cox add: 'Tickets can only be purchased at the entrance, at the foot of the steps. If the climb looks daunting, cars can be driven up to the halfway point.'

Sri Lanka's only dry-zone **arboretum** (Kandalama Rd, Dambulla; e rukraks@ sltnet.lk; ⊕ 09.00–17.00 daily) was started in 1963 on 3ha of thorny scrub jungle by a British naval officer turned tea planter, F H (Sam) Popham. It was Popham's ambition to return the savaged land he had bought to its natural state that gave birth to the arboretum. He had seen that the chena (slash and burn) method of cultivation had resulted in thorn-scrub and wild, disorderly undergrowth. Other areas of forest around Dambulla were also being destroyed due to the building of reservoirs, settlements, logging and illegal and unchecked harvesting of medicinal plants.

The arboretum's importance today is that it is Sri Lanka's only dry-zone tree-garden. (The island's three wet-zone botanical gardens have very different flora.)

Popham created it, not by drastic clearing, but by letting the area rejuvenate itself through minimal human interference. This technique has since become known as 'The Popham Method'. By gentle clearance of the scrub jungle, seedlings of the previous evergreen forest were released. These seedlings were already naturally acclimatised to cope with the harsh conditions of the dry zone and so thrived, where seedlings from outside nurseries perished.

For the first ten years, Popham lived in a thatched mud hut (seen at the entrance of the property) until moving to a granite cottage designed for him by Geoffrey Bawa. This now serves as the **visitor centre** (✆ *060 2662419*) and residence of the arboretum's scientific staff.

In 1989, a further 11ha were added and now there are more than 70 species of evergreen and deciduous trees. The arboretum opened to the public in 2005 and is easily accessible off the road to the Heritance Kandalama Hotel. Trails have been laid out through the trees and the resident naturalists are delighted to act as guides. Donations towards the upkeep, rather than an admission charge, are gladly accepted since the arboretum has no regular funding. It is managed by Ruk Rakaganno, the **Tree Society of Sri Lanka** (✆ *011 2554438*), for the Institute of Fundamental Studies that now owns it. The UK-based International Dendrology Society funded the labelling of the trees and this helps visitors identify the rare and unusual species.

Some 24km south of Dambulla, on the A9, 48km from Kandy via Matale, is **Nalanda**, considered as part of the Cultural Triangle. It was from Nalanda that Parakramabahu the Great (1153–86) advanced to defeat King Gajabahu's (1132–53) army. There are ruins there of a Hindu devale (shrine).

GIRITALE

The main feature of Giritale is its ancient tank (man-made lake or reservoir) constructed in the early 7th century. In places, the original walls of the *bund* (bank) can still be seen. The reservoir is now the centre of a nature reserve.

GETTING THERE

By train The best option by train is to go to Polonnaruwa and then switch to a local bus, since there is no railway line serving this area.

By bus Giritale is served by the No 48 bus running between Colombo and Polonnaruwa.

By road The only way by road is to turn right on to the A11 at the Habarana junction. There is a short cut along a partially unsurfaced road from Sigiriya to join the A11 at Moragaswewa.

The focal point of Giritale is the lake. There is no town – the road skirts along its shore passing just a few scattered homes, guesthouses and a few tourist hotels set in what was once a royal deer park. Resist the offers of a canoe ride; there have been drownings when wind and waves turned boisterous.

🏠 WHERE TO STAY AND EAT

🏠 **Deer Park Hotel** (77 cottages, 1 Presidential Villa) Giritale; ✆ 027 2246272; e mail@deerparksrilanka.com; www. deerparksrilanka.com. It has neither deer nor lake view, but it has everything else. The hotel derives its name from the forest's origins, as the hunting ground for ancient kings. Tame deer would be out of place given that wild animals are free to roam the nature reserve of this exotic & upmarket resort. Its theme is back to nature in pampered luxury, with 5 outdoor & 4 indoor spa pavilions, & 2 restaurants with the accent on idyllic healthful cuisine but with a couple of bars too. Serenity, buffed up with efficient service, embraces guests the moment they walk up the steps to its gracious, open-sided reception pavilion. There's a lot of walking up & down & around in this woodland garden retreat. Despite its alliance with nature, the hotel's rooms are city-slick, with bathrooms half-open to the sky as an exotic touch. The single-storey cottages are better than the duplex ones which have the bedroom upstairs & bathroom downstairs. The ultimate in environmental bliss is the 2-bedroomed villa with living rooms &, in a secret garden, its own swimming pool. The forest glade setting, with cottages around its tumbling, 3-tiered swimming pool, is eco-romantic with a manicured rural charm spliced with urbanity. **$$$**

WHAT TO SEE AND DO Birds, butterflies and tranquil nature are the attractions here. Pause in your travels to gaze at the breeze-ruffled waters of the ancient reservoir and contemplate the sophisticated civilisation that transformed the area nearly 2,000 years ago.

By the 56km post is a new addition to the scenery: a huge Buddha statue set against a black backdrop beside the lake. This was erected by the military of the area and has a small garden with a *Ficus benghalensis* planted on 14 November 2002.

The road leaves the lake, passes abandoned houses and goes deep into the woods. There is a National Wildlife Training Centre in a particularly tidy area of the forest, and that's the lot.

Just before reaching Giritale, on the road from Habarana, there is a turn-off on the right to Hingurakgoda and then on to **Madirigiriya**. The ruins of the Vatadage (pillared shelter) there and its associated buildings, set in a natural reserve, are considered enchanting. It is part of the Cultural Triangle project, 38km from Polonnaruwa. Near the signpost pointing to the lonely halt of Minneriya railway station, on the right, a squat building painted jungle-green marks the entrance to the **Minneriya National Park**. The **Minneriya Tank** (reservoir) glistens through the trees on the right of the road as it progresses through the landscape. The tank is 3,000ha in area and was constructed by King Mahasena (AD274–301), the builder of the Jetavana Dagoba at Anuradhapura.

By the road a thatched shack is stacked with mattresses, clad in gaudy ticking, and then there is a makeshift shelter with a palm-weave roof that has a sign saying it sells 'Pun'. This turns out to be rush-, reed- and rattan-ware displayed in the dignified manner of a church fête. The pieces are small enough to carry home, and each has its price marked on it.

On the left of the A11 road at the **Natural Art Workshop**, an open space with an awning, is a collection of extraordinary wooden shapes. These are roots, found in the jungle during two-week root-hunting safaris by the young people involved in the enterprise. The roots are polished and varnished and deftly carved but remain one single piece. The shapes resemble animals, birds and people. I bought a piece with four legs, a tail and a head and it stands guard, like a praying mantis, on my veranda. This art form ranges in price from Rs750 upwards per piece, and makes an unusual, if difficult to pack, memento. The workshop is the source of the items on sale at a larger outlet on the Colombo–Kandy road.

HABARANA

The virtue of Habarana is its location at the crossroads of the Cultural Triangle. Roads from here lead to Anuradhapura in the northwest and to Trincomalee in

4

the northeast. You can reach Polonnaruwa and Sigiriya easily from the junction, or head down to Matale and Kandy and on to the west coast. Perhaps because it is always on the way to somewhere else, not many rolling stones have stopped there and it boasts no monuments or dagobas.

GETTING THERE

By train The station is on the line from Colombo to Trincomalee and Polonnaruwa. It is little more than a halt and about 3km from the Habarana junction where the hotels are clustered.

By bus Bus No 48 is the best, serving Polonnaruwa and Colombo.

By road The crossroads at Habarana is one of those Piccadilly-like places where, if you wait long enough, you are sure to see someone you know. The A6 from Ambepussa to Trincomalee passes through, intersecting with the A11 from Polonnaruwa. So everyone touring the Cultural Triangle will transit this sleepy, jungly junction.

WHERE TO STAY All listings are included on the map, page 98.

Cinnamon Lodge (141 AC rooms) Habarana; 066 2270011; e lodge@cinnamonhotels. com; www.cinnamonhotels.com. The Chaaya Village shares its lakeside park setting with the more upmarket Cinnamon Lodge. The Lodge's hotel rooms are local-style villas, either ground floor with veranda or upper floor with balcony, & 4 suites which are entire villas combining downstairs bedroom & dining parlour & upstairs master bedroom, & serviced by a butler. The interior décor reflects Kandyan-style architecture, with columns & carved-wood valances, rattan & wood furniture & a concrete plinth on which rests the bed, with chunky Queen Anne-type legs, a work desk & a vanity table. There are French windows to throw open & let in breeze & light, & reproduction antique chaise longue & a stout wooden 'burgomaster' chair alongside a glass-topped table. With satellite TV for when guests are tired of watching the birds & monkeys foraging in the 11ha of parkland, rooms have 5-star amenities. The granite-walled bathrooms have both bathtub & separate glass shower cabinet with hot water. According to the hotel's publicity, 'The Lodge is laid out along the lines of the nearby Ritigala Rock temple, a meditational matrix that gently induces tranquillity.' Meals can be taken à la carte, as table d'hôte or buffets. Tucking in to the loaded buffet

counters may require a visit to the Ayurveda Herbal Treatment Centre for an oil massage or steam bath, if you are tempted to overdo it. **$$$**

Chaaya Village (106 AC rooms, 2 lodges) Habarana; 066 2270047; e village@ chaayahotels.com; www.chaayahotels.com. This is the restored & revitalised Habarana Village, the first major hotel in this area opened in 1976. Rooms are semi-detached, grouped in single-storey clusters around central paths meandering through vast tropical parkland. They are well appointed with rattan blinds shading glass walls & solid wood beds made cleverly to fit snugly into minimal space. Meals are taken as buffets, drinks in an openside bar with a view of the lake shimmering beyond. As an introduction to the lake, the hotel's new swimming pool is irresistible. It is triangular in shape, entered by 3 different level terraces of water & then tapering off into infinity. There are also tennis & badminton courts, a jungle gym & a jogging track for the super-energetic. **$$**

Acme Transit Hotel (7 AC, 3 non-AC rooms) 90 Polonnaruwa Rd, Habarana; 066 2270016; e acmetran@sltnet.lk. An appealing place to stay, not only because it has a fun atmosphere, a bar & a reputation for good local food, but also because of its great *trompe-l'œil* rustic murals décor. A snack of fish fingers (made with fresh lake fish) was superb. **$**

WHERE TO EAT AND DRINK For traditional resthouse fare, the **Habarana Heritage** (formerly Habarana Resthouse; **$**) serves rice and curry promptly at lunchtime, and also beer and arrack (though there's no bar counter). For more inspired cooking

at any time try the **Acme Transit Hotel** ($). **Cinnamon Lodge** ($$) has salad and dessert counters in a cool, glass-walled, air-conditioned pavilion to keep things fresh, and action-station pasta and seafood counters as well as roasts. For the Acme Transit Hotel and Cinnamon Lodge, see map, page 98.

WHAT TO SEE AND DO Habarana excels in elephants, being only a short drive from the national parks by the Kaudulla reservoir. There are several independent companies (and even families) who organise morning elephant safaris, or evening visits by jeep to the Minneriya and Kaudulla national parks. No advance reservation is necessary; bookings can be made either through your hotel or by simply turning up after breakfast. A safari riding on the back of an elephant (while in a basket-like saddle large enough to carry four passengers) is a thrilling way to see the jungle, and birds, at close quarters, as well as the lake when the elephants trundle in with their passengers; watch out for crocodiles basking in the sun. The safari takes about two hours with riders sitting sideways supported by a mattressed frame. (A minimum of two people, maximum four, per elephant, from US$25 for two.)

Jeep safaris penetrate much further and carry a tracker who knows the elephants' habits. Departures are at 05.00 and 15.00 daily. Charges per jeep vary according to the number of people since admission charges have to be paid. Expect to pay about US$25 per person for a jeep with four passengers, including park fee, tracker and vehicle fee, and soft drinks and fruit on the journey. Safaris can also be booked through hotels in the area.

MIHINTALE

Mihintale is regarded as the cradle of Buddhism. According to Buddhist tradition it was to this place that Prince Mahinda, son of the Indian emperor Asoka, came in 246BC to preach. He met King Devanampiya Tissa (250–210BC), whose capital was at Anuradhapura, while the king was hunting (rather surprising the king as he seemed to appear from thin air). His arrival was so propitious it resulted in the king, his family and entourage becoming the island's first converts to Buddhism.

GETTING THERE
By train There is a railway line, built in 1993, but trains run from Anuradhapura only at weekends or during the Poson season, which is the traditional time for pilgrimages to Mihintale. From Anuradhapura, the train takes the Vavuniya line, then cuts off at Mihintale Junction through flat, sparse, jungly vegetation with scarcely a house or person to be seen, to reach the new station at Mihintale. It cost Rs151 million to build the line in a period of six months. When the train runs it takes 35 minutes for the journey.

By bus Mihintale is not a destination that is visited in isolation; it is usually tagged on to a visit to Anuradhapura. There are local buses to Mihintale from the bus station in Anuradhapura.

By road It is convenient to pass through Mihintale on the way to somewhere else; either from Anuradhapura along the A12 or from Dambulla or Habarana arriving in town by the A9.

WHERE TO STAY AND EAT Mihintale has not developed as a place for overnight visitors, perhaps because of its proximity to the guesthouses of Anuradhapura. Both of the places that exist were opened during a flurry of government development of the area in 1993. There is the **Hotel Mihintale** (*10 AC rooms;* \ *025 5673680;* e *reservations@ceylonhotels.net; www.ceylonhotels.corporation.com;* $) with no bar and not much to do, while the other one, the resthouse at the railway station, no longer functions. Best to stay and eat at Anuradhapura.

WHAT TO SEE AND DO The rock at Mihintale is riddled with shrines and rock dwellings, and is the reason for visiting the area, as do thousands of pilgrims during the Poson season, usually in June. The grand stairway of 1,840 steps made of granite slabs over 4m wide leads in various flights to the summit. It is there that the king is said to have encountered Mahinda.

POLONNARUWA

Compared with the sombre atmosphere of Anuradhapura, Polonnaruwa in ruins is rather refreshing, helped by the freshness provided by the large lake, known as the 'Sea of Parakrama'. The ruins are also better preserved, being of a much later date. The ruined city was the capital from the beginning of the 11th century, after Anuradhapura was destroyed by the Cholas from southern India. It reached a brief zenith in the 12th century before being ravaged by invaders. In its prime the city, encircled by 6km of strong walls, was inhabited by hundreds of people. Now it is the preserve of monkeys and birds, interrupted by archaeologists and curious visitors.

HISTORY Dry-zone jungle covered the area with marshes where the lake is today, until about the 2nd century BC when cultivators and monks, as hermits, moved in. There is an inscription above the ledge of one cave giving evidence of this early occupation. A military garrison was there when the capital was still at Anuradhapura and in about the 6th century the area started to develop. It was known then as Pulatthinagara, named after a sage called Pulasti. Sages were Hindu holy men respected by the Buddhists; many played advisory and ceremonial roles in the Sinhalese royal court.

The area assumed a strategic importance since it commanded all the crossings over the Mahaweli River and guarded the roads to Ruhunu, the southern province. Kings maintained their armies there and King Aggabodhi IV (AD667–83) was the first king to have his country residence there. While William the Conqueror invaded England in 1066, King Vijayabahu (1055–1110) of Ruhunu captured Polonnaruwa in the same year. Although he was defeated by the Cholas, he survived many battles to return triumphant to Polonnaruwa in 1073 when he became king of a united island. Civil wars followed his death until ended by forces led by Parakramabahu, who captured Polonnaruwa and gained control of the whole island in 1161.

To that king goes the credit for developing the city. He fortified it and linked up the reservoirs to create the Parakrama Samudra, the lake that resembles an inland sea. Much of what he did remains an inspiration today. He was a conservationist who turned Anuradhapura into a wildlife sanctuary while restoring its monuments. He also restored the Mihintale Monastery; unified the orders of the Buddhist clergy, revitalising the religion; and vigorously defended his country's sovereignty, even invading India. He died in 1186 to become remembered in history as Parakramabahu the Great. It was the beginning of the end for Polonnaruwa although it remained the capital until 1293 when the tooth relic, and the capital, were moved to Kurunegala.

The jungle took over and the city's large, brick buildings were lost underneath thick tropical forest. The Portuguese in the 16th century looted what they could, then the city remained undisturbed until the beginning of the 19th century when the British rediscovered it.

GETTING THERE

By train There are two direct trains a day from Colombo Fort to Batticaloa which stop at Polonnaruwa.

The one-way fares in 2013 were quoted as Rs620 for first class, Rs340 for second class and Rs185 for third class. The station is actually at Kaduruwela, a few kilometres southeast of the ancient ruins (you'll need a local bus or a three-wheeler to get you there).

TRAIN TIMETABLE: COLOMBO TO POLONNARUWA

Train	Colombo –Polonnaruwa		Train	Polonnaruwa–Colombo	
0605	06.50	12.08	6012	09.26	15.25
6079	19.15	01.34	6080	22.25	04.55

By bus It's a long journey but it is possible by taking bus No 48-1 bound for Batticaloa from Colombo. There are also buses from Kandy and Anuradhapura.

By road Polonnaruwa is a very small town you would barely notice but for the ruins of walls and columns that line the road as you approach it. A signposted road off to the right leads to the magnificent Parakrama Samudra (the huge king-made lake, sometimes called sea) and it's better to take that than bother with seeing the town. Drive on past the resthouse to the visitor information centre by the canal to start your tour.

 WHERE TO STAY AND EAT In the 1970s, Polonnaruwa was a major transit point for visitors heading by road to the east-coast beaches of Passikudah and Kalkudah, north of Batticaloa and is likely to liven up again as new resorts are built on the east coast.

Until then, it seems a bit forlorn. While there are some wayside eateries patronised by local residents, most tourists eat in their hotels. At the other end of the Sea of Parakrama, set at the edge of the ruins, is one of the more famous of those resthouses, the Polonnaruwa Resthouse. All listings are included on the map, page 142.

Hotel Sudu Araliya (50 AC rooms) New Town, Polonnaruwa; 027 2224849; e suduaraliya@sltnet; www.hotelsuduaraliya.com. The hotel glitters with polished glass walls around its public rooms, matching its bright welcome. It has a swimming pool in its garden beside the lake & spacious, carpeted rooms with TV & minibar. **$$**

The Lake (formerly the Hotel Seruwa) (40 AC rooms) 027 2222411; e chcweb@ceylonhotels. net; www.ceylonhotelscorporation.com. The other resort is located in 3 acres of landscaped garden on the lake & is run by the Ceylon Hotels Corporation, the operators of many of the island's resthouses. **$$**

Polonnaruwa Resthouse 027 2222299; e chcweb@ceylonhotels.net; www. ceylonhotelscorporation.com. Closed at the time of writing for a much-needed facelift, its fame stems from a visit there in 1954 by Queen Elizabeth. The real attraction is its location by the 'sea' & its restaurant that protrudes over the water. The newly caught freshwater fish is delicious, although when I lunched there a few years ago the steward apologised for it not being sea fish.

Samagi Cottage Guest House (2 cottages) 49 Lakeview Gdn, Church Rd, Polonnaruwa; m 077 7587527; e info@samagivillasafari.com; www.

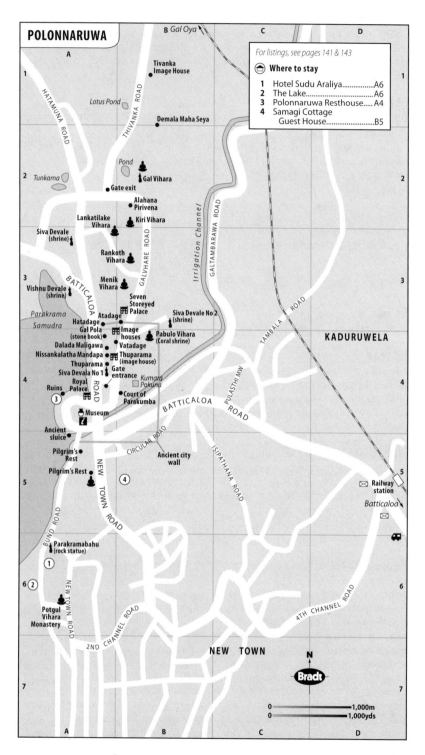

POLONNARUWA

B *Gal Oya*

For listings, see pages 141 & 143

Where to stay

1 Hotel Sudu Araliya.................A6
2 The Lake..................................A6
3 Polonnaruwa Resthouse......A4
4 Samagi Cottage
   Guest House..........................B5

HATAMUNA ROAD

THIVANKA ROAD

Tivanka
Image House

Lotus Pond

Demala Maha Seya

Pond

Tunkama

Gal Vihara

Gate exit

Alahana
Pirivena

Lankatilake
Vihara

Kiri Vihara

GALVHARE ROAD

Siva Devale
(shrine)

Rankoth
Vihara

Menik
Vihara

Irrigation Channel

GALTAMBARAWA ROAD

KADURUWELA

Vishnu Devale
(shrine)

BATTICALOA

Parakrama
Samudra

Seven
Storeyed
Palace

Atadage

Hatadage

Siva Devale No 2
(shrine)

Gal Pola
(stone book)

Image
houses

Pabulo Vihara
(Coral shrine)

Dalada Maligawa

Vatadage

Nissankalatha Mandapa

Thuparama
(image house)

Thuparama

Gate
entrance

Siva Devala No 1

Kumara
Pokuna

TAMBALA ROAD

PULASTHI MW

Royal
Palace

Ruins

Court of
Parakumba

BATTICALOA ROAD

ROAD

3

Museum

Ancient
sluice

Pilgrim's
Rest

Pilgrim's Rest

CIRCULAR ROAD

Ancient city
wall

ISIPATHANA ROAD

4

NEW TOWN ROAD

Railway
station

Batticaloa

Parakramabahu
(rock statue)

1

BUND ROAD

6 **2**

Potgul
Vihara
Monastery

NEW TOWN ROAD

2ND CHANNEL ROAD

4TH CHANNEL ROAD

NEW TOWN

N

Bradt

0 ————— 1,000m
0 ————— 1,000yds

samagivillasafari.com. P K Manjula Susantha Kumara reports this is a private cottage inn with 1 cottage having 2 twin-bedded AC rooms, & 1 with 3 twin-bedded AC rooms. It's near to the ancient city, a few mins by 3-wheeled taxi from the main road & Parakrama Samudra. There is a fully equipped kitchen, hot shower, 42in LCD TV, AC & internet. The owners run a jeep safari company & also have bicycles to rent. **$$**

WHAT TO SEE AND DO The **Museum and Visitor Information Centre** [142 A4] (✆ *09.00–18.00 except public holidays*) opened in 1999 and attempts to recreate with models the way the city looked in its heyday. It has eight sections, each one a different room linked by a long, straight corridor. Between sections, the corridor has one glass wall looking out at the flowing irrigation canal, trees and garden. The daylight makes the museum bright. There is an auditorium where a video is shown about the ancient capital. Sections are devoted to a topographical model of the city, to the palace of Parakramabahu, the Vatadage, the Alahana Pirivena and to displays of brass statues and pottery of the period.

The museum is beside the embankment of the 'sea', next to the canal, and is within easy walking distance of the Polonnaruwa Resthouse.

Impossible to miss is the **rock sculpture** [142 A6] that overlooks the reservoir. It is 3.65m (12ft) high and carved three-quarters round on the side of a boulder. While it is popularly said to be a representation of Parakramabahu the Great, it is more likely that of a great sage. It is a masterpiece depicting a strong elderly man with a thick beard and long moustache wearing a conical cap and holding an *ola* (palm leaf) book. It is a contrast to the many conventional statues of the Buddha to be seen in the ruined city.

About 100m to the south of the rock sculpture is the **Potgul Vihara** [142 A6] (Image House) Monastery. It holds a circular structure built of brick and is believed to have been built by Parakramabahu for listening to the stories of the great sage. Even though the roof of the round room – which is plastered – has collapsed, the acoustics are said to be excellent.

It is a pleasant walk some 700m northwards along the bank of the **Sea of Parakramabahu** to the other sites. This king-made lake covers an area of more than 23km². The bank (known as a bund in Sinhala) is 13.67km long and 12m high. The lake irrigates an area of more than 73km² of paddy fields, and was the source of water for the city. It was a link between two ancient irrigation systems that extended east of Polonnaruwa, via the Giritale, Minneriya, Kaudulla and Kantala tanks to Trincomalee. The king is credited with having constructed or restored 163 major reservoirs, 2,346 minor ones and 3,910 irrigation canals.

The closest of the ruins to the resthouse are those of the **baths**, which were fed by underground pipes from the lake. Between the baths and the lake is a weathered moonstone. The steps leading down to the water are ancient, as are the walls of the tank. The ancient city lies to the north of the resthouse, and the ruins on the left as you arrive on the road from Habarana are of the **Dalada Maluva**, the terrace of the Tooth Relic.

The monuments around the terrace were built at different periods. Starting with the eastern gateway by the road, are the **gatehouse**, the **vatadage** [142 A4] (a stupa shelter), the **thuparama** (image house), the **bodhi tree shrine**, the **flower-scroll hall**, the **recumbent Buddha shrine**, the **Bodhisattva image**, the **atadage** (temple), the **hatadage** (second temple), the **Gal Pola** (stone book), the **seven-storey palace** [142 A4] (Satmahal Prasada) and the **Chapter House**.

There are more than 30 historical buildings to be seen in the ancient city and its surrounds. The **Gal Vihara** [142 B2], or royal shrine, is one of the most impressive for its group of rock sculptures. It is just north of the **Alahana Pirivena** [142 B2], the monastic complex. The rock shrine includes several masterpieces of Sinhalese Buddhist art, including mythical beasts as well as seated, standing and reclining Buddha statues. The northernmost ruins are of the **flower bath** along a track in the woods, after the **Tivanka Image House** [142 A4]. On the outside of the building are some splendid lions in stucco and some boisterous dwarves.

SIGIRIYA

Sigiriya is famous for its toadstool of golden-hued granite, protruding 183m into the searing blue sky from a hot, flat wilderness of scrubland, which is transformed in the rainy season to a water garden. In the 5th century, a king domesticated the **Lion Rock**, as it is known, by building a palace atop its summit.

GETTING THERE
By train Difficult, since there is no station. The best way would be to take the train bound for Trincomalee and leave it at Kekirawa station. Built in 1925, the station serves a busy town among the paddy fields. Buses are available from there to Dambulla and thence to the rock fortress.

By bus Because of its popularity with locals as well as visitors, there is a bus service (No 48) direct from Colombo and from nearby towns, including Dambulla.

By road The main turn-off to Sigiriya from the A6 is at Inamaluwa if you are driving from Colombo. From Anuradhapura, the A13/A11 to Habarana is best and by keeping on the A11 eastwards you will come to the next junction that gives access to a road to Sigiriya. This is unmetalled for much of the way. The Lion Rock is within walking distance along the road from the first two main hotels mentioned here.

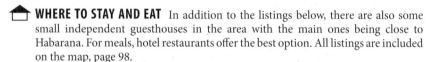 **WHERE TO STAY AND EAT** In addition to the listings below, there are also some small independent guesthouses in the area with the main ones being close to Habarana. For meals, hotel restaurants offer the best option. All listings are included on the map, page 98.

The Elephant Corridor (20 AC villas, 1 complex with 2 AC villas & garden) Sigiriya; 066 2231950; e manager@elephantcorridor. com; www.elephantcorridor.com. Along the road to Sigiriya from the Inamaluwa junction is a turning to the left marked 'for hotel residents only'. This leads to a hotel renowned in Sri Lanka for its expensive accommodation as well as for its 81ha jungle setting. When I visited, its premium, Presidential Suite in a jungle glade was quoted at US$1,550, but since that consists of 2 villas with 2 bedrooms in each & 2 swimming pools, when shared by 8 guests, the cost seems acceptable. There are 20 other detatched villas of various degrees of luxury (4 Romantic Villas each have an indoor swimming pool & 4-poster bed with mirrored ceiling), & all feature an easel & sketch

pad & binoculars as well as the usual upmarket hotel amenities. The restaurant is upstairs in the central complex with glass panels & breathtaking views of Sigiriya & the cupola of Kandalama hills. It is classically furnished with silver cutlery (even fish knives) & damask tablecloths & lends a touch of class to the scrub jungle setting. **$$$$**

Vil Uyana (25 dwellings) Rangirigama, Sigiriya; 066 4923585; e viluyana@ jetwinghotels.com; www.jetwinghotels. com. Along the road to Sigiriya is this wetland fantasy with views of the Sigiriya & Pidurangala rocks that was opened in 2006 by Jetwing Hotels. The name means 'garden of ponds' & this resort is unlike any other in Sri Lanka, combining jungle fantasy accommodation built on decks overlooking manmade waterways where crocodiles loaf. The 10 Forest Dwellings each have swimming pools & there are also 6 Marsh Pavilions, 6 Paddy Fields & 3 Water Villas clustered close together. Each villa has a separate dining deck & huge bathroom chambers & are exquisitely furnished. The central complex houses an underground wine cellar with a formidable selection of wines, an upstairs restaurant dominated by an 8m-high mural of temple legends, a cavernous bar with reproductions of the Sigiriya frescoes, a swimming pool & a viewing platform strewn with cushions. Vehicles drop guests at the entrance where buggies provide transport around the 10ha former paddy field property which is rich in wildlife. An amazing, rhapsodical place perfect for a sophisticated escape. **$$$$**

⌂ **Hotel Sigiriya** (80 AC rooms) ☏ 066 4930500; e inquiries@serendibleisure.lk; www.serendibleisure.

com. For a heady mix of environmental awareness & award-winning cocktails made from local produce, this is the place to stop. The comfortable rooms are in blocks around gardens & there is a swimming pool with a close-up of the rock. Signs display all the environmental activities (including birdwatching with a prize of a falcon T-shirt for spotting the rare shalin falcon) & even indicate where in the hotel gardens you can see parrots, mongoose, etc. The hotel has been recognised as a bird-friendly one by the Field Ornithology Group of Sri Lanka. Surprisingly for a hotel in the jungle in the Cultural Triangle, the Hotel Sigiriya barmen have also won awards in island-wide cocktail competitions. The bar has a true drinker's ambience (good stools, personable barman) in which to celebrate all the wildlife sightings, & surviving the nature trails & expeditions to an isolated rural hamlet organised by the hotel. **$$**

WHAT TO SEE AND DO Just gazing at the Lion Rock will be enough for many people since to climb it is somewhat precarious. Only windswept foundations remain to reward the stout-hearted who climb to the top of the rock's sheer face with the help of narrow, caged-in ladders that must be more than 50 years old.

Frescoes from the 5th century of bare-breasted women, acknowledged as art treasures, can be seen on the side of the rock. You reach the viewing edge by hauling yourself up an iron spiral staircase pegged to the rock's face. The frescoes, shaded from the elements by a canvas awning and smeared with cement, look better on postcards than real life. A logo to attract tourists to Sri Lanka was based on the vibrant depiction of a nubile female found in one of the frescoes, holding a flower in a classical-dance gesture.

Sigiriya was a royal citadel for 18 years, from AD477 to 495. Its creator was King Kasyapa (473–91) who left Anuradhapura and built his palace on the rock, believing it to be impregnable. And so it was, but when his half-brother Moggallan (491–508) challenged him with an army, Kasyapa came down to the plains and, when he believed the battle was lost, slew himself with his own dagger.

The summit of the rock is nearly a hectare in area. The outer wall of the palace was constructed on the brink of the rock. Gardens and ponds softened the harshness of this eyrie. The pleasure garden on the western side was studded with ponds, islets, promenades and pavilions. Underground and surface drainage systems have been discovered, adding to the remarkable achievement of this management by man of a natural phenomenon. Since that happened more than 1,500 years ago, Sigiriya deserves its listing by enthusiasts as the Eighth Wonder of the World.

If you come by vehicle, the driver will drop you at the entrance and he will obtain a receipt from the ticket office that enables him to park near where you will leave the site. If you a need a ticket solely for visiting the rock, this is obtainable from the ticket office located opposite the entrance, by a lotus pond. The cost is US$25 per person. This is checked at the entrance and again at the entrance to the climb to the summit.

There are local guides available who are not pests but genuinely interested in the history of their heritage; they delight in helping people not as fit as themselves in climbing the rock. A tip of Rs100 to Rs500, depending on your rate of satisfaction, would be appreciated. The rock is open from 07.30 to 15.30 daily. The small **museum** (*admission free*) is open from 08.00 to 17.00 daily except Tuesday.

YAPAHUWA

Yapahuwa (Rock Fortress) was the capital of the country during the reign of Bhuveneka Bahu I (1271–83). This was during the period of decline for the Sinhalese kingdom when the capital was shifted from Polonnaruwa to Dambadeniya, 29km from Kurunegala. Bhuveneka relocated the capital on the brow of a hill at Yapahuwa and today there remains a granite stairway up the face of a huge rock, nearly 100m high.

Andrew Forsyth writes: 'Visited Yapahuwa on Tuesday; museum closed. No English-speaking guide available but a wiry old gent hitched up his sarong and danced up the rocks in his flip flops as we trudged up behind. On top of the rock is a small dagoba (about 3–4m high), a raised bed that once housed a Bo tree and a small pond. View stupendous. Climb no more strenuous than Sigiriya and a lot less giddy-making. Sensible shoes recommended.'

GETTING THERE Yapahuwa is 5km from the Maho railway station on the main line to Anuradhapura, where the trains branch off to Gal Oya and thence to Trincomalee or Polonnaruwa. It does have its own railway station on the line to Gal Oya but major trains speed right through, so the best way to get there is by local train from Maho, then local bus or hired three-wheeler for the jaunt.

5

The Hill Country

There is a touch of romance and adventure in the phrase 'the hill country'. It sounds like a different world and, in Sri Lanka as in India, hill stations are unlike ordinary towns and villages. A hill station is traditionally a holiday resort, a refuge from the heat of the plains. A visit to the hill country gives a chance to see flamboyantly diverse scenery – from the arid plains of the lowlands to the pine forests and tea gardens of the hills – as well as to enjoy a change in climate and pace of life. For visitors, there is an opportunity to escape from those charmless hotel barracks walling off the beach and to 'chill out' in the much friendlier atmosphere of hill country hostelries.

The definition of Sri Lanka's hill country is loose. Kandy, at 488m above sea level, is in the hills, but it is known more for being an ancient kingdom and part of the Cultural Triangle than a simple hill station. However, the heady atmosphere of being in the hills does begin there. So for this book, I leave Kandy as the base point of the Triangle and take places southwards on the A5 road from Kandy to **Nuwara Eliya** as 'hill country'.

The road, as it climbs to **Pussellawa** through the **Ramboda Pass**, past tea gardens and woodlands, under steep cliffs and alongside plunging hillsides to valleys of paddy below, is a terrific introduction. One recent tourist study commented somewhat cynically:

> The drive to Nuwara Eliya either from Kandy or via Hatton is probably also a major
> attraction itself and may, especially for visitors who only stay one night, have a
> significance which surpasses that of their brief stay.

Nuwara Eliya is regarded as the acme of the hill country – in spirit if not in altitude – since it is 1,828m (6,000ft) above sea level, compared with Adam's Peak at 2,243m (7,359ft). However, Sri Lanka's highest mountain, Pidurutalagala, 2,524m (8,281ft), looms over the hill station but (unlike Adam's Peak) cannot be climbed due to security concerns.

Adam's Peak and its nearby towns of **Hatton** and **Maskeliya** can be regarded as on the fringe of the hill country, hemmed in by the Peak Wilderness Sanctuary. This parallels the island's south coast right along to **Halpe** and up to **Haputale**. From Haputale town you can gaze across lowland hills and glimpse the haze of the sea, if not the sea itself. The eastern rim of the hill country edges past **Ella** up to **Badulla**, and then off to Kandy. Within the area defined by the cusp of hills are colonial retreats like **Bandarawela**, the shimmering waterfalls near **Talawakele**, the wilderness of **Horton Plains**, the serenity of the **Kotmale reservoir**, the natural attractions of **Uva province** and the bungalow homes of the tea planters.

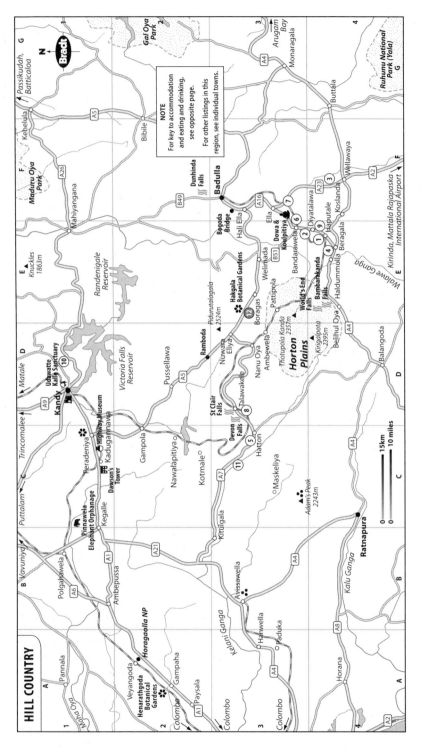

HILL COUNTRY

NOTE
For key to accommodation and eating and drinking, see opposite page.
For other listings in this region, see individual towns.

0   15km
0   10 miles

HISTORY

The history of the hill country is very much the history of Nuwara Eliya, since it was the opening up of that area to British settlement that led to the development of the hill country. However, that does not mean there was nothing there except wild animals and forest, pre-Brit. Adam's Peak has, as long as history records, been an object of pilgrimage. In Badulla, there is evidence of a 10th-century kingdom, and the Portuguese saw fit to ravage the area. Balangoda has given its name to the island's Stone Age culture.

GETTING THERE AND AWAY

BY TRAIN The prettiest parts of the hill country are best seen by train, not only because they are difficult to reach by road, but also because the elevation at which the train travels as it skirts large valleys reveals views invisible from the road.

There are three day trains (as well as a night one, though it is not a good choice if you are going for the scenery). Prospective travellers should check at the proposed departure station for the day's timetable as track conditions can cause delays and it is not unknown for the trains to be late and even cancelled completely, or to be curtailed halfway through the journey. (The moral is to carry enough rupees on the journey in case you have to bail out and find a taxi.)

The daytime journey provides the rail traveller with one of the most spectacular journeys in Sri Lanka, travelling for 290km and through 44 tunnels for 10–12 hours from Colombo to the terminus at Badulla.

Reserving seats in advance is advisable although you may be lucky enough to bag a seat in second class at the outset of the train journey from Colombo Fort station, but do not try if it is April or August (when it's holiday season time in Nuwara Eliya) or during the January to March pilgrimage season to Adam's Peak, reached by train to Hatton station.

Take a picnic lunch, plus beer if you need it since none is available on board. Sometimes you will be able to buy peanuts and *wade* (fat lentil cookies) from platform vendors, and in-season delicacies like guava and avocado pear.

Although a train journey of 290km (181 miles) from Colombo to Badulla may not seem long (especially to those used to train travel in India), do not be surprised to feel the train equivalent of jet lag, especially on the way back. Not that the train goes slow (though it does in the hills, restricted to 16km/h), but because it goes fast, particularly from Kandy to Colombo, and you will be bounced about a lot. It is probably better, as well as giving you a chance to see more of Sri Lanka without pain, to break the journey, perhaps at Kandy, rather than try the whole trip in one day.

A good way to do that would be to take an intercity train from Colombo to Kandy, and then on another day catch a train from Kandy station to Nanu Oya,

5

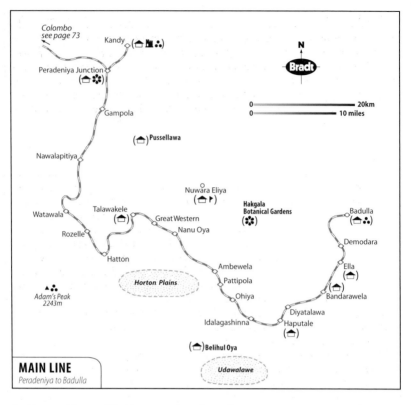

MAIN LINE
Peradeniya to Badulla

for Nuwara Eliya or Ella (for onward road travel to Arugam Bay or Tissamaharama). See box opposite for timetable.

As times and carriages may change, check at the departure station when planning your journey. (See www.gic.gov.lk, www.exporail.lk and www.rajadhani.lk.) Trains 1005/1006 and 1015/1016 resemble commuter trains and are operated by new Chinese-made Diesel Multiple Units (DMUs); they have air-conditioned first class, as well as second and third class with fans.

Peradeniya Junction has been rebuilt since it opened in 1867 but the original station has been preserved opposite the new one. It is an interesting, well-kept and pretty station, with its island platform being built as a triangle. One side is for trains to Kandy (or back to Colombo), and the other for trains to the hill country (or Colombo). The base of the triangle has park-bench seats for passengers to watch what is happening. Invariably trains pause here to wait for the single line to clear so that they can proceed safely to the next station crossing.

At **Gampola** (125km from Colombo, built in 1873) the levels reached by various floods of the Mahaweli River are recorded on the wall of one of the station buildings, with an extension on a pole showing where a flood in 1947 completely submerged the station and buildings. There is a small resthouse by the station and the bus station is opposite the station entrance. As Gangasiripura, Gampola was capital of the country from about 1344–1408. A flourishing town, it is the gateway to the tea districts of the hill country.

Ulapane is an undistinguished country town where the train stops before reducing speed gradually to cope with the winding track of the 15-minute run to **Nawalapitiya**.

This station, built in 1874, 139km from Colombo, has real railway atmosphere with lots of offices for officials (together with Colombo and Anuradhapura, it is one of the railway's three transport division headquarters), a mail room and a rather gloomy but large restaurant room. Vendors hawk rice and curry lunch packets from plastic buckets. There are restrooms, with seats, for ladies and gents. Train crews change at this station; lots of coaches are marshalled there too.

The bus station is across the road from the station entrance. It is possible to get a Colombo-bound bus from Nawalapitiya and to stop at Avissawella. This is an alternative route for returning to Colombo on the way back from the hills. After staying at Avissawella you could take a train on the (formerly narrow) broad-gauge Kelani Valley line down to Colombo.

The station booking office is open to the forecourt and nobody seems to hassle strangers since very few tourists alight here. I did once, because the train could go no further due to a landslide at Watawala. When something like that happens, there are usually buses to the obstruction where passengers can then pick up another train. Or it might be wiser to hire a minibus taxi to your destination.

A bell is rung to warn of the train's imminent departure and then it ambles through the outskirts of the town with road and shops beside the line until climbing into the wooded hills. **Inguruoya** (145km from Colombo) has a pretty platform with flowers, as befits the landscape of wooded hills and some tea gardens. **Galboda** retains its water tank for steam engines, which are now seen on this line only when chartered by steam enthusiasts.

There is more danger of being swept away by a landslide. Between Galboda and **Watawala**, the floods of 1947 resulted in a serious landslide, which was still causing trouble 45 years later. The track was washed away in June 1992 and was just being restored again when rains in June 1993 resulted in yet another landslide. There have been more since.

TRAIN TIMETABLE: COLOMBO TO BADULLA

Train	1005	1007*	1015	1045
Colombo	05.55	08.30	09.45	20.00
Kandy	08.42		12.19	
Nanu Oya	12.40	14.33	16.03	03.03
Haputale	14.15	16.08	17.36	04.55
Bandarawela	14.43	16.35	18.03	05.28
Ella	15.14	17.04	18.32	06.05
Badulla	16.06	17.55	19.23	07.10
Train	1016	1006	1008*	1046
Badulla	05.45	08.30	10.00	18.00
Ella	06.40	09.24	10.57	19.07
Bandarawela	07.11	09.55	11.28	19.41
Haputale	07.42	10.24	11.58	20.18
Nanu Oya	09.19	11.58	13.46	22.10
Kandy	12.50	16.06		02.36
Colombo	15.27	18.57	20.25	05.17

* With Exporail air-conditioned carriage with reserved seats attached daily and with Rajadhani air-conditioned carriage with reserved seats attached daily except Wednesday (Train 1007) and Thursday (Train 1008), as well as observation saloon, second and third class.

Signs urging slow speed because of 'weak sleepers' are not to prevent disturbance to those taking a light nap, but because of the condition of the track, and this causes the train to dawdle all the way to Badulla.

The ruling gradient of the line is 1 in 44, and there are actually 44 tunnels (total length 5,850m) between Colombo and Badulla. The majority of them, at this stage of the journey, are still to come.

The scenery changes from canyonesque to fir forest according to which side of the hill the track is climbing around, until the tea gardens take over after the tiny station of **Rozelle**, 165km from Colombo. The hillsides are dotted with the bright colours of the plastic capes worn by tea pluckers.

Hatton (1,271m above sea level, 173km from Colombo and built in 1884) is the centre of the tea-growing area. The most popular route to Adam's Peak, via Maskeliya, starts from this station, which is thronged with pilgrims and tourists during the climbing season (January to March).

Poolbank tunnel (at 560m, the longest in the island) comes next, an excuse for kids of all ages on the train to erupt into shrieks of mock horror as the train ambles through it. **Kotagala** interrupts the idyllic scenery of dells and brooks with its fuel tanks at the Ceylon Petroleum Corp bulk terminal. Then, with squeaking wheels, the train lurches past the swoop of St Clair Falls.

Talawakele is 185km from Colombo, 1,200m above sea level, and was built in 1884. It has a turntable overgrown with weeds, and glimpses of muddy waters winding their way through mountain gaps. After **Watagoda**, the train's wheels squeak and it slows to a walking pace through the broad hills and neat tea gardens. Then comes the grandly named **Great Western** station at 1,614m above sea level, 197km from Colombo. There is a panorama of tea bushes below and Adam's Peak in the distance. The train's progress is so slow and stately, you feel you can reach out and pluck tea yourself.

Radella is a small station dedicated to tea, and then the train heads through tunnel Number 17 and across bridges over twin waterfalls and past the tea factory of Glassaugh Estate before stopping at **Nanu Oya**, built in 1885. The main platform is the island one and if you peep into the operations room you can see the Tyer's Patent Train Tablet Apparatus, probably there since the station opened, and still used for controlling a train's progress. Without a token (tablet) from the apparatus, signifying the line is clear ahead, no trains can proceed. You alight here for **Nuwara Eliya**, 6km distant by road.

For the next part of the journey, from Nanu Oya to Bandarawela, the train wends its way through, and above, vegetation so lush and scenery so dramatic, it is one of the world's – not just Sri Lanka's – great little trips by train. It begins with views of hillsides covered with uniformly green, crew-cut tea bushes, brightened by women in red, blue and yellow plastic capes nimbly plucking young leaves, and the heady aroma of tea drying in factories.

Parakumpura is a small halt after which the mist-shrouded tea gardens begin to give way to vegetable patches between forests of fir and ferns. **Ambewela** still has the infrastructure for steam amid tall, straight fir trees, ferns, glades and babbling brooks. Hills shorn of trees for cultivation jerk you back to reality and the air turns crisper.

Pattipola, at 1,891m above sea level, is 223km from Colombo, close to the railway's summit. It is not a particularly pretty station, unless you are lucky enough to encounter a flock of red-sweatered schoolgirls chattering excitedly at the sight of the train. It is Sri Lanka's highest and heralds the passing by tunnel, Number 18, through the mountain range dividing the Central and Uva provinces. The summit is 1km after Pattipola station, marked with a signboard. It is 1,911m (6,266ft) above sea level. Another sign warns: 'Beware of rock slips'.

Ohiya (1,774m, 229km from Colombo) used to give access to Horton Plains but that road is now closed to the public. Next the train dives in and out of more than a dozen tunnels, the scenery changing with each gap from cloud-shrouded mountains to forest copses. After yet another tunnel comes the incredible station of **Idalgashina** (1,615m), amazing because of the deep, stunning views on both sides as it sits atop a ridge in the mountains, overlooking a lunar landscape and the formidable, scalloped hills of Uva. No trains are scheduled to stop at the next station, **Glenanore**, and it is not in the timetable, but it exists as a charming tea-garden halt with a lived-in look.

When the train leaves **Haputale** (1,413m, 246km from Colombo, built in 1893) you feel it has taken the wrong turning as it seems to wander down the middle of the main street, with market stalls overflowing on to the track. Then it recovers to meander through strictly ordered tea terrain. The station at **Diyatalawa** (1,331m) is spanking clean, with a pleasant forecourt and an almost military appearance; not surprising since Diyatalawa has been a military and naval training centre since British times, and also something of a health resort. There is an old cemetery there with the remains of Boer prisoners of the South African war.

The train arrives at **Bandarawela** (1,221m, 257km from Colombo) almost before you are ready. The track reached there in 1894 and for 30 years the station was the terminus. Now it is rather sleepy, with a booking office that opens 30 minutes before a train's departure.

Kinigama is reached after the train runs through the outskirts and scrubland of Bandarawela's suburbs. Close your eyes for **Heeloya**, a recently built station set in paddy fields. Cauliflowers are also grown close to the line as the train descends carefully, coming to the much lovelier station of **Ella** (built in 1918 at 269km from Colombo), if you ignore its asbestos canopy in front of the granite, cottage-like station building.

Now some fun. It begins with the train easing over a bridge of nine arches and then, at **Demodara**, where the station was built in 1921, the train turns kittenish and chases its tail. The Demodara Loop was constructed to avoid a gradient steeper than the ruling 1 in 44, so the train actually burrows under itself down the tunnel under the station.

The scenery opens up as the line follows the curve of the river to the tiny hamlet of **Uduwara**. After the high bridge by Rosette Estate, the train comes to **Hali Ella** where the station building, with its flowers and fir tree, looks like a cottage transported from the Yorkshire Dales. The final descent brings you to **Badulla** which, being 914m lower than Bandarawela, seems to have a sluggish air after the vibrancy of the hills.

BY BUS To take a bus to the hill country, decide on your destination and, for your own comfort, do the journey in stages. For example, the No 99 to Badulla stops at Ratnapura, Balangoda, Haputale and Bandarawela.

BY ROAD The road option to and from Colombo depends on your first destination. If you are going via Kandy, you take the A1 and then follow the A5 as it twists its way through the hills via Gampola and Ramboda to Nuwara Eliya. From there, the A5 continues via Welimada to Badulla. If you want to head straight for the hills, follow the road to Avissawella and then choose the A7 which will take you via Hatton to Talawakele and Nuwara Eliya, or take the A4 southwards to Ratnapura then eastwards to Balangoda. It becomes the A16 at Beragala to Badulla, via Bandarawela and Ella.

From the south and the new international airport at Mattala, the A2 from Hambantota reaches inland northwards to Wellawaya where it joins the A23 then the A16 up to Badulla, or westwards along the A4 through Beragala, then north to Bandarawela and, via Welimada, on to Nuwara Eliya.

AMBEWELA

The main reason for visiting Ambewela (halfway between Nanu Oya and Ohiya by train) is to enjoy the scenery and to stay at its luxury bungalow property.

GETTING THERE

By train The upcountry trains stop at Ambewela station, a rural halt that puts travellers in the mood for hiking and the cool, mountain climate. From the station a three-wheeler taxi will be needed to get to the Warwick Gardens bungalow, which is the reason for coming to this part of the hill country.

By bus Buses running between Nuwara Eliya and Welimada on the A5 stop at Boragas, which is the closest halt for the Warwick Gardens bungalow at Ambewela.

By road The A5 road linking Nuwara Eliya via Hakgala (for the Botanical Gardens) to Welimada passes through Boragas, where there is a turning by a Buddhist shrine on to the winding lane that leads uphill to Warwick Gardens.

 WHERE TO STAY AND EAT

⌂ Warwick Gardens (5 rooms) Ambewela; ☎ 060 2532284, (reservations) ☎ 011 2345700; e hotels@jetwing.lk; www.jetwinghotels.com. A unique place to stay, & it needs to be as getting there is a little difficult. It's off the road to Ambewela that branches off the A5 between Welimada & Nuwara Eliya at Boragas (short for Boragasketiya). Drivers need to phone the bungalow manager (m 077 3237862) for instructions about where to turn as the road climbs through plantations & forest. It is 168km from Colombo & set in a 12ha estate at 1,884m above sea level. Dubbed a 'bungalow', it is in fact a 2-storey mansion built of granite in 1880 & carefully restored by its new owner, Hiran Cooray of Jetwing Hotels & his wife, aided by architect Channa Daswatte. The architect's influence is seen in the newly created Netherleigh, a secret suite of minimalist persuasion hidden behind a curtain of Rajasthan carpets off a landing on the teak staircase to the bedrooms. The master (Warwick) suite sports a venerable 4-poster bed swathed in a plump duvet, & a restored cast-iron bathtub. There are 2 other bedrooms upstairs & a charming bedroom downstairs. This opens on to a hall with a library, a TV lounge, a drawing room with a baby grand piano & a formal, chandeliered dining room with adjacent breakfast room. Meals can also be taken in the garden or on the flagstone terrace so guests who don't want to join strangers as part of a house party atmosphere can eat in solitude. A butler is on hand, experienced cooks are in the open kitchen & the manager acts as host & guide for eco-, cultural & agricultural excursions. Rooms can be booked individually (rather than the entire bungalow) for a fascinating experience of Ceylon brought up to date in a setting of breathtaking views & utter tranquillity where the only sound is that of birdsong. **$$$$**

BADULLA *Population: 47,587 (2012 estimate)*

Badulla is the capital of Uva province, some 133km from Kandy, marking the southeast end of the hill country. It sits on a plain at an altitude of 680m and is surrounded by the high (up to 2,036m) Namunukula range of mountains with its nine peaks.

HISTORY Badulla became rather off the beaten track when trips to the east coast by foreigners were declared ill-advised. Yet it has historical connections that make it interesting enough for a visit. Former kings built temples there, including Muthiyangana, said to contain a collarbone relic of Lord Buddha. It looks modern but the core is believed to be 2,000 years old and built originally by King Devanampiya Tissa (250–210BC), first convert in the island to Buddhism. It has an ancient bell-shaped stupa and three shrine rooms with old wooden carvings.

The *kachcheri* (municipal secretariat) on a hill is built on the site of a royal palace and what was once the residence of the British administrator for the area. At the junction below the hill is a pillar with an inscription said to describe regulations of the 10th-century legal code of King Udaya III (935–38) of Rajarata. A curiosity is the huge creeper which snakes around the premises of the Kandy-period Lindamulla Pattini Devale (shrine). It is said to be at least 1km long.

The Portuguese occupied Badulla and set fire to much of it. Colonial fortifications remain, although hardly noticed, as part of the marketplace. St Mark's Anglican Church, dating from the British occupation, has a plaque commemorating the life of Major Thomas William Rogers who held nearly every government post in Badulla and was the driving force in the opening up and development of the hill country. He is remembered with shame for having boasted of killing 1,300 elephants. He is actually buried in Nuwara Eliya.

GETTING THERE
By train Badulla is the terminus of the line. The railway station was built in 1924 and is characterised by a liberal use of dark green paint. People queue for tickets in a cattle grid of guard rails until the booking office opens 30 minutes before a train's departure. There is a small lobby with park bench-type wooden seats and ornate wrought-iron railings and gates. It is all very relaxed and you suspect it has not changed much since the 1920s. There is a shed selling short eats and drinks. For times of the main trains between Badulla and Colombo, see page 151. The one-way fare in the observation car between Colombo and Badulla is Rs660; second class, Rs370.

By bus The bus station is next to the resthouse. The service between Colombo and Badulla is by route No 99.

By road Badulla is linked by four major roads with the rest of Sri Lanka. The A5 comes from Colombo via Kandy and Nuwara Eliya, and the A16 forks off the A4 from Colombo at Beragala. This is joined at Ella by the A23, which is the extension of the A2 from Colombo via Galle, Hambantota and Wellawaya. From Badulla, the A22 cuts eastwards to join the A4 to Pottuvil.

WHERE TO STAY AND EAT To experience life in a town that depends on its trading and not tourists, try the **Badulla Resthouse** (*17 rooms;* ☏ *055 2222299;* **$**). The rooms (basic with bathrooms in resthouse style) are grouped around a central garden courtyard. There is a television lounge and a bar as well as a restaurant that's good for rice and curry at lunchtime. Better though (more fun, more options) to stay in either Haputale, Bandarawela or Ella on the way to the east coast.

WHAT TO SEE AND DO The town yields a few interesting sights and has its own **Botanical Garden** set in a hectare by Race Course Road (itself a relic of colonial days). Admission to the garden, which is run by the Badulla Municipal Council, costs Rs5. As many of the plants are labelled it makes for an interesting stroll;

unfortunately the noise of foraging crows and the stench of a nearby garbage dump spoil what could be a pleasant experience.

The **Kataragama Devale** has ornate architectural features typical of the Kandyan period. At its entrance are elaborate carvings and inside the ornamental pavilion of carved pillars is a king's throne and a pair of ivory tusks donated by a 19th-century chieftain of Uva province.

Dunhinda Falls is 6km north of Badulla along the Badulla–Taldena road. There are buses (ask at the Badulla bus station for the right one) or three-wheelers. A rocky path winds through the undergrowth and there are soft-drink and snack stalls on the way. Monkeys can be troublesome. The falls (there are several small ones as well as the main one which drops 63m) are fed by the Badula Oya. The name in Sinhala suggests evaporating water, but it is the beauty of the falls that has evaporated due to the pollution caused by visitors.

On the way to Badulla on the A5 is Hali Ella, and about 10km from the town is the small village of **Bogoda** and a **unique wooden bridge**. It is a rare survival of timber architecture and engineering from the medieval Kandyan period. The supports of the bridge at its ends are three gigantic tree trunks on a rock base, and these are buttressed in the middle by two strong timber uprights. The bridge has a deck of timber enclosed by wooden balustrades. Carved pillars that were once lacquered in black, red and yellow support a roof of flat tiles.

BANDARAWELA   *Population: 65,111 (2012 estimate)*

Bandarawela, at 1,200m (4,000ft) above sea level, is overlooked by Nuwara Eliya in altitude as well as attitude. It is a town tourists drive through on their way to somewhere else. It has no 'star-class' hotels, no buildings of note, no 'season' when the Colombo crowd liven up the place, and not much happening. As if that isn't enough to make it worth visiting for the intrepid traveller, add the restorative value of its climate. The climate is governed by the monsoons and, because of its location, Bandarawela gets the benefit of both the northeast (November to January) and the southwest ones, plus being dry, even to the point of drought, in July and August. The rain keeps the hills, slopes and valleys green while the zest of the Uva breezes keeps sunny days from being oppressive. It's an invigorating, spring-like climate: good for plants, good for people.

Usually considered as second best to Nuwara Eliya as a hill station, its neighbour's popularity is Bandarawela's gain. The streets are not thronged with visitors, either local or foreign. It is a gentle, unpretentious place, an upcountry town that exists to supply the needs of the plantation workers, farmers and its hardworking inhabitants.

It is at the heart of Uva tea country; a tea that has a special quality imparted by the caressing of seasonal breezes. The undulating landscape is dedicated to tea, dominated by tall tin factories that never manage to blend into the shorn hillsides. Although the tea planters cut down the forest, wooded ravines remain. Valleys harbour paddy fields and vegetable plots.

As a town that depends on its own industry, not tourists, for survival, Bandarawela is ideal for seeing Sri Lanka at work. The town's population is mixed, with a Buddhist temple, a Hindu kovil, a Catholic church and a Muslim mosque in close proximity to each other. The post office building has its roots in colonial days, as does the Cargills shopping centre opposite; even if it has become a supermarket, it still has teak counters.

It is true that there are no hotels graded by the tourist board as worthy of stars, and I like to think that the hotels prefer it that way, so they are not overwhelmed by visitors hell-bent on star standards. Actually the town has one of the best colonial hotels in Sri Lanka, and a dozen or more comfortable bungalow guesthouses welcoming appreciative visitors.

GETTING THERE

By train Bandarawela is on the upcountry line from Colombo to Badulla, served by both day and night trains (see page 151 for timetable).

By bus The No 99 bus route from Colombo to Badulla passes through Bandarawela.

By road The town is on the A16 on the road from Haputale to Badulla, at 192km from Colombo. It can be reached from Nuwara Eliya on the A5 to Welimada and then a B road across country.

WHERE TO STAY AND EAT

Kirchhayn Bungalow (5 rooms) Aislaby Estate & Farm, Bandarawela; ☏057 4920556; e info@kirchhaynbungalow.com; www. kirchhaynbungalow.com. Bandarawela has plenty of budget-rate guesthouses & many of them, being former planters' bungalows, have charm as well as being cheap to stay in, but to live as tea planters used to do, treat yourself to a night or 2 here. The bungalow has been accommodating visitors since it was retained for guests by the owners following the nationalisation of tea plantations in 1972. It seems deliberately dated, & it is: the unco-ordinated collection of pictures on its walls & the selection of middlebrow books in its library reflect the modest tastes of British planters in the tropics. Despite taking paying guests & there being no tea planter host to entertain visitors to cocktails & dinner, Kirchhayn has the charm of a private home, not a guesthouse. Photographs show the former owner's parents picnicking in 1920s Ceylon & a note placed in each of the spacious bedrooms details the long connection of the family with Sri Lanka. Another note gives the names of the staff, & states: 'At 5pm mosquito coils will be lit & beds turned down. Also room water will be provided.' Period furniture sets the grand mood for country living where every need is foreseen by the ever-attentive staff, who can be summoned by ringing a hand bell. Drinks are set out as the sun goes down; dinner is served at a long table, course by course. The menu is chosen in discussion with the steward at the end of the previous meal & is a chance to enjoy typical planters' fare, such as roast pork followed by tree tomatoes & custard. Once when I was staying there, relaxing on the terrace with its view of lawns & flower beds, the steward

approached softly & asked: 'Would master like fresh peaches for tea?' The bedrooms are named after pioneering planters & the former owner's family. The owner's suite has French windows opening on to the lawns, & a slightly modernised bathroom. The Pyman room has crested antique twin beds, period furniture & a bright, spring-like atmosphere. All rooms have bathrooms en suite with bathtub & hot water & the price includes hearty breakfasts for 2. It takes about 30mins to drive from Bandarawela to Kirchhayn along the road to Attampitiya. The turn-off & junctions are signposted, even when the village road disintegrates into an estate track. Since there is no host (although the estate manager & his wife pop in to see everything is all right), guests are left to their own devices. The only interruption to the tranquillity is the cheerful song of birds, the chatter of tea pluckers beyond the hedge & the swish of the steward's sarong as he pads about serving tea. **$$$**

Bandarawela Hotel (33 non-AC rooms) 14 Welimada Rd, Bandarawela; ☏057 2222501; e bwhotel@sltnet.lk; www.aitkenspencehotels. com. Writing in his *Book of Ceylon* in 1908, H W Cave described Bandarawela as 'devoid of all attractions in the way of amusement'. He conceded, however, that 'there is a good hotel'. In 1929, Clare Rettie wrote in *Things Seen In Ceylon*: 'There is a good hotel & it is an excellent spot for those wishing to have a complete rest, but there are no buildings of special interest & not much to be had in the way of amusement.' Nothing has changed; the 'good hotel' described by both writers still exists: the Bandarawela Hotel is superbly reminiscent of Ceylon & Empire when tea, not tourism, ruled the hills. My own affair with the hotel began in 1980. We drove up the sweeping drive that rises grandly above the scuffle of traffic in the town. The lawn in front of the hotel's porch proved a fine place to take afternoon tea, & the service provided by the white-sarong-clad steward had a panache that matched the hotel's façade of genteel dignity. Later visits to stay for quiet weekends confirmed my first impression that the hotel is an experience in itself, & perhaps the real reason for going to Bandarawela. It is no mere transit inn to stay in 1 night on the way to somewhere else. I chose it as the place to commemorate my own half-century. It was a decision with the unexpected bonus that whenever I return there I feel I haven't got any older, as nothing has changed. The same steward is on duty, there are the same sanatorium-style, comfortable beds with brass knobs at the 4 corners, & the same hush, measured tread & lack of swank. The hotel's origins date back to when the railway line was forged through the hills from Nanu Oya to Bandarawela in 1894. Curiously, while other old hotels revamp themselves, the Bandarawela Hotel prospers because it seems never to have changed, reassuringly locked in a time warp somewhere between 1930 & 1950. This is emphasised by the uniforms of the doorman & security guard that hark back to colonial days & by the classic car & vintage motorbike parked outside. It could be considered a boutique hotel because the service is so assured & the place is utterly charming, but its room rates are too down to earth for pretension. While all the bedrooms have bathrooms en suite with hot & cold water, a link with the past is the door that opens from each bathroom to its outside garden or gantry. This was the entrance the 'lavatory coolies' used in order to clean the bathroom before there were flush toilets, & for the bath boys to bring 2 buckets of hot water per guest for the evening bath. The hairdryers & TVs in the rooms seem like interlopers. There is no dress code in the restaurant but guests will likely know by instinct that shorts & T-shirts do not match the silver service by stewards in starched tunics with brass buttons. The food, too, captures the past with starters like Scotch eggs & shepherd's pie as a main course. With its lounge heavy with chesterfields & blazing log fire in the snuggery that serves as a residents' bar, & its chalet-type frontage, the hotel guards its traditional image. Its

public bar with pool table & faded photos is worth finding: it has wood-panelled walls, heavy wooden shelves, & teak bar-stools designed for the heftiest of drinkers. It's the place to say cheers to the ghosts of those British settlers, pioneers & tea planters who patronised the hotel in its heyday. **$$**

🏠 **Cranford Villa** [map page 148] (5 non-AC rooms) 542 Kahagolla, Diyatalawa; 057 2223173; e info@cranfordvilla.com; www.cranfordvilla.com. For a different bungalow experience – it has been carefully designed for guests – try here. Set in the cantonment town of Diyatalawa & created out of a 1920s cottage, it is a spacious, peaceful place with excellent food & attendance by a resident chef & steward, & a lush, leafy garden where organic grapes are grown. Rooms are let individually but the exclusivity associated with a colonial bungalow ambience prevails. **$$**

🏠 **MF Bungalow** [map page 148] (6 non-AC rooms) Attampitiya, Pattiyagadara, Bandarawela; 057 2222618; m 072 3501919; e info@mfholifaybungalow.com; www. mfholidaybungalow.com. A 10min drive uphill past the Bandarawela bus station, this is a purpose-built holiday home, ideal for a family, a group of friends, or couples who want olde-worlde charm with modern fittings. Each room has a double & a single bed & attached bathroom including a shower with lashings of hot water. There are 3 lounges & a large dining room with valley views where a cook & staff are on hand to prepare a meal from guests' own supplies, or traditional Sri Lankan cuisine to advance order. The owner pops in every day but otherwise guests are left to their own devices to enjoy trekking through tea fields, or relaxing in the homely atmosphere where the mood music is from 1960s long-playing records. Just above basic in price because the rate includes dinner, bed & breakfast. **$$**

🏠 **Saffron Hill House** (4 rooms) 9 Attampitiya Rd, Banadarwela; 057 2222341; m 077 7908262; e indika@saffronhillhouse.com; www. saffronhillhouse.com. Saffron Hill House overlooks Bandarawela, a short drive up a road above the bus station. It was built in the 1930s as a holiday bungalow & the formal, rectangular shape of the bungalow has been softened by swirls of saffron-coloured paint. The central lounge is open on 3 sides, throwing focus onto the white & black painted fireplace. Faded photos of the original owners hang on the walls while above the picture rail on each wall is a restored mural of, incongruously, wintry landscapes. Adjoining the lounge is the formal dining room complete with oval table & scalloped, leather-backed dining chairs, another fireplace & more unusual murals. The space between the bungalow & the kitchen has been transformed into an open-sided dining gallery with a cement table on one side. 2 of the 4 bedrooms are large enough for a family of 3 in each. The master bedroom must be unique in Sri Lanka for its original, circular Art Deco furniture; even the bedheads are round. Each bedroom has a bathroom with a door to the garden & a bathtub with shower. Bathrooms are small, walled with titanium cement & with a washbasin on a concrete plinth almost blocking the entrance. With rates that are a lot lower than boutique hotels, & with a charm that is genuine, Saffron Hill House is a rare find. **$**

WHAT TO SEE AND DO Bandarawela is the closest town (5km) to **Dowa**. An example of Mahayana sculpture can be seen there in the huge unfinished Buddha image carved into the rock face. The Dowa Temple dates back to pre-Christian times. At the 13km post the **Koulpitiya Temple** has a characteristic Kandyan hipped roof, carved wooden pillars and drumming hall.

The attractions of Ella, Badulla, Haputale as well as **Diyatalawa** are within easy reach. Diyatalawa is 6km away and the site of naval and military camps. For a comprehensive programme of what to do and see in Bandarawela and Uva, look for *Day Programme: Eco Tourism in Uva*, and other publications by the Woodlands Network (*www.visitwoodlandsnetwork.org*).

BELIHUL OYA

At 160km from Colombo on the A4 to Haputale, this place is memorable for its old resthouse and the mountain stream (*oya*) that gurgles beside it. The towering mountain wall behind it is the edge of Horton Plains, 1,524m (5,000ft) above, and the stream is fed by waters from it. Belihul Oya is 570m above sea level.

 WHERE TO STAY AND EAT

⌂ **Belihul Oya Resthouse** (4 AC, 10 non-AC rooms) ☏ 045 2280156; e sales@ceylonhotels. net; www.ceylonhotels.lk. This has been a popular place for motorists to pull in for a snack or lunch for well over 50 years. It is built on the bank of the river & an open-sided restaurant annexe is a pleasant place for lunch or tea. Rooms are basic. **$**

ELLA

Situated at the junction of roads to the east, to the hill country and to the plains and coast, Ella was long a village to drive through, with perhaps a stop for tea at the resthouse. In recent years, the few pioneering guesthouses have been joined by more upmarket places as the visitor profile has changed from bargain-hunting backpackers to better-heeled nature lovers. Ella has become a destination in itself. It now has about 35 guesthouses dotted in the surrounding forest and hillsides, and a short main street vibrant with jolly cafés.

HISTORY Ella and legend are intertwined. Sita, the beautiful wife of Rama, is said to have been hidden in the caves at Ella by Ravana, King of Lanka, according to the *Ramanaya*, the great Indian epic dating to more than 1,000 years before Christ.

GETTING THERE
By train Day trains from Colombo Fort via Bandarawela stop at Ella on the outward and return journeys to/from Badulla (see page 151 for timetable).

By bus Local buses from Bandarawela stop at Ella.

By road Ella is 204km from Colombo Fort, and 12km from Bandarawela on the A16. Three-wheelers can be hired in Bandarawela to make the journey to Ella's famous gap, and also to the Ravana Falls, 5km south from Ella by the A2/A23.

⌂ WHERE TO STAY AND EAT

⌂ **Ella Adventure Park** [map page 148] (9 forest cottages, 1 treehouse, 12 riverside log cabins, 25 tents) Uva Karandagolla; ☎060 2555038; e info@wildholidays@sltnet.lk; www.ellaadventurepark.com. As you drive into its car park beside the Ella–Wellaraya road, close to the 15km post, there is no clue as to how different this hill-country resort really is. It looks like a comfortable upmarket hotel with trendy eco-décor, judging by its entrance. However, the essence of this retreat created in the forest is adventure. Outward Bound training courses are held there & tough team-building activities are laid on for corporate clients. The 12 log cabins (& 25 tents) beside the river are a long & difficult walk, climb & slither from the reception desk. The brainchild of a Sri Lankan army officer who was inspired by his nature-loving father to open the wilderness to seekers of remote peace & adventure, the park of 25ha offers many challenges: abseiling (rappelling), rock climbing, canoeing, paragliding, jungle trekking & birdwatching. A safari to Udawalawe to see elephants is available. The other side of Ella Adventure Park is luxury in the jungle. The cottages are built of granite & secluded from each other by thick foliage. There are 2 bedroom units in each cottage with a granite wall dividing their shared veranda beside a glade with its own forest-wood furniture for dining alfresco. There is even room service in the forest. The rooms are furnished in rustic fantasy style, with beds made from branches stripped of their bark, mirrors framed with creepers & lamps shaded by hollowed-out knots of wood. The shower (with hot water) is open to the sky & the water spouts from a hole in the rock. It has the nice conceit of a glass door even though there is no door to the bathroom & the entrance is covered with a canvas flap. The tree-house suite really is built in a tree & comes complete with bathroom & dreamy views of the valley & distant hills. Footpaths (with lights designed as rocks) link the cottages & treehouse with the reception & lounge areas. These are built on stilts, & the A-frame restaurant has sides of reed

curtains. This amazing retreat is suitable even for those allergic to adventure or challenges. **$$**

⌂ **Planter's Bungalow** [map page 148] (3 dbl rooms, 1 cottage, no AC) Karandagolla, Ella; ☎057 4925902; m 077 6251414; e thebungalow@wow.lk; www.plantersbungalow.com. Located above the main A23 road linking Ella with Wellaraya, this restored planter's bungalow is a treat for those who want to retreat to nature with every comfort, good food & fine conversation, if the host is in residence. At 11km south of Ella, it is reached by a turn-off up a hill beside the Karandagolla bus halt. This rural trail is being developed as an alternative road to Bandarawela but the bungalow remains isolated at the end of a fork in the road to the left just after (& above) a school building. There are 3 double bedrooms (including 1 with an enormous sitting room) & a separate tiny cottage with outside bathroom & kitchen, & rooftop dining deck. Converted by a retired Brit & his wife, this is an elegant bungalow home with superb food (the owners once ran a Michelin-star inn in Britain) in a picturesque setting at a bargain price, just above basic. **$$**

⌂ **Dream Café** (2 AC rooms, 5 suites) Main St, Ella; ☎057 2228950; e dreamcafe_ella@yahoo.com; www.dreamcafeandguesthouseella.com. The place with style to eat in Ella, with an elegant menu to match, at prices that are slightly over the top for locals but fine for tourists. Entrance is off the main A23 road to a cobbled courtyard restaurant where the genial young owner, Saminda, greets all visitors as though they are old friends. Any item on the carefully selected menu is available from 07.30 to 22.30, every day. Free internet & Wi-Fi. Inside are 2 simple rooms with attached bathroom, while at the side is a comfortable suite with bright décor, backlit local paintings & its own entrance from the courtyard. 5 spacious suites with wooden floors have been added on the 1st floor. **$**

⌂ **Ella Resthouse** (14 non-AC rooms) Ella; ☎057 2228655; e reservations@ceylonhotels.net; www.ceylonhotelscorporation.com. This is a remarkable reincarnation of the old Ella Resthouse. The stunning view between the gap in the mountain range remains, enhanced by the grandeur of the motel's new granite-walled entrance. New rooms have been added, complete with modern showers, & each has a minibar & TV. Room 304 comes with a large terrace, ideal for cocktails with a view. The restaurant is below & there are tables in a pavilion by the garden at the edge of the gap. **$**

WHAT TO SEE AND DO The Ella gap view is stunning and seen at its best from the garden of the Ella Resthouse. The Ravana Falls is a minor waterfall of 9m drop located beside the road to Wellawaya, 5km south of Ella. It is sourced by a stream that is a tributary of the Kirindi Oya and plunges over ledges into the valley close to a bend in the road. There are caves near the falls and in one of them, legend says, Sita, wife of Rama, was hidden by Ravana. Alas, all romantic associations are dispelled by the graffiti painted on the rocks around the stream and pool.

On leaving Ella in the opposite direction, heading for Badulla on the A16, the Kinellan Tea Factory is on the right, with a kiosk selling factory-fresh tea.

HALDUMMULLA

Haldummulla is a popular place to stay for a few days because of its climate, views and great trekking. The hamlet of Haldummulla is on the A4 between Belihul Oya and the road fork at Beragala, where one road goes to Koslanda and the south coast (via Wellawaya), and the other climbs up to Haputale. Driving from Belihul Oya, keep your eyes alert for the 177km post and a gated entrance up to the left to the Green Valley Holiday Resort, one of those special, secret places that Sri Lanka does so well. It's easier coming from Beragala when you'll see Green Curry Cottage (part of the complex) after 5km on the right.

 WHERE TO STAY AND EAT This listing is included on the map, page 148.

⌂ Green Valley Holiday Resort & Green Curry Cottages (1 AC lodge [3 bedrooms], 12 AC cottages) 178km post, Haldummulla; ✆ 057 5670547; www.greenvalleyholidayresort. com. The resort has grown out of the Green Cherry Café & the adjoining Mount Field Cottages. On a verdant hillside overlooking the road to Haputale, different kinds of accommodation for travellers, tourists, Sri Lankans & nature lovers in an unspoiled, eco-friendly rural setting, at various prices to suit every holidaymaker's budget. Accommodation units include a grand lodge, self-catering chalets, eco-cottages, family rooms, a dormitory & chauffeur's cottage, discreetly set in a hillside woodland, surrounded by flowers & tropical foliage where birds & butterflies hover & monkeys gambol. Ideally located as a base for discovering the heartland of Sri Lanka just 4hrs' drive from the west & east coasts, 3hrs from the new international airport in the south, & 2hrs' drive through the hills to Kandy & the gateway to the Cultural Triangle. There is a freshwater hillside rock pool fed by a cool mountain stream & a garden swimming pool overlooking the lush green valley set in 20 acres of verdant hillside gardens. Good, wholesome food freshly prepared on order (**$**). Easily reached by train to Idalgashina station & trek (with pre-arranged guide) through the forest & plantations, while the luggage goes by road, or by tuk-tuk from Haputale station. Or travel by long-distance bus (route number 99) on the A4 between Colombo & Badulla to stop at Haldummulla. **$**

WHAT TO SEE AND DO The stunning **Bambarakanda Fall** plunges 263m over a wall of rock to a deep pool, if it's been raining a lot. During a drought, it dries to a trickle, so it's best to visit between October and January. It falls through steep rocks and a forest of pines between the Welihena (1,375m above sea level) and the Bambarakanda (1,470m) mountains. The pool at its base is 15km walking distance of a motorable road off the A4 at Kalupahana.

5

World's End is Sri Lanka's largest ravine and, on the proverbial clear day when you can see forever, offers the finest view in the country. However, heat haze and mist stirred up by the monsoon can cloud the experience. The escarpment is sheer for about 328m and then slopes a little less steeply for another 1,312m. The coast on the horizon is about 80km distant. The favoured way to World's End is the trek across Horton Plains.

HAPUTALE Population: 5,559 (2012 estimate)

This town exists because of tea, and has the atmosphere of a bustling market town. The railway runs right through it and stallholders by the track scramble to clear away their vegetables when a train comes along. Only independent travellers found their way there in the past and accommodation was limited to a few basic guesthouses. That changed in 2007 when a star-class hotel (Olympus Plaza) opened, which attracts holidaying Sri Lankans as well as tourists discovering the perfect climate (crisp mountain air, bright sunny days and comfortably cool nights). The town is 181km from Colombo on the A4, and 1,429m above sea level.

You get the full impact of Haputale's precipitous location when you walk or drive from the town's main junction for 100m along the A4 in the direction of Haldummulla. You can't see the road is turning right and you feel it sails off into space over the hills and plains stretched out below.

In spite of not being on the list of mainstream tourist destinations, Haputale has a good communications centre, run by an enthusiastic Haputale resident known to travellers, tourists and residents simply as 'Loga'. He is a mine of information dispensed from his tiny internet centre in the block of shops along the road from the railway station (*Website Link, 3 Urban Council Complex, Station Rd, Haputale;* \ *057 2268612;* e *websitelink@hotmail.com or loga182001@yahoo. com*). His enterprise has broadband internet units, IDD telephone booths, and he can do technical things with CDs and computers and can advise on bus and train times and the best places to visit. He does photocopying, sells stamps, toilet paper and mineral water, and is a real travellers' friend, insisting visitors have a cup of (complimentary) tea. He also takes tourists on gentle trekking expeditions along trails he has discovered himself. This is also the place to purchase fantastically fresh tea of Loga's own brand, the Haputale Tea Garden product of orthodox as well as organic and special green tea.

HISTORY Haputale was created by the plantation industry. When coffee was profitable, cultivation was expanded into the forest-clad mountains of Dimbulla, the region around Adam's Peak, and into the forests of Haputale. By the mid 1860s, however, coffee was in decline. Some planters turned to growing tea instead, but it was not until the arrival of Thomas Lipton, who opened an office in Colombo in 1890, that tea became the reason for Haputale's development. Lipton bought up estates (including Dambatenne near Haputale) at low prices and pursued a professional approach to their cultivation. Haputale's prosperity stems from his success in creating a demand for Lipton's tea, and for creating a way to meet that demand.

GETTING THERE
By train The best trains are the morning departures from Colombo Fort station. The journey takes about nine hours from Colombo (see page 151 for the current train schedule).

By bus No 99 is the long-distance service from Colombo to Badulla, which stops in Haputale.

By road Haputale is 181km from Colombo, via Ratnapura, on the A16, on the way to Bandarawela. Access can also be made from the south of Sri Lanka (Hambantota) via the A2 and A4 to reach the A16 at Beragala.

ADVENTURE TOURISM

Those who think a visit to Sri Lanka is adventure enough will be surprised at the extent of adventure activities that are organised for visitors. There is ballooning (arranged through hotels in the Cultural Triangle and in Galle) as well as a climbing wall and rock climbing, kayaking, rafting, mountain biking and hiking. Specialist tour operators are listed on pages 19–20.

WHITE-WATER RAFTING ON THE KITULGALA RIVER This is the starter for white-water rafting enthusiasts (*Kitulgala Adventure Centre;* \ *011 2199323;* e *info@kithulgalaadventures.com; www.kithulgalaadventures.com*). There is also the Adventure Base Camp (*250 Kalukohuthanna, Kithulgala;* m *077 3069903;* e *info-campkithulgala.com; www.adventurecampkitulgala.com*), which advertises white-water rafting, outbound training, adventure sports and camping.

It takes 3½ hours from Colombo to drive to Kotmale River, where the rafting starts a few kilometres below the magnificent St Clair Waterfall. This six-hour, grade-5 river journey requires previous white-water rafting experience and is a must for any white-water rafter.

A drive of 90 minutes from Colombo is all it takes to join in three hours' rafting through bigger and better rapids (grade 4) than Kitulgala on the Lower Sitawaka River, with a swing-bridge jump of 7m into the river to get the adrenalin flowing.

CANOEING One-, two- or three-day trips by canoe are organised from the Bo-path Ella Waterfalls to the Kaluganaga on a small jungle river, with riverside campsites. This is an ideal adventure to enjoy wildlife, as well as a bottle of wine with friends, while floating down a river. Similar trips are also organised on the Kelani River, closer to Colombo. Canoeing can be arranged through the same operators as listed above for rafting.

RIDING Horseriding is available through the **Premadasa Horseriding School** (*11/12 Melder Pl, Nugegoda;* \ *011 2820588;* e *ridingschool@ premadasa.lk; www.premadasa.lk*). There are branches in the Colombo suburb of Battaramulla and in Nuwara Eliya, Kandy, Tissamaharama, Yala, Kandalama, Sigiriya, Ahungalla and Kalpitiya. The headquarters of the riding school also arranges riding holidays as well as the hiring of horses and carriages or horse carts and for the hiring of dancing, carriage and riding horses for events.

OTHER COMPANIES/ACTIVITIES Adventure sports including camping, rock climbing, abseiling and paragliding can be organised through **Ella Adventure Park** (*Uva Karandagolla;* \ *060 2555038*) (see page 160).

GETTING AROUND Minibuses can be hired from the parking place in the centre of the town, beside the railway line and level crossing. Because of the steep roads and rough surfaces, especially the estate roads, a minibus is better than a three-wheeler (which are not much in evidence at Haputale anyway).

🏠 WHERE TO STAY AND EAT

🏠 **Kelburne Mountain View Resort** (3 bungalows) Haputale; ✆057 2268029, (reservations) ✆011 2573382; e mountainview@sltnet.lk; www.kelburnemountainview.com. This resort in Haputale has more than even 5-star hotels can offer: a personal chef, butler & room boy, private bungalows with pure mountain air, hot water in the bathrooms & a view other people trek to World's End to see. It is 'private property' according to the sign alongside the unmetalled track that leads from the Haputale–Dambatenne road. The 3 bungalows, each in its own flower garden, are built at the very edge of a plateau suspended 1,300m (4,500ft) above a stippled quilt of hills & hazy plains stretching 40km to Kataragama & the south coast. The main bungalow, Aerie Cottage, has 2 bedrooms & 2 sitting rooms (the main one has a log fire on request) & a large veranda overlooking the view. The more quaint Wildflower Cottage, reached down a steep path of granite steps, has 3 rooms, 1 with bathroom en suite. Rose Cottage, at a higher elevation, is more modern, also with 3 bedrooms. Each bungalow is cosy, furnished as though belonging to a friend who has kindly lent it to you & wants you to make yourself feel at home. Meals are served in the dining room of each bungalow, or in the central pavilion, by a barefoot steward in tunic & sarong. The cooking is hearty planters' fare with a tropical flavour as British-inspired recipes have been spiced up. There is no bar so when we wanted wine, the kitchen boy ran down to Haputale to buy a bottle. For breakfast we had egg hoppers (ordered the day before to give the cook time to prepare). This is like an open crêpe with an egg fried in the middle & is served with beef curry & *seeni sambol* (a sweet & spicy onion relish). Enjoyed in the early sunshine on a terrace outside the bedroom, there could be no better start to an active day. **$$**

🏠 **Olympus Plaza Hotel** (26 rooms) 75 Welimada Rd, Haputale; ✆057 2268544; e info@olympusplazahotel.com; www.olympusplazahotel.com. A new property that is certain to make Haputale even more popular. Built on a hillside with views of Fox Hill, the Sleeping Warrior mountain range & trucks toiling up the steep roads below, the hotel has 6 floors (no lift). Rooms are on the 4 floors below the reception level & on the floor above. Entrance is on the 5th floor, where there is also a restaurant; the bar with stunning views & contemporary furniture is on the top floor. Light floods in through walls of windows that have chrome rails in front of them to stop guests stepping out into the view. The early morning sun bathes the balconies & the tea terrace at the entrance, especially welcome after a temperature drop at night. All rooms have hot water in attached bathrooms & this, being a family-run property, is an easy-going place, with rooms at the peak of the basic price range. **$$**

🏠 **Adisham** [map page 148] (2 rooms) Adisham, Haputale; ✆057 2268030. 'Lost time is never found again' says the sign at the entrance to this neo-Gothic retreat 3km from Haputale. It is used as a training centre for the Benedictine order now but was built in 1931 as the home of Sir Thomas Villiers, scion of the houses of Clarendon & Bedford. Villiers was the black sheep of a distinguished family (a grandfather was Lord John Russell, twice prime minister of Britain) who arrived in Ceylon in 1887 with US$10 in his pocket. He parlayed this modest stake into a fortune, rewarding himself by building Adisham (named after the rectory where he was born & resembling Leeds Castle in Kent), thereby expressing his nostalgia for the Home Counties & arrogance at his own success. This Englishman's castle patterned on Tudor lines is an anachronism in isolation 6°N of the Equator, surrounded by lushly wooded valleys, acres of tea bushes & cloud-shrouded mountains. Adisham is a solid folly, though, bitterly cold in winter & blissfully hot in summer. It is a grey, brooding pile of granite blocks & turret windows with teak frames. Guest rooms are in the former chauffeur's quarters over the garage converted into a dining hall. 1 has a bathroom of sorts, with cold water fed by a mountain stream. Guests can stay only by advance arrangement; day visitors are sometimes allowed to tour the lower part of the house, including Villiers's fine library. **$**

🏠 **High Cliffe** (9 rooms) 15 Station Rd, Haputale; 📞 057 2268096. The pioneering guesthouse, this used to be a haven for hippies, described in a 1980 guidebook as having '6 dorm beds at Rs7 per person ... it's an old fashioned & easy-going place'. It is still easy-going, but everything else has changed ... for the better. It is in the centre of town (on the wrong side of the rail track). It is built of granite blocks with the curious addition of a mock frontage roof-wall that makes it look like a converted cinema. A wall secludes the tiny garden from the spread of the town; a balustrade of black & white defines the entrance loggia. While the roof is green galvanise (its original tiles have long gone), the walls are solid & the windows distinctive patterns of wood & coloured panes. The dormitory beds have been thrown out, replaced with rustic-style double beds in 3 bedrooms, which have attached bathrooms & hot water. Domestic tourists have discovered High Cliffe now that the hippies are history. The management has noticed that local guests stay longer & eat all 3 meals a day there, while foreigners tend to stay overnight & then move on to another town on the travellers' trail. An annexe with 6 bright, airy & neat rooms with staggering views on the 2 upper floors has been added with a secret entrance; you sidle inside an opening in the wall to find stairs leading up past a lively bar in the old-fashioned plantation workers' style (there's a lounge bar for visitors upstairs). Snacks of fried fish are on offer with drinks by the tumbler; waiters are summoned by electric bells. **$**

WHAT TO SEE AND DO From Kelburne you can hike through the tea plantations, or down to Haputale, or scramble up a steep path to the summit of the hill behind the 20ha estate for a view of the plains and town. The bungalow that once belonged to tea pioneer Thomas Lipton can be visited on the neighbouring estate of Dambatenne. **Lipton's seat**, a viewpoint overlooking a misty canyon, is accessible by an atrocious road. It's best to go by vehicle hired in Haputale (ask the driver's assistance) as it's about a 10km distance. There is a fee payable at the entrance gate – a hike or drive of 1.3km from the summit – Rs50 'per soul' and Rs100 per vehicle.

> ### ROYAL MAIL
>
> There is a rural post office about 500m walk past the bus station on the road to Bandarawela that still has an original George VI red pillar box outside it for posting letters.

Haputale is well located for visiting Bandarawela and Diyatalawa, along a cantonment, 9km distant off the road to Bandarawela. Now the site of naval and military camps, **Diyatalawa** is where Boers and Germans were prisoners during World War I, and where military personnel came to convalesce during World War II.

Diyatalawa has a reputation as a health resort because of its salubrious and dry climate. Little of the southwest monsoon rains reach the place, although high winds do in the monsoon season. It was known as Happy Valley when it housed a rural missionary settlement founded by the Reverend Samuel Langdon of the Wesleyan Mission.

There is a small **church** on a bluff above the centre of Haputale town. It is next to the bus station, which has shaved off some of the church land. British residents from many generations are buried there and the church is administered by the St Andrew's interdenominational church in Colombo.

HATTON *Population: 16,237 (2012 estimate)*

Hatton owes its existence not just to tea but also because it is the rail gateway to Adam's Peak and thus hugely popular during the pilgrimage season.

GETTING THERE

By train As well as the regular trains serving the hill country from Colombo and Kandy, special trains run during the season (January–April) for climbing Adam's Peak. The journey by train from Colombo takes six hours to Hatton.

By bus Dedicated buses, No 18-2, serve Hatton via Avissawella and Ginigatena from Colombo.

By road It's a pleasant drive on the A7 via Avissawella and Kitulgala to Hatton, a distance of 123km from Colombo.

WHERE TO STAY AND EAT The road to Hatton leads through tea country, rolling hills of precisely shorn tea bushes. It is also the land of planters' bungalows; solid, granite block buildings sprawled atop hillocks overlooking tea gardens. The Tea Garden Hotel and Hatton Resthouse are included on the map, page 148.

The **Tea Garden Hotel** complex (*11 rooms; Colombo Rd, Watawala;* \ *051 2237236;* **$**) used to be a planter's bungalow. In appearance it still is, even though it now takes paying guests and is a managed property with staff to take care of them. Since this is no longer a planter's residence, it lacks home comforts, and a host, but nevertheless three of the bedrooms have fireplaces, as does the sitting room which also has a fine wooden floor. The bungalow is on the side of a hill, with quite a steep driveway.

Also on the way to Hatton, and on a hill, is the **Hatton Resthouse** (*7 rooms; Hatton;* \ *051 2222751;* **$**), more used to local guests than foreigners. It has a small sitting room and a dining hall where rice and curry appears quickly at lunchtime. There is a dispensary-style bar.

Hatton has come into prominence since it became the place to visit at the start of the **Ceylon Tea Trails** (*4 bungalows; 46/38a Navam Mawatha, Colombo 2;* \ *011 2303888;* e *manager@teatrails.com; www.teatrails.com;* **$$$$** *pp*), set up in 2005. This is not some kind of hare and hounds paperchase through the tea gardens but the brand name of four tea plantation bungalows that take paying guests on a room-by-room basis, and not by letting the whole bungalow (see box, pages 168–9). The leisure division of tea brokers Forbes & Walker and Dilmah Tea, the Sri Lankan company known worldwide for its premium tea, are partners in the venture.

The idea of Ceylon Tea Trails is for guests to holiday in one of the four bungalows in the famous Bogowantalawa tea district, at over 1,219m (4,000ft) above sea level. The bungalows are all run to the same exacting standards (of guests as well as of staff) and guests stay in one – or all if they like – while discovering about tea and village life, and experiencing the remarkable scenic diversity and adventure activities of the area.

From Hatton it takes about 30 minutes' drive to get to three of the bungalows, with another 15 minutes to reach the furthest, Tientsin at 8½km from Norwood Junction (a town, not a railway station). There are bright green road signs to reassure apprehensive drivers they are indeed on the tea trail. After turning right by a sign off the road to Norwood, the road passes an aqueduct that carries water for a private generating scheme on the way to the two bungalows overlooking the Castlereagh reservoir. These are **Summerville**, built in 1923 with four guest rooms, and **Castlereagh**, built in 1925 with five guest rooms and a swimming pool.

The road to the right at Norwood Junction to Upcott leads to the **Norwood Bungalow**, at 14.5km from Hatton. This was built in 1890 and rebuilt with a Mediterranean ambience in 1950. It has five guest rooms and a long, and chilly, swimming pool of blue mosaic set in the centre of its carefully mown green lawn.

The left fork at Norwood Junction is the road to Bogawantalawa. It passes through Norwood Bazaar, like a cowboy town with shops lining the main street, and then opens up to tea country again. The sides of the road are neatly planted with vetyver grass to contain soil erosion. A tea factory that thinks itself rather special has changed its name to Tea Processing Centre. A right fork leads to **Tientsin Bungalow**, built in 1939 and, at 1,402m (4,600ft), the highest of the bungalows. It has six rooms and a tennis court.

While every Tea Trails bungalow is different in character, they have been transformed, at an investment cost of Rs200 million, into designer-smart luxury. The beds are wonderfully comfortable although tiresomely draped with mosquito nets. The bathrooms have period tiles and neo-colonial fittings, including ponderous bathtubs (which you must clamber into if you want a shower) and liquid soap in dispensers. Food is prepared in the bungalow kitchen according to various table d'hôte menus. Each bungalow has a long, formal dining table where friends can dine together, and tables on patios where couples can eat privately (but it can be cold at night). A butler and stewards are on hand. The room rate per person includes morning tea in bed, all meals plus afternoon cream tea, house spirits and wines, log fires, guided walks and the run of the bungalow, its library and gardens, as well as service charge and the government taxes.

Formerly called the Yellow House, **Slightly Chilled** (*6 non-AC rooms; Dalhousie;* ✆ *051 3519430;* m *071 9098710;* e *info@slightlychilled.tv; www.slightlychilled.tv;* **$**) is as spectacularly colourful as its new name is evocative of the climate. It's an hour's ride by three-wheeler from Hatton station, down to Maskeliya then along the road to Adam's Peak (or a day's drive by minivan from Kandy). It's popular as *the* place to be based (as long as you've made advance reservations) for the climb up Adam's Peak, with great local food and an atmosphere of camaraderie.

WHAT TO SEE AND DO The reason visitors go to Hatton is to climb **Adam's Peak**. The most popular route is to travel to Hatton and then on to Maskeliya and Dalhousie (for the climb) by road. There are buses with specials operating from Hatton in the season (January–April).

Adam's Peak, 2,243m (7,359ft) above sea level, is revered by Sri Lanka's four main religions. Its English name of Adam testifies to a significance for Christians who, not to be outdone by the Buddhists, believe the image of a footprint to be found at its summit is that of Adam. Traditionally, however, the footprint-shaped indentation on a boulder at the pinnacle of Sri Pada (the Sinhala name for the mountain) represents where Buddha paused on one of his visits to Sri Lanka. Hindus have always venerated the mountain too. For them its name is Sivan Adi Padham, and calls to mind the creative dance of the god Siva. Muslims consider that the foot impression resulted from Adam standing there an age to expiate his disobedience. The Sri Lankan name of Samanala Kanda suggests it was a sacred mountain even before the advent of Buddhism. Saman was one of the four guardian deities of the island; a pre-Buddhist god.

Whatever the belief, the mountain has been a point of pilgrimage and worship for millennia. The time to climb is during January to April when the weather is calm and bright. It is traditional to climb by night (the path of uneven steps is illuminated) to reach the peak in time for sunrise. If you decide to climb, plan on resting for a couple of days afterwards as, unless you are pretty fit, your leg muscles are going to ache, making walking even a short distance quite painful.

Writing in *Sri Lanka Wildlife News*, Lynn and Peter Eastcliff described their experience climbing Adam's Peak with a group of Sri Lankan friends:

We all started off together at 1.45am but gradually became separated into two groups. At first the slope upwards was quite gradual and the path quite smooth and well maintained but as we went further the steps became more rugged and our legs started to tire. Although there were plenty of places to stop for refreshments, we tried to stop only when necessary to catch our breath or to take a short drink.

At 4.00am I felt very tired and my legs were aching from the effort of climbing the steep steps. I could easily have given up at that point as I thought there was still another two hours to go but Peter just held on to me and I struggled on. Within 30 minutes I saw the sign about removing footwear and was amazed and delighted to know we had reached the summit.

Everyone had warned us about how cold it was at the top but we did not realise how cold it would be. An icy wind blew across the top and we were soon shivering along with everyone else. At this point we decided to go back down to the last shelter and stay there until nearer sunrise.

We started back up about 6.20am and it took only five minutes so we had plenty of time to find a good place to watch the sunrise. It was spectacular to say the least. Once it was fully above the horizon we saw the mountain's shadow in the clouds below. We also visited the shrine of the 'footprint' hoping that we had not interrupted those still at prayer.

We found the journey down more difficult than expected. The climb up had taken its toll on our knee joints so it was a slow, painful process.

HOLIDAY BUNGALOWS

When plantations were denationalised in the 1990s, many of their bungalows fell vacant as modern management efficiencies and better communications were introduced, so it was no longer necessary for every tea estate to have a resident planter. Some companies have taken a leaf out of the book of hospitality and turned their empty bungalows into holiday homes. Usually these bungalows are staffed with cook/caretaker and other help. Sometimes guests are expected to take their own supplies, although some bungalows (such as the three at the **Kelburne Mountain View Resort** (see page 164) supply meals as an extra.

Also near Haputale is the **Thotulagala Bungalow** [map page 148] which, having been a circuit bungalow for touring plantation directors, is accustomed to hosting visitors. Its location some 3km from Haputale is indicated by a sign proclaiming that the area produces 'probably the finest tea'. A rocky road leads downhill to it, past thickets of tropical foliage with flashes of deep red anthuriums growing beside a lotus pond glimmering in the sunlight.

The bungalow consists of three linked pavilions with the middle pavilion as the dining room, with its own French-window access to the garden. There is a smokers' den with teak-panelled walls and a fireplace, and seven bedrooms; most have shared bathrooms and antiquated plumbing, although solar-powered hot water has been installed.

I discovered there was another reason for staying in a planter's bungalow than just to enjoy a bout of chilly nostalgia, when the bungalow's chef bounced out into the garden with a pair of binoculars. He was going birdwatching and was enthusiastic about the many varieties of birds in the vicinity. 'This is an eco-resort,' he said proudly. 'We grow our own organic vegetables in the garden.' Another plantation bungalow close to Haputale is **Sherwood** [map page 148], which is also available for renting in its entirety.

KOTMALE

Renowned today for its reservoir and production of cheese, Kotmale is an area steeped in history. It forms part of the mountainous region that Sinhalese kings deliberately left in forest so it would generate sufficient rainfall for rice cultivation in areas below.

HISTORY It was to Kotmale with its forest that the warrior king, Dutugemunu (161–137BC), fled to escape the wrath of his father. The Kandyan kings hid the sacred tooth relic in Kotmale during political instability, the last occasion being during the British occupation in 1815.

GETTING THERE
By train The nearest railway station is Nawalapitiya on the main Colombo to Badulla line.

By bus Get down at Nawalapitiya (bus No 16 from Colombo) and ask at the bus station for local buses that go to Kotmale.

By road Kotmale is 13km from Nawalapitiya on the road to Talawakele. It can also be reached on the road that turns off to the left on the Nuwara Eliya to Kandy road (A5), close to Ramboda Falls Hotel.

It takes three hours to drive from Haputale to Nuwara Eliya and past St Clair Falls, which can be seen from the neat gardens of the **St Andrew's Bungalow** [map page 148]. This is a cosy planter's home, built in 1916, with its original teak ceilings and polished wooden floors, but with modern furniture and reproduction four-poster beds in its six bedrooms.

Just ten minutes away is a more spacious bungalow, **Rosita** [map page 148], which planters pronounce as 'Rossiter'. It is a 1930s property with four bedrooms and staff quarters. The master bedroom has a fireplace and its own French-window access to wide lawns and plunging views. There are more fireplaces in the lounge and smoking den, and a grand, antique oval table in the dining room. On a clear day, the island's venerated Adam's Peak can be seen from the garden and a cairn of granite marks the viewpoint.

These four bungalows are managed by **Colombo Fort Hotels** (*53 1/1 Sir Baron Jayatilake Mawatha, Colombo 1;* \ *011 2381644;* e *salessvh@sltnet.lk; www.forthotels.lk*). Since each bungalow can sleep up to ten people they can work out very good value if sharing with a large group (**$$$$** per bungalow).

Taprospa Labookellie Villa [map page 148] (*Labookellie Estate, Nuwara Eliya;* e *info@taprospa; www.taprospa.com;* **$$$**) has the additional attraction of being next to the very popular Labookellie Tea Factory on the road to Nuwara Eliya from Kandy. Each of its three bedrooms has a jacuzzi with garden and valley view and a qualified masseur on call. Stunningly decorated and designed for comfort with the theme of 'boutique luxury in harmony with nature'.

There are several other bungalows that have recently been refurbished by their owning companies and thrown open their doors for renting by families or friends prepared to muck in together. These advertise in the *Hit Ad* magazine of the *Sunday Times* (Colombo). (See box, page 55.)

WHERE TO STAY AND EAT

Mas Villa (formerly Pahala Walauwa) (5 rooms) Kotmale; m 077 7715747; e resv@masvilla.com; www.masvilla.com. A reproduction Kandyan mansion on the banks of the Kotmale reservoir, Mas Villa is the best for country-style living. It is in an isolated & peaceful location of paddy fields & woods, reached by a private road. It has been built on the site of an ancient *walauwa* (mansion). The entrance leads into a central courtyard of wooden columns & a gallery giving access to the bedrooms, 3 standard, a suite & a master bedroom with modern amenities; there is an outdoor swimming pool, spa & mini gym. Advance reservation is essential. It is a 1hr drive (38km) from Peradeniya & 40mins' drive from Nuwara Eliya. It is 548m (1,800ft) above sea level & the temperature can be cool at night. **$$$**

WHAT TO SEE AND DO The Mahaweli Authority maintains the **Kotmale Dam View Point**, a popular attraction with touring schoolchildren. Galleries contain photographs of the building of the dam and visitors can walk out to a tower to gaze at the dam and reservoir. It was begun in 1977 as one of the four headworks (the others are Victoria, Maduru Oya and Randenigala) of the Mahaweli Development Programme for the generation of hydro-electric power by harnessing the waters of the Mahaweli Ganga. By 1995, all the headworks were completed. The Kotmale project was financed by Sweden and built by Swedish contractors with British consultants.

NUWARA ELIYA   *Population: 27,326 (2012 estimate)*

A study on how to persuade tourists to stay longer in Nuwara Eliya, instead of the customary one-night stopover, observed:

> Most foreign visitors come on package tours and, as a rule, spend one night in Nuwara Eliya only: arrivals are usually in the afternoon and departures after breakfast the following morning. Apparently tour operators consider Nuwara Eliya as a must but do not think it opportune to let their clients spend more time there than the absolute minimum.

What a shame, I thought, until I realised that Nuwara Eliya, with its hint of English resort towns of the 1950s and its uncertain climate, might not appeal to visitors from Europe. However, when Sri Lankans working in Colombo want to relax, they don't go to Kandy or the beach resorts; they head for Nuwara Eliya. There they have a different environment, natural beauty, low-cost places to stay and eat, and everyone is in a holiday mood.

PLANTATION CHURCH

High on a hill on the road to Castlereagh reservoir is the Warleigh Church, built in 1878 by British planters and maintained in perfect condition now by its sole 16 Anglican parishioners. To peep inside is to understand how the planters who gave their lives to develop the tea industry maintained the traditions of their faith. There is an old pipe organ, precious 19th-century stained-glass windows and worn, timber pews. Tombstones are testimony to those who died young, whole families buried in their adopted homeland. Some British planters, like Michael Turnbull (1921–97), who retired to Britain, even had their ashes sent back to be interred in this land they loved.

HISTORY The credit for being the first Brit to visit Nuwara Eliya goes to Dr John Davy who reached there in 1819. Dr John Davy was the brother of Sir Humphrey Davy who invented the miner's safety lamp which bore his name. He described Nuwara Eliya as 'beautiful … possessing a fine climate (certainly a cool climate) … quite deserted by man … the domain entirely of wild animals'.

Davy's guides called the place Neueraelliyapattan, which shows it was known before he arrived. There were signs of an ancient irrigation system. Sir James Emerson Tennent wrote in 1859:

> Neuera-ellia was of course previously known by the natives. It had been the retreat
> of the Kandyan kings, who fled thither from the Portuguese about the year 1610, and
> from the circumstances of its having thus become an imperial residence, 'nuwara', it
> obtained its present appellation, Nuwara-Eliya, the 'royal city of light'.

H C P Bell, the archaeological commissioner, proved in 1890 that the place was inhabited in the 10th century.

The credit for making possible the development of Nuwara Eliya (which the trad Brits still insist on calling New-raileeya) goes to two Britons: Sir Edward Barnes and Major Skinner. Skinner arrived in Ceylon in 1814, at the age of 14. Barnes came in 1819 as commander-in-chief of the forces. By the time he took over as lieutenant governor in 1820, he had already made a tour of the island and decided that what Ceylon needed was 'first roads, second roads and third, roads'.

The job was given to Skinner. With an army of experienced workmen, he spent nearly 50 years in the construction of roads and bridges. 'Until his arrival,' wrote Henry Cave in *Golden Tips* in 1900, 'there were no roads and at his departure there were 3,000 miles, mostly due to his genius, pluck, energy and self-reliance.'

During Barnes's terms as governor, from 1820–22 and 1824–31, he became enchanted with Nuwara Eliya. He built a bungalow there at his own expense (it cost him US$8,000) and entertained lavishly. With claret at US$3.15 for a dozen bottles, 'riotous folly' (as one guest described his parties) was frequent, and Barnes's enthusiasm did much to popularise Nuwara Eliya. And since it had the road access he had instigated, it rapidly became a sanatorium for enervated and convalescing Brits. Barnes Hall, as he called it when he left Ceylon in 1831, was to become the nucleus of the Grand Hotel.

Another Briton who did his bit to promote England in the tropics was Samuel Baker, who first visited in 1847 when he was 26. 'Why should not the highlands of Ceylon, with an Italian climate, be rescued from their state of barrenness? Why should not the plains be drained, the forests felled, and cultivation take the place of rank pasturage?' he wrote with empire-building enthusiasm. He returned to Nuwara Eliya seven years later to found a community of Britons and put his ideas into practice, including introducing English vegetables (grown there to this day). He stayed eight years and then went on to explore the Nile and to become Governor of Sudan.

Now Nuwara Eliya is Sri Lanka's very own hill station – the sort of institution associated with India and the days of the Raj, when the government in summer shifted from Madras to Ooty, and from Calcutta and Delhi to Simla. Nuwara Eliya was never intended as a summer capital: it has always been a cool and healthy resort, a retreat from Colombo when the heat is on.

The idea begun by the 19th-century pioneers was developed further by the British settlers during the 20th century. Planters, estate managers, employers and senior public servants concentrated on the development of the necessary infrastructure. They built their own holiday homes there, many of which have become the

The Hill Country NUWARA ELIYA

5

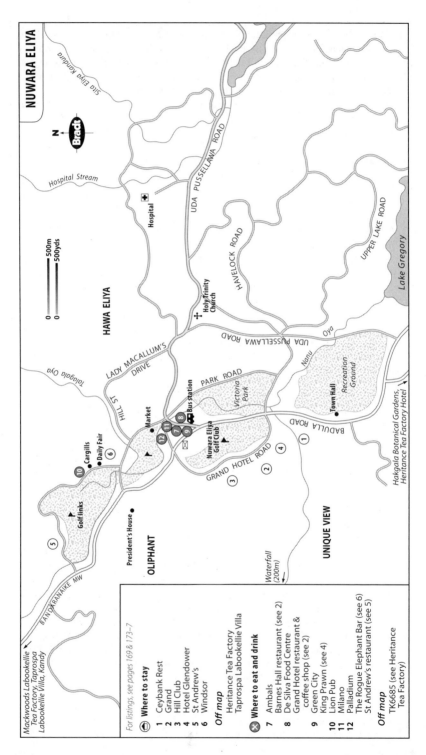

NUWARA ELIYA

For listings, see pages 169 & 173–7

Where to stay
1   Ceybank Rest
2   Grand
3   Hill Club
4   Hotel Glendower
5   St Andrew's
6   Windsor

Off map
    Heritance Tea Factory
    Taprospa Labookellie Villa

Where to eat and drink
7   Ambals
    Barnes Hall restaurant (see 2)
8   De Silva Food Centre
    Grand Hotel restaurant &
      coffee shop (see 2)
9   Green City
    King Prawn (see 4)
10 Lion Pub
11 Milano
12 Palladium
    The Rogue Elephant Bar (see 6)
    St Andrew's restaurant (see 5)

Off map
    TK6685 (see Heritance
      Tea Factory)

charming guesthouses evident today. Golf, cricket, polo, hockey, croquet and lawn tennis were played and there was hunting too. According to a 1929 guidebook, 'red deer, leopards and wild boar and birds of many varieties are plentiful'.

There were annual race meets, police sports meets, gymkhanas, horse, dog and flower shows, clay pigeon shooting and, above all, the Governor's State Ball. An old resident told me the story of one guest, a member of the Legislative Council with a limited knowledge of English who, when asked to reply to the toast 'To the guests', said: 'Your excellency, ladies and gentlemen, I have attended many balls, but I must say that I have always observed that your excellency's balls are the biggest.'

GETTING THERE

By train It is no longer possible to go all the way to Nuwara Eliya by train; you have to get down at Nanu Oya. There used to be a narrow-gauge steam railway snaking its way through the hills from Nanu Oya to Nuwara Eliya and beyond, which must have been a delightful way to travel through these scenic mountains.

The process of getting to Nuwara Eliya is simple. Local buses meet the trains at Nanu Oya station and there are also minibus taxis that can be hired in the station forecourt for the 6km drive to Nuwara Eliya. Arriving passengers also have the benefit of advice from the freelance guides who meet every train. Ask for Selvam (see box, page 179), also known as Eddie. Many boys will claim to be Selvam or his brother because he has such a good reputation. This encourages the others to give of their best, so if Selvam isn't available you could try one of his colleagues. Better to ask Selvam (*Samanpura, Bangalahatha;* m 077 6326663) in advance to meet you.

(See page 151 for details of trains to/from Nanu Oya.)

By bus There are intercity buses for the five-hour journey to and from Colombo (No 79) and also to and from Kandy (No 47) and Bandarawela/Badulla (No 31).

By road There are two ways of reaching Nuwara Eliya by road from Colombo, 170km away. Perhaps slightly quicker in time is to drive to Kandy on the A1 and then take the A5 as it twists and turns through the hills via Gampola and Ramboda to Nuwara Eliya. For a picturesque variation, from Colombo take the A4 to Avissawella to pick up the A7 via Kitulgala to Hatton and past the Devon and St Clair waterfalls and through Nanu Oya to Nuwara Eliya. There are major road links to Badulla and Bandarawela as well as a long road through tea estates to Kandy.

An alternative way is to approach Nuwara Eliya by road from the east (via the A5) or from the south by the A4 via Beragla and the A16 via Bandarawela.

WHERE TO STAY Nuwara Eliya is often cold at night – that's why hotels have log fires and no air conditioning – so remember to bring a sweater. The town is dedicated to holidaying so there is no shortage of places to stay. In fact the whole town seems to consist of bungalow-style guesthouses; however, you will find budget accommodation usually costs more in Nuwara Eliya than in less popular hill stations such as Haputale and Bandarawela. All listings are included on the map opposite.

Grand (Golf Wing 65 rooms, Governor's Wing 95 rooms) 052 2222881; e thegrand@ sltnet.lk; www.tangerinehotels.com. The doyen of the town's hotels is Nuwara Eliya's oldest, but it has new accommodation, known as the Golf Wing (\$\$\$). The Golf Wing has the panache of a major 5-star hotel; you can sense its style just by walking along its corridors, warm with the rich smell of newly polished wood. The bedrooms have dignified reproduction furniture, lending them the atmosphere of a good club. There is a health centre & sauna. The Barnes Hall Restaurant in the old wing is more like a ballroom & serves table d'hôte meals as well as buffets ($$). Snacks and fine dining are available in the coffee shop with its open show kitchen ($$), or tea can be taken on the open-sided (& heated at night) tea terrace ($) or in the lounge with deep chesterfields & a colour scheme of Edwardian maroon. There is a popular restaurant ($) specialising in Indian dishes at the hotel's gates. A Thai restaurant was rumoured at press time to be under construction (replacing the hotel's old Supper Club) and with a separate entrance at the Golf Wing side of the hotel – check the website for details. To enter the hotel is to step back in time. Its bungalow-like entrance of teak & stained-glass panels is probably part of the original Barnes Hall. You progress down the long hall with its huge flowers in tall brass pots, passing the ballroom on the right & the lounge on the left, to the reception desk. A grand staircase, which could have been built for a leading lady to make an impressive entrance, leads to 2 floors of older rooms with fireplaces & genuine period furniture. The hotel is one of the oldest in Sri Lanka because of its origins in the bungalow built by Sir Edward Barnes. When he left in 1831 it was taken over by his successor as governor & 30 years later had become a hotel. A map of 1862 shows a hotel on the site. In the complaints book of the neighbouring Hill Club, someone wrote on 18 October 1887: 'Ordered tea & toast at 4pm & waited until 4.40pm & had to go to the Grand Hotel for it.' In 1893, a guidebook quoted the cost of a double room as Rs4, hot bath 75 cents & cold bath 50 cents. Expansion became necessary with the opening of a railway line to Nuwara Eliya in 1903 (since closed), & the arrival of motor transport in 1904. Because it was built at different times, the hotel is a warren of corridors, unplanned & rambling, which lead to unexpected delights. One is the octagonal lounge with its mirrored ceiling, mirrors set in sombre walls, & mirror-topped coffee tables reflecting a contrast of colour from the flamboyant display of flowers at its centre. A corridor leads to vast loos & another winds its way to the old bar. You can tell it was created for serious drinkers by its solid-brass foot-rail & broad wooden stools. Guests congregate around a blazing log fire to be cosseted by vintage stewards bearing vintage brews. The adjoining

billiard room has 3 championship tables. The essence of the hotel is its unchanging atmosphere, even though a wine bar ($$) & a tea terrace have been added. It gives the feeling that whatever is going on outside, the Grand will quietly soldier on. $$$

🏠 **Heritance Tea Factory Hotel** (57 non-AC rooms, with heaters) Kandapola, Nuwara Eliya; ☏052 2229600; e ashmres@aitkenspence.lk; www.aitkenspencehotels.com. 'It's a crazy idea!' was one of the kinder comments made by colleagues of Mr G C Wickremasinghe when, in 1992, he proposed turning an abandoned tea factory into a hotel. Thanks to his determination the idea became a reality with the opening in 1996 of this place. Wickremasinghe's vision was matched by the talent of architect Nihal Bodhinayake & together they created a unique hotel that deserves to become as famous as Kenya's Treetops as an unusual place to stay. While the exterior of the factory has not been changed & has the customary corrugated-iron walls painted silver, & hundreds of tall, wooden casement windows, the interior is unconventional. Step inside the reception hall, once the drying room, & see an atrium latticed with steel. At its top slowly turn 2 giant wooden fans, reminding visitors that their rooms are on floors that used to be tea-withering lofts. In character with the décor is an old lift with iron-grille door & modern machinery to levitate guests gently to the 4 floors of guestrooms. Guest rooms are carpeted to dull the sound of footfalls on the original pine-wood floor that is the ceiling of the room below. Every guestroom has a built-in dressing table with wraparound mirrors. Wood is the main material used, with doors, shelves & cupboards (plenty of them) left their natural colour. The windows made from their original square wooden frames flood every room, including the bathroom, with light. Each bathroom has a bathtub, a shower, lashings of hot water & a heater. There is a tea-making facility in every room, with tea from the estate. The hotel is some 2,200m above sea level. The view from the rooms at the front is a panorama of tea; from the back can be seen hamlets, hills & forest, as well as more tea. This is countryside for hiking up & down tea-covered hills that soar skywards or plunge steeply into valleys below. In gullies between the hills, rivers of carefully tended vegetables – leeks & potatoes – seem to flow. Protected forests cap the hills & birdsong fills the air. At night, wild boar rummage in the vegetable patches while mist steals over the mountains, emphasising the cosiness of the hotel's snug interior. The main restaurant has a mobile of metal-spoked wheels under a copper canopy as the buffet-counter décor. Tea chests with original markings decorate the sides. At the far end is the bar with a collection of tea factory machinery. A fine dining restaurant ($$$) serving 7-course meals has been created out of a railway carriage, & is open to non-residents (but advance booking through the hotel's reception is necessary). In the basement, the giant generating engine remains, connected to a Heath Robinson contraption of pulleys & chains that powered the old tea rollers & sifters. The transformation is complete: the factory has become a luxury hotel of distinction. If at times it resembles a gigantic & thrilling Meccano construction, that's all the more reason for going there. $$$

⌂ **Hill Club** (36 rooms) Grand Hotel Rd; ☏ 052 2222653; e hillclub@sltnet.lk; www. hillclubsrilanka.net. Neighbour to the Grand is this gloomily Gothic pile. Set proudly in a garden on a bluff overlooking the golf course, the Hill Club likes to pretend it's not a hotel, but it is as eager for guests as its neighbours. Visitors can become temporary members, as long as the rules are observed. These have recently been relaxed with the 'Men Only' bar by the entrance becoming a 'Casual' bar; children under 16 remain banned. Such is the hushed atmosphere of the club, with its 1930s-style lounge (on the right of the entrance hall) & Monsoon Room (TV lounge), you don't expect kids there anyway. Mobile phones are banned too & gentlemen must wear a tie for dinner with a long-sleeved shirt or jacket. Ties & jackets can be borrowed from the club's stock. Dressing for dinner matches the style of the Hill Club; the waiters wear white gloves to serve. The food, however, is traditional club fare & unlikely to thrill a gourmet. Not all the bedrooms have the same comforts, but the best are cosy. From the noticeboard you learn that 'hot baths will be available between 6.30am & 10am, & from 6pm to 10pm'. The notice by the (now closed) Ladies' Entrance states: 'In the days gone by this was the original entrance through which ladies would gain progress to the Club. The main entrance was reserved for gentlemen only.' As the sign in its meticulous English implies, the Hill Club is changing. It's worth a visit before it ditches its standards altogether. $$$

⌂ **St Andrew's Hotel** (40 dbls, 5 suites, 7 family rooms) 10 St Andrew's Dr; ☏ 052 2223031; e hotels@jetwing.lk; www.jetwinghotels.com. From the same mould as the Grand & the Hill Club comes this one. It is at the other end of Nuwara Eliya with, perhaps predictably, a long view of the golf course that meanders through the town. Begun as a club bungalow by the British over a century ago, the hotel has survived many phases. Gone are the days of musty rooms, old blankets & sagging mattresses. Bedrooms in the old wing (that's the one with the crenellated towers) have been transformed with bright fabrics & white paint to banish the gloom of Edwardian furniture. The new wing of huge bedrooms, some with garrets for kids of all ages to retire to, is Swiss-chalet prim, panelled in pine & palm wood. Tea makers are available in the 5 suites. The hotel's entrance is up a broad flight of steps protected from the weather by glass, like a greenhouse. It leads to the lobby that gives access to the terraced lawns in front of the old wing & to a rambling lounge where a log fire burns on cold nights. There is a vintage billiard table (imported from Calcutta more than 115 years ago) in the old music room in the hotel's heart. The dining room ($$) has been revamped from the days when it catered for planters & their families & has a nifty show kitchen with energetic chefs displaying their skills. It is one of the few hotels in Sri Lanka with a walk-in wine cellar & guests are invited to browse & select one of the moderately priced, excellent (lots of New World) wines from its labelled racks. In response to guest interest in ecology, an Eco Room has been opened close to the billiard hall. There lectures are held for the staff to prepare them for the kind of questions guests ask, as well as to instil in them an appreciation for the town's environment. Guests get information there about the various eco-attractions of the area. $$$

⌂ **Ceybank Rest** (19 rooms) 119 Badulla Rd; ☏ 052 2223855; e ceybank_ne@sltnet.lk. The weather is often refreshingly filthy in Nuwara Eliya: cold, damp, wet & miserable; no wonder they call the place Little England. But for many visitors it's welcome after the heat of the coast & the old hostelries there match the climate. Ceybank Rest is related to the Bank of Ceylon but luckily is open to any guests, not just bankers. It's the perfect solution for tourists who want colonial style without the boutique prices of its neighbouring hotels. It's on the A5 into Nuwara Eliya within walking distance of the turn-off to the Grand Hotel & Hill Club. The spacious, wood-floored rooms & suites reflect the stylish, solid décor of the Edwardian era; bathrooms have water heaters. The charm & willingness of the staff make a stay there uniquely personalised. A feature is the 'Black Magic' bar lounge, hidden behind the reception hall. Painted a striking aquamarine with appropriate upholstery for the plump armchairs, it is a contrast to the copper ceilings (alas over-painted cream) & ancient timber floors & stairs of the rest of the building. I was delighted to discover there a barman who not only knows his drinks but also seems able to talk intelligently on any topic with bar-propping guests. Such barmen are rare in Sri Lanka; so cheers, Thivagar! **$$**

🏠 **Hotel Glendower** (9 rooms) 5 Grand Hotel Rd; 📞052 2222501; e glendower@sltnet.lk; www. hotelglendower.com. At this hotel hill country comfort has been concentrated so every guest feels delightfully at home. Although most of Glendower was built in the 1990s, it preserves the traditions of the original colonial bungalow & its location (by the golf course, the Grand & the Hill Club). More like a mock-Tudor country mansion than a hotel, it has rooms & suites with teak floors, hand-crafted polished mahogany furniture & beds piled high with fluffy woolly blankets that ensure a good night's rest. Even the quilts are filled with silk. There is a venerable 19th-century snooker table in the billiard room above the bar. While the

bar – with its solid-wood counter, stools & drink shelves made of wooden barrels – is reassuringly traditional (& has expats as regulars), it can morph into a karaoke lounge with a giant screen on demand. There is an adjoining TV lounge (no TVs in the rooms) & a more elaborate one complete with fireplace. The dining room with fireplace, tables made of slabs from a huge tree's trunk, & glassed-in breakfast loggia overlooking the road, transforms at lunch & dinner into the King Prawn Chinese Restaurant (**$$**), popular with guests from other hotels who want welcoming Chinese food as a break from standard round-trip fare. The Glendower has a warmth beyond its log fires, & is a pleasant, unpretentious place to call home in the hill country. **$$**

🏠 **Windsor Hotel** (49 rooms) 2 Kandy Rd; 📞052 2222554; e windsorhotelreservations@ dialognet.lk. Plumb in the centre of town, & looking as though it wishes it wasn't, towers this hotel. Its multi bay-windowed frontage gives it a dignity that indicates it has seen better days. But the Windsor is comparatively new, even though its better rooms are furnished with reproduction antiques & it has a large, old-style dining hall. Its courtyard is a rock garden. The Rogue Elephant Bar has all the ingredients (buttock-shaped wooden bar stools, wine rack on the counter) for a jolly booze-up. Real degenerates, though, seek out the gloomy basement bar, with entrance from the street, to sit at tables & swill Nuwara Eliya beer & local spirits. **$**

✗ **WHERE TO EAT AND DRINK** The centre of town has two streets where bars and restaurants are located. The main street, called New Bazaar Street, leads straight through town from the roundabout by Grand Hotel Road. The street veers to the left in front of the Windsor Hotel. The other road, Lawson Street, is on the left behind the shopping complex, and curves around to link up with Grand Hotel Road.

So where to go in Nuwara Eliya on a wet afternoon? If you want to join the locals, go to the **Lion Pub** close to Windsor Hotel where local beer (originally brewed in Nuwara Eliya until the brewery shifted to modern premises close to Colombo) is served.

Round the corner in the shopping arcade at the top of New Bazaar Street, you will find the **Palladium Restaurant** (📞 *052 2222879*; *$*). You can avoid walking through the downstairs saloon full of determined drinkers by taking the separate entrance to the upstairs restaurant. They serve basic local dishes. The **Milano Restaurant** (📞 *052 2222763*; *$*) is its neighbour with an upstairs restaurant specialising in Chinese dishes and with snacks available downstairs. There's no bar.

Beyond the complex of shops and back in the main street, **De Silva Food Centre** (*New Bazaar St*; 📞 *052 2223833*; *$*) has cakes and snacks on sale in its downstairs lobby and an upstairs restaurant ('Eastern and Western') with pleasant staff. **Green City** (*50 New Bazaar St;* $) is more Indian in cooking style. Next door is a vegetarian restaurant, **Ambals** ($).

The hotel restaurant most popular with non-residents is **King Prawn** (*Glendower Hotel, Grand Hotel Rd;* ☏ *052 2222501;* $$). The menu is essentially Chinese and the spiciness of the dishes suits the climate. The **Grand Hotel** (☏ *052 2222881*) has a cafeteria-style and very popular Indian restaurant ($) at its gates, which adds to the choice of where to eat, and complements the hotel's **Coffee Shop** (☏ *052 2222881;* $$).

Out of town at Kandapola and at the highest elevation (2,200m) of any restaurant in Sri Lanka, the **TK6685** narrow-gauge railway carriage restaurant at the Heritance Tea Factory Hotel (☏ *052 2229600;* $$$) specialises in set dinners with several choices (including venison) and creates an unusual dining experience, with train noises, a rocking carriage and staff in railway uniforms. Great fun as well as good food. All of the listings above are included on the map, page 172.

OTHER PRACTICALITIES

Banks There are branches of the state banks, **Bank of Ceylon** and **People's Bank** in the town as well as branches of local private banks, such as **Hatton National Bank**. ATMs are available.

Post office The town's pink/red-bricked, colonial-built post office (⊕ *08.30–17.00 Mon–Fri, 08.30–13.00 Sat, closed Sun & public holidays*) is centrally located opposite Victoria Park and the bus stand.

Medical The **Cooperative Hospital** (☏ *052 2228550*) is located at Nuwara Eliya.

WHAT TO SEE AND DO The town is fascinating in itself and many are the rewards of a casual stroll, either across the golf course on the public footpath, or on the town's pavements. You could have your fortune told by a bird that picks out a card from a pack, or shop in **Cargills**, a department store dating from the 1920s. In the grounds of the **Municipal Council building** there is a tree planted in commemoration of the coronation of King George VI in 1937. **Victoria Park** in the centre of town was opened in 1897 on the occasion of Queen Victoria's diamond jubilee. Visit in the April season to see gardens that are a riot of colourful flowers groomed for the best garden competition.

Beyond Victoria Park and past the new bus station, on the right, is the covered **market** complex (⊕ *09.00–19.30 daily*). You enter this through passageways between the shops on New Bazaar Street. It is one of Sri Lanka's most fascinating markets with a butchery and fish section as well as vegetables. Stallholders are jolly and happy to talk. The **Daily Fair** complex is on the right of the road as you walk from the Windsor Hotel to St Andrew's Hotel. It consists of a couple of narrow alleys and tiny shops, most of which are tailors or video rental shacks. The presence of a foreigner attracts good-natured banter.

The town's pink **post office** is a landmark. Beside it is a road to the **Nuwara Eliya Golf Club** (☏ *052 2222835*), a club with 3,000 members and a long waiting list. Tourists, however, can become temporary members without paying a fee if they play golf. The club's facilities include a wood-panelled bar, a dining room, badminton hall and billiard room. There is accommodation with a new wing of rooms. The club's brochure advises that 'modest cubicle accommodation for single gentlemen is also available'.

The golf club was established in 1889 and seems to coexist happily with the town that hems it in. Roads and paths have split it into four sections, adding variety. Local rules mention that 'ground under repair' covers 'hoofmarks including wild pig rootings on the cut portion of the fairway and on the putting green' and 'dung except in water hazards'.

In the grounds of the golf club are the remains of an old British cemetery. Sadly neglected, considering the role he played in the development of the hill country, is the grave of Major Thomas William Rogers. His reputation as an empire-builder is besmirched by his ruthless extermination of elephants; he claimed to have shot and killed over 1,300.

Caught in a storm in 1845 at a resthouse near Nuwara Eliya, he stepped out on to the veranda and looked up at the sky. He called to his companion, a Mrs Buller, 'It's all over now', referring to the storm. There was a flash of lightning and he fell dead at her feet. Legend has it that his grave was also struck by lightning and the tomb does have evidence of a repaired crack.

At the Anglican **Holy Trinity Church** there are many reminders of the British pioneers who built up Nuwara Eliya. Among those buried there is Lindsay Wright, who settled in the 1860s and started a mail-coach service. At one time he owned St Andrew's Hotel, and was managing director of the Grand Hotel and of what is now the Ceylon Brewery.

On the road to Kandy, at about 15km from Nuwara Eliya, you'll see a sign advertising **Mackwoods Labookellie Tea Centre** (*Labookellie Estate;* \ *052 2235806;* e *tea@mackwoodstea.com; www.mackwoodstea.com;* ⏰ *10.00–17.00 daily;* $). This is the one place to visit if you want to know about tea. There are conducted tours of the tea factory throughout the day and you can have a nice cup of tea (just pay for the chocolate cake) in the tea café and garden. The different grades of High Grown tea are displayed in a glass case on the counter. Labookellie single-estate tea (which means it has not been blended with tea from other estates) can be bought from the sales centre. The Taprospa Labookellie Villa (see box, page 169) is next to the factory, offering three bungalow rooms for visitors to stay in (**$$$**).

Begun in 1861, the **Hakgala Botanical Garden** (*Hakgala;* ⏰ *08.00–17.30; admission Rs600, reduction for students/children, vehicles extra*) is 24ha in area at 1,884m (6,182ft) above sea level. It is 10km from Nuwara Eliya along the road to Badulla. To many, it is more beautiful and interesting than the Peradeniya Gardens because it is landscaped on different levels due to its hill location. In the montane zone, at the foot of Hakgala Rock, it benefits from temperatures varying between 17°C and 30°C; December to February is cold, while April to August is warm. That's when the herbaceous borders and annual plants are in flower and when most people (more than 400,000 a year) visit. A sign at the entrance forbids alcohol and people under its influence, as well as the defacement of trees, and vehicles and musical instruments, but not children who flock and frolic on school outings with great excitement.

The original purpose of the garden was to test-grow chincona and as a result that became a profitable plantation crop (1860–80), as quinine was extracted from its bark for the treatment of malaria. The emphasis has changed to research on montane flora. The garden has a herbarium, a rose section, a fernery and a wild orchid collection.

Humbugs ($; *see map, page 148*), on the opposite side of the garden on the road to Badulla, specialises in home-grown strawberries and cream. **Horton Plains National Park** (⏰ *06.00–18.30 daily; admission charge*) is 32km by road from Nuwara Eliya to its entrance. Allow Rs4,000, which includes waiting time, for round-trip transport from Nuwara Eliya. This area of 3,159ha of plains and woodlands was declared a national park in 1988. It is a 4km walk from the entrance to World's End. For the best chance to view the ravine and not just mist, get there just after sunrise (for further details, see page 189).

PUSSELLAWA

This is a barely noticeable village that drivers pass through on the road between Nuwara Eliya and Kandy. Those who stop pop in for tea at the much expanded tiny resthouse that has become The Heritage or stay to relish rural luxury at the Lavender House bungalow, both listed on page 180.

GETTING THERE Pussellawa is a tiny town on the A5 roughly halfway between Kandy and Nuwara Eliya and easy to get to by **car**. If you're going by **train**, the most convenient station is Peradeniya on the way to Kandy (and then take a **bus** from there). Bus No 47 makes the journey along the A5 linking Kandy with Nuwara Eliya.

FREELANCE GUIDES

You will often be approached by freelance guides who have been licensed by a local authority. These are personable characters who will be able to organise what you want (information, a lobster lunch, a trip to Yala); they know everything and everybody, and can converse in several foreign languages. In Nuwara Eliya, the maestro of freelance guides is Selvam, aka 'Eddie'. In *Sri Lanka By Rail* in 1994 I wrote:

> A pleasant surprise in Nanu Oya is the presence of licensed guides (call them touts at your peril) who wait on the platform to meet tourists. While I cannot recommend them all (you'll judge their degree of shiftiness yourself) there is one whose courteous, obliging and honest service is recommended not only by tourists but by hotel managers as well. Ask for Selvam; he is short and wiry and always helpful, knows everybody and seems positively surprised when you tip him.

A decade after I first met him, Selvam was still going strong and carried a book in which guests have written comments like these:

> Trust me when I say trust your wife, child and mother-in-law to this man ... he'll make you laugh your pants off ... he is honest, and trustworthy and won't rip you off; trust him instead of the guidebooks. I promise you a good time.
>
> Stuart Morton, Sidmouth, Devon, UK.

> We hooked up with Eddie at the Hill Club and he arranged for us to do a trip to Sri Pada, a safari and then to the beach. This was good fun with interesting conversation and safe driving at a price below that quoted by other drivers in town. Eddie is a great laugh and knows the best places to stay and see.
>
> Ben Wrigley and Alison Howard, Clapham, UK.

Selvam (m *077 6326663*) still takes visitors on tours or trekking or to discover the delights of Nuwara Eliya, continuing to help visitors by making sure they have a good time.

WHERE TO STAY AND EAT

⌂ **Lavender House** (5 suites) Hellbodde Estate, Katukitula, Pussellawa; ☏052 2259928; e info@thelavenderhouseceylon.com; www. thelavenderhouseceylon.com. There is a treat in store for guests who are lucky enough to stay in the old-fashioned opulence that is the Lavender House. I fell for it when I visited in the mid 1990s when it was a smartly furnished planter's bungalow with a worn wooden shingle roof (now assiduously restored), with the remnants of an old wall with a height chart begun in 1902 with pencilled signatures of children (now carefully preserved). The restoration of the bungalow as it might have been in the 1950s (a portrait of Sir Winston Churchill glowers over the wing-back armchairs in the lounge) has been done with style by James & Gabrielle Whight, the Australian owners of Colombo's popular Cricket Club Café. The bungalow is broad & deep, built at the end of the 19th century, of exposed granite blocks & set in 3ha of terraced lawns, tea, woods & mountain views. There is a music room like a conservatory with a baby grand piano & a satellite TV concealed in an *almirah* (wardrobe). The bungalow is constructed around a split, glass-walled inner courtyard & is a warren of long passages & sumptuous suites. The dining room has walls of deep burgundy, reflecting the serious content of the attached walk-in wine chamber.

Crystal glasses sparkle on the long, locally made table for 10. A 2nd, round table is in the room's bay window, for couples. There is a choice of set menus, with singles & doubles being available on a B&B, HB or FB basis; it's not necessary to pay for the whole bungalow. Each of the 5 suites has polished wooden floors, an array of brass light switches, silk blinds & curtains, a huge fireplace (lit on request), a sitting area & a private garden with French-window access. Each bathroom is gloriously retro with a chain flush toilet with wooden seat, stand-alone bathtub with shower & lashings of hot water. Beds are smothered with duvets & soft pillows. There is a billiard room, a clay tennis court &, built on a granite platform poised above the view, an infinity swimming pool where hidden speakers send soothing music cascading around the flower arbours. It's become my favourite bungalow in the hill country, not just for its comfort but also for the fun of staying in such a well-run place. **$$$$**

⌂ **The Heritage, Pussellawa** (3 rooms) ☏081 2478397; e chcweb@ceylonhotels.net; www.ceylonhotelscorporation.com. Upgraded from its status as a resthouse but still popular for a buffet rice & curry lunch break ($) on the drive between Nuwara Eliya & Kandy rather than as a place to stay, & has a pleasant new dining room. **$$**

WHAT TO SEE AND DO The **Tea Workers Museum** (see box oppposite for details) is on the Raman Dora Estate. Otherwise, there is not much of note in the town for passing visitors.

RAMBODA

HISTORY The Ramboda Pass crept into history as a footnote to the opening up of Nuwara Eliya. Samuel Baker, later to become Governor of Sudan, tried in 1848 to establish an English village community in the hill country. Bullock wagons and elephant carts were enlisted to transport his settlers and equipment from Colombo through the Ramboda Pass to Nuwara Eliya. A letter from Baker's coachman refers to an incident in the pass:

Honord Zur,

I'm sorry to hinform you that the carriage and osses has met with a haccidint and is tumbled down a precipice and it's a mussy as I didn't go too …

A Buddhist *vihara* (image house) in the area is one of the places where the sacred tooth relic was hidden during troubles in Kandy.

GETTING THERE Ramboda is reached by **car** on the A5 road to Kandy from Nuwara Eliya (23km). The most convenient **train** station is Peradeniya on the way to Kandy, from which you can take **bus** No 47 makes the journey along the A5 linking Kandy with Nuwara Eliya.

WHERE TO STAY AND EAT It's a long, steep walk down (and worse coming back up) a track to the **Ramboda Falls Hotel** (*20 non-AC rooms; 76 Nuwara Eliya Rd, Ramboda;* \ *052 2259582;* e *rambodafall@gmail.com; www.rambodafall.com;* **$**). A tiered construction of restaurants and blocks of rooms edged into the hillside greets visitors who succeed in walking down (there is occasionally a shuttle bus). This has become popular as a lunch stop with its terrific hill and valley scenery and waterfall views.

WHAT TO SEE AND DO There are several **waterfalls** fed by small brooks that are sourced by the tributary of the Kotmale Oya. The main fall (109m) is a twin one, with two strands of water spouting over the rock ledge.

TALAWAKELE *Population: 4,087 (2012 estimate)*

Talawakele is the centre of the Dimbula tea district and is one of those hill country areas that have developed through tea. The Sri Lanka Tea Research Institute (TRI) is located at St Coombs Estate. Founded in 1925, it has a long and distinguished history of help to the tea industry. In 1946, when blister blight leaf disease was poised to wipe out the industry the way coffee had been wiped out, the TRI led the battle to beat the disease.

CEYLON TEA MUSEUMS

Even those who aren't involved with tea but simply enjoy a good cuppa will find a visit to the **Ceylon Tea Museum** (*Hantane Estate, Kandy;* \ *060 2803204;* ⊕ *08.15–16.45 Tue–Sun, closed Mon & holidays; admission Rs500*) their cup of tea. An old four-storey tea factory building has been lovingly converted, with government aid, by Dharmasiri Madugalle and enthusiasts who want to keep the history of tea alive. The museum is at the end of an 8km drive up the winding Hantane Road from Kandy (the most convenient place to stay). A three-wheeler from the Kandy railway station would cost from Rs350 for the round trip, so it is easy to visit during a day trip by train to Kandy.

The ground floor is dedicated to the 19th-century machinery used to operate a pulley-powered factory. On the first floor are items associated with James Taylor (see pages 126–7), as well as a library of old books on tea. There are shops selling tea on the third floor while the top floor has a unique high-flying catwalk (for a supervisor to view factory operations).

Another tea museum opened in 2007 dedicated to tea workers. It is housed in a converted row of line rooms, the tea workers' residences, demonstrating how the workers lived in squalid conditions. As well as documents there are artefacts such as grinding stones and even a century-old blanket (*kambali*) made of lambs' wool issued by British planters so the workers could keep warm. The museum has been set up by the Institute of Social Development, an NGO that supports plantation workers with assistance from Christian Aid and Hivos. It is at Raman Dora Estate, Pussellawa, off the road between Kandy and Nuwara Eliya.

GETTING THERE Talawakele is on the A7, 140km from Colombo by **car**; the road goes on to Nuwara Eliya, 30km distant. Hill country **trains** stop at Talawakele, the station closest to the waterfalls of Devon and St Clair.

✖ WHERE TO EAT AND DRINK

✖ **Tea Castle** Talawakele; ✆051 2222561; www.mlesnateas.com; ⊕ 08.00–18.00 daily. A modern extravaganza built as a replica castle with an emporium showcasing Sri Lanka's best teas for purchase in artistically designed containers, the Tea Castle, beside the A7 overlooking the St Clair Waterfall, serves one of the best rice & curry lunches in Sri Lanka, with rare ingredients like plantain blossoms, bitter gourd & *gotakola medun* salad. $

WHAT TO SEE AND DO The **Devon Waterfall** is 97m in height and carries water from a small tributary of the Kotmale Oya. It takes its name from the Devon Estate which originally grew coffee. From the viewpoint it is a walk of about 1km downhill through the tea plantation to reach it.

There are two waterfalls facing each other with the name **St Clair**. The bigger one (Maha Ella) has a fall of 80m, while the second one (Kuda Ella), formed by a tributary of the Kotmale Oya, falls 50m. It is set very close to the road and can be seen better from a bend on the road near the 90km post.

The **Tea Research Institute** can be visited only with special permission, which a tea-planter contact might be able to get for you. Set in 162ha, it is more like a nuclear research station to visit than one specialising in such a homely product as tea. Security guards check passes, and laboratory blocks and suburban-style residences line roads through the tea fields. There is a guesthouse for those on official visits.

right   The giant lion paws at the base of Sigiriya's granite monolith (i/S) pages 145–6

below   The enormous Ruwanwelisaya Dagoba in Anuradhapura, a sacred city venerated as the capital of Buddhism and a UNESCO World Heritage site (SS) page 132

bottom   Brightly coloured paintings decorate the sides of one of the rooms in the Temple of the Tooth, Kandy (s/S) pages 119–20

above left   A traditionally masked participant in a low country ritual folk dance (LH/C) pages 220–1

above right   Costumed drummers at a Buddhist festival, Navam Perhera, in Colombo (SS) pages 60–1

left   A tense moment during the England–Sri Lanka game at the World Cup 2011 (PB/R/C) pages 13–14

below   Monks praying at dawn at Gal Vihara Temple, Polonnaruwa (SS) pages 143–4

above   Tea plucker in the hill country around
Nuwara Eliya (SS) pages 124–5

right   One of the most fascinating markets
in the country, Nuwara Eliya's market
complex contains a butchery as well as
stalls selling fruits, vegetables and fish
(WPTB) page 177

below   Fishermen by the Weligama beach brave
the waves as they perch on traditional
poles (SS) pages 172–3

above St Clair Falls sits amid lush tea plantations in the Hill Country of central Sri Lanka (Na/D) page 152

left The late afternoon sun illuminates the landscape of Ruhunu (Yala West) National Park (SS) pages 195–7

below Waves crash against the pristine shore in Bundala National Park (SS) pages 88–9

above   Sunset creates a dynamic portrait of the drowned trees in the Yala wetlands (SS) pages 195–7

right   The vertiginous cliffs of World's End at Horton Plains provide a breathtaking view of the distant hills of the south coast (SS) pages 89–91

below   Perfectly manicured lawns and gardens are a highlight of the Royal Botanical Gardens at Peradeniya (AG/S) pages 122–3

left Male Indian peafowl (*Pavo cristatus*) (KS/MP/FLPA)

below Two young Asian elephants (*Elephas maximus*) (SS)

bottom Family of grey langurs (*Semnopithecus priam thersites*) (E/D)

above   Green bee-eaters (*Merops orientalis*) (b/S)

right   Sloth Bear (*Melursus ursinus*) (En/D)

below   Sri Lankan leopard (*Panthera pardus kotiya*) (CH/I/FLPA)

6

National Parks and Interior Towns

NATIONAL PARKS

For an island as small as Sri Lanka, the area of land dedicated to wildlife protection is considerable. Officially the island still has about 22% of dense forest cover. Of this, approximately 12% is devoted to wildlife protection. However, many of the areas are not under the direct control of the authorities, and even some that are have suffered alienation. There are 16 national parks but they are not all open to visitors. The parks convey the atmosphere of undisturbed jungle, an idea of how the island was before nature's rule was replaced by man's. While elephants roam freely in small or large herds and are the most dramatic sight, other animals can be seen.

This list is supplied by the Department of Wildlife Conservation.

Big game	Elephant (*Elephas maximus*)
	Water buffalo (*Bubalus bubalis bubalis*)
	Leopard (*Panthera pardus fusca*)
	Sloth bear (*Melarsus ursinus inoratus*)
	Wild boar (*Sus scrofa cristatus*)
Deer types	Spotted deer (*Axis axis ceylonensis*)
	Barking deer (*Munctiacus muntjak malabaricus*)
	Mouse deer (*Tragulus meminna*)
	Sambhur (*Cervus unicolor unicolor*)
Monkeys	Grey langur (*Presbytis entellus thersites*)
	Toque monkey (*Macaca sinica sinica*)
	Purple-faced leaf monkey (*Pithecus uetulus montticola*)
Reptiles	Swamp crocodile (*Crocodylus palustris kimbula*)
	Estuarine crocodile (*Crocodylus porosus menikanna*)
	Iguana (*Varanus bengalensis*)
Others	Ceylon jackal (*Canis aureus lanka*)
	Fishing cat (*Felis viverrina*)
	Civet cat (*Viverricula indica mayori*)
	Grey mongoose (*Herpestes edwadsi lanka*)
	Ruddy mongoose (*Herpestes smithi zeylannius*)
	Stripe-necked mongoose (*Herpestes vitticollis vitticollis*)
	Giant squirrel (*Ratufa macroura dandolena*)
	Porcupine (*Hystrix indica indica*)
	Indian pangolin (*Manis crassicaudata*)

Peacocks pop up frequently and you will also see the painted stork, heron, spoonbill, bee-eater, parrots and parakeets, hornbill, kingfisher and woodpecker.

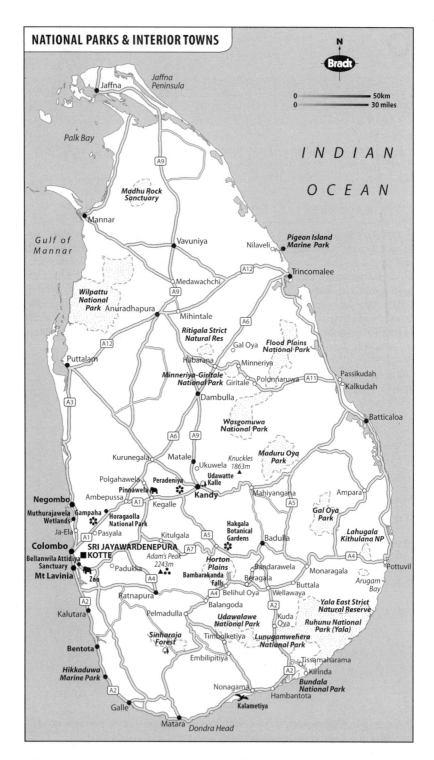

NATIONAL PARKS & INTERIOR TOWNS

N

Bradt

0 ———— 50km
0 ———— 30 miles

INDIAN

OCEAN

Jaffna

Jaffna Peninsula

Palk Bay

A9

Madhu Rock Sanctuary

Mannar

Gulf of Mannar

Vavuniya

Nilaveli

Pigeon Island Marine Park

A12

Trincomalee

Medawachchi

A9

Wilpattu National Park

Anuradhapura

Mihintale

A6

Ritigala Strict Natural Res

Gal Oya

Flood Plains National Park

Puttalam

A12

Habarana

Minneriya

Minneriya-Giritale National Park

Giritale

Polonnaruwa

A11

Passikudah

Kalkudah

A3

Dambulla

Wasgomuwa National Park

Batticaloa

A6

A9

Kurunegala

Matale

Ukuwela

Knuckles 1863m

Maduru Oya Park

Polgahawela

Peradeniya

Udawatte Kalle

Pinnawela

Kandy

Mahiyangana

Ampara

Ambepussa

A1

Kegalle

A5

Gal Oya Park

Negombo

Muthurajawela Wetlands

Gampaha

Horagaolla National Park

Ja-Ela

A1

Pasyala

Kitulgala

A5

Hakgala Botanical Gardens

Badulla

Lahugala Kithulana NP

Colombo

SRI JAYAWARDENEPURA

KOTTE

A7

Adam's Peak 2243m

Horton Plains

Bandarawela

Monaragala

A4

Pottuvil

Bellanwila Attidiya Sanctuary

Mt Lavinia

Zoo

Paduka

Bambarakanda Falls

Beragala

Buttala

Arugam Bay

A2

Belihul Oya

Wellawaya

Ratnapura

Balangoda

A2

Yala East Strict Natural Reserve

Kalutara

Pelmadulla

Udawalawe National Park

Timbolketiya

Kuda Oya

Ruhunu National Park (Yala)

Bentota

Sinharaja Forest

Embilipitiya

Lunugamwehera National Park

Tissamaharama

Hikkaduwa Marine Park

A2

Nonagama

Bundala National Park

Kirinda

Hambantota

Galle

Kalametiya

Matara

Dondra Head

The world's first fauna and flora sanctuary was established at Mihintale in the 3rd century BC by King Devanampiya Tissa (250–210BC). The **Sinharaja** rainforest is one of the few remaining in south Asia. It is also a primeval sanctuary for over 170 varieties of exotic orchid. Horton Plains appeals as a remote plateau with the island's last remaining montane forest, about 35km² at 1,500m above sea level, with a temperature of about 15°C.

There are several parks that are the habitat of the elephant, although not all of them are open to visitors. From conservationists we learn that the elephant is regarded as a flagship species. It is dubbed that because, due to its size, it requires large habitats for its survival. The idea is that by ensuring such habitats are protected, then all the other species can sail in the wake of the flagship and be protected too. Alas, that also means that as the elephants' habitat is threatened, all other species are threatened too.

The **Elephant Orphanage** at Pinnawela is a unique effort at saving threatened elephants, although this results in their domestication. The cause of elephants is promoted locally by the **Biodiversity and Elephant Conservation Trust** (*615/32 Rajagiriya Gdn, Nawala Rd, Rajagiriya;* m *077 7895700;* e *romalijj@eureka.lk; www.elephantsinsrilanka.org*), which issues a newsletter and provides education about the threats to the island's elephant population. This is estimated at 2,000; conservationists fear that most of them are doomed.

There are four kinds of wildlife reserve that are part of the conservation programme for elephants and other species. The programme actually began with the arrival of Buddhism with its basic conservation ethic. It was codified by the British when they got over their propensity to consider most four-legged animals as 'game' to be blasted to death for 'sport'. At present the reserves are:

STRICT NATURE RESERVES (SNR) These are exclusively reserved for wildlife. No entry except with permission from the Director of Wildlife Conservation himself, and this is issued only to those engaged in official or scientific work. Such reserves are Ritigala, Hakgala and Yala.

NATIONAL PARKS (NP) These parks are reserved for wildlife and a person may enter to study or observe the flora and fauna only with a permit issued by the Director of Wildlife Conservation or his appointees. There are 18 NPs declared, covering the entire range of ecosystems in Sri Lanka. Among these are the Horton Plains NP which represents the montane wet-zone ecosystems and the Hikkaduwa and Pigeon Island national parks, the only marine national parks. Not all in this list are open to the public.

1	Ruhunu (Yala)	10	Bundala
2	Udawalawe	11	Somawathiya Chaitiya
3	Wilpattu	12	Yala East
4	Wasgomuwa	13	Lahugala Kithulana
5	Flood Plains	14	Lunugamwehera
6	Minneriya–Giritale	15	Kaudulla
7	Maduru Oya	16	Horagolla
8	Gal Oya	17	Hikkaduwa Marine Park
9	Horton Plains	18	Pigeon Island Marine Park

NATURE RESERVES Nature reserves are primarily for wildlife and human activity is restricted to the conditions printed on the entry permit. Sinharaja Forest is one of the many nature reserves.

SANCTUARIES There are some 50 of these on both state and private land. Wildlife is protected but human activity that respects that is allowed. Generally no visitors' permits are required. Popular with visitors are the sanctuaries at Bellanwila Attidiya and Udawatte Kalle (Kandy), and the Muthurajawela Wetlands Centre.

ENTRY REQUIREMENTS Entry to the national parks, reserves and sanctuaries that are open to the public is possible only with a permit, obtained at the park's entrance. The fee is payable in rupees based on the day's exchange rate for the US dollar. Currently admission to the national parks for foreign adults is US$35; foreign children US$17.50. (Sri Lankans pay less.) A 15% government tax is added to the entrance fees. There is also a charge of US$5 for a tracker, who is obligatory. There is also a fee (Rs125) for the vehicle; 4x4 is recommended. There are restrictions on the number of vehicles allowed into each park at any one time (30 is the limit for Ruhunu). Passengers may get out of their vehicles only at the various specially marked locations. The best time to visit the parks is from 06.30 or from 15.30. Even parks that are usually open to visitors are closed occasionally because of the local situation at the time.

The Department of Wildlife Conservation has published an excellent booklet about the national parks (see page 312). This contains notes on **general park ethics** including the following:

- An official guide is compulsory for visitors to any park
- Walking in the parks is not allowed
- Avoid feeding animals since they are capable of finding their own food
- A forest has its own particular sounds. When in a forest why listen to any other?
- Do not talk loudly, sound the vehicle's horn nor play radios or cassette players
- Have you noticed how wonderfully animals are camouflaged in their surroundings? Wouldn't you too like to blend with the surroundings? All you have to do is to avoid wearing colours that jar on the eye; better to wear earthy colours such as brown or green.

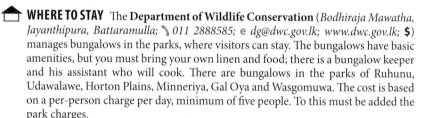

WHERE TO STAY The **Department of Wildlife Conservation** (*Bodhiraja Mawatha, Jayanthipura, Battaramulla;* \ *011 2888585;* e *dg@dwc.gov.lk; www.dwc.gov.lk;* $) manages bungalows in the parks, where visitors can stay. The bungalows have basic amenities, but you must bring your own linen and food; there is a bungalow keeper and his assistant who will cook. There are bungalows in the parks of Ruhunu, Udawalawe, Horton Plains, Minneriya, Gal Oya and Wasgomuwa. The cost is based on a per-person charge per day, minimum of five people. To this must be added the park charges.

It is important when planning to stay in a park bungalow to remember to take all you require since even a small village shop will be some miles away, and you will have to pay every time you re-enter the park. The main problem about staying in a park bungalow is that these are meant for Sri Lankans and are much in demand. Hence, finding one available is unlikely. Even Sri Lankans complain that it is difficult to rent one.

A few organisations arrange special tours that include many of the nature reserves. A pioneer is Jetwing Hotels with their ecotourism division **Jetwing Eco-Holidays** (*Jetwing Hse, 46/26 Navam Mawatha, Colombo 2;* \ *011 2381201;* e *enquiries@jetwingeco.com; www.jetwingeco.com*).

Some of the parks and sanctuaries open to visitors are reviewed below. I am grateful to **Gehan de Silva Wijeyeratne** (hereafter referred to as *GdeSW* where his research material is referenced) for permitting the use in this section of his research material, namely the pieces below on Bellanwila, Bundala, Horton Plains, Muthurajawela, Ruhunu (see page 195), Sinharaja and Udawalawe. Gehan is the author of *Sri Lankan Wildlife*, published by Bradt (see page 313 for details and also page VI for a special discount offer on this guide).

BELLANWILA ATTIDIYA SANCTUARY Bellanwila Attidiya marshes remain as a precious fragment of the once extensive marshlands around Colombo. A sanctuary since 1990, it is of major importance as a wildlife refuge as well as a flood detention area for Colombo. Although its surroundings are far from salubrious, it is rich in species and well worth a visit in its own right, not just to kill time while staying in Colombo. In the 1980s, the area was cultivated for paddy but has gradually reverted to marshland. As Colombo expands in urban sprawl, this sanctuary will become of national importance as a precious ecotourism site close to a major city.

Getting there
By train There is a station at Nugegoda on the Kelani Valley line, from which a three-wheeler would be the best way to get there.

By bus The object is to get first to the Dehiwela clocktower junction, and buses passing along the Galle road would take you there. Next take a bus (No 119 bound for Maharagama) to Bellantota junction. From there it is a walk of some five minutes to the engineer's office (see below). Another way is to go to Gansaba junction, beyond Nugegoda by bus, and then look for a bus (No 117) to get close to the site. Bus No 117 running between Nugegoda and Ratmalana passes the engineer's office every 15 minutes. Rush-hour travel can extend the journey from Colombo by an hour.

By road The landmark to make for is the Sri Lanka Land Reclamation Development Corporation Chief Engineer's office in Attidiya. From there walk along the busy Ratmalana–Attidiya road with the engineer's office on your right. On your left will be a sign indicating the sanctuary. A few yards further on is a canal. Turn left on to the left bank of the canal, passing some huts, and proceed along the canal path that crosses the marsh. At times this path can be overgrown and quite difficult. It leads to a bird observation tower. It is also possible to cross the bridge and follow the path along the opposite bank for more marsh birding.

Where to stay and eat Dehiwela is the nearest coastal point with guesthouses (see page 229); otherwise base yourself in Colombo.

What to see and do This is a superb place for birdwatching with over 150 species being recorded. A two- to three-hour session should yield around 40 species when migrants are present, including little cormorant, darter, cinnamon, black and yellow bittern, watercock, pond and purple heron, little, median and cattle egret, Asian spoonbill, lesser whistling duck, black-headed and glossy ibis, Brahminy kite, white-breasted waterhen, moorhen, purple coot, pheasant-tailed jacana, stork-billed and white-throated kingfisher, Pallas's grasshopper warbler, Loten's sunbird, blue-tailed bee-eater, brown-headed and Ceylon small barbets.

Mammals found there include otter, fishing cat and mongoose, but you will be lucky to see any of them. Other wildlife recorded include 39 species of fish,

6

52 butterflies, of which nine are endemic, and 37 dragonflies. There is at least one magnificently big water monitor in the sanctuary. It is in the same genus, *Varanus*, as the famous Komodo dragon, and is a smaller version of it. Its black-and-yellow hide is dimpled and has the appearance of armour. This is as close as you can get to Jurassic Park in real life. You may well get a bit of a scare if you suddenly encounter one on the path, but leave it alone and you'll have nothing to worry about. (*GdeSW*)

BUNDALA NATIONAL PARK Bundala National Park, comprising an area of approximately 6,200ha, had a reputation as a bird sanctuary before it was established as a national park. In the 1980s, local safari operators discovered that Bundala was a better bet for elephants than Ruhunu/Yala. Jeeps began to arrive *en masse* to see the elephant herds and subsequently it was elevated to a national park by the authorities to give control over access. It is similar to the coastal parts of its eastern neighbour Ruhunu National Park. It is a mix of scrub jungle and sand dunes bordering the sea. The beaches are an important nesting site for turtles. The lagoons within the park hold good numbers of birds and crocodiles.

Getting there Access to the park is from the A2 road between Hambantota and Tissamaharama. Access is only by vehicle. A van with a high chassis or a 4x4 vehicle is best. Jeeps can be hired from tour operators in Hambantota or Tissamaharama for about Rs5,000 per half-day safari. Nature enthusiasts should beware that most jeep drivers are only interested in showing off elephants, so it would be necessary to explain what you are looking for if you want more than that. Park entrance for foreigners is US$35 (children US$17.50) plus 15% tax and US$5 tracker charge and a further Rs125 for the vehicle. Behind the park office you can view the Embililkala Kalapuwa (tank) from a tower hide.

 Where to stay and eat Accommodation in Tissamaharama (see page 281) is probably best, so you can combine a visit to Bundala with one to the Ruhunu National Park.

What to see and do Birdwatchers can look out for the two endemics found in the park: the brown-capped babbler and the Sri Lanka junglefowl. The latter is more likely to be seen as it crosses jeep tracks. The babbler has a frustrating habit of uttering a call (it sounds like *pretee dear*) but not showing itself. The water bodies in the park hold a host of wetland birds. A successful game drive could yield upwards of 50 species, including cattle, intermediate and great egret, Asian spoonbill, black-winged stilt and yellow-wattled lapwing.

During the northern winter there are large numbers of migrants, including golden plover, large and lesser sand plovers, Kentish plover, curlew, greenshank, marsh sandpiper, little stint and curlew sandpiper.

The park has a good selection of larger animals with elephants top of the list for visitors. Other mammals include spotted deer, muntjac, Hanuman langur, jackal, black-naped hare, wild pig, water monitor and crocodile.

Unlikely to be seen by visitors because of their nocturnal habits are civet cat, rusty-spotted cat, slender loris, porcupine and pangolin.

The fishing cat is also found at Bundala. Despite being a widespread animal, little is known of its fishing technique because of its nocturnal habits. The Olive Ridley and leatherback turtles are regular visitors, whereas the hawksbill and green turtles are rare. *Bufo athukoralei*, an endemic frog, is also found in the park.

The flora consists of dry acacia scrub comprising andara, kukuruman, eraminiya and karamba. The scrub forest includes trees like maila, malittan, weera, palu, kohomba and divul. (*GdeSW*)

HORTON PLAINS Horton Plains was gazetted as a nature reserve in 1969 and declared a national park in 1988 because of its unique watershed and biodiversity values. It consists of 3,159ha. It gives access to the sheer drop known as World's End with its spectacular view (on clear days) over the distant hills and valleys to the south coast. The best time to visit is from October to April. The ticket office is open from 06.00 to 16.00, while the park itself closes at 18.00. Admission is US$25 per person.

Planter Thomas Farr 'discovered' these plains and named the area after Sir Robert Wilmot Horton, the then British governor (1831–37). The area's traditional name in Sinhala was Maha Sumanasena. Farr's hunting lodge became a resthouse known as Farr Inn, even though it could be reached only by foot. In 1999, it ceased to be a resthouse and was eventually transformed into an information centre with the addition of Horton Café but that's been closed and the old bungalow is now a small museum. The information centre serves as a good introduction about what can be seen in the park.

The sweeping plains are reminiscent of the grouse moors of Scotland. It is not hard to see why the British fell in love with the place. Interspersed among the plains are big pockets of elfin forest, with a characteristic stunted and windswept look. The trees are encrusted with lichens, colloquially referred to as old man's beard. The undulating plains have a haunting melancholy air, very different in atmosphere from anywhere else in Sri Lanka.

The plains are on a highland plateau at 2,100m above sea level. The protected area is contiguous with the Peak Wilderness Sanctuary. Sri Lanka's second- and third-highest peaks are found in the park: **Thotupola Kanda** (2,357m) and **Kirigalpota** (2,395m). There is a trail to Thotupola Kanda, which is regularly climbed. The trail for the short climb is in generally good condition. These peaks are not as conspicuous as the conical peak of Sri Pada (Adam's Peak).

As with many tropical forests, the mammals are difficult to see, although lucky visitors have seen leopard. Most visitors are content with seeing sambhur, a large kind of deer. In recent years the lichen-clad cloudforest has been dying back. Acid rain and acid mist is suspected as the possible cause. The acid probably stems from atmospheric pollution from the exhaust fumes of cars from all over the country.

The trees in the park are dominated by keena, *Syzgium rotundifolium* and *Syzgium sclerophyllum* and species from the Lauracea family. The undergrowth is dominated by dwarf bamboo in the open swampy areas. The rhododendrons are native and have affinities with those on the mountains of southern India and the Himalayas. Around half the woody species of plants are endemic. The giant ferns are a conspicuous feature and many fine examples can be seen on the road to Farr Inn from Pattipola.

Getting there
By train To Pattipola station and then a long hike.

By bus The closest point by bus is **Pattipola**, a hike of some 15km to World's End. Buses leave Nuwara Eliya for Pattipola at 07.45, 13.00 and 16.30, returning at 10.15, 14.30 and 18.00.

By road Horton Plains can be reached by any of these all-weather roads: from Nuwara Eliya via Ambewela and Pattipola (32km); from Haputale via Welimada, Boralanda, Ohiya (38km) or via Bandarawela, Boralanda, Ohiya; from Nuwara Eliya via Hakgala, Rendapola, Ambewela, Pattipola (38km). Vehicles can be hired from Nuwara Eliya to the park, where the driver will wait to take you back; expect to pay from Rs5,000, which includes the waiting time.

Approaching the park
The drive from Nuwara Eliya is on a country road leading off the A7 between Nuwara Eliya and Nanu Oya. It climbs steadily, past the Strict Nature Reserve (SNR) (no entry) that lies behind the Hakgala Botanical Gardens. It passes vegetable allotments covered with plastic sheets, and some cleared forest, and then it enters cattle country, with grassy meadows and grazing cattle on either side. At a crossroads, you will see the Ambewela Farm Shop (signposted) where balls of cheese, jars of strawberry jam and goats' milk can be purchased. The road curves around the railway line and then, in the midst of this pastoral setting, is the efficient-looking Highland Milk Products factory, with a retail outlet selling yoghurt, ice cream and bottles of ghee.

You know you are getting near Horton Plains by the hoardings on both sides of the road. These are not advertisements (although they bear the name of the sponsor) but warnings. They begin with the notice: 'No entry without permit' and then comes one that says sternly: 'No! No!! No!!! No polythene on Horton Plains.' Another states:

> The post-mortem of the untimely death of sambhur deer has revealed that the consumption of polythene has been the cause for their deaths.

Next comes:

> Have you seen a leopard yet? If you are quiet, you just might. Horton Plains is home to about 15 leopards. Loud voices and music disturbs them. Please be considerate.

Then we are told:

> Walking, riding and driving off road is extremely prohibited.

A signpost at the entrance gate points to Ohiya (11.2km), Bandarawela (52km), Nuwara Eliya (32km) and World's End (4km walk).

There is a forest of advertising hoardings by the gate with the Horton Plains Ten Commandments painted on them in three languages (English, Sinhala and Tamil). I was told by my guide, Selvam, that Sri Lankans need a lot of signs to explain to them about conduct in the park as they are not so environmentally sensitive as most foreigners. For visitors those signs are an eyesore and even their tone rather upsets the tranquillity one seeks. A huge one reads:

> Please do not:
>
> Collect any plants or animals
> Pick flowers or destroy vegetation
> Discard litter, cigarette butts and lighted matchsticks
> Disturb animals by approaching too close to them
> Light fires

Create noises or other disturbance likely to offend animals or visitors
Use radios or other musical instruments
Bring pets or plants
Carry firearms or explosives
Deface any physical features in the park by vandalism or graffiti.

Walking and birding can be done on the way to the plains without any fee being payable. Most visitors motor in from Nuwara Eliya to the entrance gate and then hike through the plains for 4km to World's End. Admission is the same as for the main parks, US$25 per foreign adult and US$12.50 per foreign child, plus 15% tax.

Where to stay and eat There are two places to stay (**Dormitory** and **Anderson Lodge**) in the park, operated by the Department of Wildlife Conservation. However, these are not a practical possibility for foreigners because of the difficulties in booking them. Staying in Nuwara Eliya is best and, if you have no transport, hiring a minibus to visit the park. The canteen by the gate serves snacks and tea, and roti in the mornings, but do not rely on it for meals.

What to see and do For birdwatchers, montane endemics include Sri Lanka white eye, Sri Lanka woodpigeon, Ceylon hill munia and dull-blue flycatcher. Other montane birds include the migrant Indian blue robin and the resident grey-headed canary flycatcher. The latter is a common bird, and its canary-like call involves a series of rapid notes fired off like a machine gun. The pied bush chat is a drab montane bird that is often seen in pairs on the plains. The male is black and white, whereas the female is a drab brown. Other birds in the park include black bulbul, bar-winged flycatcher-shrike and Indian scimitar babbler. The Sri Lanka junglefowl, which is found all over the island, may be heard uttering its familiar call.

In recent years the population of sambhur has soared, with a corresponding increase in their main predator, the leopard. Other mammals include wild boar and the highland races of the grizzled Indian squirrel as well as the highland race of the purple-faced leaf monkey. The latter has a shaggy coat, lacks the white rump patch of the lowland races and is often called the bear monkey.

The montane race of the grizzled squirrel has deep-black upper parts diffusing into the buff underparts. The lowland wet-zone race has the black and buff sharply demarcated. Other mammals include the rusty-spotted cat, fishing cat, muntjac, mouse deer, stripe-necked mongoose and otter. Feeding flocks of birds are often followed by the small, dusky-striped squirrel. (*GdeSW*)

KNUCKLES Knuckles is the mountain range north of Kandy. At Selvakanda (1,585m above sea level) is the **Pygmy Forest**. All trees are stunted to about 0.9–1½m (3–5ft) and are covered with lichens, mosses and orchids.

To reach the Knuckles range you need to drive about 27km on the A26 from Kandy, then turn left on to the road to Rangala, then on to Corbet's Gap. To get to the forest you have to drive through Bambarella Estate.

MINNERIYA–GIRITALE NATIONAL PARK Minneriya–Giritale (the full name for Minneriya) has been upgraded from a nature reserve to a national park because of its popularity with visitors seeking elephants. As it is located in the centre of the Cultural Triangle, it adds a natural dimension to a holiday gazing at ruins. Because it is not so well known, the park attracts fewer visitors, although it is a fascinating introduction to Sri Lanka's wildlife. Elephants can sometimes be seen beside the main road running close to the park.

Road signs promoting the preservation of the environment disturb the natural tangle of the scenery but one cannot help but support their message, even if they jar the senses. Elephant skulls lined up outside a forest-green building announce the entrance to the Minneriya National Park, renowned for its elephants.

Even newer as a place for observing wildlife is the **Kaudulla National Park**. There is a road off to the left, just after the lane leading to the Minneriya railway station, which gives signposted access to the park. It's a 10km drive along a country lane, deep into bush country where eagles circle and elephant watchers' huts on stilts guard paddy plantations.

Kaudulla National Park was opened as number 15 on 1 April 2002. The temperature at the park ranges from 20°C to 35°C and its elevation is from zero to 100m above sea level. Its ecosystems are dry mixed, evergreen forest, riverine forest and the Kaudulla wetland.

Fauna to be seen include elephant, leopard, bear, sambhur, hare, spotted deer, barking deer and waterbirds. Admission fee is Rs4,000 plus applicable taxes for two people. The park is open from 06.00 to 18.30 and there are trackers available for visiting vehicles, with vehicle admission charges being Rs2,500–Rs3,000.

Getting there

By train Both parks are in theory accessible from the railway station, Minneriya, close to the Minneriya park entrance. It is a halt on the line running from Gal Oya to Polonnaruwa. However, alighting there won't help much since you will need to hire a jeep to visit the parks, and there will be none at the station. If you are intent on going by train and making the parks the only places you visit (instead of combining a safari with visits to points in the Cultural Triangle) then leave the train at Habarana station, and look for a jeep to hire from there.

By bus No 48 stops at Habarana, from where you can hire a jeep.

By road The entrance to the Minneriya park is off the main road (A11) that cuts across the centre of the island to Polonnaruwa. It coincides with where the road and the railway line touch and can be seen near the Minneriya railway station signpost. Driving from anywhere in Sri Lanka, you would head for the Habarana crossroads to access the A11.

The Kaudulla NP is located around the Kaudulla tank (reservoir) to the north of Minneriya. Access is by a country road southwards from the A6, or northwards through Minneriya itself.

The Giritale (NP) part of the sanctuary is off the A11, on the opposite side of the reservoir to the National Holiday Resort.

Where to stay and eat Any of the hotels and guesthouses in Giritale, Habarana or Sigiriya would be convenient. (See pages 136, 138 and 144, respectively.)

What to see and do Naturally, elephants in the national park. For birdlife, the Giritale Sanctuary (NP) is rewarding, ranging from the sparrow-sized Tickell's blue flycatcher to the brown fish owl and the black-headed ibis. There are 70 species of bird that can be seen from the Royal Lotus and Deer Park hotels beside the Giritale reservoir, illustrated and listed in *A Selection of the Birds of Giritale* (see page 312 for details).

HORAGOLLA Previously a sanctuary, this national park was opened only in April 2005. It consists of just over 13ha and is located in Nambaduluwa village in the Gampaha district. It became a sanctuary in 1973 under protection of the Flora and Fauna Ordinance because of its rich biodiversity, and was named a park on 28 July 2004. It consists of low-country evergreen forest with a humus soil structure and has a hot temperature throughout the year.

Getting there Horagolla can be reached by travelling 35km from Colombo along the road to Kandy. At Nittambuwa the road turns to Veyangoda and after about 1km comes the Pinnagolla junction. The park office is a 6km drive from that junction. Private transport is best, since buses don't go to the park, and it's best to stay in Colombo.

Where to stay and eat There are no good options nearby, so it's best to stay and eat in Colombo.

What to see and do A variety of trees, plants and grasses cover the park's landscape. Fauna includes the fishing cat, mouse deer, fox and giant squirrel, as well as parakeets, black-headed bulbuls, barbets, Asian koels, etc. There are also pythons and cobras.

MUTHURAJAWELA Muthurajawela is an extensive area of wetlands close to the airport and Colombo that is under threat of development. Although tracts of it have been lost to the new Expressway, a part has been set aside as a conservation area. A visitor centre was opened there in 1997 which operates boat rides through the canals and rivulets in the wetland to the Negombo lagoon and back. Knowledgeable, trained guides, most of whom have at least an A-level in biology, talk visitors through the flora, fauna and history of the marshes. Although you may see more species on a visit to the Bellanwila Attidiya Sanctuary, the boat ride is an ecotourism experience not to be missed. Remember to take a hat or sunglasses as there is a lot of glare off the water.

The **Muthurajawela Wetlands** (*Bobitiya, Pamunugama Rd, Delatura, Ja-Ela;* ✎ *011 4830150;* ⊕ *07.30–16.00 daily*) has a small souvenir shop, simple conference facilities and a small activity area for children. The shop has a few publications on the fauna and flora of the marshes. Income helps to conserve the site and to continue with the educational projects. No entry fee is charged for the visitor centre. A video presentation is available in the auditorium.

The centre arranges two-hour boat rides conducted by guides. The first boat ride is at 07.30, the last at 16.00. Although not strictly required, it is advisable to telephone to make a reservation as there are only three boats available.

The boat starts from the Hamilton canal and proceeds to the Negombo lagoon. The lagoon has an area of 2,883ha and a mean depth of only 1½m. The boats then proceed to the Matiwala Bokka (literally 'Clay Pit Ditch'), which is an open area of water about 1½m deep created by the excavation of clay. Then the boat goes on to Dandugam Oya, a waterway 15m deep in places, before returning to the Negombo lagoon and back along the Hamilton canal.

Getting there
By train The sanctuary is 1km north of Ja-Ela, which is a station on the Puttalam line. Trains to and from Negombo stop there. This is an industrial area and you will need faith to believe there is a nature reserve near the station. A three-wheeler will take you the final leg of the journey.

By bus From Colombo take a bus bound for Negombo and ask to be put down at the Tudella junction, 1km north of Ja-Ela, just after the 16km post.

By road Take the highway (A3) from Colombo in the direction of Negombo and turn off to the west (seaward) at the Tudella junction, 1km north of Ja-Ela, just after the 16km post. The approach to the visitor centre is signposted, on the right, some 400m along the Pamunugama road, after you pass a freight terminal and an old Dutch canal. The A3 is the road linking Colombo with the airport and the turn-off to the airport is a further 6km along the highway from the Tudella junction. The distance from Colombo is 20km and from Negombo, 15km.

Where to stay and eat A visit would make a pleasant half-day outing from hotels in Colombo (see pages 75–80) or Negombo (see pages 227–9). There is a snack shop (\$) attached to the visitor centre.

What to see and do The birds found in the wetlands are similar to those in the Bellanwila Attidiya marshes. They include purple heron, little and intermediate egrets, black and yellow bittern, common hawk cuckoo and pied cuckoo. Favourites with visitors are the dazzling kingfishers, with common, white-throated, stork-billed and pied kingfishers likely to be seen. The black-capped kingfisher, a scarce migrant, has also been recorded. Little grebe, moorhen, lesser whistling duck, painted stork, zitting cisticola, ring-necked parakeet, greater coucal, shikra, Brahminy kite and migrant wader are other common birds in the wetland and surrounding scrub.

Other wildlife surveys of the marshes have been conducted and a fair number of species have been recorded. These include 73 fish (51 endemic), 15 amphibians (two endemic) and 37 reptiles (five endemic). The tetrapod (four-legged) reptiles include the endangered estuarine crocodile which may, with luck, be seen. A study has shown the presence of about six of them, 3–5m in length, as well as 60 smaller individuals. The snake *Gerada prevostiana* was only known from a single specimen collected about 100 years ago from the Kelani River, until a second was collected in the northern part of the marshes close to Negombo lagoon.

The endemic painted bat and the toque monkey are among the 34 species of mammal that have been recorded. Small troops of the monkey are likely to be seen on every boat ride. A lot of luck, however, is required to see the threatened otter. The marsh is also a refuge for a few threatened species including the painted bat, slender loris, rusty-spotted cat and the occasionally seen fishing cat (known locally as *kola diviya*). The jackal and the mouse deer are now rare due to loss of habitat.

Of the 129 plant species recorded, 40 are known to have medicinal properties. The banks are lined with a reed locally known as *val bata* (*Phragmites carca*). Also found is the wetland plant *Achrosticum aureum* whose tender leaves are cooked as a vegetable rich in vitamin E. As the boat glides through the rivulets, you may see a mangrove tree with green, apple-like fruits. This is *Cerbera manghas*, locally known as *diya kadura*. The fruits are poisonous. Many plants are harvested by the local folk. One is the *wetakeiya*, a kind of pandanus with thorny leaves, used to make mats. Occasionally, tidal fluctuations result in high salinity and then jellyfish may be seen in the rivulets that crisscross the marsh. (*GdeSW*)

PINNAWELA ELEPHANT ORPHANAGE (*off Rambukkana Rd;* ☏ *035 2265804;* ⊕ *daily, feeding times 09.15, 13.15 & 17.00, bathing times 10.00–12.00 & 14.00– 16.00; admission: adults Rs2,000, reductions for children & SAARC country residents*)
Not a national park, but a national treasure, the orphanage was begun in 1975 to

provide shelter and care for young elephants that had been abandoned or orphaned by their mothers. The Pinnawela Elephant Orphanage is the only one of its kind in the world. There are now over 60 elephants and some of them are founder members (there were originally seven). Older elephants are used as substitute family members for the orphans.

The best time to visit is when the elephants are being fed (bottle feeding is sometimes necessary) or when they troop off in an eager herd down a lane opposite the park entrance to the Maha Oya (river) to bathe. There are terrace cafés on the bank overlooking the river where visitors can relax while the elephants are scrubbed.

The orphanage not only has the largest captive herd of elephants in the world, it has also become the most successful breeding centre, so not all the baby elephants are orphans. It is not a zoo, but a zoo is being built nearby at Wagolla, on a 16ha site that was formerly an agriculture training centre. Animals in that zoo will be housed in landscaped sanctuaries (no cages), separated from visitors by a moat. A wildlife sanctuary and breeding centre for endangered indigenous species is planned as part of the project.

Getting there
By train The nearest station is Rambukkana, a simple one with wooden armchairs set out for passengers and a small hut selling soft drinks. The old entrance hall across the bridge to the exit has a wooden roof and resembles a Buddhist speaking-hall. A colourful vegetable market is held along the access road to the station.

By bus There is a bus service from the town centre (take the Kegalle bus) that stops at the orphanage (about 5km distant). To get there from Kandy or Colombo, take a bus that stops in Kegalle and change there for the 'Pinnawela bus'. There is also a direct service from Colombo (Nos 99/488-4).

By road At Karandapona, just after Kegalle on the A1 road to Kandy from Colombo, there is a signposted turn-off to the left to Rambukkana (13km). Note that there is no corresponding signpost if you are coming from Kandy. From Rambukkana, the orphanage is about a 5km drive past some small, privately owned elephant sideshows.

Where to stay and eat There is a **restaurant** ($) inside the orphanage. At the gates the basic-rate **Elephant View Hotel** (☎ *035 2265292;* $) has a few rooms and a first-floor restaurant from where the elephants can be viewed in safety. The skeleton of one is on display behind a curtain in the hotel's garden.

Usually guests stay at hotels in Colombo or Kandy and visit Pinnawela on the way from one city to the other (see pages 73 and 102, respectively).

RUHUNU NATIONAL PARK (YALA WEST)
This is undoubtedly Sri Lanka's most visited national park. It is a wonderful place with a diversity of habitats including scrub jungle, tanks, brackish lagoons and riverine habitat. It is simply the best park in the country for viewing animals. The park is divided into five blocks. Block 1 (Yala West), which is what visitors mean when they refer to Yala, is the only one open to the public. It comprises an area of 14,100ha and was declared a national park in 1938.

The park is closed from 1 September to 16 October every year, which is the driest season. Entry is by vehicle only. Cars can be driven along the unsurfaced main routes that run through the park but to use the side roads a minibus with a high wheelbase, or a 4x4 vehicle, will be needed. If you don't have your own transport, take a safari from Tissamaharama, where jeep operators can be found outside the Tissamaharama Resort (cost from Rs5,000). A morning run will typically be from 06.30 to 10.00, which gives a couple of hours in the park. Entry fees are standard at US$35 per foreign adult, US$17.50 per child, plus 15% and tracker fee of US$5.

Getting there
By bus The closest you can get by public transport is 11½km if you get down when the bus from Tissamaharama turns off the B422 to Kirinda. What happens then? Even if you find a three-wheeler, it won't be allowed in the park, and neither will you if you are on foot. However, there are mainline buses to Tissa from Colombo, and from there you can join an organised safari tour.

By road Tissamaharama (264km from Colombo) is reached by a turn-off eastwards from the A2, either coming from Hambantota or across the plains from Wellawaya. From there the B422 runs from Tissa to Kirinda, and the turn-off to the park is just past the 12km post. It is a drive of 11½km to the park entrance. The ticket office and the museum can be found set back from the road, on the left, about 1km before the turn-off (right) to the park entrance.

Where to stay and eat Popular is **Chaaya Wild Yala** (*60 AC rooms, 6 beach chalets; Kirinda, Tissamaharama;* \ *047 2239450;* e *wild@chaayahotels.com; www. chaayahotels.com;* **$$**), which has grown from being a bungalow resort. There is a unique place to stay – **Tree Tops Jungle Lodge** – north of the park and this is mentioned in the *Interior towns* section of this chapter (see page 205).

There are also some budget places in the town. Soft drinks are available from a canteen at the park headquarters.

What to see and do Attached to the ticket office is an interesting museum showing the development of the national park as well as models and skeletons of animals found there. In the park itself, the flora is typical of dry-season monsoon forest in much of the southern belt. Plains are interspersed with pockets of forest containing species such as palu, satin, weera, mayila, malithan, kohomba and divul. The scrub vegetation comprises andara, kukuruman, eraminya and karamba.

Two endemic birds are the Sri Lanka junglefowl and the brown-capped babbler. Very occasionally, a third endemic, the red-faced malkoha, is seen in the tall forest on the Sella Kataragama–Galge road. The park is also good for a number of dry-zone specialities like Eurasian thick-knee, great thick-knee, sirkeer and blue-faced malkohas, and Malabar pied hornbill. The park is probably the best place to see the rare black-necked stork, of which there are fewer than ten individuals in Sri Lanka. The endangered lesser adjutant is another stork to be seen in the park.

Birds seen fairly easily while on safari include painted stork, green bee-eater, pompadour green pigeon, imperial green pigeon and orange-breasted green pigeon. The park has a fine complement of wintering shorebirds as well as other attractive migrants like the common blue-tailed bee-eater and less common migrants like the Brahminy myna and rosy starling. A day's birding in the park, if it includes a visit to the Menik Ganga (river), can yield 100 species.

The biggest draws are elephant, leopard and bear. The park is one of the best places to see a variety of mammals in a single day. A game drive could show black-snaped hare, spotted deer, barking deer, mouse deer, sambhur, Hanuman langur, toque monkey (endemic), stripe-necked mongoose, ruddy mongoose, wild pig, jackal, land monitor, water monitor and marsh and estuarine crocodiles. Although large populations of buffaloes exist in the wild, it is believed that these are descendants of livestock imported from India. After dark, small Indian civets may be seen; other nocturnal mammals include the pangolin, porcupine and slender loris. (*GdeSW*)

SINHARAJA Situated in the southwest lowland wet zone and consisting of 7,648.2ha (18,899 acres), the Sinharaja Forest ranges in altitude from 300m to 1,170m. It has an average annual rainfall of 3,614mm to 5,006mm and temperatures ranging from 19°C to 34°C. Its vegetation consists of 830 of Sri Lanka's endemic species. Over 60% of the trees are endemic and there are 21 endemic bird species and a number of rare insects, reptiles and amphibians.

The **Sinharaja Man and Biosphere Reserve** was declared a World Heritage Site in 1988. It is arguably the most important site in Sri Lanka, and is internationally important for its biodiversity. The reserve encompasses some of the few remaining sizeable tracts of undisturbed, primary lowland rainforest. Despite this, much of the area frequented by birdwatchers was subjected to selective logging in the 1970s, until it was halted in 1977.

Sinharaja is also special as it is the only significant rainforest in the country that is promoted for nature watchers, trekkers and the public in general. It has been protected from over-visitation by the difficulty of access and the lack of accommodation at anything but the bottom end.

Despite it being a vast storehouse of genetic diversity, visitors may be disappointed at the approach. Turning off from **Veddagala** one travels through paddy fields and tea estates. Even at **Kudawa**, where the Forest Department office is located, there is little evidence of the rainforest, unless one wades across the river. Leaving the office, one walks past noisy village children and past paddy fields to reach the reserve boundary. Even there, paddy fields on your right don't quite make for a rainforest atmosphere. The wide, timber roads have been colonised by light-seeking, fast-growing vegetation that is dense and does not permit good views of the interior. Many casual visitors leave disappointed. Leave

ROUGH RIDE

Visitor Christine von Bulow was dismayed by the state of the safari jeeps used in Yala and suggested that I alert visitors to the dangers:

One thing I would have greatly appreciated to have known: that the safari in Yala National Park was such a bumpy ride. During the ride I twisted my back to such an extent that I had to lie down the next couple of days – and I was very worried that I might have had a disc prolapse (which in the end, luckily, I didn't). I also jumped so high in the vehicle because of the bumps that I hit my head against the roof of the jeep (no safety belts). I don't know if it's always like that at the safari – the bumpy ride seemed to be caused by elephant footsteps in mud that had dried up leaving deep, hard holes in the road everywhere – and even when the driver was kind enough to drive very carefully and very slowly and I was allowed to sit in the front where the vehicle was more stable, it was extremely uncomfortable … I know I surely wouldn't have gone on the safari had I known how it would hurt my back. So I would just encourage you to make a note on this in your guide book.

the timber road and take one of the trails for the magic of the rainforest to unfold before you. Getting caught in a rain shower may be inconvenient, but may help form a lasting impression of the place.

Visitors must register at the Forest Department office at Kudawa and pay an admission fee of Rs660. The staff will arrange for a compulsory guide to accompany you for which there is a basic fee of Rs900. The rate varies according to whether you are taking one of the trails which climb a hill, or simply staying on the main road.

Getting there Access is from Ratnapura or, from the west coast, Kalutara or Alutgama.

By train There are regular trains to Kalutara and Alutgama on the way to Galle. There are no trains to Ratnapura.

By bus From Ratnapura there are buses to Kalawana, where you should look for the 'Veddagala bus' – there are about four a day for the 15-minute journey to Kudawa. Allow two hours to travel from Ratnapura. From Kalutara or Alutgama, a series of local buses through Matugama and Agalawatta would get you to Kalawana (allow two hours), from where you take the Veddagala bus to Kudawa.

By road The objective is to get to Kudawa village where the Forestry Department has offices. This can be achieved by taking the road from Ratnapura to Kalawana, or by cutting in from the west coast via Matugama and Agalawatta. From Kalawana there is a road via Veddagala to Kudawa. It is also possible to trek on a short cut from Veddagala to Kudawa, about 4km. This short cut is on the left about 100m after you cross a large bridge on the turn-off road from Veddagala to Kudawa. Walking along the main road will also get you there. To drive in the forest, a vehicle with a high chassis is recommended.

 Where to stay and eat There are rooms and dormitories available at the Forest Department in Kudawa but these have to be booked far in advance so the independent traveller on a short visit would be better staying privately. **Forest View** (*4 rooms & dormitory; Martin Wijesinghe, Forest View, Kudawa; telegram care of Veddagala Post Office,* \ *045 5681864;* **$**) is close to the official boundary. It is 3km from the Forest Department facility at Kudawa, and 100m from the visitor centre which is above Martin's place on a hill. There are clean toilets and showers, and basic accommodation. No advance booking is necessary, but it is advisable.

The **Boulder Garden Nature Resort** (*10 non-AC rooms; Weddagala Rd, aka Sinharaja Rd, Koswatte, Kalawana;* \ *045 2255812;* e *info@bouldergarden.com; www.bouldergarden.com;* **$$$$**) comes with a health warning on its rate sheet. 'It is home to many jungle creatures and they visit our guest facilities. Our suites are thatched … wide open to the symphony of nature.' But they are elegantly furnished and have attached bathrooms. The bar is a natural cave, the restaurant under a rock. All sorts of 'strenuous expeditions' and forest trekking and birdwatching are promised, or simple relaxation in a wonderfully wild environment.

Boulder Garden is aptly named and is centred on a private estate of 4ha, nestling below a canopy of rainforest. 'Responsible environmental ethics' is practised, while another notice states 'we are located in the heart of the jungle'. It can be reached by driving southwards from Ratnapura on the road to Karawita, or eastwards into the interior from the coast at Kalutara on the road to Ratnapura.

What to see and do A staggering 64% of the tree flora in Sinharaja is considered endemic to Sri Lanka. The flora in Sinharaja is a relict of the Deccan–Gondwana flora, belonging to the Indo-Malayan realm. It comprises lowland and sub-montane wet, evergreen forests. On the east there are sub-montane Patana grasslands. The lower slopes and valleys have remnants of *Dipterocarpus* forest, with the middle and higher slopes characterised by Mesue-Doona (*Shorea*) forest.

Disturbed areas have secondary and scrub forest. A number of endemic and commercially useful plants are found. A number of forest villages are present and the villagers harvest the *wewal* (a kind of rattan) and the kitul (palm). The kitul flower yields a sweet juice from which is made *jaggery*, taken as a sugar substitute with tea. The jaggery is made into hard, dark brown hemispheres and wrapped in dried leaves for sale.

In open areas that have been subject to nutrient leaching, orchids and pitcher plants are common. Pitcher plants thrive on nutrient-poor soils as they can obtain their nitrogen from the insects they trap and therefore compete with other plants that cannot obtain necessary nutrients from the soil. Look for the pitcher plants next to the visitor centre.

Sinharaja is a paradise for birders, with a mouth-watering line-up of endemics. These include Sri Lanka spurfowl, Sri Lanka junglefowl, Sri Lanka woodpigeon, Sri Lanka hanging parrot, Layward's parakeet, red-faced malkoha, green-billed coucal, chestnut-backed owlet, Sri Lanka grey hornbill, yellow-fronted barbet, Ceylon small barbet, black-capped bulbul, spot-winged thrush, orange-billed babbler, brown-capped babbler, ashy-headed laughingthrush, Sri Lanka blue magpie, white-faced starling, Ceylon hill munia and Sri Lanka munia.

Potential splits that birders should look out for include the scaly thrush, scimitar babbler and Ceylon crested drongo (greater racket-tailed drongo). Indian subcontinental endemics include the Malabar trogon and Sri Lanka frogmouth. A host of other birds are to be seen, including the black coucal, imperial green pigeon, velvet-fronted nuthatch and yellow-browed bulbul. Raptors found in the forest include crested goshawk and besra. Oriental honey-buzzard is occasionally seen in the stretch between Kudawa village and Martin's guesthouse.

Half of the endemic mammals and butterflies are present. A few leopards are present but seldom seen, except by a lucky few. They have been seen on the main logging road, so who knows what might be around the next corner? The endemic purple-faced leaf monkey and the grizzled Indian squirrel are two mammals visitors are likely to see. Endemic lizards include the endangered rough-nosed horned lizard. Threatened freshwater fish include combtail, smooth-breasted snakehead, black ruby carp, cherry barb and red-tail goby. (*GdeSW*)

UDAWALAWE Udawalawe is fast becoming one of the most popular national parks. This is partly because it is only a few hours' drive from Colombo and partly because elephants are a sure thing. The landscape is not as exciting or as varied as Ruhunu, but with elephants available no-one seems to mind. This is not to say the park is devoid of scenery. The hills in the background across the grasslands make for a nice setting and remind travellers that the highlands are not too far away. The serious birdwatcher and wildlife buff will prefer Ruhunu as it has a much better mix of animals.

The park is a mixture of abandoned teak plantations, grassland, scrub jungle and riverine gallery forest along the Walawe Ganga and Mau Ara. It was established as a reserve to protect the catchment to the Udawalawe reservoir. It is feasible to visit on a long day trip from Colombo.

Getting there The park is in the south of the central hills of the island. It surrounds the manmade reservoir of Udawalawe, which is part of the park. On three sides it is partly in the Moneragala and partly in the Ratnapura district. The park entrance is on the minor road (B427) between Timbolketiya and Tanamalwila. The simplest approach from Colombo would be via Ratnapura.

By bus From Ratnapura a bus via Pelmadulla to Timbolketiya and Embilipitiya is what you want.

By road From Ratnapura, take the A4 to Pelmadulla and then the A18 that goes through Timbolketiya, then to Embilipitiya and on to Nonagama on the south coast. This is the road to take if you are driving from the south. From Tanamalwila in the east, on the A2 near Kuda Oya on the run to/from Wellawaya, the B427 cuts across the island to Timbolketiya. The rangers' office is at Timbolketiya for the purchase of permits. Jeeps can be hired from there and from Embilipitiya to enter the park.

Entry is by vehicle only. Open-topped vehicles are permitted (they are not allowed at Yala), which provides a more exciting safari experience. The entry rates are the same as at Yala (foreigners US$35, children US$17.50, plus 15% tax). Jeeps can sometimes be hired at the park entrance (from Rs3,000 for three hours).

Where to stay and eat Some 20 minutes' drive from the park is the **Safari Village** (*4 AC & 15 non-AC rooms; Right Bank Canal Rd, Udawalawe;* \ *047 2233201; (reservations): Kinjou Restaurant, 33 Amerasekara Mawatha, Colombo 5;* \ *011 2591728;* e *kinjoulanka@sltnet.lk; www.safarivillagehotel.com;* **$**). It has twin bedrooms with fans, mosquito nets and en-suite toilets. The rooms and toilets are kept clean, food is good and service courteous; the location is nothing to speak of. Jeep and driver can be hired for half a day, or a full day.

Located by the Chandrika Lake within easy distance of the national park is the **Centauria Tourist Hotel** (*51 AC rooms; New Town, Embilipitiya;* \ *047 2230514;* e *centauria@sltnet.lk; www.centauriaayurveda.com;* **$$**). Some rooms, much favoured by tour groups, overlook the water. The hotel does a packed breakfast for early risers. As well as safaris, the hotel can arrange boat rides and lake fishing trips. The hotel also bills itself as the Centauria Ayurveda Lake Resort since it has added seven- to ten-day ayurveda packages in a special treatment centre in its 2ha lakeside garden setting.

Cricket fans will delight in Kalu-spotting as well as wildlife sightings when they stay at **Kalu's Hideaway** (*7 rooms; Walawegama, Udawalawe;* \ *047 4922396;* e *info@ sheerholidays.com; www.kalushideaway.com;* **$$**). Kalu (Romesh Kaluwitharana) was Sri Lanka's energetic and ever-cheerful wicketkeeper/batsman for several years and has now built a chalet resort within a stone's throw of the Udawalawe National Park and the stunning Walawe Dam. Bedrooms are spacious and practical and there is a lavish use of timber. The restaurant (**$$**) is open to non-residents with no advance reservation required. Guests are encouraged to explore the locality, especially the Maduwanvala Walauwa (former home of a village nobleman), Wawulpane Caves, where there is a large bat population, the Sevangala sugar factory and the hot springs at Embilipitiya.

What to see and do On entering the park you will pass through abandoned teak plantations interspersed with grassland which has largely been created by *chena* (slash and burn) cultivation. A few economically important tree species such as satin, ebony and halmilla are present. River margins are characterised by the water-loving kumbuk trees which are easily identified by their pale trunks.

The park is good for raptors and good views can be had of black-winged kite, white-bellied sea eagle, crested serpent eagle, changeable hawk eagle, the threatened grey-headed fish eagle and the shikra. Endemics include the Sri Lanka junglefowl, the locally present Sri Lanka spurfowl, Sri Lanka grey hornbill and the endangered red-faced malkoha. Over the reservoir, numbers of Brahminy kites can be seen. Among the dozens of cormorants on the reservoir, look for the darter, or snake bird as it is sometimes known on account of its long slim snake-like head and neck. Interesting forest birds include sirkeer malkoha and blue-faced malkoha.

Look for the scarce migrant black-capped purple kingfisher at Burutha Golla Wewa. Other residents at the *wewa* (tank/lake) include stork-billed and common kingfishers, egrets, herons, white-necked stork, black-headed ibis and painted storks. Flocks of Malabar pied hornbill give themselves away by their raucous cacophony. Look out for jungle bush quails that often run across the track. A scarcer, beautiful quail is the blue-breasted quail. Two rare birds that can be seen are the grey-headed fish eagle and the internationally endangered lesser adjutant. Adding a touch of colour are the Indian rollers and Asian paradise flycatchers. A game drive can yield up to 100 species when migrants are in.

Among the mammals likely to be seen are the endemic toque monkey, Hanuman langur, spotted deer, wild pig, black-napped hare, ruddy mongoose and sambhur. Rarely seen mammals include the stripe-necked mongoose, muntjac, pangolin, giant flying squirrel, jungle cat, porcupine and the nocturnal slender loris. The endemic golden palm civet has also been recorded. Leopard is present but rarely seen. (*GdeSW*)

UDAWATTE KALLE The following quotation and information are extracted from a pamphlet prepared by GLRC Jayawardena:

> Udawatte Kalle is a vast virgin primeval forest … where hidden streams are found trickling under tree ferns, and the mountain terrain, undisturbed by man, covered with verdant impenetrable jungle, is clothed at its highest points with mist.

The Udawatte Kalle Forest is situated in the middle of the town of Kandy and is the only forest in the middle of a city. It is located behind and above the Temple of the Tooth. Its elevation is 1,600m and the temperature around 28°C to 30°C. The forest gets its rain from the southwest and northwest monsoons and the usual annual rainfall is 2,500mm to 3,000mm.

The sanctuary covers 104ha and has more than 150 species of plantlife growing. The forest was once part of the royal palace and protected as a forest reserve. However, soon after the British conquest of the Kingdom of Kandy, the British made Kandy their military headquarters for the Kandyan province. Protected forests like Udawatte Kalle were cleared for the purpose of erecting military barracks and redoubts. Then parts of the forest were taken over to build the governor's residence, schools, homesteads and coffee plantations.

In 1856, Udawatte Kalle was declared a reserved forest by the British authorities. However, the Forest Act did not become law until 1885, with the Forest Department being set up in 1887. On 1 January 1898, Udawatte Kalle was finally officially proclaimed as a forest reserve.

The sanctuary is open from 08.00 to 17.30 daily; the entrance fee for foreigners is Rs600, children under 12 pay Rs300.

Getting there The sanctuary is behind the Temple of the Tooth, so first you must skirt around that by walking up D S Senanayake Veediya, the main road that flanks the Queen's Hotel. A right turn into Kande Veediya takes you eastwards towards the sanctuary and the paths that meander through it. The easiest way, so you save your energy for walking in the sanctuary, is to take a three-wheeler taxi from your hotel to the sanctuary entrance.

Where to stay and eat Any central Kandy hotel is within a short distance of the sanctuary (see pages 111–18).

What to see and do There are some intriguing paths to explore the forest, among them one called Lady Horton's Walk, which was later constructed as a road. It begins by the side of the gate of the president's pavilion and zigzags its way to the pond where it branches left and circles a major part of the forest. Gregory's Path (almost covered by jungle) starts near the bamboo trees by the pond and climbs the hill ending at Lady Gregory's Seat. It was constructed by Governor Gregory between 1873 and 1877. Byrde's Lane continues from the seat to join Lady Horton's Walk.

The best times for birdwatching are from 06.15 to 08.30 (but the sanctuary is not officially open that early) and from 16.30 to 17.30. Some 30 species can be seen. The forest is the natural habitat for every rare endemic orchid, while some exotic ones have become naturalised. There are also some relief patches of natural forest. The puswela is one of the unique features of Udawatte Kalle. This plant would have existed many years prior to the British occupation, for perhaps 200 to 300 years. It extends over 3–4ha and is also found in Sinharaja and Ratnapura, but probably nowhere else in the world. Over 40 ferns and flowering plants are found in the sanctuary.

Mammals include squirrel (*Funammbulus palmmarumm*), porcupine (*Hystrix indica*) and monkey (*Macaca sinica*). Insects in the forest include many species of moths and butterflies; cockroaches, mantises, leaf and stick insects; termites and white ants; dragonflies; bugs, beetles and midges; mosquitoes and flies. The average visitor mainly notices the butterflies, of which 32 species have been recorded, out of 242 species found in Sri Lanka.

Other interesting sights are the Garrison Cemetery (see page 121), Lovers' Walk complete with ferny alcoves and drooping willows, and the pond. Originally the pond was where the folk of the court, the kings and queens, bathed. A pot of gold coins is supposed to lie hidden somewhere in the murky green waters and is guarded by a serpent with glowing red eyes. Some say the pot of gold surfaces once every year, and yet others say they have seen the serpent. More haunting is the tale about those who hunted for the gold and never returned.

THE INTERIOR TOWNS

Visitors usually pass through the towns of the interior without stopping, unless for lunch, while on the way to somewhere more exciting. Hence, whatever accommodation is available is usually intended for locals. However, every town is likely to lead to happy, unexpected discoveries, so some of the major ones are included here. Towns are listed in alphabetical order.

AMBEPUSSA At 60km from Colombo on the A1 to Kandy, Ambepussa is at the fork in the road where the A6 begins its journey northwards to Kurunegala and eventually Trincomalee. Above the town is a devale (shrine) dedicated to the goddess Pattini. Some 6km away, off the main road at Dedigama, is a stupa erected by King Parakramabahu (1153–86) to mark the spot where he was born.

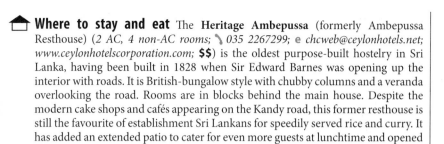

Where to stay and eat The **Heritage Ambepussa** (formerly Ambepussa Resthouse) (*2 AC, 4 non-AC rooms;* \ *035 2267299;* e *chcweb@ceylonhotels.net; www.ceylonhotelscorporation.com;* **$$**) is the oldest purpose-built hostelry in Sri Lanka, having been built in 1828 when Sir Edward Barnes was opening up the interior with roads. It is British-bungalow style with chubby columns and a veranda overlooking the road. Rooms are in blocks behind the main house. Despite the modern cake shops and cafés appearing on the Kandy road, this former resthouse is still the favourite of establishment Sri Lankans for speedily served rice and curry. It has added an extended patio to cater for even more guests at lunchtime and opened access by steps direct from the main road parking area.

On the opposite side of the road and part of the same Ceylon Hotel Corporation group that operates the resthouse is an elaborate snack bar called **Avanhala** (\ *035 5671803*). Rice and curry is available there at lunchtime as an economically priced buffet meal (**$**), and savoury pastries and cakes all day. It has a juice bar as well as a bar serving alcohol, and good, clean toilets, so it is a popular stop on the drive to or from Kandy.

AVISSAWELLA The railway station beside the road heralds the approach to this busy town, 47½km from Colombo on the A4. This road turns right at Avissawella to go via Ratnapura around the outer rim of the hill country to the east coast. The A7 starts at Avissawella bound for the hill country. At the fork in the roads is the site of the historic **Sitawaka**, said to have been the place where Sita (Rama's wife) was kept in captivity by Ravana, a prehistoric king. There is a ruined temple by the river, begun by King Rajasingha (1581–93) of Sitawaka but never completed. The town itself is without even a hint of the past.

Getting there

By train The train journey to Avissawella is still as fascinating as when it was served by narrow-gauge (2ft 6in) line, with a couple of trains hauled by steam or baby diesel locomotives chugging through cluttered suburbs and tranquil byways twice a day. Now it is a twin broad- and narrow-gauge line with regular commuter trains clattering through the landscape.

A survey for the railway was carried out in 1896 with the result that a break in gauge (all other lines were then broad gauge) was introduced when the narrow-gauge line was laid to Avissawella in 1902. The service was extended further inland to Yatiyantota in 1903, then to Ratnapura in 1912 and to Opanaike in 1919. Because the extensions were not 'economically viable', they were dismantled in stages, beginning in 1942 and ending in 1977.

In 1938, the whole line was recommended for closure and in 1975, it was decided to run a passenger service only to Homagama. Somehow the link to Avissawella survived, although by 1990 it was reduced to one train a day in each direction. This was hauled by a diminutive steam loco (No 220 class J1, type 4–6–4T Hunslet-built in 1924) or by a 1949 diesel.

The laying of the dual track, capable of taking both broad- and narrow-gauge trains, was begun in 1991. The track was broadened by the addition of a third rail, keeping the two rails of the narrow gauge in place. This was done so the regular narrow-gauge service could run while the line was being converted.

Although it is no longer served by steam and the narrow gauge is broad, the Kelani Valley line, as it is still known, is still a great little trip by train. The train starts at Colombo Fort station and then, after a stop at Maradana, begins its journey by following the single track which detaches itself from the web of main lines to

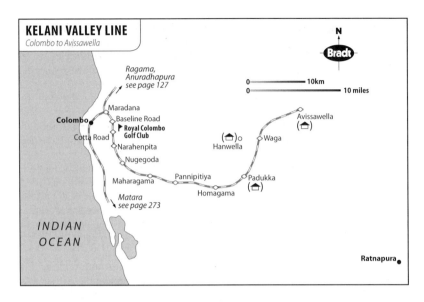

KELANI VALLEY LINE
Colombo to Avissawella

N

Bradt

Ragama,
Anuradhapura
see page 127

0 ——————— 10km
0 ——————— 10 miles

Maradana
Baseline Road
Colombo
Royal Colombo
Golf Club
Cotta Road
Narahenpita
Nugegoda

Avissawella
(⌂)

(⌂)o Waga
Hanwella

Pannipitiya
Maharagama
Homagama

Padukka
(⌂)

Matara
see page 273

INDIAN
OCEAN

Ratnapura•

disappear down a narrow funnel formed by two side walls, overhung with trees. This opens out as the train trundles alongside the crowded streets of Colombo's fringes, passing under the eaves of overhanging roofs of houses bordering the track. After a stop at Baseline Road station, the train runs on to Cotta Road where flowers entwine the trellis roof shading the old platform.

Then the train emerges from the suburbs into a vast expanse of green: the golf links of the Royal Colombo Golf Club. Regular golfers sigh with resignation as the train cuts across the course, while newcomers rub their eyes in disbelief at this unexpected hazard to their play. The scenery becomes rural until palm-thatched cabins beside the line give way to the neat villas of Nugegoda.

At Homagama, the new booking office has a sign displaying the times and stops of all trains to and from Colombo, and a bridge linking the platforms, as this station is an important one where some trains terminate and originate. From there the Avissawella train dawdles across shimmering paddy fields which give way to wild orchards of mangoes, breadfruit, areca nut, coffee and cocoa. At Padduka the station is close to the centre of town and there is a typical country-style resthouse with garden and veranda. The journey continues through woods and tea and rubber plantations, with hills in the distance glimpsed through tangled vegetation. Betel leaf and croton (a tropical bush with coloured, skewer-like leaves) grow in profusion by the line and cottages with gardens full of flowers look idyllic.

TRAIN TIMETABLE: COLOMBO TO AVISSAWELLA

Colombo–Avissawella		Avissawella–Colombo	
08.30	11.19	05.10	07.27
16.10	18.30	05.45	07.47
16.35	18.48	06.25	08.44
17.15	19.34		
20.00	22.23		

Avissawella's new station building opened in 1997, on the opposite side of the track to the old one, and beside the main A4 road. Because the line serves commuter traffic, the main flow of trains is into Colombo in the morning, and out in the evening. The schedule of direct trains is in the box opposite. Schedules can change for various reasons and it's advisable to check operations before trying to travel.

By bus There is an intercity service (No 122 to Ratnapura) every ten minutes from Colombo to Avissawella, as well as a slower service (No 677) via Hanwella.

By road Avissawella is linked to both Colombo and Ratnapura by the A4.

Where to stay and eat The **Avissawella Resthouse** (*8 rooms; Main St, Avissawella;* \ *036 2222299;* **$**) has a mixed reputation. It has a bar and can do rice and curry lunches for groups but the rooms are basic and sometimes without water. It is difficult for a resthouse to seem inhospitable; this one does its best. It is five minutes' walk from Avissawella railway station. If you plan to catch the early train to Colombo, allow time to wake the resthouse gatekeeper so you can get out, or you may have to climb over the wall.

Dehiowita is 7km after Avissawella, on the road to Kitulgala. Here you will find the **Picturesque Mountain Inn** (*10 AC, 18 non-AC rooms; 503 Tembiliyaya Estate, Dehiowita;* \ *036 2230194;* **$**). It is one of those privately run hotels that seem to have grown little by little. It has narrow stairs (a lot of them) and small basic bathrooms. However, there is hot water, and a television in every bedroom. There is a swimming pool in an adjoining lot reached by a bridge.

BALANGODA Although it looks no more than a fairly busy market town today, Balangoda has given its name to *Homo sapiens balangodensis*, since it was in this area that skeletons of Stone Age men, dubbed 'Balangoda man', were found. The Stone Age culture is believed to have existed in the island until about 500BC when it was overwhelmed by a more sophisticated culture from India. However, pockets of Balangoda man could have remained in the unexplored wilderness of the district for another 1,000 or more years.

The town has a population of 13,589 (2012 estimate) and lies astride the A4 road between Ratnapura and Haputale, 143km from Colombo. There is no local monument to its importance in the history of the country but it does give an experience of the small-town life of Sri Lanka today.

Where to stay and eat Reached by a turning uphill off the main road in the centre of town is the **Balangoda Resthouse** (\ *045 2287299;* **$**) run by the Urban Development Authority. This is one of those places tourists are usually steered past (to more modern, garish establishments) but it maintains the traditions of obliging service by an old retainer, and rice and curry lunch produced with a flourish from a rural kitchen. A canopied pavilion has been added on to the back of this bungalow-style hostelry for a massive influx of guests but usually there's just a posse of lawyers and some local travellers enjoying distinctly local fare at budget rate.

BUTTALA At a T-junction on the A4 with links via Monaragala to the east and via Pelwatte and Wellawaya with the hill country, there is a road to the south from the hamlet of Buttala to the Yala (Ruhunu) National Park. That is the way to the eco-incredible **Tree Tops Jungle Lodge** (*5 clay huts;* m *077 7036554;* e *treetopsjunglelodge@gmail.com; www.treetopsjunglelodge.com;* **$$**). With emphasis on creating as little disturbance as possible to the jungle in which it is located, while also creating employment for the impoverished villagers of the area, this private nature reserve has been opened to those who really want nature in the raw.

Accommodation is in typical jungle mud huts and treetop shelters; food is cooked over a wood fire. Villagers are the staff, including a band of nightwatchmen as this is elephant country, north of the Ruhunu National Park. A minimum stay of three days is recommended. Since there is patchy email in the jungle, the management request enquiring guests to be patient for a reply to any emailed reservations. The website is an excellent introduction to this novel project.

Also at Buttala, the **Kumbuk River Eco Lodge** (*2 chalets for 8 people in each;* \ *011 5523140;* e *info@kumbukriver.com; www.kumbukriver.com;* **$**) features a mammoth thatched and open-sided eco-villa in the shape of an elephant and is set in 4ha by the waters of the Kumbukkan Oya, bordering Yala. This is a good place for groups intent on having a fun adventure rather than for those seeking traditional comfort.

GAMPAHA The reason for going to this town 32km from Colombo is to see the Henarathgoda Botanical Gardens. It has a population of 9,889 (2012 estimate).

Getting there
By train Most trains (but not the intercity) to Kandy from Colombo stop at Gampaha station, 32km from Colombo. On leaving the station, cross over the bridge to the other side of the railway line where buses and three-wheelers are available for the short run to the gardens.

By bus There are buses (No 200) from Colombo to Gampaha. From Gampaha, you need a bus headed for Minuwangoda. The gardens, a contrast to the paddy-field plains of the area, are located at Asgiriya, down a signposted road to the left of the bus stop (tell the conductor where you want to be dropped so you don't miss it).

By road Gampaha is off the main A1 road to/from Kandy, reached from the junction at Yakkala along the A33.

What to see and do
Opened in 1876, the 15ha **Henarathgoda Botanical Gardens** (⊕ *08.00–18.00 daily; admission Rs600*) at 11m above sea level are a well-cared-for combination of imported exotic trees, a fernery (where the toilets are hidden) and a plant nursery. The island's first rubber plantation was begun here. Cars and pedal bikes are allowed, but it is small enough to make strolling pleasant; a haven for courting couples; hardly ever a tourist.

HANWELLA Only 29km from Colombo on the A4, this is the place where the last king of Kandy met his destiny: defeat and exile by the British. Where the resthouse stands by the river, there was once a Dutch fort. Nowadays the town's attraction is as a snack- or toilet-stop on the way north.

Where to stay and eat The **Hanwella Resthouse** (*8 rooms;* \ *036 2255042;* e *sales@ceylonhotels.net; www.ceylonhotels.lk;* **$**) provides basic stopover accommodation as well as meals for travellers. Explore its small garden bordered by the Kelani River and you will see a venerable jak tree. This was planted by the Prince of Wales in 1875 to commemorate his visit to Ceylon.

With an ancient name meaning 'rest pavilion providing shelter for travellers' is **The Ambalama** (*6 non-AC cottages, 8-room non-AC block; Ambalama Leisure*

Lounge, Ihala Hanwella; ☎ 036 2253388; e contact@ambalama.lk; www.ambalma.lk; **$$**), only 29km from Colombo on the High Level Road, 100m after the road meets the Low Level Road *en route* to Ratnapura.

This is one of the new generation of restaurants/guesthouses that is low-cost but stylish and, according to its publicity, 'combines nature with a bit of history, culture and tradition thrown in'. This translates into a super place to stay. It begins with the roadside restaurant (**$**) built on a wooden deck, with log tables and an antique dumb waiter, and buffet rice and curry served in clay pots, as well as an inexpensive à la carte menu. The real waiters are quiet too but look around and you'll discover the Wakkalama Ginger Café cocktail hut, the Pinthaliya beer deck and four guest cottages on stilts.

Each cottage is defiantly rustic (water for the shower spouts from rocks or a clay pot) with a traditional theme, such as Potter's Cottage, Blacksmith's Workshop and Teacher's House (with upstairs bunks for kids). Each one has a private balcony, living area, queen-size bed and cute accoutrements. They are set in wetlands and nature abounds; but there is a swimming pool and a kiddies' park as well. A real find if you want to escape the crowd (except on local holidays when Sri Lankans make the most of it too).

KEGALLE Over halfway to Kandy (78km from Colombo) on the A1 road, Kegalle is a busy town of approximately 17,962 (2012 estimate) that can be reached only by road since the railway bypasses it. There are some ancient sites (cave dwellings) in the vicinity. It is close to the Pinnawela Elephant Orphanage (see page 194).

Getting there To get here by **car**, take the road to the left off the A1 shortly after leaving Kegalle on the way to Kandy. Getting here by **train** is not a sensible option since the nearest station, Rambukkana (the one that's closest to the Pinnawela Elephant Orphanage), is a cross-country rural bus ride away. Regular **buses** (No 1) link the town with both Colombo and Kandy.

🏠 **Where to stay and eat** For a fine place for lunch on the drive to or from Kandy with an excellent bar (even quarter-bottles of wine) and fast-paced service, there is **Salika Inn** (*20 rooms with fans; 118 Colombo Rd, Kegalle;* ☎ *035 2222876; e salikainn@sltnet.lk; www.salikainn.com; $*). Rooms are available but are actually pretty basic, more suited for the domestic traveller (**$**).

KITULGALA Get to Kitulgala and it won't be long before someone tells you that the movie *The Bridge on the River Kwai* was filmed there. This picturesque village at 86km from Colombo is about halfway to Nuwara Eliya on the A7. Hence it is a popular lunch halt on the road journey, and new places with rooms have opened in recent years. The river is the Maskeliya Oya, a tributary of the Kelani Ganga. A large habitable cave at Belihena, near Kitulgala, yielded stone artefacts during an excavation, suggesting a date not older than 10,000BC, which aligns this area with the Balangoda culture (see page 205).

The town probably takes its name from the kitul palm tree that grows in the area. The sap drawn off the kitul palm can be used for toddy, an effervescent cloud-coloured drink. It thickens to become treacle and is delicious when mixed with curd. It can be boiled down to make jaggery, a naturally sweet fudge that rural folk like to nibble with plain (that's without milk) tea.

Getting there The town is reached by **car** on the A7 linking Avissawella (via the B1 and A4 from Colombo) with Ginigathena on the way to Hatton and Nuwara

Eliya. By **train**, take the Kelani Valley Line, which terminates at Avissawella, from where there are frequent **buses** (No 23) to Kitulgala. From Colombo, look for bus No.16, which does the run to Nawalapitiya via Avissawella and Kitulgala.

⌂ Where to stay and eat

Forget about the movie and surrender to the jungle at **Rafters Retreat** (*10 log cabins, 3 rooms; Hilland Estate, Kitulgala;* ☏ *036 2287589;* e *channape@sltnet.lk; www.raftersretreat.com;* **$$**). You'll have no idea what's in store if you drive unannounced, like I did, through the imposing gateway next to the turn-off to the Kitulgala Resthouse (on the right as you come from Colombo). The drive leads to a great walauwa (mansion) complete with deep veranda, wooden shutters and hints of a bygone era.

The red rafts stacked in a shelter behind it give a clue to the 'adventure' side of the enterprise, since this is a base for white-water rafting expeditions on the Kelani River. The walauwa itself is not open to the public, but there are three guestrooms in an annexe. The surprise, however, is the log cabins on the riverbank, reached by a path through the jungle.

The movie recalled here is *Tarzan*. Creepers form the guide rails, the steps into the cabins are tree branches, the furniture is made of slabs of wood, the bed from branches lashed together with creepers. If you ever dreamed of retreating to a treehouse, here are some; sheer jungle fantasy with the river rushing below. As if that wasn't enough, look for the bathroom and toilet. In one cabin you have to lift up a trapdoor in the floor and climb down a tree ladder. The toilet, set into a plinth of dry clay, has a wooden seat and an overhead chain flush.

With cabins that are the antithesis of everything five-star, Rafters Retreat seems the ideal place for back-to-nature poets and painters, and not just for athletic mountain bikers and white-water rafters. It's one of those places for getting in touch with your soul.

The more conventional stopover, usually just for lunch though, is **Kitulgala Resthouse** (*4 AC, 15 non-AC rooms; Kitulgala;* ☏ *036 2287783;* e *chcweb@ ceylonhotels.net; www.ceylonhotelscorporation.com;* **$$**). It has become so popular for lunch that the dining room overlooking the Kelani River has been enlarged to accommodate groups. Old stills from the *River Kwai* movie hang on the walls and the video can be bought there. Rooms are river-facing, and the new ones have glass-cabinet showers.

Kitulgala has another surprise, the **Plantation Hotel** (*8 AC rooms; 250 Kalukohutenna, Kitulgala;* ☏ *036 2287575;* **$$**). If it didn't have a large sign a couple of kilometres further along the road, you would miss it since, from the outside, it looks like a rather swish private house. Its glass doors open on to a small but neat reception area that gives access to rooms prettily appointed and with lots of mirrors, and bathrooms with glass-cabinet showers. It is all designer smooth.

The modest entrance conceals a multi-level complex of two riverside restaurants and a bar. A notice tells you of a connection with the Open International University for Complementary Medicines and a bookcase contains the works of the late owner, author and doctor Anton Jayasuriya. The staff are very obliging and it seems a fun place to stop for a lunchtime rice and curry buffet (**$**) or a night by the river.

There's an even better surprise away from the main river at a small hostelry run by the same people behind the Plantation Hotel. The **Royal River Resort** (*4 rooms; Eduru Ella, Kitulgala;* ☏ *036 4920790 or 011 4934923;* **$$$**) is grandly named but it's so special that one can forgive its delusion. Set deep in lush wilderness with only four rooms around a swimming pool fed by a gushing mountain stream, it is the perfect place for escaping life's cares. That's if you can find it, since it seems deliberately hard to get to. It lies at the end of a winding track (*Beli Lena Rd*) that leads off the A7 away from the river between the Kitulgala Resthouse and the Plantation Hotel, close to the 38km post. Overhung with gigantic ferns, the road climbs ever upwards, dives under kitul trees, straddles streams and then disintegrates, splitting into two separate surfaced tracks just wide enough for a vehicle's wheels. There, as all hope of finding the place is lost, at the base of a gully on the left of the trail, is a cluster of cottages astride boulders washed by a flowing torrent. Around a corner a door, set into a short wall by a parking space for three cars, opens to a bijou pavilion surmounting a path rambling a long way down through an orchid garden.

This extraordinary complex has rooms with balconies in two separate blocks (one by the river with French windows opening on to the bracingly cool pool, the other atop the kitchen with river view) and needs no background music, although there is a piano in the lounge, because of the joyful cacophony of the raging river. Rooms are bright with sunlight bursting through windowed walls, but furnishings and bathrooms are basic and there's a touch of eccentricity in the décor. Meals are refreshingly neither fancy nor expensive, prepared in a galleried kitchen where guests in the pool can look up and see the chefs at work. Open to non-residents for meals (**$$**), this is a great retreat for a partying friends. Red Dot Tours (see pages 20 and 21) has more information and photographs of the resort on its website: www.reddottours.com.

What to see and do By crossing the river (there is a makeshift ferry), you can visit the rainforest on the far bank. According to Gehan de Silva Wijeyeratne, among the host of birds found only in Sri Lanka are to be seen the enigmatic red-faced malkoha and the dazzling blue magpie. The observant naturalist will also see a number of endemic lizards, amphibians and fish.

KURUNEGALA Kurunegala is the capital of the Northwestern province, with a population of 30,314 (2012 estimate). This embraces northwestern villages and includes the coastal area from Puttalam to Chilaw and down the coast to the Negombo border with the Western province. Kurunegala was the capital of Sinhalese kings for a little over 50 years in the 13th and 14th centuries, starting with King Bhuveneka Bahu II (1293–1302).

The outstanding feature of the town is the enormous rock formations dominating the skyline around it. On top of the one close to the bus station is a temple containing a replica of the footprint at Adam's Peak. The rock can be climbed and gives a magnificent view of the surrounding countryside and the lake. The rocks have been named in Sinhala after the animals whose shapes they are supposed to resemble, such as tortoise, elephant and goat. The shapes can be seen more clearly from the train as it leaves Kurunegala for the north. The town is the centre of a flourishing coconut industry.

Getting there

By train Kurunegala is on the Northern line, the first major stop after the line begins at Polgahawela. The line reached Kurunegala in 1894. The station is 15 minutes' walk from the town centre, represented by the bus station and the resthouse.

By bus As evidence of its importance as a trading town, Kurunegala can be reached from all parts of Sri Lanka by bus. Nos 5 and 6 serve it from Colombo while other services are from Horowpotana (15-16), Anuradhapura (15-17 and 57-5), Panadura (17-1), Kaduruwela (48-8), Hingurakgoda (48-9), Horiwila (48-11), Meegaswewa (48-24), Toduwawa (48-25), Welikanda (48-27), Trincomalee (49-1; Rs77 and Rs155 luxury), Vavuniya (57-2), Wilachchiya (57-16), Kegalla

(507), Rambukkana (508/509), Warakapola (533), Kekirawa (548), Galnewa (548-1), Dambulla (549), Wewala (549-1), Galkiriyagama (549-4), Sigiriya (549/499), Matale (556) and Ankumbura (564).

By road At 94km from Colombo, Kurunegala is at an important crossroads, where the A6 from Ambepussa to Trincomalee (on the east coast) meets the A10 from Kandy to Puttalam (on the west coast).

🏠 **Where to stay and eat** Alas, the Rajapihilla Resthouse by the Kurunegala bus station has closed down and lies shuttered and neglected. Perhaps it will be revived again, which will delight a British visitor who wrote to the *Daily News* in 1991 that it was 'an architectural jewel which if protected ... can still lend serenity to Sri Lankans and world travellers alike'. Formerly the abode of a colonial administrator, it is overwhelmed by the buses and other vehicles that park in front of it during the day.

Its closure led me to discover a more modern hostelry, the twin hotels **Seasons** and **Diya Dahara** (*8 rooms; 7 North Lake Rd, Kurunegala;* ✆ *037 2223452;* **$**). The accommodation part is in Seasons, which has a tall and grand entrance to which the rooms do not live up; it is popular with locals and shows evidence of many honeymoons. Across the road, the Diya Dahara caters for tourists stopping for a low-priced lunch or a drink in the garden by the lake, and has its price list prominently displayed, suspended from a huge shade tree. Boys lurk by the lake to tempt tourists to part with money while they do magical things with a lotus bud.

MAHIYANGANA This is probably the oldest of Sri Lanka's many capitals. It is reputed to have been a city with wide streets and handsome houses extending for a mile along the bank of the Mahaweli Ganga. Now it is known as the town to visit if you want to see Veddahs, the descendants of the island's aboriginal inhabitants. It is 188km from Colombo and some 70km east on the A26 from Kandy.

Its location between the northern and southern kingdoms caused it to be visited by kings and their armies, such as Dutugemunu (161–137BC) and, over 1,000 years later, Vijayabahu (1055–1110). Access to Kandy from the backdoor port of Trincomalee was through the town. The dagoba is supposed to be the oldest in the country and is regarded as one of the holiest of Buddhist monuments. Tradition has it that the dagoba was erected while Buddha was alive (he is believed to have visited during a Veddah festival) and contains locks of his hair.

A settlement of Veddahs is **Dambana**, 10km from the town, and the Veddah village is advertised as one of the attractions close to the **Mahiyangana Resthouse** (*7 AC, 3 non-AC rooms;* ✆ *055 2257304;* **$**), which is basic, although refurbished in 2000 and overlooking the Mahaweli River. Any visit to gaze at the Veddahs necessarily involves payment of a certain amount of rupees and can be a degrading experience for both visitor and visited.

MATALE This town, located 25km north of Kandy, is in the Cultural Triangle but is usually passed through. Although in the earlier days of the Kandyan kingdom it was a principality, Matale's connection with the cultural glory of the past is slight. It is now known as a prosperous planting district and a progressive town and has a population of approximately 40,859 (2012 estimate).

About 8km away is **Aluvihara** where a gathering of 500 monks committed the doctrines of Buddha to writing, on talipot palm leaf parchments, in 88BC. Previously the doctrines had been handed on orally from teacher to pupil.

Contemporary Matale began with the erection of a fort by the British in 1803. Matale is a bustling town with a high number of pastry-shop cafés.

Getting there

By train Matale has its own railway line with a service linking it to Kandy (see map, page 103). This branch of the main line from Colombo was opened in 1880. Soon afterwards, H W Cave in his book *Golden Tips* (actually about tea, not hints on premium travel) commented that Matale 'is the most northerly district cultivated by Europeans and at present the utmost point to which the railway extends in this direction.'

It has remained the utmost point and the traveller has to resort to bus to get from there to Dambulla or Sigiriya.

Since this is a rural line in the classic tradition, with landscapes of paddy fields terraced in curves and richly wooded hillsides, no-one expects the train to hurry. At the beginning it eases slowly out of Kandy station to rattle over a level crossing on the town road, and then to plunge into the countryside north of the city.

Three minutes later it stops at **Asgiriya**, the first of 17 halts on the line. The next station, reached after another three-minute run, is **Mahaiyawa**, built like a pavilion with a colonnaded veranda all around it. **Katugastota** station is also pavilion style. Look up to the left just after crossing the magnificent river bridge and you will see, where the road and the track cross at the Katugastota level crossing, a tree weighed down, not with fruit but with fruit bats, also known as flying foxes.

There seems to be no place to buy tickets at **Mawilmada**, which is like a bus shelter on a brief stretch of platform. Many of the stations on this line have no staff, just a nameboard.

After the main crossing station of **Wattegama**, the train meanders at much less than the permitted 32km/h through forests of tall trees. Wheels squeak as it tackles an incline before running into **Ukuwela** station, another colonial pavilion. A trio of halts at intervals of three minutes comes next before the train pulls into Matale.

Matale, at 369m above sea level, is 146km from Maradana station. The station, and the staff, have the charm of a leisurely forgotten lifestyle and you get the impression, from the dilapidated condition of the rolling stock, that the line is regarded as a backwater.

By bus There is an intercity service (No 8) linking Colombo with Matale without changing in Kandy.

By road Matale is 26km from Kandy on the A9, which is the road to take to reach the Cultural Triangle crossroads at Dambulla. It is 47km to Dambulla from Matale.

Where to stay and eat
Matale is one of those towns tourists pass through, in this case on the way to the towns of the Cultural Triangle, which is where you should go to stay. However, there are several jolly good pastry shops in the town for a lunch break.

What to see and do
The **Aluvihara Temple** is a complex of image houses, meditation cells and monasteries. The Fifth Buddhist Council was held there and the doctrine inscribed in 88BC. The task took over three years to complete. There are other temples in the Matale vicinity. At the **Dambarawa Temple** is a collection of tiny wall paintings including one, of Sujata milking a cow, which is

considered a masterpiece of 19th-century art. The temple shrine dates to 1780. The **Sri Muttumari Amman Temple** is famous for its festival during the Hindu New Year (April), when the goddess Mari Amman is taken in procession along the streets and there are fire-walking sessions.

At Malleheva village some 40 families are engaged in mat weaving using local sisal. The weaving is done on a *poruwa*, the simplest weaving apparatus in the world. A mat of average size is about 1.8m by 0.9m (6ft by 3ft); these mats are known as Dambara mats. Reed trays and baskets are also made there.

MONARAGALA This is another of those towns one drives through on the way to somewhere else. It has a troubled recent history, suffering both from southern and northern terrorism, which kept it off-limits to all but locals for many years. It is on the way to the east coast and is also accessible from the deep south. It has a population of approximately 10,853 (2012 estimate).

Getting there

By bus Since it is at a crossroads linking all parts of Sri Lanka, Monaragala is well served by buses. Bus No 98-2 serves it from Colombo and No 14 from Kandy. There are also services available linking the town with Mulatiyana (25/363), Matara (35-3), Ampara (909), Batticaloa (909/887), Kalmunai (98-9) and Akkaraipattu (98/10).

Where to stay and eat The **Monaragala Resthouse** (*6 rooms; Main St, Monaragala;* ✆ *055 2276815;* **$**) has a rough rustic charm. The rooms are basic although it has a rather grand reception hall complete with fishpond. Surely unique is its bar set in the garden, consisting of a faux-wooden complex of awnings and tables and stools actually made out of cement, painted and carved to resemble wood. At night it glitters with fairy lights.

PASYALA At 44km from Colombo, on the Kandy road, Pasyala marks a crossroads. To the south is a road through the countryside that is used by vehicles coming from Kandy whose drivers want to avoid Colombo on their way to the west coast. It used to be the location of a reproduction 1940s rural village called Pasgama, reviewed in the first edition, but that closed down in 2004.

Getting there

By train A train that stops at Veyangoda on the line to Kandy or the north is the only method of getting to Pasyala by rail. From Veyangoda take a bus or three-wheeler to Nittambuwa, on the Kandy road, and then continue for about 4km to the Pasyala junction and turn right.

By bus Look for a No 1 bus bound for Kegalle or Kandy, or Kurunegala (No 6).

By road The drive from Colombo (or Kandy) is along the Colombo–Kandy road to the Pasyala junction. This is 4km after Nittambuwa if coming from Colombo, and just after the stalls where girls sell cashew nuts if you are driving from Kandy. Coming from the west coast, the country roads via Horana, accessed from Kalutara, and from Hanwella link up with the main road (A1) at Pasyala.

Where to stay and eat Pasyala is a place to drive through (or to stop to buy cashews) with nowhere to recommend for staying or eating.

What to see and do Cadjugama is the hamlet where belles wave at passing motorists to entice them to buy cashew nuts, adding charms to the Kandy road near Pasyala. The girls display their wares in thatched kiosks and dress in the brightest blouse and skirt they can find. Drivers love to stop and flirt, but it's nuts to expect anything other than, well, nuts.

Some of the cashew girls have done so well they have progressed from thatched kiosk to tiled-roof pavilion and then to a glass-fronted shop. Such a girl is Jayanthi who runs a cashew shop at 72 Kandy Road, Pasyala (on the left driving to Kandy, after the 46km post) and she has a photograph album showing her progress over the years. Her husband offers three kinds of nuts (plain, salted and with chilli) for tasting and the shop has drinks, and a toilet, too.

POLGAHAWELA Tourism might have reached other places in the interior but it has had little impact on Polgahawela, a typical Sri Lankan town that gets along nicely under its own steam. And steam is what helped develop the town because of its importance as a railway junction.

Getting there

By train Polgahawela is a junction station where trains to the north leave the line to the hill country. It is a major station with spasmodic activity but is otherwise rather dreary. The exit, over a bridge and through the booking hall, leads to the wrong side of town. It is more convenient to walk the platform's length to the level crossing at the end to reach the town centre. At the other end is a resthouse with a veranda view of the track, and not much else to recommend it.

The station has five platforms and marks the end of the double track from Colombo. All trains to and from Anuradhapura, the hill country and Kandy (except for the intercity) stop there. However, trying to make a connection from one line to another (say from Anuradhapura to Nanu Oya) is neither convenient nor practical.

By bus Bus No 6 passes through on the way to Kurunegala.

By road From Colombo it is 75km to Polgahawela on the A1 to Kandy, branching off to the A6 at the Ambepussa junction. The road crosses the Maha Oya (river) and turns right to run alongside it, bypassing the town of Alawwa, famed for its betel-leaf market. Polgahawela is also linked to the A19 with Ranwala on the Kandy road, and by the A6 to Kurunegala.

Where to stay and eat An unusual place to eat at or stay in is **Gajamadara Walauwa** (*3 rooms; 75 Kurunegala Rd, Polgahawela;* \ *037 2244159;* **$**). This mansion (walauwa) was built in 1884 as the home of local notables and is typical of the late Victorian style with portico, broad veranda and huge rooms. Conversion in 1998 changed it to a guesthouse with a bar pavilion in the garden. It is named after the tree (*madara*) to which elephants (*gaja*) traditionally bowed. There is one struggling to grow in its garden.

What to see and do The brochure for the Gajamadara Walauwa carries an intriguing note:

For those guests with a fancy for outdoor diversion, a hike to the sylvan hillside of Yogamuwakanda flanking the hotel complex on one side will be an exciting experience ... known to have been an important stronghold of Sinhalese kings of the late medieval period – with its idyllic atmosphere and wide array of tropical fauna and flora worthy of the ardent admiration of environmentalists and nature lovers will make the rest of the world seem far away from you. Hiking arrangement and guidance will be provided by the management.

RATNAPURA Most people visit Ratnapura for one thing: **gems**. Even its name means 'City of Gems'. However, unless you are an expert, be wary of what you are offered in the streets of the town. While men may sidle up to you and unwrap a leaf of tissue-paper package containing gems at a remarkably low price, how do you know if you are buying a gem or a chip of polished beer bottle? The advice on gem purchase is to buy only from reputable dealers, either in Ratnapura or Colombo or in a popular holiday resort like Bentota.

To help you know what is what, there is a **National Museum** (🕘 *09.00–17.00 Tue–Sat, closed public holidays; admission Rs300*), a **Gemmological Museum**, the **Ratnapura Gem Bureau and Museum** and also the **workshops** of many jewellers open to the public. There was a proposal in 2001 for a gem and jewellery centre to replace the ruins of the fort that was the administration centre of the Dutch and British. A government minister was quoted as saying he was 'more interested in the practical importance of the fortress as a gem and jewellery centre for the people of Ratnapura than in its sentimental value as a museum piece'.

The countryside surrounding Ratnapura is dotted with thatched awnings marking the location of an active gem mine. They look crudely built but they follow a traditional design that enables the near-naked miners at the bottom to pass up gem-bearing gravel to the top. This gravel is known as *illam*. It is washed in shallow reed baskets that allow the mud and water to fall away, leaving the heavier gravel. This is sifted thoroughly for gemstones. Small ones are sold directly to dealers, while larger ones are auctioned.

The auctions are almost silent affairs as the bidding is done by a complicated system of handholding and finger-tapping. Proceeds are shared according to a traditional formula with 20% going to the owner of the land where the mine is located, 20% to the owner of the pump that keeps the mine workable and 10% to the holder of the licence to mine. The workers involved share the balance, and also share half their income with their own backers.

One of the many names for Sri Lanka was Ratnadipa, island of gems. A great ruby given to the Queen of Sheba by King Solomon is said to have come from the island. A gem adorning the Ruwanwelisaya Dagoba at Anuradhapura was described in 1293 by Marco Polo as 'a flawless ruby a span long and quite as thick as a man's arm'. The British crown contains a 400-carat blue sapphire known as 'Blue Belle' that was mined in the then Ceylon. Also from Ratnapura, but wrongly

---

GEMS

The **National Gem and Jewellery Authority** (*25 Galle Face Terrace, Colombo 3;* ☏ *011 2325364;* e *gemautho@sltnet.lk; www.srilankagemautho.com*) is a government institution. Jewels and gems purchased in Sri Lanka can be tested there free of charge although there is a charge on certificates guaranteeing authenticity as well as for valuations and identification. The gemstones found in Sri Lanka are alexandrite, amethyst, aquamarine, cat's eye, garnet, moonstone, ruby, sapphire, spinel, topaz, tourmaline and zircon.

named the 'Star of India', is the 563-carat blue sapphire on display at the Museum of Natural History in New York.

The most popular gem is the blue sapphire since the ruby has gone out of fashion. Other gems to be found are garnet, quartz, spinel, topaz, tourmaline, zircon and the devastatingly attractive cat's eye. No emeralds or diamonds (except the Matara diamond, another name for zircon) are found, although imported diamonds are cut and polished for export. Because the cutting and polishing of stones was almost entirely in the hands of Muslims, the medieval Chinese called gems from the island 'Mohammedan stones'.

Getting there

By train There is no longer a rail service and Avissawella, the terminus of the Kelani Valley Line, is the nearest station from which buses ply the A4 to Ratnapura.

By bus Bus Nos 3-6 and 122 provide direct services from Colombo.

By road Ratnapura is 101km from Colombo by the most direct route. The A4 from Colombo via Hanwella and Avissawella is the major road. This also links Ratnapura with Balangoda and across the edge of the hill country to Wellawaya. It is also possible to drive south from Ratnapura via Pelmadulla and the A18 past Udawalawe National Park to Nonagama on the south coast between Tangalle and Hambantota. There is a road (A8) linking Ratnapura with Pandadura (69km) on the west coast, passing through Horana (where there is a pleasant resthouse to stop for snacks or lunch).

Where to stay and eat Ratnapura is actually a good place to stay, not just if you have gems in mind, but also for exploring the region. Its bustling town style provides a contrast to days of nature watching. However, because actual demand for accommodation in Ratnapura is low, the cost and standard of accommodation matches that demand.

The **Ratnapura Resthouse** (*10 rooms;* ℡ *045 2222299;* **$**) sits atop a hill above the town and preserves a basic, old-fashioned outlook. Good for lunch, as long as it's rice and curry.

There's a different view of the town from **Nilani Lodge** (*5 AC, 5 non-AC rooms; 21 Dharmapala Mawatha, Ratnapura;* ℡ *045 2222170;* e *nilanihotel@yahoo.com; www.nilanihotel.com;* **$**). This small hotel attached to a gem outlet spreads over three floors; bathrooms have hot water. It is opposite the Bank of Ceylon.

Out of town, the **Kalavathi Holiday and Health Resort** (*4 AC, 14 non-AC rooms; Polhengoda village, Ratnapura;* ℡ *045 2222465;* **$**) is on the private estate of a gem merchant. It emphasises ayurveda herb baths, massages and something billed as 'jewel therapy' among its attractions. Jeeps are available for Sinharaja Forest tours.

What to see and do Attractions close to the town are its lush scenery, rivers and waterfalls, tea and rubber plantations, and wildlife. It is two hours' drive to the 300km² **Udawalawe Wildlife Sanctuary** (NP) where more than 400 elephants roam. The **Sinharaja Forest** begins 30km to the south. The town is at the foot of **Adam's Peak** (see page 167).

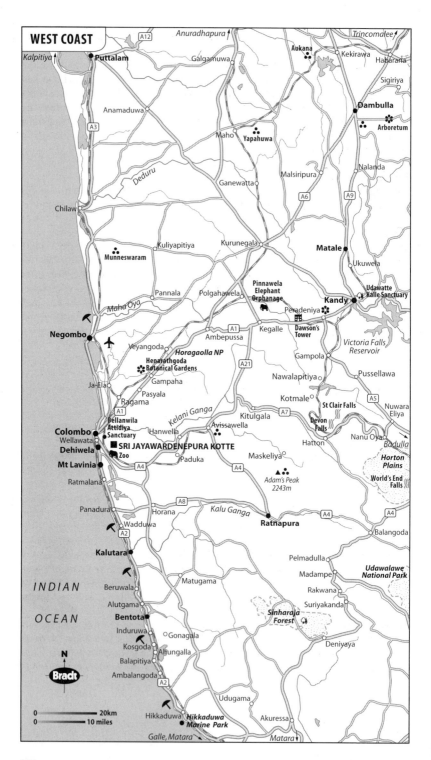

7

The West Coast

The west coast means beaches. While there are some beaches near the airport, to the north of Colombo around the former fishing village of **Negombo** and much is planned for the beaches of **Kalpitya** in the northwest, the best start about 60km south of Colombo. There is variety to the beaches too. At Negombo they are still the preserve of fishermen, and red sails in the sunset is a reality. Local folk use the beaches for their daily work and hotel gardens shimmer down to the sea without barricades.

There is a feeling of being a laid-back (literally) spectator as one lies in the sun and others get on with the work. At night, in the beachside bars and restaurants, there is an attempt at after-beach action.

The beaches on Colombo's southern rim, from **Dehiwela** up to **Mount Lavinia**, are where Colombo residents do their thing. Early morning joggers and, in the late afternoon, strolling families people these beaches. Although there are seaside hotels in **Wadduwa** and **Kalutara**, the beaches there are less than perfect. Swimming can be dangerous, and holiday life looks inwards as guests use the hotels' swimming pools and don't go out much.

Beruwala's beach is a fun stretch with lots of people-to-people contact, although guests are usually package tourists on a budget. At **Bentota** the atmosphere is more upmarket, even staid. The beach is a gorgeous broad swathe of sand yet is often near-deserted as guests disport themselves by hotel swimming pools instead of in the surf. The contrast comes with **Hikkaduwa**, renowned for its downmarket *après-plage* nightlife, worn beach and slight sense of sleaze.

The prudent visitor heading for the beach will remember three things: (1) the sun's rays are deceptively mild; even on a cloudy day they can burn a tender skin. Visitors should always use some form of sun protection; (2) some of the beaches shelve rapidly and the sea can have a nasty undertow, so never swim when red warning flags are flying, and always take care; (3) boys lurk to offer all sorts of services so do not tempt them by leaving anything on the beach when you go swimming or walking. However, the beach boys have their own code of ethics and if you are considered a client of one, the others won't bother you. They can be very helpful for the independent traveller (see box, page 218).

Because of the various warnings from tour agency staff who meet guests at the airport, from guides conducting tours and from the management of beach hotels, many guests feel apprehensive about leaving their hotels to eat or shop away from the hotel premises. Alas, these warnings are more in the hotels' interests than the guests'. Hotel managers want you to patronise their outlets, not go out for a lobster dinner in a shack on the beach, or for a booze-up in the bar across the road. Tour guides want you to buy from where they take you so they get a commission.

Even if you visit Sri Lanka as a member of a tour group on a pre-paid package holiday with everything included, you don't have to do what you're told! You can eat independently in the restaurants close to the resort to try dishes especially prepared for you (instead of mass-produced tourist fodder). You can seek out bars that sell drinks without the hotel's colossal mark-up, and with the company of locals instead of other tourists. And you can shop in the local town where there is a greater choice than in a hotel's souvenir and gem stores.

Hoteliers might disapprove of this advice but in fact the restaurants, bars and shops which have sprung up around their hotels add to the holiday experience. They merit a visit even if you are 'jes-lookin' and don't buy anything. You will be pleasantly surprised at how helpful are the Sri Lankans you meet in the west-coast beach areas. They might address you in German, since Germans used to make up the majority of visitors, and they want to make you feel at home. If you reply in English, they will switch immediately.

BEACH BOYS

My advice to a beach boy was to address a stranger in English first, not German. I told him that German tourists won't take offence if they are greeted in English in Sri Lanka, but British tourists would not take kindly to being spoken to by a Sri Lankan in German.

However, the tourist demographic is changing; no longer are white-skinned tourists bound to be German or British; they could be Russian or from other mid-European countries. Indians, too, are discovering the west coast, although those who come on cheap flights find Sri Lanka more expensive than they expected, and hence skip hotel extras to forage in local supermarkets and share meals in wayside cafés.

Generally, a holiday at the west-coast resorts will be a restful experience. There is no nightlife beyond the bands hired to fill in the gap between dinner and bedtime. There might be a show of some kind: a desperate conjuror, a manic fire-eater, an energetic drum-and-dance troupe. Early to bed is easy. Many beach hotels also have ayurveda centres where guests can enjoy rejuvenation therapy or a spa. Where there is television in the bedroom, don't expect much, unless it is satellite television.

It's not just the beaches that make the west coast attractive for a holiday. Surprisingly perhaps, traditional rural life survives close to beach resorts. While the presence of foreigners on holiday has resulted in the construction of luxury hotels and guesthouses lining the island's shores, down palm-shaded byways off the beaches village life continues at its own tempo.

Signs of post-2004 tsunami recovery are everywhere along the west and south coast. It first becomes evident after **Kalutara**, where the railway line crosses the road by the coast at **Paiyagala**. What used to be a wall of houses along the narrow strip between the road and shore has disappeared and the rubble cleared to leave coconut palms and a breezy view of the shore.

All the way down south, wherever the Galle road edges the coast and houses were destroyed by the tsunami, it seems amazing that there ever were buildings on such a precarious and slim spit of shore between the road and high-water mark. It's sad that it took a tragedy to open up ocean vistas that haven't been seen since independence and the land rush to settle on any empty space.

It's at Paiyagala that the railway begins its flirtation with the road, touching it and then wandering off parallel as the road runs along the shore to **Beruwala**. An ancient mosque overlooks the Beruwala harbour where the fish market fascinates those visitors who get up early enough to observe the unloading and auctioning of each day's catch.

Although there are some hotels at the end of lanes leading off the Galle road around Kalutara, the beach resorts become more noticeable where they border the road on its way from Beruwala to Alutgama. There are major package-holiday resort properties there as well as small, independent owner-run hotels on the banks of the lagoon at the mouth of the Bentota River.

The topography has changed and the mouth of the river broadened. Its magnificent sweep is seen clearly from the road bridge across the Bentota River. That's where the railway crosses the road again to run alongside the beach from Bentota until Induruwa. As if bored by this, the railway responds to the lure of the road and crosses it once more to resume its progress southwards. On the beach side of the road there are dozens of informally run guesthouses that, even in 2013, were offering rooms with attached bathrooms for around Rs3,000 (**$**) a night for two people.

The beach glistens by the side of the road where there is no space for houses and the view of the sea beyond the palm trees is enchanting. At **Balapitiya**, a safari by boat into the hinterland pierced by the Madu Ganga, with calls at the many islands and sightings of exotic birdlife, is popular with visitors and locals alike.

The main road along the west coast to Galle vies with the railway line for the best views of sprawling golden sands. The road and the railway track cross each other often, the clatter of trains and the rush of traffic accompanied by a chorus of waves surging up the seashore.

Coconut groves, paddy fields, colonial mansions, rural homesteads, village shops, antique shops and craftsmen are to be found on the land side of the road. They add an extra dimension to a beach holiday.

While many village families have sons and daughters who are employed in the modern beach hotels, home life beyond the tourist belt remains remarkably unchanged. Villagers are still neighbourly, joining in each other's festivities, helping with village improvement projects, and practising crafts and a lifestyle handed down for generations.

The main tourist area of **Bentota** (62km south of Colombo) is fringed by villages nestled in coconut groves, each one revealing a fascinating glimpse of rural life, within a few minutes' walk of major hotels.

Coconut palms provide the material for traditional crafts as well as for villagers' livelihoods. *Gokkala* is an ephemeral but artistic craft involving the making of elaborate designs from young, green palm fronds. Nimble-fingered villagers fashion the split fronds into headdresses or decorations for community occasions. Since these creations soon wither away, they are not made as souvenirs, but for villagers' own delight.

Stroll from the beach hotels along the southern bank of the Bentota River, and you can witness a thriving village industry: the production of coir. Even with today's preference for synthetic fibres, coir is still in demand for yarn.

The husks of coconuts are soaked for days in pens in the shallow waters of the river, then beaten with wooden mallets to extract the brown fibrous threads. These are dried in the sun and then spun by village women into rope. Loose coir is used as the stuffing for mattresses whose natural ingredients make them environmentally correct.

Village houses range from the rustic wattle-and-daub hut with roof of palm thatch, to simple buildings with a veranda, wooden columns and a clay-tiled roof. These have wooden shutters and bars on the windows, instead of glass panes and air conditioning. Cool air flows into the house through ornately carved wooden transoms.

Life in coastal villages, like Bentota and **Balapitiya**, further south near the tourist resort of Ahungalla, centres around a river. Where there are no bridges, children have to paddle themselves to school in slender, dugout canoes. River fishing is done using sunken wooden fences to form funnels that lure fish and freshwater prawns to bamboo cages, where they can be netted from the water with ease.

At **Beruwala**, a coastal settlement whose origins reach back to the 1st millennium when Muslim traders landed there, the old harbour has been extended as an anchorage for deep-sea fishing boats. These motor into the harbour after several weeks at sea to unload large tuna and shark on the quayside for auction. Smaller boats, which go to sea in the evenings, return in dawn's early light with rockfish. The fish auction, held in the open air, begins at dawn and is over by breakfast time. Visitors can pay a fee to enter the harbour and watch.

On the beach by **Induruwa**, near the 68km post, are fishing boats that look as old as time. Called *paruwa*, these boats are made to a traditional design out of tree trunks bound and stitched together with coir rope. They carry a dozen men to row and cast the nets that are gradually drawn into the shore, where the fish are gathered up and carried off by villagers.

In the **Kosgoda** area there are some independent turtle hatcheries run by villagers. Before ecological concern, eggs laid by turtles on the beach would be scooped up by villagers to eat. At the urging of environmentalists, several villagers have set up hatcheries by the beach, collecting the eggs to re-bury them until they hatch, instead of eating them. The baby turtles are given a chance to grow in a protected environment until released into the sea by tourists who pay a contribution for the enterprise.

Village markets are an irresistible attraction for visitors. On Mondays, there is a major one at the town of **Alutgama**, on the northern bank of the Bentota River. For a more intimate insight into village life, the Tuesday morning market at **Gonagala**, 2km inland from the Galle road up the Kaikawala road at the junction between the 67km and the 68km posts, features exotic fruits and intriguing vegetables. Rice and curry is a staple of Sri Lankan cuisine, and paddy fields, whose harvest yields rice, line the hinterland as the Galle road heads south.

Another staple is bread. For visitors, sampling a loaf of hot bread baked in a wood-fired oven is a memorable treat. Sometimes bread can be bought from vendors riding bicycles with wooden panniers, looking like bedside cupboards, stuffed with loaves and freshly baked cakes.

Itinerant vendors are common along the coast. Salesmen can be seen walking along the road carrying tables and chairs on their heads; man-powered carts sell fish or vegetables; and strolling craftsmen offer to repair rattan chairs and cane blinds at home. Ice cream sellers on bicycles call children by blowing on horns, while lottery-ticket sellers ring bells vigorously to attract attention. The fish salesman's lusty shout of '*maalu, maalu!*' (fish, fish!) brings housewives hurrying out of their homes to buy.

From tiny shelters built with plaited palm-frond thatch, known as *cadjan*, wayside vendors entice motorists with bunches of golden-hued coconuts called thambili. They chop off the top, stick in a straw, and sell it as a natural and refreshing drink. Other common sights close to modern resorts are housewives scavenging for wood for cooking fires, and herdsmen driving buffaloes to graze.

The area between Bentota and **Ambalangoda**, 20km further south, is rich in local crafts. Goldsmiths have worked there for generations, growing prosperous catering for the tourist trade. The methods used are time-honoured; gold is still smelted and poured by hand in back-garden workshops.

Mask carving is a traditional craft of this area, producing the grotesque and fanciful masks used in devil-dance rituals. The masks are carved out of a wood that is light enough to be worn throughout a night-long dance performance. Each mask is hand-carved and painted with symbols according to what demon it is supposed to frighten away. Sales have boomed as visitors buy the masks to take home as provocative interior design statements.

The odd sight of a pair of men sawing wood over a pit beside the road heralds the district around Ambalangoda devoted to woodwork. To saw a huge tree into planks, the trunk is positioned over a pit. One man crouches on a frame above the opening of the pit, while the other stands below, smothered in sawdust. The two men pull the large-toothed saw blade backwards and forwards until the trunk is reduced to boards, used for building or turning into furniture.

The wood-turners and cabinet-makers of Ambalangoda have become renowned worldwide for their skill in making reproduction antiques. Using ancient tools and wood seasoned by months of exposure to the weather, they can copy any design, producing colonial-style furniture that is exported to Europe, the USA and South America.

The making of batik is another village craft that has benefited from foreign demand. Bolts of cloth are put through several stages of waxing and dyeing in village workshops. Designs done by untutored but talented village artists result in bright wall hangings, dress and shirt lengths, and sarongs. Batik is popular for souvenirs because of its exotic, colourful patterns and light weight, which makes it easy to pack.

Lace making is practised in villages further south, within walking distance of hotels at **Galle** and **Unawatuna**. Called pillow lace because it is woven by hand around pins popped into pillows, items range from exquisite doilies to intricate tablecloths. Housewives hunker down on their verandas to join in sessions of gossip while their fingers set the shuttles of cotton weaving almost faster than the eye can see.

To discover more than could be learned from sunbathing on the beach, or by taking a guided tour by air-conditioned coach, you need only amble along the inland byways from the coast. There you will find villagers who are pleased to share the joy of their craftsmanship, and their gentle rural lifestyle.

GETTING THERE AND AWAY

BY TRAIN Details of trains to the west-coast beach resorts north of Colombo (Puttalam, Chilaw and Negombo) are given under the resort headings.

The easiest way to get straight to the beaches south of Colombo is by train. Some of them stop at Bentota, a popular resort, so all you have to do is alight at the station, cross the bridge and stroll on to the beach. Ideal for a day trip, or when you want to find a guesthouse by the beach for a few days. Since the line was built (in 1877–90) to serve local traffic and now brings commuters into Colombo in the morning and takes them out again in the afternoon, the best trains to aim for are the ones that operate outside those peak hours. Otherwise you will have to stand all the way.

All the Coast line express trains run to Galle, and some to Matara. However, if you are bound only for Wadduwa or Kalutara, you might like to try one of the local passenger trains that stop at every halt on the way. The west-coast trains start at Maradana, so if you want a seat on a popular train it is best to board there before the train fills up at Colombo Fort station.

The journey along the west coast begins with the train creaking slowly out of Fort station, allowing latecomers to scramble aboard. It is still gathering speed as it runs through **Secretariat Halt** in front of the Colombo Hilton. (In the morning rush hour, commuters drop off there to go to nearby government offices.) Then it turns southwards, passing the bilious green waters of the Beira Lake and the shanties on the embankment, with the Taj Samudra Hotel in the distance on the right. On the left comes the venerable Castle Hotel (a drinking den) with its pink, Victorian façade.

Kompannavidiya (Slave Island) is a commuter halt, a grim-looking station. Passing under the Galle road bridge, with the Cinnamon Grand Hotel on the left, the train reaches the sea. The view from there, up to Mount Lavinia, is of couples courting under the shade of umbrellas in crannies in the rocks, and of rubbish dumps at the sea's edge. Litter is scattered willy-nilly for this is the backyard of the southern edge of the city.

Kollupitiya (Colpetty) has a wall obscuring the sea in front of the platform; it is the closest station to the US Embassy and the Indian High Commission. The ticket office is on the island platform, reached by a bridge from the entrance, 100m from the Galle road. Next is **Bambalapitiya** station, another charmless one with concrete pillars and asbestos roof and a vast wall preventing a view of the sea. The ticket office is on the island platform and this is a major halt for commuters. The Majestic City shopping complex is between the station and the Galle road.

Wellawatta and **Dehiwela** come next, both stations serving the busy commercial and downmarket residential areas. After Wellawatta, the beach scene improves with fishing catamarans drawn up on the sand. The stretch from Dehiwela to Mount Lavinia has thatched beach huts between the railway line and the beach serving as snack bars.

Mount Lavinia station has an old-style booking office, spacious with wide arches and a high roof. Train times are chalked on a blackboard, giving arrival and departure times from Fort station as well. From its exterior it is like a rural station, tucked away down a leafy lane and beside the Mount Lavinia Hotel. There are four platforms to serve the double track, with a linking footbridge. The view of the beach is blocked by a wall running the length of the platform, and by the back of a wing of the hotel.

The domestic airport is located at **Ratmalana**, whose station is in the typical suburban mould. The carriage and locomotive repair workshop is at Ratmalana. The next major station is **Moratuwa**, 20km from Maradana. It has its booking office off a busy forecourt and a snack bar on the main platform (there are three other platforms). Furniture making is a thriving industry in this heavily populated town. Bolgoda Lake is part of the waterway embracing Moratuwa, extending from Mount Lavinia to south of **Panadura**, which is the next station.

The tourist strip begins at **Wadduwa**, another charmless station with an asbestos roof and small package hotels between the railway line and the sea. Three kilometres further down the line is the only station without a name. In 1953, the station was dubbed 'Train Halt Number One' because the people of the area it serves (Potupitiya and Waskaduwa) could not agree which town it should be named after.

Kalutara North is easily recognisable by the vines trailing over its roof and the potted plants along its platform, an example of how a little-used station can be brightened up to delight passengers. **Kalutara South** is the main station for Kalutara, just after crossing the Kalu Ganga (Black River). A prominent landmark is the large modern (and actually hollow) dagoba (stupa). Do not be alarmed at the sight of passengers tossing coins out of the window in its direction. It is customary for Buddhists passing the dagoba and the Bo tree by the road to make an offering of money to ward off bad luck during their journey.

The district is known for its basketware, for its rubber plantations and for its mangosteens (a delicious seasonal tropical fruit). The main toddy-tapping and arrack-distilling area starts there, which is why many of the coconut palm trees beside the railway line, right up to Hikkaduwa, have no nuts. The line crosses the main road to Galle at **Payagala South** station to wend through palm groves alongside the road, which runs beside the rural belt of the south as the scenery takes on a greener hue.

Beruwala station is inland where more mass-market hotels line the beach. Only a few trains stop there though. The next station, **Alutgama**, is a major one where slow local passenger trains from Colombo, and from Galle, terminate. It consists of a single, long island platform with a bridge connecting it to the roadway entrance. The ticket office is on the platform. The station still preserves facilities for steam engines with a water tower and a turntable and is occasionally used by the *Viceroy Special* steam train.

Bentota railway station was built in the 1970s especially for the National Holiday Resort. A bridge from the platform crosses the beachside road to bring you to the picnic pavilions by the public area of the beach. There is an inexpensive hotel (*Hotel Susantha Garden;* **$**) beside the sole station platform, with steps down into its gardens and rooms (see page 239).

The stations get prettier after Bentota with nothing much happening to them since they were built a century ago, apart from the addition of roofs of asbestos sheeting over the platforms. Between the next two small stations of **Induruwa** and **Maha Induruwa**, if you can tear your eyes away from the sea view, look inland at the houses and you may see a rambling cottage with a sort of dormer window in its attic, in a coconut grove on a bluff overlooking the railway line. That is where I live – probably the first time a guidebook author has listed himself as a tourist attraction!

Along the coast, near Induruwa and before **Kosgoda** station, are a few turtle hatcheries. If you are bound for Sri Lanka's first five-star beach resort, Heritance (formerly Triton), **Ahungalla** is the station, but it is served only by slow, local trains, and is rather lacklustre. The next station, **Balapitiya**, retains the railway atmosphere of its British styling, enhanced by potted plants and its location on the bank of a broad river. Watch carefully after the station for the train to cross the river. You are now on an island with no road access, only the railway bridges at both sides. It has several houses, most of which get flooded when the river rises. It takes about two minutes to cross it by train. Then more palm groves and houses of red-tiled roofs until the train reaches **Ambalangoda**. The station reflects its 19th-century origins.

Hikkaduwa is the station for the beggars to get on or off; they know that's where the tourists are. Exit at the southern end of the platform for quick access to the bus station and three-wheeler park.

BY BUS No 2 buses (both intercity and stopping buses) ply the Galle road from Colombo down the west coast to Galle and then along the southern coast to Matara. Northwards along the west coast, it's bus No 4 on its way via Puttalam to Anuradhapura.

BY ROAD The journey by road is simple. Hit the Galle road in Colombo and just keep going southwards. The start will be frustrating because of heavy, ill-disciplined traffic, especially when school is out and minibuses herd around school gates to pick up kids. The peak time to avoid commuter traffic used to be from 16.00 to 18.00 but now the Galle road remains chock-a-block with traffic at any time during daylight hours. The journey from Colombo to Dehiwela and Mount Lavinia will be slow, speeding up only after Moratuwa.

The road cuts through Kalutara with a side road and shops on either side, then settles into a more rural scene, although with plenty of shops and houses. After

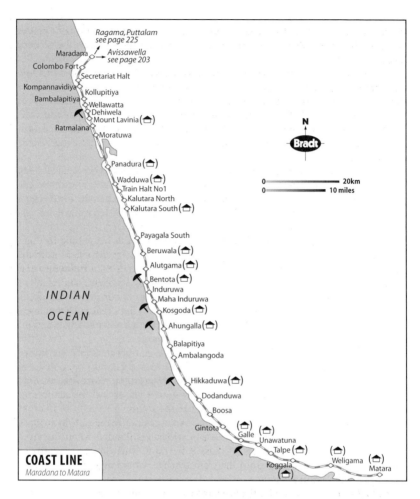

COAST LINE
Maradana to Matara

a right-angled bend at Alutgama and across the bridge over the Bentota River, the scenery brightens and you feel you are at last in holiday country. There are hotels on the sea side of the road, and villas on the land side. The route becomes more interesting, tempting you to stop at antique warehouses, mask workshops, turtle hatcheries and art galleries on the way to Ambalangoda. The rash of signs advertising guesthouses and restaurants means you have arrived in Hikkaduwa.

A new option for driving to the south is to take the Southern Expressway bound for Galle, although this involves a drive of about an hour from the centre of Colombo inland through city traffic to the suburb of Kottawa, where the Expressway begins. Then it's full speed ahead to the coast via exits to Alutgama, Ambalangoda and Hikkaduwa (see page 248).

BEACH RESORTS (Listed from north to south)

The term 'west coast beach resorts' is customarily used to describe those south of Colombo, but the newest resort area on the west coast (Kalpitiya) is developing to the north of Colombo and the oldest tourist resort (Negombo) is also north of Colombo.

KALPITIYA Kalpitiya – and the development of it – is being proclaimed as the future of tourism in Sri Lanka. Because it is on the northwest coast, at the northern tip of the lagoon stretching for some 35km north of Puttalam, it was in the war zone and escaped development. That has changed with gusto. The Kalpitiya Integrated Tourism Report Project was launched in 2008 but it was only in 2010 that proposals led to concrete agreements being signed.

The Kalpitiya Tourist Zone was established, spreading over 2,023ha (5,000 acres) of land including 14 islands in the Dutch and Portuguese bays of the Kalpitiya lagoon. At the time of writing agreements had been signed with developers to lease Vellai and Ippanthivu islands to build five-star hotels with 200 rooms. In the Puttalam lagoon, 17 islands are to be developed in the second stage.

A report in the *Sunday Observer* (Colombo) in September 2010 states, enthusiastically if a little bizarrely, that 'all hotels will have yacht marinas, watersports centre, golf course and gaming resorts, leisure resort, camping and caravan locations, eco-resorts, underwater worlds, caretaker resorts, bird sanctuaries, aquariums, nature museums and water parks'.

The same report admits that Kalpitiya is 'dry and arid' and that 'isolation blends with the gracefulness of nature' but adds 'it is going to get a touch of beauty'. The area is fringed with mangroves and is one of the few places in Sri Lanka to see the dugong. Whales and dolphins inhabit the waters and the area is rich in birdlife.

To keep track of what's planned and what's happening, visit www.sltda.lk/ kalpitiya. Development, even with the best of intentions, takes time and although accommodation is available at Kalpitiya in makeshift guesthouses, the area has yet to capture the energy and ambience of a true holiday resort. There were also reports of legal action being taken against unauthorised construction with a consequent delay in development of the area. At press time, the **Dutch Bay Resort** (*www.dutchbayresorts.com*) was set to bring luxurious accommodation to the area.

Getting there Access at present is by road from Puttalam.

PUTTALAM With a population of 45,401 (2012 estimate), Puttalam, the northern terminus of the coastal railway line, 131km from Colombo, has the air of a forgotten frontier. It is at the end of a drive or train ride past the lagoon and fishing hamlets outside Chilaw to **Bangadeniya** and **Madurankuli**, and through windswept flats to **Palavi**. It is possible to drive from Colombo to Anuradhapura via Puttalam, but it is not the scenic route.

Getting there

By train The railway line to Puttalam was begun with the building of a branch from **Ragama** which reached **Ja-Ela** in 1908. Negombo railway station was officially opened in 1909 and the line reached Chilaw in 1916, then up to Puttalam ten years later. The track from Bangadeniya to Puttalam was removed in 1943 as the rails were needed due to shortages caused by World War II. It was relaid, with new station buildings, in 1964.

Only slow, sometimes very slow, trains serve the line now, stopping at every one of more than 40 stations on the way. To make the 133km journey from Colombo Fort more fun (it can take six hours), it is better to overnight on the way at Negombo. Since none of the trains has catering, except for itinerant vendors of peanuts and prawn croquettes, take a picnic. It helps pass the time. Only a few of the trains have loos, which may mean you will have to break the journey, or dash out to find a station toilet (you'll probably wish you hadn't) when the train is unloading freight that ranges from clay pots of curd from the south to sacks of seeds.

By bus Bus No 4 (occasionally with an intercity service) goes to Puttalam on the way to Anuradhapura.

By road The A3 coastal road actually begins in Peliyagoda, after crossing the Kelani Ganga where it is called the Negombo road. It is 126km long. At Puttalam the A3 vanishes and the A12 begins, crossing the country via Anuradhapura to Trincomalee, a distance of 179km.

CHILAW At Chilaw, 80km north of Colombo, sea breezes billow over the lagoon, ruffling fishing boats moored close to the railway station. It is a colourful, if sleepy, town and the shore is only five minutes' walk from the station. The resthouse, with access to the beach, is basic in rate and comfort and does not double its price at the sight of a tourist. In fact, tourists are rare and although the town has a beach (and a population of 26,714), it's a bit bleak. The **Munneswaram Temple** with renowned Tamil inscriptions is a place for pilgrims.

NEGOMBO This is the closest coastal town to the airport (5km away), and its hotels and guesthouses sprang up to cater for the demand by passengers stopping for a break during long-haul propeller flights on their way to Australia. Before that it was an important centre in the cinnamon industry and was occupied by the Portuguese and then, from 1644, by the Dutch. A canal built by the Dutch connected Colombo via Negombo with Chilaw, and it is possible to cruise on the backwater canals as a change from lazing on the beach. There is a broad lagoon that provides good fishing. In 2012, the town had a population of 127,754.

The town has a leisurely air about it and one feels it is a modest, unambitious place, content at being overlooked by tourists who head for the better beaches further south. It is a pleasant cross between the two extremes of its southern counterparts, Bentota and Hikkaduwa. With scores of restaurants and raucous bars, it is livelier than Bentota but not as sleazy as Hikkaduwa. However, the beach is not as clean or as broad, and the sea not as blue, nor the vegetation as lush as in the resorts further south.

Yet a renaissance is underway. Hotels are being tarted up and re-branded as boutique properties and the Hamilton Canal running at the back of the town has been cleaned up so it can become a tourist attraction.

Getting there
By train There are frequent trains from Colombo Fort to Negombo throughout the day, since it is on the line to Chilaw and Puttalam. Depending on where it stops, the journey can last from 35 minutes to an hour and 35 minutes. The train follows the main line up to Ragama where it branches northwards. Three halts and 20 minutes later it stops at the industrial area station of Ja-Ela, then it passes through the developments leading to the free-trade zone at Seeduwa and around the airport. The train gives a good view of the runway at the old station of Katunayake. Next is Negombo.

Attempts have been made at the station (rebuilt in 1978) to make it look attractive. Outside is a huge, silver-painted statue of a buxom fishwife, with a fish rampant in her hand.

By bus The bus station is a five-minute walk south of the railway station. There are frequent buses to Negombo from Colombo's central bus station. Nos 4–11 (to

Chilaw) and 4–7 (to Puttalam) pass through. From Negombo No 1/245 goes to Kegalle and Kandy and No 34–10 cuts across the island to Trincomalee.

By road The Negombo road (A3) is the link with Colombo (40km); it's a busy road as it is the main access to the airport. There is a branch off it that sweeps into the southern part of town past the bus station and up to the ruins of the old Dutch Fort. Through the town, past the fish market, the road leads into Lewis Place, the downtown hotel area, and then up to Ethukala, where the beach accommodates the main concentration of hotels.

Getting around There is no shortage of three-wheelers, many parked near the station forecourt and bus station. You'll need one to get to the hotels if you come by train or bus.

Where to stay Negombo began its tourist life as a transit town accommodating passengers *en route* to and from Australia by air. Although it has now become a destination in itself with boutique guesthouses and mass-market hotels, Negombo still has the air of being a place where people stop while on the way to somewhere better. All listings are included on the map, page 228.

⌂Jetwing Lagoon (55 rooms & suites) Pamunugama Rd, Thalahena, Negombo; ☏ 031 2227272; e resv.lagoon@jetwinghotels.com; www.jetwinghotels.com/jetwinglagoon/. Sri Lanka's first hotel built specifically for 1960s tourists reopened in 2012; situated at Thalahena about 20mins' drive south of Negombo in a commanding location between the huge lagoon & the sea. The original building was one of the first designed by the Sri Lankan architect Geoffrey Bawa (1919–2003) who had a major influence on Sri Lankan contemporary architecture, particularly hotels, with simple lines & innovative nooks & crannies. The impact of the building style is apparent immediately on arrival with a stunning view of the longest swimming pool in Sri Lanka (100m) extending down the centre of the cup of a U-shaped plaza, with rooms & gnarled pathways on each side. The hotel's rooms include some impressive 2-bedroom suites with terraces overlooking the lagoon. It is a hallmark of Bawa hotels that the convivial centre of camaraderie, the bar, is unlike those of traditional hotels. The 2 bars, by the pool & between the hotel's 2 restaurants, are no exception. The furniture does not encourage lingering & bottles are hidden from view. The water activities are good, with lagoon boat trips, kayaks for rent, water skiing & tours to & along the Negombo canal & visits to the Negombo harbour & to the Muthurajawela Wetlands Sanctuary. **$$$**

⌂ The Beach (75 AC rooms, 3 suites) Ethukala, Negombo; ☏ 031 2273500; e resv. beach@jetwinghotels.com; www.jetwinghotels. com/jetwingbeach. A stylish option for a night before departure or a night on arrival, this is the new face of hospitality in Negombo. Converted out of the Royal Oceanic Hotel, the property is spacious with huge public areas & grand bedrooms; the suites have butler service & an interior courtyard bathroom. The Beach seems to be halfway between a package hotel & a boutique one; it's the star of Negombo & tries its best to make its setting sparkle. The revamp

> **READER'S PICK**
>
> Reader Margaret Sheldon has reported that north of Negombo, **Villa Araliya** (*154/10 Poruthota Rd, Kochichikade;* ☏ *031 2277650;* e *villaaraliya@sltnet.lk; www. villaaraliya-negombo.com;* **$$–$**) 'has a magnificent complex of apartments for short- and long-term letting, all built to the highest standards, with a very beautiful swimming pool; good restaurant although menu limited. I enjoyed returning a second weekend.'

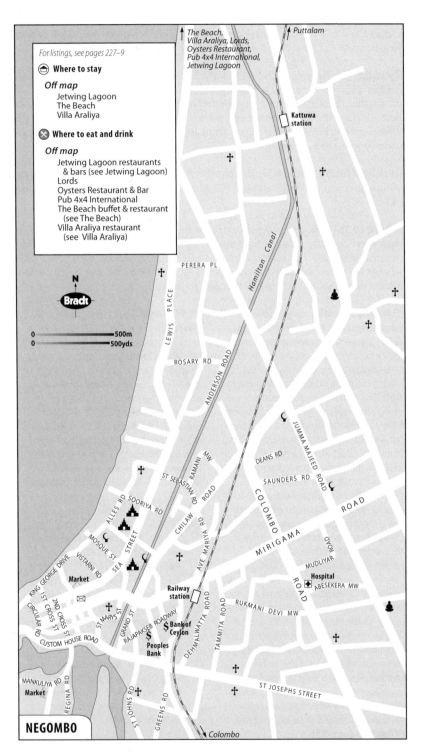

For listings, see pages 227–9

🏠 **Where to stay**

Off map
Jetwing Lagoon
The Beach
Villa Araliya

⊗ **Where to eat and drink**

Off map
Jetwing Lagoon restaurants
& bars (see Jetwing Lagoon)
Lords
Oysters Restaurant & Bar
Pub 4x4 International
The Beach buffet & restaurant
(see The Beach)
Villa Araliya restaurant
(see Villa Araliya)

The Beach,
Villa Araliya, Lords,
Oysters Restaurant,
Pub 4x4 International,
Jetwing Lagoon

Puttalam

Kattuwa
station

Hamilton Canal

PERERA PL

LEWIS PLACE

Bradt

N

0   500m
0   500yds

ROSARY RD

ANDERSON ROAD

JUMMA MAJEED ROAD

DEANS RD

SAUNDERS RD

COLOMBO ROAD

ST SEBASTIAN RD

RAMANI MW

CHILAW ROAD

ALLES RD

SOORIYA RD

MOSQUE ST

SEA STREET

VISTARNI RD

KING GEORGE DRIVE

1ST CROSS ST

2ND CROSS ST

CIRCULAR RD

CUSTOM HOUSE ROAD

ST MARYS ST

GRAND ST

Market

**Railway
station**

AVE MARIYA RD

MIRIGAMA

MUDLIYAR ROAD

Hospital
ABESEKERA MW

RAJAPAKSEB ROADWAY

$ **Bank of
Ceylon**

$ **Peoples
Bank**

DEHMALWATTA ROAD

TAMMITA ROAD

RUKMANI DEVI MW

MANKULIYA RD

Market

REGINA RD

ST JOHNS RD

GREENS RD

ST JOSEPHS STREET

NEGOMBO

Colombo

228

has introduced chunky wooden furniture into the bedrooms & bathrooms with walls entirely of glass, giving an air of space to counteract the low ceilings of its construction in 1987. Each room has a view of the pool, beach & ocean. Management is the usual high calibre of Jetwing Hotels with such innovations as a choice of welcome drinks (iced tea, wood apple juice or king coconut water) & a meal preference form (low fat, vegetarian, etc) to fill in on check-in. There is a fine dining room for à la carte or table d'hôte dining ($$) as well as a buffet restaurant. $$$

✖ Where to eat and drink

Negombo's main street, actually in the hotel strip known as Ethukala crowned by the Beach Hotel, throbs with action at night, which is perhaps why people stay there. During the day, though, restaurants and bars are quiet as guests (and staff) get over the frivolities of the night before. Menus are innovative as are the lurid cocktails, and prices are reasonable.

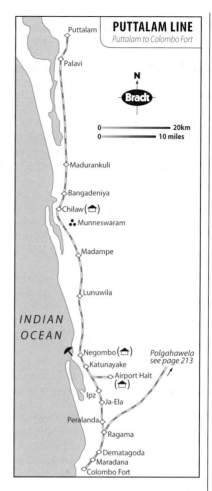

✖ Lords 80B Poruthota Rd, Negombo; m 077 7234721; e martin@lordsrestaurant.net; www.lordsrestaurant.net; ⏰ 10.30–23.30 daily. British themed (& owned) with roadside bar & restaurant, & an art gallery, specialising in a combination of seafood & more mundane snacks in a party atmosphere. $$
✖ Oysters Restaurant & Bar 94 Poruthota Rd, Negombo; ☎ 060 2615933; ⏰ daily. Long established under venerable bougainvillaea boughs, justly famed for low-priced seafood, burgers &, in its beer garden at the back, for pizzas at night. There's an AC music bar too. $$
✖ Pub 4X4 International 74 Poruthota Rd,

Negombo; ☎ 031 4874900; ⏰ daily. Seats are stone benches, & décor is quad bikes at this trendy roadside pub that includes George's Dining Bar & Grill. Daily specials, seafood & bar snacks. $$

What to see and do

Visit **Muthurajawela** (see page 193) for a boat ride through marsh and waterways. There is diving to see shipwrecks and reefs. From Dutch days there are the canals, churches and the Negombo Fort. Negombo is not the place for great diving but watersports are advertised as being available through **The Pearl** (13 Poruthota Rd, Negombo; ☎ 031 4927744) or through beach hotels.

WELLAWATA In a run-down extension of Colombo previously known for its drinking shacks on the beach has sprouted **Global Towers Hotel and Apartments** (23 AC rooms, 45 apts; Marine Dr, Colombo 6; ☎ 011 2591000; e info@globallanka.com; www.globallanka.com; $$). A review of this appears on page 77, since it is more likely to be favoured by visitors needing a good place to stay near Colombo by the newly fashionable Marine Drive than because of its beach, which is more popular with exercising urbanites.

DEHIWELA This is a heavily developed suburb 10km south of Colombo and the only reason for going there is to visit the zoo since the beach suffers from its crowded environment.

Getting there

By train Slow trains to/from Colombo stop at Dehiwela station, from where you could walk, catch bus Nos 176 or 118 or take a three-wheeler into Hill Street, the other side of the Galle road, to link up with Dharmapala Mawatha for the zoo.

By bus From Colombo Port take bus No 101 to Dehiwela Junction and then catch bus Nos 176 or 118 to go directly to the zoo.

By road To drive to the zoo from Colombo: after crossing the bridge over the Dehiwela canal, look for Dharmapala Mawatha, second on the left, turning inland. Follow this road past Jayasinghe Park, on the right, up to the zoo, on the left.

Where to stay and eat Since the zoo is so near to Colombo (and to Mount Lavinia), accommodation and restaurants are best found in those places; there is a restaurant and snacks available in the zoo itself (see page 95 for details).

What to see and do The **National Zoological Gardens** (*Anagarika Dharmapala Mawatha, Dehiwela;* ☎ *011 2712752;* e *zoosl@slt.lk; www.colombozoo.gov.lk;* ☉ *08.00–18.00 daily; admission charge*) is gradually being upgraded. Once known as the largest zoological gardens in the region, with animals in artificial habitats instead of cages, it is receiving a facelift to make it better for animals as well as humans. There is an upgraded restaurant ($) for snacks and light meals in the zoo complex. There are a number of activities on different days: elephant rides on Saturdays (*14.30–16.00*); pony rides on Sundays (*14.30–16.00*); sea lion shows (*16.00–16.15 daily*); and elephant shows (*16.30–16.55 daily*). This is one of those places, like so many in Sri Lanka, where foreigners pay more for entrance than Sri Lankans: in this case Rs2,000 for a foreign adult, Rs1,000 for a foreign child. (It's Rs100 for local adults; Rs30 for kids.)

MOUNT LAVINIA Only 12km from the centre of Colombo, this is the closest dedicated beach strip to the city. Still called Galkissa by its residents, the area takes the name of Mount Lavinia from the house built there by Sir Edward Barnes (Governor 1820–22; 1824–31). Tales are many about who – or what – Lavinia was, but since Barnes was known as a libertine (he sired one bastard son in Nuwara Eliya) it is possible she was one of his mistresses. However, some claim the origin of the name is a plant, called *levinia*, common throughout the island. The beach north of the hotel, with its view of distant Colombo, is usually busy with local residents enjoying a stroll. The southern end is quieter with sunshades for hotel guests.

Getting there

By train Slow trains stop at Mount Lavinia station, from where it is a short walk to the Mount Lavinia Hotel and the beach on the other side of the track.

By bus There are many buses heading down the Galle road, especially Nos 100, 101 and 102.

By road From Colombo, the Galle road conveniently forks (all other roads leave it at right angles) into Hotel Road to the right, well marked with signboards to guesthouses. This road runs past St Thomas College and links up with beach access roads, then curves around to Mount Lavinia Hotel.

🏠 **Where to stay** The **Mount Lavinia Hotel** (*210 AC rooms & suites; 100 Hotel Rd, Mount Lavinia;* ✆ *011 2711711;* e *info@mountlaviniahotel.com; www. mountlaviniahotel.com;* **$$$**) used to be visited solely because of its connections with the past. Established as a hotel in 1877, it maintained colonial standards and was famously featured as the hospital in *The Bridge on the River Kwai*. A wing was added in 1983 and gradually it has undergone modernisation to turn it into a mainstream hotel that just happens to have an old heart. Now you'll have to look carefully to see where the old has withstood the new. It has a splendid air to it and several surprising theme restaurants, as well as gourmet events with visiting chefs from abroad. There is a deck-style swimming pool with views that embrace the coast.

There are many budget-rate **guesthouses** in the area and this is a popular place for independent travellers who want to be close to the action.

✖ **Where to eat and drink** There are some definitely dodgy places to eat so choose wisely. A restaurant that opened in 2001 set a trend for improvement, making the beach the place to go again. Called **Golden Mile Restaurant** (*43/14 Mount Beach, off College Av, Mount Lavinia;* ✆ *011 2733997; www.jaysonsholdings.com;* **$$**), this is primarily for seafood and fish but serves steaks and chicken too. Its name comes from the old nickname for the beach.

Under the same ownership as the Glendower in Nuwara Eliya (see page 176), it shares that hotel's easy sophisticated ambience. The generous use of good wood that is a feature of the Glendower is in evidence in Golden Mile; the bar is decorated with 22 different kinds of tropical timber and tables are polished wooden slabs. The restaurant bills itself as 'a log station on the beach'. The upmarket décor is matched by good-quality food and obliging service. It's a great place to go in the evenings and its prices are not much more than at fast-food outlets, but the food is served quickly and is top-notch.

WADDUWA The railway line hugs the coast at Wadduwa, about 35km from Colombo, and it has to be crossed to reach the hotels and guesthouses that have managed to establish themselves along the coast. All, of necessity, have swimming pools since the beach isn't very inviting.

Getting there
By train The railway station is served mainly by slow trains.

By bus Bus No 400 serves Wadduwa on the way to Kalutara.

By road The Galle road runs through Wadduwa with only the signboards pointing to the coast to indicate there are hotels in the vicinity.

🏠 **Where to stay and eat** In addition to these listings, there are also beach shacks and wayside cafés, but the below places are the only ones recommended.

🏠 **Reef Beach Villa** (7 AC suites) 78 Samanthara Rd, Wadduwa; ✆ 038 2284442; e brendan@reefvilla.com; www.reefvilla.com. Unbelievable. A haven of fantasy that begins with a drive off the Galle road & across the railway line south of Wadduwa station through a miniature botanical garden. But even the impressive, exotic entrance doesn't prepare the visitor for this unique hotel, created by Brendan O'Donnell & his partner Bernadette Barker over 4 years before its opening in 2009. Every suite is palatial with debonair décor that says emphatically that it is 'fit for a Maharajah'. Ceilings of Kerala terracotta tiles soar while hand-crafted floor tiles of a 12th-century pattern are cool underfoot. Beds are antique Jacobean 4-posters from Calcutta & much of the furniture is based on original East India Company designs. The bathrooms are bliss, graced by Venetian-style mirrors, each with a bathtub hewn from a single block of granite & a granite waterfall shower. There is a garden swimming pool with a view of the beach & sea, & pavilions for dining on menus prepared to guests' demands. Lavish & comfortable, this is tropical tranquillity of superior quality, & it's also great fun. **$$$$**

 Blue Water (100 AC rooms) Thalpitiya, Wadduwa; 038 2235067; e reservations@ thebluewatersrilanka.com; www.bluewatersrilanka.com. Built on utilitarian lines, a contrast to the homely clutter of colonial properties & in keeping with the modern mode of clean lines & dramatic vistas. With top-range rates the hotel relies on minimalism for its appeal. It is the closest 5-star beach hotel to Colombo but is dedicated to pre-booked tourists rather than those who just want to drop in for a meal or a drink. **$$$**

KALUTARA Kalutara is 42km from Colombo, located at the lagoon-like mouth of the Kalu Ganga, along which boats and rafts used to float from Ratnapura. It was once a popular resort for Colombo's colonial residents and earned the sobriquet 'Richmond of Ceylon' because of its similarity to that Thames-side town. It was temporarily the capital of King Wickrama Pandu (1042–43) ruling from the Ruhunu region. In 1655, it was captured by the Dutch, who built a fort on the site of a Portuguese one that replaced the original Gangatilaka Vihara, which the Portuguese demolished. In 1797, the fort was ceded to the British. It has a population of 39,615 (2012 estimate).

The river was known to Arab sailors who took shelter in its lagoon during the southwest monsoon. **Kalutara North**, where the hotels are, is divided from **Kalutara South** by the river, linked by road and rail bridges. On the southern bank, between the road and the railway line, is a Buddhist shrine under a venerable Bo tree. On the opposite side of the road is a huge white dagoba that glints in the sunlight. The dagoba, built in the 1960s, has a painted interior. Outside the shrine, which has inherited the name of Gangatilaka Vihara, are several collecting boxes into which passing motorists drop coins as a token-offering for a safe drive.

Getting there
By train The main station is Kalutara South, just after the line crosses the wide expanse of river. It takes an hour by semi-express train from Colombo.

By bus Bus No 400 departs every 30 minutes from Colombo's central bus stand.

By road The road sweeps through Kalutara South as a dual carriageway and then crosses the railway line by **Paiyagala South** station to cruise along the edge of the beach. This maritime stretch was planted with coconuts on the orders of King Parakramabahu II (1236–70) to serve the needs of the increasing population of the then Ruhunu, and also for export. As a legacy, the area today is the main source of the country's arrack, the spirit distilled from the sap of the coconut palm, known in its raw form as toddy.

 Where to stay and eat Unfortunately, Kalutara is poorly served for independent restaurants since the package hotels cater for full board clients.

🏠 Royal Palms Beach Hotel (118 AC rooms, 5 suites) De Abrew Dr, Waskaduwa, Kalutara North; 📞034 2228113; e royalpalms@tangerinehotels. com; www.tangerinehotels.com. Eclipsing the few hotels in Kalutara, this is a sister & neighbour of the moderate-rate Tangerine Beach Hotel. All rooms have balconies or patios & sea or garden views. There is an agreeable attitude by staff, which makes this large beach resort inviting. It is 40km by road from Colombo. **$$$**

🏠 Halketha (2 non-AC cottages) near Mathugama, Kalutara; m 077 6321787; www. halketha-matugama-sri-lanka.lakpura.com. Perfect for getting away from it all, just 2 cottages, with a central dining pavilion, set in a privately owned 4ha (10 acre) rubber estate. It's the kind of place that I was at first selfishly reluctant to review in case it gets fully booked when I want to stay there again. Never mind; it's a treat that visitors will enjoy after a surfeit of ruins, beaches & Sri Lanka's mad traffic. The drive there involves getting from Kalutara to Mathugama town centre. By the roundabout & bus station take the Naboda road to the left for 1km. At the sign (in Sinhala) announcing Major Sudeera Premadasa Mawatha, it's a right turn to drive 3km through paddy fields. After a sign marking Vogan Estate, the road runs through a glade of rubber trees & out again. Then there's a sign on the right by a gate announcing Halketha. A lane leads through tea bushes up to a mud wall with a thatched awning & an ancient wooden entrance with a low transom. Step through this into a garden of rubber trees, tea bushes & neat crannies of flowers. There are 2 cottages: Surangana for romantics & Kasyapa for families, both furnished caringly with appropriate local antiques but without the ostentation of boutique properties. Meals are by arrangement. FB prices will make you gasp with delight. The ideal hideaway to laze away in rural solitude. **$**

Other practicalities
Medical
✚ **New Philip Hospital** 📞034 2222888

What to see and do Mangosteen are offered for sale beside the road on the outskirts of Kalutara. The fruit is traditionally associated with the area and was described lyrically by Major Raven Hart in his 1964 book, *History in Stone*:

> It would be worth walking the 26 miles from Colombo for a good mangosteen. There is no fruit in the world to equal it: it peels almost as easily as a banana, with no loose juice to dribble down your chin or squirt into your eye, and serves you with little segments like orange-pips but separated for you, each a mouthful; and it tastes like Heaven.

However, other than the aforementioned accommodation, Kalutara is a commercial town with little to interest the tourist passing through.

BERUWALA Spelt Beruwala or Beruwela, this was known to ancient mariners as Barberyn. It has a lighthouse on an island off its shore and there is a flourishing fishing harbour. It is one of the first ports used by Arab traders from the 9th century and has on its rocky headland a mosque, **Kechimalai**, whose existence goes back 1,000 years. By the 19th century, Beruwala had developed into a thriving port for the shipment of cinnamon. From Beruwala to Hikkaduwa, hotels used by tour operators for package groups wall off the coast, but there are, mercifully, dozens of independent low-cost guesthouses squeezed between gaps, as well as some high-priced boutique hotels. It has a population of 35,312 (2012 estimate).

Getting there
By train There is a station at Beruwala but only slow passenger trains stop there. Best to take an express to Alutgama and pick up a three-wheeler at the station to drive you back to Beruwala.

By bus Bus No 400 will get you there; intercity buses will drop you on request.

By road Beruwala is 55km from Colombo. The hotels are off the Galle road on the way to the next town of Alutgama.

Where to stay At the time of writing, the three major hotels and some minor adjoining ones, including **Eden Hotel and Spa**, **Riverina Hotel** and **Tropical Villas**, were closed and were being pulled down or refurbished under a scheme to create a resort of over 400 bedrooms.

However, two hotels (Riverina and Beyroo) have been completely and pleasantly rebuilt into the modern, Turkish-themed (well, lots of colourful mosaic tiles breaking up expanses of light grey concrete walls and columns) **Cinnamon Bey Hotel** (*198 AC rooms, 2 suites; Moragalla, Beruwala;* ✆ *034 2297000;* e *reservations@cinnamonhotels. com; www.cinnamonhotels.com;* **$$$**). The entrance is impressive with a separate lattice-screened reception lounge and a massive central lobby like a plant-filled amphitheatre/piazza with views of the swimming pool and ocean. There are 170 superior bedrooms complete with work desk, plug points and sliding wooden lattice doors to the shower and toilet in the main wing, and 28 deluxe rooms with bathtub and broad balcony with exclusive access to a private swimming pool, plus two huge, exotic suites with plunge pools. As well as the bright main restaurant there are six others offering a range of Asian-fusion, Japanese, Arabic, grill and spa cuisines. The newest hotel on the west coast, it is agreeably modern, bringing a refreshing style and caring service to the conventional Sri Lankan beach hotel.

Where to eat and drink On this stretch of road from Kalutara, with so many small hotels, it is hard to find a decent independent restaurant or bar. Best to head to Alutgama or Bentota (see below and page 237, respectively). If you have a Sri Lankan friend or trusted driver/guide, ask him to take you into the **Beruwela Resthouse**, a haunt of boozing fishermen, for some fresh fried fish snacks.

What to see and do The fishing harbour at Beruwala is the place to see caught fish being landed on the quayside before breakfast and the intricacies of auctioning the catch. It costs foreigners Rs25 entrance. Other attractions are as outlined in the sections on Alutgama (see below) and Bentota (see page 237).

ALUTGAMA Alutgama is not a pretty town (it means New Town in English) but it does mark the end of the built-up area before the road crosses the Bentota River and the scenery brightens. It is 61km from Colombo and exists as the place you go through on the way to somewhere else.

Getting there
By train All express trains stop at Alutgama, which is also the terminus for some slow passenger trains from north and south. See the box opposite for the times of the main trains plying the west coast between Colombo and Galle (* indicates Monday to Friday service; + indicates Sunday service only). Before planning a journey by rail, these times should be checked with the stationmaster of the departing station as schedules change unexpectedly.

From the station there is access to the independent small hotels to the north of Alutgama, and to the hotels of Beruwala. Walk over the bridge and down to the exit where there will be a turmoil of three-wheelers, each one eager to take you. If you want to walk to Bentota do not leave by the exit but walk to the southern end of the

Train	8050	8040	8086	8056	8058	8096*	8760*	8766*	8775
Colombo	06.55	08.35	10.30	14.25	15.50	16.45	17.25	18.05	19.30
Alutgama	08.26	09.53	11.48	15.40	16.47	17.49	18.31	19.26	21.16
Bentota	08.30	09.56		15.45			18.34		21.23
Ambalangoda	08.52	10.18		16.05	17.08	18.09	19.10	19.49	22.07
Hikkaduwa	09.05	10.29	12.22	16.16	17.19	18.20	19.30	20.01	22.26
Galle	09.26	10.49	12.42	16.31	17.34	18.37	20.03	20.23	22.55

Train	8311	8327*	8097*	8059	8057	8085	8053+	8039	8051
Galle	03.40	05.00	05.50	06.55	07.25	11.15	13.45	14.45	15.30
Hikkaduwa	04.10	05.29	06.06	07.09	07.37	11.34	14.06	15.04	15.49
Ambalangoda	04.26	05.49	06.17	07.20	07.52	11.45	14.24	15.16	16.00
Bentota	04.47	06.25			08.12		14.48	15.38	16.27
Alutgama	05.05	06.28	06.48	07.41	08.15	12.11	14.52	15.41	16.31
Colombo	06.51	07.42	08.08	08.43	09.30	13.30	16.34	17.20	18.05

platform and jump down on to the track. It's about a 500m walk along the track to the rail and road bridges over the Bentota River and so to the beach.

By bus The bus station is a short walk (five minutes) from the railway station. Bus No 400 supplies the service, with intercity buses leaving Colombo every 30 minutes.

By road Traffic on the Galle road has to slow down to pass through Alutgama because of the commerce of the place. It may not look much but there is a certain prosperity, given the number of hotels nearby and, hence, employment and sales opportunities.

Getting around There are three-wheeler taxis on every corner and junction from Beruwala onwards, wherever there is a possibility of a hire, not just from tourists but from locals too. They are so useful for getting around and the fare can be negotiated since they don't have meters. There are also air-conditioned minibuses outside hotels, ready to be hired for a round trip of several days or just an excursion to Brief Garden or to Colombo. Since the drivers usually speak only a little English, it is customary to take along a local freelance guide (OK, beach boy if you don't like me being politically correct) who knows his way around and will arrange everything.

Where to stay and eat The town runs parallel to the inland bank of the lagoon. Hotels on the opposite bank, by the beach, are classed as being in Bentota. A few small independent hotels with an Alutgama address border the town side of the lagoon – many have watersport centres and are good for arranging diving and fishing as well as for river tours and jet skiing. All listings are included on the map, page 240.

Thumbelina Apartments (7 apts) 88 Welipenna Rd, Alutgama; 034 2275607; e nebula@dialogsl.net; www.nebula88.com. Close to the bus & train station at Alutgama on the access road

to the Southern Expressway. Built on 2 floors above the Nebula speciality supermarket, with quick access to the banks, post office & shopping centres, these self-catering apts are not only located within reach of all amenities, they are also beautifully situated beside the Bentota River. Entrance to the apt block is street side, next to the Nebula Supermarket, & access is restricted to resident guests by key. Each of the 7 apts has its own front-door access from the 1st- or 2nd-floor landing. There are 6 luxury studio apts with a broad balcony with a view of the Bentota River & each apt has a double bed, AC, a kitchenette with fridge, cooking facilities, kettle & crockery & cutlery. There is also a settee & dining table & chairs made out of grained coconut timber, a TV & free Wi-Fi. In the en-suite bathroom there is a power-shower with hot water, hair-dryer & bathroom amenities. A 7th, larger apt, perhaps more suitable for the business visitor, has a long view of the main street of Alutgama, busy during the day but quiet at night. For all apts, bed linen & towels are refreshed every 2 days. Housekeeping service, included in the room rate, is carried out each morning. A washing machine & ironing facilities are available communally as are extra kitchen facilities such as a storage

refrigerator, a gas oven, & a landing lounge. Amazingly, for such convenience & quality, it's inexpensive. **$**
✗Pier 88 88 Welipenna Rd, Alutgama; ✆034 2275607; e nebula@dialogsl.net; www. nebula88; ⊕ daily. Concealed behind the Nebula supermarket in Alutgama, Pier 88 (Nebula Garden Restaurant) is set on the banks of the Bentota River surrounded by colourful bougainvillaea bushes & reached through an archway of tropical blossoms. There are tables in the fan-cooled library parlour entrance (free Wi-Fi) while kiosks & tented pavilions provide shade for the rustic tables & chairs cooled by the river & sea breeze. The menu includes sandwiches, soups & salads with typical Sri Lankan dishes like rice & curry & fresh fish & seafood, & traditional fare like pasta, pickled pork knuckle & mixed grill. The service is swift & courteous & the prices are unbelievably low, much cheaper than hotels & guesthouses in the area. Beers, wines & cocktails are available. **$**

What to see and do

What to see and do A private house and landscaped garden open to the public, **Brief Garden** (✆ 034 2274462; ⊕ 08.00–17.00 daily; admission Rs1,000) manages to combine an elaborate European layout with a tropical wilderness. It was an 81ha rubber estate when it was acquired in the 1920s by a barrister from funds made from a legal brief. His son, Bevis Bawa, decided to make his home and garden there in 1929, gradually selling off the rubber lands to reduce it to manageable proportions. On his death in 1992, his six houses and the garden were inherited by his employees, one of whom, Doolan de Silva, runs Brief, and also creates gardens for many of the country's new hotels.

In the early 1970s, in response to requests from tourists who began to stay in Bentota, Bawa opened the garden to the public. It is a landscaped collection of several small gardens each leading to another, whether by paths, steps or vista. There are over 120 different types of trees, countless plants and bushes, and only a few flowers in the 2ha garden. Visitors are encouraged to linger and enjoy the tranquillity, since it is not a garden to walk through smartly just for the sake of ticking it off on the list of 'what to see'.

The ramble through the garden finishes at the house where Bawa lived. It's a fascinating place, not just for its unexpected design that leads visitors downstairs to a door out to the car park, but also for the *objets d'art* within. Pride of place is a weatherworn mural by Australia's famous artist, Donald Friend. It shows many local scenes and people, including an image of Bevis Bawa lying full length in a planter's chair directing some planting. 'You didn't do the garden,' Friend told him. 'Your gardeners did.'

There is a gallery of old photos of Bevis Bawa showing him as a man whose strong face must have deterred dissent. He was an ADC to four governors before leaving the colonial service to do things 'here and there' as de Silva explained. He was tall and debonair and attracted the attention of Vivien Leigh when she was filming in Sri Lanka. The gossip was that she fancied him. 'Nonsense,' said Bawa, who had a Rolls-Royce. 'She just likes the car.' When asked by an eager journalist what was the plan of the garden, Bawa replied: 'No plan. It's just a happening.'

A visit to Brief is to see how one man's inspired happening has become a unique heritage for Sri Lankans and visitors to enjoy. It takes only 30 minutes from Colombo along the Southern Highway to reach the Welipenna junction on the way to this extraordinary garden of Eden, then a further 15 minutes to the approach to Dharga town and a Bo tree shrine marking the differently named Ambagaha Handiya (Mango Tree Junction).

Turn right there (or left if you are coming from Alutgama, 9km away) until a dignified signboard with lettering like the writing on a legal brief, directs drivers to the right. Then the road disintegrates to a country trail until a retired fountain marks a crossroads. The extreme left fork leads through carefully manicured bushes to Brief – and its garden paradise.

BENTOTA This was the halfway house between Colombo and Galle in coaching days. There was a resthouse near the mouth of the Bentota River, which was infested by crocodiles, and local oysters were to be had for tea. Now the resthouse has been replaced by the Bentota Beach Hotel and the mouth of the river, which forms a long lagoon, is used for jet skiing and banana raft riding. The crocodiles have gone and there are no oysters, but in season the rocks yield mussels. Trips by motorboat and outrigger canoe up the river through the mangroves are possible.

Bentota is 62km from Colombo and begins on the southern side of the Bentota River, which is also the border between the Western and Southern provinces. In Sinhala, it is Bentara and the river is the Ben Ganga. There is no real town, just a few local and souvenir shops beside the Galle road.

When the area's potential for tourism was recognised a National Tourist Resort was created embracing the beach-frontage land for a structured 40ha complex. Here the early commercial architecture of Geoffrey Bawa is in evidence with a shopping arcade longing for customers, and a toytown-type square complete with bank, post office, police station and resort-authority bungalow. It's rather soulless. The railway station was built to give access to the beach. A pond, shaped like a map of Sri Lanka, was created from a swamp beside the Galle road.

The area's history has been overwhelmed. The Galapatha Temple, 1km inland by an offshoot of the river, was built 600 to 900 years ago. The Portuguese built a fort, which the Dutch took over, and then the British turned it into the resthouse.

Getting there

By train Slow trains stop at Bentota's station as it has become absorbed into the railway network and it is used more by locals than tourists. Some semi-express trains also stop there. For train schedules, see under Alutgama (page 235).

(As always when planning a railway journey, check the times from the station in advance as they are subject to change.)

By bus Intercity buses passing through Bentota will only stop if the fare for the full journey (Colombo to Galle or vice versa) is paid. Local buses from Alutgama serve Bentota on their way south.

By road The Galle road opens up after crossing the river bridge. A turning to the right, immediately after the bridge, and over the railway line, leads to a side road serving the beach hotels. The next right turn off the Galle road, by the pond, is the road to Pitaramba, an old village that retains its character despite the tourist hotels

Because of the high proportion of hotel guests who have booked a two-week stay in Bentota and then decide to make a short tour – called 'a round trip' locally – car and minibus (van) drivers are to be found wherever guests are staying. The drivers all speak a bit of English (so no guide is needed, although sometimes guests take along the freelance guide they have met on the beach for company) and have a fixed-price tariff.

Prices, however, are not constant as they have to be revised every time there is a fuel hike or a new tax to take into account. At the time of writing, expect to pay upwards of Rs12,000 a day for a chauffer-driven car or minibus, or the quoted fixed price to a tourist destination and back. You don't have to worry about meals or accommodation for the driver on the journey as the establishments will provide these. The driver, however, will expect a nightly allowance while on tour of Rs500 and extra according to waiting time and any extra kilometres over an agreed amount.

Some enterprising drivers/guides will create (at a day's notice) an entire package for guests that includes transport and hotels and even admission charges (to places such as the Elephant Orphanage, Kandy Temple, etc). This is a good way to set your own itinerary instead of being confined to organised tours.

around it. A road to the right around the pond leads to a mini town square, the police and railway stations, a branch of the Bank of Ceylon, the post office and the Golden Grill Restaurant (see page 241).

The Bentota district extends for another 6km along the Galle road to include the beach area of Induruwa. Here the road runs alongside the ocean. Between the 67km and 68km posts, look inland to see a rambling cottage built in 1903, set on a bluff in a coconut grove overlooking the railway line, the road and the beach. That's where I live.

 Where to stay Bentota has accommodation to suit everyone but, because the British built the railway line along the beach, trains rumble through the holiday landscape. They don't run at night though.

At the other side of the headland straddled by Vivanta by Taj, the broad strand of beach has a few independent, small villa-type hotels (see Paradise Road The Villa Bentota and Club Villa below and opposite). These are accessible from the Galle road by turning down the signposted lanes to the right that lead to them. All listings are included on the map, page 240.

⌂ Paradise Road The Villa Bentota

(15 AC rooms) Mohotti Walauwa, 138/18-22 Galle Rd, Bentota; \ 034 2275311; e reservations@ villabentota.com; www.paradiseroadhotels.com. With its rooms & suites all impressively furnished thanks to the genius of Shanth Fernando, the man behind the fabulous Paradise Road lifestyle stores & the Gallery Café & Tintagel Hotel in Colombo, this villa hotel is both over the top & laid-back. The décor is the wow factor & does much to make

up for its location, with a railway line between its privacy & the beach, but it has 2 delightful swimming pools & a rarefied atmosphere. Originally designed by Geoffrey Bawa, it has all his trademarks of columns & pure white austerity, brightened with a striking collection of Sri Lankan art in its gallery corridors. It has metamorphosed from a listlessly run property into an address of distinction & is not to be confused with Club Villa next door. The courtyard-like Villa Café ($$$) is open daily for lunch & dinner & to non-residents with advance reservation. **$$$$**

⌂ **Vivanta by Taj** (162 AC rooms) Bentota; ☎034 5555555; e vivanta.bentota@tajhotels.com; www. vivantabytaj.com. This was formerly the Taj Exotica Hotel, found at the end of the road running parallel to the railway line & the beach (past the upgraded package-tour hotels: Avani, formerly Serendib, & The Surf, formerly Lihiniya Surf). At least this hotel is a change from the gaunt architecture of some of its neighbours, although it seems rather more suited to the Bahamas with its exaggerated grandeur. Rooms are on 4 floors & have balconies with sea or garden view. There are speciality restaurants (seafood **$$$**; an excellent Chinese restaurant with a chef from China **$$$**) as well as the usual facilities for guests in groups. The bar doubles as a bingo hall on some nights. The hotel spreads its wings where there was once a coconut grove on a bluff (bulldozed away) & commands views of the beach north & south. **$$$$**

⌂ **Bentota Beach Hotel** (130 AC rooms, 3 suites) National Holiday Resort, Bentota; ☎034 2275176; e bbh@keells.com; www. johnkeellshotels.com. A pioneering beach hotel dating from the 1970s (with 1999 renovation), still setting the standards for resort hospitality. Each room has the extras expected by tourists: central AC with in-room control, TV, room safe & minibar. Set in 4ha of gardens by the beach & lagoon, the hotel is spacious enough so that even when full 'guests can find their own place in the sun'. The freshwater swimming pool meandering through the garden attracts many visitors, while the active head for the sports & live-entertainment centre that is part of the hotel complex. Behind the formidable granite bastions of the hotel is a pretty courtyard-pond, & a bar, lounge & vast dining hall with sea views. There is an escape from the scrums around the buffet by going to the à la carte restaurant downstairs (**$$$**). Simple menu, good food prepared in a show kitchen, & a good wine list too. By the time you read this the hotel might have been revamped again to emerge as the Cinnamon Beach, as part of the rebranding of the properties of the local Cinnamon hotel chain, Keells. **$$$**

⌂ **Club Villa** (17 AC rooms) 138/15 Galle Rd, Bentota; ☎034 2275312; e clubvilla@sltnet.lk; www.club-villa.com. Another Geoffrey Bawa-inspired hotel, next door to Villa Bentota, this has an exclusive ambience similar to its neighbour but with less intensity, & costs several dollars less. **$$$**

⌂ **Nisala Arana** (6 non-AC suites) 326/1 Circular Rd, Kommala, Bentota; ☎034 4287079; e info@nisalaarana.com; www.nisalaarana.com. On the Galle road, just after a yellow-painted antique shop & a purple-painted bar, take the turning off to the left, turn left where the road forks to the right to Elpitiya, & then left again where a stupa heads a T-junction. A long, grey wall & gates made from railway sleepers embrace Nisala Arana. Here are 3 antique-style cottages, each with a pair of suites set in 2ha of landscaped gardens with an ancient temple for meditation, a sparkling swimming pool & an open-sided dining pavilion. It's dubbed 'an abode of peace' & is ideal for absorbing sheer tranquillity & for a break from the beach. **$$$**

⌂ **Aida Ayurveda & Holistic Health Resort** (28 AC rooms) 12A Mangala Mawatha, Galle Rd, Bentota; ☎034 2271137; e aida1@sltnet. lk; www.aidaayurveda.com. Don't be put off by the formality of its name: this is a hotel with a difference, in design as well as character. Access is by the lane that is the 1st turn-off on the left after crossing the river. About 50m down on the right is the wellbeing part of the complex, a delightful airy, modern hotel building with garden vistas & a 1st-floor swimming pool. This is exclusive to guests taking the various ayurveda revitalisation programmes, & is a haven by the river. On the other side of the road is Aida's restaurant (**$$**) which also has more guestrooms. **$$**

⌂ **Hotel Susantha Garden** (18 rooms, 6 with AC & self-catering apts) National Holiday Resort, Bentota; ☎034 2275324; e susanthas@sltnet. lk; www.hotelsusanthagarden.com. A popular guesthouse that has come up in the world, but still retains its informality & low prices. This adjoins the Bentota railway station & is accessible by steps from the platform (& hence the beach) or by driving in from the village square. Its rooms are built around a garden & it is one of those independent places that Sri Lankans do so well. Guests are left to their own devices & there are no rules or set meal times. The restaurant (**$**) is popular with non-residents too. Margaret Sheldon wrote to say that she loved staying at Susantha's & would like to return. 'In half a day I managed to fit in 2 good meals, a trip to Brief Garden, a massage, buying some jewellery & best of all, getting a lovely suit made for me, all through the hotel at bargain prices.' **$**

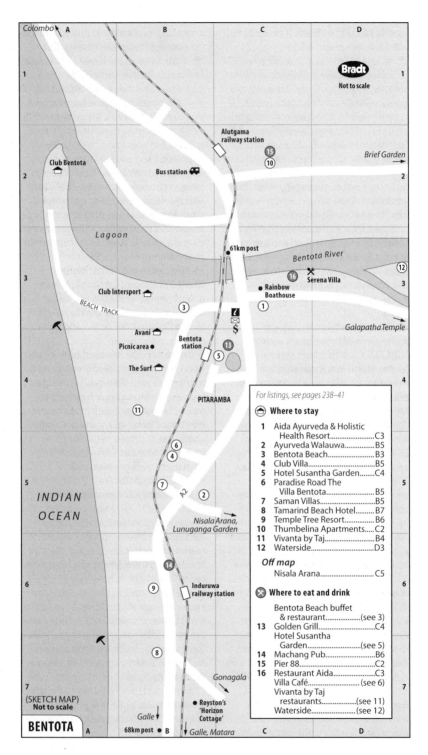

Colombo ← A

Alutgama railway station
15
10

Brief Garden →

Club Bentota

Bus station

Lagoon

61km post

Bentota River

16 ✕ **Serena Villa**

12

Club Intersport

BEACH TRACK

3

• **Rainbow Boathouse**
1

Galapatha Temple →

Avani

Picnic area •

Bentota station

13

5

The Surf

PITARAMBA

11

6
4

INDIAN OCEAN

7
A2
2

Nisala Arana, Lunuganga Garden →

14

9 **Induruwa railway station**

8

Gonagala →

(SKETCH MAP)
Not to scale

BENTOTA

Galle ↓
68km post • B

• **Royston's 'Horizon Cottage'**

↓ *Galle, Matara*

Bradt
Not to scale

✗ Where to eat and drink Bentota is not known for the finesse of its cuisine and only has a few independent restaurants worth visiting. The two top hotels, Bentota Beach and Vivanta by Taj, cater for non-residents (with advance reservations) in their à la carte restaurants with predictably high prices and formula dishes. Genuine exotic culinary delights, however, can be had at The Villa Café (see *Paradise Road The Villa Bentota*, pages 238–9) with imported meat as well as local fish and a lavish sundae made with spun jaggery (like candy floss and made from kitul palm treacle). All listings are included on the map opposite.

✗ Golden Grill National Tourist Resort, Bentota; 🕻034 2275455; 🕐 daily for lunch & dinner. You'll find this restaurant beside the pond, next to the Bank of Ceylon. There is a terrace for dining overlooking the pond & the Galle road, & a good menu of grill & seafood items, as well as local dishes on demand. The service is excellent with young, bow-tied & knowledgeable waiters & the food, whether Western or Eastern, comes quickly. It's extraordinarily good value & a happy place to dine with everything run so smoothly, & very popular with Sri Lankans too. It's at the top of my list of Sri Lanka's best restaurants for good value & a good time. A great wine list too, with only a modest mark-up; a rare find in a tourist area. The wedding-hall décor is genuine; it is often used for wedding receptions by local couples. $$

✗ Restaurant Aida 🕻034 2275398; 🕐 daily for lunch & dinner. Opposite Bentota Beach Hotel, this is by the river & above a gem workshop behind one of Sri Lanka's foremost gem & jewellery shops, Aida Jewellers. Tables are open-air or in individual pavilions overlooking the river. It has a bar, a fair selection of wines, & a menu of standard dishes that over the years have proved to be the most popular choice of visitors. As well as the usual seafood there is shark on the menu; however, there is no pork. $$

✗ Waterside Yathramulla, Bentota; 🕻034 2270080; e reservations@bentotawaterside.com; www.bentotawaterside.com; 🕐 daily for lunch & dinner. New, & with a refreshingly different menu. Although it has very comfortable, chintzy rooms (*6 AC rooms; $$$ – unusually, the B&B rate here includes all taxes & service charge*) with splendid views of the river & the swimming pool (reserved for residents), it is Waterside's restaurant that is popular with non-residents, both for lavish lobster or king prawn lunches & for dinners with novel starters, steaks & scrumptious desserts. The brainchild of an English woman who's lived in Spain & saw a gap in the market for a better style of dining in an elegant, tropical setting, with obliging service & carefully prepared food, Waterside attracts guests from the beach hotels who come by boat along the Bentota River, or by road down village lanes. Tim & Marion Gowing, who went there on my recommendation, liked it so much they returned a 2nd night. Definitely worth a try, even if only to sample dishes that are a contrast to the regular fare at the resorts. $$

✗ Hotel Susantha Garden National Holiday Resort, Bentota; 🕻034 2275324; e susanthas@ sltnet.lk; www.hotelsusanthagarden.com; 🕐 daily for lunch & dinner. Basic-priced dishes & drinks served in the fun setting of a busy tropical garden behind the Bentota railway station platform. $

Other practicalities

Bank There is a branch of the **Bank of Ceylon** [240 C3/4] (and an ATM) used to dealing with foreigners in the mini town square in front of the railway and police stations.

Medical Several doctors in the area are familiar with tourist complaints and they can be contacted through the hotels or guesthouses.

Post office A post office [240 C3] (🕐 *07.30–1700 Mon–Fri, 08.30–13.00 Sat, closed Sun & public holidays*) where the staff know the cost of postage to foreign parts is in the mini town square.

Tourist information An official tourism information centre [240 C3] (⊕ *09.00–16.15 Mon–Fri, closed w/ends & public holidays*) is at the entrance to the Bawa-designed, open-sided shopping corridor leading from the Galle road to the mini town square.

What to see and do Trips to see the wildlife in the mangrove trees that line the Bentota River can be arranged at **Rainbow Boat House** [240 C3] (✆ *034 2275383*) which is on the left of the Galle road immediately after crossing over the bridge from Alutgama. Boats with helmsman/guide can be hired by the hour. A whole-day cruise inland includes a visit to a village for a special rice-and-curry lunch and even a local wedding ceremony. Crocodiles can be seen, as well as water monitors and a rich variety of birdlife.

There are several **turtle hatcheries** privately run as sanctuaries on the road south, between Bentota and Kosgoda. Turtle eggs are collected from the beach by local people who sell them to the hatcheries, instead of eating them. The eggs are buried in the sand at the sanctuaries until they hatch. After the young turtles have grown sufficiently, they are returned to the sea, often sponsored by tourists paying to release them on a special occasion, such as 30 turtles on a 30th birthday.

Geoffrey Bawa, who died in 2003, aged 84, was Sri Lanka's most famous and revered architect. He was self-taught and lived near Bentota at a place he named **Lunuganga**. He loved its isolation, where he could work without disturbance, and potter about in the bungalow's garden while thinking of a detail of one of his architectural masterpieces. He was the younger rother of Bevis Bawa, who created Brief Garden (see page 236).

Bawa bought Lunuganga in 1949 when his prowess as an architect was still unknown. It was a rubber plantation on a 6ha peninsula surrounded by the waters of the Dedduwa Lake. It had a typical robust and characterless plantation house that was to become the focal point of the garden. Bawa named the estate himself, its meaning of 'Salt River' referring to its location.

Bawa began his transformation of the plantation and abandoned paddy fields by ruthless pruning, felling of trees and even training the branches so they would grow into more interesting shapes. He created not an ornamental garden but a fantasy of light and shade, of water and space, of green and brown, of dips and mounds, with vistas framed by doorways and arches and soaring views punctuated by the classic form of a perfect jar or a Grecian statue.

Lunuganga became legendary over the years as people heard of Bawa shaving the top off a hill so that he had a better view of the lake, of burying a road so it passed through a miniature canyon unobserved from his patio, and of the pavilions he built in the woods to look as though they had been there for years.

He commanded that a stupa, which protruded on the forested horizon, be painted white and that an eyesore of an abandoned government pumping house on the opposite bank be roofed in tiles and painted mustard, all at his expense. To preserve the natural environment, and the view from his patio, he bought the 7ha island of Honduwa in the lake and dedicated it as a bird sanctuary.

He worked hard over the years while designing landmark buildings (such as the Bentota Beach, Heritance Kandalama, Heritance Ahungalla and Lighthouse hotels) to create this garden within a garden. He succeeded to the extent that Lunuganga is both an extension and a reflection of the countryside that contains it.

Bawa had his favourite walks and viewpoints that visitors can now enjoy, while they marvel at how he moulded nature to fashion the landscape he wanted. Curiously, although he became such a famous and much-imitated architect, the buildings in the garden have a rustic simplicity. Visitors can peep into his house where the atmosphere owes a lot to venerable and sometimes eccentric pieces of furniture, including kerosene-powered fans and religious statues from Europe.

A tour of the garden starts with an introduction by the resident architect and then a guide escorts visitors along terraced walks, up and down steps and hills, past water gardens and down to the lake, through woods and around the outside of buildings rich in patina, for an impression of Bawa's vision of the perfect garden. It is even more impressive as the source of the architect's inspiration and genius.

Lunuganga is appropriately difficult to find and has no signposts. It lies just south of Bentota, reached by turning left off the Galle road to drive down the Elpitiya road and right at the Dedduwa junction, after the 3km post. The right fork, after a bakery on the left, leads to another fork where the mud road on the right, by a post on which someone has daubed '14', gives access to the entrance gate.

Lunuganga is open to visitors daily (⏰ *09.00–17.00, admission Rs1,250*). At certain times of the year, it is possible to stay in one of the six guest rooms of the house (📞 *034 4287056;* e *lunuganga@sltnet.lk; www.geoffreybawa.com/lunuganga-country-estate/introductionpage;* **$$$$**).

INDURUWA
The sea side of the Galle road at Induruwa where it runs southwards from Bentota to Hikkaduwa has been colonised by pastry shops opened optimistically to cater for passing traffic (but which have sparse business as through-traffic takes the Southern Expressway) and small guesthouses with boutique property pretensions.

🏠 **Where to stay and eat** Between Bentota and Kosgoda there are several guesthouses, on both the beach and land sides, that operate year-round, surviving on walk-in customers. **Tamarin Beach Hotel** (*Galle Rd, Kaikawala, Induruwa;* 📞 *034 2270560;* **$**) is painted yellow, puce and purple and is located between the 67km and 68km markers by the road junction that leads to the lane to my house. It's clean and with basic beachside accommodation and a local-style bar with drinks and snacks (**$**) served in the garden by the beach.

🏠 **Saman Villas** (27 AC suites) Aturuwella, Induruwa; 📞 034 2275435; e resv@samanvilla.com; www.samanvilla.com. Accommodation is in individual mini villas on a small cliff with a swimming pool that seems to soar out over the beach. 7 of the villas have their own swimming pools too. There's a gentle feeling of class about the place, as well as one of seclusion. Its location means it's a 3-wheeler ride into Bentota when you want to eat out. It was Sri Lanka's first boutique hotel when it opened in 1995, & the management's philosophy is to let its discerning, affluent guests do what they want, with breakfast & other meals served at any time of day, in the open-sided restaurant (**$$$**) or in the villas. **$$$$**

🏠 **Temple Tree Resort & Spa** (10 suites) 660 Galle Rd, Induruwa; 📞 034 2270700; e info@templetreeresortandspa.com; www.templetreeresortandspa.com. Opened at the beginning of 2008 on a quiet section of the beach,

with a shallow swimming pool along its length, it has suites in its 2 upper floors of engaging wood & cement design, with bathrooms as long as the bedrooms. The restaurant (**$$$**) & adjoining bar are open-sided, giving a view of the pool & garden. In spite of the broad & always closed wooden gate closing off the hotel from the Galle road, it is open to non-residents, bringing a touch of fine dining to this area where pastry shops are more common. **$$$$**

🏠 **Aida Ayurveda Holistic Health Resort** (10 rooms) 📞 034 2271888. This is a beachside hotel with distinctive salmon-pink walls that opened in Feb 2002 close to the 67km post on the Galle road, & is a sister of the one in Bentota, with all-inclusive rest-cure packages including specials as detailed by the hotel's ayurveda specialist. **$$**

🏠 **Southern Star Hotel** (8 AC rooms) Galle Rd, Galboda, Induruwa; 📞 034 2227466. A good cheapie right on the beach. With a swimming pool (open to non-residents for a fee) in its entrance compound & a patio restaurant ($) beside the beach, this is low enough in price to make it suitable for long-staying visitors on a budget, as well as popular with locals on a weekend outing or celebrating a wedding. $

✗ **Machang** Galle Rd, Warahena, Induruwa; ⏲ 11.00–14.00 & 17.00–23.00 daily. Part of a newly introduced chain of local brewery-sponsored pubs, this branch of Machang (meaning 'brother-in-law' but also used colloquially in Sinhala to address a best friend) serves spirits & cocktails as

well as its trademark draught beers. It specialises in food cooked behind the bar counter in woks by agile chefs producing cheap but good local delights such as *kunkun* (a kind of spinach) & garlic, black pepper pork curry & manioc, & hot butter mushrooms. There are other branches of this industrially decorated (cement floors & exposed beams) pub throughout Sri Lanka but this rates as the best with cheap cocktails, a pool table & even a sea view. Popular with locals as well as visitors. (It's on the land side of the Galle road between the 64km & 65km markers.) $

AHUNGALLA This village has grown because of the presence there of the **Heritance Ahungalla** (formerly Triton Hotel) (*154 AC rooms; Ahungalla;* \ *091 5555000;* e *ahungalla@heritancehotels.com; www.heritancehotels.com;* **$$$**). This was Sri Lanka's first five-star beach hotel and has a magnificent approach through an avenue of palm trees around a large pond, which is reflected in the swimming pool visible from the open entrance terrace with the sea glistening beyond it. It has another swimming pool in its newer, northern wing. It has been revamped with more glitz and glamour and a new fine-dining restaurant (**$$$**) commanding a dramatic view and serving some of the best fare on the coast. There is also a café (**$$**) with a decent menu and good service, a nightclub, and a main dining room where most meals are buffets.

Just a kilometre further south is **Villa Ranmenika** (*12 rooms, 2 suites; Galle Rd, Ahungalla;* \ *091 2264251;* e *ranmenike@sltnet.lk; www.villaranmenika.com;* **$$**), one of Sri Lanka's best-kept secrets and an agreeable place to stay any time of the year, no matter how rough the sea or sticky the air. Set in what once was a wilderness of bushes and weeds that has been transformed over 15 years into a delightful tropical garden, not with artistic finesse like the Bawa brothers' creations, but with a love for the lushness of manicured nature. On the land side of the Galle road (near the 75km post), this hotel, privately run by a Swiss lady, is hidden by a plethora of palms and crotons gathered around a huge swimming pool (23m x 13m and 2¾m at its deepest) always sparklingly clean. Rooms, equipped with everything needed, spread across two floors with some ground-floor ones opening onto their own miniature garden. The inner courtyard is pure fantasy: faux rocks and pretend timber and a pond brimful with plump, leaping red and silver fish. It's an ideal base to explore the west coast and to retreat from it too since so few people seem to have discovered Ranmenika's gentle charm. Without lavish boutique extravagance, it is amazingly inexpensive to stay; meals and snacks are available on demand ($).

Between the Heritance Ahungalla hotel and Villa Ranmenika, at the end of a short lane on the beach side of the main road is **Daniel's Pub** (*46A Galle Rd, Ahungalla;* ⏲ *11.00–14.00 & 17.00–23.00 daily except Poya days; $*). It's hidden behind a couple of shops but well signposted; it's a bit dark inside with the bar counter in a cage but with two kinds of draught beer available. Imported and local spirits are sold by the bottle at off-licence prices and there are lots of tables to sit down and enjoy the local atmosphere. The only snacks seem to be chips or fried egg. A great place for escaping hotel refinement and associating with locals.

BALAPITIYA The town straddles the road and has grown as tourists have discovered the area and guesthouses and small resorts have opened up. The main reason, though, for visiting it is for a river safari on the Madu Ganga.

Where to stay and eat There are some riverside guesthouses and snack stations, but most visitors stop only for the river tour, not overnight. Some new hotels were under construction at press time.

What to see and do Although there have been motorboats putt-putting up and down the Madu Ganga (river) carrying curious visitors since 1977 when Jayantha De Silva of the **Green Lagoon River Safari Boat Service** (*193 Galle Rd, Balapitiya;* ⤷ *091 2257638*) started operating, the river remains a wonderful discovery. Prawn breeding and fishing, and a timber mill or two as well as coir-manufacturing cottage industries, are the main forms of income, and a welcoming smile still greets visitors instead of a riverbank stall selling tacky souvenirs.

There are seven boat operators grouped on both the land and sea sides of the road bridge (where boatmen wave at passing cars to show they are available for hire). Prices are negotiable according to the season and time of day but a cruise of around two hours can cost about US$20 per person. It is best to take a trip early in the morning, into the sunrise, when birds (lots of cormorants) and the prawn fishermen (dropping nets into the reed baskets at the end of bamboo-fenced funnels) are busy. Water monitors nudging along the banks and leaping purple-faced leaf monkeys with attractive black and grey markings are common sights.

ANTIQUES ROADSHOW

Adding to the fun of a drive on the west-coast road, between the 63km marker at Bentota and the 86km marker at Ambalangoda, there are several ramshackle villas whose verandas are stacked with solid teak doors and frames, centuries-old wooden chests and granite grinding stones. These are treasure troves for local interior designers seeking mahogany wardrobes and carved four-poster beds. A peep inside the villas, looking behind the statues, curved ebony and rattan couches and planters' long-armed chairs, can reveal more convenient-to-carry collectibles.

The search could begin in Bentota where De Silva Antiques is housed in a former village headman's house painted an eye-catching mustard yellow. The heady scent of burning incense mingling with the warm aroma of furniture polish creates a distinctive smell redolent of a revered past. The villa is laid out like a museum with exhibits neatly grouped together, labelled with historical information and stored in glass showcases. But unlike a museum, you can handle the exhibits as everything is for sale, and the price is marked in US dollars (not in code), so potential purchasers know it isn't inflated the moment they express interest in a piece. Yes, the price is negotiable according to the volume of business.

Just after the next town of Balapitiya a dilapidated house almost hidden by long grass is the home of Sudath Antiques where old furniture fills two floors. Copies of pieces are made for export in the backyard of the house. At Rajapaksa Antiques just before Ambalangoda there are sometimes to be found curious items like a diamante evening bag and an Art Deco flower basket made entirely of cowry shells. Serendib Antiques in Ambalangoda has old black-and-white photographs from colonial days as well as furniture.

Even if you don't buy anything a visit to the antique coast of Sri Lanka gives an insight into the country's intriguing history.

There are 64 islands (some of them inhabited but with access by outrigger canoe or motorboat) in the river, including a tiny one with an abandoned shrine room, one whose only building is a temple with hospitable monks and another where an old couple who live in a mud hut spend the day stripping bark off branches to make cinnamon quills. Notices in Sinhala alert people to keep the river free of garbage and, with its lush mangrove forests on either side, a safari on the Madu Ganga is a pleasant encounter with river life.

AMBALANGODA Masks, puppets and reproduction antiques are the products of the Ambalangoda area (population 21,573; 2012 estimate). The making of masks and puppets has its roots in folk craft. The exorcism rituals of low-country folk-dancing demands demon-faced masks to scare away the devils. The grotesque and garishly painted carved wooden monstrosities have become souvenir items. Puppet pageantry is another entertainment form that used to be practised in the area and old puppets turn up in antique shops.

Perhaps it was the skill of the Ambalangoda mask and puppet makers, as well as an appreciation of ancient traditions, that has resulted in Ambalangoda being

TAKING THE TUK-TUK TOUR   *Bianca Perera*

'This area not coming tourists many,' my driver, Jagath, said as we bounced along an unmade road with a vista of mountains in the distance looming over paddy fields glistening in the sunlight. He was right. Although Bentota has been home to a National Tourist Resort for 30 years, few are the tourists who venture inland to discover the beauty and traditions of the Sri Lankan way of village life. He told me that few tourists want to explore the village environs just a few minutes' drive from their hotels. 'They prefer to go on organised round-trip tours, yet we have tea and rubber, traditional crafts, wildlife, historical temples and …', he paused as though overwhelmed by what he was saying, '… everything!'

I met Jagath when I decided to explore beyond my beach hotel. He is the owner of one of the ubiquitous three-wheelers (or tuk-tuks as they have become familiarly known). A tuk-tuk might not be the best vehicle for seeing the scenery because of its low roof and rolled-up blinds which means having to crane forward to peer out. It was also a bumpy journey due to the amount of pot-holes on the country lanes. The advantage is that tuk-tuks can go anywhere, and that's how I found places inaccessible to motor vehicles.

We paid a visit to the obligatory temple, Galpatha, 1km inland by an offshoot of the river. A carved gateway and an inscription recording the gift of lands and slaves to the monastery on the site recalled its 12th-century origins. I was fascinated by the different architecture in the villages, ranging from crumbling mansions over a century old, 1930s Art Deco houses, squat residences from the 1960s and pretentious villas built by the newly rich. Alongside them were village houses, some made of mud, and tiny wooden shops with platforms displaying shiny vegetables.

There were vast open plains, which Jagath explained were abandoned paddy fields where saltwater seepage had made paddy growing impossible. Instead the reeds used for mats and baskets were grown there and dried on the roadside before being dyed and used for weaving. Paddy is still grown in Bentota and is threshed and dried beside the road before being taken to the mill and emerging as rice.

The buffaloes in the paddy fields each had a white egret to groom them. There were cormorants perched on branches over shallow ponds, where kingfishers the centre of a flourishing antique industry. When I first visited Ambalangoda in 1980, it was possible to buy genuine antique furniture (I bought a 19th-century wooden baby-cradle, which I use as a bar). The demand both at home and overseas for colonial furniture, like planters' chairs (with long extending arms), almirahs (wardrobes), four-poster beds and cabin trunks, led to enterprising dealers setting up workshops to make copies of the genuine pieces. These are exported as colonial reproductions to Europe and the USA, but who knows what they are called by the time they reach the market.

Getting there
By train The express trains to and from Colombo all stop at Ambalangoda. (See the Alutgama section for the timetable, page 235.)

By bus Route No 2 serves Ambalangoda from Colombo.

By road Ambalangoda is a bustling town 85km from Colombo and 13km from Hikkaduwa further south. The fork to the right on approaching the town on the A2

swooped and purple and white lilies grew in profusion. There were black monkeys gambolling in the trees while dragonflies hovered and butterflies flitted over tea bushes. Tea? Yes, there are small tea gardens close to Bentota so tourists don't have to go to the hill country to see how it is grown. One smallholding we passed had rubber trees, coconuts, coffee, cocoa, breadfruit, jak-fruit, pepper and cardamom growing beside the road.

In season toddy is tapped from the tops of coconut trees, and wooden barrels of this effervescent beverage beloved by villagers are mounted on stands awaiting collection. Sometimes a toddy tapper can be induced to let visitors try toddy as it comes fresh from the tree. Driving along a footpath through the vegetation we came to a cinnamon garden where the workers were happy to demonstrate cinnamon peeling and how the oil is made. At a coir factory close to the river, coconut husks were being transformed into rope and mattress stuffing. I saw the balsa trees used for mask making and witnessed the village mask carver at work. I spotted an abandoned granite mill used for making coconut oil from copra. The smell of freshly baked bread enticed us to stop at the village bakery where bread is baked in the traditional manner in an old wood-fired brick oven.

The highlight of the hinterland tour was the journey on a hand-pulled ferry across the Bentota River. Only pedestrians, motorbikes, bicycles and tuk-tuks can use the ferry – motor vehicles have to cross the river by the bridge on the Galle road at Bentota. Passengers helped the ferryman haul on the rope that pulls the raft across the broad sweep of the river. On the southern bank there is a shelter for passengers to wait out of the sun. It was built as a memorial to a villager, a soldier who died in 1995.

There are crocodiles deep in the river, but we saw shaky, single-hull canoes drifting along it, each with a fisherman perched in its stern. The atmosphere was serene and timeless and evocative of real Sri Lankan village life. For me, the tuk-tuk tour added a new dimension to my holiday in Bentota that an organised coach tour could never match.

from Colombo takes you down the side road parallel to the coast, where there is a resthouse. There are many antique showrooms and workshops (usually with old timber stacked outside in the garden to weather) on the Galle road from Beruwala to Hikkaduwa, but the ones at Ambalangoda are the pioneers, both in finding the genuine articles and in reproducing them. Ambalangoda is also linked by a feeder road to the Southern Expressway.

Where to stay and eat There are no hotels in Ambalangoda, but there are a few budget guesthouses, informal places advertising 'ROOMS'. Most tourists who've come this far prefer to press on and enjoy the holiday atmosphere of Hikkaduwa.

What to see and do The privately run mask and puppet museums are interesting, and also have items for sale. The antique shops specialise in furniture with some old brass, and don't have many small items that are easy to take home. However, they are experienced in shipping goods overseas.

HIKKADUWA
Hikkaduwa was known from the 1930s for its excellent bathing and as a charming fishing village. It was the invasion of young independent travellers in the 1960s which sparked development and earned it the nickname 'Hippy-kaduwa'. Now it has rather a 'Benidorm' air to it, with its main street and the beach lined with hotel blocks, guesthouses, fast-food outlets, bars and discos. Its coral gardens, viewed from glass-bottomed boats, are no longer fabulous. About 10km inland, at Baddegama, is the island's first Anglican church, built in 1818.

Getting there
By train Express trains to and from Colombo stop at Hikkaduwa. (See the Alutgama section for the timetable, page 235.)

By bus The bus station is at the northern end of the strip of town and is well served by buses from Colombo and Galle.

By road At 97km from Colombo, Hikkaduwa is 19km from Galle. The A2 road curves along the profile of the coast after Ambalangoda, revealing the ocean and slithers of beach between villas, temples and cake shops. The harbour marks the entrance to Hikkaduwa and next comes the commercial part with railway station, road inland to Baddegama, and the bus station, also on the left. Then the tourist strip starts, nicely overwhelmed by the town and hinting at lots of fun after dark. A feeder road links Hikkaduwa with the Southern Expressway.

The Chaaya Tranz Hotel (also known as the Cinnamon Tranz) sticks up like a dark thorn on the headland beside the beach, and then the road sweeps past several hotels with Coral in their names (reminiscent of the time when the village was famous for its corals, unfortunately now mostly dead) and restaurants with funny names like Fixi Foxi and Living Lobster. Quaint, small guesthouses line the road right down to Dodanduwa. Finally the road settles down to cruise along the coast and passes through Boosa, marked with a long wall on the land side of the road, behind which is a timber yard and a prison camp and where there used to be a popular racecourse in colonial days.

Getting around There are minibuses and three-wheelers at every corner so there is no difficulty in getting transport for local trips, such as inland to Baddegama. But the joy of Hikkaduwa is being able to walk its length, either along the beach or the roadside, from one end to the other.

Where to stay Hikkaduwa has the widest range of places to stay of any town in Sri Lanka. El cheapo guesthouses are there in plenty and many are the likely lads lounging around, eager to guide you to one. There is so much choice you can cheerfully decline what you are first offered if it doesn't suit you, and look for somewhere else.

Chaaya Tranz (144 AC rooms, 6 AC suites) Galle Rd, Hikkaduwa; 091 02277023; e reservations@johnkeellshotels.com; www. chaayahotels.com/chaayatranz.htm. With its gimmicky name, now renamed as the Cinnamon Tranz, this renovated beachside hotel has transformed accommodation in Hikkaduwa, offering luxury in colourfully decorated rooms (shades of deep pink prevail) pitching this former happy hippy haven upmarket to a conventional but lively beach resort. Its rooms are bright & spacious, every one with a broad sea-view balcony, glazed grey clay tiles, plenty of power points (Wi-Fi is free), & rain & handheld showers in the neatly equipped bathrooms. With a signature restaurant, The Crab ($$$), often packed with non-residents who pop in for dinner using the Southern Expressway for quick access from Colombo, daily rice & curry buffets & dining in the wine cellar with adjacent cigar bar, Chaaya/Cinnamon Tranz provides a seamless, sophisticated holiday for locals & foreigners alike. **$$$$**

Coral Rock by Amaya (32 AC rooms) 340 Galle Rd, Hikkaduwa; 091 2277021; e coralrock@ amayaresorts.com; www.amayacoralrock.com. Cheek by jowl with the A2 coastal highway roaring through

---

TURTLES

The Turtle Conservation Project (TCP) has produced a leaflet about the turtles of Sri Lanka. Five (all of them endangered) species come ashore to nest, as they have done for millions of years. They are the green turtle (*Chelonia mydas*), the loggerhead (*Caretta caretta*), the hawksbill (*Eretmochelys imbricata*), the leatherback (*Dermochelys coriacea*) and the smallest of them all, the Olive Ridley turtle (*Lepidochelys olivacea*).

While there are several 'turtle hatcheries' along the west and south coasts, their objective is more commercial than ecological, with the releasing of turtles in daytime to please tourists, in return for a fee per turtle that is sent scuttling across the beach to certain doom. The TCP is a genuine, UNDP-funded conservation project that started a pioneering conservation programme at Rekawa in 1996. The aim is to protect sea turtles in their natural habitat while providing an alternative source of income to local people formerly dependent on the illegal collection of eggs.

The TCP initiated its second conservation programme in Kosgoda in August 2003, to conserve the five species of turtle and their nesting habits in a 1km stretch of beach, through community participation and education, according to a leaflet about its Turtle Watch initiative.

This is not a typical commercial hatchery with turtles or hatchlings in a tank. The TCP conducts research 24 hours a day throughout the year and acts to prevent egg poaching. Tourists are invited to visit the turtle beach at night under the auspices of TCP researchers to see the nesting and laying process. A fee is charged and this helps support the turtle nest protection and awareness programme.

The Turtle Watch starts daily at 20.00, at the TCP Beach Hut on Kosgoda Beach, behind the Kosgoda Beach Resort. It is a thrilling – and even humbling – experience. For more details contact the **Turtle Conservation Project** (*389 Godagama, Kosgoda;* 091 2264765; e *tcpsl@sltnet.lk; www.tcpsrilanka.org*).

The West Coast BEACH RESORTS

7

The average age at which women in Sri Lanka marry has risen to 26. There are advertisements in the Sunday newspapers advertising for brides/grooms. This is not a lonely hearts column but part of the ancient tradition of arranged marriages which assures that couples are matched through horoscope, cultural identity and social status.

The central feature of a Sinhalese wedding is the *poruwa* wedding ceremony. Foreigners who come on special wedding-package tours can also be married in this fashion. A registrar attends such a ceremony and issues a certificate confirming marriage. The following description has been supplied by the **Bentota Beach Hotel** (see page 239), which is a favourite venue for visitors who stay there, especially to get married in the local style.

The poruwa is a decorated marriage platform used for the bride and groom to stand upon until the traditional wedding ceremony is completed. In accordance with ancient Sinhalese rites and customs, the platform is prepared by covering it with a clean white cloth and placing rice, five kinds of medicinal herbs, a coconut and a few coins on it to bring blessings and prosperity to the couple.

Four pots adorned with coconut flowers, upon which four oil lamps are placed, are kept on the four corners of the poruwa. The lamps are lit before the ceremony starts, to give protection and to invoke blessings upon the couple by the gods in charge of the four zones. The traditional marriage ceremony is officiated by a *Gurunnanse*, or Master of Ceremonies.

Traditionally, the groom is first escorted to the right side of the poruwa. The bride is escorted to the left. With the reciting of *ashtaka* (stanzas) the couple will get on to the poruwa together. The ashtaka are eulogies composed in Sanskrit calling upon the gods to invoke blessings and good wishes on the couple.

Once the couple are on the poruwa, seven sheaves of betel leaves are given to the couple to drop on the dais of the poruwa. This act represents unity, friendship and co-operation. The offering of betel leaves to elders by the couple is considered a gesture of great respect and is done on special occasions.

The little finger of the right hand of the bride and the little finger of the left hand of the groom are tied together with a blessed thread and water is sprinkled on the hands, which denotes Oneness. At this stage, four girls dressed in traditional half-sarees chant *Jayamangala Gatha*, a set of stanzas used only for special occasions, wishing the couple well in health, wealth, prosperity and happiness. Rings are exchanged.

During the chanting of stanzas blessing the couple, bride and groom are led off the poruwa, with both putting their right foot forward. Then the couple light the oil lamp together, depicting unity and for prosperity. The entire ceremony is accompanied by the beating of drums.

Hikkaduwa so it's only a step from the kerb to reception. A staircase leads to the 2 upper floors of 16 sea-view & 12 roadside rooms, while 4 other rooms open on to the pool terrace. The rooms, small like a ship's cabin & with a tiny, shipshape bathroom with a glass cubicle rain shower, have large flat-screen TV, minibar & tea maker, a small wardrobe & safe, single wooden chair & counter, & smooth, grey cement floors & brilliant white décor. There is a lounge open to the sea breeze on both floors providing extra space. The balconies of the sea-view rooms overlook the beachside, stone-paved terrace, a third of which is occupied by a long, narrow swimming pool. The hotel's restaurant, off the reception lobby, serves all meals as buffets & there is a cosily cushioned bar from which cocktails of bright hues, & promotional pricing, are served by keen stewards to sunbathers lounging by the pool. An option if you don't want to stay at the top but want to be in the centre of both the Hikkaduwa action & the price range. **$$**

🏠 **Nippon Villa** (25 AC rooms & apts) 412D Galle Rd, Wewala, Hikkaduwa; 📞 091 4383095; e nipponvilla@emailsrilanka.com; www. nipponvillabeach.com. Owned by a friend of mine who worked his way up from being a waiter in Bentota, this is the sort of place where guests feel at home. Its bright colour scheme of saffron & dark blue, & gleaming columns around an inner courtyard giving a view, from the street, of the sea, are alluring. The proprietor, Piyal Gunarathna, has learned over the years what visitors want, & so has added a super bar lounge with a pool table, as well as a swimming pool overlooking the beach. This is a friendly, informal, fun place, as well as convenient to get in & out of. **$$**

🏠 **Nature Resort** (10 *cabanas*) Pathana, Hikkaduwa; 📞 091 4383006; e nature@slt.lk. A dream for the ecotourist comes true by Hikkaduwa Lake at Nature Resort. There is a large signboard at the junction of the Galle & Baddegama roads, just as you enter Hikkaduwa. Drive 2km down this road to another sign on the left. The road there climbs & then you drive down a track to an opening in the mangroves. A boardwalk raised on wooden posts over a swamp leads through the mangroves to the bank of Hikkaduwa Lake. The shelter there, made entirely of heavy, matured timbers, with a wooden floor & table slabs of tree trunks, is a bar & seafood restaurant. This is the starting place for a waterborne safari to see dozens of species of birds, including migratory duck & cranes, & to visit uninhabited islands that are natural wildlife sanctuaries. The soothing tranquillity is enchanting. Accommodation is in wooden cabins built over the lake. **$**

✕ **Where to eat and drink** There are so many restaurants in Hikkaduwa, getting a meal – whether it's rice and curry or lobster and chips – at a reasonable rate is simple. You could easily stay in Hikkaduwa for your whole holiday and not have to eat in the same place twice. However, once you discover **Restaurant Refresh** (*384 Galle Rd, Hikkaduwa;* 📞 *091 5058108;* e *refresh@sltnet.lk;* ⊕ *daily;* **$$**), you'll probably have every meal there. Since the menu has over 300 items on it, it's possible to do so without getting bored.

And the choice is amazing, from super-fresh seafood to delicious oddities like stuffed eggplant. You can even get blue margaritas from the bar. It benefits from swift and practised service and substantial portions. Although food is in the moderate price range wines are expensive, but at least wines are available. Stop there any time of day when you're driving through Hikkaduwa to be assured of a warm welcome. It's on the beach and it's worth eating there even if it's raining.

Other practicalities
Banks Hikkaduwa has branches of the state banks of **Bank of Ceylon** and **People's Bank** and other major private banks like **Hatton National Bank**.

What to see and do
Going **diving** to see underwater life used to be the reason for going to Hikkaduwa and there are several scuba-diving outfits licensed to teach PADI courses. These are popular with young beginners since it is possible to stay in Hikkaduwa at around US$25 a day for board and lodging, and spend the rest on diving lessons (from US$450 for a certificate course). There are glass-bottomed boats to see the coral.

If you like museums, there is a small private one at the home of **Priyantha Antiques and Museum** (*25 Galle Rd, Hikkaduwa*) where everything can be bought. It is a cut above the antique furniture reproduction workshops on the road from Beruwala to Hikkaduwa because it has small items as souvenirs of old Ceylon, such as keys, bottles, puppets and brassware. There are also some fascinating old farming implements.

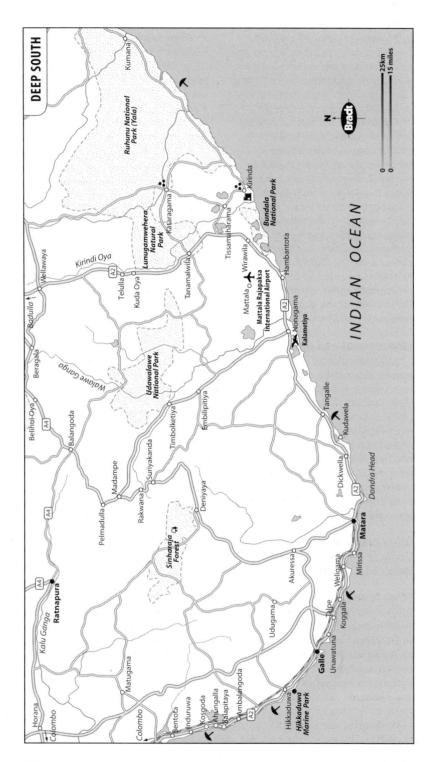

DEEP SOUTH

INDIAN OCEAN

8

The Deep South

The deep south, as it is called to distinguish it from the southern part of the west coast where the older beach resorts are, faces Antarctica. The Dondra Head lighthouse, near Matara, is Sri Lanka's most southerly point, less than 6° from the Equator. The next land mass in a straight line would be that of the South Pole.

Because it took so long (at least five hours) to drive to the deep south from the airport, before the advent of the Katunayake and Southern Expressways and the opening of the second international airport near Hambantota, and because of the war, investment in hotel infrastructure along the south coast east of Galle was slow. Instead private villas built, or rebuilt, by foreigners for letting to other foreigners opened with the result that the southern coast became a bazaar of boutique properties. The situation is changing as, remarkably, swathes of beaches are being discovered and major developers are moving in.

Until the new southern airport becomes an accepted gateway to the country, only a few organised tours take in the deep south region since its attractions are considered inferior to those of the Cultural Triangle and hill country. Yet the south has culture, history, temples and shrines, arts and crafts, tea plantations, colonial mansions, nature parks and wildlife, and broad, clean beaches.

Instead of sacred cities, it has an 18th-century fort that is a living World Heritage Site; instead of hills it has sandy coves. Even so, the south is usually low down on a visitor's list of places to visit. That is a shame, because even a day trip from Colombo to Galle is enough to discover another facet of this incredible gem of a country.

HISTORY

Some 500 years before the birth of Christ, the rulers of the various regions of Sri Lanka, which they were colonising and cultivating (and whose natural resources they were trading), saw the division of the island into three. According to Tennent in his 1859 book *Ceylon*:

> All to the north of the Mahawelli-ganga was comprised in the denomination Pihiti, or the Raja-ratta, from its containing the ancient capital and the residence of royalty; south of this was Rohano or Rohunu, bounded on the east by the sea, and by the Mahawelli-ganga and Kalu-ganga, on the north and west … The third was the Maya-ratta, which lay between the mountains, the two great rivers and the sea, having the Dedera-oya to the north, and the Kalu-ganga as its southern limit.

Tennent suggested that the southern region of Ruhunu got its name from the 12th-century name for Adam's Peak. He wrote:

The district of Rohuna included the mountain zone of Ceylon, and hence probably its name, *rohuno*, meaning 'the act or instrument of ascending, as steps of a ladder'. Adam's Peak was in the Maya division but Edrisi, who wrote in the 12th century, says that it was then called El Rahoun.

The rulers of Ruhunu were obliged to co-exist with the Kingdom of Anuradhapura until King Dutugemunu (161–137BC) attacked from Ruhunu and overthrew the Tamil ruler, Elera. Ruhunu had been settled by ancient Sinhalese about the same time as the capital, but never rivalled Anuradhapura or, later, Polonnaruwa in power. There have been few excavations to uncover the ruins of Ruhunu, although the Maha Thupa in Tissamaharama (the ancient capital of Ruhunu) dates from 2BC. Near the inland town of Monaragala, at Maligawila, there is a fallen statue of Buddha, 10m high and carved from a single stone, which dates from the 7th century.

Ruhunu seems to have served as an alternative kingdom, becoming a refuge for defeated kings from the north or for rival claimants to the throne. Events in the north affected the south and with the death of the Indian pirate Magha (who had conquered Polonnaruwa and become King Kalinga Vijayabahu, 1215–36) city civilisation declined.

Agriculture and trade through its ports became the south's mainstay and it was trade that opened the southern door of the island to foreign domination. The Portuguese arrived in Galle in 1505 (apparently by accident; the fleet was heading for the 'money islands' of the Maldives) and gradually developed trading links. In 1588, King Rajasingha I (1581–93) of Sitawaka laid siege to the Portuguese in Colombo which resulted in them gathering in Galle where they built a small fort out of palm trees and mud. They called it Santa Cruz, later extending it with a wall and watchtowers, three bastions, and a fortalice to guard Galle harbour.

Their influence spread through the south, with Christian conversions beginning in 1543 and the sowing of seeds to start Sri Lankan family trees with names like Pereira and Fernando. From their base in Galle, the Portuguese took over the southern littoral and infiltrated throughout the island, imposing Christianity.

They were dislodged by the Dutch in 1656, who went on to consolidate their presence in the south by building the 36ha fort at Galle on the site of the original Portuguese one. They followed the Portuguese pattern of capitalising on the trading activities of the south. Their influence was considerable and many of their buildings remain, as does their style of formal furniture adapted to tropical living. They also introduced the term (although not the practice behind it, as that had come in with the Portuguese) of 'burgher' for the offspring of miscegenation.

Galle, and hence the south, was conceded by the Dutch to the British on 23 February 1796. For a while Galle and the south flourished under British administration. It began to decline in the mid 19th century with the development of Colombo as the island's capital and main port.

GETTING THERE AND AWAY

BY AIR Following the opening of the Mattala Rajapaksa International Airport near Hambantota (see page 279) in March 2013, SriLankan Airlines introduced some flights that carry domestic passengers to the south from the main international airport at Katunayake. Although with the advent of the Southern Expressway (see page 256) flying to Mattala made no sense when trying to get to Galle from Colombo, the air link has opened up the south for passengers who wanted to transfer to the deep south (or even the hill country) without driving through Colombo.

BY TRAIN A frequent train service links Colombo with the south and there are many Sri Lankans who commute to work from Galle, even though the journey takes well over two hours each way. The southbound express trains terminate in Matara, which gives a chance to see at least part of the deep south, from Galle to Matara, from the train window. The line is understandably popular with visitors since it runs south along the western coast, beside the Indian Ocean, and serves the main beach resorts. If you plan your trip properly, you will even be able to get a seat. If possible, travel against the commuter flow of traffic. The early morning trains into Colombo are packed with office workers; that's the time to get a train south, not in the afternoon when the office workers are homeward bound.

A luxury carriage has been introduced by Rajadhani Blue Train (*www.rajadhani. lk*), a company that operates a single air-conditioned carriage attached to Train 8050 from Colombo and Train 8051 from Matara with reserved seats and refreshments served to the seats, and a clean toilet. While reservations and payment can be made online, the printout has to be verified and the reservation confirmed through a visit to one of the company's agencies throughout the country. The times listed in the box below for daily trains between Colombo and Matara were correct at press time. However, times may be changed and special services operated at weekends and on holidays, so it is advisable to check at the departure station for the latest update.

For the best coastal views on trains from Colombo, sit on the right, facing the engine. While most visitors prefer to gaze at the beach and the sea, which starts about ten minutes after the beginning of the ride, a seat on the other side of the carriage gives views of town and village houses and glimpses of Sri Lankans at ease. It is a pleasant, relaxing journey, with some inspiring seascapes, along a line that first reached Galle in 1894 and Matara a year later.

Galle is 20 minutes from Hikkaduwa and you know you are getting there when the palm trees give way to suburbs. It is a terminus, although some trains reverse out to continue to **Matara**. The through trains stop for about ten minutes while the engine is detached from the front and, if no other engine is available, reverses to the other end of the train. So if you want to keep on the sea side, it is time to cross over the vestibule and sit on the other side so you are still on the right of the train, facing the engine.

Sometimes an express becomes a slow train between Galle and Matara, stopping at every station. Even for the enthusiast of train travel, and of rural scenes, this can become wearying as there are 14 stops, and sometimes long waits in sidings for incoming trains to cross.

TRAIN TIMETABLE: COLOMBO TO MATARA

Train	8050	8040	8086*	8056	8058	8096	8766
Colombo	06.55	08.35	10.30	14.25	15.50	16.45	18.05
Galle	09.26	10.49	12.42	16.31	17.34	18.37	20.23
Matara	10.53	11.50	13.50	17.48	18.20	19.30	21.33

Train	8097	8059	8057	8085*	8039	8051
Matara	04.55	06.05	06.10	10.15	13.35	14.10
Galle	05.50	06.55	07.25	11.15	14.45	15.30
Colombo	08.08	08.43	09.30	13.30	17.20	18.05

* Train 8085/86 runs to/from Vavuniya, via Colombo and Anuradhapura to Matara.

Passing through a tunnel after Galle the train assumes a leisurely pace through coconut and palmyra groves with only occasional glimpses of the sea. **Unawatuna** station gives no hint of the delightful beach within 15 minutes' walk (across the main road). It is a major halt for tourists seeking the sun and fun of this romantic atmospheric cove.

The booking office at **Talpe** is built of granite and it is easy to imagine how it looked a century ago when the line was built. Gradually the scenery changes to flat scrubland and then to the industrial landscape of the Free Trade Zone at **Koggala**, with lagoon, airstrip and new factories. A succession of halts consisting of concrete huts and a short stretch of platform follow until the scenery grows lusher and the line wends inland and comes back to reach **Weligama**.

All the platforms on this line are single ones on the southern side of the track. A surprise is the sight of verdant paddy fields as the train approaches **Walgama**, which makes it resemble main-line scenery. Then there is a gentle build-up of houses and the train comes to the end of its journey, entering Matara station, 158km from Colombo.

BY BUS There are frequent, and very fast, intercity air-conditioned buses from Colombo to Galle. Look out for bus No 2 which has a luxury service to Galle and to Matara. Less frequent are buses going deeper to the south. However, there are local services linking the small coastal towns. An option is to take a bus from Colombo Fort to the suburb of Kottawa and there catch an air-conditioned bus that speeds along the Southern Expressway to Galle.

BY ROAD The opening of the Southern Expressway (a toll road) in 2012, has put Galle and the deep south within much easier driving distance. People will claim they can now drive from Colombo to Galle in less than one hour. That might be true from the northern entrance to the highway, at Kottawa, but getting to Kottawa from the centre of Colombo can take 45 minutes or more.

The wonder of the Southern Expressway is that it exists at all. For years there were rumours about it being built and then suddenly it was there – a dual carriage highway that cuts a swathe through plantations and abandoned land, with only a few houses in sight and a marvellous vista of the interior of Sri Lanka that motorists had never seen before. At press time there was news of an extension being built that will eventually reach Hambantota.

The rules about driving on the Southern Expressway are rather strict, with no stopping anywhere, except at the exits or at the roadside (both sides) cafés that are about halfway along the highway at Interchange No 5. The cafés are actually snack-bar counters (and even a local souvenir shop) in a mall (⏲ *24hrs*) with a supermarket, ATMs and a vehicle insurance counter; toilets but no filling stations (and no alcohol).

Access to the north end of the expressway (at Kottawa) is possible by road from Maharagama, Nugegoda, Colombo, Ratnapura, Avissawella and Homagama. (Planned for a 2013 opening was an expressway link from the main international airport at Katunayake to Kelaniya, thence to Kottawa.) After 5.9km on the expressway, there is an exit to (or entrance from) Kesbawa, Piliyandala, Colombo, Horana, Ingiriya and Ratnapura.

Exit No 3 at 13.7km links Bandaragama, Panadura, Horana, Ingiriya and Ratnapura with the expressway, while No 4, at 34.8km, is progressing away from the suburbs to Nagoda, Kalutara, Matigama and Agalawaththa. By the 46km mark are the two malls and the link to Alutgama, Matugama and Agalawaththa.

After another 21km (at the 67.6km post), there are links to Elpitiya, Karandeniya, Batapola, Ambalangoda and Balapitiya. Then comes Exit No 7 at 79.8km for the beach resorts of Hikkaduwa and Baddegama, and also Nilhena and Udugama. At 95km, Exit No 8, turn right for Galle and Galle Fort, and left to join the A2 bordering the southern coast.

The traditional way by road to Galle and on through the deep south was by the A2. That starts in Colombo and cuts along the coast, flirting with the railway line so much you lose count of brief encounters with level crossings. It has the coast to itself after Matara and only turns inland at Hambantota when it strikes out across the plains deep in the interior.

The distance by the A2 from Colombo to Galle is 116km (coincidentally, this is the same distance travelled by the A1 to Kandy). From Galle it is 45km by road to Matara, and 124km to Hambantota. Hambantota northwards to Wellawaya is another 80km. While it is possible to drive the 260km from Colombo to Tissamaharama in one day, this would not give much time for sightseeing. An overnight stay in Galle not only breaks the journey but also gives you a chance to walk the ramparts and explore the most fascinating fort city in the whole of Asia.

From Galle, the road has its share of views and unexpected attractions, although not as many as on the road to Kandy. It heads out of Galle along the promenade overlooking the industrial harbour, and then skirts around the port to head eastwards along the coast. Almost immediately comes a chance for souvenir shopping. There are a few shops specialising in pillow lace where women with dextrous fingers fashion beautiful placemats and tablecloths.

The road misses the no-longer-secret beach and cove of **Unawatuna** but you still need to find the right side road to get to it. (Look on the southern side of the road for the sign indicating Amarasinghe Road and Thambapanni Leisure or, if you miss that turn, go down the lane by the antique shop, signposted to Unawatuna Beach Hotel.) Unawatuna has lost none of its raffish charm and the bay with its kiosks and cafés continues to attract those who don't want their holiday organised. It seems that every house in the village has rooms to rent. It's easy to sense the intrigue and appeal this pretty cove has for visitors who want to pretend they are beachcombers.

Approaching the next resort of **Koggala**, the scenery degenerates because of the presence of the old airstrip and the new Free Trade Zone. The stilt fishermen, featured on so many postcards and photographs of Sri Lanka, have moved to Koggala from Weligama. There are a dozen of their perches sticking up from the waters of a rock pool originally blasted there by Britons based at the Koggala airstrip in the 1940s. A visit to the Martin Wickremasinghe Folk Museum makes a pleasant break during the long drive south.

Much of the beach here is hidden behind the high walls of private villas. At **Mirissa**, around the 151km post, there are more cabanas and rooms suitable for the independent traveller. It has become popular with budget travellers of a certain age but unfortunately does not always seem as hospitable to tourists as other beaches in Sri Lanka.

Matara, the next main town, has become so busy with local commerce it can take 30 minutes and more to drive right through it. Perhaps it is because the railway line terminates at Matara that the visitor feels he is leaving the rest of Sri Lanka behind and heading into the unknown. The A2 plays hide and seek now with the ocean as it meanders eastwards along the southern coast. On the land side comes the campus of the University of Ruhunu, its red-roofed buildings standing out starkly on a plateau. The Dondra lighthouse blinks on a promontory and the road settles down for a long haul.

On the way to **Dickwella**, roadside vendors sit beside makeshift tables on which are perched jars of cashew nuts. Unlike the damsels of Cadjugama on the Kandy road, these vendors make no effort to flag down drivers. One feels it's not part of their nature to be pushy. Even the water spouting up from the blowhole at **Kudawela** sometimes seems to be having a lazy day. Occasionally a token spurt of water booms through the rocks as if to hint what commotion it could cause if it were in a playful mood.

The approach to **Tangalle** along the coast reveals enticing sea views reminiscent of Cornwall with its picturesque coves and gaily coloured fishing boats bobbing at anchor in the harbour. After the tangle of Tangalle's narrow streets, the A2 threads its way through another change in landscape; tropical suburbia gives way to wide-open plains. There are wayside stalls selling melons and, as another clue to the produce of the area, small piles of clay bricks awaiting customers.

Down one unmarked and unsurfaced village track, the luxurious Amanwella Hotel has opened with hillside villas above a dreamy white-sand beach. More prosaic, the resthouse at Tangalle overlooks the harbour where jaunty fishing boats are moored.

To follow the road as it twists inland on the way to **Hambantota** is suddenly to enter a more rural part of the country. Wood apple and papaya are offered for sale beside the road and the signs are in Sinhala, not English. Outside Hambantota stalls selling ceramic statuettes and gaily painted clay fruit wait for customers. A new road bypasses the town and there is very little to be seen from it of the massive development taking place in the area.

After Hambantota houses have clusters of clay pots hanging outside them to advertise they have fresh curd for sale. Real curd is made by swilling a clay pot with buffalo urine before filling it with the buffalo milk to curdle into curd. Curd gourmets insist on sticking a toothpick into the curd to judge how thick it is. Good curd should be solid like butter, not soft like yoghurt.

While the A2 continues northwards through a flat, uninteresting landscape to Wellawaya, the gateway to the hill country, a road to the right takes you to Tissa, as **Tissamaharama** is affectionately known. You will find your vehicle being followed by young men in jeeps, while others in jungle greens lounge under trees eyeing you speculatively. This is safari country and the jeep operators and their crews are looking for business. Better to get established in a guesthouse or hotel and check the going price for jeep hire before committing yourself. (See box, page 197, for a guest comment on safari jeep travel.)

From Tissa, the road to **Kataragama** presents another aspect: there are so many wayside stalls offering fruits and crafts, you feel you have diverted into a church bazaar. Particularly fascinating are the fibreglass models of wild animals and, since this is forest land, there are also carvings of animals, and plant stands, made from wood found nearby. Finally, at Kataragama, with its resthouses and local hotels awaiting pilgrims to the shrine, there is a chance for some soul-searching at the end of the drive through the deep south.

GETTING AROUND

Distances are too far to base yourself in, say, Matara, and travel to Galle on one day and Tissa the next. If you have time to explore the whole area, and the stomach for local buses, then local buses are in fact the best way to get around. Spend some time in Galle or Unawatuna, and then take a train to Matara. A bus can take you from there to Tangalle, and other buses serve Tissamaharama and Kataragama. It is possible, and perhaps more prudent given the reckless way buses are driven, to hire three-wheelers from Matara station that could take you all the way to Tissa and even Yala National Park (170km).

RESORTS *(Listed from west to east)*

GALLE Although the city of Galle is a thriving metropolis with a population of 99,478 (it is the capital of the Southern province), it is Galle Fort that attracts attention, and around which the history of the area is spun. That mysteries are hidden behind the sombre grey walls of the fort is no surprise. Those brooding hulks of stone – shipped as ballast and hauled into place by slaves from Africa – dominate this coastal city, walling off a small peninsula and guarding the harbour. For four centuries there has been a fort here; it was the thin end of the wedge driven by European invaders to open up their conquest of the island. Portuguese, Dutch and British – following the sea lanes of Arab traders – lived and died in the fort. The Dutch forbade their maritime pilots ever to leave its walls in retirement, in case they divulged the secrets of the port's approaches to enemies.

Even when the fort's battlements are brightly lit at night, there hovers a sense of foreboding, as though ghosts of soldiers past are waiting only for the light to dim so they may march again along its ramparts. As dusk gathers, its narrowed streets and cloistered inner courtyards of shuttered mansions echo softly with the murmurings of bygone evenings. The fort is steeped in history; you will sense it from afar and feel its spell from the moment you pass through its gates.

The fort is the best-preserved colonial sea fortress in the whole of Asia. The main entrance is ten minutes' walk from the Galle railway and bus stations, its ramparts looming gaunt against a peerless blue sky as you walk across the esplanade, created by the British from reclaimed land when they decided to broaden the peninsula's link with Galle town. In 1873, they tunnelled through the embankment that connects the Star, Moon and Sun bastions to create a road access. Although it is recognised as No 200 on UNESCO's World Heritage List, entry to the fort costs nothing, and residents and visitors pass freely through its two gateways.

Galle is believed by some scholars to be the Tarshish of Old Testament history, the great emporium of the East with which the ships of Tyre and Phoenicia traded, to which King Solomon sent his merchant vessels and to where Jonah fled from the Lord. In 1344, the great Arab traveller Ibn Battuta observed Moorish vessels in the harbour. The peninsula was then an entrenched settlement in the lowland territory of the Kandyan kings and remained so until the Portuguese – who first saw Galle in 1505 – invaded in 1589.

They built bastions, embankments and a small fortress to guard the harbour. The Dutch took it after a fierce battle in 1640 and stayed for 156 years, adding ramparts and more bastions around the edges, and churches, houses and streets within the walls, together with a complex network of underground channels which enabled the sea to flush away the sewage. They ceded it to the British.

Entrance was then by a drawbridge. Now the moat is filled in and the British coat of arms adorns the outer wall of the Old Gate, with the crest of the Dutch East India Company, dated 1669, on the inner side.

There are 473 houses in the fort, every one counted by the staff of the Archaeological Department which maintains an office in a converted Dutch building opposite the Old Gate, and which pursues a vigorous campaign to restore and preserve the fort's architectural heritage. About 50 of the present buildings pre-date the British occupation, with a further 104 constructed pre-1850.

The Deep South RESORTS

8

The streets are of Dutch and British colonial houses, adapted by local builders to tropical living with colonnaded verandas and ornate gables, giving glimpses through open doors of plant-filled courtyards. Styles of Art Deco from the 1930s, and earlier Art Nouveau, are represented too, with peculiarly Sri Lankan touches, together with the brash frontages of modern houses built before tight planning regulations were enforced.

The distinctive buildings, with their mysteriously shaded interiors, give the fort its intriguing character; its mild-mannered inhabitants are its soul. However, not surprisingly, Galle Fort has been discovered by the 'Arts & Crafts' clique of expatriates (many are British) and several properties have been relentlessly restored, replacing the fort's seedy charm with a pseudo-poshness.

Lighthouse Street and Church Street are the main thoroughfares, both different in character. The lighthouse, which used to stand at the end of the street to which it gave its name, was burned down in 1936, and a new one erected on the opposite bastion. There is a bank, some shops and a tea room where the street begins, then schools and swanky private residences. Church Street boasts grander buildings, beginning with the fort's tallest, the Amangalla, formerly famous as the New Oriental Hotel, and the 18th-century post office building. A belfry tower, originally built in 1701, still has its bell. Opposite stands Queen's House, which carries the date 1683 above its doorway. As the street has become fashionable and attracts affluent young visitors, boutique stores – as well as hotels – have opened up selling stylised art and trendy bits and pieces.

Pedlar Street, formerly known as the Street of Moorish Traders, is the only artery linking the western ramparts to the eastern. Appropriately enough, given its name, it appears noticeably busier than its neighbours.

Leyn Baan Street leads to the busiest area of the fort, the courts. Lawyers in ill-fitting black suits can be seen sauntering across the paved square that separates the District Court on the sea side and the Magistrates' Court on the other. Their ancient, book-lined chambers line one side of the square. A wall on the sea side carries a worn inscription: 'Aker Sloot 1759'. Behind it grows the island's oldest breadfruit tree, and cannons point out to sea in the garden.

At four in the afternoon, the fort begins to lapse into a lethargy matured over centuries. The streets are silent but the ramparts, and the patch of beach below the lighthouse, are lively with people. A few boys offer ancient coins, coral or lacework for sale, but seem more interested in chatting with their friends. Sunsets from the ramparts, near the Buddhist temple, are spellbinding. Then darkness descends quickly, and suddenly the ramparts and the streets are deserted. 'It is as though a film director has shouted "Cut",' said an expatriate American who has a house on Rampart Street. 'The light goes and everyone just disappears.'

Perhaps they leave because at nightfall Galle Fort seems to slip back in time. Not a sound disturbs the empty streets, houses are shuttered and, although the modern Victorian-style street lanterns shine, they cannot banish all the ghostly shadows. You can walk the streets in safety, but however many times you visit, you'll never completely know the fort and all its secrets.

Getting there

By train The major trains serving the west coast from Colombo and Matara stop at Galle (see timetable, page 235). At **Galle station** [262 B3] there are four platforms, with restrooms on the right of the ticket barriers. The cafeteria is best avoided. Tickets are collected as you leave the platform, or clipped as you enter. There is a kiosk selling newspapers in English in the booking hall. A plaque commemorating the laying of the foundation of the new railway station in 1965 is by the ticket office. Train departure times are shown on clocks and there are loudspeaker announcements.

By bus The main bus service (No 2-1) runs frequently between Colombo and Galle. There is also an air-conditioned express bus service (route No EX-01) operating between the Colombo suburb of Kottawa (take bus route No 138 from Pettah to get to Kottawa bus station) and Galle, along the Southern Expressway. The journey takes about one hour. Seats can't be reserved so if the bus is full, wait for the next one; it should be along in 20 minutes.

By road The A2, either from Colombo along the west coast or from the east along the south coast, is Galle's main road link to the rest of the country. (See page 256 for full details of the link to Galle via the new Southern Expressway.)

Getting around Galle Fort is easy to explore on foot and is about ten minutes' walk from the railway and bus stations. There are three-wheeler taxis available at the railway station for driving to the hotels. Any foreigner will have to bargain fiercely to get the best fare.

 Where to stay and eat In addition to the listings below, several small cafés and sophisticated souvenir shops, many run on behalf of foreigners, have been opened in Galle Fort to cater for day visitors to the fort. All listings are included on the map, page 262.

Amangalla (33 AC rooms, chambers & suites) 10 Church St, Fort, Galle; ☎091 2233388; e amangalla@amanresorts.com; www.amanresorts.com. In 2003, the venerable (& decidedly dilapidated) New Oriental Hotel (NOH) closed for complete remodelling & eventually reopened as Amangalla. The first hotel in the elite Aman group in Sri Lanka, it manages to combine a confident elegance of style but without the decadent ambience that gave the original hotel such character. Affectionately known as the NOH, the hotel was neither new nor oriental. There was a building on the same site in 1684, put up by the Dutch to house army officers, & later this was occupied by officers of the British 83rd Regiment. The original barracks was incorporated in the hotel, which was first licensed to operate as an inn in 1865. The Regency-style building, with sandstone walls 1m thick & ceilings 6m high, had vast suites with wooden floors on each of its 2 upper storeys. These have been carefully renovated & upgraded with rain-showers & designer bathtubs, & slim line furniture complementing the chunky 4-poster beds. Visitors are still encouraged to pop in for tea or a drink on the ornately tiled veranda, as they did in the old days. The lounge, complete with grand piano, has its original wooden floorboards, now highly polished & immaculately clean, with the restaurant at one end where an antique wooden sideboard has been restored & retained. Hidden in the hotel's interior are the bedrooms & chambers, suites & a Garden House, & a huge 21m x 10½m swimming pool with terraces & cabanas. The Baths – a spa with pools & sauna – has been created in the old vaults. With high prices for Sri Lanka, Amangalla – & its sister hotel Amanwella at Tangalle (see page 277) – are part of the new trend in Sri Lanka for top-range boutique hotels of character to attract those who demand (& can afford) the best. **$$$$**

Doornberg/The Dutch House (4 suites) 18 Upper Dickson Rd, Galle; ☎091 4380275; e info@thesunhouse.com; www.thedutchhouse.com. This was built in 1712 & its outside wall & entrance veranda look appropriately antiquated. Its huge bedrooms come with colonial-period furniture including Edwardian-style bathtubs. Columned cloisters enclose a sun-drenched lawn, with frangipani blossoms floating in clay pots & a path that leads to a lower-level swimming pool. **$$$$**

Galle Fort Hotel (3 AC rooms, 9 AC suites) 28 Church St, Fort, Galle; ☎091 2232870;

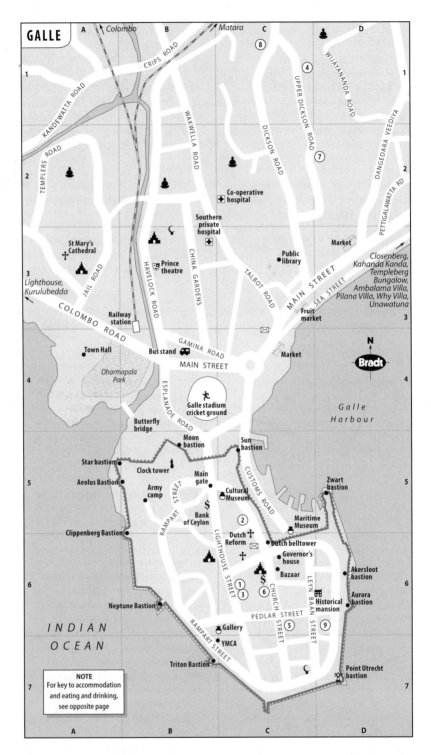

GALLE

A ↑ *Colombo* B ↗ *Matara* C D

CRIPS ROAD

KANDEWATTA ROAD

TEMPLERS ROAD

WAKWELLA ROAD

CHINA GARDENS

UPPER DICKSON ROAD

DICKSON ROAD

WIJAYANANDA ROAD

DANGEDARA VEEDIYA

PETTIGALAWATTA RD

St Mary's Cathedral

Prince theatre

Co-operative hospital

Southern private hospital

Public library

Market

Closenberg, Kahanda Kanda, Templeberg Bungalow, Ambalama Villa, Pilana Villa, Why Villa, Unawatuna

Lighthouse, Kurulubedda

JAIL ROAD

HAVELOCK ROAD

Railway station

COLOMBO ROAD

GAMINA ROAD

MAIN STREET

Bus stand

TALBOT ROAD

MAIN STREET

SEA STREET

Fruit market

Market

N

Bradt

Town Hall

Dharmapala Park

ESPLANADE ROAD

Galle stadium cricket ground

Galle Harbour

Butterfly bridge

Moon bastion

Sun bastion

Star bastion

Clock tower

Main gate

Cultural Museum

CUSTOMS ROAD

Zwart bastion

Aeolus Bastion

Army camp

RAMPART STREET

Bank of Ceylon

②

Maritime Museum

Clippenberg Bastion

LIGHTHOUSE STREET

Dutch Reform

Dutch belltower

Governor's house

Bazaar

Akersloot bastion

Neptune Bastion

① ③ ⑥

CHURCH STREET

LEYN BAAN STREET

Historical mansion

Aurora bastion

INDIAN OCEAN

RAMPART STREET

Gallery

YMCA

PEDLAR STREET

⑤

⑨

Triton Bastion

Point Utrecht bastion

NOTE
For key to accommodation and eating and drinking, see opposite page

262

e info@galleforthotel.com; www.galleforthotel.com. In Feb 2005, another major renovation was completed, turning an abandoned Dutch mansion near the old NOH, dating back to 1695, into a boutique hotel. In 2007, the Galle Fort Hotel won a UNESCO Heritage Award, the most prestigious conservation award ever made in Sri Lanka. This was important as there has been criticism by locals of the gentrification of buildings in Galle Fort by foreigners. However, following the collapse of many buildings over the last 3 decades, it is apparent that without foreign investment paying for restoration there would not be much left of the original buildings in the fort to admire. Australian film producer Karl Steinberg & Malaysian investment banker Chris Ong were the geniuses behind this enchanting hotel although they have since sold it. They described the hotel as: 'about passion. It was done with love.' It also happens to be fun, as well as reasonably priced for what it offers, & it delivers, being half the room rate of its competing nouveau boutique properties along the coast. All rooms have AC & king-size beds. The Portuguese barrack room features a deep sunken terrazzo bath for 2. In the bathroom of 1 suite the shower spouts high from the roof, like a waterfall. In another, a wardrobe opens up to reveal a washbasin, & a shutter in another reveals

---

GALLE

For listings, see pages 261–5 & 269

---

sunlight streaming in from a hidden atrium. 1 delightful suite is furnished with antique Chinese & Peranakan fittings, & the loft suites have a 4-poster bed & a large parlour & bathroom below. It's not necessary to stay at the hotel to enjoy its eccentricities & colonial grace & charm, since there is a bar & veranda café (**$$**) open to non-residents, with exquisite food served in the dining salon (**$$$**) enhancing the hotel's appeal to the discerning. **$$$$**

Kahanda Kanda (9 suites) Anugulugaha, Galle; \091 2286717; e info@kahandakanda.com; www.kahandakanda.com. Featured with awe in glossy magazines worldwide. Off a country lane heading inland 9km east of Galle, this was originally built as the owner's private, fantasy residence following his purchase of an abandoned 5ha tea plantation in 2000. He has since created a retreat of suites in the original bungalow & vast guest pavilions, with a stunning swimming pool, ponds & 2 recreational pavilions, with furniture made locally to the owner's design & contemporary fittings by in-vogue Sri Lankan designers. Staying there is to feel at one with the 'in-crowd' who adore its sense of secure tranquillity. **$$$$**

Lighthouse Hotel (60 rooms, 3 theme suites) Dadella, Galle; \091 2224017; e lighthouse@lighthouse.lk; www.jetwinghotels.com. This is on the outskirts of Galle, on the approach from Colombo. With a façade as formidable as the Galle Fort's, this is an architect's concept that combines the nautical with the historical & seems, only incidentally, to be built as a hotel. The entrance with flagstones & walls of granite is like a medieval underground car park, a contrast to the bright sunshine outside. A stairway – with a banister that is to be looked at, not clutched, since it comprises a jagged tableau in brass & copper of heroic historical episodes – spirals up a rotunda crowned with a glass dome. There is a lift for the faint-hearted. There is more history depicted in the bar with its batik ceiling of 18th-century coats of arms. The nautical image of the public rooms, with wooden decks & wood-&-rattan chairs, is disturbed by white concrete columns stark against the blue of the sea seen through the wooden-framed windows. Bedrooms are a flourish of pastel colours & boast 'wooden Dutch beds', a teak writing desk, & a picture window with wooden shutters framing a view of the ocean. Heavy wooden doors slide open to a large bathroom of wood & granite. One of the maxims of travel writing is that if a review of a hotel or restaurant witters on about the décor, then usually the food isn't any good. At Lighthouse, the opposite applies: the food is gourmet class, & it is complemented by commendable service & a fine wine cellar. The hotel was Sri Lanka's first resort to pitch its advertised prices high (then US$250 for a double) & its success prompted others to follow. As part of the activities offered to guests, & mentioned here to give an idea of what to see, there is a tour to Rumassala (15min drive) for a nature walk to an isolated beach. 'On the drive back,' says the brochure, 'note the very picturesque statue of Lord Buddha in the far distance, followed by a stop at a lace-making factory & a silk-producing factory.' A tour is also organised to a low-country tea estate & factory. $$$$

🏠 **The Sun House** (5 rooms, 2 suites) 18 Upper Dickson Rd, Galle; ☏091 4380275; e info@thesunhouse.com; www.thesunhouse.com. At the other side of the fort, a short drive up from the bustle of town, is a remarkable haven of sophistication at the Sun House. This is a place to stay of a different ilk: a 5-star boutique hotel created in a 1860s hilltop colonial mansion overlooking the harbour & fort. Its approach up a road of suburban-style houses to an unprepossessing gate in a wall gives no inkling of the idle splendour awaiting within. There are 5 double rooms with antique 4-poster beds & a suite that takes up the whole 1st floor of the main building. There is a comfortable drawing room combined with a library, loggias for dining, a swimming pool, & a team of gentle staff in sarongs. Food, prepared to guests' wishes with supplies bought fresh that day in the fish & vegetable markets, is exquisite. The Sun House is owned by an Asia-based Englishman & guests feel they are privileged invitees in an elegant private house, & the temptation to do nothing but be pampered is almost irresistible. The Sun House is part of the Taprobane Collection & also manages with superb style the Beach House at Tangalle & the villa on Taprobane Island at Weligama &, across the road from the renovated Sun House, known as Doornberg. $$$$

🏠 **The Fort Printers** (5 suites plus 5 suites in an annexe & 3 in the mansion opposite) 39 Pedlar St, Fort, Galle; ☏091 2247977; e theprinters@sltnet.

lk; www.thefortprinters.com. This boutique hotel in the centre of Galle Fort was a printers' before it was transformed into a hotel in 2004, & before that it was a pioneering school. The building, originally an 18th-century mansion, was adapted to house the original Mahinda College, which opened there in 1892 at the instigation of The Buddhist Philosophical Society founded by Colonel Olcott. The primary classes were held downstairs & the higher classes & the principal's quarters were upstairs. That pattern has been followed in the modern renovation, with the Prefect's Suite being downstairs & the Headmaster's Suite, & former classrooms, now bedrooms, known as Geography, History & Art, upstairs. The spaciousness of the ground-floor area has been converted into living spaces that flow from one to the other. Tables for dining are set up on the street veranda & in the courtyard too, since the hotel is open for non-residents to enjoy refined versions of wholesome local cuisine ($$). Surprisingly there is a lap pool with frangipani petals floating in it in the courtyard shielded by a high sandstone wall. A doorway through the sandstone wall gives access to the newest wing: 5 rooms converted out of a building with stout columns & deep veranda with low overhanging roof, typical of practical, colonial architecture designed to be cool, before the advent of AC. Another new extension lies at the other side of Pedlar Street with 3 self-contained rooms & an auxiliary kitchen where guests can fend for themselves if they want. That should suit the independent-minded visitors who want a private retreat in the fort. $$$

🏠 **Closenberg Hotel** (16 AC, 4 non-AC rooms) 11 Closenberg Rd, Magalle, Galle; ☏091 2224313; e closenberghtl@sltnet.lk; www.closenberghotel.com. Off the highway to the east, just out of town, the road beside the entrance to the harbour leads up to this hotel. It was built in 1858 as the home for the British agent for P&O lines, on the site of a Dutch fort that guarded the bay. The villa has 4 large colonial-style rooms at its centre, surrounded by a veranda for wining & dining. An extension of charming rooms has been built on the side of the cliff looking away from Galle. A pool was under construction at press time. Managed with panache by the gregarious father & dapper son of the owning family, with occasional theme evenings to enliven the essential Sri Lankan traditions, this is a great place to stay, packed with atmosphere, nimble stewards who've been there decades & with hearty Sri Lankan food. **$$**

⌂ **Templeberg Bungalow** (6 non-AC rooms) Kaduruduwa, Loressakanda, Wanchawala, Galle; m 077 7108477; e templebergplantation@ gmail.com; www.templeberg.com. A former plantation bungalow built in 1864 converted into a guesthouse atop a 5-acre coconut plantation, this has a master suite with attached bathroom, 3 family rooms sharing a bathroom & a detached cottage of 2 rooms linked by a bathroom. Solitude for relaxing or creative adults (the Templeberg Fellowship is awarded annually to Australian writers to spend a month in the cottage). An abandoned lotus pond has been converted into a water-filled space with boulders as seats for chilling out as the sun sets. Meals prepared with locally sourced ingredients are taken in the semi-open parlour with a view of the inner lawn. To get to Templeberg leave the Southern Expressway at the Galle exit then turn left at the first set of traffic

lights into the Akuressa road. After driving about 300m, take the first lane on the left, which leads uphill to the plantation gates & the curving drive up to the bungalow. Creative peace. **$$**

⌂ **Kikili House** (5 AC rooms) Lower Dickson Rd, Galle ☏ 077 7300175; e info@kikilienterprises. com; www.kikilihouse.com. Bills itself as a '5-star boutique B&B guesthouse', & since it is run by the dynamic Henri Tatham who looked after Sun & Dutch House hotels for 10 years, guests can expect to be wowed. It's colourful & comfortable & Henri & her partner Kokila are enthusiastic hosts & provide more than just breakfast if required. There's free Wi-fi & solar power; the house is located a short way from & above Galle town. **$$**

⌂ **Thenu Rest** (1 AC, 3 non-AC rooms) 12 Hospital St, Fort; ☏ 091 2246608. Like staying in a family home; clean & chintzy, with free internet for residents. Opposite the old Dutch Hospital & next to a police post. **$**

Other practicalities

Banks The two state banks, **Bank of Ceylon** [262 B5] and **People's Bank**, have branches in Galle Fort as well as in the town, and there are also branches of the major private banks.

Post office There is an old post office in Galle Fort (near Amangalla Hotel) [262 C6], as well as the main post office in the Main Street (Matara Road) [262 C4].

Medical The **Hemas Southern Private Hospital** [262 B3] (☏ 091 2222187) is a private hospital in the centre of the town with a cadre of specialist doctors serving private patients from the west and south coasts.

What to see and do The reason for going to Galle is to see the **fort** [262 A/D5–7]. It is easy to walk around its ramparts or along its streets, but don't forget there can be cars and other traffic during the day. On the right after entering through the main archway is the **clocktower** [262 B5] and various vaults and access up a slope to the ramparts. If you turn left you can walk to the Amangalla Hotel and to the **cultural museum** [262 C5] next to it. This was once part of the hotel and is a bit dull.

There is a Christian church at the other side of the hotel, built in 1775 on the site of a Portuguese Capuchin convent. Opposite stands a Dutch **belltower** [262 C6] whose bell was tolled hourly in the 18th century, timed by an hourglass. A walk down the road by the belfry will bring you to the original archway entrance leading up from the sea. A **national maritime museum** [262 C5] has been opened within the fort wall.

Opposite is the fort's village green, now paved over, with the law courts and administration buildings around it. Hospital Street leads off it to the **lighthouse** [262 D7] that, if you meet the right caretaker in the right mood, you might be permitted to climb. From the top there is a splendid view of red-tiled roofs and purple bougainvillaea bursting from the concealed gardens of hidden courtyards. The **rampart walls** are riddled with a warren of cells, and gaps through the

The Galle Fort Hotel has produced an interesting leaflet and map, based on an aerial photograph, describing a walking tour of the fort which starts at the hotel with a walk up Church Street to the Dutch Reformed Church with 300-year-old gravestones and family crests. The belltower, post office and Dutch Commander's House across the road formed the centre of the Dutch VOC company's rule of the fort. The leaflet continues:

Follow the Dutch Spice Warehouses down the hill. At the VOC crest on the wall, go through the gate, look back at the English crest on the other side before walking along the jetty where you can see the original Portuguese Black Fort on your right. Come back through the Fort Gate and cross the Law Court Square. The crowds that gather on weekdays are attending the Magistrate's Court where you can see cases in progress through the huge Dutch windows. Cross the lawns and walk past the old Dutch Hospital to the Lighthouse where you can climb down for a dip at the Fort Beach.

Next to the Lighthouse is the Powder Magazine with its stone roof. This is where the Dutch stored the gunpowder for the cannons which capped the bastions to protect from sea attacks. On your right is the Mosque. As you continue along the next section of the rampart you will be offered handmade lace, carvings and old coins. At Flag Rock the boys will dive from the lookout for a few dollars.

Continue along the ramparts to the Bhodi Tree and Temple where you are welcome to see the lying Buddha and a quaint diorama of the first monks in Sri Lanka. Please leave a small donation. Continue to circle the front section of the Ramparts and Bastions until you finally weave your way along a narrow wall to bring you to the Belltower and back down Church Street to the hotel.

battlements to turrets, like pepper pots, protruding at strategic corners. Solid half-moons in the grass mark the foundations of gun emplacements.

The oldest residential building in the fort, built in 1763 and which was in ruins until restored in 1992, is the **Historical Mansion** [262 D6] (*31–39 Leyn Baan St;* \ *091 2234114;* ⏱ *09.00–18.00 daily*). The original Dutch architectural pattern was followed in the restoration and a clay and coral mixture was used in the construction of its walls. A section has been left unplastered to show how. The main rooms are over 10m high and the walls are nearly a metre thick. The ancient well, in the garden courtyard, has been reconstructed with limestone and coral.

The house contains a private museum of antiques, jewellery, pottery, coins, porcelain and old weapons collected over a 35-year period by the owner. There are also demonstrations of traditional hand cutting and polishing of gemstones, and of lacemaking. The front of the house is devoted to rooms where the gems, jewellery, brass and copper knick-knacks and handicrafts, as well as antique items, can be bought.

After the fort was ceded to the British in 1796, the moat was filled in and an esplanade created where before there was a narrow causeway. This is dominated now by a test-match-class **cricket pitch** [262 B4] outside the fort gates, with a super view of the play available from anywhere along the ramparts.

UNAWATUNA This bay, with its sandy beach and sea suitable for bathing year-round, was developed without anyone noticing, except for those independent travellers who discovered it and wanted to stay there, and enterprising locals who let them, by turning their homes into guesthouses. Perhaps that's why it seems to have a more laid-back sun-and-fun atmosphere than any other Sri Lankan beach resort. It has been acclaimed as one of the world's ten best beaches but even its most ardent fans would find that hard to believe if it is judged solely on its sun, sand and sea quality. However, if the rating is based on availability of locally and informally run beachside cabanas serving fresh seafood platters and exuding an atmosphere of easy conviviality, then Unawatuna scores very high indeed as a lazy-days tropical haven.

Unawatuna is for the traveller on a low budget who wants somewhere reasonable to stay, without hassles, away from the main road, the railway line and mass-market tourist factories. It is the kind of place where you don't make reservations in advance but turn up and take pot luck.

There are several small guesthouses (many unrecognised by the tourist board) with rooms starting at US$20 for two, and beachside restaurants with fancy names like Lucky Tuna. There are also some colonial bungalows, which help balance the appeal of the area. However, Unawatuna seems likely to lose its carefree character as the heavy hand of officialdom tries to slap it into conformity.

Getting there The simplest way is by train to Galle and a local bus or three-wheeler for the ten-minute ride along the A2 to the turn-off to the beach. There is also a railway station at Unawatuna from which you could walk to the beach area.

Where to stay

Coco Bay (12 rooms) 10/4 Roomassala Rd, Unawatuna; 091 2250560; e info@cocobayunawatuna.com; www. cocobayunawatuna.com. Off the main road to Unawatuna, with bright, bold & brash décor with white columns broken up by colourful blinds & crimson & lime green silk upholstery, this new property faces its own beach with views of Closenberg Bay & Galle Fort. Boats shuttle to Jungle Beach, an isolated cove between the hotel & Unawatuna. Almost Caribbean in its sheer holiday ambience, but no buffets so no weekend crowds, nor beach lurkers. Well-appointed rooms with jacuzzi & pillow menus. **$$$**

Unawatuna Beach Resort (63 AC rooms) 091 4384545; e reservation@ubr.com.lk; www. unawatunabeachresort.com. Acquired in late 2012 by a company with British/Sri Lankan connections & good ideas to move the resort upmarket so it's less of a packaged free-for-all & more of a fun & safe place to enjoy Sri Lanka, this is the biggest hotel in Unawatuna. It is another of those hotels that started off small & had to expand to meet demand. Hence its rooms are of several styles (all being refurbished), with the family ones being grouped around their own swimming pool. The dining area & bar adjoin the beach; meals & drinks can be served on the beach as well as on the dining terrace. What's nice

about UBR is the lack of formality & its location, literally at the edge of where it's all happening. (Just follow the path through the shacks along the beach to find out.) **$$$**

Joe's Bungalows (8 AC rooms) Unawatuna Beach; 011 2507848; e joesbungalow@ jolankagroup.com; www.joesbungalow.com. Right at the edge of the beach at the eastern corner of the Unawatuna Bay was formerly the private seaside retreat of Joe Amirthalingam, chairman of Jolanka Resorts. There are 4 neat & clean bedrooms each with attached bathroom & solar-power hot water in the rain showers & a sitting room in the main bungalow with a cute attic bedroom with sea-view Juliet balcony above it. There is an open-sided sea-view restaurant (**$**) & beachside jacuzzi as well as a 2-bedroomed villa in the complex, & 2 self-contained chalets across the road. **$$**

Villa Gaetano (3 AC rooms) Susimawatta, Atharagoda, Unawatuna; 077 348047; e gjhapuarachchi@gmail.com; www.villa-gaetano.com. This is a new concept in Sri Lankan accommodation: a homestay guesthouse. It's the home of a charming young couple, Melani & Chrishan, who both have hospitality & Ayurveda training, & welcome guests as family friends. The villa is set in an acre of papaya & banana orchards with a swimming pool & even a fishing pond, as well as opportunities for jogging & hiking, yet it is close to the Unawatuna railway station & about 2km inland from the beach. **$**

🏠 **Thambapanni Retreat** (18 AC rooms) Yaddehimulla Rd, Unawatuna; 📞 091 2234588; ✉ thambapanni@sltnet.lk; www. thambapannileisure.com. At the edge of the downmarket muddle that characterises Unawatuna. It's up a narrow lane at the eastern end of the bay away from the beach, to where uniformed security guards scrutinise every potential visitor. This is done to preserve the exclusive zone of peace that prevails there. This is a hotel favoured by discerning couples, not the partying young. The entrance gates frame a flower-bedecked scene with a meandering swimming pool in front of the main house & rooms defying logic as they cling to the cliff face. Many guests use their balconies for dining, with deep views of the sea in the distance over the tops of palm trees. Hammocks are slung on these balconies & coffee tables are adapted antique doors. The room interiors feature timber floors, 4-poster beds & bathrooms that are a delight of coloured cut-&-polished cement, with bathtub of peacock blue & walls of Mediterranean umber. Rooms in the main house have less charm but nevertheless this retreat delivers enjoyable seclusion even though it's close to the raffishness that characterises Unawatuna. **$$**

✖ **Where to eat and drink** The beach at Unawatuna has a variety of low-cost eateries where anything from a hamburger to a lobster supper, or a cool beer to a bottle of champagne, can be found. The most popular is **Lucky Tuna** (📞 *091*

Bianca Perera

A new element to a holiday in Sri Lanka is staying in a private home. I don't mean renting a room in someone's house or checking into a guesthouse, but renting a villa in its entirety. There is something blissfully seductive in waking up in a sumptuously furnished bedroom between crisp cotton sheets, head on downy pillows, and glimpsing through the window the glint of the sun on the patio swimming pool. Even more enticing is knowing that the pool is exclusive to oneself and family. The pleasure of staying in a villa is that it isn't shared with strangers.

The other joy, especially if you are holidaying with the family, is that there is no housekeeping to worry about. Everything is done by trained villa staff on demand. The welcome greeting 'make yourself at home' couldn't be more appropriate. Even in my wildest dreams, my own home is not like those luxury villas in the south. They are owned by expat Sri Lankans and foreigners who have invested money to build holiday villas for themselves. Because these villas are actual homes, they have been created to be a joy and a comfort to their owners rather than being utilitarian in furnishings and ambience. They all share evidence of their owners' good taste.

While some villas have been converted out of existing properties, others are new. All exhibit features familiar in smart Sri Lankan properties: high ceilings, open shutters to let the breeze flow through, good wooden furniture including antiques, private patios and that wonderful atmosphere of knowing one can do exactly what one wants.

Luxury living includes staff who are always obliging and eager to help. Even if one's request isn't what they're used to, they'll do their best to satisfy. Catering depends entirely on what guests want and if madam insists, as I did, in helping out in the kitchen, that's accepted.

When we packed up to leave after a weekend of pretending we were the wealthy owners of our beachside villa, we felt we had found a second home. And it was a cost-effective way of having a holiday with family and friends. Had we all stayed in a beach hotel it would have cost more and wouldn't have been so much fun, nor would we have had such keen attention paid to our every desire.

4380346; e *luckytuna@hotmail.com*; $). This well-designed two-floored open-sided restaurant on the beach attracts guests even from other resorts because of its fresh seafood and an amazing dish described as 'mixed seafood spring roll' that looks like a deep-fried rolled-up pancake and is indescribably delicious. There are some beach-view rooms ($) too for those who want to linger after the partying. The proprietor, Lalith Nagasinghe, loves to party and is a man of many parts, happy to advise strangers on where to find a room, a bottle of wine or even a house to rent for the season.

Also fun is **Wijeya Beach** (*Dalawella, Unawatuna;* \ *091 2283610;* e *mahendrawijesena@yahoo.com; www.wijeyabeach.com;* $$). Rave comments from most people who manage to find this beach-shack-style restaurant (look for the tiny sign on the roadside wall, about 2km east of Unawatuna), mostly because of its superb crisp pizzas cooked in a wood-fired oven with locally inspired pizza dough. Its seafood menu is innovative too and even features locally farmed oysters and French champagne at amazingly low prices. No need to book; if it's crowded there are tables on the beach. Service that would seem frustratingly amateurish elsewhere at Wijeya's fits even sophisticated guests' relaxed mood perfectly. There are a limited number of rooms ($) if you don't want to go home. Ever.

While prices depend on the villa size and location, and the time of the year, a villa rental usually starts from US$250 a day. **Olanda International** (*30 Leyn Baan St, Fort;* \ *091 2234398;* e *info@olandavillas.com; www.villainsrilanka.com*) act as letting agents for several prime properties when their owners are not in residence. Another agency with a similar website address (*www.villasinsrilanka. com*) represents villas in the Galle district, as well as in Kandy and Bandarawela. A specialist in the niche market of attractively designed villas for independent guests is **Sri Lanka In Style** (\ *011 2396666;* e *info@srilankainstyle.com; www. srilankainstyle.com*).

Among the villas and mansions that take paying guests are **The Fort House** (e *enquiries@theforthouse.com; www.theforthouse.com*). Behind the Galle Fort Hotel, there is **41 Lighthouse Street** [map page 262] (*3 rooms;* e *41@ lighthousestreet.com; www.lighthousestreet.com*), with striking black-and-white tiles and an interior swimming pool. **The Ambassador's** [map page 262] (*5 suites;* e *enquiries@edenvillasonline.com*) is designer luxury.

Beyond Galle along the south coast there are at least a score of villas to choose for a longish stay. **Pilana** [map page 262] (*5 rooms;* e *Saratoga@netvigator.com*) is 6km away from Galle on a hillside; it has a swimming pool and deep veranda. Near Thalpe 700m inland from the coast is **Why** [map page 262] (*7 rooms;* e *whyhouse@ hotmail.com; www.whyhouseresort.com*) which features Italian cuisine. By the ocean is **Ambalama** [map page 262] (*4 rooms;* e *davegerard@attglobal.net; www. ambalamabeachhouse.com*) with 'Balinese pool, chef and houseboys'.

At Weligama, **Amapola** (*4 rooms;* e *information@weligama.net; www.weligama. net*) boasts an infinity pool by the beach.

Further to the east along the south coast, around Tangalle, there are several villas available. **Kadju House** (*4 rooms;* e *info@kadjuhouse.com; www.kadjuhouse. com*) is set in a cashew grove. **The Colony** (*4 rooms;* e *info@thecolonysrilanka.com; www.thecolonysrilanka.com*) is new with a pool, by the beach and run by a lovely British couple.

There are several places run by congenial Sri Lankans that help give Unawatuna its unique appeal that induces guests to return for a few weeks year after year. Repeat visitors and locals hope that rumours of Unawatuna being 'cleaned up' by the authorities don't come true, destroying that edge that makes it so appealing.

KOGGALA A big surprise when driving along the south-coast road from Galle is, at Koggala, to be confronted with a gleaming blue-painted Sri Lankan Air Force plane, number SCM 3101, near the 130km post. It is parked by the sea, at the end of the runway that forms the Koggala airport, run by the SLAF. It is in the grounds of an open-sided restaurant ($) called **Catalina**, after the type of flying boat that Air Commodore Birchall was piloting when he took off from Koggala and spotted planes from Japan heading for Ceylon. The alarm he gave spoilt the surprise attack and was, according to Sir Winston Churchill, 'one of the most important single contributions to victory' during World War II.

Getting there Stopping **trains** between Galle and Matara halt at Koggala, which is on the main A2 road. Local **buses**, or even three-wheeler taxis, from Galle are available.

⌂ **Where to stay and eat** The area was plunging steadily downmarket for years, with a nasty wall lining the length of the beach side of the road and keeping the happy campers enjoying cheap, all-inclusive holidays away from the rest of the world. Now that has changed as the most successful of the package resorts (Club Horizon) was sold and torn down. In its place at the end of 2006 opened a resort that could be the future of Sri Lanka's beach hotels. **The Fortress** (*53 AC rooms & suites; Koggala, Habaraduwa;* ☏ *091 4389400;* e *info@thefortress.lk; www.thefortressresortandspa.com;* **$$$$**) has spacious stylish teak-floored rooms equipped with the latest gadgets including plasma television, Bose speakers, mini telephone and a pre-programmed iPod.

Designed like a fortress, effectively walling off the beach, entry is through massive wooden doors reminiscent of the doors that used to guard the entrance to Galle Fort. Inside, a vast garden courtyard is lined with stout columns, cloisters and a first-floor gallery. Ground-floor rooms give access to the beach while first-floor rooms have a balcony. Beds are huge and blissfully comfortable; bathrooms open-plan, no doors, with huge stand-alone jacuzzi bathtub and separate rain showers. A garden swimming pool overlooking the beach runs the length of the hotel. Despite its grandeur, the atmosphere is casual, with meals served on a wooden deck by the pool, in the air-conditioned café or the 'Surf & Turf' themed wine cellar (*open to non-residents too;* **$$$**).

Another option is **Joe's Bungalows** (*Kathaluwa, Koggala;* ☏ *011 2507848;* e *joesbungalow@jolankagroup.com; www.joesbungalow.com;* **$$**), part of the Jolanka Resorts group that includes bungalows in Unawatuna, Yala and Jaffna and a chalet village in Habarana. The main bungalow is over 100 years old but properly modernised, although bristling with oriental antiques. Located a couple of kilometres inland from the coastal road, it has a master bedroom off the columned veranda and a second bedroom with bathroom across the hall, as well as a dining room and attic television gallery. A second building by the river has a dining gazebo and two bedrooms upstairs as well as a private boating deck. There is a garden swimming pool completing the tranquil charm of the place.

What to see and do Adjoining The Fortress there is public access to the beach and the unusual facility of a **swimming pool** formed by the sea flushing in and out of a basin in the rocks. This is not a natural phenomenon but another legacy of the British. The pool was created by the detonation of two anti-submarine depth charges by members of the Royal Air Force stationed at RAF Koggala in 1947. This left many jagged edges on the bottom of the hole which, over the years, have been covered by sand, making it a pleasant place for locals to bathe, next to the Fortress enclave.

A refreshing sea breeze blows away the cobwebs normally associated with museums at the **Martin Wickremasinghe Folk Museum** (*Koggala;* ⏰ *09.00–17.00 daily; admission Rs200*) 8km from Galle. Who, you are bound to ask, is Martin Wickremasinghe? When told he was a Sri Lankan writer you are quite likely to sigh with boredom and drive on past. Don't. The museum is worth a visit both for the incredible collection of village artefacts pleasantly presented in a building mercifully bereft of gloom and academic seriousness, and also for the chance to see how life was a century ago in a prominent villager's house.

The museum is located in 3ha of delightfully landscaped grounds off the coastal road between Galle and Matara. It is clearly signposted, opposite The Fortress. A three-storey glass-fronted building, housing the Melco supermarket and Golden Chef Chinese Restaurant (beer available) on the land side of the road, marks the turn-off. Galle–Matara buses stop nearby and the nearest railway station is Koggala. Three-wheelers park near the entrance.

It is a short walk along a path through a field to the modern building housing the folk museum. The exhibits are objects associated with village life and now seldom seen, such as a sandboard on which children learned to write, gourd shells used for carrying water and cowbells made of wood. There is a section devoted to pottery, another to puppets and, in pride of place, a gallery of wooden masks. I found especially intriguing the re-creation of a village kitchen with its clay walls, smoke-charred ceiling and wooden cooking implements.

A further walk along a path lined with indigenous trees, all labelled for easy identification, brings you to the original house where Martin Wickremasinghe (1890–1976) was born. You can find out more about him in the gallery dedicated to his achievements behind the house, where photographs of him and copies of his books and manuscripts are on display.

It is the house itself that gives an insight into rural life a century ago. Luck played an important part in its preservation. During World War II the Allied Forces took over the area, which included the hamlet of Mahalagama, which had about 1,000 dwellings. The residents were given 24 hours to vacate the village so a military airbase and camp could be set up. (The airstrip which served RAF Koggala survives to this day.)

While most of the homes were demolished, the Wickremasinghe residence was spared to accommodate military personnel. After the war the area had a sense of desolation that can still be felt as all the trees were cut down and no-one lived there. In 1962, the property was returned to the Wickremasinghe family, and the house where he was born eventually became Martin Wickremasinghe's retreat.

The house has been renovated to its original design, with the square clay tiles over 170 years old still forming the floor. The roof is typical of old village houses, with red clay, tubular tiles and no asbestos reinforcement. You can peep into the author's room where his spectacles are on the bedside table and his clothes in the cupboard, and you wonder if he will return any moment from a stroll on the beach. He won't; his ashes are scattered on the grass sward, with its headstone of natural rock, beside the house.

The museum, the house and the estate are maintained by a private trust. It is seldom visited by foreigners. However, for an insight into Sri Lanka, as well as for a gentle morning out, it is definitely worth dropping in.

WELIGAMA The drive to Weligama is brightened by the sight of fishermen who perch upon sticks in the shallows, dangling rods in the water and angling for photographers. If you pass early enough you will see them actually fishing instead of posing, which some of them are prepared to do for a fee in the midday sun. Previously a quiet transit stop on the A2, Weligama was about to have a Marriott Hotel – under construction at the time of writing. The town has a population of 24,159 (2012 estimate).

Getting there There is a halt served by stopping trains between Galle and Matara, and a local bus or three-wheeler can also be used since this is on the main A2 highway.

 ## Where to stay and eat

Taprobane Island (4 rooms) e info@ thesunhouse.com; www.thesunhouse.com. If your ultimate in holiday fantasy is to stay on your own island, the one in the bay opposite the Weligama Heritage (formerly the Resthouse) can be rented. Now known as Taprobane Island, it was called Yakinige Duwa, which means She-Devil's Island. Then it became known as Count de Mauny

Island after it was taken over by the expatriate count & aesthete in the 1930s. He converted this scrub-covered islet into an exquisite garden with an open-sided house. Another expatriate, the American writer Paul Bowles, lived there a couple of decades later. **$$$$**

Robin Hill (3 suites) 39 Kandewattha, Weligama; m 071 4174714; e info@robinhill.

TREKKING

There are a dozen established routes for trekkers and they give a varied insight into the country. The treks are not arduous and ordinary sports shoes (hiking boots are too heavy) are adequate. It is also wise to begin trekking in the early morning, before the sun becomes too hot, and all walks should be completed before sundown (unless you plan to camp). Although there are small grocery shops (boutiques) throughout the countryside, it is wiser to take a picnic lunch than to rely on local supplies. Walkers should also carry their own water (at least two litres) with them, since available natural water may be unfit for drinking.

In the introduction to *Trekker's Guide to Sri Lanka* (see page 313), a book which every trekker should obtain, the authors warn: 'Even the most intrepid walker will find the attentions of village children at some point distracting. Earlier visitors seem to have left the impression that strangers equal school pens, or bonbons, or money!'

The book details walks beside temples, tanks and paddy fields; through tea estates; by salt, fish and mangrove ponds; and even early morning city walks in Galle and Kandy as well as Colombo. It is safe to walk alone or with a companion in most districts, but do seek local advice first. While villagers will give directions this will usually be to the nearest bus stop, since it is regarded as odd for a visitor to want to walk along a country footpath when there is a bus service.

Many of the hill country hotels, particularly The Heritance Tea Factory Hotel at Kandapola (see page 174) have tracker guides on call. In the Haputale area, ask for Loga (see page 162) who leads an exciting trek from Idalgashina railway station down through the forest to Haldumulla. Based in Kandy, freelance guide Ravi comes highly recommended (see his impressive website: *www.srilankatrekking.com*).

lk; www.robinhill.lk. To stay at Robin Hill is to experience gracious Sri Lankan living at its best, with flavourful curries made from home-grown organic ingredients slow cooked on an open cinnamon-wood fire. This mini mansion is more than a century old beside the road leading to the area's main attraction, the 6th-century rock carving of Kusta Raja. In a welter of wooden furniture & tall classical columns are frivolous touches like busts sprouting plants. Suites are grouped around a garden courtyard & air conditioned by nature's breezes. On one side is a large suite with 2 bedrooms & attached outdoor shower/toilet while opposite is a 2-storey suite with a ballroom on the ground floor (the bathroom's outside) & a massive antique-furnished bedroom above. Absolutely charming. Advance reservation is essential. **$$**

🏠 **The Heritage** (10 rooms) Weligama; ⤷041 2250299; e chcweb@ceylonhotels.net; www.ceylonhotelscorporation.com. Back on the main road, on the land side, the Ceylon Hotels Corporation operates this hotel, which was formerly a resthouse, so good for lunch. **$$**

What to see and do Just over a kilometre away from Weligama, at Walliwala, there is a 9m-high rock wall **statue** said to be of Kusta Raja, a prince who was cured of leprosy and reputedly planted the island's first coconut grove.

MIRISSA A sense of what's in store is inspired by the number of large, ugly billboards that herald the approach to the town of Mirissa, a contrast after the discreet charm that is Galle Fort. The road runs through Mirissa so it is easy to avoid the bay that has become the poor-man's Unawatuna, which places it pretty low on places to be. However, it is popular with surfers and low-budget package holidaymakers and with those who want to experience the new money-maker for the south coast: whale watching (see box, page 284). If you fancy being herded with a group on boats that patrol the ocean in search of whales to chase, then check out **Paradise Beach Club** (*140 Ven Gunasiri Mahimi Mwatha, Mirissa;* ⤷*041 2250623;* e *mirissa@sltnet.lk; www.paradisemirissa.com;* **$$**).

MATARA This town of 47,420 (2012 estimate) bustles with prosperity and purposeful people (there is even a brand-new 'financial services' building near the railway station).

Then, in the midst of progress, there are buildings from another age: the tiny Star Fort, the people's dispensary rugged with classic columns, and the Galle Oriental Bakery in an old manor building, its eaves laced with so much fretwork it could almost be a gingerbread house. Beside the electronic equipment stores are those dealing in discarded items: one shop carries the sign 'Dealers in gunny bags and empty bottles'.

History Matara is the gateway to the Ruhunu, the southern territorial division of Sri Lanka whose people, even today, have a reputation for freedom, independence and enterprise. In ancient times the Ruhunu was a kingdom ruled from Magama, the present Tissamaharama. Circumstances made the Ruhunu a district of resistance and refuge as many a Sinhalese prince fled there from the northern capitals to regroup his forces. Vijayabahu I (1055–1110) spent his boyhood in exile in Panakuduva, now known as Pasgoda, in the Matara district. From there he led his army to the north and was crowned king at Anuradhapura.

However, it was because of the trading in elephants and spices that Matara became known overseas. In the time of the Sinhalese kings, wild elephants were corralled and brought to stockades on the banks of the Nilwala River where they were tamed for export. There were elephant stables close to what is now the Matara Resthouse. Spices were an easier export and the area is still renowned for citronella and lemongrass cultivation. It is also the source of the Matara 'diamond', in fact a white zircon (no diamonds are found in Sri Lanka) that was used in local jewellery. It is a versatile gemstone; when found with a pink tint the Matara diamond passes as a ruby.

The coming of the Portuguese to Matara resulted in the razing to the ground of its temples but the first fortification of Matara was by King Dharmapala (1551–97), with the aid of the Portuguese. The Dutch built the main fort, part of which remains, and also the Star Fort, now restored. Today, Matara still exudes a feistiness, communicating to strangers a sense of being a more interesting town than first appearances would suggest.

Getting there

By train Matara is easy to get to by train from the north, from Kandy, from Colombo, and Galle, although the new high-speed track has not reduced the journey time significantly. (See box, pages 46–7, for train times.)

By bus There are long-distance intercity buses (No 2) to Matara from Colombo and also from Kandy (No 2-7). Bus No 31-1 links Matara with Nuwara Eliya and bus No 32-2 serves Matara from Badulla. There are also local buses from both Galle and villages deeper south (like Tissamarahama).

By road Matara is on the A2, 160km from Colombo and 45km from Galle. The highway is good from Colombo, although the standard of driving is not; expect a long, stressful drive. There is now an option of taking the Southern Expressway which cuts out the dawdle down the west coast. It is also possible to drive from Matara to the interior along the A24, which becomes the A17, to reach Deniyaya and the Sinharaja Forest Reserve.

Getting around Bullock hackeries, 19th-century passenger traps, were commonplace in Matara's streets up to the mid 1990s, when they were slowly sold off to hotel designers. You will see many, polished and parked, inside hotel lobbies, but probably not on Matara's streets any more: they wouldn't survive the traffic.

⌂ Where to stay and eat

⌂ **Matara Resthouse** (16 rooms, some with AC) ☎041 2222299. Matara town is poorly served for accommodation but on the waterfront of the old fort are rooms in a block beside the garden & in a new block on the left of the resthouse, also facing the sea. Basic furnishing. It is owned by the Urban Development Authority (UDA) & in 1999 was refurbished, not to make it modern but to emphasise its colonial charm. However, reader John Cox found it 'badly run & dirty'. **$**

What to see and do The **Star Fort** is in the town centre, on the western bank of the Nilwala River that bisects Matara. Opposite it are the Matara general hospital and the urban council buildings, and it is almost concealed by the daily commerce going on around it. 'Fort' is perhaps too grand a name for what was built as a redoubt, a polygonal fortification without flanking defences. There had been a rebellion against Dutch rule (in place since 1656) in the south, 1760–61, and the fort of Matara was attacked and seized. This resulted in the panic construction of this miniature fort ordered by then governor Van Eck (who was later to occupy Kandy briefly). Its design was functional with watchtower and cells. Its thick walls were built of coral and it is distinguished by a picturesque gateway, which still stands, with the date 1763 and the inscription VOC (Vereenigde Oost-Indische Compagnie – United East India Company).

The fort's effectiveness was never tested since it was ceded by treaty (not capture) to the British following the surrender to them of Colombo in 1796. With their emphasis on infrastructural development, the British used the fort as the office of the district engineer. Its aesthetic value was recognised in 1914 by the Commissioner of Archaeology who ordered its preservation. In 1965, it was taken over as the town's first library. It has now been re-restored and is open to visitors.

Although no longer used as a market, what is still known as **Nupe Market** is an odd public building that seems both at home and out of place on the outskirts of Matara. Its design attempts to combine an open-sided, covered space suitable for a tropical market with the stature demanded by its imperial gift. At first glance it looks like something from medieval England, wanting only walls to be a baronial hall. That's because of its local tiled, pitched roof with three tiny conical towers and gabled entrance.

The supporting wooden frame of the roof is elaborate and edged with lavish latticework. It is 15m in height and supported by massive white stone pillars, typical of the British period when the imperial stamp was impressed on public buildings. The floor plan is in the shape of a T with the upper bars of the T facing the highway and providing the entrance. One wing would have been for the vegetable market, the other for meat and fish. The stem of the T was probably for the sale of textile and household items. After falling into disuse as a market, the building was abandoned for many years before restoration took place and it was used spasmodically as a youth training centre.

On the way to Tangalle, 6km from Matara, is the **Dondra Head lighthouse**, 54m high, warning ships of the country's southern tip. Hand-painted signs point off the main road down country lanes that lead to Sri Lanka's southern tip. Boys with rods fish off huge boulders battered by the sea while the lighthouse stands serenely in a carefully tended garden of lawns and palm trees. It is not possible to climb the 196 steps to the top, but its immaculate exterior, painted off-white, with wooden windows a Tuscan yellow, inspires a shiver of wonder at its survival. Beyond it, in a cleft in the coastline, bright blue fishing boats bob in a surreally turquoise sea.

The ancient Buddhist temple there, destroyed by the Portuguese in 1588, was mentioned by Ptolemy. Tennent records that in its pristine grandeur the complex was so vast it had the appearance of a city, richly decorated and with roof plates of copper. The Sinhalese name was Devinuwara (City of the Gods). Ibn Battuta visited what he called Dinawar in 1344 on his way from Adam's Peak to Galle.

The temple was dedicated to the god Vishnu and the Portuguese saw it as the most celebrated and greatest pilgrim goal of all in the island, after Adam's Peak. Now all that remains is a modern temple and Buddhist statue as the centre of a bustling town, also known as Devundara. The temple in its present modern form is a place of pilgrimage at the time of the Esala full moon.

At the roadside beyond the town, women sit waiting for drivers to pause and buy cashew nuts from jars perched on makeshift tables, and later there is a cabin dedicated to selling sea shells. A stack of clay bricks bound with coir rope hanging from a tree acts as a sign for a brick-makers' kiln. A tractor trundles along loaded with bales of coir, rope made from the fibre of coconut husks. Another is piled high with jak-fruit, a village staple resembling a cross between breadfruit and durian in appearance. Broad plains of paddy, from which rice is harvested, line the land side of the road, golden strands of beach on the other.

DICKWELLA This town, 180km south of Colombo and 22km east of Matara on the road to Tangalle, began to attract visitor attention in the 1980s when a beach hotel for Italians (currently closed for redevelopment) was opened. Nothing much has happened since. As if to make up for its lack of historical monuments, the tallest Buddha statue in the island was erected in the vicinity in 1970.

What to see and do A sign points the way inland to the **Wewurukannala Maha Vihara** about 1km down the road to Beliatta off the Dickwella main road. This is a temple of unusual flamboyance in contrast to the surrounding greenery and is where a seated Buddha statue as tall as the Dondra lighthouse confronts the world clad in dazzling colour. A building containing a staircase behind the statue allows visitors to climb eight flights to the statue's head and to view vivid depictions of events in Buddha's life. The statue, reputed to be the tallest one of a seated Buddha in Sri Lanka, reflects the era in which it was built, the psychedelic 1970s.

Drive 6km beyond Dickwella on the road to Tangalle and you will see a signpost at Kudawela pointing to the **blowhole**, 1.1km towards the sea.

In February 2002, the Sri Lankan Tourist Board announced a plan to develop the blowhole as a tourist attraction, with a stairway, a viewing platform and modern parking area, at a cost of Rs3 million. It still awaits sprucing up. Known in Sinhala as 'Hummanaya' (say it slowly and it imitates the sound of exploding water), this is a curious phenomenon of nature. When the sea is rough, water gushes through a fissure in the overhanging cliff and shoots through the blowhole, high into the air. The approach to it is through a fishing village where men repair bright red nets in front gardens. Enterprising villagers let cars park in their compounds for a fee, while visitors trek 500m along a concrete slab path, up a worn flight of stone steps, along a path to beach level, then climb up to the cliff top to gaze at the spout. An admission fee (Rs50) is levied by the local council and visitors are urged to buy fish snacks from stalls along the trail.

To be candid, at some times the visit there can be a disappointment. It has stirred up local controversy, with one letter to the press from a Sri Lankan complaining about:

> ...so many women and children forcing us to park in their compound for a fee as high as Rs25 ... next along a path a group of men demanded Rs20 from each tourist for walking across their private property, further on the way up many engaged in selling fried fish also demanded a fee unless we bought fried fish from their outlets.

Turn towards the sea by the sign close to the 187km marker that announces the Marawela Beach Resort for immediate access to an old bungalow that can be rented in its entirety for self-catering holidays. **Sethsiri Bungalow** (*3 rooms; Marawela Beach, Moraketiara, Nakuluwagamuwa;* e *rohangunaratna@yahoo.com; www. sethsiribungalow.com;* **$**) has one bright bedroom off the enclosed entrance veranda, a master bedroom with large bathroom and new wooden floor, and a second bedroom with small bathroom. There is a parlour with television and dining on the veranda. The kitchen is fully equipped. A path through the garden of coconut palms leads to Breadfruit Alley, a narrow trail where breadfruits grow, between the high walls of two neighbouring properties, to the vast beach.

TANGALLE No longer a quaint village on the coast as its old houses have been replaced by concrete boxes, Tangalle is a scruffy town of 11,258 (2012 estimate) by the 198km post on the A2 highway that runs from Colombo via Galle to Hambantota and beyond. The highlight for early risers is to witness the fishing boats unloading the previous night's catch and the auctioning of it at dawn at the small harbour just below the Tangalle Resthouse.

Although it was originally built in 1774 and a colonial bungalow, with a bar, remains on the site, the resthouse's guest rooms are in an adjoining bleak block building next to the police station. Its redeeming feature is its view of a small cove and beach where locals enjoy sea bathing.

The town itself is unattractive with a busy covered vegetable market and some stalls selling fish behind it. The town's playing field where kids practise cricket all day is behind the market and a local bar overlooks it – buy drinks from the cage downstairs and consume them in the 'Chinese' restaurant upstairs.

Getting there

By train The nearest station is at Matara, 35km away, where three-wheelers and minibus taxis can be hired to drive to Tangalle.

By bus There are intercity buses (No 2) from Colombo and Galle and also from Tissamarahama further east. Bus No 32-4 runs a dedicated service to Tangalle from Colombo. There is also a service, No 32/49, between Tangalle and Trincomalee. Local buses run from Matara.

By road On the A2, the town is 196km from Colombo and at least six hours' drive from the airport. However, it is about an hour's drive from the Mattala Rajapaksa International Airport, north of Hambantota (see page 279).

Where to stay and eat There are some beachside cafés to the west of the town on the way to what used to be the most interesting hotel architecturally in the area, the genuinely retro (1970s) Tangalle Bay Hotel, with rooms straddling the sides of the cliff running down to the shore. However, at the time of writing, it was closed for refurbishment.

Amanwella (30 rooms) Bodhi Mawatha, Wella Wathura, Godellawela, Tangalle; 047 2241093; e amanwella@amanresorts.com; www.amanresorts.com. Down an unsurfaced village lane to the sea, between the 193km & 194km posts, is this astonishing new resort. The entrance is marked by high walls through which can be glimpsed a thicket of stark, black square columns complementing the palm trees of its coconut-grove location. A rectangle of grass, edged with an open-sided walkway, blocked by the wall of the library (with internet) at the end, & with an ill-lit bar lounge on the other side, shows the influence of Geoffrey Bawa on its Australian architect (then Sri Lankan resident Kerry Hill). The view of the rectangular 45m², green-tiled swimming pool poised above the beach & breezy sea is breathtaking as water flows over its sides. Staff swish around greeting everyone ceaselessly with *ayubowan* as though it means 'Hi!' The accommodation is in villas strung out in 3 tiers along the hillside, & each one has its own rectangular swimming pool. The rooms are glass-sided with no curtains, partial privacy from prying eyes in the villas above being obtained by drawing the latticed screens. Locally sourced fittings & furniture of darkly grained palm wood, & wooden-board ceilings under ancient clay tiles, create a comfortable elegance contrasting with the harsh abundance of dappled terrazzo. TV would be out of place in such a refined atmosphere but a lot of time could be spent exploring your enormous room with its open-plan bathroom, in finding the hairdryer & where to plug it in, & in learning to operate the light & AC controls. Towels are placed conveniently everywhere, including 1 on a hook outside the shower room, & there are thoughtful touches like his-&-hers slippers. The hotel is somewhat isolated but the food served in the restaurant is so good (& appropriately priced: **$$$**), & the place so relaxing, guests are unlikely to want to pop in anywhere else. **$$$$**

Turtle Bay Hotel (7 AC suites) Turtle Bay, Kalametiya; 041 7887853; e info@turtlebay. lk; www.turtlebay.lk. By the 214km post on the Tangalle–Hambantota highway, close to the

Kalametiya Bird Sanctuary. Gaze from the hotel's swimming pool on a bluff & the long sweep of beach seems deserted, with nary a building in sight among the palm trees. Land all along this coast has been sold for development but meanwhile this brand-new boutique resort has the view to itself. Unlike Sri Lanka's other boutique beach hotels, this one has an agreeable lack of formality, being run by young Sri Lankans who delight in giving guests what they want, whether it's breakfast at 16.00 or giant prawns for brunch. There is a Bawa-like austerity in the thicket of white square columns spoiling the view of the horizon from the ground-floor restaurant, but this is relieved by colourful mosaic tiles & thoughtful décor. There are 5 huge (40m²) suites on the upper floor, each with an oversized luxurious bed (no mosquito nets), big bathroom, wooden floors & tea/coffee maker. TV only on request. There are 2 ground-floor rooms opening onto the pool & garden. Each room is named after a species of turtle, & turtles come to hatch on the beach by moonlight. An ayurveda spa completes the charm of this refreshingly relaxed resort. Very popular with British guests; advance reservation is essential. Great value for money too. **$$$$**

⌂ **Buckingham Place** (12 suites & rooms) Wellawathugoda Rd, Rekawa, Netolpitiya, near Tangalle; 047 3489447; e reservations@ buckinghamplace.lk; www.buckinghamplace.lk. To the east of Tangalle, & named after its owner, Nick Buckingham, this is neither regal nor formal but a joyously addictive, sturdily built place to stay with suites & bedrooms in brightly decorated units tucked away in woodlands by an empty,

rugged beach. Bicycles & canoes for village & lagoon exploration are available. With wining & dining in a central pavilion usually developing into convivial evenings, guests quickly become attuned to a carefree lifestyle (the Big Village Breakfast is served all day) & a genuine camaraderie. Meals of refined cuisine, with reservations in advance, are available for non-residents too with advance reservation (**$$$**). An additional delight is that the room rates for this boutique-style hotel are lower than in popular tourist factories. **$$$**

⌂ **Ranna 212** (54 rooms) Kahandamodera Rd, Ranna; 047 4934999; e info@ranna212.com; www.ranna212.com. The number in the name of this beachside establishment refers to the distance in km from Colombo. The town of Ranna is on the A2 (13km from Tangalle) with the resort hidden several km through scrubland down a village track. Rooms are spacious with tiled wooden floors & high timber roofs in villas built facing each other around a swimming pool & a central grass piazza. The bathrooms are relentlessly minimal with matt grey cement walls & floors & even a cement bathtub, with separate glass-walled shower & a pair of washbasins. This is the pioneering hotel in the area in the first phase of a 120-room project with overwater cottages, a spa & restaurants which were under construction at press time. It would suit families with children who could play on the long, deserted beach, watch turtles laying their eggs in the evening, & explore the surrounding wilderness. Being about an hour's drive from the new international airport at Mattala, it makes a good starting point for a holiday for passengers landing there. **$$$**

What to see and do Get up early to see the day's catch being unloaded at the quayside in Tangalle's fishing harbour. Fish are auctioned, gutted and cut up on the dock to be carried by pedal cycle and motorbike to eager customers in inland villages.

Beyond Tangalle a diversion of 16km inland yields a place of great importance in the historical fabric of Sri Lanka. **Mulkirigala** is a gaunt, grey, natural rock monolith soaring 106m from jungly vegetation into the sky. A cave retreat of Buddhist monks, possibly dating back to 130BC, its importance stems from a chance discovery there of the key that unlocked the secrets of the *Mahavamsa* historical chronicle.

The *Mahavamsa* was known to contain the story of the island, but its Pali verse was untranslatable. In 1826, George Turnour, a Ceylon-born British scholar of Sinhala and Pali, climbed the rock with a learned monk and found an ancient parchment *tika*, or commentary. This contained the code that enabled him to decipher the *Mahavamsa*. Today there is a post office at the base of the rock, and visitors can climb barefoot past the caves with paintings and images up to the dagoba (domed shrine) perched on the summit. There is an admission fee and guides lurk, eager to elaborate on the rock's history.

On the road to Hambantota, on the sea side, can be found the almost forgotten bird sanctuary of **Kalametiya**. In his book *Seeing Ceylon*, R L Brohier wrote of the vast shallow lagoon 'surrounded by swamp with succulent subaqueous plants' which lies between the A2 and the sea. You can still hear 'the repeated mewing calls of the lightcoloured Jacanas with their pheasant-like tails' that he describes, and peacocks can be seen strutting beside the mud trail. This leads through the sanctuary and past an overgrown wartime landing strip to the shore.

HAMBANTOTA Although Hambantota is the town with the most inhabitants on the southeastern coast (the population in 2012 was 12,071), and boasts the new developments of major road infrastructure, a deep-water commercial cargo and transhipment port and an international airport, it seems a quiet place. The beaches, too, are not as rewarding as those to the west. Saltpans were a prominent feature of the landscape before the tsunami. In the days when steamships made regular voyages around the island, Hambantota was one of the ports of call. In early British times a Malay regiment was stationed in the area, and the descendants of those soldiers make up a large proportion of the Muslim population.

The town is about to emerge from somnolence as it is the focus of the government's development of the south. As though to compensate for the industrialisation and urbanisation, attention is being paid to the natural beauty of the area. A 122ha (300 acre) Botanical Garden is being created at Mirijjawila near Hambantota, and Ussangoda, adjacent to the Kalametiya Bird Sanctuary, was declared the country's newest national park in 2010.

The area is considered unique due to its red earth and short vegetation. Ussangoda is 350ha in size and consists of both scrub jungle and a plateau on the sea side that drops 18m (60ft) over a rocky escarpment to the sea below. It is believed the area was struck by a meteorite in ancient times, hence its barren and unusual landscape.

The visual arts are also being acknowledged in the Hambantota district with the building of a tele-cinema park, Ranmihithenne, with permanent film sets and accommodation on 95ha (235 acres) of state land, opened in 2011.

Getting there

By air There are international and domestic flights to **Mattala Rajapaksa International Airport** less than 30 minutes' drive from Hambantota.

Sri Lanka's second international airport opened there to much pomp and ceremony in March 2013. There were lots of press articles about it (the total cost was US$209 million; it was built with financial assistance and expertise from the Chinese government; it covers 2,000 acres; and is able to process one million passengers annually, capable of handling A380 aircraft). It's actually a compact, passenger-friendly airport located within easy reach of Sri Lanka's hill country (Nuwara Eliya 94km), wildlife park (Yala 53km), the east-coast surfer hangout of Arugam Bay (110km), and the southern coastal resorts from Hambantota to Galle. It lies 122km from Galle along the A2 and then inland from Hambantota along a grand dual carriageway that gives access to the airport turn-off after about 25km. Wild peacocks lurk in the wilderness and a giant metal sculpture of one guards the approach to the airport.

From the entrance to the airport terminal, there is one broad corridor for departing and arriving passengers linking to the public concourse and an interior open courtyard, behind a large statue of Buddha, where the public can watch aircraft movements. Departing passengers are processed in the check-in lounge on the left wing, from where domestic passengers access the departure lounge while international passengers take an escalator to the first floor for immigration formalities. The departure lounge has huge windows making it bright and pleasant to use; the seating for waiting passengers is polished chrome chairs and pastel-shaded armchairs.

There is a small Business Class lounge but at press time only soft drinks and snacks were available in it. At press time too duty-free shopping counters, run by Dufry, were scheduled to open for departing and arriving international passengers. Two air bridges serve two aircraft at a time with departing passengers taking the upper level and arriving international passengers the lower level to emerge at immigration and customs. Domestic arrivals follow another channel. All passengers emerge into a bright arrivals hall forming the right wing of the airport and then access the main red-carpeted corridor to the exit.

After the first few weeks of opening, the airport was seeing an average of two aircraft a day and was served by SriLankan, Mihin Lanka, Fly Dubai and Air Arabia, providing direct flights to the Middle and Far East. Other flights were to Colombo's main international airport at Katunayake for onward connections.

The new airport is very impressive, and a contrast to the undeveloped plains of the surrounding countryside. While the airport will bring employment and development, it also makes air travel easier for residents of the area, and seems to herald the future development of the south. Together with the new deep-water harbour and the super highways constructed to access them, these are the first massive major infrastructure developments in Sri Lanka since the 19th century when Governor Barnes declared the solution to prosperity and peace was 'roads, roads, roads' and then, in 1867, the railway network was begun. It can give perceptive visitors an eerie feeling of being witness to a valiant vision intended to change the demographic of Sri Lanka during the next decade.

By bus Bus No 32-1 links Colombo with Hambantota.

By road Hambantota is 238km from Colombo. The A2 from Matara in the west and Tissa in the east serves Hambantota. It is also possible to drive there from Ratnapura on the A18 which joins up with the A2 at Nonagama, just after the 220km post. That road provides access to the Udawalawe National Park (see page 199).

Where to stay and eat

There is a rush to upgrade existing accommodation and build new hotels to cater for guests who want to take advantage of the new ease of access via the international airport to the previously neglected beaches of the deep south. At press time, guests wanting to stay close to the airport usually opted for accommodation at appropriate standards to suit them in or near Tangalle.

Hambantota Resthouse (15 rooms) Hambantota; ☎047 2220299. Located on the brow of a hill that overlooks the beach, this is one of the traditional resthouses originally built to accommodate travelling colonial officials, now run by the Urban Development Authority & operated by a private company. The development of the area around Hambantota has led to an improvement in standards as rooms, public toilets & the verandas are clean & pleasant, having become pretty grotty in the past. The original wing is vintage Art Deco in design & has fine views of the fishing harbour. This is the place to eat in Hambantota as it has a licensed bar (drinks are served on the lawn or verandas) & a restaurant ($) where prices are designed for locals, as is the fieriness of the rice & curry. A bargain is the seafood mixed grill platter of prawns, 2 kinds of fish & crab that, in 2013, cost only Rs750. **$**

⌂ Lotus Chalets (4 chalets) Canal Rd, Migahajandura, Sooriyawewa; m 077 7352450; e lotuschalets@gmail.com; www. lotuschaletscom. Perhaps the oddest near-airport accommodation you'll ever find, just 15mins by road from the Mattala Rajapaska International Airport. Created in a *chena* (a wilderness area cleared for cultivation) amidst thickets of manioc plants & furrows of sweet potatoes are 4 chalets. 1 has AC, with exterior walls covered in coconut leaves & roof hidden under a passion-fruit creeper; the other 3 are made with breeze blocks disguised with mud & with roof of palmyra thatch – no asbestos or galvanised tin sheeting. Rooms are basic with mud-plastered walls & cement floor, but with comfortable locally made timber bed; power point, fan & east-facing veranda. Attached bathrooms have tiled floor &

are decorated with jungle green daubs. At night peacocks mewl, frogs croak & crickets chirp like a jungle movie soundtrack. Food is cooked using farm-grown produce on demand. A natural, rural haven, perfect for a first or last night in Sri Lanka for passengers using the Mattala airport or for cricket spectators (it's only 5mins from the new test match stadium). **$**

✗ Min Rong Restaurant 108/1 Siribopuya, Hambantota; m 077 4893368. In a converted, modern residence on the right of the new road into Hambantota town, this Chinese restaurant is the real thing, catering for the many Chinese residents of the area. Run by the personable Mr Lu, the restaurant has an amazing menu ('Dry Pot Pig Stomach') with huge portions, & delicious dumplings at remarkable prices. Clean & great fun. **$**

What to see and do

The **bird sanctuary of Bundala** (see page 188) is 16km from Hambantota on the A2 to Tissa. Flamingos pop in during the northeast monsoon and elephants can be seen during times of drought. A further 18km brings you to the **Wirawila Sanctuary** where aquatic birds as well as jungle ones including hornbills are drawn to the Wirawila and Tissa tanks (reservoirs).

TISSAMAHARAMA

This town is familiarly known as 'Tissa'. It was the capital of the southern kingdom of Ruhunu from 3BC. During the following century King Kavantissa created the reservoir and built palaces, temples and dagobas. The ruins of them all have yet to be revealed. It was the site of the monastery of King Tissa of about 150BC. As Magama, its ancient name, this was the southern capital for 2,000 years. The reservoir teems with birdlife.

Getting there

By bus There are intercity buses from Colombo (No 32) as well as local ones from towns along the A2, and from Wellawaya to the north.

By road You branch off the A2 at Wirawila to get to Tissa, a distance of 268km from Colombo. It is 30km from Hambantota. The A2 from here goes through the plains to Wellawaya and then up to the hill country, so Tissa is a popular place to stay on a round-trip tour of coast and hills. In fact, the usual route is to see the hill country first and then descend along the A2 to the coast.

Getting around

A safari jeep is the favourite mode of transport here and you will need one if you plan to go to Yala or Bundala. Otherwise, there are three-wheelers for short drives. Usually visitors are so tired after driving to Tissa they are happy not to go out but to eat where they are staying, and go to bed early so they can catch an early morning safari.

⌂ Where to stay

Aside from the recommended options listed below, there are several basic-rate guesthouses, many with attached jeep for the inevitable safari, in and around Tissa open to walk-in guests.

The Safari (formerly Tissamaharama Resort/Resthouse) (50 AC rooms) `047 2237299; e chcweb@ceylonhotels.net; www.ceylonhotelscorporation.com. Previously a resthouse upgraded to a resort & now restored again to provide more upmarket quality rooms for visitors to the south, it lies on the banks of the reservoir, with superb views. Run by the Ceylon Hotels Corporation (now part of the revitalised Galle Face Hotel group), it can be expected to maintain a standard acceptable to visitors as it shakes off its downmarket resthouse image. Safaris are easily arranged there. **$$$**

Priyankara Hotel (30 AC rooms) Kataragama Rd, Tissamaharama; `047 2237206; e priyankara@ sltnet.lk; www.priyankarahotel.com. Tucked behind a hedge on the opposite side of the Kataragama road to the lake. It boasts a view of paddy fields. Despite its low room rate, the image of the hotel is good taste: it shows immediately you step into its long lobby. The receptionists wear ties with the hotel's stylised logo (resembling a contented bird on its nest?). Grey & blue is the theme of the hotel, from the staff's neat uniforms to the floor tiles. Access to the rooms is by a staircase behind the tiny bar counter. The bedrooms (all AC) are well appointed & have tiled floors, dark furnishings & bathrooms blessed with hot water. All have balconies. The restaurant is a gracious-looking room, completing the image of the hotel as a charming spot for a couple of nights. **$$**

Lake Side Tourist Inn (11 AC, 9 non-AC rooms) Akurugoda, Tissamaharama; `047 2237216. Close to the reservoir, this is a smart & popular resthouse-style place with very low room rates. Rooms are in blocks off the garden while the bar, restaurant & reception are in the main building. A lake boating service, as well as a safari jeep, can be arranged by reception. **$**

What to see and do Most people who stay in Tissa are bound for some sort of safari but you don't need a jeep to see the birdlife on the reservoir. A desolate place called **Kirinda** is a 10km drive from Tissa and it is there that Viharamahadevi (the queen after whom the Victoria Park in Colombo was renamed in 1958) was washed up on shore after being cast adrift from Colombo by her father, the King of Kaleniya. She was taken as queen by King Kavantissa and became mother of the conquering King Dutugemunu (161–137BC).

For most, the only reason for staying in Tissa is to be in position for a morning safari to Yala, or at the end of an evening one. Entry fees at the park are US$25 per person, plus tax of 15% and a service fee for the obligatory tracker. (See page 186.)

KATARAGAMA The god of Kataragama is the war god and is held in awe, making this town with his temple a place of pilgrimage, not just at the Esala full moon time, but whenever a believer – Buddhist or Hindu – wants a blessing for a new venture, even for something as mundane as a new vehicle.

Situated on the left bank of the Menik Ganga, this is primarily a Hindu shrine. According to tradition, King Dutugemunu (161–137BC) developed the original shrine to fulfil a vow following his successful overthrow of the Tamil ruler, Elara, at Anuradhapura. This shrine is dedicated to Skanda, the Hindu god of war, also known as Kali Yuga Varatar, or Subramanya or, in India, Karititaya. He is said to have come to the island to fight the enemies of the gods and, having defeated them at Velapura, today's Kalutara, settled down at Kataragama.

The present temple is enclosed in a great compound with a large avenue down which it is approached by devotees bearing offerings of flowers and fruit. Time and tradition, and perceived effectiveness, have made this one of the holiest places in Sri Lanka. Many southerners, convinced of the deity's benign influence, journey to Kataragama for a *puja* (offering) at the time of embarking on new plans for the future.

The ritual traditionally involves a bathe in the Menik Ganga (dubbed 'The River of Gems'), the wearing of clean clothes (usually white), then a walk of several hundred metres to the temple. The temple is simple, a quadrangular white building with carved wooden doors at the east-facing entrance. Inside, the walls are coated with the soot of centuries of burning oil lamps and candles. Part is curtained off, accessible only to the priest in charge.

A walk of about 800m from the god Skanda's shrine brings you to a **dagoba** (Kirivehera) dating from 1BC and a **mosque**. Muslims join Buddhists and Hindus in the respect for this sacred city. During festival time, the place is thronged with crowds, each engaged in its own form of worship. At other times, the main street where all the eateries and local hotels are found seems surprisingly deserted.

Getting there

By bus The main bus route from Colombo is No 32. Local buses serve this sacred city from neighbouring towns.

DIVING AND WATERSPORTS

The leading diving and watersports operator is **LSR (Lanka Sportreizen)** (*PADI Licence 18526;* \ *011 2824500;* e *LSRdive@sltnet.lk; www.LSR-srilanka. com*), with watersports centres on the east and west coasts; a cottage site in Uwa Kuda Oya; the Catamaran Beach Hotel in Negombo, the Water Garden Hotel (*www.lsrhotels.com*) in Belihul Oya, the sea-side Marina Hotel in Bentota and a new marina and luxury villa property at Passikudah.

Diving at all the popular sites can be arranged through this company, which also has fins, masks, snorkels and diving gear for sale or hire. PADI-certified lessons are available.

Bentota, at the centre of Sri Lanka's sun-soaked strand of beach that stretches from north to south, from Colombo to Galle, provides diving that is good from November to March: the seabed is sandy and the depth from 10m to 35m, ideal for underwater exploration; gentle for beginners, satisfying for experienced divers. Gaining in popularity is the beauty of diving (May to October) from Passikudah Beach where LSR provides diving courses for guests of Maalu Maalu Hotel, at these prices:

Resort course: inclusive of 2 pool sessions, 1 open-sea dive, 1 log book, 1 certificate: US$150.
PADI International Open Water Diver course: inclusive of video sessions, 4 pool sessions, 4 open-sea dives & international licence: US$475.

While diving off the west coast, southwards from Beruwala down to Unawatuna and along the coast to Tangalle and the famed Great and Little Basses, is rewarding, night diving near Hikkaduwa to see lobsters and grinning parrotfish, etc, is great fun. The east coast has some exceptional sites, especially off Pigeon Island at Nilaveli. ✓

Also less expensive than in other popular holiday resorts are various watersports. **Sunshine Divers** in Bentota (m *077 7941857;* e *srisunshinedivers@yahoo.com; www.srisunshinedivers.com*) offers a complete service in watersports: water skiing, jet skiing, surfing, windsurfing, tube and banana-boat rides and deep-sea fishing. Deep-sea fishing is with their own 32ft Boston Whaler boat complete with rigging for catching tuna, barracuda, king fish, blue marlin and other game fish. They do not fish in dolphin waters. All fishing trips are led by a master fisherman who has an unrivalled knowledge of the deep. Sunshine Divers is a partnership of five brothers, sons of a fisherman, who were born by the sea at Bentota.

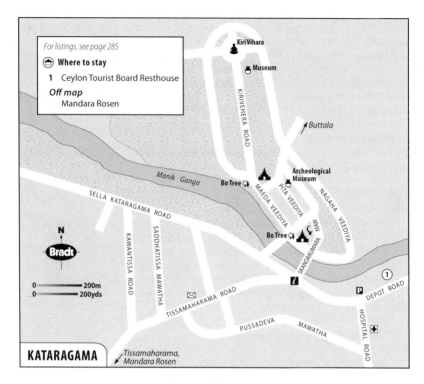

For listings, see page 285

Where to stay

1 Ceylon Tourist Board Resthouse

Off map
Mandara Rosen

Kiri Vihara

Museum

KIRIVEHERA ROAD

Buttala

Manik Ganga

Bo Tree

Archeological Museum

SELLA KATARAGAMA ROAD

MAEDA VEEDIYA

PITA VEEDIYA

NAGAHA VEEDIYA

N

KAWANTISSA ROAD

SADDHATISSA MAWATHA

Bo Tree

SKANDAKUMARA MW

0 — 200m
0 — 200yds

TISSAMAHARAMA ROAD

DEPOT ROAD

1

P

PUSSADEVA MAWATHA

HOSPITAL ROAD

KATARAGAMA

Tissamaharama,
Mandara Rosen

By road The distance from Colombo, along the A2 to the turn-off to Tissa, is 283km; from Tissa, 16km. Driving from the north, via Wellawaya, a turn-off to the right at Tanamalwila leads to Sella Kataragama and on to Kataragama.

WHALE WATCHING

Whale watching has become a bit of a craze, especially among Sri Lankans who like to crowd into motorboats and cruise the Indian Ocean off the south and west coasts for a few hours in search of whales. It is not cheap, nor does it seem to be a very environmentally friendly pursuit. However, if you decide to go on a trip, some operators include:

Raja and the Whales m 071 3331811; e RajaAndTheWhales@gmail.com; www.rajaandthewhales.com
Sri Lanka Navy m 077 7323050; e sinwhalewatching@gmail.com; www.whalewatchingnavy.lk
Sri Lankan Expeditions 011 2199323; e info@srilankanexpeditions.com; www.srilankanexpeditions.com
Whales Sri Lanka Tours m 077 7445549; e whaleslankacustomercare@googlegroups.com; www.whalessrilanka.rezgo.com
Whale Watching Mirissa m 071 3121061; e whalewatchingmirissa@gmail.com; www.whalewatchingmirissa.com
Whale-watching-Mirissa m 077 6376714; e info@whale-watching-mirissa.com; www.whale-watching-mirissa.com

🏠 **Where to stay and eat** The main street is full of places to stay since pilgrims usually spend at least two nights for their devotions. Both listings are included on the map opposite.

🏠 **Mandara Rosen Hotel** (52 AC rooms) 57 Detagamuwa, Kataragama; ☎047 2236030; e rosenr@sltnet.lk; www.rosenhotelsrilanka.com. On the road to Kataragama from Tissa, slow down at the sign advertising Harro's Pastry Shop to see a sturdy granite wall & high, wrought-iron gates. This is the entrance to this remarkable hotel, another in Sri Lanka's galaxy of extraordinary star-class properties in out-of-the-way places. The location is one of its attractions: on the doorstep of Kataragama & not far from the wildlife park at Yala & the parks at Bundala & Udawalawe. The hotel enhances its rather ordinary surroundings with creative architecture. A glass-walled pavilion acts as the reception lobby & gives a view of the swimming pool spanning the interior courtyard. (The boast is that the pool has an underwater music system.) For the active, there is a gym; for the shopper, a boutique stuffed with saris. The rooms are on 2 floors, lined up alongside a narrow garden, the upper floor presenting an avenue of balustrades defining its gallery. These rooms have the ambience & amenities typical of a city hotel: AC, 2 double beds, TV, minibar, minisafe, etc. The main restaurant ($$) functions in a separate glass-walled pavilion & also on its garden terrace, a popular place for visitors to dine. It has a view of 2 representative images of Sri Lanka: a fort wall typical of Dutch architecture, & a pond built on the lines of a Sigiriya water garden. **$$$**

🏠 Ceylon Tourist Board Resthouse (45 rooms) Kataragama; ☎047 2235227. Welcomes foreign as well as local tourists & charges them the same low rate with rice & vegetable curry dinner for 2 included. Rooms are basic but comfortable. The resthouse is set in 2ha bordering the Menik Ganga. Since this is a sacred area, there is no bar; alcohol & smoking are banned & no meat is served. The busiest times are weekends, & the months of Apr, Jul–Aug & Dec. **$**

YALA Yala is the place most visitors think of when planning to see wildlife in Sri Lanka; it is a simple name to remember and, like Kandy, trips off the tongue easily. Yala National Park is actually two national parks: east and west. It is the western one, real name **Ruhunu National Park**, which is open to visitors. For purists, it is already overcrowded, and jeep jams when elephants are spotted are customary.

'Safari' is a marketing word. A safari here is nothing like the long drives through a game reserve in Africa. It simply means a morning or afternoon being bounced around in a jeep over scrubland tracks, in the hope of seeing elephants (likely), leopards (perhaps) and bears (unlikely). There are no indigenous human inhabitants (as with the colourful Maasai in Kenya) herding cattle and glowering. A safari in Sri Lanka is something different to do during one's holiday, not the main purpose of it.

Getting there
By road While you can drive yourself to and around the park (as long as fees have been paid and you have the obligatory tracker), it is not advisable. A jeep, hired in Tissa or through your hotel, is best.

🏠 **Where to stay and eat**

🏠 **Cinnamon Wild** (formerly Yala Village) (68 AC rooms) Kirinda, Tissamaharama; ☎047 2239450; e reservations@cinnamonhotels.com; www.cinnamonhotels.com. With 60 safari-type chalets, each with its own veranda, & 8 timber beach chalets & a huge swimming pool created around forest trees, this is an 'eco-resort', with guests asked to 'take your garbage home'. It has a resident naturalist & jeeps are provided for safaris. **$$$**

🏠 **Elephant Reach** (35 AC rooms) Yala Junction, Kirinda; ☎047 5677544; e elephantreach@sltnet.lk; www.elephantreach.com. This is a new jungle resort. Guests are housed in AC chalets or standard rooms with all modern conveniences & wild animals as the neighbours. There is an AC restaurant & a Tree Tops stair bar, along with a swimming pool & safari jeeps with trackers on hand. **$$$**

9

The Eastern Seaboard and the North

TRINCOMALEE *Population: 99,135 (2012 estimate)*

The best-known town on the eastern seaboard, Trincomalee is seeing a return of tourists to enjoy the beaches to its north. The island's longest river, the Mahaweli Ganga, flows into the sea at Matur in the south of Trincomalee's great bay. The bay is said to be one of the world's best natural harbours, a view expressed by Admiral Lord Nelson who recalled it as 'the finest harbour in the world' having visited there in 1775 as a midshipman on board HMS *Seahorse*.

It was the home base for the combined east Asian fleets of the Allied Powers during World War II. It has 53km of shoreline and, surrounded as it is by hills on three sides and protected by islands in the bay, it seems like a landlocked inland lake. It is actually the fifth-largest natural harbour in the world. However, even though a lot of shipping of tea for export was done through the harbour, it has never realised its full potential as a commercial port.

Trincomalee is the capital of the Eastern province, which has a coastline of 326km from its northern boundary by the Ma Oya at the Kokkilai lagoon, 9° from the Equator, down to Ruhunu and the Southern province. The town is built on the neck of a peninsula less than a third of the way down the province's coastal boundary. This curves down from north to south like a parrot's beak, securing China Bay between itself and the mainland.

HISTORY The very nature of its harbour indicates that Trincomalee would have been used as a port in ancient times. On the eastern precipice of what became Fort Frederick is a Hindu shrine at Swami Rock where the Temple of a Thousand Columns is believed to have existed hundreds of years BC. This was demolished by the Portuguese after they took possession of Trincomalee late in their time in Sri Lanka, in 1622. What they didn't topple over the cliff into the sea, they used for their own fortifications.

The Portuguese stayed until ousted by the Dutch in 1639. During the Dutch tenure, the French occupied some islands in the bay in 1672 but didn't stay long. During the Dutch occupation, an English emissary landed near the north of the Mahaweli River in 1762 and visited the King of Kandy. Trincomalee was often used as the back door for foreigners' missions to the Kandyan kingdom.

Another emissary from Britain turned up in 1782 – when Britain was at war with Holland – with a force that occupied the harbour. The emissary went to Kandy to seek the co-operation of the new king, Rajadhi Rajasingha (1782–98) against the Dutch, but was rebuffed. He was also pretty miffed when he discovered on his return to Trincomalee that the French had taken over and his garrison had been transported to Madras. Trincomalee returned to Dutch possession in 1783. The fort there became the first to fall to the British in August 1795, capitulating after a siege lasting three weeks.

There was much discussion during the 19th century among the British administration about the future of the harbour. Sir James Emerson Tennent, colonial secretary of Ceylon 1845–50, wrote in *Ceylon*, published in 1859:

> On comparing this magnificent bay with the open and unsheltered roadstead of Colombo, and the dangerous and incommodious harbour of Galle, it excites an emotion of surprise and regret that any other than Trincomalie [sic] should ever have been selected as the seat of government and the commercial capital of Ceylon.

Tennent saw that the reason Colombo had become the commercial capital was because the Portuguese and Dutch had made it so, only through their need to be close to where cinnamon was grown, since that was their prime purpose for being in the island. He argued strongly that since the reason for Colombo being the capital and principal port was no longer valid, Trincomalee would be a better prospect for development.

GETTING THERE Although there are occasional military and police roadblocks, getting to Trincomalee is no longer the hassle it was when security was tight. I spent my second night in Sri Lanka in 1980 in Trincomalee and adored it so much I camped out in a run-down guesthouse on the beach there for several months. I was delighted when I visited there again in 2013 to find the guesthouse is still in operation, although under a different name (Club Dive Paradise) [290 A1].

By train At press time there was only one direct train a day running between Colombo and Trincomalee and that is only at night.

However, from Colombo on Thursday, Saturday and Sunday this train has an Exporail air-conditioned luxury carriage attached to it with advance reservation possible; it operates from Trinco to Colombo on Friday, Sunday and Tuesday. Prices quoted on the company's website (*www.exporail.lk*) are Rs1,900 single, Rs3,800 return, including dinner/tea and coffee.

The service used to be known as the BTLR (Batticaloa–Trincomalee Light Railway), which actually begins at Maho, the junction station 136km from Colombo where the Northern line to Anuradhapura branches off to Gal Oya and Trincomalee.

After stopping at **Habarana** station, which is a walk of about a kilometre from Habarana town and the road junction, the train halts at Hathareskotuwa, a halt in the middle of nowhere and not even on the map

Gal Oya station (224km from Colombo) was built in 1926 and the line bifurcates here for Trincomalee. The other fork allows trains to go to the station for Polonnaruwa and on to Batticaloa. A mark on the wall of the gents' toilet shows the level reached by floodwater in December 1957. Station staff and 400 passengers were marooned then but salvaged provisions, including a case of whisky, from the goods wagons and survived on that and food drops until rescued. The new station building was built in 1970.

TRAIN TIMETABLE: COLOMBO TO TRINCOMALEE

Train	Colombo–Trinco		Train	Trinco–Colombo	
7083	21.00	05.10	7084	19.30	04.05

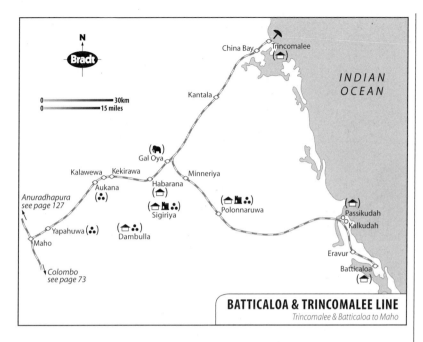

The train resumes a staid and steady pace through dry flatlands as it heads northeastwards, passing several stations on the way. When there are daytime trains, the view as the train approaches **Kantala** is of the bund (bank) around the 1,912ha Kantale Lake, the source of water for Trincomalee. Curd in clay pots and peanuts are offered for sale by various vendors at the station. The plains are swept by a cool breeze blowing in from the sea as the train creeps into **China Bay** for a short stop. From its window you can glimpse first a temple, then a church and then, of course, comes a kovil (a Hindu temple) and a mosque. In season (May to October) the sea shimmers like the Caribbean and the barren hills surrounding the bay make you feel you are in the Virgin Islands. Five more minutes to go before the train reaches Trinco [290 A1].

By bus The intercity bus No 49 makes the journey from Colombo to Trincomalee [290 B2]. There are bus services to Trincomalee from Tangalle, Negombo (No 34-10), Kandy, Kurunegala (No 49/1) and Anuradhapura (No 835).

The usual comments about the stress and perils of bus travel apply on this route, but more so. While the road from Habarana eastwards to Trinco is reasonable, but bumpy, the bus can occasionally be stopped at police checkpoints. It is better to forget about going by bus and let the train take the strain, if hiring your own transport is not an option.

By road Trincomalee is 257km from Colombo. Access from the south is by the A6 road, which branches off the A1 where it forks into two at Ambepussa, 62km from Colombo. The road leads through Kurunegala (see page 209) and Dambulla (see page 133) before reaching the junction with the A11 at Habarana.

There is scrubland on both sides of the road and the railway can be seen running parallel to it until it veers away at Gal Oya. When I travelled on the road I was idly watching a clump of boulders about 15m away, between the road and the railway line, when I saw them move. I blinked. We stopped the minibus, reversed, and

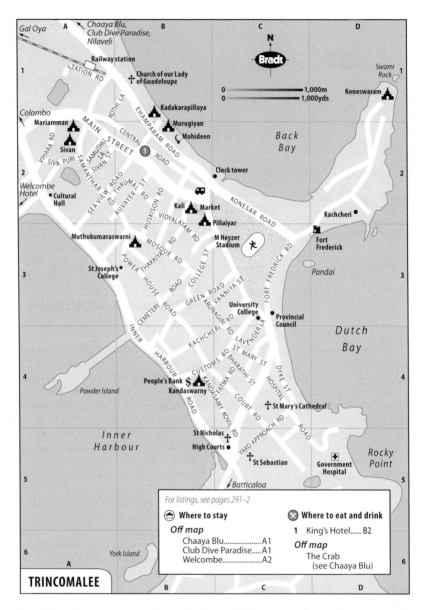

TRINCOMALEE

Map labels:
Gal Oya · Chaaya Blu, Club Dive Paradise, Nilaveli · Railway station · STATION RD · Church of our Lady of Guadeloupe · Kadakarapillayai · Koneswaram · Swami Rock · Colombo · Mariamman · KOTHI LA · EHAMPARAM RD · Murugiyan · Mohideen · Back Bay · MAIN STREET · CENTRAL ROAD · Sivan · VIHARA RD · SIVA PURI · SAMUTHU LA · SAMANTHAR RD · SIVAN ST · THRUMAL ST · AUVAYER RD · Clock tower · KONESAR ROAD · Kachcheri · Welcombe Hotel · Cultural Hall · SEA VIEW ROAD · HUSKISON RD · VIDYALAYAM RD · Kali · Market · Pillaiyar · M Heyzer Stadium · Fort Frederick · Muthukumaraswarni · MOSQUE RD · THAKKIYA RD · COLLEGE ST · Pandai · POWER HOUSE ROAD · St Joseph's College · CEMETERY ROAD · GREEN ROAD · VANNIYA ST · University College · Provincial Council · FORT FREDRICK RD · Dutch Bay · INNER HARBOUR ROAD · ARUNAGIRI RD · KACHCHERI RD · LAVENDER LA · ST MARY ST · BHARATHI ST · DIKE ST · HOSPITAL RD · Powder Island · People's Bank · Kandaswarny · KANDASAMY KOVIL RD · CUSTOMS RD · FATMA ST · COURT RD · YARD APPROACH RD · St Mary's Cathedral · Inner Harbour · St Nicholas · High Courts · St Sebastian · Government Hospital · Rocky Point · Batticaloa · York Island

N · Bradt · 0 — 1,000m · 0 — 1,000yds

For listings, see pages 291–2

Where to stay
Off map
Chaaya Blu A1
Club Dive Paradise A1
Welcombe A2

Where to eat and drink
1 King's Hotel B2
Off map
The Crab
(see Chaaya Blu)

found ourselves staring at a dozen elephants of all sizes, quietly standing in the bush and minding their own business.

The scenery on either side of the road from Habarana to Trincomalee is mostly bush and scrub, with occasional flocks of goats and scrawny cows. There are lots of roadside vendors, with often no more than an upturned box on which to display their produce: fat pots of curd, bottles of honey, fruit or neatly stacked firewood.

As the road approaches Trinco the countryside gets greener and gradually more built up. Then the highway is swallowed up by the town's narrow streets, packed with vehicles and people and with shops overflowing on to the pavement. The residents of the town go about their daily duties normally; the policemen, when asked for directions, are friendly in the British bobby-on-the-beat manner. The town, too, apart from the occasional boarded-up store, resembles most commercial towns in Sri Lanka, with colourful saris on sale at drapers, blue and red plastic buckets and basins at hardware shops, and massive provision trucks blocking the roadways.

GETTING AROUND Dozens of three-wheeler taxis meet the train on arrival at Trinco and it is expected that a foreigner will bargain for a good price. It's an easy town to walk around, as well as fascinating to peer into the shops.

WHERE TO STAY The main reason for travelling to Trinco is to enjoy the beaches at Uppuveli and Nilaveli. Be warned, however, that these beaches are pleasant only during the May to October season and, even then, have to be shared with crows and stray dogs. If you read that the beaches of the east coast are better than those of the south and west of Sri Lanka, don't believe it. They have neither the sand quality, the beautiful bays, the ambience nor the after-beach activities of, say, Unawatuna or Bentota. However, the upgrading of hotels and guesthouses with swimming pools has been done with a view to making the area a year-round destination.

The beach runs northwards for some 16km up to Nilaveli, and has only recently regained attention after its heyday in the late 1970s. The Nilaveli Beach Hotel is in operation again after battering by the war and the tsunami and other smaller hotels are opening up in the area. All listings are included on the map opposite.

Chaaya Blu (81 AC rooms) Uppuveli, Trincomalee; 026 2222307; e reservations@johnkeellshotels.com; www.chaayahotels.com. Chaaya Blu has been created out of the former & somewhat forlorn Club Oceanic. The transformation isn't just the addition of mirror mosaic walls & glittering disco balls in the lobby; it's like a brand-new hotel with a deliberate retro touch. Blue denim is everywhere as a practical upholstery fabric, as blinds, as breeches for the staff uniform topped with bright shirts with a palm-tree motif. From the lobby there is a boardwalk past the huge swimming pool to the beach, with rooms (confusingly called chalets) in blocks of 4 on one side, & beach rooms on the other. Entrance to the new rooms is from a private veranda or terrace & with walls & furniture of white with orange cushions galore & a denim half-counterpane on the bed; each room is as bright & as cheerful as the hotel's sunny setting. The food is delicious, whether as a buffet in the main restaurant or à la carte in the speciality Crab Restaurant ($$$), open to non-residents, which concentrates on dishes like crab Caesar salad or fragrant crab curry. Bar & restaurant prices include service charge & taxes so there is no sudden surprise tacked on to the end of the bill. With the opening of the hotel, Trincomalee could become a year-round destination now that it has a hotel that rivals fabled (& expensive) Maldives island resorts for style, fun & sensational cuisine. $$$

Welcombe Hotel (23 AC rooms) 66 Lower Rd, Orr's Hill, Trincomalee; 026 2222373; e info@welcombehotel.com; www.welcombehotel.com. The premier place to stay close to town (too far to walk though, as it's in the residential area on a peninsula jutting out into the Inner Harbour) used to be the glamorous colonial hostelry (built 1937) known as the Welcombe Inn. By the 1980s it had slipped as a fashionable place to stay (as beach resorts opened) & become the rather forlorn – but cheap – Seven Islands Hotel. When I visited it after an absence of 22 years to compile the first (2002) edition of this guide I was appalled to see the havoc wrought by military occupancy during the troubled 1990s which left only 7 ground-floor rooms habitable while those on the upper floor were roofless & abandoned. The portico entrance remained & its lobby hearkened back to the sparse architecture of the 1930s, but its real charm was to be found in the saloon bar. It had walls panelled in Burma teak & a quarter-moon bar counter of the same wood. Its windows opened on a central pivot & were latticed with wood. In 2004, that colonial wreck was transformed into – & reverted to its old name of – the Welcombe Hotel, & became a

Jetwing-managed hotel. Now it is independent again. The transformation does not look comfortable as it has involved introducing a blatantly modern element with a green metal roof & a startling construction of metal poles dominating the entrance & supporting a monstrous sun terrace. Inside, glass walls & tiled floors have chased away the musty gloom of the long corridors & the whole place has been tarted up with lashings of bright colour, orange being predominant. Actually, the stewards – who are wonderfully polite – add a touch of gaiety with their orange tunics & sarongs. The rooms have been relentlessly refurbished & the 4 suites, with contemporary 4-poster beds & broad balconies, are good value. Fortunately, the unique 1930s bar has survived with the addition of a pretty prospect of the lawns & sea seen beyond the corridor's exterior glass walls. By 2010, the garishness of its modernisation had weathered & blended with the ambience of the old style that suits its superior location. **$$**

🏠 **Club Dive Paradise** (6 rooms with fan) French Garden, Uppuveli; m 077 7728266; e cdp. french@yahoo.com. This has been created out of what used to be called Pragash French Garden (where I first stayed in 1980), a few mins' walk along the beach from Chaaya Blu, but a lot further than that in comfort & trendiness, at about a tenth of the price. With its doors, walls & shutters painted bright reggae colours, Club Dive Paradise is reminiscent of the hippy era of the 1970s. There are only 6 small guest rooms, basic in amenities with metal frame beds with a single, slim pillow, & attached shower & toilet cubicle. The paradise part is waking up in the morning & flinging open the shutters to a brilliant sunrise. The club part of the name doesn't mean membership is required but refers to the exclusivity of being a guest at the place. The atmosphere is so laid-back, the staff of amiable youngsters either relax in the hammocks spun between palm trees, jog along the beach, or jig around to music. They respond to guests' requirements only when absolutely necessary, & that's the way guests like it since they are all young at heart & happy to do things for themselves. Food, freshly caught or straight from the Trinco market, is prepared whenever guests are hungry. The guesthouse & diving are under the direction of Eric Fernando, one of Sri Lanka's most experienced divers who runs dive centres in Bentota (at the Surf Hotel) & Nilaveli (at the Nilaveli Beach Hotel). Eric knows reefs & wrecks that make diving with him a special thrill as he introduces guests to paradise underwater. For me, staying at Club Dive Paradise was like returning to the old days when beach holidays were easily affordable – & we weren't fussy about shortcomings. It's a living reminder of what simple holidays by the beach used to be. **$**

🍴 **WHERE TO EAT AND DRINK** For sensational crab, go to **The Crab** (**$$$**) at Chaaya Blu [290 A1]. Otherwise prospects are limited to where the locals go. If you have come this far, you are bound to be used to local food by now, so no problem. Dive in the nearest dive. The **King's Hotel** (**$**) [290 B2] in Trinco is not a hotel but a seedy place with a warren of rooms for serious drinkers of arrack and local beer. Foreigners are regarded with amazement, but insist on local food and you might find a tasty snack of fried fish. All of the above listings are included on the map, page 290.

WHAT TO SEE AND DO The town has a laid-back atmosphere, continuing the feel of the Caribbean. Fishing boats are hauled up on the beach behind the fish market in the centre of town by the **clocktower** [290 C2] and the abandoned watering hole of yore, the Trinco Hotel. Opposite is the compound containing the daily **market** [290 B2]. Emerge from the main-road side of the market, and opposite is the **bus station** [290 B2]. Resist the soft drinks made of lurid orange, green, blue and yellow water sold from vendors' colourful stands.

A hot walk along the road (or try a three-wheeler) beside the bus station leads to **Fort Frederick** [290 D3]. The gate bears the date 1676 above its arch. Entrance is free for the walk to the summit of the hill for a view of the natural harbour. Behind the temple there is the **Swami Rock** (121m high) [290 D1] and the ruin of the monument to the Dutch girl who is supposed to have flung herself into the sea from the rock as her lover sailed away.

Andrew and Susan Beasley, who honeymooned in Trinco in September 2004, reported that they hired a three-wheeler in Trinco town for a city tour of an hour. They had a most amazing drive around seeing sights, including Fort Frederick and the public hot-water baths (where they bathed too), took part in a Hindu temple festival and had sweet tea and snacks provided by the driver at a local eatery. The tour took 2½ hours and included returning them by a beachside jungle path to the Club Oceanic, now Chaaya Blu. This trip can still be done as part of an independent tuk-tuk tour.

PASSIKUDAH AND KALKUDAH

Accessible down one of the many roads on the left side leading to the coast from Valachchenai, these neighbouring beaches that still haunt the minds of old Sri Lanka hands are coming alive again. They were renowned as potential beach playgrounds before a cyclone in 1978 blew the dreams away, and then what little tourist infrastructure there was disappeared during 25 years of civil war. Following the end of the war Trincomalee and its beaches to the north, and the unspoilt beaches of Passikudah and Kalkudah to the south, and further down the eastern seaboard around Pottuvil and Arugam Bay, are at last being developed.

GETTING THERE

By train There is actually a train halt at Kalkudah but this is not served by Colombo/Batticaloa express trains (see pages 295–6), only by local trains, so best to go to Batticaloa and take a taxi for the 30-minute drive north back to Passikudah or Kalkudah.

By bus There is a bus service (No 48-1) from/to Colombo.

By road For tips on road travel, see pages 49–50. Batticaloa is 30km south of Passikudah, and can also be reached by the A11 from Polonnaruwa and the A15 from Trincomalee.

WHERE TO STAY AND EAT

Maalu Maalu Resort & Spa (32 chalet rooms, 8 suites) Passikudah; 065 7388388; e info@maalumaalu.com; www.maalumaalu.com. The pioneering beach resort on the tranquil bay of Passikudah opened in 2011 after the decades-long separatist war ended. By the end of 2013 it was being challenged for the tourist dollar by slick, new conventional hotels not open at press time but designed to wall off the beach. Chandra Wickramasinghe, the chairman of the owning company of Maalu Maalu, had a vision of creating not another tourist factory but a hotel that encompassed local traditions. Maalu Maalu works beautifully because of its intriguing design (elegantly simple, palm thatch, A-frame cottages with palm wood floors), superb beach setting, huge swimming pool & fine locally inspired cuisine & (rare in some mainstream Sri Lankan hotels) swift, obliging & knowledgeable staff. Sure, it's a 6hr drive from Colombo, but the roads are good. The entrance reveals a small reception desk & a glorious panorama of a swimming pool seeming to float off into the sea, edged with thatched cottages with downstairs & upstairs rooms, some with attic bedrooms for kids. Each room is supremely comfortable with fans as well as AC, a working desk & tea/coffee set-up, deep pile beds & huggable pillows. Behind the palm wood screen backing the bed is a wardrobe & 2 doors opening onto a huge bathroom, complete with bathtub & separate shower. 8 of the rooms are classed as suites & have extra refinements including jacuzzi & cluster plunge pool. 2 beach bars are converted from abandoned fishing hulls, the open-sided restaurant with sarong-clad waiters features both buffets & à la carte menus. In the season of Apr–Oct, the sea resembles a shallow lagoon ideal for lazy swimming in contentment, but the hotel is popular off-season too. 'Maalu Maalu' (actually a fish vendor's cry) is the phrase to remember for a perfect beach holiday in Sri Lanka. **$$$**

While hotels will soon have blocked off Passikudah Bay from reality, the next-door cove of Kalkudah is slower to take off and mostly features guesthouses stranded inland. **Coco Ville** (*Kalkudah Bay;* m *077 9057986;* e *jimmijve@yahoo.com;* **$$**) advertises beachfront private chalets with air conditioning, minibar/mini pantry and satellite television.

For action and independent drinking dens and local cafés, visitors should venture further south to Batticaloa.

BATTICALOA

The east-coast town of Batticaloa (population: 92,332; 2012 estimate) is becoming more interesting now that the strife has settled, the NGOs moved on and new places are opening up. However, it remains a town and not a tourist resort, even though one new hotel opened late in 2013.

HISTORY The Sinhalese name for Batticaloa is Madekalapuwa, or muddy lagoon. The Portuguese had a strong presence in the island when, in 1602, a Dutch fleet appeared off Batticaloa and a Dutch general went to Kandy in an effort to win a foothold on the island. Visits via Batticaloa and Trincomalee by the Dutch to the King of Kandy infuriated the Portuguese who built a fort in Batticaloa in 1628. It was described then as: 'a square structure with four bastions of ancient design, armed with a dozen iron cannon, and its garrison consisted of a captain and 50 soldiers, with a gunner, 20 inhabitants, a chaplain, a church and a magazine of stores and ammunition'.

In 1638, the Dutch arrived and took the fort. They called Batticaloa 'a vile, stinking place' and handed the fort over to the Sinhalese in 1643, when it was demolished. In 1665, the Dutch again occupied Batticaloa but they surrendered it to the British (who had just taken Trincomalee) in September 1772. The British didn't stay long but the process of surrender by the Dutch to the British was repeated when the British arrived in Trincomalee in 1795 and secured the maritime provinces.

In 1848, Tennent visited Batticaloa and described the old Dutch fort as 'a grim little quadrangular stronghold ... surrounded by a ditch swarming with crocodiles'. He was impressed by the healthy and sizeable coconuts grown there, which he attributed to 'a soil sandy and pervious, a profusion of water from the fresh lake on the one side and the sea on the other ... a warm and genial sun and timely rains'. He was intrigued by Batticaloa's renowned Singing Fish but decided the noise – 'like the gentle thrills of a musical chord, or the faint vibrations of a wine glass when its rim is rubbed by a wet finger' – came from 'mollusca ... not fish'.

GETTING THERE

By train The railway line to the east was laid in the 1920s because of the strategic importance of Trincomalee harbour. The line was built from Maho via Gal Oya (1926), reaching Trincomalee in 1927, with a branch to Batticaloa being completed in 1928. The rails used were light, hence the railway was called the Batticaloa–Trincomalee Light Railway (BTLR).

Commenting on the tortuous route taken for the laying of the lines, a railway general manager wondered if it was due to construction costs being paid for on

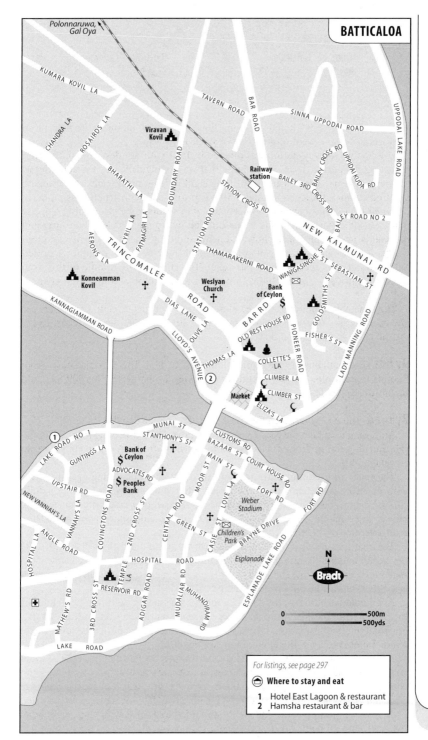

Polonnaruwa,
Gal Oya

KUMARA KOVIL LA
CHANDRA LA
ROSAIRDS LA
BHARATHI LA
CYRIL LA
FATMAGIRI LA
BOUNDARY ROAD
TAVERN ROAD
BAR ROAD
SINNA UPPODAI ROAD
UPPODAI LAKE ROAD

Viravan
Kovil

Railway
station

STATION CROSS RD
BAILEY 3RD CROSS RD
BAILEY CROSS RD
UPPIDAI KUDA RD
BAILEY ROAD NO 2

AERONS LA
TRINCOMALEE ROAD
STATION ROAD
THAMARAKERNI ROAD
WANIGASINGHE ST
ST SEBASTIAN ST
NEW KALMUNAI RD

Konneamman
Kovil

Weslyan
Church

Bank
of Ceylon

GOLDSMITHS ST

DIAS LANE
OLIVE LA
BARD RD
OLD REST HOUSE RD
FISHER'S ST
LADY MANNING ROAD

KANNAGIAMMAN ROAD

LLOYD'S AVENUE
THOMAS LA
PIONEER ROAD

COLLETTE'S
LA

CLIMBER LA

Market
CLIMBER ST
ELIZA'S LA

MUNAI ST
ST ANTHONY'S ST
CUSTOMS RD
BAZAAR ST
COURT HOUSE RD

LAKE ROAD NO 1
GUNTINGS LA

Bank of
Ceylon
ADVOCATES RD
MOOR ST
MAIN ST

UPSTAIR RD
VANNIAH'S LA
Peoples
Bank
FORT RD

NEW VANNIAH'S LA
ANGLE ROAD
COVINGTONS ROAD
2ND CROSS ST
CENTRAL ROAD
GREEN ST
CASIE ST
LOVE LA
FORT ST
Weber
Stadium

HOSPITAL LA
HOSPITAL ROAD
Children's
Park
BRAYNE DRIVE
ESPLANADE LAKE ROAD
FORT RD

MATHEW'S RD
3RD CROSS ST
TEMPLE LA
RESERVOIR RD
ADIGAR ROAD
MUDALIAR RD
MUHANDIRAM RD
Esplanade

LAKE ROAD

N

Bradt

0 ————— 500m
0 ————— 500yds

For listings, see page 297

⊜ **Where to stay and eat**

1 Hotel East Lagoon & restaurant
2 Hamsha restaurant & bar

The Eastern Seaboard and the North   BATTICALOA

9

TRAIN TIMETABLE: COLOMBO TO BATTICOLOA

Train	Colombo–Batticaloa		Train	Batticaloa–Colombo	
0611	06.05	14.20	6012	07.15	15.25
0679	19.15	04.00	6080	20.15	04.55

a mileage basis. He is quoted as saying that the railway 'followed the path of an intelligent cow' and went round every obstacle in its way.

The current railway station was opened in 1981 with nondescript architecture reflecting the period, then one of hope that was extinguished by the activities of the next 28 years. There is an astonishing sight in front of the railway station: an inspired colourful Rococo fountain. This extraordinary construction is modern, crowned by a gorgeously ample mermaid, who seems to be strumming a guitar made out of a plaster fish. She is surrounded by leaping fish and bare-breasted mermaids and is probably showered with spouting water when the fountain works. A frieze around the wall of the pond at the base of the fountain is dotted with pairs of jolly mermaids in bas-relief. The effect in the middle of this drab town is uplifting and every bit as impressive as the colonial fountain of cherubs in Kandy.

The timetable should be checked closer to your journey time to see if there are any changes. The one-way fare was quoted in 2013 as Rs760 for first class; Rs420 second class; and Rs230 third class.

By bus The main bus service from Colombo is No 48-1. There are also buses from Badulla to Batticaloa (No 30), Kandy (Nos 41/48), Monaragala (Nos 909/887) and Vavuniya (No 86-1).

By road The A15 runs down the coast from Trincomalee to Batticaloa.

An option is to take the road (A6) to Habarana whether driving from Colombo (via Kurunegala) or from Trinco, and then turn on to the A11 for Polonnaruwa (see page 140).

The road from Polonnaruwa to Batticaloa has signs suggesting grazing cattle, with an artificial insemination centre just after Polonnaruwa and then a milk chilling centre, but there were no cows to be seen when I made the journey. The railway line runs alongside the road by viaduct and actually shares a bridge with the road, over one of the many rivers.

The road passes close to **Welikanda** railway station and then dips and soars down dale and uphill through plains. At **Oddamavadi**, a prosperous little town, the road and the railway line share a narrow bridge on the way to **Valachchenai**, which is the turn-off for the rapidly developing beach resort of **Passikudah**.

At **Chenkaladi** the road is joined by the A5 that snakes up through the interior for 150km from **Badulla**, providing a way to reach Batticaloa from the hill country. The road into Batticaloa runs by a vast lagoon, giving the flavour of the town where a sign announces it as 'The Land of the Singing Fish'.

It is also possible to drive to Batticaloa northwards via **Pottuvil** from the beach at **Arugam Bay**, along the A4 as it runs along the east coast. Another way, from the south coast, is to take the A2 from Hambantota to Wellawaya then Monaragala (see page 212) and Ampara to link up with the A4 at Karativu, halfway between Pottuvil and Batticaloa. The road is wide and well maintained and lined with shops as it eases into the centre of Batticaloa town.

GETTING AROUND Batticaloa, known familiarly as Batti, is a busy, bustling town with little concern for visitors. The foreigners seen on bicycles or in huge air-conditioned jeeps bearing official emblems are attached to NGOs or foreign missions. A bicycle is a good way of getting around since the town is flat, but there are plenty of three-wheelers for visitors.

WHERE TO STAY AND EAT Batticaloa, by any stretch of the imagination, is not a place in which one would willingly stay. It's a fishing town and, although the lagoon front has been smartened up with garishly painted concrete benches, the guesthouses are basic. Far better to stay in one of the splendid new hotels by the sea at Passikudah or in guesthouses in the plains around Kalkudah, about 25 minutes' drive to the north, and then pop into the town to explore when beach life palls. Both listings below are included on the map, page 295.

Newly opened in 2013 is **Hotel East Lagoon** (*40 AC rooms; Lake Rd No 1, Uppodai Lake Rd, Sinna Uppodai, Batticaloa;* ✆ *065 2229221;* e *info@hoteleastlagoon.lk; www. hoteleastlagoon.lk;* $$$–$$) with stunning views of the lagoon and the sea beyond. It offers several styles of rooms with furniture and fittings imported from China, TV and Wi-Fi (surcharge), as well as a swimming pool and dining room open to non-residents for tourist-standard fare.

There is a bar with food: **Hamsha Restaurant and Bar** (*4 Lloyds Av, Batticaloa;* $) overlooking the waterfront and two bridges crossing the lagoon. It's not the place the fastidious would like, being a rooftop (reached up an unlit flight of steps and fenced in with chicken wire) rowdy bar but great for boozing and low-budget eating, with fresh devilled lagoon prawns and delicious mixed fried rice.

ARUGAM BAY

HISTORY At the beginning of the 1970s, this bay attracted the attention of intrepid travelling surfers and the legend grew during the 1980s and 1990s, when the area was unsafe for visitors, that it was a fantastic place for surfers. A participant in the Sri Lanka Airlines Champion of Champions British Pro-Surfers Association (BPSA) Surf Contest, held there, raved about the bay, 'I would say it's the perfect wave. It's long, consistent and good for a lot of turns.'

The area itself is part of the ancient Ruhunu kingdom and there are still temple ruins and forgotten shrines to be found in the vicinity. Notable is the Madu Maha Vihara on the coast by Pottuvil, the main town. It lies amid sand dunes and is said to mark the place where Queen Vihara Maha Devi and her entourage were washed ashore, and not at Kirinda. The ruins remaining are of a brick boundary wall of an image house with lots of tall stone pillars like sentries guarding a well-preserved statue of a Buddha and two Bodhisattva figures.

Arugam Bay is a great, curving swoop of coast with a dull beach that has been home – and toilet – to generations of fisherfolk. It comprises three small hamlets. **Ulle** is the main one, situated at the corner of the bay with a few Sinhalese families, and the village has both a Sinhalese and a Tamil school. **Perie Ulle** has mostly a Muslim population and a mosque and Muslim school, as well as a sub post office. The third village, **Sinna Ulle**, is also Muslim. It was the Muslim community who began offering accommodation to the young surfers who first arrived during the summer of 1971. The only accommodation then was a resthouse; before the tsunami the bay bristled with guesthouses, most of them quite horrid.

The first tourists didn't surf much, preferring the solitude of a bay undiscovered by other visitors: a sort of embryo Hikkaduwa or Goa. They used to ride out lazily on tyre tubes although some did surf, using planks found locally. Eventually serious surfers, hearing about Arugam Bay on the travellers' grapevine, turned up bringing their surfboards with them. Since they were an undemanding lot, they were happy with makeshift arrangements staying in local homes, and the grubby quality of the beach didn't deter them.

What little expansion of infrastructure to cater for these athletic young foreigners did develop was put on hold during the troubles of the 1980s and 1990s. Those lost years give Arugam Bay an air of being on the verge of being the next 'in' place. That ambition was washed away in the tsunami. Now, in spite of its isolation, distance from the mainstream and limited season (May to September), the hope is that Arugam Bay will at last become a popular resort for the mainstream tourist. But a lot has to be done. As a sign of its recovery, the BPSA surf contest is now an annual event attracting crowds of surfers and international publicity.

GETTING THERE

By bus Pottuvil is the gateway for Arugam Bay and the main bus is the No 98-4 from Colombo. There is also a service from Matara, No 35/303.

By road The town to head for, whether driving down the east coast from Batticaloa along the A4, or on the A4 via the interior town of Monaragala, is Pottuvil. Turn right at the town; Arugam Bay is about 2km south of Pottuvil.

On the drive from Colombo (314km distant, about 12 hours' driving) via Ratnapura and Wellawaya, the scenery changes subtly after passing through Monaragala, about 250km from Colombo. The harshness of rural life becomes obvious, with people living in thatched mud huts and selling jak-fruit to each other by the wayside. Labourers load sugarcane on to carts pulled by tractors; the earth is dry and dusty. The A4 forks because of the important-looking road to Ampara near the 286km post and is surfaced all the way to Pottuvil.

The road heads through scrubland pocked with anthill funnels. The only activity by an apparently abandoned military checkpoint was the lazy grazing of elephants and the lolloping of grey langur monkeys. We passed a building blasted with bullet holes then slowed to allow a mongoose family to file across the road. We were close to the Lahugala National Park, now reopened for visitors, where bears and jackal roam.

There are fields of brilliantly verdant paddy, edged with talipot trees, on the approach to Pottuvil. This is a frontier town, its sole street bustling with business.

After crossing the broad new bridge that gives access to Arugam Bay, it's possible to drive the length of the town's main street without realising there are hotels on the beach at the end of sandy lanes leading off the main road.

Arugam Bay has reverted to being the kind of place where the visitors are young, dazed, and keep their money in purses around their necks. It makes Hikkaduwa look old-fashioned. Is it the new Hikkaduwa? It has survived because of the backpackers and surfers who managed to get there. Now, even so long after the tsunami and being off-limits for years, it still awaits serious development.

By train There are no train services to Arugam Bay, and none are planned at present.

WHERE TO STAY AND EAT

Stardust Beach Hotel (14 non-AC rooms) Arugam Bay, Pottuvil; 063 2248191; e sstarcom@ eureka.lk; www.arugambay.com. The legendary Stardust Beach Hotel has opened up again. Its pioneering Danish owner was swept away by the tsunami but the Danish connection, & the pioneering, remains. As do many of the independent guesthouses that have long struggled to survive & been rebuilt since the tsunami. Advance bookings aren't necessary as Arugam Bay is the ultimate independent traveller destination, rewarding those who make the journey there with an unplanned, laid-back holiday lifestyle & an effortless mingling with the local community. Cabanas **$**; new wing **$$**

⌂ **Tsunami Hotel** (10 rooms with fans) Arugam Bay; ☏063 4923373; m 077 6642991;

e hotel@tsunamihotel.com; www.tsunamihotel. com. Opened with an ill-fated name in 1999, this beach hotel was wiped out in the 2004 tsunami (a wall of photographs shows the damage) but has reopened with the same name & the same totally laid-back, carefree atmosphere. Rooms are basic: 2 built of concrete blocks have hot water while the others, built of local timber with thatch roof, have showers. There is a beachside restaurant with food (naturally the fish is good) prepared on demand. There are hammocks in the garden & Wi-Fi connectivity. **$**

WHAT TO SEE AND DO Surfers. Arugam Bay is a long right-hand point/reef that breaks at the headland in front of the bay. Being the best swell magnet of all the points in the region, the waves at the point range between 2ft and 6ft (0.6–2m). On a good day it provides a clean wall that barrels in the sections and gives a surfer a 400m ride right through to the inside.

Beyond Arugam Bay a drive of 18km through paddy fields and scrubland leads to **Panama**. This one-street town commands the entrance to a stretch of sand dunes deeply shelving to the sea. It is an isolated, wild place, of the same ilk as the more hospitable strand of jungly dunes further south along the coast at Yala.

The **Kudumbigala Hermitage** is 10km south of Arugam Bay. It consists of a large rock complex of ridges and huge granite boulders. In ancient times, a cave-dwelling hermitage of Buddhist monks was located there.

Close to the national parks of Yala East and Lahugala, the **Okanda Devale** is an ancient Hindu shrine dedicated to the god Skanda-Murugan. The shrine is on a rocky outcrop overlooking the sea. It is an important place of worship for pilgrims undertaking the annual walk from Jaffna all the way along the coast to Kataragama.

JAFFNA *Population: 88,188 (2012 estimate)*

Geographically Jaffna is not part of the tourist circuit and it is only the curious, or those with ancestral Jaffna connections, who would want to go there. But Jaffna is certainly worth the visit if you have time even if the only reason is to see a part of Sri Lanka closed for a couple of decades through war. Since the war ended, Jaffna has been developed and is now as busy as Colombo's southern suburbs like Wellawatte.

However, in front of the massive construction work being undertaken to implant supermarkets and apartment blocks, some of the cars parked by the building sites are classic Morris Oxfords and other 1950s motorcars still used as taxis. There is a politeness, too, and foreign tourists don't attract the attention they would even in Colombo. No-one seems concerned and even customers in the least salubrious of eating and drinking places seem unperturbed at foreigners amongst them.

Restrictions on foreigners visiting Jaffna were removed in 2011 and all that became necessary then was to submit passports for checking at the military post by the road at Omanthai, about three hours' drive from Jaffna. Passports, as identification, are needed for foreign passengers taking flights there.

HISTORY The Jaffna Peninsula is almost an island, being connected to the mainland by the narrow Elephant Pass. Jaffna is 396km from Colombo, not far in modern

9

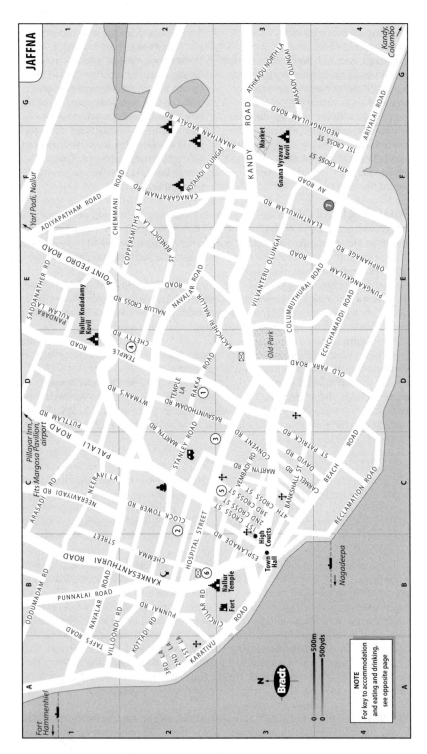

JAFFNA

Fort Hammenhiel

Yarl Padi, Nallur

Pillayar Inn,
airport

Fits Margosa Pavilion,

ADIYAPATHAM ROAD

CHEMMANI ROAD

POINT PEDRO ROAD

SADDANATHER RD

PANDARA KULAM ROAD

COPPERSMITHS LA

ST BENEDICT LA

KOTAIADI OLUNGAI

CANGARATNAM RD

ANANTHAN YADALY RD

Nallur Kndadamy Kovil

TEMPLE LA

CHETTY RD

NALLUR CROSS RD

NAVALAR ROAD

RAKKA ROAD

KACHCHERI NALLUR

RASAVINTHODAM RD

WYMAN'S RD

TEMPLE LA

STANLEY ROAD

MARTYN RD

PALALI ROAD

PUTTLAM RD

NEERAVI LA

ARASADI RD

NEERAVIYADI RD

CLOCK TOWER RD

CHEMMA STREET

KANKESANTHURAI ROAD

PUNNALAI ROAD

NAVALAR ROAD

ODDUMADAM RD

TAFFS ROAD

VILLOONDI RD

KOTTADI RD

PUNNAI RD

3RD LA

2ND LA

1ST LA

KARATIVU

HOSPITAL STREET

CIRCULAR RD

Nallur Temple

Nallur Fort

ROAD

Town Hall

High Courts

ESPLANADE RD

1ST CROSS ST

2ND CROSS ST

3RD CROSS ST

4TH CROSS ST

MARTYN RD

TEMBADI RD

CONVENT RD

DAVID RD

ST PATRICK RD

CAMEL ST

BANKSHALL ST

BEACH ROAD

RECLAMATION ROAD

Nagadeepa

Old Park

OLD PARK ROAD

COLUMBUTHURAI ROAD

ECHCHAMADDI ROAD

PUNGANGKULAM ROAD

ORPHANAGE RD

ROAD

VILVANTERU OLUNGAI

ELANTHIKULAM RD

KANDY ROAD

Market

Gnana Vyavar Kovil

AV ROAD

ATHIKADU NORTH LA

ARASADY OLUNGAI

NEDUNGKULAM ROAD

ARIYALAI ROAD

1ST CROSS ST

4TH CROSS ST

Kandy, Colombo

N

Bradt

0   500m
0   500yds

NOTE
For key to accommodation
and eating and drinking,
see opposite page

300

terms, but its distance from the main towns of Kandy and Colombo (and the short sea passage to India) isolated the peninsula from Sri Lanka in ancient times.

From 1983 when the conflict between the Tamils in the north and the Sinhalese in the south escalated into a civil war that lasted until 2009, Jaffna was off-limits to tourists. That does add to its interest for visitors today since the residents of Jaffna are not bothered by foreigners gaping at their temples and enthusiastically shopping for mangoes and palmyra products in the markets.

Of course, history plays its part in the making of Jaffna's identity. Sir James Emerson Tennent, colonial secretary (1845–49), writing in his history *Ceylon* published in 1859, noted:

> Jaffna is almost the only place in Ceylon of which it might be said that no-one is idle or unprofitably employed. The bazaars are full of activity, and stocked with a greater variety of fruits and vegetables than is to be seen in any other town in the island. Everyone appears to be more or less busy; and at the season of the year when labour is not in demand at home, numbers of the natives go off to trade in the interior.

Tennent stated that:

> Jaffna has been populated by Tamils for at least two thousand years, the original settlement being [about] 204BC' and refers to 'the occasions on which they carried on wars with the Sinhalese kings of the island.

The Portuguese took forcible possession of Jaffna in 1617, deposing the last sovereign of the Malabar dynasty. They were eventually expelled by the Dutch in 1658. Although it lasted only 40 years, the Portuguese influence was considerable, especially with the introduction of the Roman Catholic religion, attested by the number of churches they built. 'These remain,' observed Tennent, 'to the present day, having served in turn for the missionaries of three nations: Portugal, Holland and England.'

JAFFNA
For listings, see pages 303–4

🛏 **Where to stay**

1	Blue Haven	D2
2	Gnanams	C2
3	Green Grass	C3
4	Jaffna Heritage	D2
5	Lovusi	C3
6	Tilko Jaffna City	B2

Off map
Fits Margosa Pavilion.................D1
Fort Hammenhiel........................A1

✖ **Where to eat and drink**

7 A Taste of Jaffna.........................F4
Green Grass Hotel
  drinks kiosk.......................(see 3)
Tilko Jaffna City Hotel bar
  & restaurant.....................(see 6)

Off map
Fits Margosa Pavilion restaurant
  (see Fits Margosa Pavilion)..........D1
Fort Hammenhiel restaurant & bar
  (see Fort Hammenhiel).................A1

The Dutch were compelled to cede their possessions in Ceylon (which included Jaffna) to the British in 1796. Under the British, missionaries extended their activities providing a good selection of schools, as well as opening up communications, with the arrival of the railway line to Jaffna in 1905, and to Talaimannar in 1914. This connected with the ferry service to India (now disbanded) that cut down the cost, and the time, of importing Indian labour for the burgeoning tea industry in the south, giving the Jaffna Peninsula the status of a gateway to the country.

(For more on the crisis that developed from 1983, see pages 8–9.)

GETTING THERE

By air There are currently three flights a week from the local airport [300

D1] (Monday, Wednesday and Friday) between Colombo (Ratmalana) and Jaffna (Palaly) by small fixed-wing propeller aircraft operated by **Helitours**, a division of the Sri Lanka Air Force (*395 Galle Rd, Colombo;* ✆ *011 3144944;* e *helitours@slaf. gov.lk; www.airforce.lk/ pages.php?pages=helitours_sri_lanka_air_force*). The flight takes just over one hour; with a round-trip fare, at the time of writing, of Rs19,100.

Helitours no longer has the monopoly on the route; a private company, **Fits Aviation** (formerly Expo Aviation) (*6 Joseph Lane, Colombo 4;* ✆ *011 2555156;* e *reservations@fitsair.com; www.fitsair.com*) operates between Ratmalana and Jaffna (Palaly) with a daily service from Colombo by a nifty (single engine) Cessna Grand Caravan 208B aircraft.

Being a private operation it has none of the intimidating feeling of flying with the air force and is more comfortable. The seating is A (aisle) BC in three rows; the fourth row, a banquette at the back, has plenty of leg space. There is no divider between passengers and the two pilots, which makes the flight even more exciting, especially when a recorded voice squawks 'Traffic!' and passengers crane anxiously to spot nearby flying aircraft.

The flight, at around 8,000ft, takes only 75 minutes with the round-trip fare, at the time of writing, being Rs29,000. A free shuttle bus meets passengers to take them into Jaffna town, and there is a similar free service for the flight's departure.

Fits Aviation organises special packages for two- or three-day/night tours that include the airfare to Jaffna and back, airport shuttle in Jaffna, half-board hotel accommodation, and air-conditioned vehicles with English-speaking guide (*www. jaffna.travel*).

By train Work was still underway restoring the rail link between Colombo and Jaffna at press time, when trains were reaching Kilinochchi. There are daily trains, with reservable seats in the observation car, from Colombo to Anuradhapura and also to Vavuniya and then on to Kilinochchi. From there it would be necessary to hire a minivan or take a bus.

There is also a daily air-conditioned luxury carriage service by Exporail (*www. exporail.lk*) attached to Trains 4003 (departs Colombo 16.20; arrives Vavuniya 21.16) and 4004 (departs Vavuniya 05.45; arrives Colombo 10.25), which would entail an overnight stay in Vavuniya for onward travel between Vavuniya and Jaffna. (For other trains to Vavuniya, see box, pages 46–7.)

By bus Buses going to Jaffna start at the Central bus station near Colombo Fort railway station and depart at 07.00, 20.00, 21.00 and midnight, stopping in the centre of town [300 C2]. There are also privately operated air-conditioned luxury buses plying the route. The journey from Colombo to Jaffna by bus takes about 11 hours. It is not recommended unless you really want to see how Sri Lankans cope with such a long (and even noisy if the television is playing videos) journey.

By road The journey by road is excessively tedious as well as long and even in 2013 the highway was still being rebuilt with consequent delays when the traffic was restricted to one-way for 20 minutes at a time. For those determined to go to Jaffna independently by road the first stage is to get to Anuradhapura for an overnight stop before joining the A9. The A9 highway is 325km long and the longest highway in the country, connecting the central city of Kandy with the northern tip of Jaffna.

The shortest road route is actually from Colombo via Puttalam, but the road is not so good. The best road is Colombo to Kurunegala (via the A1 and A6) and then on to Anuradhapura although this is subject to heavy traffic on the Kandy road to the Kurunegala turn-off. Another route is from Colombo via Ja-ela, Ekala, Padeniya and Talawa to Anuradhapura. The A9 road goes from there via Vavuniya (an alternative overnight stopping place) to Jaffna.

GETTING AROUND Bicycles are the main form of transport, and can be borrowed from guesthouses. There are three-wheelers, mini cabs and some classic car taxis that can be hired to visit the popular sites. It is also possible to hire minivans with an English-speaking driver or guide for touring around the peninsula. Rates range upwards from Rs2,000 a day (*www.jaffna.travel*). Tilko Travels at Tilko Jaffna City Hotel (see details below) also operate day tours from Rs3,500.

WHERE TO STAY Accommodation is in guesthouses or the above-mentioned City Hotel. Be prepared for what a cautionary email from one hotel management said: 'Tourism in Jaffna is in early stage, so is the hotel industry. Maintenance and management are Herculean tasks as most of the staff are novices.' Novices, perhaps, but everyone seems keen to do whatever is required when reminded about it. All listings are on the map, page 300.

Fits Margosa Pavilion (6 rooms) Channakam, Jaffna; ℡021 7390490; e fitsmargosa@fitsair.com; www.jaffna.travel. One of those rare hotels in Sri Lanka that's worth the visit for itself, not just because it's on the Jaffna Peninsula. The 6 bedrooms have elegant boutique-hotel accoutrements (brushed cement floors & cement-block beds) some with open-roofed bathrooms, but none of the pretension of 'arts & crafts' boutique bungalows of the south. Food is conscientiously prepared to be full of flavour (& not too spicy for tourists unless requested) & served in the charming inner courtyard. The relaxed but willing attitude of the staff enhances the pleasure of staying there as the attention is friendly & genuine making guests feel perfectly at home. An excellent base for exploring the Jaffna Peninsula. **$$$**

Fort Hammenhiel (4 rooms, 1 cell) Karainagar, Jaffna; ℡011 3818215; e fff@navy/lk; www.forthammenhiel.navy.lk. Possibly Sri Lanka's most unusual hotel, a 330-year-old, octagonal Dutch Fort isolated in the middle of a lagoon, only reached by boat. It's called Fort Hammenhiel, apparently because the Dutch saw the tiny island's resemblance to the heel of the ham, which was how the Dutch viewed Sri Lanka (when tipped on its side as it was often mapped). Run by the navy, with guests required to register with an armed sentry at the gate to the navy compound – where there is also a restaurant & bar – it has 4 luxury suites complete with boutique hotel extras plus satellite TV, minibar, & 24hr room service by navy personnel. There are also pallets in a cell with outside, but modern, shower/toilet, barely converted from the days when the fort was a prison for revolutionaries & naval miscreants. Prison uniforms & caps are available on the pallets for cell guests. Fort Hammenhiel is a beautiful conversion of an Architecturally Protected Property into a luxury hotel with, as one guest has said approvingly, 'honest hospitality'. It has a courtyard garden, good for BBQs, sunrise & sunset decks, & assorted activities like snorkelling, diving, windsurfing & jet ski & boat trips to neighbouring islands. It lies 21km by road & causeway (& navy motorboat) from Jaffna. **$$**

Jaffna Heritage (10 rooms) Temple Rd, Nallur, Jaffna; ℡021 2222424; e gmstpholdingsleisure@gmail.com; www.jaffnaheritage.com. It's a fancy name but without much atmosphere although it does have alfresco dining & a small swimming pool. **$$**

Tilko Jaffna City Hotel (43 AC rooms) 70/6 K K S Rd, Jaffna; ℡021 2225969; e info@cityhoteljaffna.com; www.cityhoteljaffna.com. A typical city hotel in the town centre with AC rooms of various grades but all rather claustrophobic. A pioneering venture by a Jaffna resident who returned from a successful career as a property developer in London to help create a new Jaffna. Good buffet food in the restaurant & a modern bar. **$$**

Blue Haven (10 rooms) 70 Racca Rd, Jaffna; ℡021 2229958; e bluehavenjaffna@gmail.com;

www.bluehavenjaffna.com. With 10 spacious AC rooms (also with ceiling fan, telephone & plug points for laptop & portable kettle), this guesthouse in a residential suburb has a swimming pool & a pleasant, informal atmosphere. Basic bathrooms but with hot water. **$**

🛏 **Gnanams Hotel** (32 AC rooms) 299/301 Clock Tower Rd, Jaffna; ☎021 2220630; e gnanamshotel@gmail.com. Built around a garden courtyard with a restaurant at the back, but no bar, this is in the budget range with small rooms. **$**

🛏 **Green Grass** (52 rooms) 33 Aseervatham Lane, Hospital Rd, Jaffna; ☎021 2224385; e greengrassjaffna@gmail.com; www. jaffnagreengrass.com. With newly built rooms added, this is a warren-like property down a side road with old features like a central kiosk for drinks service, a dated swimming pool & lots of cement décor. **$**

🛏 **Lovusi** (12 AC rooms) 584 Hospital Rd, Jaffna; ☎021 2221326; e greengrassjaffna@gmail.com. Convenient location, a budget version of its sister property, Green Grass. **$**

✕ **WHERE TO EAT AND DRINK** The hotel restaurants at Tilko Jaffna City Hotel (**$$**), Fits Margosa Pavilion (**$$**), and the shoreside one serving Fort Hammenhiel (**$**) are good for Jaffna dishes such as Jaffna crab and black mutton. At the many Muslim-operated eateries (**$**) in the town the food is robust and spicy. Dishes are set out in glass display cabinets so it's easy to point out what you want and it's served quickly on a plate swathed in cling foil for easy cleaning.

There are some new restaurants too, but they are disappointing for an authentic Jaffna experience. A place called **A Taste of Jaffna** (*101 Main St, Jaffna;* ☎ *021 2221322;* **$$**), with its chairs wrapped in upholstery and ribbons more suited to a wedding reception, seems designed for tourists, both local and foreign.

Bars exist. I found two wonderful seedy drinking dens where strangers sit around tables in individual rooms swigging Sri Lankan beer or local spirits from half bottles. Those places might not suit visitors of a nervous disposition, although customers keep to themselves. I experienced an example of that courtesy when the drunkard sitting beside me quietly turned away to vomit in a corner, so I wouldn't be upset. I did move to another room. The Green Grass Hotel has a central kiosk in its inner courtyard where bottles can be purchased for more sophisticated drinking, while there is a fine modern cocktail bar at the Tilko Jaffna City Hotel.

WHAT TO SEE AND DO You may well ask. The landscape from **Omanthai** is flat and uncultivated with the scrub jungle taking over. There are signs of life starting again, but the detritus of war is still depressing. The chemical factory at **Oaranthan** is a mere shell and derelict. On reaching Elephant Pass, what were familiar landmarks – the fort and resthouse – are no longer there, even though a signboard points to where the resthouse once stood.

On the road journey to Jaffna, after Elephant Pass, watch carefully for wayside sellers of palmyra toddy, a similar effervescent (or repulsive according to your taste) beverage to the coconut palm toddy that is the popular poor-man's tipple in the south. Expect to pay around Rs50 for a plastic water bottle filled with it (but take your own bottle).

The **Jaffna Fort** [300 B3] has its ramparts smashed and all the buildings within it – King's House, the jail, the Old Dutch Church – were flattened by shells and are being rebuilt. Every tour of the city includes the **library**, initially established in 1935, burnt down in 1981 and rebuilt in 2004. It stands tall

---

FIRST TO THE POST

The original Jaffna **post office** [300 B2] was one of the first six to open in Sri Lanka; it's located in the centre of town.

and white against the skyline, as does the **clocktower**, which is 130 years old, near the library. The **Nallur Temple** [300 B2/3] is still worth a visit and closes at 18.00 unless there is a ceremony. The bazaars in town are alive and buzzing with activity; Stanley Street and Main Street have foodstuffs and Jaffna products like palmyra baskets, jaggery and mangoes.

Nagadeepa, a Buddhist shrine, can be reached from the pier at **Punkudutivu** [300 B4], from where a ferry plies at regular intervals. Historical Hindu temples abound. At **Uduvil,** 22km from the Chunakam junction, there is the intriguing sight of the **Kantharodai** archaeological site where a grass meadow is stippled with tiny stupas that are believed to be tombs. One of most dynamic sights is the **Keerimalai Tank**, a walled bathing tank invariably filled with happy youths, right by the sea but fed with fresh water from an underground stream.

The scruffy **Casuarina Beach** is some 33km from Jaffna town on the Karainaga road. With its whispering casuarina trees and long stretch of sand washed by shallow sea, this is a popular bathing place. A long causeway where prawn nets and straw-hatted fishermen define the lagoon on one side and the ocean swirls on the other, leads to **Kayts** where the large houses have all been destroyed.

A navy compound, known as *SLNS Elara* is located at the southwestern tip of **Karaitivu**, 21km from Jaffna town. An armed sentry at the compound gates registers visitors who come to dine at the modern restaurant complex built on the shore, run by the navy and open to guests. The 330-year-old octagonal Dutch fort, **Fort Hammenhiel** occupies a small island [300 A1] a short boat ride away which is now open to visitors (see page 303). Legend says that it gained its odd name as the Dutch occupiers thought the tiny island resembled the heel of a ham, which was how they viewed a chart of Sri Lanka (when tipped on its side as it was often mapped). It was formerly a prison and a quarantine station before being transformed into to one of Sri Lanka's most unusual hotels.

An astonishing sight beside the road at Maruthanar Madham resembles a huge jolly green giant. This **statue** was recently rebuilt in front of the temple named for it and is of Anjaneyar whom Jaffna Tamils consider as one of their gods. It is also known as Hanuman, the very revered monkey god, and the god Ram's right-hand person. Legend has it when Ram's wife Sita was abducted by Ravan to his home in Sri Lanka, Hanuman went over and set fire to Lanka with his tail and rescued Sita. Ravan is seen as a demon in India, but worshipped in Sri Lanka.

The District Secretariat of Jaffna has published a booklet *Tourism Jaffna* that lists 60 sites of interest to tourists, with brief directions of how to get there and when are the festival times for pilgrims. It can be purchased from reception at the Tilko Jaffna City Hotel [300 B2].

With Jaffna accessible to visitors, Sri Lanka now has yet another attraction to add to the main established sites, providing a fascinating insight to an island worth visiting for a holiday again and again.

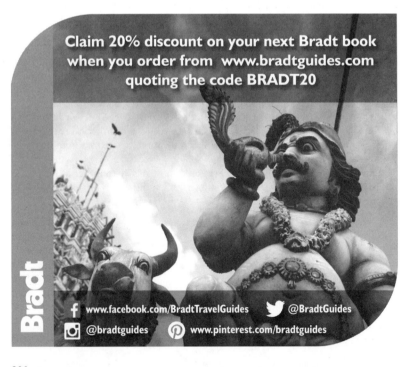

Appendix 1

LANGUAGE

Three languages are spoken in Sri Lanka: Tamil mainly in the north, east and plantation interior; Sinhala mainly in the west, south and centre; and English island-wide. Since English is widely spoken and understood – most Sri Lankans delight in trying out their English on tourists – the list of useful phrases featured below is short but they should serve the needs of travellers when and where English is not understood.

Both Tamil and Sinhala have their own alphabets, and for correct pronunciation and conversation the language enthusiast should purchase phrasebooks produced in Sri Lanka; they are available everywhere, even in village bookshops, The phrases below have been translated from Sinhala and Tamil in an effort to arrive at an approximation of how the words are pronounced. Other sources may give other spellings.

USEFUL PHRASES

	Sinhala	**Tamil**
Traditional greeting	*ayubowan*	*vanakkam*
Good morning	*subha udhasanak*	*kaalai vanakkam*
Good evening	*subha sandhavak*	*maalai vanakkanm*
Good night	*subha rahthryak*	*nal iravu*
Goodbye	*gihilla ennam*	*poittu varen*
Welcome	*sadarayen piligannawa*	*nalvaravu*
How are you?	*kohomada?*	*eppadi sugam?*
How much is it?	*keeyada?*	*evvalavu?*
Thank you	*istuti*	*naandri*
Please	*karunakarala*	*thayavu seithu*
What is your name?	*oyage nama mokadde?*	*ungada peyar enna?*
My name is	*mage nama*	*en peyar*
Where do you live?	*oba koheda innay?*	*neenga enga irukinga?*
Where are you from?	*oba kohendha?*	*nienga varrienga?*
I'm from …	*mama … ven*	*naan … irundhu varean*
Nice to meet you	*oba dhanagana labema sathutak*	*ungalai santhithathil magalchi*
Far	*aathah*	*tuuram*
Near	*langa*	*arukkil*
Doctor	*dostara*	*waithiyan*
Hospital	*rohala*	*aspithri*
Bank	*bankuwa*	*vangi*
Post office	*thapal kantoruwa*	*anjal aluvelaham*
Happy birthday	*subha upan dinayak*	*pirandha naal valthukal*

	Sinhala	**Tamil**
Happy New Year	*subha nava vasarak*	*inniya putthaandu valthukal*
Enjoy (for meals)	*vinoden kanna*	*nanraaga saappidunka*
I love you	*mama oyata adareyi*	*naan unnai kadalikiren*
Yes	*o-u*	*ama*
No	*naha*	*illai*
I don't understand	*mata therenney naha*	*ennakku vilanga illai*
I'm lost	*mama ataarmang wella*	*enakku vazhi theriyala*
Right	*dakuna*	*valathu*
Left	*vama*	*idathu*
Do you speak English?	*oba ingreesi kathaa karanavadha?*	*neenga English pesuviengala?*
Sorry	*mata samavenna*	*mannikkanum*
Closed	*vahala*	*mudapatulladhu*
Open	*arala*	*thranduladhu*
One	*eka*	*onnu*
Two	*deka*	*rendu*
Three	*tuna*	*moonu*
Four	*hatara*	*naalu*
Five	*paha*	*indhu*
Six	*haya*	*aaru*
Seven	*hata*	*ealu*
Eight	*ata*	*ettu*
Nine	*namaya*	*onbadhu*
Ten	*dahaya*	*patthu*

GREETINGS The Sinhala greeting *ayubowan* derives from three words: *ayu* (long life), *bo* (much) and *wan* (let it be) and means: 'may you live long'. It is used as a greeting, accompanied by palms held together at chest height on formal occasions. A more common greeting, the equivalent of 'hi' or 'hello', is *kohomada*. It is said in the manner of 'how are you?' and an answer is not expected, although it may bring the response: *ohe innava* or *varadak nee*, meaning 'fine'.

Appendix 2

GLOSSARY

ambalama	a wayside pilgrims' shelter
arrack	Sri Lanka's whisky; an alcohol drink distilled from *toddy* (the sap from a coconut tree)
Ayurveda	traditional herbal treatment
bhikkhus	Buddhist monks
Bo tree	*Ficus religiosa*; a tree with spreading branches worshipped by Buddhists
Buddha	The Enlightened One
bund	bank of a reservoir (tank)
Burgher	a Sri Lankan with Dutch ancestry
cadjan	a fence or wall of palm leaves
chaitiya	a shrine
coir	fibre spun from coconut husks
dagoba	(also *stupa*) an onion-shaped, domed building erected as a Buddhist shrine
devale	a shrine
ella	rivulet or stream
ganga	river
illam	gem-bearing gravel
jaggery	palm sap sugar, like fudge
kachcheri	local government secretariat
kovil	a Hindu temple
nirvana	the state of unbeing to which every Buddhist aspires. (Reader Richard Jones elaborates: 'Nirvana (or Nibbana in Pali) is a very difficult word to translate simply into English, but I would suggest the word "unbeing" has a rather negative meaning, whereas the Buddha described it as the "highest happiness". Perhaps something such as "The Enlightened state, release from all suffering and conditioned existence, the goal of all Buddhist practice"'.
ola	dried palm leaf used for writing with a stylus
oruva	a wooden dugout canoe with outrigger
oya	a stream or small river
paddy	unhusked rice; the rice plant
pandal	a decorated illuminated hoarding
pansala	a Buddhist temple
perahera	a grand procession
pirivena	a teaching monastery where young monks receive monastic training

Poya	lunar phase
puja	religious offering
roti	unleavened bread
SAARC	South Asian Association of Regional Cooperation (comprising Afghanistan, Bangladesh, Bhutan, India, Maldives, Nepal, Pakistan and Sri Lanka)
sambhur	an elk-like deer
samudra	inland sea or large tank
sangha	monks
stupa	a domed building erected as a Buddhist shrine
tank	a manmade reservoir
thambili	a golden-hued (king) coconut containing liquid
toddy	fermented coconut sap
tuk-tuk	a three-wheeler taxi, trishaw, auto-rickshaw
Veddahs	descendants of aboriginals
vihara	image house
walauwa	ancestral mansion
wewa	manmade reservoir (or *tank*)

Appendix 3

FURTHER INFORMATION

BOOKS Many books about Sri Lanka are only available at bookshops in Colombo and some are listed here. The Sri Lankan sections in Colombo bookshops will have many others.

General

Arjuna's A–Z Street Guide Arjuna Consulting Co (Pvt) Ltd, Dehiwela, 2006. Maps showing every street in Colombo and suburbs, and also in Kandy, Galle, Nuwara Eliya, Anuradhapura, Polonnaruwa, Trincomalee, Batticaloa and Jaffna.

Arjuna's Atlas of Sri Lanka Arjuna Consulting Co (Pvt) Ltd, Dehiwela, 1997. A fascinating atlas with lots of text and maps on topics as varied as gem deposits, industrial employment and banking.

Barlas, Robert and Wanasundera, Nanda P *Culture Shock! Sri Lanka* Times Books, Singapore, 1992. A deep explanation of cultural mores.

Cave, Henry W *Golden Tips* London, 1900. Beautifully produced with late 19th-century photographs, a general guide as well as details on tea production.

Daswatte, Channa *Sri Lanka Style: Tropical Design and Architecture* Photographs by Dominic Sansoni, Periplus Editions (HK) Ltd, Singapore, 2006. A superb collection of stunning photographs on vernacular and colonial inspirations, island eclectic, and contemporary interpretations of houses, retreats and resorts with an erudite and delightful text by brilliant young architect Channa Daswatte. A must-have souvenir book celebrating the distinctive style of architecture designed for Sri Lanka living.

Ellis, Royston *The Grand Hotel* Colombo, 1991. Celebrating the centenary of this venerable hotel, out of print.

Ellis, Royston *Seeing Sri Lanka By Train* Ceylon Tourist Board, Colombo, 1994. An illustrated pamphlet about rail travel.

Ellis, Royston *Sri Lanka By Rail* Bradt, 1994. Now out of print, this guide to train travel can still be found in Colombo bookshops, or through the internet.

Ellis, Royston *The Tea Factory Hotel* Colombo, 1997. About the Hethersett tea factory and how it became a hotel, out of print.

Ellis, Royston *On the Wings of Freedom: Sri Lanka at 50* Explore Sri Lanka/Business Today/Department of Information, 1998. Published for Sri Lanka's golden jubilee of independence.

Ellis, Royston *The Sri Lanka Story* Colombo, 2003. A souvenir coffee-table book.

Ellis, Royston *The Growing Years* Colombo, 2004. Commemorating the 150th anniversary of the founding of the Planters' Association of Ceylon.

Ellis, Royston *20 Years Uncovered: The MAS Story* Colombo, 2008. Commemorating 20 years of the MAS group, a pioneer in ethical garment manufacturing in Sri Lanka.

Handbook for the Ceylon Traveller Studio Times, 1983. Lively contributions by several authors on all aspects of Ceylon/Sri Lanka.

Hands on Colombo Colombo, 2004. Contains contact details of practically every enterprise in Colombo grouped under categories, such as libraries, movers and packers, and sports. An invaluable guide for the long-term visitor.

Hulugalle, H A J *Guide to Ceylon* Lake House, Colombo, 1969. As the island used to be.

Lewcock, Robert, Sansoni, Barbara and Senanayake, Laki *The Architecture of an Island* Barefoot (Pvt) Ltd, Colombo, 1998. A massive and wonderful book containing stories, sketches and photographs of 95 examples of Sri Lankan architecture.

Meyler, Michael *A Dictionary of Sri Lankan English* Colombo, 2007 (*www.mirisgala.net*). A self-published volume by an English teacher who first stayed in Sri Lanka in 1985 and who has worked since 1995 at the British Council in Colombo where he teaches a beginner's course in colloquial Sinhala. With some amazing examples of Sri Lankan English culled from Sri Lankan authors with sources quoted, making an entertaining read as well as a useful reference book.

Roberts, Norah *Galle: As Quiet as Sleep* Colombo, 1993. Details of Galle and the town's personalities of the past.

Health

Wilson-Howarth, Dr Jane *Bugs, Bites & Bowels* Cadogan, 2009

Wilson-Howarth, Dr Jane and Ellis, Dr Matthew *Your Child Abroad: A Travel Health Guide* Bradt, 2005

History

A Guide to Anuradhapura Central Cultural Fund, 1998

A Guide to Polonnaruwa Central Cultural Fund, 1998

Baldwin, Jan *Colombo Heritage* Lake House, Colombo, 1984. Sketches and notes on some colonial buildings of character.

Bandaranayake, Senake *Sigiriya* Colombo, 1999. A pictorial guide.

De Silva, K M *A History of Sri Lanka* Oxford University Press, Delhi, 1981. Detailed and fascinating with a list of all Sri Lanka's rulers.

Tennent, Sir James Emerson *Ceylon* 2 vols, Tisara Prakasakyo Ltd, Colombo, 1977 (reprint of first edition, 1859). Even though it was written nearly 150 years ago, contains a wealth of fascinating detail that's still relevant.

Natural history

Banks, John and Judy *A Selection of the Birds of Sri Lanka*, 1980; *A Selection of the Butterflies of Sri Lanka*, 1985; *A Selection of the Animals of Sri Lanka*, 1986, Lake House, Colombo. Three illustrated booklets ideal for quick identification of puzzling species.

Department of Wildlife Conservation *A Guide To The National Parks Of Sri Lanka* State Printing, Colombo, 2001. Packed with information and maps about the first 14 national parks.

Dirckze, Jan *A Selection of the Birds of Giritale* Colombo. A delightful booklet by the general manager of the Royal Lotus Hotel, Giritale.

Kautzsch, Everhard *A Guide to the Waterfalls of Sri Lanka* Tisara Prakasakayo Ltd, Colombo, 1983. Lists 92 waterfalls with details of how to get to them.

Miththapala, Sriyanie *What Tree is That?* Ruk Rakaganno, Colombo, 1999. A layperson's guide to some trees in Sri Lanka.

Ratnayake, H D and S P *Common Wayside Trees of Sri Lanka* Royal Botanical Gardens, Peradeniya, 1995. With photographs and details of Sri Lanka's trees.

Ratnayake, H D and S P, Sumithrarachchi, D B *Beautiful Wild Flowers of Sri Lanka* Royal Botanical Gardens, Peradeniya, 1995. With photographs and details of Sri Lanka's wild flowers.

Trekkers' Guide to Sri Lanka Colombo, 1994. An invaluable booklet with maps and information on estate and city walks, and walks beside temples, tanks and paddy fields.

Wijeyeratne, Gehan de Silva *A Birdwatcher's Guide to Sri Lanka* Colombo.

Wijeyeratne, Gehan de Silva *Sri Lankan Wildlife* Bradt, 2007. An absolutely fascinating book with superb photographs and an ideal companion to this guide.

Wijeyeratne, Gehan de Silva *A Photographic Guide to the Birds of Sri Lanka* New Holland, 2008. Two detailed books to fascinate both the beginner and the experienced birdwatcher.

WEBSITES It is surprising how many websites there are devoted to Sri Lanka, or a particular part of it. Type 'Sri Lanka' in the Google search box on the internet, and you will be rewarded with 570,000,000 entries. I have listed hotel websites in the guide. Here are some others to peruse for particular information:

www.books-maps.com/lk Database of maps, aerial photos, site images and guidebooks and where to buy them

www.colombopage.com News of Sri Lanka

www.dailymirror.lk A newspaper website with breaking news posted throughout the day

www.dailynews.lk A newspaper website

www.island.lk A daily newspaper website

www.lacnet.org For emails of daily news bulletins

www.lanka.net Extracts from news reports and general information

www.lankalibrary.com Virtual library and information on Sri Lanka

www.lankapage.com News about Sri Lanka

www.priu.gov.lk Official website of the Government of Sri Lanka

www.roystonellis.com/blog For a weekly update by this book's author on life in Sri Lanka

www.search.lk Links to websites about Sri Lanka

www.srilankainstyle.com How to enjoy the country in style

www.srilankaluxury.com Concentrates on unique accommodation, rustic as well as luxury

www.srilankan.aero SriLankan Airlines site, with timetable

www.srilanka.travel The official website of the Sri Lanka Tourism Development Authority

www.sundaytimes.lk Enter 'Royston Ellis' in the search box to see some of the many articles on Sri Lanka and little-known places to stay written by the author of this guide

www.theacademic.org Lanka academic newspaper

Index

INDEX OF ADVERTISERS